Yurugu

Yurugu

An African-centered Critique of European Cultural Thought and Behavior

by Marimba Ani

(Dona Richards)

Africa World Press, Inc.

P.O. Box 1892
Trenton, New Jersey 08607

Africa World Press
P. O. Box 1892
Trenton, NJ 08607

Text Design by Jonathan Gullery
Cover Concept and Design by Aziza Gibson-Hunter
Cover Artwork by Amurá Oñaā
Interior Mask Drawings by Smith-Chinyelu

Library of Congress Cataloging-in-Publication Data

Ani, Marimba
     Yurugu : an african-centered critique of European cultural thought and behavior / Marimba Ani.
        p. cm.
     Includes bibliographical references and index.
     ISBN 0-86543-248-1. – ISBN 0-86543-249-X (pbk.)
     1. Europe–Civilization. 2. Ethnocentrism–Europe. I. Title.
CB203.R5   1992
940' .01–dc20
                                     91-71027
                                        CIP

TABLE OF CONTENTS

Charts

Introduction

PART I - THOUGHT AND ICONOGRAPHY
Chapter I - *Utamawazo*: The Cultural Structuring of Thought

Chapter 2 - Religion and Ideology

Chapter 3 - Aesthetic: The Power of Symbols

PART II - IMAGE AND NATIONAL CONSCIOUSNESS
Chapter 4 - Self-Image

Chapter 5 - Image of Others

PART III - BEHAVIOR AND ETHICS

Chapter 6 - Rhetoric and Behavior

Chapter 7 - Intracultural Behavior

Chapter 8 - Behavior Towards Others

PART IV - IDEOLOGY

Chapter 9 - Progress as Ideology

Chapter 10 - Universalism: The Syntax of Cultural Imperialism

CONCLUSION
Yurugu: The Incomplete Being

Author's Note

According to the Dogon people of Mali, in West Africa, Amma, the Creator, ordained that all created beings should be living manifestations of the fundamental universal principle of complementarity or "twinness." This principle manifests itself as the wholeness which is created when female and male pairs join in all things. Such pairing establishes equilibrium, cooperation, balance, and harmony. Amma therefore equipped each being with twin souls - both female and male - at birth. But in one of these primordial placentas the male soul did not wait for the full gestation period to be born. This male being was known as Yurugu (Ogo), who arrogantly wished to compete with Amma and to create a world better than that which Amma had created. With his fragmented placenta he created Earth; but it could only be imperfect, since he was incomplete, that is, born prematurely, without his female twin-soul. Realizing that he was flawed and therefore deficient, Yurugu returned to Amma, seeking his complementary female self. But Amma had given his female soul away. Yurugu, forever incomplete, was doomed to perpetually search for the completeness that could never be his. The Earth, he had defiled in the act of self-creation, was now inhabited by single-souled, impure and incomplete beings like himself. Yurugu's descendants, all eternally deficient, originated in an incestuous act, since he had procreated with his own placenta, the representation of his mother.

Dedication

To my mother,
Delphene Douglas Richards
And to my daughter,
Delphene Djifa Atsufi Fumilayo Douglas Richards,
in whom her spirit has been reborn.

In the tradition of Afrikan Ancestral Commemoration,
This book is dedicated to the Egun of the Maafa
Who trusted in us, their descendants, to carry out the Victory
For which they sacrificed so much.

It is for all Afrikan people, therefore,
Who have fought for the simple Truth -
Race First!

And it is especially for those who do not understand
the meaning of that Truth.

For those Afrikans who would be seduced into the
labyrinth of academia,
this book was written to free your minds,
 that your spirits might soar,
and you would become Warriors and Fundi,
rather than professors of white power.

It is for and to our Youth
who must believe in the power of their Africanness
So that they will be able to destroy
And to rebuild with African vision.

Introduction by John Henrik Clarke

In this book, Professor Dona Richards has opened up a Pandora's box called racism that will not be easily closed by the creators of racism or its victims. What she is saying will have to be seriously considered if the reader of her words is ever to know peace. This is a pioneering and ground-breaking work dealing with a neglected aspect of European culture. Most books about Europeans deal mainly with what Europeans think of other people. In this book Professor Richards has analyzed the European influence on the world based on what they think of themselves and how this thought affects most of the world.

Without saying it, she has emphasized that for the last 500 years the world has been controlled by a form of European nationalism. They have created a concept called the "cultural other" that has influenced their vision of themselves and other people in their contact with Africans, Asians, and people of the Pacific Islands. They have declared most things primitive that they could not understand. They have laughed at the gods of other people. This cruelty was compounded when, through propaganda and the misuse of the Bible, they taught other people to laugh at their chosen gods and adopt the god of their conqueror.

I have referred to this as the manifestation of the evil genius of Europe. They were the last branch of the human family to emerge into that arena called civilization. In their conquest of the minds of most of mankind they have been able to convince themselves and others that they were indispensable to civilization, and without them it would not have existed.

What the European has forgotten and made his victims forget is that over half of human history was over before most of the people of Africa and Asia knew that a European was in the world. The emergence of Europeans or white people as the handlers of world power and their ability to convince millions of people that this is the way things should be is the greatest single propaganda miracle in history.

In the 15th and 16th century Europeans not only colonized most of the world, they colonized information about the world. They developed monopoly control over concepts and images. The hallmark of their colonization in this regard was the colonization of the image of god. After a number of years under European domination, the slaves and the colonial subjects of the Europeans would not dare to mention the word god in a language of their own creation or visualize god through the lens of their culture.

The political and social sciences and other academic disciplines used to explain human existence and to prophesy the possibilities of progress came under European control. The Christian church in many ways became the handmaiden of European world domination and to some extent it still is.

> When in 1492 Columbus, representing the Spanish monarchy, discovered the New World, he set in train the long and bitter international rivalry over colonial possessions for which, after four and a half centuries, no solution has yet been found.
>
> *Capitalism and Slavery*
> Eric Williams, University of North Carolina Press, 1944

The above statement indicates the arrogance of the Europeans in the expansion beyond their shores on the lands of other people. Since the re-emergence of Europe in the 14th and 15th century to the present day, part of what I refer to as their evil genius is their ability to drain the diseased pus of their political sores on the lands of other peoples. With consistency they have attempted to solve their problems at other people's expense. The European has a grab bag of rationales for seizing the land and resources of other people in order to justify their domination.

Prior to the period that I'm referring to, the people of the world were not referred to by their color. Therefore, the concept of a white people is a creation; the same is true of black people, of yellow people and brown people. The concept of race that now plagues the whole world is an artificial European invention. Professor Ashley Montagu has referred to it as man's great myth. While the word race and the concepts around it are artificial, the effects of its creation are *real.* The application of this concept has affected the lives of most of the people of the world. It was part of the basis of the slave trade and of the colonial system that followed. In their textbooks, travelogues, and sometimes in their interpretation of the Bible, the European has said or inferred that they were the only people in the world who created anything that deserves to be called a culture. Europeans destroyed more culture and civilizations than they built. They have studied people without understanding them and interpreted them without knowing them.

Professor Richards in her book asks this revealing question:

What is the relationship between the way in which Europeans conceive of the world and the way in which they relate to majority peoples? Put another way: What is the relationship between the dominant modes of European thought and the dominant modes of their behavior towards others?

If the people in Africa and Asia and the former European colonies are to emerge into full independence, statehood and world responsibility, they will have to answer the above question creatively and in their favor. Then, in a collective sense, they will have to participate with others in a world that can be free, that can recognize European influence without accepting European dominance.

Inasmuch as there are not enough soldiers in Europe to hold down five empires of people that outnumber the population of Europe, the victims of European aggression need to ask, "How did they do it?" The European conquest of the mind of most of the people of Africa and Asia is their greatest achievement. With the rise of independence movements and millions of people demanding the right to rule themselves, the European monopoly of the minds of most of mankind was over. Imperialism and colonialism will not die easily. The former colonial subjects of Europe are fighting to regain what slavery and colonialism took away—mainly their self-confidence and the image of god as they originally conceived him or her to be.

In order to understand the new information and revelations in this book, the readers might have to approach it as carefully as the writer has. This will be an intellectual experience that has its own reward.

John Henrik Clarke
April, 1992

Incantation

(Taught to me by Armah and Kambon)

Two thousand seasons of restless sleep
Beneath the destroyers' fragmented image
We used their definitions of ourselves
To disconnect our consciousness
Lines drawn in denial of deeply textured souls
Okra/Ka/Se
Life/Force/Energy
Nyama.

They knew even as we slept
That our spirit was more powerful
Than their white death.

In our will-less sleep
We have allowed the Earth to be defiled.
The wake of two thousand seasons
Of Spiritless matter...
Destroyers' work.

Confusion in Maafa aftermath
Within our lost knowledge
Enemies have blurred the line
Between us and them.
Are we destroyers ourselves?

No - We are the Springwater
Compelled by Ancestral consciousness
Egun/Nsamanfo
Issuing from Ani's womb
We divine a victorious destiny
Ifa/Odu.

We are awakening,
Announcing ourselves, self-determining
With Nubian will
Crystal vision
Shaping a new reality
Ancient genius rediscovered
So Dayi - The Clear Word.

Balancing the scales
Restoring spirit to matter
The Whole completed
Made cosmic again.

Rhythm is the key to the Way
Alternating Death with Life
Joining us to each other.
We are the Healers.
The Victory is ours!

We call upon Onyame, Olodumare, and Amma
Invoking the Nommo-power of Blackness
Carried in the genes of Race Memory
Hesse!

Ancestors and Children to be born
Keys to the circles of connectedness
and clarity
Africa redeemed
The universe in harmony
Return and move forward
To the Way
Of a natural order
African World Order
Resplendent reflection of Ma'at.

Ase!

Acknowledgement

*Tiko Ba Si Igi Le Hin Ogba Ogba Ma Nwo**

To Whom Praises and Thanks are Due:

I live close to my ancestors, and most particularly to my mother. I thank them everyday for the blessings that they continually bestow. My responsibility to them is what this book is about. It helps to fulfill the oath that I took, by having been born African, to avenge their spirits. I acknowledge them here for giving me life, for my connection to the Universal Life Force (Ntu), for being my collective consciousness, and for the spirituality with which I think.

This work has been mandated by the Maafa, the great suffering of our people at the hands of Europeans in the Western hemisphere. It is hopefully a partial solution to what Professor John Henrik Clarke has identified as "the imprisonment of a people to image." The minds of African people are still crowded with the image of Europeans as superior beings. This is a condition which locks our will and freezes our spirit-force. Professor Clarke has said that we must "instill will into the African mind to reclaim itself." That is what he has done for me. In turn I have attempted here to establish a basis for the demystification of the European image, so that our collective conscious will can once again be activated.

I owe my awakening and growth towards a Pan-African, Nationalist consciousness to Professor John Henrik Clarke, who allowed some of us as young people who worked with SNCC to literally sit at his feet in his Brooklyn apartment in 1965-66 and drink of his wisdom and knowledge concerning the history of the Pan-African world. This close contact with Professor Clarke tapped my African center and I developed a passion for the realization of the Pan-African vision.

After my experience with SNCC (the Student Nonviolent Coordinating Committee) in Mississippi, and some travel in the Motherland, I began graduate studies in anthropology. That contra-

---

* "If fence does not have props it will collapse." (Yoruba Proverb)

diction led to a dissertation meant to uncover the roots of anti-Africanism and European imperialistic consciousness in the discipline of anthropology. The research began what has to become a 20 year sojourn through the bowels of European thought, leading to the conclusions of this work.

Professor Clarke was later to come back into my life as a mentoring force. When I finished graduate school in 1975 he brought me into the Department of Black and Puerto Rican Studies at Hunter College. He then advised me to write articles on aspects of my analysis and helped me to get them published.

Perhaps, more than any single person in the African world community, Professor John Henrik Clarke has stimulated young people of African descent to search for an African-centered truth. I take this opportunity to express my love and gratitude, and to acknowledge the genius of this master teacher; this molder of minds. For a great teacher is one who can point in his sunset years to hundreds of younger African people who owe their ideological commitment and political development to his/her inspiration. Ase!

The specter of continuing the research, indeed of developing an African-centered paradigm within which to place Europe for critique, was awesome. I was certainly tempted to let this project go. And then in 1979, Molefi Kete Asante introduced himself to me, asking that I write an article for a book that he was doing. My acceptance of this task resulted in *Let The Circle Be Unbroken*. But his work *Afrocentricity* in 1980, gave me and countless others the affirmation we needed to move further towards the vision. It was the African-centered perspective stated boldly in print by an African author. Molefi articulated what others had implied and what their work had meant. He stated what we were feeling.

It was this same Molefi Asante who, one day when he was visiting New York, pulled out a dusty manuscript and began to read. I subsequently mailed more chapters to him. He read all 686 pages, writing comments in the margins. When he finished he was enthusiatic, saying, "Marimba, you must publish this!" It was the first time that anyone had taken the time to read the entire work, and he made me believe in the necessity of its completion.

I rewrote every chapter, did an elephant amount of new research, and developed a theoretical formulation which I used to make sense of what I had found. It was a painful and exhausting ritual. This was a process that I would not have completed had my brother Molefi and Professor Clarke not stayed on my case: Professor Clarke saying whenever I would see him, " When are you going to finish that book!"

Asante Sana to my daughter, Djifa, who has also sacrificed, suffered, worked on, and thought about this book. More than anyone, she has shared this experience. Her 16 years have been the years of this manuscript. She has lived through it with me. This in itself was an ordeal for her. She has collated pages, processed words for indexing, and listened while I explained and worked out concepts. Her thoughts and perceptions have been invaluable. She has suffered long weekends grounded in our apartment while I worked. Closer to me than anyone else I know, she "shares my space." And I thank her for hanging in. Her faith and love kept me going. Djifa, Nina kupenda!

My students at Hunter, especially those who participated in our seminar on Critical Theory during the spring of 1993, have been exposed to the concepts presented here. Their insights, reactions, critical comments, and enthusiasm has encouraged me to finish. I am indebted to the nurturing relationship which we have shared.

Linda and Jessica started me off with typing "almost" final drafts. It is to Herriot Tabuteau that I owe so much. He "saved me" when I did not know how I would be able to get the manuscript typed. A pre-med student, who could work on the computer (having written and published his own book at the age of 16), he processed the entire manuscipt efficiently and with great care. It was a critical juncture for me. Herriot also gave me critical feedback on the ideas and concepts that it contained. I thank the Nsamanfo (ancestors) for bringing us together on this project.

Nichelle Johnson, a young friend, former student, and organizer of the Daughters of Afrika at Hunter College, worked with me on the endnotes, bibliography, index, and proofreading. Her spirit was just what I needed. She is careful, precise, and thorough. Asante Sana, Nichelle!

I thank Andre Norman for being patient enough to introduce me to the MacIntosh, as he has done with so many of our people. That skill made my editing so much easier. I thank him for allowing me to invade his family's apartment for specific "computer help" that I needed. His is a nurturing spirit.

Adupwe to the Egun for sending my spiritual brother, Amurá Oñaā who is always able to visually manifest what I see and Amurá, Medasi for your help with the charts of explanation.

We collectively thank the Ancestors for the genius of Al Smith who brought African judgement to this work through mask symbolism. Al, thank you for your supportive energy and friendship.

The following people helped in various invaluable ways; James Conyers, Carole Joy Lee, Persheen Maxwell, Geyuka Evans, Mark

Staton, and Spencer Forte.

To Patricia Allen, my editor, I must give more than thanks. I offer my understanding. I apologize for the volume of this work. It required months of laborious work. I know that the task was exhausting. Yet Patricia went through it several times, making extensive, painstakingly thorough editorial comments. She has helped me to strive for excellence in the presentation and form of this work, but I am responsible for any problems of style which remain.

Had it not been for Kassahun Checole's judgement that this book was worth publishing, it may never have "seen the light of day." Asante Sana, Kassahun.

I give thanks to my cousin, Sandra Lawrence, for keeping our family together while I immersed myself in this project. I also thank my father, Franklyn Richards, and the other members of my personal family and lineage, for their support during this endeavor.

Medasi to my sister Gerri Price for our friendship. She supported me in this project without even knowing about it, for she taught me about the Victory in confronting the enemy which is ultimately only fear.

And finally, I want the African world to know how grateful I am to my sister and brothers, Aziza (Claudia) Gibson-Hunter, Jawara Sekou (Keith Hunter) and Kobi Kazembe Kalongi Kambon (Joe Baldwin), for their African-centeredness, for their love for me and for African people, and for their consistent encouragement and imani (faith) in this project. They share the vision.

To You All, Asante Sana!

Marimba Ani
(Dona Richards)

Glossary

Asili

The logos of a culture, within which its various aspects cohere. It is the developmental germ/seed of a culture. It is the cultural essence, the ideological core, the matrix of a cultural entity which must be identified in order to make sense of the collective creations of its members.

Utamawazo

Culturally structured thought. It is the way in which cognition is determined by a cultural *Asili*. It is the way in which the thought of members of a culture must be patterned if the *Asili* is to be fulfilled.

Utamaroho

The vital force of a culture, set in motion by the *Asili*. It is the thrust or energy source of a culture; that which gives it its emotional tone and motivates the collective behavior of its members. Both the *Utamawazo* and the *Utamaroho* are born out of the *Asili* and, in turn, affirm it. They should not be thought of as distinct from the *Asili* but as its manifestations.

Cultural Other

A conceptual/existential construct which allows Europeans to act out their most extreme aggression and destructiveness, while simultaneously limiting their collective self-destruction on a conscious level.

Rhetorical Ethic

Culturally structured European hypocrisy.It is a statement framed in terms of acceptable moral behavior towards others that is meant for rhetorical purposes only. Its purpose is to disarm intended victims of European cultural and political imperialism. It is meant for "export" only. It is not intended to have significance within the culture. Its essence is its deceptive effect in the service of European power.

First World People   African descendants throughout the world.

Majority Peoples   The members of the indigenous core cultures of the world regarded collectively, excluding the European minority.

Nationalism   Ideological commitment to the perpetuation, advancement, and defense of a cultural, political, racial entity, and way of life. This use of the term is neither limited to, nor determined by the boundaries of a "nation-state" as defined eurocentrically.

European Nationalism   All forms of thought and behavior which promote European Hegemony/global white supremacy.

White Nationalism   An expression of European nationalism which identifies caucasian racial characteristics with superiority and African racial characteristics with inferiority.

Cultural Imperialism   The systematic imposition of an alien culture in the attempt to destroy the will of a politically dominated people. The mechanism of cultural imperialism causes cultural insecurity and self doubt within the dominated group. Separated from their ancestral legacy, they lose access to their source of political resistance.

Scientism   The ideological use of "science," defined Eurocentrically, as an activity which sanctions all thought and behavior; that is, science becomes sacred, the highest standard of morality.

Objectification	A cognitive modality which designates every-thing other than the "self" as object. This process mandates a despiritualized, isolated ego and facilitates the use of knowledge as control and power over other.
Desacralization	The alienation and objectification of nature. In this view, nature becomes an adversary. This approach to reality originates in unnatural-ness.
Materialization	This begins with the separation of spirit and matter. This separation, in turn, results in the denial of spirit (despiritualization), the loss of meaning, and the loss of cosmos (interrela-tionship).
Despiritualization	The denial of spiritual reality. The inability to experience spirit. Objectification used ideo-logically results in the desacralization and despiritualization of the universe.
Reductionism	The reduction of phenomena to their most simplistic manifestations. This occurs when the mind is not able to apperceive deeper, more textured levels of meaning. As a cogni-tive deficiency, it prevents comprehension of metaphysical truths.
Reification	This occurs when theory is used as law rather than metaphor and when process is replaced by factual manipulation. Reification is the hardening of dynamic, vital truth into dead-ened dogma.
Lineality	The interpretation of phenomena as being made up of unidimensional, separate entities arranged in sequential order. This conception is necessarily secular and results in desacral-ization. It denies circularity and the spiral of organic development. It prevents transcen-dence of ordinary time and space, thereby

denying ancestral ontological experience.

Dichotomization	A mechanism which accompanies objectification. It is the splitting of phenomenon into confrontational, conflicting parts. It facilitates the pursuit of power over other, and is therefore suited to the European *Asili*.
Spirit	The creative force which unites all phenomena. It is the source of all energy, motion, cause, and effect. As it becomes more dense, it manifests as matter. It is the meaningful level of existence.
Spirituality	The apprehension of cosmic interrelationship. The apperception of meaning in existence, and the degree to which one is motivated by such meaning. Spirituality is one's ability to relate to the metaphysical levels of experience. It unites thought and feeling and thereby allows for intuitive understanding. This cognitive /affective sense is transmitted through collective ancestral relationship. The absence of spirituality is an ancestral legacy.
Yurugu	A being in Dogon Mythology which is responsible for disorder in the universe. This is a being conceived in denial of the natural order, which then acts to initiate and promote disharmony in the universe. In African Cosmology such a being is deficient in spiritual sensibility, is perpetually in conflict, is limited cognitively, and is threatening to the well-being of humanity.

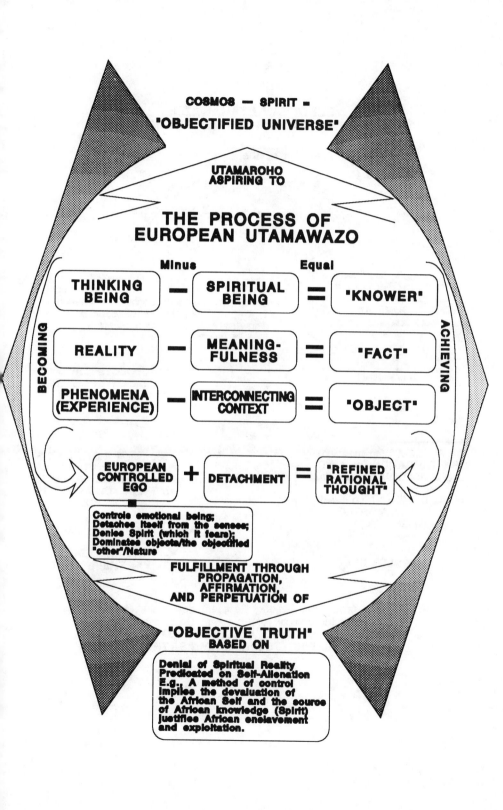

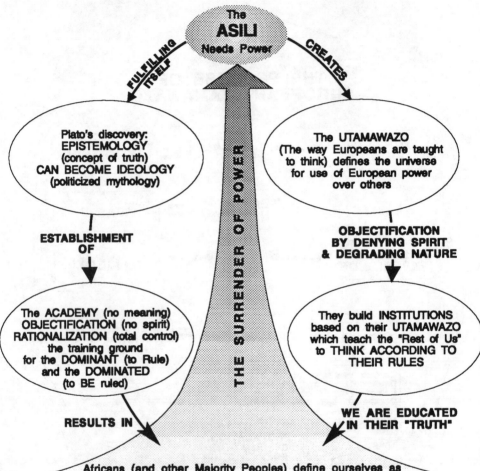

EUROPEAN UTAMAWAZO:
MIND CONTROL FOR WORLD DOMINATION

The
ASILI
Needs Power

FULFILLING ITSELF

CREATES

Plato's discovery:
EPISTEMOLOGY
(concept of truth)
CAN BECOME IDEOLOGY
(politicized mythology)

The UTAMAWAZO
(The way Europeans are taught
to think) defines the universe
for use of European power
over others

ESTABLISHMENT
OF

OBJECTIFICATION
BY DENYING SPIRIT
& DEGRADING NATURE

THE SURRENDER OF POWER

The ACADEMY (no meaning)
OBJECTIFICATION (no spirit)
RATIONALIZATION (total control)
the training ground
for the DOMINANT (to Rule)
and the DOMINATED
(to BE ruled)

They build INSTITUTIONS
based on their UTAMAWAZO
which teach the "Rest of Us"
to THINK ACCORDING TO
THEIR RULES

RESULTS IN

WE ARE EDUCATED
IN THEIR "TRUTH"

Africans (and other Majority Peoples) define ourselves as
"inferior objects" of European Domination:
WE ARE TRAINED TO ACCEPT THE SYSTEM OF
GLOBAL WHITE SUPREMACY AS "TRUTH"

Christianity as a Core Mechanism of the European Asili for the Achievement of EUROPEAN WORLD DOMINATION

European Imperialism

Birth of European National Consciousness

Expansion of the European Cultural Self

Monotheistic Ideal

Monolithic European Control

POLITICAL AGGRESSION

Elaboration of Materialism and Individualism

European Religion

ASILI

CHRISTIANITY

Ideological Preparation for Capitalist Order

PROSYLETIZATION

Patriarchal
Nature identified with "Sin" and "Evil"
Nature to be controlled,
Rationalistic -- denial of Spirit,
Fear of Blackness,
Whiteness defined as "good"
Identifies with the (unnatural)
European Self

Intensification of European
"WE"/"they" dichotomy

Christian

Exploitation Destruction Domination

of the "Heathen"

EUROPEAN AESTHETIC AND EUROPEAN DOMINANCE

NTU -- Universal Life Force

Separation from Nature, Rhythm --

"Perfection" = Non-Spiritual, External, Material Realism

COGNITIVE

Abstract/Distant
Pure
Rational
Elementary
or Superficial

Pleasure =
Technical Control

Displeasure =
Nature

Anxiety =
Spirit, Can't Be Controlled

European Aesthetic
Causes Self-Hatred
Inferiorization and Rejection
of the "Non-European" (natural) Being

AFFECTIVE

Linear
Angular
Antiseptic
White

POLITICAL

EUROPEAN CULTURAL EGO AND WORLD DOMINATION

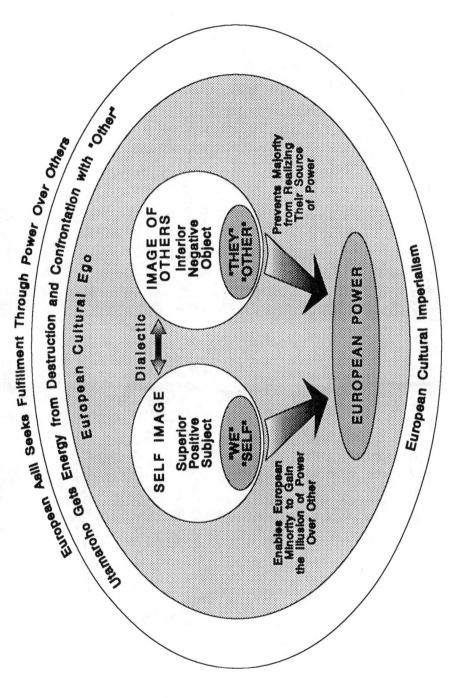

EUROPEAN BEHAVIOR AND ETHICS
IN RACIAL AND CULTURAL DOMINATION

ASILI -- Lacks Spirit -- Seeks Power

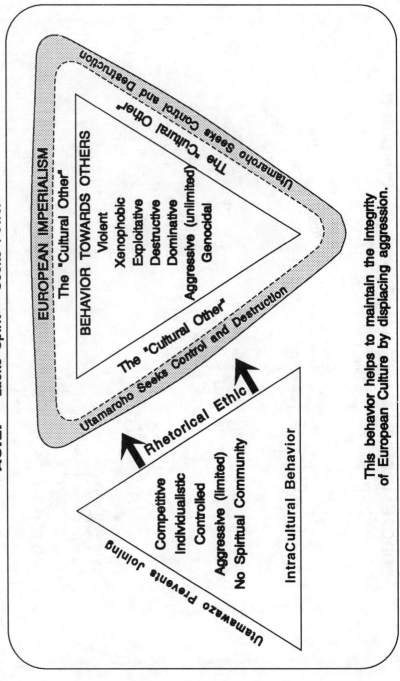

This behavior helps to maintain the integrity of European Culture by displacing aggression.

THE IDEOLOGY OF
EUROPEAN WORLD DOMINATION

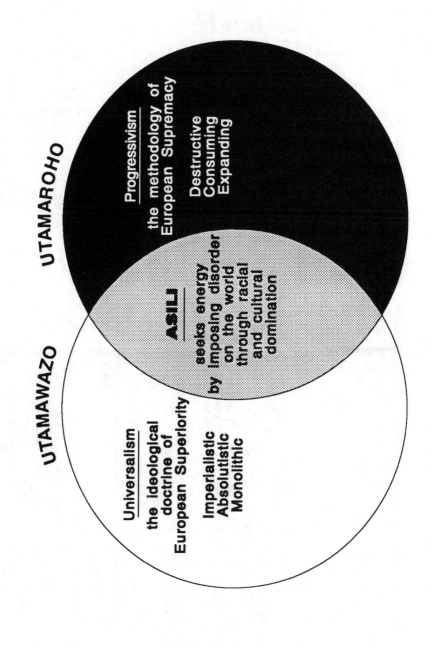

UTAMAROHO

Progressivism
the methodology of
European Supremacy

Destructive
Consuming
Expanding

ASILI
seeks energy
by imposing disorder
on the world
through racial
and cultural
domination

UTAMAWAZO

Universalism
the ideological
doctrine of
European Superiority

Imperialistic
Absolutistic
Monolithic

TANGLE OF EUROPEAN CULTURAL PATHOLOGY CREATES SYSTEM OF EUROPEAN WORLD DOMINATION

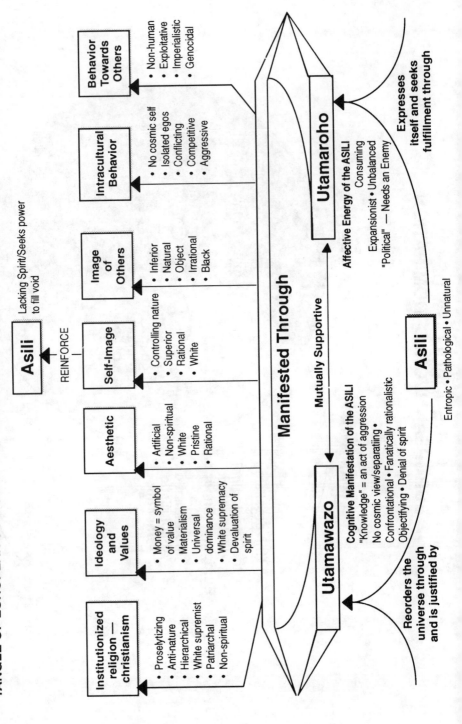

Introduction

Bolekaja!*

This study of Europe is an intentionally aggressive polemic. It is an assault upon the European paradigm; a repudiation of its essence. It is initiated with the intention of contributing to the process of demystification necessary for those of us who would liberate ourselves from European intellectual imperialism. Europe's political domination of Africa and much of the "non-European" world has been accompanied by a relentless cultural and psychological rape and by devastating economic exploitation. But what has compelled me to write this book is the conviction that beneath this deadly onslaught lies a stultifying intellectual mystification that prevents Europe's political victims from thinking in a manner that would lead to authentic self-determination. Intellectual decolonization is a prerequisite for the creation of successful political decolonization and cultural reconstruction strategies. Europe's political imperialistic success can be accredited not so much to superior military might, as to the weapon of culture: The former ensures more immediate control but requires continual physical force for the maintenance of power, while the latter succeeds in long-lasting dominance that enlists the cooperation of its victims (i.e., pacification of the will). The secret Europeans discovered early in their history is that culture carries rules for thinking, and that if you could impose your culture on your victims you could limit the creativity of their vision, destroying their ability to act with will and intent and in their own interest. The truth is that we are all "intellectuals," all potential visionaries.

This book discusses the evolution of that process of imposition, as well as the characteristics of cultural beings who find it necessary to impose their will on others. It is not a simple process to explain, since the tools we need in order to dissect it have been taken from us through colonial miseducation.[1] It is necessary to begin, therefore, with a painful weaning from the very epistemological assump-

---

Bolekaja is a Yoruba term meaning, "Come on down, let's fight!" See Chinweizu, Onwuchekwa Jemie and Ihechukwu Madubuike, *Toward the Decolonization of African Literature,* Vol. I, Howard University Press, Washington D.C., 1983, p. xii

tions that strangle us. The weaning takes patience and commitment, but the liberation of our minds is well worth the struggle.

My chosen field is African-centered cultural science — the reconstruction of a revolutionary African culture. I teach Pan-African studies. The experience convinces me more and more, however, that teaching Pan-African studies well means teaching European studies simultaneously. To be truly liberated, African people must come to know the nature of European thought and behavior in order to understand the effect that Europe has had on our ability to think victoriously. We must be able to separate our thought from European thought, so as to visualize a future that is not dominated by Europe. This is demanded by an African-centered view because we are Africans, and because the future towards which Europe leads us is genocidal.

Chinweizu describes himself as an "occidentalist"; Iva Carruthers calls for the study of "Aryanology."[2] These African-centered scholars have made contributions to the demystification of European thought and behavior; the African liberation movement is indebted to them. And there are others (far too many to be mentioned here); *Ankobia** who are paving the way for an African-centered social theory. In the spirit of Cheikh Anta Diop and Bobby Wright there comes Ayi Kwei Armah, Kwame Agyei Akoto, Kobi K. K. Kambon (Joseph Baldwin), Molefi Kete Asante, Ifi Amadiume, Frances Cress Welsing, Wade Nobles, Jacob Carruthers, Amos Wilson, Na'im Akbar, Kariamu Welsh-Asante, Maulana Karenga, Linda James Myers, Aziza Gibson-Hunter, Asa Hilliard, Ngugi Wa Thiong'o, K.C. Anyanwu, Cedric Robinson, C. Tsehloane Keto, Haki Madhubuti, Abena Walker, and others; a vanguard that is codifying the language of African-centered analysis. The standards for bold African affirmation had already been set by Harriet Tubman, Nat Turner, Ida B. Wells, Anna Julia Cooper, Edward Wilmot Blyden, Marcus Garvey, Carter G. Woodson, George James, John G. Jackson, Chancellor Williams, Yosef Ben Joachannan, John Henrik Clarke, Malcolm X, and the names we cannot mention, the names we do not know, the hundreds of political prisoners and prisoners of war, who have spent out their youth since the early 70's in jail. Most of all, the intellectual tradition of African affirmation cannot be separated from the spiritual force which exists in every African person, as they sing and make music and protect their families and raise their children. Academia— a European misconception—has no place for us. African-centered

---

* *Ankobia* is a Twi term that identifies those who lead in battle, setting the standard for courage and commitment.

social theory is the collective creation of every aspect of our history of struggle and victory. It began when we began; challenged by the first invaders of the Motherland. It received new life from the Middle Passage. It was shaped during the crucible of the Maafa. And now encompasses the visions, thoughts, and creations of every African soul; every mother and father, every child. These are the names I would list.

I have attempted a comprehensive critique of the European tradition, but the degree to which the minds of people of African descent (especially our youth) are freed to envision a victorious African future will be the judgement of its success. The critique will be called "racist" by Eurocentrists, but it was not developed for them. And as Aziza Gibson-Hunter says, "'racism' is the fire ignited by the Europeans; our response is only the smoke." And though the "liberals" would have it otherwise, there is no way to extinguish a fire without experiencing the smoke. Europeans have made the fire; we will put it out.

Thesis and Process

To be of African descent and to study anthropology is to be struck by the pervasive anti-Africanism of the discipline. And if one then approaches the discipline critically, it emerges as a tradition of Eurocentricism, functioning to satisfy the needs of the European ethos. The critique of anthropology led me right into the belly of the beast, as I discovered how deeply it was embedded in the bowels of the European cultural/historical matrix. I had no alternative then but to embark on a critical study of the totality that is European culture; to lay bare its ideological underpinnings, its inner workings, the mechanisms that facilitate its functioning.

Anthropologists, through their use and abuse of the culture concept have inhibited this necessarily critical process. They have generally ignored the political implications of culture by deemphasizing its ideological function. They have typically focused their attention on supposedly "simple" and "isolated" non-European societies. Through this conventional use of the culture concept these societies have been theoretically and superficially abstracted from the political contexts in which they exist. This use allows anthropologists to ignore the implications of European exploitation, while the conditions of colonialism and neo-colonialism provide them with their "objects" of study.

Anthropology is not simply a "child of imperialism."[3] It is a manifestation of the European ethos. This is why very few anthropologists study themselves, i.e., their own cultural backgrounds. Their politically superior position allows them to study others, but not to *be* studied. The few who do study Europe do so in isolated bits and pieces (Nordic myth, peasant society, folk culture). Even "urban anthropology" does not approach European culture as a totality. A Eurocentric social science cannot be used to critically examine the European cultural tradition. Yet there is no reason the concept of culture should not be used to study the extraordinary character of European imperialistic behavior. In fact, the African-centered perspective makes it compelling. Fortunately, this perspective has separated me from the tribe of European anthropologists.

Our present endeavor requires the "de-Europeanization" of the culture concept. It must be made relevant to the political needs of those who have been victimized by Europe,[4] and Europe must be brought into focus as a cultural entity. By emphasizing the ideological function of culture, it is possible to make sense of the intimidating confusion and superficial complexity of the European experience. Understanding culture as ideology allows us to approach European culture in such a way as to make it a visible, extremely cohesive and well-integrated phenomenon, in a sense more "simple" than we might suppose. Beneath its deceptive heterogeneity lies a monolithic essence; an essence that accounts for the success of European imperialism. This is not to say that this endeavor is an easy one. But that should not dissuade us. Its difficulty makes it all the more imperative, all the more urgent.

Wade Nobles defines culture as "a process which gives people a general design for living and patterns for interpreting their reality." Its "aspects," he says, are ideology, ethos, and world-view; its "factors" are ontology, cosmology, and axiology; and its "manifestations" consist of behavior, values, and attitudes.[5] These are the aspects of European culture that we will bring into focus in this study. Let us see how culture and ideology "fit" together; how an ideological emphasis in the interpretation of culture is more consistent with its meaning and significance. If we look at the phenomenon of culture, we are impressed by the following characteristics:

1. It acts to unify and to order experience, so that its members perceive organization, consistency, and system. In this respect it provides a "world-view" that offers up orienting conceptions of reality.

2. It gives people group identification, as it builds on shared historical experience, creating a sense of collective cultural identity.

3. It "tells" its members "what to do," thereby creating a "voice"

of prescriptive authority.[6] To its members, culture *re*-presents values (which they themselves have created together out of shared experiences) as a systematic set of ideas and a single coherent statement.

4. It provides the basis for commitment, priority, and choice, thereby imparting direction to group development and behavior; indeed, it acts to limit the parameters of change and to pattern the behavior of its members. In this way culture helps to initiate and authorize its own creation.

5. It provides for the creation of shared symbols and meanings. It is, therefore, the primary creative force of collective consciousness, and it is that which makes it possible to construct a national consciousness.

6. For all the above reasons, it impacts on the definition of group interest and is potentially political.

Willie Abraham's understanding of the nature of culture is helpful in our study, and he perceptively acknowledges its applicability to the examination of European development:

> Culture is an instrument for making . . . cooperation natural. Its success depends on the extent to which it is allowed to be self-authenticating. Though it allows for internal discussion . . . the principles of decision in such discussions are themselves provided by the culture. By uniting the people in common beliefs and attitudes . . . culture fills with order that portion of life which lies beyond the pale of state intervention . . . . It fills it in such a way as at the same time to integrate its society, on the basis of common reactions, common actions, common interests, common attitudes, common values. It creates the basis of the formulation of a common destiny and cooperation in pursuing it. If one looks at the West one finds that this use of culture is well-developed. It is what is involved, when one hears it said that this or that belief will destroy a certain way of life, and that that way of life must be defended no matter what the cost.[7]

The ideological thrust of culture is inescapable. It boldly confronts us. Culture is ideological since it possesses the force and power to direct activity, to mold personalities, and to pattern behavior. This recognition implies a theory of culture. Raymond Betts puts it this way: "Ideology is here used in a cultural sense, to denote the verbal iconography by which a people represents itself in order to achieve communal purpose."[8] Leonard Barrett says that ideology is "the spiritual and intellectual foundation of group cohesion."[9] Both culture and ideology are extremely political in nature, since they are about the definition of group interest, the determination of group destiny and common goals. Political behavior is simply behavior that issues from an awareness of group definition as distinct from other groups. We think politically when we assess our group interest in relation to the interests of other groups and determine whether those interests are compatible with or in opposition to ours. We act politically when our behavior and strategies reflect those assessments. Cultural identification and ideological commitment are bases for political consciousness. With this "repoliticized" understanding of culture we are prepared to begin our study of Europe.

The approach of the study must be, of necessity, holistic and synthetic. Exhaustive ethnographic description of European culture is of limited value even if it were feasible. The attempt to achieve detail would only serve to divert our attention from ascertaining the fundamental nature of the culture. The successful approach to the analysis and synthethic understanding of European culture demonstrates its organicity, discovers the relationships and interdependencies between its various aspects. As with any culture we look for consistency and pattern. Idiosyncrasy and anomaly are only useful in that, through contrast, they help us to recognize what is characteristic. This is revealed through an ideological focus and a methodology by which we search for the interrelationships between the dominant modalities through which the ideology of the culture expresses itself. European culture, like culture universally, is an ongoing process in which meaning is created and reaffirmed. The apprehension of meaning in the culture and the mechanisms through which it is reinforced are critical concerns of this study.

This endeavor is facilitated by the identification of "themes," which, as Morris Opler called them, are "dynamic affirmations" that act to determine behavior and to "stimulate activity." The translation of a theme into behavior or belief becomes its "expression."[10] Again there is an ideological focus. Suddenly the complexity (vastness) of European culture becomes approachable. We are in pursuit of the "explanatory principles" of the culture.[11] Through an axiological focus (values) the pivotal axes of the culture are clarified, and through an emphasis on synthetic functions we apprehend unity beneath the surface diversity (heterogeneity) of Europe. Looking beyond the superficial for that which has ideological significance, we have sought the modes of standardization and the mechanisms of legitimization. It is these aspects of European culture that give it order, and order is the most forceful attribute of culture. Indeed, the present study reveals that the impressive European order, its overwhelming consistency, and the force of its ideology, give it an incomparable degree of power. The two-pronged question, "why" and "how," determines the method and approach of our inquiry. We have approached significant cultural creations and behaviors by asking: Why do they exist? How are they made forceful? These are the questions of ideology.

The divisions and subdivisions through which the study is presented are, to a great extent, superficial. They have been created for convenience and to aid us in the perception of a reality that we generally experience as one forceful totality, not in analyzable parts. The order of presentation is not meant to imply a lineal or hierarchichal relationship between these "parts," for they overlap in a way that defies compartmentalization, and their relationship is circular and reticular.

In all cultures there is the taken-for-granted, assumed, and habitual aspect that though generally less visible than others, and rarely explicit — exerts the most profound influence on its members. This is precisely because it functions on such a deep level. According to Edward T. Hall these "hidden controls" become habitual responses that are experienced "as though they were innate." [12] Anthropologists talk about world-view as that aspect of culture that functions to replace presented chaos with perceived order by supplying the members of a culture with definitions of reality with which to make sense of their surroundings and experiences; it is the meaningful organization of experience, the "assumed structure of reality."[13] This "deep structure" of culture, as Wade Nobles has called it, has a most powerful influence on the shape of the culture and the thought-patterns of its members.[14]

This is only one of the reasons that this study begins with a discussion of European thought; there is another. European culture is unique in its use of cultural thought in the assertion of political interest. While the logic of any culture, in the sense of what its members are taught to accept as "making sense," may become for them part of an assumed reality, Europeans have used their "cultural logic" in an effectively aggressive manner: (1) The culture "teaches" its "logic" and world-view to the ordinary participants, who then assimilate it, assume it, and push it beneath the surface, from where it influences their collective behavior and responses. (2) Then "special" members of the culture — regarded as "intellectuals," "scholars," "theorists" — retrieve the assumptions of this world-view and represent them as the tenets of a universal system of thought, one that presents standards of logic, rationality, and truth to the world. These are considered the seminal theorists of the culture, when actually their ideas simply reflect the assumed reality of the mainstream culture. The manner of their presentation is, however, authoritative. (3) In this way the European world-view takes on ideological force not only within, but *outside* the culture, since it can be imposed as universal, speculative, and self-conscious. (4) At the same time, its parochial and axiological character remains well-hidden and camouflaged beneath a pseudouniversalism.

This is the most difficult aspect of European culture. But once understood it is the key to the ideological thread that runs from one mode, one theme, one characteristic to another. The thought process is consistent, reflecting the consistency of the ideological thrust that must be laid bare. It is part of the nucleus of imperialism. Chapter 1, which begins Part 1 of this work, attempts to characterize the epistemological and ontological themes of European thought in order to establish a context in which to place the other dominant modes of European culture. To approach Europe critically, we must first understand that the language of European value is the language of an abstract scientism. Our task, in short, is to throw into question precisely what is assumed to be beyond question in European culture, namely, its scientific epistemology. By doing this we succeed in bringing European ideology into view so that it can be recognized in other patterns and creations of the culture. The ideological implications of the epistemology become a decoding tool for the critical interpretation of culture.

Chapter 2 reviews institutionalized religion as a system that sacralizes the ideology, achieves internal social and political order and imperial authority vis-à-vis other cultures. Chapter 3 discusses aesthetics as an expression of value. European conceptions of beauty and European principles of pleasure reveal a further statement of the ideology and the collective psyche. The theme of universalism rears its head, since the discussion of "art" is used by Europeans as a tool of imperialism. This concludes Part I, which leaves us with an understanding of the mental, philosophical, and aesthetic habits that act to support a particular style of behavior.

Part II, (Chaps. 4 & 5) examines the images and concepts of self and "other," which support the discussion in Part III: the patterns of behavior within European culture (Chap. 7) and towards others (Chap. 8). Chapter 6, which begins Part III, discusses the relationship between what Europeans want us to believe they are doing and what actually happens. It is very important to understand this breach between word and deed, as it were, since people from other cultures often make costly political errors because of the lack of this rhetorical and hypocritical component in their own culture. They misinterpret European language and fail to predict European behavior. They are always therefore shocked by the intensity of the hostility and aggressive nature of that behavior.

Part IV closely examines the themes of "progress" (Chap. 9) and "universalism" (Chap.10) in European ideology. Together they are the cutting edge that intellectually and culturally disarms the victims of European domination. The study concludes by offering an interpretation of European culture that relates its extreme rationalism to its intensely imperialistic behavior towards others. The various themes, modes, and patterns under discussion converge to form a single monolithic reality. Imperialism emerges as the overwhelming persistent theme of this critical statement, which demonstrates how epistemology, axiology, aesthetic, iconography, and behavior all link together in such a way as to form an impressively solid and supportive network, girding the quest for European power.

Evidence

Once we have discerned the explanatory principles of European culture, we discover many varied sources of information. They include the historical record of European behavior, both from the viewpoint of those with whom Europeans have interacted and from the viewpoint of Europeans themselves. The emphasis, however, in terms of information-gathering, is on the various vehicles of European self-expression, in the belief that it is by looking at the statements, behavior, and modes of expression of those who have considered themselves European that we can begin to get at what "European" means. It emerges then as a desired "way of being" for a particular group of people. Our ethnographic sources are those vehicles of self-expression that reveal how Europeans see themselves and their culture; i.e., what they would like to be and how they wish to appear to others. We can then understand the logic of the behavior implied by these ideas, using the record of European behavior towards others.

Western European literature is also a very valuable source of information. I have used European social theory because there is so much axiology to be found hidden in its jargon and in the thought patterns that emerge from it, and I have occasionally used the literature of white nationalism, as it manifests crucial aspects of European ideology and the European self-image and image of others. Often I have used and referred to the words and ideas of those philosophers and theorists who are considered Europe's seminal thinkers. This discussion is in part a synthesis and affirmation of previous African-centered critiques of Europe as well as a recognition of those critical voices that have been largely ignored by the European tradition. These critiques also become a source of information.

However, the most important source is my own experience of the culture. Experiencing the intellectual core through its academies, feeling the weight of its oppression because of my Africanness, I have been both semiparticipant and "observer," amassing evidence of the nature of the European reality through direct confrontation. The advantage of being African is that it has allowed me to penetrate European culture from a "non-European" frame of reference.

Concepts and Terms

Ultimately the liberation of our thought from its colonized condition will require the creation of a new language.[15] Those involved in the development of African-centered theory are steadily moving towards that goal. At this stage we are prepared to create new concepts to facilitate our approach to the subject matter, which fit the methodology demanded by our critique. To understand and to explain the nature of European culture, we need a concept that is both analytical and synthetic. This concept must enable us to explain the European experience as a product of European culture and to explain the culture (thought, behavior, institutions) as a product of its ideological core. Indeed, any culture must be understood in these terms.

Robert Armstrong discusses the idea of a "primal consciousness" as "the code of awareness that instills each person, causing him to inherit and in turn to help constitute his culture, dictating the terms under which the world is to be perceived and experienced. . . ."[16] This consciousness acts as a "generative germ"; it is thus "the causative factor of culture." This "preconceptual," "preaffective," "prespatial," and "pretemporal" factor functions to maintain the integrity and homogeneity of the culture. Armstrong calls it the "mythoform."[17] Armstrong's approach to what he calls "humanistic anthropology" is far in advance of Eurocentric social science, and "mythoform" opens up more liberating possibilities than the traditional European anthropological paradigm. As he presents it, mythoform links the unconscious and the conscious expressions of culture. In terms of consciousness, then, we could say that the cultural process is from mythoform to mythology to ideology. But we have to extend Armstrong's conception. Mythological systems present synthesizing symbols that help to collectivize the consciousness of persons within the culture, at the same time stating preconscious, hidden experience in a more outward modality. Mythology creates ikons out of collective unconscious experience. Ideology is an intensely self-conscious extension of this process, which began with preconscious "mythoform" (if we are to accept Armstrong's term). Ideology involves the more intentional use of the sacred ikons of the culture for political purposes, that is, for the survival, defense, and projection of the culture. Ideology is mythology politically interpreted.

These facts of the presentation of culture can be understood as experiential actions (intellectual, emotional, spiritual) in a consistent process. Each cultural activity leads to or grows out of the other when all the causal circumstances are present. The process moves from the preconscious (mythoform) to the conscious (mythology) to the self-consciousness (ideology). But this is neither a hierarchical nor a strictly unidirectional process. Ideology is not necessarily the "highest" stage, except in a political context. (Unfortunately our reality has become dominated by political definition, and we have no choice but to give more attention to this facet of life.)

The ideological aspect of a culture can have two thrusts: (1) It is in every culture — giving direction to the lives of its members and to their group creations; (2) It gives the culture momentum. But in some cultures the ideology is also outward, seeking to project the culture, assuming a competitive and hostile posture towards other cultures. All cultures do not have an intensely developed ideological statement in this last sense. The lack of an aggressive ideology seems to be related to the lack of the perception of a threatening "outside" world, the inability to perceive other cultural groups as "the enemy." In European culture, the outward ideological thrust, the aggressive stance, is developed more intensely than in any other culture. As we examine the culture, we find that its dominant modes of expression reveal an almost fanatically political or confrontational consciousness in which all cultural phenomena that are "other" or different are considered hostile to the group interest. The heightened political awareness begins in the preconscious mythoform; the bio-cultural origins.

We need yet another concept, one that combines mythoform, mythology, and ideology in one causal atom, so to speak. In the present study I have introduced the concept of *asili*, a Kiswahili word that is used in several related ways to mean "beginning," "origin," "source," "nature" (in the sense of the "nature" of a person or thing), "essence," and "fundamental principle." It can also be taken to mean "seed" (i.e., origin) and "germ" (i.e., the source or initiating principle

of development). All of these meanings fit the idea I am attempting to
convey, and I have taken the liberty of using *asili* as a term and fashioning it into a conceptual tool that the nature of this present study
demands.

   Asili as a conceptual tool for cultural analysis refers to the
explanatory principle of a culture. It is the germinal principle of the
being of a culture, its essence. The idea of a seed, the ubiquitous analogical symbol in African philosophical and cosmological explanations, is ideal for our purposes. The idea is that the *asili* is like a
template that carries within it the pattern or archtypical model for
cultural development; we might say that it is the DNA of culture. At
the same time it embodies the "logic" of the culture. The logic is an
explanation of how it works, as well as, the principle of its development. Our assumption then is that the *asili* generates systematic
development; it is a statement of the logos. The *asili* of a culture is formulative, and it is ideological in that it gives direction to development. It accounts for consistency and pattern in culture, also its
tenacity. The *asili* determines cultural development; then the form
that the culture takes acts to maintain the integrity of the *asili*. It acts
as a screen, incorporating or rejecting innovations, depending on
their compatibility with its own essential nature. It is as though the
asili were a principle of self-realization. It is a compelling force that
will direct the culture as long as it remains intact: i.e., carried in the
"cultural genes." In order for the culture to change (and this includes
the collective thought and behavior of those within it), the *asili* itself
would have to be altered. But this would involve a process of destruction and the birth of a new entity. Cultural *asili*(s) are not made to be
changed.

   Obviously the introduction of this concept implies a theory of
culture. This theoretical framework has certain advantages. First, the
assumption is that every culture has an *asili*, since it is the germinating seed of cultural formation, and that *asili* is determined by the
collective, fundamental nature of its members. Second, the *asili* of a
particular culture can be identified and consequently its inherent
nature delineated. Third, this presents us with a powerful tool of
explanation, since we have a concept that helps to explain the
organicity, structure, and development of any culture: *Asili* accounts
for its driving force, telling us "what makes it tick."

   Asili is a synthesizing concept in that it allows us to explain and
to see the way in which the various aspects of a culture relate and
how they cohere. This critical relationship takes place within the ideological matrix of the culture, the *asili*. Rather than being limited by

a lineal process, we always come back to the center; the *asili* is our reference point; explaining cultural phenomenon within the context of a specific cultural tradition. *Asili* has an ideological focus, since it is concerned with that which compels and demands particular forms and content of expression. *Asili* allows us to recognize culture as a basic organizing mechanism that forges a group of people into an "interest group," an ideological unit. This is the case even when the descendants of an original culture and civilization have become dispersed in other areas of the world; as long as they are connected through a common *asili,* they constitute a diaspora, manifesting the continued life of the civilization. *Asili* allows us to distinguish the peripheral, the anomalous, and the idiosyncratic, and at the same time *asili* allows us to interpret patterns of collective thought and behavior (in terms, of the cultural *asili*). *Asili* is both a concept and a cultural reality. If we assume it (the concept), then it helps to explain a culture in terms of the dominant and fundamental principle of its development (its reality).

Asili, then, will enable us to understand and explain the behavior, thought, and creations of a people in terms of the origin and logic of their culture. In this case, it enables us to understand European thought and behavior as being part of an ideological whole. European religious philosophy and aesthetics become particularized in the context of the European *asili*. It remains now for us to determine the content and nature of this particular *asili*. Once we have done that, European culture becomes explicable as an ideological totality. This does not mean, however, that a definitive *asili* is conveniently visible for us initially; rather its nature emerges from the most forceful characteristics of the culture as they are "felt" through confrontation and observation. It is a question of the perception of emphasis, focus, and priority. These gel into our conception of *asili* as the seed, which is then understood as being the formulative germ. But *asili* is not an idea, like Armstrong's mythoform. It is a force, an energy that asserts itself by giving direction to and placing limits on cultural creativity. *Asili* is the primary determinative factor of cultural development and an essential explanatory principle of cultural theory.

In the present study, I have used two other concepts to complement the *asili* concept. I have borrowed other Kiswahili terms to connote the ideas in question. *Utamaduni* means "civilization" or "culture"; *wazo* means "thought"; and *roho* is "spirit-life." I have created the concept *utamawazo* to convey the idea of "thought as determined by culture." And I have introduced *utamaroho*,[18] slightly more difficult to explain, as the "spirit-life of a culture," also the "collective personality" of its members.

Utamawazo is very close to what is meant by "world-view," but it has more of an ideological emphasis than the way we usually use that term. Gregory Bateson's "eidos" is similar, but again, there are differences. In his book *Naven,* Bateson introduces the concepts "eidos" and "ethos" as tools for investigating what he calls "cultural structures," a collective term for the coherent logical scheme of the culture. This is somewhat like our *asili.* The investigator can determine the "scheme," he says, by "fitting together the various premises of the culture."[19] Eidos is "a standardization of the cognitive aspects of the personality of individuals," and, again, the "cultural expression of cognitive and intellectual aspects of personality." Ethos refers to the emotional aspects of cultural behavior; "the system of emotional attitudes which governs what value a community shall set upon the various satisfactions or dissatisfactions which the contents of life may offer."[20] Bateson offers an explanation of how this process works:

> The culture into which an individual is born stresses certain of his potentialities and suppresses others, and it acts selectively, favoring the individuals who are best endowed with the potentialities preferred in the culture and discriminating against those with alien tendencies. In this way the culture standardizes the organization of the emotions of individuals.[21]

A really valuable aspect of Bateson's approach is the concept of "standardization" as "the process by which the individuals in a community are molded to resemble each other in their behavior."[22] Interestingly enough, he says that the concept of ethos can be "valuably" applied "even to such enormous and confused cultures as those of Western Europe."[23] If we look at the way in which Bateson explains the process through which the ethos is standardized from an African-centered perspective, we can understand that the "discrimination" against those of us with African "tendencies" is, in a sense, a natural result of the standardization process that functions in European culture. The culture "chooses" the personality-styles that "suit" it, just as our personalities have been influenced by the African *asili.*

Utamawazo, thought as determined by culture, is Bateson's eidos in that it focuses on the way in which culture acts to determine collective cognitive style. It refers to the thought patterns of a group of people who are culturally related, in so far as these thought patterns have been determined by the culture. *Utamawazo* is like "world-view" in that it stresses the significance of metaphysical assumptions and presuppositions about the nature of reality, and the way in which the culture presents its members with definitions and conceptions with which to order experience. *Utamawazo*, however, places more emphasis on conscious mental operations and refers to the way in which both speculative and nonspeculative thought is structured by ideology and bio-cultural experience. *Utamawazo* allows us to demonstrate the ideological consistency of the premises of the culture and to identify those premises as they tend to be standardized expressions of a single cultural entity. Julian Jayne uses the expression "collective cognitive imperatives,"[24] and this is very much what we mean by *utamawazo*. It focuses on epistemological definitions in the belief that as culture acts to fix definitions of truth and truth-process, the culture constructs a universe of authorization that rejects and incorporates ideas with reference to a cultural predisposition in intent and style. And, what is more, the *asili* adds dimensions of purpose and direction, that are forceful. *Utamawazo*, then, cannot be understood unless it is placed in the context of *asili*. *Utamawazo* accounts for perspective.

Wade Nobles defines the ethos of a people as "the tone, character, and quality of their life, its moral and aesthetic style and mode. It emerges as a set of guiding principles that define the underlying attitude they have toward themselves and their world."[25] Karenga defines ethos as "the sum of characteristics and achievements of a people which define and distinguish it from others and gives it its collective self-consciousness and collective personality."[26]

Utamaroho, like ethos for Nobles, accounts for "attitude," "character," and "aesthetic" in a collective sense, but it does not include the "guiding principles" that have a determinative function; that would be closer to our *asili*. In terms of Karenga's use of "ethos," *utamaroho* does include the idea of "collective personality," but it is not in any way self-conscious. *Utamawazo* has a self-conscious expression, even though it originates in the meta-conscious *asili*, but *utamaroho* remains on an unconscious level of feeling. *Utamawazo* is cognitive in expression, while *utamaroho* is affective. *Utamaroho* is many things at once. It is a concept that denotes the way in which the *asili* acts to forge a collective response among the members of a culture to life and to the world as they confront it. But this response, in the sense of *utamaroho*, is not thought out or planned. It is more of an instinctive reaction caused by their "spirit." Used this way "spirit" refers to the essential nature of a being. It is the idea that a person, (or as it is in this case), a culture, or group of people possess an immaterial (nonphysical) substance that determines their unique character or "nature." But the physical and nonphysical essence is here linked as it is in the concept of a "gene" which carries "memory."

We speak of *utamaroho* as we might speak of "temperament" and "character" and emotional response. These may sound like the terms of psychology, but *utamaroho* is not "individual"; it is collective. The question of relationship between culture and personality is not a new one. The fairly recent "psycho-historical" studies assume a Freudian posture for the most part, using psychoanalytical theory to analyze cultural developments in the context of historical circumstance.[27] The "culture and personality" school of anthropology is much older, its theorists attempting to discover the ways in which culture influences the personality of its members. They have usually emphasized alternatively world-views or "patterns" (Benedict) and/or "configurations," "themes" (Opler), and language (Mead) as these phenomena act to determine the style of the culture in question. Spengler (1926) talks rather obscurely about the "soul-image" of the Western European as being "Faustian."

Utamaroho does not categorize the ethos(es) of cultures into types, as previous ethnological theories may, but, as inseparable from *asili*; it focuses on the uniqueness of a particular culture with respect to its emotional rather than cognitive patterns. While the character of a culture's *utamawazo* is expressed most obviously in literature, philosophy, academic discourse, and pedagogy, *utamaroho* becomes more visible in behavior and aesthetic expression whether visual, aural, or kinesthetic. At the same time *utamaroho* is the inspirational source from which the *utamawazo* derives its form, for *utamawazo* is not simply "thought," but "forms of thought." The *asili* defines the *utamaroho* (spirit) and gives form to the *utamawazo*. The *asili* is in turn energized by the *utamaroho* (life-force). *Utamawazo* (thought), *utamaroho* (spirit-life), and *asili* (seed), influence, reinforce, and build on each other in a circular process and in a reality that precludes their rigid distinction as "cause" or "effect." This circular process and synthesis is culture itself. It would not be possible for one of these cultural phenomena to contradict another within the same cultural experience. By their very definition they are supportive, compatible, reaffirming, and mutually generative. They are the interlocking pieces of one ideological system.

Utamaroho is a special part of this process, since it is the energy source for all of the culture's collective forms. The *asili* is the seed, the origin, but once in existence, the *utamaroho* is the vitality of the culture. It guarantees its continued life. The *asili* compels the culture to fulfill itself, but it does so through the form of its *utamawazo* and the life of its *utamaroho*. The *utamaroho* of a people is a force made powerful through its collectiveness. The unique character of the culture — its accomplishments, limitations, brilliance, institutions, and posture vis-à-vis other cultures — are spirited by its *utamaroho*. But the *utamaroho* must be continually regenerated by the institutions, creations, and patterns of thought and behavior in which it is reflected. The *utamaroho* (collective personality) of the people will be warlike, if the *asili* demands war for its fulfillment, its self-realization. The *utamaroho* will be spiritualistic or materialistic, creative or controlled, depending on the nature of the *asili* of the culture. The *utamaroho* will be an indication of the kinds of activities that are pleasurable and desirable for the members of the culture. It will determine what they consider to be beautiful and, to some extent, how they move and speak. The axiological aspects of culture will be related to its *utamaroho*, which significantly accounts for motivation in a collective sense. The *asili* is the seed that produces a force. The force is the *utamaroho* of a people. It is the collective personalization of the *asili* and represents the possibility of its continued existence. The *utamawazo* is the thought modality in which the people's mental life must function in order for them to create and to accept a culture that is consistent with the originating *asili*.

Utamaroho and *utamawazo* are extremely forceful phenomena in the European experience. They are brought together in the *asili*, the root principle of the culture. Neither the character of the European *utamaroho* nor the nature of its *utamawazo* are alterable unless the *asili* itself changes. Understood this way, the culture is the unfolding of principles already implied in its originating process. But the *asili* concept does not imply its own cause. Chapter 8 reviews other theories of the origin of European behavior. My theoretical discussion, however, is limited to a delineation of how the culture works, not what caused the *asili* to come into being. These three concepts allow us to approach and understand European culture as a unique product of its fundamental aspects. They become intensely political concepts as European culture is intensely political, and they cohere in the ideological thrust of the culture. Thus, with their introduction, we have properly politicized the idea of culture by giving it an ideological focus.

There are a few more terms, although they do not represent new concepts, that should be discussed for the sake of clarity, so that my use of them will be understood from the onset. It would seem absurdly academic to ask the question, What is "European?" Much of what passes for information in the academies is simply one long panegyric of the European experience. In these instances, there never seems to be a problem identifying what is meant by "European" or "Western." Norman Cantor reveals his Eurocentric perspective as he introduces his three-volume work *Western Civilization: Its Genesis and Destiny,* while using the rhetoric of academic "objectivity":

> Most of us are products of the Western heritage, and our traditional ways of thinking about historical events have been shaped by the forces that molded much of Western culture. In all our modes of thought, we inevitably show the impress of the Western heritage. We imbibe our ethics, religions, philosophy, science, art, and literature from families, schools and a social and intellectual environment which in turn have been formed by centuries of growth and development.[28]

He feels comfortable talking about "the basic foundations of our civilization," and goes on to ask the following question:

> How and why did the West attain intellectual, economic, and military preeminence in the world by 1900? Why does the history of the West, in spite of many retrogressions and failures, appear to be a story of progress toward new forms of thought and art toward the achievement of greater and greater wealth and power?[29]

He continues:

> Some qualities of European thought and social life are unique. Other civilizations have merits that the West lacks, but certain ideas occurred only to Europeans, and certain techniques were discovered and applied only by them.

For Cantor the fundamental problem to be addressed by students and teachers of Western civilization is, "Why and how did the distinctive ideas and institutions of the West develop?"[30] Toynbee answered that only the West responded to challenges, and that the West was marked by its creative vitality. According to Cantor, "Thus far no scholar has offered a full and thoroughly satisfactory explanation of the development of the unique qualities of Western civilization." That is precisely the objective of the present study, though not from the same perspective as Cantor's. As to what he means by the "West," Cantor says specifically, "the countries of Western Europe and the branches of Western civilization found in North and Latin America."[31] And he has made it clear that in his view Europeans are the people responsible for "Western civilization."

This is the kind of definition that is assumed as we make our way though the plethora of undergraduate required courses, texts, television, and even movie spectaculars that deal with "Western civilization" Eurocentrically. But when an African-centered critique of Europe is attempted, suddenly it becomes, if not invisible, an evasive entity of uncertain definition and demarcation. Once when I made a comment about the "European world-view" a colleague asked me to which of the "many" world-views represented in the European tradition, I was referring. Though he had praised the tradition consistently, now he argued that it was not uniform, nor did it represent a single reality. But European nationalism, so strong and so pervasive, is created not by diversity, but by the perception of unity. This is R.H. Tawny's perception:

> The societies composing Europe are in varying degrees the heirs of the first great age of Western civilization; nor was the partnership dissolved when that age was wound up. Greek philosophy and literature, Roman law; the long adventure of Christian missionaries; the medieval church; feudalism; the Renaissance, the Reformation and Counter Reformation; the Revolution — all these and much else have reacted to them. Their religion, their literature and art, their science, their economic systems are a cosmopolitan creation, to which all have contributed and all are in debt. Such things, it is true, do not in themselves create unity, but create the conditions of it. They cause Europe, amid all its feverish jealousies and terrors, to be a single civilization, as a contentious family is still a family, and a bad state remains a state. They make its culture one, its crimes domestic tragedies, its wars civil wars.[32]

This is the cultural entity under examination in the present study.

I have used the term "European" most consistently in this study, but I consider it to be interchangeable with "Western," "Western European," and "European American." Oswald Spengler talks about "Western-European-American," which he considers to be the only culture in the phase of "fulfillment."[33] What is "European," like other cultural phenomena, is in part an intuited whole and therefore does not lend itself to simplistic "scientifically" rigorous definition. Yet the term is understood and used by academicians, theorists, and lay people alike. The definition of any particular culture is not a lineal process, but a necessarily circular one. We begin with the assumption of the cultural phenomenon of "Europeanness" that lends itself to description and explanation, because we have already perceived and experienced (felt) it to be such. In the process of describing what we perceive, we hope to give it the definition it already inherently pos-

sesses. But this does not lead to any kind of lineal or temporal priority, nor is it "seen" in the same way that a material object is "seen."
What is European will forever be, in part, a product of how it is experienced. To abstract these reactions from its definition would not
only be impossible, but would leave very little of value or relevance.

What is European is not simply a group of characteristics, and
to attempt to enumerate such characteristics would not only mis-
represent my intention, but would leave this study open to obvious
criticism. Any one or a number of the generalized characteristics that
will be discussed as European can be found to some extent in other
cultures. And a discussion of the etiology of "Europeanness" using
such an approach would be further complicated by the fact that it has
been one of the more significant manifestations of European chauvinism to claim cultural creations that can be shown to be of non-
European origin. The contradiction in this attempt is obvious, since
the self-conscious identification of the cultural entity that would be
referred to as "Western" occurred chronologically much later than
many of the institutional developments with which Europeans choose
to identify. As cultural traditions go, the "West" is, after all, quite
young and biologically or racially Europeans are, of course, the "new
boys on the block." Individual characteristics do not identify them
as being "European": rather it is the way in which they are combined,
and the fact that they are reinforced throughout culture, that fuses
them into an ideological force. It is only in the context of European
culture that the identified themes take on ideological significance. It
was this realization that led me to the concept of *asili*, as the organizing and meaningful center of culture.

With this understanding and objective in mind, we need not
become involved in the argument as to what cultural institutions are
"European inventions," and "how much" or "how little" a particular
culture has "contributed to the progress of civilization." These are
merely the polemics of European chauvinism, and they become significant only as ethnographic data in this study. For part of the definition of what is European is to be found in those things with which
those who call themselves Western or European have traditionally
chosen to identify, and, similarly, the way in which they view themselves in relation to other peoples. What is presented herein is a
unique configuration of characteristics that are combined in such a
way that the emphasis, priorities, and manifested behavioral tendencies form an experienced cultural/historical reality that has traditionally been referred to as "Western European," "Western," or, as
we shall refer to it, "European."

A product of modern Europe civilization, studying any problem of Universal History, is bound to ask himself to what combination of circumstances the fact should be attributed that in Western Civilization, and in Western Civilization only, cultural phenomena have appeared which (as we like to think) lie in a line of development having *Universal* significance and value.[34] [his itallics]

Max Weber has asked the "right" question for Eurocentric reasons and therefore cannot offer an answer that is useful to us. The key to the African-centered answer lies in his parenthetical statement — "as we like to think." That is the only element that is universal about "Western civilization." Its *utamaroho* ("we like") and its *utamawazo* ("to think") combine in a manner dictated by an *asili* that causes the culture to consistently project itself in universalistic terms. This tendency is specifically discussed in Chap. 10, but it is a recurring theme throughout the book.

Is European synonymous with "modern?" Is it, after all, a stage in universal cultural development? The answer depends on one's perspective. The question is, therefore, moot. Part of the difficulty is with the definition of terms. The significant point from an African-centered perspective concerns what happens if we say that European culture merely represents what will be the eventual form of all cultures. The answer is that there is no possibility for a viable critique of what Europeans have created, because there is no other ("non-European") perspective. Other ideologies become impotent, because to identify "Europeanness" as an inevitable stage in "non-European" development is to say that they ("non-Europeans") do not exist — certainly not as directives, as influences, or as agents of change.

Most of the potentially valuable critiques of European culture — of which there are a precious few — have suffered from a common malady. Since they syntactically make European culture into a representation of a universal stage in human development, they are left with no place to look for solutions or creative alternatives. "Western" problems become the problems of "modern man" in these critiques. Thereby they are superficially universalized, and Africans must become "modern" before they can even deal with them. Europeans are, in this view, the only ones with the authority to criticize their culture, and the criticisms they make and the solutions they find are said to have universal significance. European imperialism, in this way, is not seen as the product of the behavioral patterns of a particular cultural group nor of certain kinds of people, but rather of the "natural" tendencies of all people at a particular period of cultural development. The argument continues: "Every culture becomes European as it becomes more modern," so there is really only one valid culture, and the only ideological alternative is the "more-than-modern" one.

To be useful, "modernity" has to be redefined, so that, for instance, we can speak of modern African dress or modern African art using an African-centered frame of reference. Presently, the concept of modernity is much too Eurocentric to be either practical or of theoretical value in a critique of European culture. We must begin with the assumption that Europeanness is not inevitable. And since we wish to describe "a certain mode of cultural being as opposed to "a certain level of history,"[35] European development is a product of European ideology. Consequently, it represents a particular view and approach to the world — as partial as any other. And, as any other ideological construct, it can theoretically, therefore, be rejected, critiqued, or replaced. This is not to say that the rejection of Europeanness is an easy task, or that Europe does not give the illusion of being ubiquitous. But the question of the universal validity of European forms must not be confused with the successful expansionism of European culture. And the resistance to Europe, as it is now defined, can only be achieved through a commitment to that resistance. Those who begin with the assumption that they are simply dealing with the character of "modernity" are doomed from the start, for they have already accepted the terms of European ideology.

Some problems in terminology arise in referring to other cultures. The term "non-European" is used reluctantly because of its usual negative connotations, and because it implies a Eurocentric frame of reference. But in this case it is appropriate since the focus of the study is Europe exclusively: So that what is "other" is indeed a negation of what is "European" (i.e., "non-European"). This fact not withstanding, I have felt more comfortable using other terms, and they require some explanation. The term "First World" is used to refer to the descendants of the oldest civilizations known to us: Africa and its Diaspora. "Primary cultures" is also used in this way. Europeans in this sense represent a secondary, derived, and younger people. I have sometimes borrowed Chinweizu's term from the title of his book, *The West and the Rest of Us* (1978) and refer to those of us who are not European as "the rest of us." And I have referred to these "other" peoples and cultures as "majority," since Europeans and the culture they have created represent a small "minority" when viewed in the world context.

"Nationalism" as a cultural phenomenon is a very significant aspect of European culture and therefore of this study. Nationalism in this sense is not limited by the concept of "nation-state," rather it refers to the commitment on the part of the members of a culture to its political defense, its survival, and its perpetuation. In the case of Europe it also involves a commitment to its supremacy, to its expansion, and to the destruction of other cultures. European nationalism is therefore dangerous to the rest of the world. But it is very important to understand that this does not mean that nationalism is a negative phenomenon universally. It is indeed "natural" to be centered in one's culture and to seek to preserve it. That is part of the essence of culture. But the content of European nationalism becomes problematical: (1) because it implies imperialistic aggression; and (2) because it is usually not recognized as the expression of group interest, thereby making it difficult for other groups to defend themselves against its effects. An important objective of this work, therefore, is to make European nationalism recognizable as such.

Perspectives and Objectives

This study was not approached objectively. It is not possible to be objective towards Europe: Certainly the victims of its cultural, political, and economic imperialism are not objective, if they are sane. And Europeans cannot be "objective" about their own cultural history. The question, then, becomes: What could objectivity possibly mean in terms of human mental attitudes? The implications of the concept of objectivity are discussed critically in this study and elsewhere.[36] It is a concept that acts to mystify Europe's victims: one of the most effective tools of European ideology.

The claim to an absolute ultimate truth is a psychological necessity for the European mentality. And since we have accepted it, it is an edict that has constrained most of us who have been trained in European academies. But African-centeredness breaks that hold by recognizing the truth as a process in which we immerse ourselves because of a commitment, not to some universal abstraction, but to a certain quality of life. From an African-centered perspective, we understand truth to be inseparable from the search for meaning and purpose — the unique concern of human consciousness. As African scholars, it is our responsibility to create systematic theoretical formulations which will reveal the truths that enable us to liberate and utilize the energies of our people. In this view, the self-determinist, the revolutionary, and the scholar are one, having the same objective, involved in the same truth-process. The claim that we make is not to a spurious "objectivity," but to honesty. I, therefore, have made no attempt to camouflage either my relationship to Europe or my goal in undertaking this study.

As Wade Nobles says, the types of questions we ask are influenced by the culture to which we belong.[37] Theory is born out of commitment and intention. Every theorist puts part of herself (or himself) into the theoretical formulations and conclusions that she (or he) produces. But that does not make them any less valid. When dealing with the social sciences, theories gain validity when viewed in relationship to one's frame of reference, one's center. That center is culturally meaningful only when it issues from a collective consciousness. The view of Europe presented herein will be convincing only to the extent that one is freed of European assumptions and Eurocentric ideological commitments. But that is not because of any weakness in the arguments or evidence presented. The record speaks for itself. Ultimately validity is judged in terms of interest. This theory of European culture is valid to the extent that it helps to liberate us from the stranglehold of European control.

This study represents a view of European thought and behavior that grows out of protracted personal confrontation with European culture, out of an awareness politicized by means of African consciousness, and made intellectually positive through a grounding in African-centeredness. "Afrocentricity" is a way of viewing reality that analyzes phenomena using the interest of African people as a reference point, as stated by Asante[38]. African-centeredness provides the theoretical framework within which the dominant modes of European expression have been set for analysis here-in. This process establishes a system for critical evaluation. Its standards are severe. Its questions uncompromising.

The most insidious expression of European nationalism is manifested in the process of codification through which behavior and thought patterns have been standardized by validating theoretical formulations provided by European academia. We need only to decode its workings in order to understand the mechanisms of supremacy and break its power. The objective of this study is to place the European experience under scrutiny in order to reveal its nature. We turn the tables by transforming "subject" into "object," and in the process we are ourselves transformed into victors rather than victims. We emerge from the yoke of European conceptual modalities that have prevented us from the realization of the "collective conscious will" of our people.[39] Our objectives are, specifically:

1. to demonstrate the relationship between European thought, the nature of European institutions, European anti-Africanism, and European imperialism;
2. to remove the cloak of universalism from European choice,

    value, particularism, European interest and Eurocentricism;

3. to examine and expose expressions of European nationalism;
4. to understand the *asili*, or fundamental germinating principle of European cultural development; and thus
5. to provide a tool for the explanation of European thought and behavior as part of a consistently patterned ideological construct.

    This is achieved through an ideological focus that recognizes Europe as the powerful monolith that it is. The compelling question this study asks and answers is: What accounts for European power and Europe's successful domination of the world? The objective of this book is our liberation from that control, so that we can indeed reclaim ourselves and what belongs to us, and in the process, transform the universe, thereby reestablishing primary equilibrium. The intent is to speak with the voice of African nationhood and to be inspired by the collective vision of our people and our ancestors.

PART ONE

THOUGHT AND ICONOGRAPHY

. . . unconnected consciousness is destructions
keenest tool against the soul.
—Ayi Kwei Armah

Chapter I
Utamawazo:

The Cultural Structuring of Thought

Archaic European Epistemology:
Substitution of Object for Symbol

The African world-view, and the world-views of other people who are not of European origin, all appear to have certain themes in common. The universe to which they relate is sacred in origin, is organic, and is a true "cosmos." Human beings are part of the cosmos, and, as such, relate intimately with other cosmic beings. Knowledge of the universe comes through relationship with it and through perception of spirit in matter. The universe is one; spheres are joined because of a single unifying force that pervades all being. Meaningful reality issues from this force. These world-views are "reasonable" but not rationalistic: complex yet lived. They tend to be expressed through a logic of metaphor and complex symbolism.

Rob the universe of its richness, deny the significance of the symbolic, simplify phenomena until it becomes mere object, and you have a knowable quantity. Here begins and ends the European epistemological mode. What happened within embryonic Europe that was to eventually generate such a radically different world-view? What part did Platonic thought play in this process? Whether or not all of Western philosophy is "but a footnote to Plato," certainly his influence on the European style of speculative thought and ultimately on the *utamawazo*—the general premises and assumptions of the culture—has been formulative and seminal. Any discussion of the nature and origin of European epistemology must focus on, if not begin, with Plato. This is not to say that he was not influenced by the pre-Socratic African philosophies that preceeded him.[1] But what Plato seems to have done is to have laid a rigorously constructed foundation for the repudiation of the symbolic sense—the denial of cosmic, intuitive knowledge. It is this process that we need to trace, this development in formative European thought which was eventually to have had such a devastating effect on the nontechnical aspects of the culture. It led to the materialization of the universe as conceived by the European mind—a materialization that complemented and supported the intense psycho-cultural need for control of the self and others.

Contrary to our image of the philosopher as being otherworldly and remote, even irrelevant (Aristophanes, *The Clouds*), Plato appears to have been very much aware of himself as a social and ideological architect. His success was eventually overwhelming. The power of his ideas is evidenced by the way in which they have contributed to the growth and persistence of a new order. This is precisely the power of the Euro-Caucasian order: its ability to sustain and perpetuate itself. Plato's innovations were ultimately incorporated into the culture because they were demanded by the *asili*.

The dialogue the *Republic* is Plato's ideological justification of the State he wishes to bring into being. What we witness in the dialogue can be viewed epistemologically as the creation of the object. In previous and disparate world-views, we see a knowing subject intimately involved in the surrounding universe. The acquisition of knowledge involving immersion in this universe until, through sympathetic participation, meaning is revealed, expressed, and understood via complex and multidimensional symbols. But in the "new" epistemology we exchange symbols for "objects." The creation of the object requires a transformation of the universe, no longer experienced but rather, "objectified." This transformation is achieved through a changed relationship of the knower to the known. In the *Republic,* Plato performs this feat: a psycho-intellectual maneuver by which the subject is able to separate her/himself from the known. This separation is at once the key that opens the way to "knowledge" as conceived by the European and the key that locks the door to the possibilities of the apprehension of a spiritual universe.

Two things occur, one effecting the other. First, the psyche undergoes a transformation: Slowly the "self" is perceived differently from before; then, the universe to which that self relates is perceived differently, because the nature of the relationship is changed. The self is no longer a cosmic being, instead it becomes "the thinking subject."

The Greek word *psyche* indicates an understanding of an autonomous self distinct from everything surrounding that self. The primary function of this self becomes the "knowing" and "thinking" of scientific activity, which is no longer connected to "intuiting." According to the Platonic view the highest endeavor is philosophy, and therefore the most valuable person is the philosopher, the lover/seeker of "truth," the one who "thinks" best. Other functions and human activities are devalued. This new self becomes fiercely isolated from its environment. Why autonomous, distinct, and isolated? Because this "thinking being," if it is to be capable of scientific cognition, must be, most of all, *independent.*

In Eric Havelock's analysis (developed obviously from within the confines of the European world-view) the dominant mode in pre-Platonic Greece was the poetic, exemplified by the epic of which Homer's writing is so representative. The success and appeal of Homer's epics depended on the identification of the audience with the characters and plot. His works were memorized and recited, and they rested on the strength of oral expression. When successfully dramatized they evoked emotional response from an audience that felt itself to be personally involved with the subject matter. This, according to Havelock, was an "unsophisticated," nontechnological mode that would prevent the development of a "reflective, critical" psyche. "The doctrine of the autonomous psyche is the counterpart of the rejection of the oral culture." [2] In his view Plato was the visionary, mainly responsible for the transition from the Homeric, oral mode to the literate, critical mode. The "old" poetic represented the "habit of self-identification with the oral traditions." It represented emotional interrelationship. In other words the success of the poetic mode rests with the ability to forge the world into a phenomenal universe, an experienced reality. Within this context the self is dependent on its experiences. The crux of the matter for Havelock and Plato is that this dependence lodges us hopelessly in the concrete, unable to break loose from each instance reaching beyond to an abstract statement. Havelock says that Plato was arguing for "the invention of an abstract language of descriptive science to replace a concrete language of oral memory."[3]

According to the new epistemology, in order to be capable of critical thought, we must be independent from that which we wish to know: uninvolved, detached, remote. Clearly, what this allows for is *control.* First, we achieve control of the self, the self no longer able to be manipulated by its context. In fact, it is a self without context (which in African terms makes it a self without meaning, a "nonself").

This idea of control is facilitated by first separating the human being into distinct compartments ("principles"). Plato distinguishes the compartments of "reason" and "appetite" or "emotion." Reason is a higher principle or function of woman/man, while appetite is "more base." They are in opposition to one another and help to constitute, what has become one of the most problematical dichotomies in European thought and behavior. This opposition results in the splitting of the human being. No longer whole, we later become Descartes' "mind vs. body." The superiority of the intellect over the emotional self is established as spirit is separated from matter. Even the term "spirit" takes on a cerebral, intellectualist interpretation in the Western tradition (Hegel).[4]

As *we* understand it, Plato's "reason" is the denial of spirit. Reason functions to control the more "base appetites" and "instincts." The European view of the human begins to take shape here. It is a view that was to grow more dominant through centuries of European development and that was to become more and more oppressive in contemporary Western European society, where there is no alternative view offered. For Plato, self-mastery, like justice in the State, is achieved when reason controls:

> . . . in the human soul there is a better and also a worse principle; and when the better has the worse under control, then a man is said to be master of himself; and this is a term of praise; but when owing to evil education or association, the better principle, which is also the smaller, is overwhelmed by the greater mass of the worse—in this case he is blamed and is called the slave of self and unprincipled . . . look at our newly created State, and there you will find one of these two conditions realized; for the words "temperance" and "self-mastery" truly express the rule of the better over the worse . . . the manifold and complex pleasures and desires and pains are generally found in children and women and servants, and in the freemen so called who are the lowest and more numerous class . . . . Whereas the simple and moderate desires which follow reason, and are under the guidance of mind and true opinion, are to be found only in a few and those the best born and best educated . . . . These two . . . have a place in our State; and the meaner desires of the many are held down by the virtuous desires and wisdom of the few.[5]

Dichotomization and The Notion Of Harmony

The Platonic view sacrifices the wholeness of personhood in order to set the stage on which the epistemological foundations of the European view will be played out. Cognitive styles were being molded or at least anticipated. This codification suited an *utamawazo* that was the realization of the cultural *asili*. Plato had layed an elaborate trap. Once the "person" was artificially split into conflicting faculties or tendencies, it made sense to think in terms of one faculty "winning" or controlling the other(s). And here begins a pattern that runs with frighteningly predictable consistency through European thought, continually gathering momentum for ages to come. The mind is trained from birth to think in terms of dichotomies or "splits."[6] The splits become irreconcilable, antagonistic opposites. Holistic conceptions become almost impossible given this mindset. First the dichotomy is presented, then the process of valuation occurs in which one term is valued and the other is devalued. One is considered "good," positive, superior; the other is considered "bad," negative, inferior. And, unlike the Eastern (Zen) conception of the Yin and the Yang or the African principle of "twinness" (Carruthers refers to this as "appositional complementarity"[7]) these contrasting terms are not conceived as complementary and necessary parts of a whole. They are, instead, conflicting and "threatening" to one another.

The process of dichotimization in the European *utamawazo* is of great significance, for it is this dichotomized perception of reality on which the controlling presence (imperialistic behavior) depends. The *utamaroho,* which needs to control, is dependent on the antagonistic oppositions presented by the cognitive style (*utamawazo*) of the cultural myth (mythoform). Realities are split, then evaluated, so that one part is "better," which mandates its controlling function. This, we will see, is a pattern throughout Platonic thought. Moreover, it is a pattern that develops consistently as a continuing characteristic of the European *utamawazo* grounded in the nature of the originating *asili*. Robert Armstrong says it this way,

> Dualities abound, constituting our civilization. Our religion is premised upon good and evil, and indeed could not exist were it not for the presence of evil which endows it with meaning and efficacy. We analyze the unitive work of art into form and content; and we construct a logic based upon right and wrong. Our languages are of subject and object . . . Our science is one of the probable versus the improbable, the workable as opposed to the unworkable, matter and anti-matter... all revealing more of the nature of the scientist's mind than of the actual nature of the physical universe.[8]

He continues,

> We see the world as delicately constituted of both terms in an infinite system of contrasting pairs, and bound together by the tension that exists between them. To be sure one term in each case is, by

definition, of greater value than its opposite . . .

In large measure then, the myth of the consciousness of western Europe is the myth of bi-polar oppositions.[9]

Armstrong foreshadows a basic premise of this study as he relates this polarizing tendency to the structure of the Euro-American state, its religious ideas, and its international posture.

It is not inevitable that there should inexorably be a division of the world into friend and foe with the result that the history of foreign policy in recent years at least is more accurately to be characterized in terms of our determination to identify and to perpetuate enemies than to create friends. [10]

We have already completed the circle, for it is possible to trace this tendency of conceptualization and behavior from classical Greece. The theme is confrontation. The mode is control. Page duBois refers to this as the "polarizing vision" based on "confrontation between opposites," which she identifies as being adumbrated in the art and architectural style of the "metopes" of Athens. In duBois' analysis, Greek thought about "difference" (barbarian/Greek; female/male) was analogical and became hierarchical as a response to political crisis following the Peloponnesian War.[11]

The thrust of her study (*Centaurs and Amazons*) is significant in this discussion for two reasons: (1) because of its recognition of the ideological significance of the style of Greek speculative thought and (2) because it affirms our recognition of those cognitive characteristics that distinguish the developing European *utamawazo* from previously established traditions.

When is it, in Greek thought, that "appositional" relationships become "opposites?" When does it become necessary to perceive pairs as being in polar opposition and exclusive, rather than as complementary and diunital?[12] This may be the point of origin of the European consciousness. I suspect that the need occurs at a much earlier point in the archaic "European" experience. Classical Greece was merely an important phase of standardization. It had inherited a particular *asili,* already carrying the cultural genes.

DuBois believes that the shift from polarity to hierarchy corresponded to "the shift from the democratic city of the fifth century to a period in the fourth century of questioning the *polis* as a form."[13] The origins of the initial splitting tendency itself are important in this study, however, because it may be neither "natural" nor universal to perceive the universe in terms of "self" as opposed to "other,"[14] and the ideological significance of that distinction and the implied relationship between those two beings is the point at issue.

As duBois points out, the "Greek male human" defined himself very much in terms of opposition to what he was "not"—"barbarian female animal." This brings us closer to the origin of a nascent "European" consciousness. She asserts that, "The Greek male struggled against imaginary barbarism, bestiality and effeminization."[15] In her view the opposition between self and other did not always imply superior/inferior relationship. But certainly the Greek/male/human thought it was better to be *that* (superior, i.e., Greek/male/human). And this perceived separation gave Plato, then Aristotle, the polarizing mechanism with which to work. It was already present in the Greek consciousness, a consciousness resting on an *utamaroho* that had a predilection for postures of superiority and dominance. Polarity was necessary for the hierarchy that followed. DuBois refers to the hierarchical structures as a "new ordering" based on a "new logic," one that establishes the "Great Chain of Being" based on "relationships of superiority and subordination."[15] But Platonic conceptions represent a formalized ideological statement of hierarchical thought, the terms of which were already present in the Greek mind. We agree on the significance of these formulations, however. "Hierarchical ideas of difference formulated by Plato and Aristotle continue to define relations of dominance and submission in Western culture and in philosophical discourse today."[16]

This brings us to yet another related and salient feature of the European *utamawazo*. It does not generate a genuine conception of harmony. An authentic idea of harmony cannot be explained or understood in this world-view. "Harmony" is mistakenly projected as rational order, an order based on the mechanism of control. What Plato recognizes as "harmony" is achieved when the "positive" term of the dichotomy controls (or destroys) the "negative" term/phenomenon/entity: when reason controls emotion, both in the person and in the state. (In the African and Eastern conceptions, harmony is achieved through the balance of complementary forces, and it is indeed impossible to have a functioning whole *without* harmonious interraction and the existence of balancing pairs.)

A theory of the universe, a theory of the state, and a theory of human nature are implied in Platonic epistemology.[17] Justice, or the Good, is achieved when the "best" controls the "worst." The universe is ordered through such control. In the State, the "highest" control the "lowest." The person is constantly at war within himself and is not properly human until his reason controls his emotion, i.e., men were to control women. The political implications of this consistent and unified theory are not difficult to extrapolate. Plato has already described what for Europe becomes the "Ideal State," one in which the human being who has gained control of himself in turn controls those who haven't (women, of course, were perceived as not having the necessary control). It would follow that the universe is then put in order by the nation of people who are "higher" (controlled by reason). It is also significant that Plato indicates that the "higher" tendencies will always be "less" in number and the "lower" of greater mass. This rationalizes an ideology of control by the few within the State and world dominance by a small racial minority.[18] If indeed this splitting of the person is artificial, inaccurate, and undesirable—if indeed emotion is an inseparable part of the intellect and of human consciousness—then this new epistemology ("mental habit") can be interpreted as a justification of what was to be manifested as European racism, nationalism, and imperialism. The group that has the power to enforce its definition of "reason" so that it becomes the most "reasonable," consequently has a mandate to control those whose reasoning abilities are judged to be less (and so there is a need to "measure" intellectual ability: enter I.Q. mythology).

On the level of epistemology we have seen that this splitting of the human being facilitates the achievement of that supreme mental state (of being) that in European culture has come to be identified with the ability to *think,* at least to think rationally. Unless the intellect is separated from the emotions, it is not possible to talk about them distinctly, to concentrate on gaining knowledge by controlling or eliminating the emotional relationship to a given situation, thing, or person.

Reification Of The Object:
Devaluation Of The Senses

In establishing this new epistemological mode, Plato used his imagination: He *created* a reality. Hypothesis became theory. He demonstrated brilliance, perception, and vision. He must have known what he wanted the future to look like, taking into consideration the political and ideological needs of his society. But when theory that originates in imagination becomes more than a useful epistemological tool for specific tasks associated with scientific investigation, it can become dangerous, because it can indeed obfuscate the reality it is attempting to clarify and distort the cognition it is attempting to perfect. Plato's theory of knowledge became eventually reified into an ideological statement with political implications. His creation was to become a determinant and support—a foundation and an inspiration—for the dominance, intensification, and valorization of one tendency in European behavior to the detriment of other inclinations. The need to control and to have power over others ascended to a position of priority. It became an obsession, always struggling to negate whatever humanism existed in the culture, because of the *asili*.

The universe presents itself naturally as cosmos, as "subject" to which we are linked as "subjects"; ancient African cultures viewed the world so, and the early Greeks inherited this view. According to Havelock, Homer's success rested on the identification of the reader or listener with the subject matter of his epic.[19] The human being of these ancient civilizations was a cosmic being (and remains so for that matter in the contemporary African world-view). Plato wanted to change all that. He was proposing a "revolution" in thought. This "revolution" was necessary in order to satisfy the European *utamaroho*. Perhaps he should have said, Let us *pretend* that the universe is not subject, but object; that we are not a part of it; but separated from it; and let us do this solely for the purpose of experimentation, in order to see what implications such a conception might have. But he didn't say let's pretend. Rather, he said authoritatively that in order to "know" we must be dealing with "objects." The way that we create "objects" is by totally detaching ourselves from what it is we wish to know. By eliminating or gaining control of our emotions we can become aware of ourselves as thinking subjects, distinct from the contemplated object. Through this separation, this remoteness, this denial of cosmic relationship, we achieve "objectification." *That* is a necessary achievement if we are to be capable of scientific cognition. To think properly about an object, to gain knowledge of (mastery over) an object, *we must control it*. We can only do this if we are emotionally detached from it. And we gain this emotional distance from the "object" by first and foremost gaining control over ourselves; that is, by placing our reason (intellect) in control of our emotions (feelings).

Vernon Dixon discusses a "descendant" epistemological view easily recognizable as Platonic in definition.

In the Euro-American world view, there is a separation between the the self and the nonself (phenomenal world). Through this process of separation the phenomenal world becomes an Object, an "it." By Object, I mean the totality of phenomena conceived as constituting the nonself, that is, all the phenomena that are the antithesis of subject, ego, or self-consciousness. The phenomenal world becomes an entity considered as totally independent of the self rather than as affected by one's feelings or reflections. Reality becomes that which is set before the mind to be apprehended, whether it be things external in space or conceptions formed by the mind itself.[20]

The key is "control." Clearly, reason is positive, valued, "higher"; emotions are negative, devalued, "more base"—because they have a tendency to control us. Such control is an indication of powerlessness. To understand the self as a cosmic being is to be powerless. It is politically unwise and undesirable; it is morally reprehensible. Better people are "more reasonable," less emotional. This is what Plato implied. This is the essence of his "authoritative utterance." And what he said was prophetic, nay prescriptive, for those who were "emotional" (spiritual) indeed were to be rendered powerless.

Here then is the concept of an "object," fiercely isolated from time, place and circumstance, and translated linguistically into an abstraction and then put forward as the goal of a prolonged intellectual investigation.[21]

The above is Eric Havelock's description of the process of objectification. In his view this separation of the self from the remembered word introduced a new cognitive mode and allowed the Greeks to "gain control" over the object and thereby, so we are told, eventually to "escape from the cave." Or at least their leaders (the philosophers) escaped and the descendants of the philosopher kings (Europeans). It is very important that we place this process in proper historical context. The "European" had not yet "developed," but Plato had helped to construct a yardstick by which the "true European" would be measured. The vicious and violent internecine war against the "barbaric" tendencies in archaic Europe would go on into the eleventh century (and of course beyond, on a lesser scale, but none the less vigilant). This was a war to ensure a particular world-view, which, as we shall see, was complemented by the institutionalized manifestation of religion identified with European culture.

It is a testament to Plato's success that Havelock speaks for the contemporary European academician in his unquestioning praise of Plato's work. Approximately 2500 years after his concepts were introduced as "new" to the Greeks and as "radical" and "revolutionary," they are still part of the "taken-for-granted," underlying, presuppositional foundation of European scholarly thought and of the cognitive aspects *(utamawazo)* of the culture as a whole. While Plato had to argue for the validity of these concepts, Havelock can uncritically extol their virtues and therefore Plato's contribution to European thought. Havelock is convinced of the correctness and appropriateness of Platonic epistemology just as he is convinced of the superiority of the "Platonic Man" in relation to the "Pre-Platonic" or "Homeric Man." We will see that Havelock is talking about a supposed superiority, a mental, even moral superiority. This is *assumed* just as the superiority of European civilization is assumed because of the overwhelming success of European scientific-technological pursuits.

For Havelock, as well as for Plato, the cave or the world of the senses is presented as a world of illusion. But this implies that Plato's theory of ideas and objectification allows one to escape to reality. Yet neither raises the question of the illusion of "objectivity," the illusion of control. This *illusion* has indeed facilitated the "real" growth of the scientific-technological order and the ascendance of the European world, but that should not allow us to mistake it for the only "reality." In one sense the history of European thought has been based on the use of metaphor as literal description. It is as though with Plato, the limitations of the written "word" were forgotten; the complexity of the symbolic mode was abandoned for the simplicity of unidimensionality. The symbol became the object. And this manipulation paid off. It has enhanced the ability to have power over others.[22]

Superiority of the Platonic epistemology is aided by dichotomies that become grounds for invidious comparisons, further justification for control mechanisms. The contrast of "knowledge" and "opinion" becomes another such dichotomy for Plato. Once it is established as a statement of value it is used by Europeans to devalue alternative epistemologies, modes of cognition, world-views, therefore cultures, and even "religions," as we shall discuss in subsequent chapters.

Havelock accuses the Homeric poets of only being able to deal with "opinion." The term "accusation" seems appropriate because it is deemed "lowly" and "unfit," even immoral for rational man to function in this way. The Homeric poets were, according to Havelock, writing prior to the great Platonic Revolution that taught people (only the superior ones) how to think. In the Platonic state of mind one is equipped to deal with "knowledge." Why? Because the mind in this state has separated itself from "the object." Much of Plato's argument centers on this object. It is in one sense the nature of the object that determines the validity and truth of statements made about it. There are "proper" objects of knowledge, and then there are those that are "improper" or inadequate.

A related dichotomy on which Plato's argument depends is that between "perception" and "knowledge," where perception fairs about as well as mere opinion. In the *Theatetus* Socrates argues that perception is of the body in which exist the senses. The senses are like "instruments"; the sense organs must necessarily "specialize," as it were. Socrates says that one cannot "hear" through the eyes, nor "see" through the ears, and so on. He makes much of the fact that the appropriate preposition is "through" and not "with" when we are dealing with the "body" and with perception.[23] What Socrates gets Theatetus to agree to is that things that the body perceives are "separate," and that it is only the "mind" that can relate these things, can compare them, can say whether they exist or don't exist. According to Socrates we perceive "through" the senses (body), while we reflect or know "with" the mind. Theatetus, like Protagorus and other Sophists, had argued that perception *was* knowledge. Socrates "proves" that it is the mind that "unites" our ideas about the objects we sense. We "think" with our minds.

Again the genius of Plato: Another characteristic dichotomy—an architectonic one, culminating in the infamous Cogito, ergo sum of Descartes about twelve centuries later—is born as "mind" is separated from "body." The "splits" that we have mentioned are worked out in such a way that they deny and prevent interrelationship. They do this on a cognitive level, a semantic level, and through the "logic" on which they are based. The splits then move to the level of culture, world-view, and belief. They begin to effect experience, because although they may not be accurate, they limit people's ability to experience the universe as an integrated whole. It is the essence of "traditional" medicine that the person be considered as a whole being. Richard King argues that in the African conception, not merely the "brain," but the entire body is the human "computer." In that sense, we also "think" with our sense organs, which perhaps helps to explain "genius" on the basketball court.[24]

Evidently, Plato did not anticipate problems resulting from such artificial separations as the mind/body dichotomy. His concern was with providing an edifice of "logic" that could be used at once as an unquestioned foundation of "truth" and to discredit other views. This was necessary because the other views were seen as being "competitive," since they could lead to divergent forms of social organization. Plato was concerned solely with the intellectual habits and behavior of those who would be participating in the new society. He does not seem to have been concerned with the quality of their lives. There had to be a standard for the definition of truth. The Sophists were a tremendous threat with their arguments that opened the way to a form of relativity. Plato had to establish dogma. The dogma that he argued for not only discredited other epistemologies, it established a hierarchy in which certain kinds of people (the overwhelming majority) were inferior. His arguments were ultimately effective. They succeeded in influencing centuries of subsequent European development, as other formidable European minds joined his ranks. As such, his ideas helped to reveal the *asili* of European culture.

Page duBois' perspective renders a very different view of Plato's revolutionary alteration of the Greek literary mode from poetic analogy to the more precise language of discourse, different from that of Havelock. This change served the purpose of preparing minds to accept a new state order; a radically altered internal structure. duBois says,

> Once Plato's project of *diaeresis,* of division and categorization, was explicitly acknowledged, the focus of discourse shifted away from reasoning through analogy, from the Greek/barbarian distinction, to internal divisions, towards hierarchization which rationalized differences inside the troubled city. Plato denied the utility of the Greek/barbarian polarity, turned his attention to male/female difference, but concentrated finally on reasoning based on subordination and dominance.[25]

It is as Havelock suggests, a new mode for the development of a new consciousness. But while for Havelock this represented an unquestioned "good" and the creation of the "critical" mind, for duBois the move to discourse from the poetry and more poetic prose of the fifth century was made necessary by the elaborated, detailed *logos,* language appropriate for articulating new relationships. She says of the Platonic view,

> Every logos—that is, every argument, every rationalization, every discourse—should be subject to the same type of subordination and hierarchy, as well as organic connection, as the body described at its moment of creation in the *Timaeus.*[26]

In other words, the structure of Platonic discourse itself forced those who used it to accept a particular concept of social order. Brilliant! In the very syntax of our speech as we learn the English language, the justification of our "inferiority" is embedded, and, what is more, *we accept that fact as we "master" the language.* (And it is not accidental, given the nature of European cultural history, that the word *master,* which designates the male gender, means "to gain control over.") Indeed this analysis of Platonic thought is not merely an academic exercise. It helps to expose the oppressive and repressive forms within European and Euro-American culture that shackle Africans, other "non-Europeans," and to a lesser extent, women. Why is it that speech in European-derived societies is the mark of status in the culture? And why is it that African people in America and the Caribbean have maintained such distinct language styles? Here we have the intuitive resistance to a change in consciousness. The creation of African-influenced languages in circumstances of oppression can be understood as a force that insists on the maintenance of an ancestral world-view.

> But this, I think, is what you would affirm, at least, that   every discourse (*Logos*) should be constituted like a living being, having its own body (*Soma*), so as to be neither headless nor footless, but having a middle as well as extremities, which have been written so as to be appropriate to each other and to the whole.[27]

DuBois says that Phaedrus' discourse "moves from head to foot, from the middle to the extremities and returns finally to the whole. The form of the argument exemplifies the patterns of subordination and control which it defends."[28] DuBois perceives the almost fanatical consistency and thoroughness in Plato's attack on the traditional social reality. Every thrust is part of a directed methodology that seeks to guarantee the nature of its result.

This is, indeed, the genesis of Western scientific thought; not of science itself. Plato set the mold, neither for a critical method, nor for authentic critical thought with which Europeans proudly identify themselves, but for a method of thinking, discourse, argumentation, and organization that would guarantee social control by people (men) like himself. His genius was in understanding that to do this sucessfully he had to influence the style of thought, language, and behavior of all human beings, i.e., their total experience. As we learn to think "Platonically," we are convinced that that is the only correct way to think. The mode of the academy is still at the base of social control. Gregory Vlastos remarks of Plato,

> . . . his views about slavery, state, man and the world, all illustrate a single hierarchic pattern; and . . . the key to the pattern is in his idea of *logos* with all the implications of a dualist epistemology. The slave lacks logos: so does the multitude in the state, the body in the man, and material necessity in the universe . . . . Order is imposed on them by a benevolent superior: master, guardian, mind, demiurge . . . the common title to authority is the possession of *logos*. In such an intellectual scheme, slavery is natural: in perfect harmony with one's notions about the nature of the world and of man.[29]

We are witnessing the uniquely European phenomenon: the process by which epistemology becomes ideology. Jurgen Habermas seems to be arguing that this is a universal historical process by which one world-view supercedes and devalues another.[30]

Plato sought to construct a world made up totally of conceptual reality. In this world there was little room for sense perceptions. They occupied a very inferior position. He wanted the citizen to become more and more acculturated to this conceptual reality. Doing so meant that the citizen's senses were trusted less and less, until European culture ended up at one end of the spectrum of which Africa might be at the other. Europeans are not trained to use their senses nor to be "perceptive" (in so far as that is taken by them to mean "non intellectual"), whereas Africans relate to the universe using sense perceptions as highly developed tools—media, if you will—that are a valued part of the human intellectual apparatus.[31]

Sensations, says Socrates, are given at birth. Not only that, but they are given to animals as well as men. And they are natural. All of which functions to devalue the senses and sense perception in the European world-view. A very strong theme in European moral and political philosophy is the idea that human beings are superior to other animals and that they must protect that superiority in order to be truly "human." Knowledge in the Platonic view is long and slow in coming. One has to work for it. Is it "natural" to human beings? In a sense it is only cultural. The senses are afterall only instruments, and what causes perception to be inferior to knowledge is the nature of its "object," (the all-important concept of the "object.") The objects of perception do not have the true reality that the objects of knowledge must possess.[32]

The senses, perceptions (what is natural to the human) function only in the world of appearances and therefore are below the line that separates "adults" from "children" in Platonic thought. Our senses can only tell us how things "seem" to be. True knowledge, on the other hand, relates to the "real world" of "ideas." We are then above the line and are doing important things. Anyone can do what is natural and stumble around the cave in darkness. Light and dark are two sides of this value dichotomy, irreconcilable opposing forces. Since light becomes the metaphor for truth. The mind, it seems, exists *behind* the organs through which we perceive. And only the mind is capable of making judgements. Sensing is easy and immediate. Knowledge comes only through difficult reflection—part of a "long and troublesome process of education."[33]

But why was it so important to debase the senses in this way?

Why did Plato so persistently and unrelentingly drive home the definition and confines of this epistemological mode? It was an epistemology that implied a social, ethical, and even political theory. Plato's epistemology did indeed eventually become the foundation for a form of social organization that would facilitate domination of the many by the few. It helped to create a world-view. The epistemology took on ideological implications in Plato's presentation and his commitment to its assumptions. His dialogues were ammunition for the proselytizers who would follow until the assumptions of his epistemology became the assumptions of a cultural tradition. These epistemological assumptions translated into an ideological statement in the civilization that would claim them as tradition.

> That which is apprehended by intelligence and reason is always in
> the same state; but that which is conceived by opinion with the help
> of sensation and without reason is always in a process of becom-
> ing and perishing and never really is.[34]

Friedrich Juenger says "being" is good, valued, and intelligent. "Becoming" is devalued, inferior, irrational. In Plato's ideology, "Reason establishes itself as absolute, dominates all other modes of apprehension, understanding. . . . It refuses to admit of any concepts not established by itself. . . . All non-intellectual concepts are held to be unreasonable, and are discarded."[35] In this statement, Friedrich Juenger points to the ideological, absolute and uncompromising thrust of Platonic conceptions.

Theory of Humanness

A theory of the human being has already been implied in our discussion of Platonic conceptions. We, as humans, are not whole beings, but rather made up of parts that are in continual conflict with one another. We are made up of "reason," "intellect," and our "better natures," which are constantly seeking to control our desires, appetites, emotions and to put our "senses" to proper use. The better part must control the "baser." According to Eric Havelock, Plato "discovered" the "psyche" that came to refer to the "isolated, thinking self." The self was no longer conceived as a cosmic being, that is, a being that experienced itself as intimately involved with other beings in the cosmos. A "cosmic self" implies that the reality of self is phenomenally part of other realities presented as a result of sentient, conscious, and spiritual coexistence in the universe. Cosmos itself refers to the universe as a unified, interrelated (organic) whole. Havelock is saying that "pre-Platonic" Greece understood the self in this way. That makes historical sense, since Greece developed out of its cultural and intellectual association with early African traditions.

The African and Native American world-views have similar cosmic concepts. Their intellectual traditions and thought-systems rest on the assumption of cosmic interrelationship. These conceptions form a basis of communal relationships as well as a sympathetic relationship with the natural environment. How would such a conception of the human being interfere with the ground rules of Platonic epistemology? Why was it essential that he cast doubt on the validity of such conceptions? A cosmic being must be whole. In such a being reason and emotion cannot be experienced as disparate, unconnected, and antagonistic. *A cosmic self cannot objectify the universe.* The more "intelligent" such a self becomes, the more it understands language as merely metaphor. This idea is common to the thought-systems mentioned. The highest, most profound truths cannot be verbalized, and one reaches for the dimension beyond the profane word where the *meaning* of the symbols becomes clear. But for Plato the "cosmic self" is incapable of knowing; it can only perceive, sense, intuit, and have "opinions." (The ascendancy of the so-called "left-brain.")

Plato establishes instead the "autonomous, thinking self." According to Havelock, this "self" or "psyche" is a thing or entity capable of not only scientific cognition, but of moral decision.[36] Plato not only put forth the idea of the "thinking self"—an idea which must have predated him—but he simultaneously discarded other aspects of our "human" beingness as invalid or unworthy (unreal) and declared this superconceptual function—this totally cerebral activity—as the *essence* of humanness. Therein lies its uniqueness, strangeness, and significance all at once. He had proferred a new theory of humanness (man/woman). Much later, caught in the throes of evolutionary theory, it became very important in European thought to emphasize those characteristics that were thought to separate and distinguish "humans" from animals. "Intelligence," of course, was key; the essence of man/woman. (For Michael Bradley it is the "discovery of time.")[37] Using Platonic conceptions and elaborating them, intelligence took on a particular definition.

Scientists have talked in terms of two parts or "hemispheres" of the brain for some time. The left hemisphere is believed to control certain kinds of thought processes, while the right hemisphere controls other kinds of thought processes.[38] The implications involved are important to this discussion and will be discussed later. A related point to be made here is that while all cultures and all people involve both "hemisphere-modes," so to speak, in "normal" functioning, cultures and therefore their members can value one style of cognition over another. In such cases one will be emphasized and encouraged, while the other is not. A person will be rewarded for thinking in the valued mode, and such habits of thought will be reinforced in the formalized learning and socialization processes. The same person will be "punished" for thinking in the "devalued" mode, and will "fail for doing so."

In nineteenth century Europe, in which unilinear evolutionary theory reigned, European scientists said that the left hemisphere was "major," because it was associated with "thought" and "reasoning," which set humans apart from animals. The right hemisphere was labelled "minor" and less advanced or less evolved. It had a "lower" capacity, dealt with "emotion," and had to be directed by the left hemisphere. Clearly this was a nineteenth century version of the Platonic conception, which split man/woman into reasonable and emotional tendencies, superior and inferior faculties, and mandated the dominance and control of the emotional as normative state of being. And so "order" and "justice" were achieved. Plato stated the case for this kind of order in the person and, by extension, in the State. Nineteenth century evolutionists were giving "scientific" backing to the same kind of imposed "order" among the world's cultures, with the more "reasonable" (higher and rational) cultures controlling the more "emotional" (lower and less advanced) ones.

*The point that is critical to this analysis of European thought and behavior is that Platonic theory and epistemology and its subsequent development, enculturation, and reformulation provided the most effective ideological underpining for politically and culturally aggressive and imperialistic behavior patterns on the part of European people precisely because the argument was stated in *intellectual* and academic "scientific" terms.*Plato not only helped to establish a theory of the human that would valorize "scientific" cognition to the exclusion of other cognitive modes, but he established the Academy. It has since become a characteristic of European culture that association with academia represents association with truth, superior reasoning capacity, and impartiality or "objectivity"—this also means a lack of commitment to anything other than the supposed "abstract truth." What Platonic conceptions allowed for, consequently, was that the most politically motivated acts (e.g., wars of aggression, racially based slavery) could be justified in what passed for a-political, "scientific" terms; the terms of a supposed "universal truth," the eternal, unchanging "idea." This was not necessarily the Platonic objective, but it is the use to which this conception was put within

Very important !

the confines of European culture, molded by the needs of the European *utamaroho*. The *asili*—demanding power—made appropriate use of the "universal truth" idea.

The task here is to lay the groundwork for a comprehensive analysis of European thought and behavior by examining related aspects of Platonic theory in terms of their ideological significance in subsequent European development. This analysis ends and begins in synthesis which is the *asili* demonstrating the consistency and cohesion, the monolithic character, of the tradition under scrutiny.

Plato's theory of humanness is a crucial aspect of his over-all theory. He successfully creates an illusion of the isolated self, and so, in twentieth century European (Euro-American) society, this self is indeed experienced as the psyche. This conception of the autonomous thinking self has locked the European into a narrow and limiting view of the human. It precipitated a kind of spiritual retardation in which painful isolation and alienation either incapacitates participants in the culture or makes them extremely efficient competitors, aggressors, and technocrats (technicians). In the *Theatetus,* Socrates uses the term "soul" as synonymous with "mind." Given the Platonic conception of significant mental faculties, this means that the soul became identified with cognitive thought, with "cold" calculation, with a lack of emotion and a denial of feeling and sensation. What theory of the human being does this imply? And what kind of *utamaroho* and behavior develops in a culture that accepts such a theory? If I am right in suggesting that these Platonic conceptions did indeed become normative and then tremendously powerful as cognitive models, and if we can accept the relationship between *utamawazo* (cultural cognitive character) and *utamaroho* (affective characteristics) as being intimate and co-generative, then clearly a model begins to emerge of patterned thought and behavior reinforcing each other as they develop.

In the *Theaetetus,* Socrates talks about the soul perceiving under its own "power." He makes the distinction between the body and the soul or mind. *Through* the organs of the body we perceive "hardness," "cold," "red," etc., but *with* the mind (soul) we "reflect," make judgements, and "think" about "likeness," "difference"—things that require knowledge of the "forms" or of "being." The soul reflects with its own "power," and the objects that it perceives are universal. Universality emerges as superiority and value. In the chapters which follow, the attribute of universality will be traced along the road of European ideology as it develops and hardens into the framework of the culture.

What is it that the soul, mind, or psyche has that the body and senses do not? Clearly it is control and with control comes power as in "the ability to dominate." The desire (need) for control and power are the most important factors in understanding the European *asili.* We will see that the sensation of controlling others and of therefore having power over them is the most aesthetically, psychologically, and emotionally satisfying experience that the culture has to offer. It therefore satisfies the *utamaroho.* It is the pursuit of these feelings and this state of being that motivates its members. The sensation of control and power is achieved in many ways in European culture, but what is significant here is that in its earliest and formative stages, Plato laid the basis for its achievement through an epistemology that rejected the poetic participation, thereby gaining "independence" (Havelock) from poetic involvement in order to both "create" and to apprehend the proper object of knowledge. The "object" was in this way controlled by the mind that contemplated it. With this knowledge came power, because the world could begin to be understood as being comprised of many such objects capable of being manipulated by the knower, the knower who was aware of himself (women didn't count) as knower and as being in complete control. The "pre-Platonic" man, in this view, was powerless, lacked self-control and was indeed manipulated by the myraid of emotions he was made to feel by the images around him. Such is the picture that we are given.

We cannot overstate Plato's significance precisely because we find European theorists and scholars making the same argument, painting the same picture in the twentieth century. Henri and H.A. Frankfort are concerned here with the distinction between ancient, "primitive man," and "mythopoeic" thought on the one hand and "modern," "scientific" man, and "scientific thought" on the other:

> Though (mythopoeic thought) does not know dead matter and confronts a world animated from end to end it is unable to leave the scope of the concrete and renders its own concepts as realities existing per se.[p.14]

> . . . the procedure of the mythopoetic mind in expressing a phenomenon by manifold images corresponding to unconnected avenues of approach clearly leads away from rather than toward, our postulate of causality which seeks to discover identical causes for identical effects through-out the phenomenal world. [p.20]

> . . . mythopoetic thought may succeed no less than modern thought in establishing a coordinated spatial system; but the system is determined not by objective measurements, but by an emotional

recognition of values.[39]

Not only does Plato's epistemology bring control accompanied by power, but also its attendant theory of (hu)man produces the European conception of the authentically moral being. For Plato, with rationality comes the power to make moral decisions, and only this new "autonomous thinking self" (Havelock) can properly be the seat of moral decision. This position, however, represents a confusion between the spiritual and the scientific/rational. Having equated human potential with an abstracted rational faculty, Plato takes us out of a humanly defined social context as the ground or determinant of our being. He then places us back into an artificial social construct that is now a reflection of his abstract concept of the "good" and of the "true"; a denial of the lived and experienced reality. But in fact, our concepts of morality must reflect our ideas as well as our feeling about proper human interrelationship. The "rational" person is not necessarily the "moral" person. It may be "rational" (efficient) to think in terms of selective breeding, cloning, and extermination in order to produce the "master race." It is neither spiritually nor morally compelling to do so. Plato seemed to be hinting that scientific method would generate "right" action. But war in the twentieth century is both rational and irrational at the same time. European horror movies in which mad scientists do crazy things are expressions of this seeming contradiction. Yet that personality is a "logical" extension of the Platonic equation of the moral and the rational.

This argument has been expanded, refined, and camouflaged in the terms of "modern" European "critical" philosophy. Jurgen Habermas seems to be arguing for a kind of universal language of "communicative rationality," in which social/cultural beings rely on their own intellectual examination of issues as the basis for judgement, as opposed to relying on their cultural traditions as a source of validation of choices/actions.[40] This for Habermas would be part of the process of "rationalization" and can lead to authentic moral behavior or at least a criterion for determining such. His own language is that of European philosophic discourse of the 1980s; the Platonic model honed to cerebral perfection. It is "rationality" at its most impressive calling for a universal rationalism as the basis for "rational action orientations"[40] and rationalized social order. Habermas uses Piaget's theory of cognitive development in relation to the valued process of "decentration," in which *a priori* cultural definitions are devalued in the determination of "truth" and right action. While he allows for the problem of a "utopian" view and cautions us against "the imperatives of a one-sided rationality limited to the cognitive-instrumental," he insists that "the decentration of world understanding and the rationalization of the lifeworld are necessary conditions for an emancipated society."[41] To approach the rational is to do away with difference. Here lurks the same *utamawazo* that is uncomfortable with ambiguity. There is a difference between the arguments of Plato and those of Habermas (who emphasizes process as opposed to reified ideal), but the differences are not cultural/ideological. These two philosophers represent variations—one more refined, more liberal, more recent than the other—of the same *utamaroho.*

In his theory of (hu)man and of the State Plato succeeds in exorcising human and social reality of its problematical and ambiguous character. He does this by creating his own reality in which the mathematical abstraction reigns. "Real" truth, he says, is what we do *not* experience. It is unchanging *being.* Our experience is not real, but constantly changing, *becoming.* What this allows him to do is in fact to create an "unreal" reality in which ambiguity, creative imagination, and uncertainty of human truth is superficially eliminated. Of course, there is no such thing as "unreal" reality, so in truth the problematical still exists. Plato's Republic is a *theoretical structure.* His theory of the human is unrealistic. It leaves out some essentials of humanness and so as a model to be imitated has a tendency to create Marcuse's "one-dimensional man." Each of us is suited to one task or mode of participation in the State. The Philosopher-King and Guardians will be able to determine our proper place and so our destiny, very neat, very simple. The Republic is modelled after the "good," an abstract unambiguous, unchanging, monolithic reality. In order for it to work, people within it would have to be convinced of the theory of the human on which it rests. Stanley Diamond explains why the artist was seen as a threat to the State;

> The artist does not believe in abstract systems; he deals with felt and ordered emotional ideals and believes order is attained through the contradictions, the tense unities of everyday experience. Thus, the artist himself may be unstable, a changeling, and this is a threat to any establishment.[42]

On the other hand, the mathematician would fair much better as Plato's view of the ideal man for the Ideal State. He emphasizes mathematics in the curriculum for the guardians. For him "mathematics" has the shape of truth and can provide the solution to all problems. Here again a particular concept of human nature is implied. And if people were in fact not like this, he would make them so. He would fashion their minds to think the way they had to think to make his plan work. He would train them with the "syntactical condition of the mathematical equation," because "numbers drag us toward Beingness."[43] In other words there were changes that he had to make in the cognitive habits (*utamawazo*) of the participants in the culture if he was to succeed in the creation of the new order.

The New Dominant Mode

The birth of the archaic "European" *utamawazo* was accompanied and supported by the introduction of the literate mode as the dominant and valued mode of expression in the culture. The written mode preserved communication in an ever-increasingly precise form in what was to become "Europe." Writing had been used much, much earlier in other cultures, but as in the Kemetic MDW NTR (ancient "Egyptian Hieroglyphs"), it involved forms that symbolized much more than sounds or objects. The MDW NTR contains transformational symbolism that embodies African conceptions of universal and cosmic truths.[44] It is an indication of the nature of the European world-view and of course an example of the intensity of European cultural nationalism that European scholars so consistently characterize the MDW NTR of Kemet as being merely "concrete."[45] This form of "reductionism" is an effort to oversimplify ancient African writing, the earliest form of writing. It is an effort to make the MDW NTR appear conceptually limited and sometimes contradictory. In truth, the MDW NTR was too complex for Plato's purposes. He needed a modality that robbed the symbols of their "symbolic," their esoteric content. They had to be disengaged from the cosmos.

It is important to understand the process by which the literate mode became dominant in the culture and to understand exactly what is meant by the "literate mode" in this context. Although for many centuries to come it was inaccessible to most of the population, it still had a valued place in nascent, archaic, and feudalistic European society, and so greatly effected the shape of the culture. We are describing a process of development, and because the development had a "direction" does not mean that other characteristics were not identifiable. The poetic or, as Henri and H. A. Frankfort call it, the "mythopoetic" continued to exist among the vast majority of the population, but it was relegated to a devalued position, implying inferiority of intellectual capacity. That is why "the primitive," defined Eurocentrically, is always associated with a lack of writing, and this is called being "*pre*-literate."

In nascent Europe the literate mode had ideological force. Remember that according to Platonic epistemology we must achieve objectivity in order to know and that in his terms this is achieved by causing our reason to dominate our emotions, which in turn gives us control. We gain control over that which we wish to know, therefore creating an "object" of knowledge. The mode of preserved communication (which had characterized most cultures and which would prevail in Greece centuries after Plato), was the poetic, the oral, and to some extent the symbolic mode, although Greek culture was not nearly so well developed in that regard, borrowing from other cultures their sacred and religious concepts. This mode relied on the identification of the knower with the known, on powers of memorization, and familiarity of the listener/participant with the subject-matter being used. The symbolic modes of the more ancient and developed civilizations also required apprehension of abstractions, but these were not the rationalistic abstractions that would come to dominate in European thought.

In the analysis of Eurocentric theorists it was this memory, this emotional identification and "involvement" caused by the poetic, "oral," and "Homeric" mode that had limited "pre-Platonic" man. This characterization thrusts us into yet another "split," another dichotomy of invidious comparison. And with this another aspect of the supposed "superiority" of the European rears its head. The "pre-Platonic" man (Havelock's term), whom Homer's epics represented and whom they addressed, was in trouble according to Havelock. He is described as being "nonliterate," which of course has much more ideological force than just saying that he preferred the poetic form. It surfaces as a weakness and inability to conceptualize, a negative characteristic. It devalues him as a person. This "nonliterate," "pre-Platonic" person also picks up a host of other characteristics, which, in the European world-view, are either valueless or absolutely negative. Havelock describes the "Homeric man" as being in a "sleeping" state, as though drugged. His mind is governed by "uncritical acceptance," "self surrender," "automatism," "passivity of mental condition," "lavish employment of emotions," "hypnotic trance," "complacency." He uses "dream language" and is the victim of "illusion." He is in the "long sleep of man" and is even "lazy."[46] Why is Havelock so hard on those whom he places in intellectual opposition to Plato? It is as if this stage in Greek history or European development must be destroyed; certainly thoroughly repudiated. We will see in subsequent chapters of this study why these are precisely the terms that Europeans use to describe and demean other cultures,

cultures that are labelled "primitive." And these are the terms they use to characterize the abilities of children of African descent and other groups who are seen as lacking cultural and racial value within the societies in which Europeans dominate. In fact, European academies "create" such nonminds.[47] In each of these instances, including Havelock's critique of the mental habits of humankind "before" Plato, the statements made have ideological significance. They are supporting a chosen way of life, a set of beliefs. The objective is to establish the "way of life" as superior to all which either preceeded it or that is different from it. It is the ideological nature of Platonic epistemology that makes this possible: an epistemology dictated by the European *asili,* carried in the cultural genes.

For Plato, the poet does not appeal to the proper "principle" in the person or to the proper part of his or her soul. And so the poet would not be able to help in the task of lifting us out of the darkness of the cave and correcting our ignorance towards the "light" of truth. The poet obstructs the proper functioning of reason and does not help us to gain control over our emotions.

> The imitative poet . . . is not by nature made, nor is his art intended, to please or to affect the rational principle in the soul; but he will prefer the passionate and fitful temper, which is easily imitated. . . his creations have an inferior degree of truth . . . and he is . . . concerned with an inferior part of the soul; and therefore we shall be right in refusing to admit him into a well-ordered State, because he awakens and nourishes and strengthens the feelings and impairs the reason. As in a city when the evil are permitted to have authority and the good are put out of the way, so in the soul of the man, as we maintain, the imitative implants an evil constitution, for he indulges the irrational nature which has no discernment of greater and less, but thinks the same thing at one time great and at another small he is a manufacturer of images and is very far removed from the truth.[48]

Plato's argument with the poets is that they do not foster the view of the State and of the "good" of which he wants to convince people; of which they must be convinced in order for them to play their parts well. The Republic is perfect because it is absolute. But what if human realities are not absolute? Suppose there are ambiguities endemic to human existence? Plato solves this problem by simply "eliminating" the ambiguous nature of our existential reality, by pretending that it isn't there. Who, after all, is creating "illusion" and who is dealing with "reality?" The philosophy underlying the *Republic* says that human beings fit into neat categories, that they are each suited to specific tasks by nature, and will be happiest doing that for which they are best suited and that such is best for the order of the whole. Isn't that convenient? Plato doesn't need the poets "messing" up this picture—they won't help him sell his myth.

If the poets and the poetic in us is bad and backward, certainly the other side of the coin is that our better, more rational natures are brought out by the literate mode, the substitution of object for symbol. When the literate mode dominates, we nurture a new and different mindset. That is the important thing. That is the significance of Plato's work. Contrast Havelock's characterization of this "new" man with that of the "old." The new man is governed by "self-conscious critical intelligence," "individual and unique convictions," a "critical psyche," "inner stability," "inner morality," and "calculated reflection." He is "self-governing," "emancipated," "reflective," "thoughtful," "self-organized," "calculative," "rational," "self-generated," "awakened," "stimulated," "thinking abstractly," and "autonomous." In the rhetoric of European value the deck is clearly stacked. This "new" person is *smart!* What we see is the epistemological basis of the conviction that literacy renders progressiveness and that when the literate mode becomes valued and finally dominant, we have a "higher" form of culture in terms of European ideology. So that in a meeting on general education at Hunter College in New York City in 1984, it was assumed that to educate our students we must teach them about "Western" European civilizations, since that is where human beings learned to be "critical," indeed to "think."

But the European is certainly not very "critical" if that means questioning the European world-view as Plato inspired its configuration. The world of literacy, it is believed, is a world of objectivity, a world of "impartial" truth. Oral media is "subjective." In it personality is merged with tradition. How do we change this? "The fundamental signs enabled a reader to dispense with emotional identification . . . ."[49] Plato urged a move away from "emotional involvement," "unquestioned precepts," and "imitation." (Today Habermas urges us away from predecisive validity claims based on cultural tradition.[50]) Plato supposedly introduced "technical" learning "on the highest level of consciousness."[51] So while Plato is seeking to produce minds capable of the "highest" form of thought, "nonliterate man" emerges as being barely able to "think" at all. Indeed, we cannot be sure that he is even "conscious." And, what is more, this epistemology is seen to have moral implications as well. The literate participant of the ideal state is more moral because his ethics are subject to questioning, criticism, and analysis, while the earlier Greek ethic was not. (Of course, once the "questioning" takes place in the Socratic dialectic, not too much more "questioning" is necessary.) Within the logic of European nationalism these ideas were to be later echoed in nineteenth century evolutionary theory where Victorian culture was judged as the "highest" form, representing a more objectively valid moral state, the assumption being that European values were arrived at "critically" and "rationally" and were therefore universally valid. This was a legacy from the "enlightenment," so-called.

Plato had set the stage for important ingredients of the European self-image. He sees himself as a critical being, rational and in absolute control. His mission is to control and rationalize the world, and this he achieves through the illusion of objectivity. Plato himself must have been something like this. Stanley Diamond draws a portrait:

> He was it seems, a man of a certain type, incapable of tolerating ambiguity, intuitive in his conviction of an objective, superhuman good . . . . He believed in logic with the cool passion of a mathematician, and he believed, at least abstractly, that the perfectly just city could be established, through perfectly rational and perfectly autocratic means.[52]

The desacralized written mode allowed the object to be "frozen," reified into a single meaning; Kemetic MDW NTR is not of this nature:

> The ordinary consideration of the Egyptian symbol *reduces* it to a primary, arbitrary, utilitarian and singular meaning, whereas in reality it is a synthesis which requires great erudition for its analysis and a special culture for the esoteric knowledge that it implies.[53]

R. A. Schwaller De Lubicz characterizes the MDW NTR in the following way, distinguishing them from the merely literal mode: "symbolism," which is a mode of expression, he distinguishes from the "symbolic," which is the application of a "state of mind," or, again, a "mentality." "Symbolism is technique; the symbolic is the form of writing of a vital philosophy ."[54] "The symbol is a sign that one must learn to read, and the symbolic is a form of writing whose laws one must know; they have nothing in common with the grammatical construction of our languages. It is a question here, not of what might be called "hieroglyphic language," but of the *symbolic,* which is not an ordinary form of writing." De Lubicz is concerned with describing "the principles that govern the symbol and the symbolic in the expression of a vital philosophy, not a rationalistic philosophy." He says that there "exists no *hieroglyphic language,* but only a hieroglyphic writing, which uses the symbol to lead us toward the symbolic."[55] The significance of these passages is that it affirms my belief that the MDW NTR of Kemet does not represent a "primitive" form of secular or profane script and is not therefore "pre-European." Rather, it represents a quite different view of reality—a mindset that sought to understand the universe as cosmos, therefore careful not to attempt the separation of spirit and matter. So that when we speak of the literate mode as championed by Plato, we mean to stress a unique definition and use of that mode: one devoid of the "symbolic" in De Lubicz' sense. This writing lacked something. It was only able to deal with "one-dimensional realities," and as Diamond says,

> It reduced the complexities of experience to the written word . . . with the advent of writing symbols became explicit; they lost a certain richness. Man's word was no longer endless exploration of reality, but a sign that could be used against him . . . writing splits consciousness in two ways—it becomes more authoritative than talking thus degrading the meaning of speech and eroding oral tradition; and it makes it possible to use words for the political manipulation and control of others.[56]

It was not that this literal mode represented or led to higher truths, but that the *claim* was made that it did and that it gave the illusion of having done so, making this medium useful. It worked! It helped to control minds, values, and behavior, just as any media does, but in a new and for some a "desirable" way. The written language was more impressive than speech. Platonic epistemology achieved this once it was valued. Then speech came to imitate this writing, which was no longer "magical," sacred, and truly symbolic. The permanence of the written word gave it ideological strength. Written dialogues, written laws, and strangely enough, written prayers—the sacred reduced to profane "scriptures"; all of this became evidence, for the European, of the superiority of his/her culture.

Lineality and Cause: Scientism and "Logic"

Consistent with this literate modality as frame of reference, there is an association between the "critical mind" and the "logical mind" in Platonic epistemology, which idealized objectification and insisted on the literate mode as valued technique and further enhanced the idea that there was only one correct method of reaching truth, and that was via "logic." This idea of "logic" is presented as though it were a guarantee that conclusions would have absolute, verifiable truth. Anything else was mere opinion, subject to the whims of human nature. Logic helped one to maintain one's "objectivity" (emotional distance). The statement below, from a contemporary introductory textbook by H. L. Searles, demonstrates the ideology of Platonic epistemology. According to the author, the study of logic should enable students to:

> ... develop a critical attitude toward the assumptions and presup-positions which form the background of his own and many others' arguments in such fields as politics, economics, race relations, and other social sciences, where the facts are not fully verified but con-tain elements of tradition, preference and evaluation.[57]

Habermas wrote in 1987, that we must form a reflective concept of "world" so that we can have access to *the* world.[58]

Searles statement sounds like those of Havelock comparing "pre-Platonic" and Platonic "man" or like those of Plato debasing the poets in relation to the State order. Searles can only make these statements sound reasonable because Plato had argued so well such a long time ago, when Europe was not even in its infancy but in the last stage of a gestation, that perhaps began as a mutated conception in the Eurasian steppes (Caucasus). Searles statement is an excellent exam-ple of the longevity and ideological strength of the Platonic influence. It is a statement of Platonic epistemology, now taken for granted because it is etched into the European world-view and *utamawazo*; it is assumed. Plato, however, had to argue for its supremacy, fighting the Sophists, the powerful ancient mystery systems, ancient Kemetic (Egyptian) science, philosophy, religion, and other philosophical and ideological possibilities. He had to change the mental outlook of the culture. His task was to shape an *utamawazo* that would suit the *uta-maroho* of those who would come to identify themselves as European. The psychological habits of the poetic or "mythopoeic" mode had to be replaced by the illusions of the literate mode. By the time Searles is writing some twenty-five centuries later, these habits are so ingrained that Europeans are not even aware that the "logic" that they are taught cannot explain Zen philosophy, African ontology, or existential, phenomenal reality. They are not aware of the fact that it is neither "total" nor "universal." Edward Hall says it this way:

> ... in his strivings for order, Western man has created chaos by denying that part of his self that integrates while enshrining the parts that fragment experience ... Western man uses only a small fraction of his mental capabilities; there are many different and

legitimate ways of thinking; we in the west value one of these ways above all others—the one we call "logic," a linear system that has been with us since Socrates. . . . Western man sees his system of logic as synonymous with the truth. For him it is the only road to reality.[59]

While I am arguing for the seminal nature of Plato's work and its powerful influence in the formulation of the European *utamawazo,* I do not want to give the mistaken impression that his work was very influential at the time of his writing. Only a tiny fraction of the Greek populace followed, had access to (i.e. was literate and privileged) or was convinced of this new epistemology. And its accessibility was to remain restricted for many centuries to come. But what makes it so important is that those few who did have access and who were convinced were also those who set the intellectual and ideological patterns for the civilization that would follow. It was as Plato wanted it to be—the few made decisions for the many. The "logical" ones led those who "could not reason well."

According to Havelock, Plato was looking for the "syntax of true universal definition." Platonic epistemology allowed one to choose between the "logically and eternally true" and the "logically and eternally false," whereas the poetic mode did not.[60] Plato identifies the "logical" with the "eternal," while the poetic is seen as being temporally limited, all illusion. But now some Europeans are discovering what other cultures have always known: verbal -linear logic is only one aspect of our consciousness, one part of our cognitive apparatus. As humans we have other tools that are global and intuitive. But within European culture these have almost been put out of commission, made inoperable, deformed by a civilization whose epistemology ignored them and considered them almost "inhuman," certainly "uncivilized." Deficient in the ability to grasp cosmic reality, organic interrelationship, Europeans were deprived of the source of a different kind of power, which comes from joining. They turned, therefore, to those forms of intellectual manipulation which seemed to yield power over others; the nature of the *asili.*

The dominance of written codification is accompanied by other conceptual habits that support it and that it supports. Epistemology meets with ontology as concepts of space and time begin to adhere in theories of humanness, knowledge, and truth. Lineality in European thought has all of these implications. It is present in the nascent European conceptions of purpose and causality; in the secularization of time that puts emphasis on historicity in the culture; in the teleological thrust of European religious, philosophical, and ideological thought. These characteristics are all related, but their visibility as dominant themes emerge at different times in the development of the culture. They are introduced here briefly, so that we can pick them up later as recognizable themes contributing to the over-all configuration of European thought (*utamawazo*) and behavior.

Dorothy Lee, in *Freedom and Culture,* tells us that European culture codifies reality in a lineal manner. She bases her conclusions on comparisons with specific "non-European" cultures that she finds have "nonlineal" codifications of reality. Her work helps to elucidate the assumption of lineality in the European *utamawazo*. In European culture reality is codified — understood, perceived, organized — in lineal, sequential relationships. Events are viewed in terms of temporality.[61] The line underlies the European aesthetic apprehension of the given. Its presence is taken for granted in life, and in all academic work. Teachers, says Lee, are always drawing them on blackboards. She goes on to say that "progress" is the "meaningful sequence," "where we see a developmental line, the Trobriander sees a point, at most a swelling in value." Europeans "take pleasure and get satisfaction in moving away from a given point ... the Trobriander finds it in the repetition of the known, in maintaining the point; that is in what we call monotony."[62]

Lee has hit on the ideological significance of lineality in European thought. Change or movement away from the point in a lineal direction toward another imagined point as far as that line can extend (the future) is "progress" as it is defined in European culture. This conception becomes the basis for willed cultural behavior. "Progress," as we shall see in Chap. 9, is the idea that initiates change, that gives supposed supremacy to the culture, and that justifies exploitation of others. This idea of progress rests on the assumed reality of the line. All things are reduced to sequential relationship on a line: one dimensional and unidirectional. This time line joins the points of "past," "present," and "future," where the function of past and present is to give value to the future by virtue of inviduous comparison, and then the future is used as a standard by which to evaluate the value of the present and the past. The future reigns supreme. Any form of cultural behavior is justified in the pursuit of this never attainable future. And any culture whose *utamawazo* does not allow for the abstract yet oppressive future of the progress ideology is thought to be doomed to failure. John S. Mbiti, writing from a Eurocentric perspective, has this to say about African religious thought:

> So long as their concept of time is two dimensional, with a Sasa (present) and a Zamani (past), African peoples cannot entertain a glo-

rious "hope" to which mankind may be destined. . . . Here African
religions and philosophy must admit a defeat: they have supplied
no solution. . . . Do religions become universal only when they have
been weaned from the cradle of looking towards the Zamani (past).
. . and make a breakthrough towards the future, with all the (mythological?) promises of "redemption?". . . . It is in this area that world
religions may hope to "conquer" African traditional religions and
philosophy,. . . by adding this new element to the two dimensional
life and thinking of African peoples. Only a three-dimensional religion can hope to last in modern Africa which is increasingly discovering and adjusting to a third dimension of time.[63]

Sadly, while African himself, Mbiti strives so hard to take on an
alien *utamawazo* that he loses sense of African metaphysical conceptions. The African conception of time is not merely "profane" or
ordinary, but also sacred. Indeed it is the European lineal conception
that is *one* dimensional. This is one of Mbiti's most obvious errors.
Past, present, and future are meaningful only as relationships in a lineal sequence, necessarily unidimensional. They do not represent
three dimensions. In the African conception, sacred, cyclical time
gives meaning to ordinary, lineal time. The circle/sphere adds dimension to the line as it envelops it. The sphere is multidimensional, and
it is curved. Sacred time is not "past" because it is not part of a lineal construct. The ancestors live in the present, and the future lives
in us. Sacred time is eternal and therefore it has the ability to join
past, present, and future in one space of supreme valuation. This is
what Mircea Eliade has called hierophany.[64] Rituals that express
sacred time, connecting it with ordinary experience and punctuating
life, restate and affirm values, beliefs, and symbols, thereby placing
daily existence in a meaningful sacred context. African societies do
not need an abstract European concept of the future to give their
members "hope."[65] The European idea of progress is not a universal
statement of meaning.

What Mbiti is probably getting at, however, has nothing to do
with religion per se, but rather has to do with technology and its
place in the society. Indeed, technological success (European-style)
depends in part on the assimilation of a lineal concept or secular
concept of time, as the most meaningful or ultimate temporal reality.
Friedrich Juenger makes this point. He says that for the European,
time like the "future" becomes a force that dominates human life.
This is certainly not the spiritually enlightening concept that Mbiti
makes it out to be. Time, in European society, serves the technological order, and as such is nonhuman and mechanical.[66] The cosmic

is the enemy of the technological or so it becomes in the European experience. Juenger refers to this mechanical time as "dead time," and identifies its symbol as the clock. For Newton, time was an absolute, while to others it is a mental construct that relates our experiences and ideas. Newtonian time, says Juenger, is linear, uninterrupted, inexorable motion.[67] Neither we nor our experiences effect it.

Time in European culture loses its phenomenal character and is instead experienced as absolute and oppressive. Once again we have a concept created by human beings, reified than used against them. Within the logic of European development this process is necessary, because mechanical time is a precondition for the triumph or ascendance of European science and technology. They are the supreme values because they are "progress." Several theorists (Juenger, Mumford, Joel Kovel, and others) have made the connection between the establishment of watchmaking in Geneva in 1587 with the ascendancy of Calvinism there in the sixteenth century. Calvin intensified the importance of the idea of predestination.[68] While preparing people for salvation in heaven, Calvinism trained them for assembly-line production on earth. In Juenger's words:

> It ["lifeless time"] can be split and chopped up at will, something that cannot be done with life time or with the organisms living in it: seeds, blossoms, plants, animals, men, organic thoughts. This is why technology works with fragments of time, . . . and . . . employs time—study experts—men who watch over the rational exploitation of lifeless time. . . all these are methods which subject live organisms, partaking of vital time, to a mechanical, lifeless time.[69]

Because the dominance of lineal conceptions has lead to Europe's overwhelming technological success does not mean that there are not other viable conceptions. All objectives are not technological/scientific. There must be other "times." Lineal time fails spiritually. It pushes us constantly towards anxiety and fear. The European is always asking him/herself, even while she/he rests: Where am I going? What will become of me? Lineal time is one dimensional because it has neither depth or breadth, only the illusion of length. It leads to evolutionary theories. Reality is perceived as the continuous development of one entity through necessarily temporal stages. One stage is more "evolutionarily advanced" than the one it follows, since they are arranged or "unfold" in a temporal sequence. The concept is based on assumed lineal connections. The connections exist in the minds of those who share a European *utamawazo* (cognitive style); they are not universal realities. Evolution cannot be "seen." What is experienced is "difference." The continuity is the theoretical aspect. Evolutionism posits that it is the same entity that changes and therefore "develops." In spite of its obvious theoretical short-comings, evolution persists as a European metaphysical assumption—not just a theory. The assumption is maintained because it suits the *utamaroho* leading to power over others, not because of its accuracy.

Marshall McLuhan says that "all media are active metaphors in their power to translate experience into new forms.[70] Edmund Carpenter affirms that the written media encourages linear conceptualization; "The spoken word came to imitate writing," and this "encouraged an analytical mode of thinking with emphasis upon lineality."[71] The written mode as understood in ancient Greece was a nonpoetic mode that suited a secular view of human events. In the subsequent development of European culture lineality became dominant until the lack of a cyclical, multidimensional notion of time became a reflection of the profanation or secularization of the world as seen by Europeans. The contemporary spiritual malaise that we witness in Euro-America and in Europe, I would argue, is linked in part to narrowly based lineal conceptions, as well as to other features of the European *utamawazo* and world-view. The assumption of lineal time is an ontological prerequisite to the European idea of "progress" and that of unilinear evolution. The valorization of the written mode encourages and supports these conceptions. It is linear, it accumulates, and it has physical permanence. Therefore, to the European mind, it gives the impression of "truth": objective and eternal. In nascent Europe people could begin to talk about the "correct historical perspective" (Havelock), and in retrospect, Europeans looking back on their development see this as an advance aided by the syntax of the written word. "Chronology," says Havelock, "depends in part on the mastery of time as abstraction." The participants in "oral culture" do not have this sense. Mircea Eliade's view, like that of Dorothy Lee and Juenger, is very different from Havelock's. Instead of viewing nonlineal conceptions as symptoms of "backwardness" and "ignorance," he sees them as being indicative of a theory of humanity in opposition to, perhaps deeper than, that of the European. He finds, "in this rejection of profane, continuous time, a certain metaphysical "valorization" of human existence."[72]

The European conception of history was secular—ostensibly to separate it fiercely from "myth." To them this was another mark (indication) of superiority—accurate, written history as opposed to "inac-

Glossary

Asili

The logos of a culture, within which its various aspects cohere. It is the developmental germ/seed of a culture. It is the cultural essence, the ideological core, the matrix of a cultural entity which must be identified in order to make sense of the collective creations of its members.

Utamawazo

Culturally structured thought. It is the way in which cognition is determined by a cultural *Asili*. It is the way in which the thought of members of a culture must be patterned if the *Asili* is to be fulfilled.

Utamaroho

The vital force of a culture, set in motion by the *Asili*. It is the thrust or energy source of a culture; that which gives it its emotional tone and motivates the collective behavior of its members. Both the *Utamawazo* and the *Utamaroho* are born out of the *Asili* and, in turn, affirm it. They should not be thought of as distinct from the *Asili* but as its manifestations.

Cultural Other

A conceptual/existential construct which allows Europeans to act out their most extreme aggression and destructiveness, while simultaneously limiting their collective self-destruction on a conscious level.

Rhetorical Ethic

Culturally structured European hypocrisy. It is a statement framed in terms of acceptable moral behavior towards others that is meant for rhetorical purposes only. Its purpose is to disarm intended victims of European cultural and political imperialism. It is meant for "export" only. It is not intended to have significance within the culture. Its essence is its deceptive effect in the service of European power.

First World People   African descendants throughout the world.

Majority Peoples   The members of the indigenous core cultures of the world regarded collectively, excluding the European minority.

Nationalism   Ideological commitment to the perpetuation, advancement, and defense of a cultural, political, racial entity, and way of life. This use of the term is neither limited to, nor determined by the boundaries of a "nation-state" as defined eurocentrically.

European Nationalism   All forms of thought and behavior which promote European Hegemony/global white supremacy.

White Nationalism   An expression of European nationalism which identifies caucasian racial characteristics with superiority and African racial characteristics with inferiority.

Cultural Imperialism   The systematic imposition of an alien culture in the attempt to destroy the will of a politically dominated people. The mechanism of cultural imperialism causes cultural insecurity and self doubt within the dominated group. Separated from their ancestral legacy, they lose access to their source of political resistance.

Scientism   The ideological use of "science," defined Eurocentrically, as an activity which sanctions all thought and behavior; that is, science becomes sacred, the highest standard of morality.

Objectification	A cognitive modality which designates every-thing other than the "self" as object. This process mandates a despiritualized, isolated ego and facilitates the use of knowledge as control and power over other.
Desacralization	The alienation and objectification of nature. In this view, nature becomes an adversary. This approach to reality originates in unnatural-ness.
Materialization	This begins with the separation of spirit and matter. This separation, in turn, results in the denial of spirit (despiritualization), the loss of meaning, and the loss of cosmos (interrela-tionship).
Despiritualization	The denial of spiritual reality. The inability to experience spirit. Objectification used ideo-logically results in the desacralization and despiritualization of the universe.
Reductionism	The reduction of phenomena to their most simplistic manifestations. This occurs when the mind is not able to apperceive deeper, more textured levels of meaning. As a cogni-tive deficiency, it prevents comprehension of metaphysical truths.
Reification	This occurs when theory is used as law rather than metaphor and when process is replaced by factual manipulation. Reification is the hardening of dynamic, vital truth into dead-ened dogma.
Lineality	The interpretation of phenomena as being made up of unidimensional, separate entities arranged in sequential order. This conception is necessarily secular and results in desacral-ization. It denies circularity and the spiral of organic development. It prevents transcen-dence of ordinary time and space, thereby

denying ancestral ontological experience.

Dichotomization A mechanism which accompanies objectification. It is the splitting of phenomenon into confrontational, conflicting parts. It facilitates the pursuit of power over other, and is therefore suited to the European *Asili*.

Spirit The creative force which unites all phenomena. It is the source of all energy, motion, cause, and effect. As it becomes more dense, it manifests as matter. It is the meaningful level of existence.

Spirituality The apprehension of cosmic interrelationship. The apperception of meaning in existence, and the degree to which one is motivated by such meaning. Spirituality is one's ability to relate to the metaphysical levels of experience. It unites thought and feeling and thereby allows for intuitive understanding. This cognitive /affective sense is transmitted through collective ancestral relationship. The absence of spirituality is an ancestral legacy.

Yurugu A being in Dogon Mythology which is responsible for disorder in the universe. This is a being conceived in denial of the natural order, which then acts to initiate and promote disharmony in the universe. In African Cosmology such a being is deficient in spiritual sensibility, is perpetually in conflict, is limited cognitively, and is threatening to the well-being of humanity.

curate" orally transmitted mythology. Yet this concept of history rests on a conception of time that is not validated by phenomenal reality. "Time" in this view moves ceaselessly towards some point never reached in the "future." This sense of *telos* is an important aspect of European mythology. It gives meaning to European life. "Purpose" is taking humankind into the "future." Yet this peculiarly European conception of the "future" creates more serious problems for the members of the culture than it can possibly resolve. Ironically it is this "future" approached by the ever present line of time through which the European seeks fulfillment, but at the same time assures her/him of never *being fulfilled.* The "future" in this conception represents unattainable perfection. It is an abstraction that is unreachable and, therefore, is unknowable.

What is unknowable for the European causes anxiety. The European psyche needs the illusion of a rationally ordered universe in which everything can be known. Yet European mythoform creates an unknown and unknowable future whose only relationship to the past and the present is that it determines them and cannot be determined by them. This antagonistic situation causes emotional confusion, anxiety, and fear for the European. Yet this oppressive future cannot be avoided, because the clock moves him/her toward it at an uncontrollable pace, which seems to move faster and faster. All of this is an effect of the limitations of lineal, secular time. It is neither phenomenal nor sacred nor spiritual. Participants in the culture have only one recourse against the fear: science. (The purchasing of "insurance" is another attempt to escape the fear, but it does not work.) Science becomes a force conjured up to battle another powerful force. (Like a battle of "Gods.") Science predicts! It prepares Europeans for the future. It is through science that they seek to relieve their anxiety by gaining control over what controls them. It is therefore dictated by the *asili.* It works only up to a point. Failing in the end to provide fulfillment, for, after all, the European conception of science is above all secular and rests on alienating, literate, rationalistic, linear concepts. The monster that the Europeans have created—this abstract and oppressive future—continues to threaten, to intimidate, to frighten. Everything is thought to move inexorably towards this future, a movement that imparts value (progress), and yet the perceived destiny is fear-producing. Thus, lineality is despiritualizing, while simultaneously contributing an essential ingredient to the structure of the mythoform. It helps to create the illusion of the superiority of European culture for its members, and therefore fits the *asili.*

All purpose becomes "final cause." While it may be a mistake to view Aristotle as an especially creative or intuitive mind, and history suggests that he "borrowed" (to use a euphemism) much from the ancient Kemites ("Egyptians"),[73] Aristotle does exhibit a particular manifestation of the Platonic influence and therefore needs to be considered in this examination of the development of the European *utamawazo*. His formulation both intensified and foreshadowed two epistemological and ideological tendencies that became crucial themes and identifying characteristics of the European world-view: the assumption of cause and scientism (science as ideology). The Aristotelian typologies, in their emphasis on particular aspects of Platonism, had tremendous influence on medieval thought and laid the groundwork for subsequent definition of the rationalistic endeavor, an endeavor that became the European obsession.

For Aristotle, "metaphysics," or the science of "first causes," is the "divine" science. It is the "first philosophy," the study of the principles of other sciences. It is divine by virtue of the fact that the nature of divine thought is that it must necessarily have "itself for its object."[74] Metaphysics, that which is beyond the physical, is indeed the "place" for the discussion of "cause," since cause is a concept, a way of making sense of observed and experienced phenomena, that cannot itself be observed and is not inherent in that phenomena. We can see "effects." We cannot see their "causes." Cause is a metaphysical concept. Yet with all of the European emphasis on this concept of cause, they end up by lacking a true "metaphysic," because of the "success" of a materialistic world-view.

The concept of cause is the basis of a tradition of European science that deals exclusively with the physical and in which the metaphysical is debunked as "mystical" and antiscientific. De Lubicz argues that there is no "cause" until it produces an "effect" and that that relationship is by no means certain since any number of conditions may effect the potential "cause," thereby changing its "effect" from what we would have rationally thought it would be.[75] Yet European science is predicated solely on the predictability of the relationship between cause and effect and treats this relationship in a totally mechanistic way. It is a science that has attempted to materialize a spiritualistic concept, just as from an African-centered viewpoint, it has attempted to materialize a spiritual universe. But the "discovery" of cause and the formulation of universal laws of causation are seen from the Eurocentric viewpoint as representing progress. Henri Frankfort sees it as the transformation of the "mythopoeic" to the "scientific" mind:

Just as modern thought seeks to establish causes as abstract functional relations between phenomena, so it views space as a mere system of relations and functions. Space is postulated by us to be infinite, continuous, and homogenous - attributes which mere sensual perception does not reveal. But primitive thought cannot abstract a concept "space." [76]

And this experience consists in what we would call qualifying associations. Primitive thought naturally recognized the relationship of cause and effect, but it cannot recognize our view of an impersonal, mechanical, and lawlike functioning of causality. . . the category of causality. . . is all important for modern thought as the distinction between the subjective and the objective. . . science. . . reduces the chaos of perceptions to an order in which typical events take place according to universal laws. . . the instrument of this conversion from chaos to order is the postulate of causality.[76]

Cultures prior to European classical Greece most certainly *did* order events in terms of universal laws, and impersonal, external cause is not the only possibility for conceptualizing causality. What Frankfort portrays as a weakness is certainly only a difference. It is the European *asili* that transforms "abstract," "impersonal" conceptions of reality into an advantage, because the *asili* defines the goal as "power over other," and it is in this sense that African and other conceptions appear to be defeated.

Frankfort's statements are characteristic of Eurocentric scholarship as it attempts to draw the line between European civilization and what came before it. (This kind of "before" can of course also be contemporaneous—that is the effectiveness of European evolutionary theory and ideology in combination.) Again we can see the importance of Plato. From the terms that Frankfort uses he may as well be drawing the line that separates the "cave" from the world of ideas.

But there are other interpretations of the implications of the concept of causality. Kwame Nkrumah, in his book *Consciencism* (1964), makes an attempt to synthesize "external causality" with the African concept of causality, which he characterizes as "internal." Cedric X. Clark, however, delves deeper into the spiritual implications of these two views. He implies that Nkrumah was attempting the extremely difficult, if not the impossible. For Clark these two views of causality represent different axiological modalities and different levels of consciousness. European culture glorifies the ego in the context of individualism, while African culture minimizes the ego for the sake of a sense of oneness and group identity. Europeans therefore constantly attempt "to demonstrate independence from the forces of nature" and are "reluctant to acknowledge the fact that (they) along with everything else in the Universe have been caused," while for Africans "everything in the Universe is related, is dependent and is caused," including themselves; they believe that "things happen because they *do*."[77] In Clark's analysis, the European "why," which is different from the African "why," issues from a consciousness that remains locked in to the "lower order" of spatial-temporal dimensions. African consciousness, on the other hand, functions more on the level of spirituality that becomes the meaningful dimension. (Leonard Barrett makes a similar point with regard to the African conception of illness.[78] This different emphasis in the conception of causality is, in Clark's view, "the manifestation of a totally different state of consciousness" in which the African is able to move beyond ordinary time and space to a higher level on which events can become meaningful in terms of cosmic or universal causation.[79]

Yet the idea of cause is problematic even within European logic. Of Aristotle's four kinds of causes, "material," "formal," "efficient," and "final," the final cause is crucial for our analysis. According to Aristotle the final cause of an object, thing, or phenomenon is its purpose, the end for which it exists. In his view determining the final cause of an object or phenomenon is the most important objective of science. At the same time this tradition rigidly separates science and belief. Yet the idea of final cause can only be understood to be a belief! The belief in the idea of "final cause" gives to European thought its strong teleological character. It leads to an assumption that everything that exists, exists for a purpose, and that purpose is the most important thing about it. This idea manifests itself in ideologies as diverse as Judeo-Christian thought and Marxian analysis, and perhaps finds its ultimate expression in the idea of progress, a critical component of both of these traditions. European science therefore states what must be taken as an act of faith (the belief in cause) in an absolutist and deterministic manner. Clearly, the result is dogma and its purpose is ideological: "scientism."

What should be method only becomes ideology, which rests on the following myths, according to Carl Spight: (1) that science is fundamentally, culturally independent and universal; (2) that the only reliable and completely objective language is scientific knowledge; (3) that science is dispassionate, unemotional, and antireligious; (4) that logic is the fundamental tool of science; and (5) that the scientific method leads systematically and progressively toward the truth.[80] The function of science in European culture becomes that of establishing an invulnerable source of authority that cannot be challenged. In relation to other cultures it has the role of establishing European givens as "universal" truths, European culture as somehow the most rational, and the rational model of the universe as the only accurate view. This has led to what De Lubicz calls "a research without illumination." For him the basis of all scientific knowledge or universal knowledge is intuition. Intellectual analysis is secondary and will always be, at best, inconclusive. The African world-view: Spirit is primary!

The European definition of science is not the only way of defining what science should be. For Hunter Adams, science is the "search for unity or wholeness within or without *all* human experience" [Adam's italics][81] and for Wade Nobles, "science is the formal reconstruction or representation of a people's shared set of systematic and cumulative ideas, beliefs, and knowledges (i.e., common sense) stemming from their culture. . . ."[82] The definition of European science reflects the European consciousness, and the style of thought generated by that consciousness has become ideological. In this role it is identified as "scientism." Nobles warns us: "Thus the danger when one adopts uncritically the science and paradigms of another people's reality is that one adopts their consciousness and also limits the arena of one's own awareness."[83]

Aristotle's role in setting the stage for the development of scientism as a European attitude toward truth and value was significant. For him the world became a hierarchy of beings in which each realm fulfilled a purpose for the realm "above" it. This was a world-view in the making, a world described in terms of telic relationship. The crucial mechanism was "cause." But causality is not the only way of relating phenomena. The tyranny of mechanical causation in European thought precludes the perception of cosmic interrelationship, identification, meaningful coincidence, complementarity, and the "circle." Aristotle's insistence on the idea of cause was necessary if people were to accept "purpose" as the essence of the universe. "Purpose" is an essential ingredient of the progress mythology and the technical obsession that would develop subsequently in European culture. It is impossible to worship "efficiency" without a prior emphasis on mechanical causation and materialistic purpose. All of these conceptions require a lineal modality. The regenerative and renewing cycle interferes with and cannot be tolerated by this view. (De Lubicz talks about the "closed, self-renewing Osirian cycle" of ancient Kemet.[84])

In the African world-view it is the eternal cycle of life that offers the possibility of transcendence, of harmonious interrelationship, of wholeness, integration, and authentic organicity. The concept is spiritually satisfying. The European, on the other hand, is perceptually and phenomenally (experientially) limited by his lineal conception of reality. There is no link between past, present, and future save a "causal" link. There is no sacred time. History is limited to the secular. Even the most meaningful religious image in the European tradition—that of the Christ—is only seen to have value in so far as it can be placed within an "historic" sequence. It does not have a sacred validity, but a *secular* one. The dominance of lineal models perhaps helps to account for the spiritual malaise of European societies.

Edward Hall believes that the alienation of the European from nature is related to the dominance of lineality in the European worldview. "We live fragmented, compartmentalized lives in which contradictions are carefully sealed off from each other. We have been taught to think linearly rather than comprehensively."[85] "It is not that linear relationships don't help to order certain aspects of experience, but they will not alone generate a holistic view."[86] By insisting on the dominance of one mode the European has lost sight of the whole. But this was necessary! Just as the mode of objectification *had* to be elevated to supremacy in order for the "right" people/minds to achieve control. Lineality was fundamental to the system of "logic" that Aristotle introduced, which was thereafter equated with truth. Vernon Dixon quotes from the *Metaphysics:*

> It is impossible for the same thing at the same time to belong and not to belong to the same thing in the same respect; and whatever other distinctions you might add to meet dialectical objections, let them be added. This, then is the most certain of all principles. . . . [87]

Dixon characterizes European (Aristotelian) logic as "either/or logic," which is based on the laws of contradiction, the excluded middle, and laws of identity. He says that "either/or logic has become so ingrained in Western thought that it is felt to be natural and self-evident." He contrasts European logic with what he calls the "diunital logic" of the African world-view, in which things can be "apart and united at the same time." According to this logic, something is both in one category and not in that category at the same time.[88] This circumstance is unthinkable given the European world-view.

One problem evidenced repeatedly when Europeans look at "non-European" or what they consider "pre-European" cultures is their misunderstanding of the relationship between the one and the many, between unity and diversity. For people other than Europeans these exist simultaneously and are not seen to be contradictory. The European most often views these conceptions as examples of the inability to think "logically." Levy-Bruhl referred to the "pre-logical" mentality. This is because Europeans *needed* to be able to say that there was only "one road to reality," and that road could then be controlled by one culture, one civilization, one type of person—yes, even one race. And what unfolds in these pages is the way in which that control, that power, was achieved: the necessity of the monolith! The *asili* of European development allows us to understand these "eidological" (Bateson) developments as preparation for the putting in place of the powerful monolithic state culture that has become Europe.

Supremacy of the Absolute, the Abstract, and the Analytical

In the *Republic*, Glaucon and Adimantis are seeking abstract "virtue" as opposed to "virtue" always attached to a concrete situation. Havelock again sees this as part of the backwardness of "Homeric" as opposed to "Platonic" Greece. In the former modality, one only learned of concrete instances of virtues. The Platonic "revolution" in thinking was not only to "separate the knower from the known," but also to introduce a special kind of abstraction that was to become identified with European thought. In the *Euthyphro,* a similar concern arises. Socrates convinces Euthyphro that he cannot "recognize" piety when he sees it, because he has no "idea" of it. Euthyphro's actions are therefore, according to Socrates, plagued by "inconsistency." It is above all permanence and consistency that are achieved through Platonic abstraction, the "unchanging" form to which all things subject to change can be referred. But is this not merely an illusion—at best an operational method? Situations such as the one with which Euthyphro is confronted will always arise in the human condition. There will always be times when one's duty to the Gods and one's duty to one's father conflict. Having an "idea" of piety will not necessarily help one to make the right decision—if, indeed, one exists. Fanatical commitment to such an "idea" tends to result in moralistic, self-righteous, and antihumane postures. "Piety," after all, has to do with meaning and value and as such is necessarily attached to the "human," the existential and the concrete. Plato invents the "Idea" which is other than human, and what he claims to achieve by doing so is to rid "truth" of the ambiguity that is inherent in the human. The *Republic* itself is such an "Idea" or "Form." It is a state of perfection that solves human problems by eliminating them. In the *Republic* the ambiguity and inconsistency of the concrete disappears as it is replaced by the Platonic abstraction: "the Idea of the Good."

The fact is that the existence of "piety" and "virtue" as abstractions, and as intellectual "objects" distinct from the "knowing self" must be demonstrated. It cannot be assumed. The only convincing argument is that the illusion of objectification and the use of such abstractions may, under the proper circumstances, be handy tools with limited applicability. It is unreasonable to accept them as ontological givens or as being necessary for all kinds of "knowing," as Plato argues. But then, he must make this argument, because his intent is not only philosophical but also ideological, i.e., social and political.

Havelock has only praise for Platonic epistemology. For him it represents "advance" in human intelligence. The object that the knower knows must be an abstraction. It must be the quality in isolation, the "thing in itself." The Platonic forms are of this nature (yet certainly impossible to imagine). According to Havelock:

> The abstracted objects of knowledge as known and as stated, are always identical with themselves—unchanging—and always when statements are made about them or when they are used in statements, these statements have to be timeless.[89]

What is it that the knower "knows?" Only these abstracted identities. According to Plato they have greater reality than concrete instances, because they are more "permanent." Yet it would seem to us that the concrete has greater reality: the material as manifestation of spirit. Havelock says of Plato, "He tries to focus on the permanence of the abstract whether as formula or as concept, as opposed to the fluctuating here today—gone tomorrow character of the concrete situation." Plato skillfully creates the illusion of "permanence." He draws the notorious "line" to separate the invisible from the visible, the "intelligible" from that which can only be sensed or felt; and those things (ideas) that "are" from that which merely "seems to be." In Plato's writings, "Ideas" and "Forms" are written with capitals and so adumbrate the written symbolization of the European "God," while things in the sensual world, opinions, and poetry are written in the lower case—just as are the "gods" of people who are not European.

In his obsession with the abstract and the absolute, Plato has borrowed from the teaching of the Mystery Schools that preceded him and from which he learned. (There are also Eurocentric scholars who say that it was the other way around: that traditions attributed to ancient Egypt actually came later and were influenced by Plato.[90]) He has taken the idea of a sacred, eternal, symbolically stated truth, approachable only through spiritual enlightenment, and he has secularized and distorted it for ideological use. It is interesting that the mysteries of the universe for Plato become profane, as the esoteric becomes exoteric, and at the same time deceptively elitist. While it is an epistemological system that everyone is forced to relate to, only the very special few are capable of knowing the "Ideas," and so must teach and rule the rest. Again the creation of power.

This idea of the Platonic abstraction raises an interesting point. It is important that all of us be able to see relationships between particular events and phenomenon and that we "understand" or organize them. We want our children to be able to think "conceptually," i.e., to feel comfortable with concepts that can be used to make sense of things, to solve problems. We don't want them to be forever limited to the familiar circumstance, unable to apply a concept to a "new" situation or problem. There is also the very simple cultural reality that in all societies and cultures people *must* abstract from experience in order to organize themselves, to build and to create and to develop. Abstraction has its place. It is not a European cognitive tool (methodology), but a "human" one. Contrary to European thought, it did not begin with Plato or the Greeks.

Plato separates the world into two parts—or rather creates two worlds: the world of "appearance" and the world of "reality." This separation has continued to characterize European scientific thought. For Stanley Diamond this is problematical as "concepts become real entities rather than metaphors and as such have power over people." Concepts become reified. This, indeed, appears to have been Plato's objective. Plato "isolates the abstract from the concrete (and) the intellectual from the emotional."[91] However, as Diamond points out, the Platonic abstraction is but one kind of abstraction and it is this style that has become entrenched in European thought:

> . . . every linguistic system is a system of abstraction; each sorting out of experience and conclusion from it is an abstract endeavor; every tool is a symbol of abstract thinking; indeed, all cultural convention, all custom is testimony to the generic human capacity for abstracting. But such abstractions are indissolubly wedded to the concrete; they are nourished by the concrete, and they are, I believe, ultimately induced not deduced. They are not, in short, specifically Platonic abstractions, and they do not have the politicized psychological connotations of the latter.[92]

Diamond has perceived the significance of the Platonic style of abstraction. It is ideological in intent. Its role is to establish epistemological authority and, of course, other kinds of authority can then be derived from and supported by it. The special nature of this rela-tionship in European development will unfold in the chapters that fol-low. Those colonized by Europe (as well as Europeans themselves) are taught that Platonic abstraction *is* abstraction and that because their thought-systems are not based on such abstractions, they are incapable of thinking "abstractly." This is merely one aspect of Europe's assault on the rest of the world.

Certainly abstraction is valuable in specific situations, when rea-soning about certain kinds of things, e.g., concepts of "opposite," "sameness," "difference," etc. But we all know that there are very few instances in which these abstract categories can be applied accu-rately and without qualification to concrete realities. Plato knew this and so therefore called reality as we know it "unreal." He says that it is only our perception that is contradictory, not "Reality" (with a cap-ital "R"). Perhaps my major argument with the Platonic argument is the dictum that the mode of abstraction must be applied to our moral conceptions and our relationships with each other, or as Kant puts it, our "judgements." The Kantian imperative is, after all, morally and existentially irrelevant. To be meaningful it must be applied to con-crete human situations and be qualified and conditioned *by* those sit-uations. The use of abstract "universal" formulations in the European experience has been to control people, to impress them, and to intim-idate them. These formulations have political significance not moral or ethical significance. They do not help people to live better. That is why Eric Havelock is wrong when he implies that the Greeks were capable of living more morally *after* Plato's influence. And that is why, despite the ascendancy of European scientific thought, European cul-ture is in many ways *less* moral than the majority of cultures that have an authentically moral base.

Abstraction is then a tool that all people use to integrate them-selves into their environment and to organize their thinking and their knowledge. Clearly the Platonic emphasis that grew to dominate European thought, behavior, and social organization did not have this purpose. Alvin Gouldner's interpretation is closer to mine than that of most European scholars:

> Plato's effort to find transcendental universal Ideas which he pos-tulates to be real is probably related to the very practical problem confronting the Greek morality of his time: finding a common ground among diverse beliefs and establishing a basis for unifying them, of composing competing claims and values so that all need not be treated relativistically, as if they were of equal value. The development of universal definitions may, then, not only have

emerged from the disinterested stirring of an idle curiosity anxious to think more clearly for its own sake, but also as a response to the crisis of Greek moral and belief systems. On a sociological level, it is in effect an effort to identify a hidden ground among warring views and a rhetoric serving to win consent to a method aimed at producing concensus.[93]

Even in its tentativeness, Gouldner's portrayal of the implications of Platonic philosophy, and importantly of Plato's motives, is refreshingly honest in its lack of ordinary European chauvinism. The implications that Plato's intentions may have been more than "academic" is strangely sacrilegious in a thoroughly secular society. Perhaps the Sophists were the most effective critics of the Platonic Order from those among the "ancestors" of the European. They apparently presented the greatest threat to his new state, as they attacked it at its epistemological base. So they come out to be the worst moral villains, since immorality is equated with relativism. Lewis Richards says:

According to the philosophy of the Sophists there does not exist any objective truth, only beliefs. "Man is the measure of all things," said Protagoras. There may be many contradictory opinions about the one and the same thing and all of them equally true. The wise man is he who can change the opinions of the many through the art of persuasion. This explains how they believed that they could prove "the wrong logic as the right one and the right as the wrong one."[94]

We would do well to look more closely at the writings of the Sophists from an African-centered perspective. It would seem that they were dangerous, because if one believed them, the painstaking "arguments" in the Platonic dialogues might not hold water. Things are not necessarily what they are made to appear. In contemporary Euro-American society the skill that pays off is that which enables one to make aggression look like "defense," oppression look like "freedom," and cultural imperialism look like "enlightenment." The Sophists, we are told, were dangerous because they "undermined the concepts of religion, family, the state and moral behavior." (But isn't this what Plato had to do?) "They taught that religion was an invention of the philosophers, that Gods were the creations of man, and that the laws were passed by the strong for their own protection. The danger of such teachings to society was vast. The young people especially were apt to become influenced and ruined."[95]

But, in fact, Platonic views were to lead to monolith and imperial control, while the Sophists seem to have had a more pluralistic view, recognizing the validity in cultural diversity and world-view. In Gouldner's words, this recognition leads them to:

> . . . a critique of the conventional distinctions between Greeks and barbarians, aristocrats and plebeians, slaves and masters, viewing these as artifices contrary to nature, and, indeed, viewing the gods themselves as men's own invention. The diversified customs and beliefs they encounter lead some Sophists to conclude that when men disagree about institutions, laws, or customs, it does not necessarily follow that some of them must be right and others wrong; and that there is not necessarily any one unvarying standard of truth by which the validity of social beliefs can be judged. Institutions and laws, from this standpoint, have to be evaluated in terms of the differing conditions that prevail in different communities.[96]

Obviously this would not do at all. This epistemological stand was incompatible with the Platonic objective. No wonder Plato spends so much time "refuting" the Sophists in his dialogues. The Sophist's view did not yield power, did not suit the demands of the European *asili* and was therefore rejected as an epistemological model.

To understand the function of the abstract-absolute modality is to understand European development and its relationship to alternative patterns of development, that is, to other cultures. An effective critique of European culture must trace its development from one critical juncture to the next, at which point the need to solidify new orders has always been met by another dogma, another ideological statement of European supremacy. This process leads towards ever more intense despiritualization and greater control.

The culture that Plato has initiated is not a good one for the creative mind nor for those who are not European. In light of this interpretation, Plato's anger towards the Sophists makes more sense. They become enemies, almost the symbol of evil because of their rejection of the rational. To state explicity that man was the measure of all things, as Protagoras said, was to undermine the new order. Of course, the Platonic view implied the same thing, but he limited it to "rational man," and he defined "reason." Once the new "measure of man" had been decreed, it couldn't be changed. Well over one thousand years later in the same tradition, Saint Simon and others would echo Plato's edict. They would say that the new society should be derived from principles of rational thought. Absolutism was a corequisite for the realization of such a state. The Sophists had said that there could be many and contradictory opinions about the same thing and all of them true! What blasphemy! Worse, sedition!

Arthur O. Lovejoy uses the phrase "metaphysical pathos" in a way that seems to bring together Gregory Bateson's "eidos" and "ethos" into one idea. A sense of the eternal gives aesthetic pleasure to the European mind, says Lovejoy.[97] The idea of immutability and pure abstractness are pleasing to the European *utamaroho*. Lovejoy says of Platonic thought:

> Having arrived at the conception of Idea of Ideas which is a pure perfection alien to all the categories of ordinary thought and in need of nothing, external to itself, he forthwith finds in just this transcendent and absolute Being the necessitating logical ground of the existence of this world. . . . And if any reason for the being of the sensible world was to be found, it must necessarily, for Plato, be found in the Intellectual World, and in the very nature of the sole Self-Sufficing Being. The not-so-good, not to say the bad, must be apprehended as derivative from the Idea of the Good, as involved in the essence of Perfection. The self-same God who was the Goal of all desire must also be the Source of the creatures that desire it.[98]

The experiencing of the sacred and the eternal, as opposed to profane and secular time seems to be essential for human spiritual fulfillment or at least satisfaction. But in majority cultures this experience is achieved in other ways. The power of ritual drama as a cultural mechanism capable of restructuring ordinary categories of time and space is profound, startling, and impressive: a different kind of transcendence indeed from the artificial construct that serves as the basis for rational thought. This is not a transcendence in which we participate existentially. Ritual drama, on the other hand, acts to transform the psyche to redefine reality for a special moment. It becomes a phenomenal reality. The European conceptual framework treats phenomena as objects and so takes away the power of experienced reality. As Norman Brown has said, "Secular rationalism is really a religion."[99]

William James is a European philosopher who appears insane when viewed in terms of European philosophy, because of his refusal to accept its long standing tradition, his rejection of the European *utamawazo*. James critiques what he calls "monistic idealism" or the "philosophy of the absolute." He says that it is essentially "nonhuman"; "[it] neither acts nor suffers, nor loves nor hates; it has no needs, desires, or aspirations, no failures or successes, friends or enemies, victories or defeats." "Absolutism," he says, dictates that nothing in this life is real. "The great claim of the philosophy of the absolute is that the absolute is no hypothesis, but a presupposition implicated in all thinking, and needing only a little effort of analysis to be seen as a logical necessity."[100] James' own "pragmatic" conception of truth is as follows:

> True ideas are those that we can assimilate, validate, corroborate and verify. False ideas are those that we cannot. . . . The truth of an idea is not a stagnant property inherent in it. Truth *happens* to an idea. It *becomes* true, is *made* true by events. Its verity *is* in fact an event, a process: the process namely of its verifying itself, its veri-*fication*. Its validity is the process of its valid-*ation*. [James' italics][101]

Plato would not have had any patience for James' "pragmatism" and neither has the European tradition. It does not "fit" the ideological needs of this minority culture. Does not "suit" the other dominant modes of the culture. It does not satisfy the power needs of the *asili*.

The synthetic mode yields cosmic conceptions. The European world-view has succeeded in leaving the culture with no authentic cosmology, no true metaphysic. Everything is physical, material, and separate. The ultimate approach to knowledge is objectification and analysis. Willie Abraham talks about the European "tendency to rip things apart."[102] There are some things, he says, that cannot be "divided" without destroying their integrity. It would seem that the human would be one of these. The European scientific approach tears human beings to shreds in order to understand them. The essentialist view assumes man/woman to be irreducible. The analytical mode splits things up. Remote and absolute abstraction is made applicable to the here and now through an analytical methodology. What seems to have occurred very early in European development was a predilection for one of the cognitive methods that we as human beings were capable of employing. The absolute, the abstract, and the analytical suit the European *utamaroho*, an *utamaroho* that needs the sensation of control.

Empirical evidence supports this intepretation. As mentioned previously, early on in the history of European scientific thought, language-related skills, and methods of "knowing" were associated with a portion of the brain that was labelled "major," while the portion that generated other types of responses was called "minor," and as is indicated by the semantic relationship of these two terms, the "minor" was thought to be "less developed" than the "major." This was natural or "cultural," given the predilection of the European mind for unilinear evolutionary models that allow for the comparison of phenomena on a "progressive" scale. Later, however, in the 1960s experimentation on the brain, it was discovered that both hemispheres of the brain, the "right" and the "left" were involved in "higher" cognitive functions and that these two halves were not in opposition or antagonistic to one another as the European world-view would predispose one to think, but that their functions were complementary. Each hemisphere, according to "split-brain" theory, is fashioned to "different modes of thinking, both highly complex."[103] The term "mode" here is very important. It is the *Kuntu* of African philosophy: the manner in which a thing is perceived, apprehended, made intelligible, and expressed. It is the modality and as such it effects the contours of what we receive, perceive, and experience. It is "media" and therefore has a complex and intimate relationship to communication. The *Kuntu* can do much to determine, limit, portray, distort, or enrich the phenomenon being presented.

Roger Sperry at the California Institute of Technology has carried out investigations to further the understanding of the "bimodal" nature of our brains. His work has produced the following information: (1) that there is a connecting "cable" of nerve fibers between the two hemispheres of the brain; (2) that when this cable is severed each hemisphere operates independently; (3) and that each hemisphere perceives its own reality, but that this reality is only partial or incomplete without that of the other hemisphere. The intact brain has a "corpos callosa" (connecting body) that facilitates communication between the two hemispheres and so unifies the thinking/feeling being. The principles expressed are those of an African cosmology in which we have the fundamental "twinness" of the universe; the complementary functions of opposites that cooperate to form the proper working of the whole. But our notions of what constitutes intelligence have been molded by the minority Western European world-view, and so we have difficulty thinking holistically in this regard, since the European world is predicated on first separation, dichotomization, and then "dominance" of one of the opposites.

The two hemispheres are now known as "left" and "right." The left hemisphere is thought to function in a verbal, analytical mode, while the right hemisphere is nonverbal, global, or "synthetic," spatial, complex, and intuitive. Clearly just as the latter was previously known as the "minor" function, it has consistently and systematically, even—one could say—institutionally, been devalued in European civilization/culture. It is rarely even recognized as being a source of "intelligence." It is neither "tested for" nor encouraged. Intelligence in European society has been identified with the cognitive mode that is generated and controlled by the left hemisphere of the brain. Hunter Adams prefers to talk about "cultural styles of knowing" rather than splitting the brain in this way.[104]

Perhaps the most recent vintage of this Eurocentric view, "scientifically" stated, is to be found in the work of Julian Jaynes. His theory is that human consciousness as "we" know it did not begin to develop until the Second century before the Christian Era! This means that the Great Pyramid of Gizeh and the calculations involved in its creation, the medicine, mathematics, chemistry, and state organization of ancient (Kemet) Egypt, not to mention Sumeria, were all accomplished without "consciousness." "A civilization without consciousness is possible." [105] Jaynes' theory is interesting and ultimately of the classical Eurocentric genre, while on the surface giving the impression of being unique and innovative. It is a new variation on an old theme. For Jaynes, consciousness has the following features: (1) "spatialization." (2) "Excerption" - we only "see" a part of any particular thing. It is ironic that he should say this since it is the left-brained European modality that keeps people from comprehending globally. (3) "The Analog 'I'" which allows us to imagine ourselves doing things, i.e., "The Metaphor 'Me.'" Of this feature of consciousness, Jaynes says, "We can both look out from the imagined self... or we can step back a bit and see ourselves." (4) "Narratization," from which "we are constantly seeing ourselves as the main figures in the stories of our lives." (5) "Conciliation," "bring[ing] things together as conscious objects."[106] According to Jaynes, human beings in ancient times could speak, write, listen, read, learn, make decisions, think, and reason, but were not "conscious":

> . . . consciousness is an operation rather than a thing, a repository, or a function. It operates by way of analogy, by way of constructing an analog space with an analog "I" that can observe that space, and move metaphorically in it. It operates on any reactivity, excerpts relevant aspects, narratizes and conciliates them together in a metaphorical space where such meanings can be manipulated like things in space. Conscious mind is a spatial analog of the world and mental acts are analogs of bodily acts.
> *Consciousness operates only on objectively observable things.*[italics added.][107]

He takes Havelock's view one step further, "There is in general no consciousness in the *Iliad* . . . . The beginnings of action are not in conscious plans, reasons, and motives; they are in the actions and speeches of gods. . . .The Iliadic heros had no egos."[108] Why were these ancient people not yet "conscious?" According to Jaynes, it was because of the structure of their brains, which had two distinct "chambers." They used only one part for speaking, thinking, learning, etc. The other was used for the "voice" of the "gods." In other words, ancient human beings were told what to do by "voices" in their heads. "Voices" told them to build pyramids and civilizations. They took these voices to be the authoritative speech of divine beings, and so they obeyed. One question that comes to mind is: What *couldn't* they do? Well, says Jaynes, they were not capable of "introspection." (One has only to read the ancient Kemetic texts to know that he is mistaken.) And they could not be "self" directed. The voices of the bicameral mind were a form of social control; the last stage in the development of language, a development that made civilization possible. In the bicameral stage of "civilization," "the language of men involved only one hemisphere in order to leave the other free for the language of gods."[109] It seems that one of the things that led Jaynes to the development of his theory was his observance of schizophrenics. He tells us that schizophrenic hallucinations are like the guidances of the gods in antiquity. Stress is the instigation in both instances. During the eras of the "bicameral mind" the stress threshold of human beings was lower, like that of schizophrenics today.[110] Stress, he says, comes from decision making, and that is what caused hallucinations of the gods. Jaynes writes:

> . . . the presence of voices which had to be obeyed were the absolute prerequisite to the conscious stage of mind in which it is the self that is responsible and can debate within itself, can order and direct, and that the creation of such a self is the product of culture. In a sense, we have become our own gods.[111]

Jaynes' theory is quite physiological. The difference between "conscious" and "unconsciousness" human beings, or rather "preconscious" human beings, lies in the structure of their brains. The two temporal lobes of the bicameral brain connected by the tiny "anterior commissure" across "which came the directions which built our civilizations and founded the world's religions, where gods spoke to men and were obeyed because they were human volition,"[112] became the "modern" brain with the right and left hemispheres as we know it. The left hemisphere, according to Jaynes, contains the "speech areas" ; the supplementary motor cortex, Broca's area and Wernicke's area. The latter is the "most indispensable to normal speech." This coupled with his feeling that the right brain is "largely unnecessary,"[113] led him to conclude that the right brain is a "vestigial" remain of the "chamber" of the voices of the gods in ancient times. These "voices" that caused past civilizations to be built were afterall only "excitations" in what corresponds to Wernicke's area on the right hemisphere of the contemporary human brain.

But cultural/environmental changes were to cause physiological changes in the brain. Writing and trade interfered with the "voices." Writing no longer stressed the auditory, and trade meant interaction with other groups of people who were hearing "other" voices, which at the very least was confusing. The gods also failed in the "chaos of historical upheaval."[114] The result was "consciousness." The result is also a continued valorization of the left-brain cognitive modality by the European. Beneath the complexity and ingenuity, even intellectual creativity of Jayne's theory of consciousness, are quite visible the earmarks of the European *utamawazo* as well as its ideological tendencies: Universal, unilinear evolution, "progress," and the intellectual superiority of European culture is assumed. The differences between earlier civilizations and those that came later are understood invidiously: "contemporary differences between the hemispheres in cognitive functions at least echo such differences of function between man and god as seen in the literature of bicameral man."[115]

For Jaynes the process has not ended; it couldn't. "Evolution" does not stop; after all "progress" is not reached. That is the beauty of these ideas for the European mind. And so he imagines us to be still in the throes of "transition" from the grip of the bicameral mind, still fighting the authority of the gods, or their "voices"—even though now we can only "read" their voices (except for those of us who are "schizophrenic.") Jaynes never says what "we" are moving towards. Is it toward a one-hemisphered brain? The illusion will then become the reality, and that is truly psychotic. I agree with Jaynes on one point. We see the same thing, but we see it from different perspectives. "Science" has become secularized; its view of the human, profane. And as this happens people (Europeans) search for the loss "authorization" of the gods past.[116]

But typically Jaynes has falsely "universalized" a cultural phenomenon. He is describing European science and the European malaise. In his view "we" are going through a necessary stage in the march towards "enlightenment," which, if I interpret him correctly, results when human beings "realize" that there is nothing more than themselves, that they can look to no greater authorization for their decisions. This leads to the ultimate and total desacralization of the universe. (Thank goodness Europe represents only a small minority of the world, given the nature of the European conception of the human!)

But there are other views of the modalities of human consciousness. Erich Neumann offers a Jungian-influenced conceptualization, to some degree reminscent of the right-brain/left-brain distinction. His distinction is between "matriarchal consciousness" and "patriarchal consciousness." Matriarchal consciousness is prior, is linked to the "moon spirit" and "moon time," as it is grounded in natural and cyclical rhythms; it is intuitive and becomes "impregnated" with ideas, rather than "willing" them. Understanding in this modality is not divorced from feeling. It involves natural processes of transformation, so that knowing and comprehending affect the knowing being. Matriarchal consciousness is also associated with the still darkness of night that is pregnant with growth.

Patriarchal consciousness relates to "daylight and sun." It is associated with independently willed thought. Neumann says however, that it is self-deceptive, "interpreting itself as an absolutely free system." It is "highly practical," efficient, and quick to react. It followed matriarchal consciousness in development, detaching itself from the unconscious.

> We see processes of abstraction, which assist in the free disposal and application of ideas and . . . lead to the manipulation of abstractions like numbers in mathematics and concepts in logic. In the psychological sense such abstractions are in the highest degree without emotional content.[117]

In "patriarchal consciousness" the knower is not affected by what is known; rather the knower controls the idea. While matriarchal consciousness involves "affect-participation," "the abstract thought of patriarchal consciousness is cold in comparison, for the objectivity demanded of it presupposes an aloofness possible only to cold blood and a cool head."[118]

For Neumann, as opposed to Jaynes, both modalities represent forms of consciousness, even though one is linked closely to the unconscious. But in an African-centered view this is not negative, since it allows us to be in tune with a universe in which we participate as one form of being. Clearly *both* forms of consciousness are necessary. They complement one another. The whole brain has two halves. Perhaps European culture has been molded by a Platonic, "patriarchal" consciousness, and seeks to destroy "matriarchal consciousness" because of the destructive, confrontational nature of the European *utamaroho*. "Matriarchal consciousness" represents a loss of control in the European view. And as it struggles to resurface even

European feminists fight against it.

When Plato deified the "patriarchal consciousness," he reified "form" that inhibited the further "transformation" ("matriarchal consciousness") of the human spirit. As a result European culture does not allow its members to become complete ("full-term") human beings (the symbolism of *Yurugu*). Jaynes may be correct but only with regard to the European. Maybe they will succeed in the elimination of one of the hemispheres of their brains, therefore being forever off balance, in a state of perpetual disequilibrium. (Or is that, in fact, how they came into being?) This is certainly a description of the culture.

According to Levy-Bruhl, who offered an earlier version of Eurocentric theory, "logic" began with "civilized" thought, based on the principle of contradiction. "Primitives" made use of "prelogical," "collective representations." The mode of participation contradicts the European emphasis on recognition of discrete entities. In anthropological theory this cognitive style of thinking has been called "primitive," "native," and sometimes "folk." But aren't we really dealing with two different world-views, which in turn, generated different epistemological and ontological conceptions? Indeed, the objective of this discussion has been to scrutinize the "taken-for-granted" aspects of European culture or "mind," which is afterall a minority phenomenon,[119] so that they can no longer be assumed to be "universal": two (or more) world-views rather than two developmental stages of human thought as Levy-Bruhl, Julian Jaynes, and countless other European theorists would have them.

The African metaphysic, the Native American and Oceanic "majority cultures" (it is safe to generalize here), all presuppose a fundamental unity of reality based on the organic interrelatedness of being; all refuse to objectify nature, and insist on the essential spirituality of a true cosmos. What became known as the "scientific" view was really the European view that assumed a reality precluding psychical or spiritual influences on physical, material being. This view also resulted in the elimination of a true "metaphysical" concept and of an authentic cosmology. David Bidney says that,

> Levy-Bruhl . . . exhibited an ethnocentric prejudice in assuming that only the positivistic, antimetaphysical position current in his time was logical as well as scientific and that metaphysical postulates were a priori prelogical as well as prescientific.[120]

Desacralization of Nature:
Despiritualization of the Human

From the outset, let me say that, in discussing these European conceptions we will have a problem with gender terminology. First of all, it is awkward, but nonetheless important to refrain from the use of "man" to refer to "human" as the European has done in discourse. Second, the confusion is further complicated by the fact that when discussing the European, I will be talking about European men for the most part, because Plato,and those who followed in his wake, ignored women and did not include them in their self-concepts of "philosopher," "king," or "the European," and that is why they could refer to themselves collectively as "European Man." In one sense we *are* talking about ideas that effected and were adopted by European women, children, and men. The issue, then, becomes complicated, and the reader must indulge me as I attempt to deal with these problems generated by the European world-view.

The way the European is taught to view nature and his/her proper relationship to it is particularly important, because it is, in part, the consequences of this conception that are most distinctive of European culture. European ontology generates a conception of nature and the human, and of reality.

What is the implicit idea of nature and its significance that emerges from Plato's dialogues? Alvin Gouldner says:

> In Plato's view . . . ends are not resident in nature but in the universal Ideas or eternal Forms which transcend nature, in which nature only imperfectly "participates" and apart from which it is inherently disorderly. From his standpoint, therefore, nature cannot be controlled by the external influence of some regulating end or design.[121]

Elsewhere Gouldner talks about the ideas of those who were to restructure the society:

> On conceiving of all nature as intrinsically hostile or indifferent to mind—having, that is, an abiding disposition toward disorder—the planners'proposed changes are felt to be made and maintained only against nature, not with its cooperation. From Plato's standpoint, mind and reason, and therefore orderliness are not in but above nature and need to master it.[122]

Nature emerges as the world of becoming, the sensate world of a lower order than "being" and, therefore, to be always controlled,

conditioned and moulded in accordance with the absolute and perfect ideas that issue from the "World of Being." And the human being,
insofar as he is part of this imperfect nature, which only "imitates" but
cannot "be," must be controlled and moulded as well.[123] What begins
to emerge is a view of nature and of the human that places them in
opposition to one another, by virtue of the fact that only that part of
the human being which is other than nature (the rational) is superior
to it. This idea of the basically hostile relationship between "human"
and nature, in which the human seeks continually to control nature
is characteristically European. It runs through European culture lineally (in a chronological historical sense) and collaterally or synchronically in that it has both effected the course of European
development and informed the collective behavior and social constructs of the culture.

The Christian view of nature again exhibits the influence of
Plato's idea of the disorderly and chaotic, even hostile "nature" that
must be controlled. The "pattern" or "design" (standard) to which
Gouldner refers, is what the Christian uses to measure the morality
of other peoples and to mould them. Katherine George comments on
the Christian view of nature as evidenced in reports of newly "discovered" lands in the sixteenth century:

> The dominant attitude in these accounts conceived of civilization-
> Graeco-Roman civilization in particular- as an essential discipline
> imposed upon the irregularities of nature; as nature -blind nature-
> without restraint and guidance, runs to monstrousities, so culture
> without civilization runs to disorder and excess.[124]

> Raw nature, "fallen" nature, which for the Greek was disorder, is for
> the Christian even worse: it is sin.[124]

Rheinhold Niebuhr attempts to present a more "modern" explanation of Christian concepts, a more philosophically and politically
attractive interpretation in terms of contemporary European
lifestyles than that offered by the Church's scholastic heritage. The
results of an astute mind wrestling to make Christian ideas into both
something distinct from and simultaneously appropriate to the
European *utamawazo*, and to rescue the Church from the more bar-
barous tendencies in European history are most interesting. Niebuhr
is fighting a losing battle, for to separate Christian ideology from
European cultural imperialism would be to forge an entirely new religious statement. This, of course, he cannot do since he is intent on
demonstrating the way in which his philosophical interpretations are

rooted in the origins of the Christian idea. (Unconsciously, perhaps, it is precisely the European heritage that he wants to claim.)

Though Niebuhr's style and subtlety make his ideas appear to be unfamiliar at first, it is possible to recognize, if we know how to look, a characteristically European interpretation of the relationship between "human" and nature:

> Human existence is obviously distinguished from animal life by its qualified participation in creation. Within limits it breaks the forms of nature and creates new configuration of vitality. Its transcendence over natural process offers it the opportunity of interfering with the established forms and unities of vitality as nature knows them. This is the basis of human history, with its progressive alteration of forms, in distinction from nature which knows no history but only endless repetition within the limits of each given form.... Since man is deeply involved in the forms of nature on one hand, and is free of them on the other; since he must regard determinations of sex, race and (to a lesser degree) geography as forces of ineluctable fate, but can nevertheless arrange and rearrange the vitalities and unities of nature within certain limits, the problem of human creativity is obviously filled with complexities.[125]

and finally Niebuhr says,

> Nature and spirit both possess resources of vitality and form. The resources of nature may be more negative. The vitalities of nature and its forms may be the indispensable presuppositions of human creativity rather than its active agents; but they cannot be disregarded. . . the vitalities and unities of nature may play a more negative part in human destructiveness than those of spirit. The natural impulse of sex is, for instance, an indispensible condition of all higher forms of family organization as it is the negative force of destructive sex aberrations. In the same way the natural cohesion of tribe and race is the foundation of higher political creations as also the negative determinant of interracial and international anarchy.[126]

In spite of Niebuhr's continual qualifications, the view of the relationship between "human" and nature that he offers is ideologically consistent with and characteristic of European thought. The relationship to nature is one of arrogance and exploitation as opposed to awe, respect, and harmony. Put simply, nature is not to be trusted. The human only trusts her/his rational faculties that are not natural, but "cultural." One ends up in conflict with one's nature, which represents the devalued circle of repetition as opposed to the valued line of historical progress. To which category does "god" belong?

The concepts of nature, of reality, of "the human," and of truth are intricately bound one to the other and inextricably entwined in the "specialness" or seen another way, the "otherness" of the European world-view. It is a particular view of nature that allows for European science, a "science" which is predicated on an epistemology that involves the separation of the human from itself in order to isolate and valorize the seemingly peculiar human ability to rationalize.Thus as the concept of the human becomes limited, so does the concept of reality. Theodore Roszak places emphasis on Francis Bacon and René Descartes for this European tendency, while I have begun with an emphasis on Plato.

> . . . domination remains the object; Bacon never deviates from his conviction that "the command over things natural—over bodies, medicine, mechanical powers and infinite others of this kind—is the one proper and ultimate end of true natural philosophy."[127]

Roszak's work critiques "objectification," "reductionism," "alienation," and power in European thought in unparalleled fashion:

> . . . what Baconian-Cartesian epistemology did was to bestow high philosophical status upon that act of alienation by insisting that it provided our only reliable access to reality. Far more directly than it encourage callous behavior, this ennobling of the alienated psyche has progressively degraded every other form of awareness human beings possess.

> once we elevate such a psychic mode to the highest cultural dignity, identifying it as the only intellectually productive way of addressing the universe. . . There will be knowledge, power, dominion without limit. We are licensed to unravel all mysteries and to remake the world- including human nature itself.[128]

Roszak's view of the "psychic mode" that makes European science possible is radically different from Eric Havelock's, who praises Plato for ushering in a new modality. Indeed, it was Plato, and others who followed, who laid the groundwork on which Bacon and Descartes could erect their theories. Roszak speaks of Bacon and his disciples:

> They had found the great truth: break faith with the environment, establish between yourself and it the alienative dichotomy called

objectivity, and you will surely gain power. Then nothing—no sense of fellowship or personal intimacy or strong belonging—will bar your access to the delicate mysteries of man and nature. Nothing will inhibit your ability to manipulate and exploit. This is the same power we gain over people when we refuse to honor their claim to respect, to compassion, to love. They become for us mere things on which we exercise power. Between ourselves and them there is no commerce of the feelings, no exchange of sentiment or empathy.[129]

Roszak has stated almost poetically what became the cutting edge of the thesis of this study: that European epistemology is symbiotically related to European imperialism. The objectification of the human and the natural allow one to treat both as "things." Peoples and cultures that refuse to regard themselves and nature as spiritless are considered "stupid."

Roszak's concept of "reductionism" explains why life must be taken out of nature in order to facilitate the method:

Reductionism flows from many diverse sources: from an overwhelming desire to dominate, from the hasty effort to find simple, comprehensive explanations, from a commendable desire to deflate the pretentious obscurantism of religious authority; but above all from a sense of human estrangement from nature which could only increase inordinately as Western society's commitment to single vision grew ever more exclusive. In effect, reductionism is what we experience whenever sacremental consciousness is crowded out by idolatry, by the effort to turn what is alive to a mere thing.[130]

In discussing European cosmology, Arthur Lovejoy isolates certain ideas or principles that in his view have been seminal to European philosophy. These ideas find their origins in Plato and can be traced through their various expressions in the subsequent history of European thought. He concludes that there have been basically three ideas so closely associated in European intellectual history that they together have produced "one of the major conceptions in Occidental thought"; expressed in a single term they are represented by (1) the "Great Chain of Being."[131] Two of the generative aspects of this idea taken in isolation have been the "Principle of Plenitude":

. . . not only for the existence of this world, but for every one of its characteristics, for every kind of being which it contains—in strictness, indeed, for each particular being—there must be an ultimate reason, self-explanatory and "sufficient."

... and (2) the "Principle of Continuity":

> ... there are no sudden "leaps" in nature; infinitely various as things
> are, they form an absolutely smooth sequence,,in which no break
> appears, to baffle the craving of our reason for continuity every-
> where.[132]

These culminated in "two great rationalistic ontologies of the
seventeenth century" and in the argument for optimism. According
to Lovejoy, the idea of an "ontological scale" in combination with
Aristotle's zoological and psychological hierarchies produced a third
principle of "unilinear gradation" that was grafted to the two principles of "plenitude" and "continuity."[133]

Lovejoy is concerned with tracing the "historic sources" of these
cosmological and ontological ideas. He says that the principles underlying the Chain of Being conception and its related groups of ideas—
"plenitude," "continuity," and "gradation"—owed its genesis to Plato
and Aristotle and its systematization to the Neoplatonists."[134]

> The scale of being, as implied by the principle of expansiveness
> and self-transcendence of "The Good" becomes the essential con-
> ception of the Neoplatonic cosmology.[134]

Difference of kind automatically implied difference of value,
which generated "diversity of rank in a hierarchy."[134]

As we move toward a theoretical model for the explanation of
European cultural imperialism, Lovejoy has given us food for thought.
Clearly one of the outstanding characteristics of the European world-
view is its treatment of "difference," and perhaps what developed
was an *utamaroho* that related to perceived "difference" intensely,
xenophobically, and aggressively defensive. This relationship could
have been both caused and effected by a world-view that scaled difference in terms of relative value: an *asili* that demands power.
Accompanied by the mode of objectification, this encourages an ideology and political behavior that allows Europeans to feel justified in
treating "different" peoples as devalued objects. Since the world-view
has ideological strength, other world-views were (are) political
threats, and so cultural aggression is necessary whereby the
European world-view is imposed on "different" peoples. This theoretical model will be restated throughout this study. Its main thrust
is the insistence on the intimate and causal relationship between (*utamaroho*), ontology, eidos, epistemology (*utamawazo*) and politi-
cal/cultural behavior in the European experience.

Lovejoy says that Aristotle, in *De Anima,* suggests a hierarchical arrangement of all organisms, an idea that had a great influence on subsequent philosophy as well as natural history. The hierarchy was based on the "powers of the soul" possessed by an organism: those of plants were nutritive, those of "man" were rational. Each organism possessed the powers of those below it on the scale as well as its own additional and definitive "power."[135] Ultimately this results in a universe that constitutes a hierarchy with the most "natural" of beings occupying the lower positions of rank and the most "spiritual"—God and the angels—as the highest and "upper" beings. The human is unique in that he is both nature, flesh, and spirit and therefore among (animate) beings he is the most "rational" and therefore the "highest." The use of the term "spirit" is somewhat problematical. Niebuhr, Hegel, and Aristotle use it very differently from my use of the term. Their use connotes intellect and the rational, as opposed to nature. In my view spirit *is* nature and human as well as "supernature." It is the metaphysical. It accounts for human moral sense, commitment, value, and emotion: for human creativity and culture. It constitutes the substratum out of which the intellect is born and by which it is properly grounded.

Platonism, Christian theology, and the Chain of Being cosmology all contain a conception of the human as not being at home in the natural world. They are not "at peace" with themselves because of the "dualistic" nature—the coexistence in the person of two conflicting essences; "the flesh and the spirit." Lovejoy says, of the concept of the human being's place in nature generated by the "Chain" idea;

> ... torn by conflicting desires and propensities; as a member of two orders of being at once, he wavers between both, and is not quite at home in either. He thus has, afterall, a kind of uniqueness in nature; but it is an unhappy uniqueness. He is, in a sense in which no other link in the chain is, a strange hybrid monster; and if this gives him a certain pathetic sublimity, it also results in incongruities of feeling, inconsistencies of behavior, and disparities between his aspirations and his powers which render him ridiculous.[136]

And when the "spiritual" entities are removed from the picture—as they usually are once the cosmology is constructed—what is left is a hierarchy with human beings at the top looking down over nature (their own special kingdom). Lovejoy quotes from a textbook of scholastic philosophy of the Middle Ages: "As man is made for the sake of God, namely, that he may serve him, so is the world made for the sake of man, that it may serve him."[137] Once "god" is postulated to give the impression of spiritual priority and the feeling of intellectual satisfaction that comes to the European mind from an absolute first principle, "he" is eliminated and, for all practical purposes, the human being becomes this god. Page duBois says,

> it must be remembered that not only barbaroi, foreigners were seen by Plato to be deprived of reasoning ability. Women and slaves as well as animals formed part of a "chain" which descended from the Idea of the good, from god. The hierarchy which Plato fixed among kinds endured for many centuries and still operates in Western discourse about difference . . .

> The clarification of ideas of superiority and inferiority in terms of sexual, racial, and species difference is an important step in the history of Western philosophy and of social relations of dominance and submission for those who follow in the tradition.[138]

The European conception of nature, the cosmological consequences of this conception, and the place that the human being has in this cosmology are all significant ingredients of the European mythoform. Herein are raised several critical ontological issues that relate to European thought, behavior, and value (ideology). Europeans assume a very special place for "themselves" in the universe and at the same time feel "uneasy" in that universe. If there is anything "natural" in them it is opposed to and in conflict with what is considered to be the most valuable part of them. This line of thought (and it must be kept in mind that it is among the deepest, most conscious—i.e., reflective—as well as unconscious assumptions of European belief, has several cultural implications. First, the European ascribes to the abstraction "man" priority in the universe, and throughout the history of European civilization there has been the tendency to translate this idea concretely into that of the priority of European "man" in the universe of "men" (humans). As other "nonrational" creatures exist to serve "man," so other, "less rational" people exist to serve European "man" (and women, of course, must serve them, since they are the least rational of the Europeans). This theme in its more blatant forms is pejoratively referred to in contemporary parlance as "racist" thought, and characterized as an aberration of "illogical" minds, in an effort to separate it from the best of the European tradition. But, to the contrary, such thought is "normal," even understandable and quite "logical," if one accepts the givens of the European *utamawazo*. The argument would go something like this: The European "man" is the most rational of people. It is within him that the natural and the pathological are best controlled. Other people are closer to beasts in the Chain. The European, therefore, serves the rational plan of his god by guiding and controlling other people. American presidents always talk in terms of the American mission abroad being that of bringing "freedom" to all people. Anti-American revolutionaries are always equated with "barbarism," while America is seen as defending "civilization." These terms and arguments are all based on the same mythoform.

We have seen that the European conception is that of human beings at war with themselves and with their natural surroundings. This feeling is both reflective and productive of the "will-to-power" and the desire to control nature and other people and what is natural (emotional) in themselves. They have no place in a harmonious relationship to their environment since their conceptions do not allow them to experience the peace that such a relationship offers. Niebuhr says that the "essential homelessness of the human spirit is the ground of all religion."[139] What happens when that religion is inadequate? Unable to achieve peace and security from spirituality, the European seeks fulfillment in the will-to-power, in "mastery over" rather than "harmony with." Their effect on the world is one of discordance. Imperial ambitions and the structures they dictate are the symptomatic expression of a lack of spiritual peace. A being who is not at peace with itself, not at home in the universe, is compelled to disrupt that which surrounds it—to refashion and control that universe. The European seeks peace in human-made, imposed order, and, of course, does not find it. And so the imperial pursuit continues infinitely, as well as the pursuit of "progress." This as a malaise finds its origins even before its crystallization in Platonic culture, which was perhaps a result of a latent "ice-age" *utamaroho*. While Platonic conceptions facilitated the institutionalization of the European *utamaroho* and European supremacy in the world, there are other "pre" and "non" platonic expressions of this same *utamaroho* in the warrior mythology and behavior of Northern Europe in its "pre" -Christian experience. While the devaluation of nature may have been intellectualized by Plato, we find its "religious" expression in early Hebrew thought. (See Chap. 2.)

The objectification of nature is what allows for its exploitation and rape. In other cultures nature is experienced subjectively, as are other human beings. The European seeks the perfectly rational order—an order that has no place for the natural (as irrational) and that is the embodiment of the human nightmare. In majority cultures there appears to be an intuitive and sophisticated grasp of the implications of the exploitation of nature and of the creation of an antagonistic relationship between human and nature. The contemporary ecological discussion is pitifully naïve when expressed in terms of "detergents with low phosphates" and the recycling of paper. The real implications for ecological sanity touch the deepest beliefs of the European and the philosophical basis of their culture, as Theodore Roszak points out in *Where the Wasteland Ends*. The question is whether it is possible for them to alter their concept of nature and of their relationship to it. Such a change would, of course, imply corresponding changes in the total conceptual apparatus offered by the European world-view and would therefore involve many other aspects of European culture and ideology with which the concept of nature interrelates. (See Chap. 2.) The *asili* of the culture would change. The culture would cease to exist as it is now known. It would be a different "set" with different members.

Willie Abraham, in *The Mind of Africa,* suggests that there are two main views of human nature: They are the "essentialist" view and the "scientific" view. These two views help to provide the philosophical and ideological bases of two correspondingly different types of culture. The "essentialist" view is that "there is a constant element in man which is irreducible, and is the essence of being a man." African civilization, Abraham believes, is "essentialist in inspiration."[140] In the "scientific" view, human nature can be altered; the human can be resolved into elements; and it is possible to predict and control human reaction. "The scientific view depends on analysis, disintegration and then control of selected variables."[141] In this view it is possible to analyze human "material" into elements and then rearrange them according to a desired dominant principle. What are the implications of these distinctions for the "construction" of cultural models? Abraham characterizes European culture as "rationalistic" (scientific), and Akan culture (which he says is paradigmatic for African civilization), as "metaphysical" (essentialist).

"Humanism" in European discourse is usually assumed to represent the highest and most politically disinterested or "universalistic" approach to the human. In reality "humanism" has generally implied the typically European deification of the rational and the ascent of the human being to supremacy in the universe by virtue of her/his rational faculties. It is the intercultural implications of this line of reasoning that become politically significant. Abraham says:

> . . . . the essence of humanism consists in the replacement of God the creator with man the creator. . . . Culture in the age of enlightenment meant cultivation of the reason. . . . The idea underlying

rational humanism is a rational one. It was already involved in Aristotle's account of man as a rational animal and the democratic political theory which he based on this idea. The idea is that *we* cannot think it accidental that we possess reason. . . to humans, this is a defining characteristic. This is what should be meant by calling reason a capacity, or a faculty, or a disposition, rather than a sequence of episodic acts.

The cult of rationalism is so deeply imbedded in European ontological and epistemological conceptions that it leads even to a "rationalistic ethics":

Since the sensibilities were held to be subject to the reason. . . ethics and aesthetics were both accepted as being rationalistic. The culmination of this was in Kant's rationalistic ethics, which founded the validity of moral and aesthetic judgments on commands of reason."[142]

This, of course, is the working out of the Platonic imperative. It is the development of a theme. Abraham observes that in European culture, "art is identified with reality, supernature with nature itself, (and) ideals with mere truths." The artist may not have been banished from the State, but in serving the State he/she came to accept the Platonic conception of the "true." His creation began to reflect the rational order. On the other hand, in the Akan theory of the human," spiritual factors are primary," which contrasts sharply with European conceptions. For the Akan, says Abraham, the human being is "an encapsulated spirit, and not an animated body as the Genesis story has it."[143] This conception of human nature extends beyond the three-dimensional finite existence of the human being as conceived in Europe, which is one of the reasons European anthropologists have so misunderstood the African concept of Ancestor Communion. The African ancestors are not gods, but spiritual extensions of human beings on earth, representing another stage of human development. Eric Havelock discusses the Platonic model:

The parables of the Sun, the Line and the Cave have been offered as paradigms which shall illuminate the relationship between ideal knowledge on the one hand and empirical experience on the other, and shall suggest to us the ascent of man through education from the life of the senses towards the reasoned intelligence.[144]

This ontological metaphor is so powerful that it has strongly influenced the European's perception of his own place in the universe. It has enabled him to speak of "high" and "low" cultures. In the former, people are closer to the "light" of civilization, while those in the latter wallow in the "darkness" of ignorance, aware only of what they "feel." Havelock describes the view of humanness offered in the *Republic* (compare it with Abraham's earlier description of the Akan conception of the human being):

> Here the conception of that autonomy is now elevated to a plane where the soul attains its full self-realisation in the power to think and to know. This is its supreme faculty; in the last resort its only one. Man is a "thinking reed."[144]

According to Havelock, this new definition of the human psyche that Plato sought to encourage signified not "man's ghost or wraith, or a man's breath or his life blood, a thing of sense and self consciousness," but "the ghost that thinks," that is capable of "moral decision" and of "scientific cognition"... something unique in the whole realm of nature.[145] It is not, after all, that the European considers human beings to be unique and special that is surprising, for each category of beings in the universe is unique and special; it is the importance that he attaches to this uniqueness that is so characteristically different. The epistemological mode that Havelock has described, that which became characteristic of European culture, presupposes a rationalistic concept of the human, whose proper function is not to feel, but to overcome feeling with "thought." Thought is only properly so called when isolated from feeling and when based on "objectification"; that is, separation of the "self" from the contemplated "object." Human nature is above all and most properly rational. This rational faculty gives humans power and independence. In the *Laws,* Plato says of "man":

> Human nature will be always drawing him into avarice and selfishness, avoiding pain and pursuing pleasure without any reason, and will bring these to the front, obscuring the juster and the better; and so working darkness in his soul will at last fill with evils both him and the whole city. [146]

And Plato's definition of human "freedom" would be realized when man is totally "rational"; that is, when "reason" rules "passion."

The height of arrogance is approached in the rationalistic conception of being and of the human. The European conceives of his god in his own image and not the reverse. Lovejoy says:

> Man is the creation in which God fully becomes an object to him-

self. Man is God represented by God. God is man representing God in self-consciousness. Man is God wholly manifested.

Europeans assume that their god created the universe according to the logic of scientific rationalism, their own invention. "The history we are to review is thus among other things, a part of the history of Western man's long effort to make the world he lives in appear to his intellect a rational one."[147] The Christian formulation of the European tradition is also, as we have pointed out, consistent with this conception of the human being. Lovejoy says,

> The recognition of the fact that man is a creature not in harmony with himself was not, of course, due primarily to the influence of the notion of the Chain of Being. Other elements of Platonism, and in Christianity the radical Pauline opposition of "flesh" and "Spirit," had made this dualistic theory of human nature one of the ruling conceptions in western thought.[148]

Again what we see is a consistent conception of human nature reinforced in the various modalities of the culture, making possible the most successful technico/scientific collasus in our experience. Friedrich Juenger says, "An advanced state of technology is accompanied by mechanical theories of the nature of man."[149] It would seem that in subordinating existential humanity to the machine, the European would end up with a low estimation of human worth. And of course, paradoxically, there is in a real and tragic sense, a corresponding devalorization of the human. But the European with political astuteness and ideological consistency deals with this problem by lowering his estimation of *other* people, thereby rationalizing his aggressive and demeaning behavior towards them. At the same time the part of him that might have been sensitive, and emotional, was also demeaned. Ontologically, the European sees himself as perfect through the perfection of the machine; he becomes the perfect machine. The efficiently operating machine becomes an extension of his ego. Its power to "make" and "produce" is his power. Since all knowledge was linked to the object, eventually this would effect ontological definitions as well: only the object existed. Plato's epistemology is also an ontology. The "True" is that which exists—"Being." Everything else is "becoming" or later "non-being." Ironically this led from an "idealist" philosophy to a materialist view of reality, since the only thing that existed was that which could be objectified. Spirit could not be made into object, could not be controlled so as to be known—it was not valued. Therefore it did not exist. Objectification led to materialization where matter, studied "scientifically" was all that was left. Even human psychology and relationships would be governed by mechanical and physiological causation (Freud). Objectification leads to inorganic relationships.

The rationalistic conception of the human leads inevitably to the machine and to the technological order. A materialistic conception of the human is what rationalism becomes in the existential "acting-out" of culture, for rationalism denies human spirituality. It is only matter in isolation that ultimately has significance for the European mind; it is only matter that can be made to appear perfectly rational. So everything must be materialized. The European view of the human is rationalistic/materialistic, and the European concept of being involves the perfectly ordered universe—with meaning and value being derived only from this rationalistic material base. Scientific rationalism leads to technological rationalism; organization for efficiency.

Lovejoy's concluding comments present one of the most theoretically devastating critiques of the main currents of European philosophical thought. Of the "rationalist ontology" of Europe, he says:

> In so far as the world was conceived in this fashion, it seemed a coherent, luminous, intellectually secure and dependable world, in which the mind of man could go about its business of seeking an understanding of things in full confidence, and empirical science, since it was acquainted in advance with the fundamental principles with which the facts must, in the end, accord, and was provided with a sort of diagram of the general pattern of the universe, could know in outline what to expect, and even anticipate particular disclosures of actual observation.[150]

His estimation of the Chain of Being idea and its implications:

> the history of the idea of the Chain of Being—in so far as that idea presupposed such a complete rational intelligibility of the world—is the history of a failure . . . . The experiment, taken as a whole, constitutes one of the most grandiose enterprises of the human intellect. . . *as the consequences of this most persistent and most comprehensive of hypotheses became more and more explicit, the more apparent became its difficulties; and when they are fully drawn out, they show the hypothesis of the absolute rationality of the cosmos to be unbelievable. . . .* [italics added] It conflicts, in the first place, with one immense fact, besides many particular facts, in the natural order—the fact that existence as we experience it is temporal. A world of time and change—this, at least, our history has shown—

is a world which can neither be deduced from nor reconciled with the postulate that existence is the expression and consequence of a system of "eternal" and "necessary" truths inherent in the very logic of being. Since such a system could manifest itself only in a static and constant world, and since empirical reality is not static and constant, the "image" [as Plato called it] does not correspond with the supposed "model" and cannot be explained by it.[151]

Lovejoy sees that rationalism admits of "rational" contradictions, and that in the attempt to exclude all "arbitrariness," it becomes "irrational." He says that the world of "concrete existence" is a "contingent" world and as such is the negation of "pure logic." "Will," he says, "is prior to intellect."[152] But if such is the case, why would Plato, Aristotle, and so many of their descendants spend so much time trying to prove the opposite, indeed, living as though the opposite were true?

Clearly, European forms of thought have worked, and they have worked well. The theorists had ideological commitments to a social order that would facilitate the rule of certain kinds of people. The *utamawazo* described in this chapter became a tool. The tool was so successful in one kind of enterprise that its shortcomings in other areas could easily be overlooked. Just as its definition of the human was one that encouraged the manipulation of human beings, but ignored "the human" at the same time. "The utility of a belief and its validity are independent variables"[153] The ethnological study of European thought demonstrates the power of its conceptions in the service of the expansionistic, confrontational, domineering *utamaroho, not* their truth or universal validity.

Alternative Models

But this is, after all, merely a description of the European *utamawazo,* and Europe represents a fraction of the world's ideological and cultural creations. There are other possibilities. Vernon Dixon contrasts the European-American and African "axiological worldviews" in the manner in Figure I (overleaf):[154]

The African universe is personalized, not objectified. Time is experienced. There is no infinite abstract and oppressive future; it grows organically from the past and present. Value is placed on "being" rather than "doing."[155] The universe is understood through phenomenal interaction, which produces powerful symbols and images, which in turn communicate truths. "Diunital logic" indicates that in African thought a thing can be both A and not A at the same time. Though Dixon does not say so explicitly, what he calls "diuni-

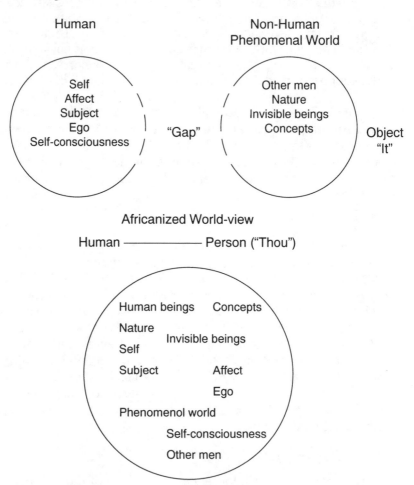

Figure I: Euro-American World-view

Africanized World-view

tal logic" can be understood as the recognition and affirmation of the ambiguity and multidimensionality of phenomenal reality. What is contradictory in Euro-American Aristotelian logic is not contradictory in African thought. The European *utamawazo* cannot deal with paradox.

This is not the place to discuss in depth the world-views of majority civilizations. It is appropriate, however, to make some obvious observations about what African, Amerindian, and Oceanic majority thought-systems have in common to the exclusion of European thought. All of the views mentioned are spiritual in nature, that is, they have spiritual bases and thereby reject rationalism and objectification as valued epistemological modes. Obviously, they do have rationalistic and pragmatic aspects but these do not dominate. These views generate an authentic cosmology, the interrelatedness of all being. They reject Aristotelian logic as the primary path to ultimate truth, while recognizing the symbolic and not the literal mode as appropriate for the expression of meaning. Most clearly these peoples share a vision of a harmonious order achieved through balance, as they seek to understand and maintain that order. We who have been educated in European societies have grown up assuming that it is only with the triumph over such world-views that "true knowledge" begins. Yet, what should strike us as students of culture is the fact that of all the world's civilizations the European *utamawazo* worldview is the strangest (the minority view); it is most conspicuous in its materialism and rationalism. Max Weber called this "universalism." By what logic does anomaly become the norm? Obviously with the introduction of ideology and value-judgement. Weber mistook overwhelmingly successful cultural aggression for "universalism." The European world-view is far superior to the others mentioned in its ability to generate material accumulation, technological efficiency, and imperial might. That does not make it universal.

Fortunately, these are not the goals of all of humankind, nor the definition of all cultural *asilis* and other views of reality have led many to construct different models, to envision the possibility of new and different functional definitions. We have already seen that African-centered theory is moving towards new definitions of sciences.[156]

In *The Sacred Science,* De Lubicz offers an interpretation of ancient African philosophy. He calls it "Pharoanic Theology." It is a "sacred science" because it is concerned with "revealed" knowledge and with the "beginnings of things." It is founded on an irrational basis and therefore not a rational science. It rests on the assumption of a "common energetic origin to all bodies," an ultimate spiritual source "which alone is able to animate matter," "an undefined cosmic energy." De Lubicz recognizes two irreconcilable mentalities based on the separation of two concepts; one that "points to a kinetic energy immanent in matter," and the other that "calls upon an undefined cosmic energy."

With absurd reasoning, our science sees in the universe nothing but a closed circuit, an agglomerate and a decomposition of the self same matter. Such a view is certainly less reasonable than admission of an undefined source of energy which becomes matter, although the latter solution poses a purely metaphysical problem.

From there it is but a very small step to seeing a divine principle in
the harmony of the world.[156]

The interpretations of both De Lubicz and Jaynes are antithetical: One understands the ancient Kemites to have had a heightened
consciousness; the other says that they had no consciousness. That
is because of the difference in perspectives. In De Lubicz's view, the
materialist mentality splits from the spiritualist beginning with
Xenophanes in the Eleatic school of philosophy, ca. 530 before the
Common Era. With the split comes the beginning of the separation
between science and religious thought and ritual. These are
dichotomized in European thought so that "rationalistic religion" in
Aquinas, Leibniz, et al. approaches the absurd, as great minds wres-
tled with the search for "scientific" and materialist proofs of the existence of the most spiritual of beings. Even now Christian thought
suffers from a doctrine that overlooks the contradiction inherent in
a "faith" based on secular historicity. European science ascended on
the demise of spiritual religion.

In the early schools of what was to be considered "Greek
Philosophy," the teachings of "Pharoanic Science" are evident, and
what continued to be developed as "science" was heavily influenced
by what had preceded in Kemet (ancient Egypt). What began to
change, however, was the approach and attitude of objectification.
The new forms had a different *utamaroho* (spirit life). The definition
of the *utamawazo* became critical. The Greeks, unable to grasp the
spiritual principle at the base of the "sacred science," simplistically
"anthropomorphized" the cosmic truths. Their religious response
resulted in the reduction of African philosophy, as expressed through
the symbols of the Neters, through the attribution of "physical char-
acter(s) to metaphysical principles."[157] According to De Lubicz, those
who rejected this adulterated version of ancient mysteries sought
truth through an extreme rationalism. Two tendencies developed in
archaic Europe: One group claimed a body of religious ritual whose
base they could not understand; the other group took the pragmatic
scientific aspects and developed them into a science without meaning. This is the chronic European split between faith and reason,
which was to intensify throughout the centuries of European development. Rational doctrine led to the denial of the divine, the sacred.
Yet rationality alone could never reflect cosmic truth and ironically
could not give spiritual nor ultimate intellectual satisfaction. This
had been understood in Kemet and is still understood outside of the
European tradition. As De Lubicz argues, there must always be mystery involved; "an irrationality at the origin which makes rational

philosophical construction impossible."[157] It is almost as though people outside of the European tradition (the majority) make up a collectivity who recognize and are comfortable with the tiny bit of "mystery" at the beginning and at the end. This view originates with human beginnings in Africa. Ayi Kwei Armah writes in *Two Thousand Seasons:* "We have not found that lying trick to our taste, the trick of making up sure knowledge of things possible to think of, things possible to wonder about but impossible to know in any such ultimate way."[158]

There are several theorists whose work touches on the striking difference between the European world-view and that of the majority; several who do not presume this to be an indication of the superiority of "Western civilization," that is, who do not approach the comparison eurocentrically. Often such theorists will contrast Eastern philosophies with those of Europe. Fritjof Capra, in *The Tao of Physics,* attempts to reconcile Western science and Eastern mysticism. In the process he characterizes these two views of reality, just as Dixon has done with the African and Euro-American views. In Capra's discussion, the Eastern view comes out on top: the Eastern (and early Greek) view is organic. All things are perceived as being interrelated and different manifestations of the same ultimate reality. The basic unity of the universe is the key to understanding phenomena, and one's aim becomes that of "transcending the notion of the isolated self, and to identify oneself with the ultimate reality." Spirit and matter are joined. Causal forces are intrinsic properties of matter.[159] One is struck again and again with the familiar sound of this characterization. It is almost identical to our description of the African world-view. How many of us have been compelled to ask, why the European world-view is the only one that differs so drastically from those of majority cultures. The European solves this problem by inventing the concept of "modernity," based on progress.

The following is Capra's characterization of "Western philosophy," in contrast to the "unifying" philosophy of the Milesians the ancient Indian and Chinese civilizations:

> The split of this unity began with the Eleatic school, which assumed a Divine Principle standing above all gods and men. This principle was first identified with the unity of the universe, but was later seen as an intelligent and personal God who stands above the world and directs it. Thus began a trend of thought which led, ultimately, to the separation of spirit and matter and to a dualism which became characteristic of Western philosophy.[160]

Capra, like De Lubicz, places the origins of this tendency in the Eleatic school. The tendency becomes a dominant theme and much later hardens in the philosophy of René Descartes, who further divides reality into "mind" and "matter." The results were the greater fragmentation of the universe in which we perceive "a multitude of separate objects and events." The mind having been separated from the body is given the task of controlling it. The human being is split into a "conscious will" that opposes our "involuntary instincts." The European experiences a mechanized universe constructed to deal with a world made up of mutually hostile parts.[161] This results as we have seen, in their being alienated from nature, while "physics" prior to the eleatic school did not include a word for "matter" "since they saw all forms of existence as manifestations of the 'physics,' endowed with life and spirituality." Capra says that the "roots of physics, as of all Western science, are to be found in the first period of Greek philosophy in the sixth century B.C., in a culture where science, philosophy and religion were not separated."[162] He is almost right. But his error becomes glaring when viewed from an African-centered perspective. Capra must know that Thales et al. did not grow from "nothing." As George James, and others have pointed out these "early" Greeks learned their "science" philosophy and religion from the civilization of the "sacred science." In those times everyone travelled to Egypt (Kemet) and studied there. Capra's omission of Africa in his comparison of philosophies is blatant.

Vine Deloria, in *God is Red,* contrasts the Native American worldview, which is "religious," with Western philosophy as expressed in Christianity. In the world-view of the Native Americans, all living things share a creator and creative process and, therefore, relate to one another.[163] Their spiritual quest is to determine the proper relationship that people have with other living things. The universe manifests life energies, "the whole life-flow of creation." The person is dependent on everything in the universe for his/her existence. Rather than the determination to subdue nature (European world-view), "the awareness of the meaning of life comes from observing how the various living things appear to mesh and to provide a whole tapestry."[163] We have seen that Europeans have problems with difference (Page du Bois). The Western "fragmented view is further extended to society, which is split into different nations, races, religions, and political groups." This results in conflicts that are an essential cause of present "social, ecological and cultural crises"[161] (Capra). This as opposed to the Native American approach that says that "in differences there is the strength of the Creation and that this strength is a deliberate desire of the Creator."[164] Both these and a host of other writers have talked about the European's "alienation from nature" as opposed to the idea of the "identity and Unity of life" in which symbolism expresses reality.[165]

This cursory glance at different thought-systems is necessary, not only to demonstrate the possibility and existence of alternative world-views, but also to bring attention to the chauvinism in European interpretations of these world-views. We have seen repeatedly that European epistemological and ontological definitions are placed, by European theorists, in the context of "advanced" intellectual and cognitive development, as compared with what they call "ancient," "primitive," or "prescientific" thought. What this interpretation does is to preclude the viability of alternative definitions of reality, in so far as these same theorists represent a successfully aggressive culture that has the means to impose its interpretations on others. Let me bring home the point emphatically that this imposition was made by equating "European" with "modern" or "scientific" and all other cultures with "pre-European" or "primitive." According to Henri and H.A. Frankfort:

> The ancients, like the modern savages, saw man always as part of society, and society as imbedded in nature and dependent upon cosmic forces. For them nature and man did not stand in opposition and did not, therefore, have to be apprehended by different modes of cognition. . . natural phenomenon were regularly conceived in terms of human experience and [that] human experience was conceived in terms of cosmic events. . . the fundamental difference between the attitudes of modern and ancient man as regards the surrounding world is this: for modern, scientific man the phenomenal world is primarily an "It"; for ancient—and also for primitive—man it is a "Thou."[166]

The Frankforts have camouflaged their cultural nationalism in universalistic terms. (No wonder there is no "modern god" for the European.) In this study, we have made European culture the focus, and therefore interpretations such as these become ethnographic data to be explained in terms of the European *asili*. They enable us to understand the nature of the European *utamawazo* and *utamaroho*. The question becomes that of why there is a need for Europeans to view themselves in a superior evolutionary position *vis-à-vis* other cultural selves. We will continue to address this question and others in the chapters that follow.

The Character of the European *Utamawazo*

We should not leave this discussion with the impression that Platonic thought ushered in vast and immediate changes in the nature of European culture. To begin with there was, in a sense, no "Europe" in his time. But in another sense, what we have identified as the European *asili,* the seed of the culture, had already been planted. The planting of this seed had to have taken place in the early days of Indo-European tribal development, where there was already a very definite *utamaroho,* or even earlier with the first homosapiens to inhabit the Eurasian Steppes and the Caucasus region for a long enough period to have become "non-African."

This means that Plato's work was all the more important in the definitional process of the *utamawazo,* because it had been prefigured in the germ of the culture, necessary if the *asili* was to be realized. It means as well, that as the culture, through its members, fought to assume a particular definition, it was developing according to a code already in existence, somewhat in the sense that we think of a particular combination of genes as determining a particular human form. The seed struggles to develop. The germ insists on fulfilling its formulative role. European history is a history of bloody internecine wars and battles fought to maintain a particular character and to eliminate opposing influences: "heretics," "infidels," "barbarians." It is a history of aggressive behavior towards other cultures. All difference threatens the realization of the *asili.* It is like a child's struggle to be born. The battle is fought because the *asili* exists, and Platonic thought is so significant (determinative) because it suited the *asili.* His epistemological theory helped in the formulation of an *utamawazo* that complemented the *asili.*

With Plato, epistemology became ideological. What is more, contrary to what some have claimed, Platonic conceptions did not make knowledge accessible to the masses through its desacralization.[167] What he did was to ensure that, at least until the "Gutenberg Galaxy," the few would have no threat from the many, because the many did not have access to the intellectual life of the State. This was due to the ascendancy of the literate mode coupled with the lack of printing and mass-production technology, as well as the fact that only the privileged few were trained to be "literate" in this sense. Plato's plan was foolproof; because even when the European masses gained access centuries later, the mechanisms of control were so tightly structured that the assumptions they had to assimilate in order to be considered "educated" guaranteed that they would think the way he had planned. It was as though his hand reached through centuries of cultural existence, as the European cognitive style (*utamawazo*) became an extension of Platonism. Not only all European intellectuals but *all* intellectuals would be trained in the academy (Plato's legacy), a testament to the success of European cultural imperialism. The Academy has preserved a cultural tradition, a race of people, and a dominant society. No matter the internecine controversies and so-called political revolutions that might occur, the Academy ensures that the ideological infrastructure will remain intact.

The emergent theme is power. What begins to develop from this initial discussion is a portrait of the European *utamawazo* as responding to an *asili* that is power-seeking. A particular definition of power presents itself in the search for European predilection, temperament, and need. Power is here defined, not as the "power to do," which results from the giving and receiving of energy from forces in the universe and through interaction with these forces as they manifest themselves in the various modalities of natural being; it is instead defined as "power over" and is predicated on or rather originates in separation. This is the fanatical European objective. "Power to do" seeks balance and harmony. "Power over" functions only through the modality of control. It precludes cosmic, communal, or sympathetic relationship. It is essentially political and materialistic.

The *asili*-seed of the culture prefigures, then dictates, the development of structures, institutions, "arrangements,"[168] that facilitate the achievement of power-over-other. The forms that are created within the European cultural experience can then be understood as mechanisms of control in the pursuit of power. That is what they all have in common. That is the key to their cultural explanation. The ideological base of the culture is the will-to-power.

The *utamawazo* or culturally structured thought reorders the universe into relationships that "prepare" it for the illusion of control. Separation must come first. The *asili* forces its own self-realization through the cognitive structure of the *utamawazo* in the following manner:

Dichotomization. All realities are split into two parts. This begins with the separation of self from "other," and is followed by the separation of the self into various dichotomies (reason/emotion, mind/body, intellect/nature). The process continues until the universe is composed of disparate entities.

Oppositional, Confrontational, Antagonistic Relationships. The self "knows itself" because it is placed in opposition to "other," which includes the natural and affective part of the self. This "self-awareness" is the origin of European consciousness. "Other"—that which is perceived to be different from the self—is threatening, therefore establishing an antagonistic relationship between all entities that are "different." This presents a principle of confrontational relationships in all realities. Indeed, cognition itself is made possible through confrontation.

Hierarchical Segmentation. The original splitting and separating mental process assigns qualitatively different (unequal) value to the opposing realities of the dichotomies and a stratification of value to all realities within a given set or category. This process of valuation and devaluation is accompanied by that of segmentation and compartmentalization of independently derived entities. The effect is to eliminate the possibility of organic or sympathetic relationship, thereby establishing grounds for the dominance of the "superior" form or phenomenon over that which is perceived to be inferior: the power-relationship. Abstracted from the larger whole, these opposing realities can never be perceived as either complementary or interdependent.

Analytical, Nonsynthetic Thought. The tendency to split and segment makes the European comfortable with the analytical modality in which realities are torn apart in order to be "known." This is an essential process within all cognitive systems on one level of understanding. But since organic interrelationship discourages the hierarchical thought patterns necessary for confrontation, control, and power, it becomes impossible, *within* the parameters of the European *utamawazo*, to comprehend the whole, especially as a cosmic reality. Culturally this tendency inhibits the movement to a higher, more synthesizing level of understanding. It is on the level of synthesis that opposition would be resolved, and given the fundamental premises of this cognitive system, there would no longer be any basis for knowledge: power-over-other.

Objectification. With these characteristics of the *utamawazo* an autonomous self has been created. This autonomous self is gradually identified with "pure thought." The conceptualization of "pure thought" is made possible by a cognitive emphasis on *absolutism* and *abstractification*. The self as emotionless mind creates the proper "objects" of knowledge through the act of controlling that which is inferior to it in a phenomenal sense. In this sense, everything that is "other" than the thinking self is objectified and is therefore capable of being controlled by that self; as long as the knowing self is careful to remain affectively detached. Therefore, through the mode of objectification, knowledge becomes a mechanism that facilitates power-over-other.

Absolutist-Abstractification. This also mandates the universalization as well as the reification of truths. This universalization is not to be confused with the inductive search for authentic principles of a cosmic reality; that is discouraged by the limited analytical and segmenting mentality. It is instead, a universalism dictated by the need to use epistemology as a power tool and as a mechanism of control.

Rationalism and Scientism. Extreme rationalism is not reasonableness; quite the opposite. It is the attempt to explain all of reality as though it had been created by the European mind for the purposes of control. It is the belief that everything can be known through objectification and that the resulting presentation of reality is an accurate picture of the world. If all of reality can be explained in this way, then we as thinking beings have control over everything. Intense rationalism is the ultimate experience of control for the European mind. Ideologically, it justifies the control of the European self over others.

Scientism is the merger of religion and rationality. Here the European god becomes the great scientist and the rationalist pursuit is the criterion of moral behavior. The need to experience control creates a scientistic *utamawazo* in which predictability and rationality help to defend the knowing self against any possible threat from the unknown. Intuitive knowledge is devalued and mistrusted since it is only possible through cosmic self-awareness; it does not guarantee control, it does not help to create the illusion of power-over-other. The intuitve modality is not uncomfortable with mystery.

Authoritative Literate Mode. The written symbol becomes authoritative utterance, enabling the European mind to further objectify reality as it universalizes European control. Reductionist symbols set in a nonsymbolic lineal modality help to further alienate the knowing self from its authentically affective environment. More control, more power. Conceptual lineality further secularizes the axiological aspects of the culture thereby linking it as well to the process of objectification.

Desacralization. This is a necessary by-product of all of the characteristics of the European *utamawazo*, as nature is alienated and objectified and approached with a *quantifying mentality,* that views the universe as material reality only, to be acted upon by superior "mind."

The characteristics outlined all issue from and result in the illusion of a despiritualized universe. European power is the negation of spirit, just as European control is threatened by the recognition of spirit. All of these characteristics when understood ideologically, that is, in terms of the nature of the European *asili,* yield the possibility of power and create the illusion of control. The pursuit of power is the nature of the European *asili*. The *utamawazo* is one manifestation of the *asili*. It is created to assist in the realization of the *asili*. What remains to be demonstrated is the way in which these characteristics encourage the development of a technical order and imperialistic behavior towards other cultures. We must explain how the *utamawazo* couples with the *utamaroho* (energy force) to support the ideological thrust (*asili*) of the culture: the quest for dominance. The *asili* makes each aspect of the *utamawazo* political in its use (application), every action motivated by the *utamaroho*, both defensive and aggressive: the assumption of a confrontational reality.

We have identified the *asili*-logos and source of the culture; it is a seed that once planted dictates the logic of cultural development. In the chapters to come we will use this concept to explicate the relationship between the dominant modes of the culture, following the path along which the logos of the *asili* leads.

I am the way, the truth, and the light. No one comes
to my Father but through me.
— John 14:6

There was a third white destroyer: a missionary who wanted
to replace all knowledge of our way with fables even our chil-
dren laughed at then. We told the white missionary we had
such fables too, but kept them for the entertainment of those
yet growing up - fables of gods and devils and a supreme being
above everything. We told him we knew soft minds needed
such illusions, but that when any mind grew among us to adult-
hood it grew beyond these fables and came to understand that
there is indeed a great force in the world, a force spiritual and
able to shape the physical universe, but that that force is not
something cut off, not something separate from ourselves. It is
an energy in us, strongest in our working, breathing, thinking
together as one people; weakest when we are scattered, con-
fused, broken into individual, unconnected fragments.
— Ayi Kwei Armah

Chapter 2

Religion and Ideology

A Point of Departure

Religion is integrally related to the development of ideology in
the West. For that reason and because of the unique nature of
European culture, it is critical to make clear what I mean by "religion." This is important because what is identified formally in the
European experience as religion often has very little to do with what
is understood generally as "the religious" in a phenomenological
sense.[1] This discussion focuses on the European experience of religion as a formalized institution existing in relation to the other institutions of European culture, as opposed to "religion" as the
expression of beliefs about the supernatural world and as the basis
for ethical behavior, or as a determinant of value.

It is critical as well to distinguish between "religion" and "spirituality." Spirituality rests on the conception of a sacred cosmos that transcends physical reality in terms of significance and meaning. At the same time spirituality enables us to apprehend the sacred in our natural, ordinary surroundings: They become elements of a symbolic language. Religion refers to the formalization of ritual, dogma, and belief, leading to a systematic statement of syntactically suprarational tenets that may or may not issue from a spiritual conception of the universe. Most often it functions to sacralize a nationalistic ideology.

If one looks for a sense of the supernatural, the sacred, or extraordinary in European culture, undoubtedly the only area of experience that approaches the "religious" in this sense is that of "science." It is only what is considered to be science and scientific method that is regarded with the awe and humility that in other cultures represents the "religious attitude." Scientism, as such, is not the focus of this immediate discussion, but rather the institutionalized set of ideas and practices that Europeans refer to as "religion." Scientism will enter the discussion only as it functions normatively to provide the models or paradigms of European theology.

The other sense of "religion," i.e., beliefs concerning the nature of the human and the universe, have been discussed in Chap. 1 as metaphysical conceptions. The authentically normative European ethic is treated in a later section of this work. Such beliefs are not easily recognizable if one makes the mistake of looking for them only in what is labeled "religion" in an avowedly secular society. The two uses of the term will overlap occasionally, as has already become apparent in the previous chapter, and will do so more in the following discussion as we observe the way in which the themes of European epistemological and ontological premises find expression in the formalized religious statement of European culture.

To say that a culture is "secularly" based in European social theory is primarily to associate it with what in the terms of European ideology is the phenomenon of modernity. But an ethnological understanding of European culture using the concept of *asili* leads to a conclusion that is more far reaching than that understanding of "secular" would imply. We are not simply discussing the separation of Church and State. The relationship of European religion to other aspects of the culture is symptomatic of a persistent despiritualization and desacralization of experience and can be shown to be a characteristic of "Westerness" since its archaic stages. The European *utamawazo*, *utamaroho*, and European ideology determine the nature of the formalized religious statement in the West rather than the reverse. That is what it means for a culture to have a "nonreligious" base. It means that the formal religious statement merely *reflects* fundamental metaphysical concepts and ideology. It is not their source. It is not identical with them as is the case in traditional and classical African and Islamic cultures. This secularization of European culture begins with the institutionalization of European religion. It begins with the Church.

This discussion begins, therefore, with the Platonic influences on the development of European institutionalized religion, its Judaic origins, and its solidification in the ideology and organization of the early Christian Church. Later we will discuss the ideological significance of European paganism. Throughout this treatment, however, our focus is on European institutionalized religion as a manifestation of the European *utamaroho*, *utamawazo* and ideological commitment. The concept of *asili* particularizes this "religious" statement, and exposes its legitimization of European behavior.

The Platonic Influence

For the most part, whatever dramatic imagery and spiritual profundity are traditionally associated with what is called "Christianity," originate in chronologically "older" cultures,[2] cultures that existed as established traditions centuries before the crystallization of archaic Europe or the establishment of Christianity. We are discussing here what Europeans isolated as valued characteristics of a proper religious statement. I will take the liberty of using the term Christianity to refer specifically to its European manifestations; that is, to the "European" uses and responses to the religious ideas presented by earlier cultural-ideological traditions. For, having changed the emphases and offering different interpretations, Europeans can indeed be credited with the creation of a formulation that uniquely responded to the needs of their cultural selves. In this sense, which emphasizes the ideological uses of religion (the *asili* approach), European Christianity was a "new" phenomenon.

The dialogues the *Euthyphro*, the *Apology*, and the *Republic* are all to some extent concerned with the problem of the moral justification of an individual's choice of action (*Euthyphro, Apology*) and of the State (*Republic*). In the *Euthyphro*, Socrates succeeds in convincing Euthyphro of the logical inconsistency of his appeal to "that which the gods love" as the criterion or definition of "the pious act." According to Socrates, Euthyphro's problem is that his gods are many, unpredictable, and, like men, fallible. Sometimes they do not agree with one another as to what "pleases them." And since they are

"many," what pleases one may not please another. Socrates demonstrates to Euthyphro that in looking for a proper "first principle" it is
necessary to go beyond the gods to something prior to them as a reference point. "The gods love what they love *because* it is holy," and
not the reverse. This priority is, of course, a logical one.

In the *Apology,* Socrates accounts for his actions by saying that
they were divinely inspired: He was *made* to act as he does; he was
compelled to "ask questions," an activity that apparently is threatening to the authority of the State. Socrates becomes the nemesis of
the State as he demonstrates to the young Athenians that the politicians are the least wise of its participants. The point that we are concerned with is the way in which Socrates defends his actions. By
identifying his behavior as having been made "necessary" by the
order of the gods, he is, in fact, saying that he cannot help being
Socrates, that he cannot help being as he is. Socrates is being charged
with "impiety," and it is therefore necessary that he brings the gods
to his defense; but more than that, *he does so because of the nature
of that which he is defending.*[3] Socrates is, after all, defending an entire
"way of life"; not merely one specific or concrete action which, in
Platonic terms, is Euthyphro's mistake. To do this he must appeal to
something that is outside of, greater than, independent of, that life;
something to which it can be referred. The moral principle of justification for "all actions" cannot be in terms of anything "human," for
that would be inconsistent, ambiguous, and imperfect, as Euthyphro
was made to see. Socrates' appeal can only be made to the divine; that
which is beyond space and time, that which "created" him.

> Now the duty of cross-examining other men has been imposed upon
> me by god; and has been signified to me by oracles, visions, and in
> every way in which the will of the divine power was never intimated
> to anyone. [Plato, *Apology,* 33]

> God orders me to fulfill the philosopher's mission of searching into
> myself and other men. [Plato, *Apology,* 28]

It is not that Socrates has suddenly become a priest. It sounds as
though he is describing "the religious" in experience; the creation of
meaning through transcendence beyond the ordinary, beyond the
profane. But, if this were the case, clearly it would not represent a
"new" human activity, nor a new conception of religion. Euthyphro
has been in the habit of doing precisely that. In the Platonic view, the
nature of this "god" or "principle" that Socrates seeks is an extension
of the human. It is not "greater than" nor "outside" the ordinary.

Rather it is a logical necessity of human reason, that is, reason as Plato defines it. Socrates is talking about an absolute, unchanging reference point: the grounding of reason.

Both Euthyphro and Socrates appeal to the gods for the justification of their actions that are being challenged. But Socrates makes it clear that the logic of Euthyphro's argument is defective. Euthyphro does not make effective polemical use of the authority of the gods, while Socrates, in his own defense, uses the divine to construct a logically rigorous argument for the moral validity of his actions. This brings us directly to a critical component of European religion. It is the "syntax of the mathematical proposition," in Havelock's words, that becomes the model for the moral precept and idea. In this way the European "monotheistic ideal" comes into being, and its religious statement becomes rationalistic. The arguments of the *Euthyphro* and the *Apology* make the assumption that there is but one system of logic, one mode, and this comes to appear "logical" within the epistemological confines of European culture. Plato identifies the "good" with the "true," and for him this means that the *morally* true has as its methodological model the *mathematically* true. That is why it is important that the Guardians be trained first in "the art of number":

> The knowledge at which geometry aims is knowledge of the eternal, and not of aught perishing and transient . . . then geometry will draw the soul towards truth, and create the spirit of philosophy, and raise up that which is now unhappily allowed to fall down.

> And all arithmetic and calculation have to do with number?

> Yes.

> And they appear to lead the mind towards truth?

> Yes, in a very remarkable manner.

> Then this is knowledge of the kind for which we are seeking, having a double use, military and philosophical; for the man of war must learn the art of number or he will not know how to array his troops, and the philosopher also, because he has to rise out of the sea of change and lay hold of true being, and therefore he must be an arithmetician.[4]

The *Republic* is an "ideal" state because it is best and therefore what a state should be; but it is also "ideal" in the sense that it does not and cannot concretely exist. The ideal state is itself a "Form" to be participated in, approximated, imitated, but never consonant with the becoming, that is, the experienced. The Republic is not in any way limited by the particular circumstances of human experience. Just as in the European conception, the philosophic and ethical "progressiveness" of the Christ image lies in its presentation of a model of moral perfection, to be imitated but never reached. So the Republic represents the perfect order towards which the European state must continually "advance." As "idea," as "normative model," it is not simply modeled after the "good," it is the embodiment of the "good." The problems in the *Euthyphro,* the *Apology,* and the *Crito* are created by the discrepancy in the world of becoming between the "moral" and the "natural." This problem is eliminated in the *Republic;* the State becomes totally moral because it is totally rational. Virtue is identified with "objectification"; spirit is reduced to matter and the ability to manipulate it.

This mode of thought that has worked so well to produce the kind of technical and social order that Europeans desire has also created a moral and spiritual disaster. The formal religious statement has taken on the form of the rational state and has left Europeans no access to the necessarily spiritual reservoirs of human morality. This tendency has intensified over the centuries; until now, when the West is faced with tremendous self-doubt.

But the point to be made here is that the epistemological model in which the Platonic abstraction was born (the normative "absolute") underlies the expression of the "monotheistic ideal," the "rational religion" syndrome, and written codification as values in the formalized Judeo-Christian religious statement.

Stanley Diamond succinctly states the reason for the "monotheistic ideal" as well as the reason for its failure as a religious vehicle in one sentence. "Absolutely pure monotheism exists in the realm of mathematics, not religion!" Precisely! And that is why it became the European ideal, since ("logically") pure monotheism can be understood as an attempt to express the Platonic abstraction as the necessary justification of all moral propositions. When European theologians took up from where Plato left off, they should have realized that they would be forever plagued with the dilemma of reconciling what should have remained two distinct philosophical-epistemological modes; Plato had mistakenly identified them as one.

Diamond says that this tendency toward the integration of mental and emotional life and the development of the "exalted and positive ethical idea" implies "progress" to the European mind and has become one of the shibboleths of European culture. But this is a slippery point, if one is unfamiliar with the mode of ancient philosophy. For the Kemites (ancient "Egyptians"), other Africans, and many contemporary "non-European" peoples, there is an authentic integration of science, philosophy, and religion. The difference between these two kinds of "integration" is that one reduces spiritual reality to matter, while the other understands spiritual reality as the fundamental integrative principle of all being. The European view results in the desacralization of the universe and, by extension, the despiritualization of morality.

Monotheism for the European becomes a characteristic of superior philosophical belief. It is not important here that other cultures exhibit religious concepts that philosophically imply the spiritual priority of a single creative principle and that the idea of monotheism, of course, came to the West from other experiments with it. Even in European culture, where it is discussed so much, the "high god" concept is not experienced as an "unknown featureless quantity" that never changes: Several gods are called by one name, and they are personalized. But what *is* significant in this discussion is that absolute and "pure" monotheism is expressed as an ideal or value in Western European cultural chauvinistic expression, and that it serves as a basis for the devaluation of other cultures. In addition the expression of this ideal is, in part, a legacy of the Platonic abstraction.

Havelock's observation on the developmental relationship between the written media or "literate" mode and "objectification" as a dominant or preferred epistemological mode can be used to understand the uniqueness of the European, Judeo-Christian religious tradition. Religion, to be superior and worthy of the "civilized," had to be "knowledge" and have the nature of the eternal truth of logic. Its written codification helped to give it this character and so became to European's evidence of "true religion." (A student in my African civilization course vehemently protested that Christian belief was superior because it was "documented.") Where else but in the European mind would it seem so compelling that the "self" be separated from the "religious object" in order to achieve a proper religious statement. It could instead be argued from a different perspective that it is the very point at which the "individual" self and the experience of the "other" *defy* distinction that a sense of the religious is born. But for Europeans, even this experience has to be understood rationally, which ultimately robs them of the ability to recognize it. George Steiner says,

The classic and the Christian sense of the word strive to order real-ity within the governance of language. Literature, philosophy, law, the arts of history, are endeavors to enclose within the bounds of rational discourse the sum of human experience, its recorded past, its present condition and future expectations. The code of Justinian, the *Summa [theologica]* of Aquinas, the world chronicles and com-pendia of medieval literature, the *Divina Commedia*, are attempts at total containment. They bear solemn witness to the belief that all truth and realness—with the exception of a small, queer margin at the very top—can be housed inside the walls of language.[5]

The European formalized religious statement was made to fit the conceptual mode that had become aesthetically pleasing to the European mind because of the Platonic influence, the diligence of Aristotle, and the nature of the *Utamawazo*. Arthur Lovejoy has this to say regarding Plato's relationship to the subsequent religious for-mulations:

The interpreters of Plato in both ancient and modern times have endlessly disputed over the question whether this conception of the absolute Good was for him identical with the conception of God. Stated thus simply, the question is meaningless, since the word "God" is in the last degree ambiguous. But if it be taken as standing for what the Schoolmen called *ens perfectissimum*, the summit of the hierarchy of being, the ultimate and only completely satisfying object of contemplation and adoration, there can be lit-tle doubt that the Idea of the Good *was* the God of Plato; and there can be none that it became the God of Aristotle, and one of the ele-ments or "aspects" of the God of most philosophic theologies of the Middle Ages, and of nearly all the modern Platonizing poets and philosophers.[6]

Plato's influence was most heavily felt in the early formulative work of Augustine, and Aristotle's influence was directly manifested in Aquinas and the Scholastics in their conceptions of the "self-mov-ing Mover" and of "Final Cause," but most importantly in their labo-rious attempts to "prove" the existence of their god. These efforts become pathetic when it is understood that the need for "proof" itself is symptomatic of the human failing of the culture. Aristotle, in this way, becomes himself the "prime mover" of the "religion and ratio-nality syndrome" that continues to plague European theology.

The Judaic Heritage

In Judaism we find the first conscious formalized and institutionalized statement of certain critical characteristics of European culture, tendencies, and values that intensified as the culture became an ever increasingly identifiable ethno-historical entity. This does *not* include the Qabbala, which is non-European in both a spiritual and a racial-cultural sense. In fact, a caveat to this discussion would be to raise the question of to what extent our knowledge of Judaism is determined by the tradition of the Khazars, who were *converted Jews,* and their descendants the Askenazim and contemporary European Jews. (See Arthur Koestler, *The Thirteenth Tribe,* 1976.)

Judaism is much more than a "religion" as that term came to be used in the European experience. It is a political and cultural ideology. It has within it the germ of a model for social organization designed for the energetic development of technological efficiency. It is the prelude to a cultural configuration that emphasizes that aspect of the human experience. The characteristics that can be identified within this tradition combine to give the culture of the early Hebrews the particular socio-technological direction that later became a definitive component of the Western European tradition.

The Judaic tradition is associated with a cultural tool that is generally termed "codification" in relation to the social norms, sanctioned behavior, and religion of the Hebrew people. The term "codification," however, properly refers to the systematic arrangement and preservation of certain aspects of culture. All cultures possess methods and media (songs, mythology, art, poetry, ritual) that act to standardize in this way; therefore, all peoples "codify" what they consider to be the valuable and necessary facts of their tradition.[7]

It is specifically the use of the medium of the written word in this respect that, in European parlance, is connoted by the term "codification" and that, in the minds of Europeans, is so reverently associated with their cultural heritage. Through the use of the written word culture becomes recorded, and this recording becomes an impressively cumulative activity, giving the impression that the culture itself is more cumulative and therefore within the logic of this same value system, evolutionarily superior to cultures that codify their traditions through other media.

Writing, of course, first developed neither in the context of Judaism nor any other part of the European cultural tradition. So that it is not merely the presence, knowledge, or "possibility" of this medium that is critical in identifying the peculiarity of the European configuration. More subtly, it is the way in which this tool figures in

the culture in question that is important here. In the European tradition writing takes on the features of a dominant value within the belief
system of the group. It is not merely a tool among tools. The medium
of the written word is so valued that it can itself impart value, much
as religion does to the entire fabric of traditional cultures. Without the
written media, how could the European "God" and all the pronouns
referring to "Him" be capitalized?—a primary European expression of
reverence. The same is true of Plato's "Forms." The act of writing and
its importance become ideological in function. They become a frame
of reference that acts to determine and, in many respects, limit the
mode of perception of those caught up in this structure of values. We
have already pointed to some of the implications of "lineality" in the
European *utamawazo* as it relates to the written media. (See Chap. 1
of this work.)

The point to be made here is the way in which this valued activity related to other Western tendencies of the European *asili,* already
prefaced in early Judaic culture. When written expression becomes
a dominant value, words become binding through writing, and values
are perceived laws. Laws preserved through written codification are
more impressive to the European mind than mere "values." This circular process helps to maintain order in lieu of those mechanisms
that would be binding in other cultures. Written laws became the
mark of European religion. The literate mode helped to impart the
illusion of historicity and therefore of "universal truth."

Written codification is necessary for the development and
growth of a certain kind of ideology and a qualitatively distinct style
of organization; not necessarily more complex, but in many ways
more oppressive to the human spirit as it forces human activity to be
increasingly technologically oriented. The Kemites (Egyptians) possessed a system that allowed them to keep written records thousands of years before the Hebrews. They also had a larger and more
technologically accomplished culture. And for these reasons, Kemet
might at first appear to be the ethnological precursor to the crystallization of European culture.

But Kemetic civilization is sacredly based, and its religion more
cosmic, mythic, and symbolic in intent. The mathematical, astrolog-
ical, astronomical, and philosophical knowledge of the Kemites, even
the material colossus that was Kemet, were products of a total conception of the universe as spirit. It is for this reason that Kemet still
remains a puzzle to the European mind. The African apprehension of
the universe as cosmic harmony simply represents a philosophic
approach that defies the European world-view. What is relevant here

is the difference between the uses of written codification and its value-place in Kemetic and Hebraic culture, respectively. What was written in the *Book of the Coming Forth by Day ("The Book of the Dead")* was to be buried with the dead and was intended for their benefit and use. But the philosophical essence of spiritual knowledge (which included science as well as theology) was represented by the Priest "schools" or Mystery Systems, and could only be transmitted orally—reserved for a small circle of initiates.

Written expression of these teachings was prohibited for two reasons: They were "secret," and they were "sacred." Writing, on the other hand, imparts two things to its content: (1) it publicizes, reveals, and spreads its content in a way that other (pre-electronic) media cannot (one never commits to writing that which one truly wishes to remain private); it "makes public" its content in this way. (2) The written media "profanes." Initiates into this system of spiritual wisdom pledged themselves to secrecy. This was interpreted to mean the prohibition of writing down what they had learned. It was only when individual Greek, Persian, and Ionian students (Socrates and Plato no doubt among them) gained access to Egyptian schools, and political control of Egyptian civilization, that acts of sacrilege were performed, acts that in the nascent European ideological framework of ancient Greece were compelling. As early as this in the European experience, the culturally exploitative use of the written media seems to have been recognized and utilized. And the European interpretation of these priestly Kemetic teachings became much of "Greek Philosophy" through the many strokes of many, many pens, as George James explains (1954). In this view we could almost say that classical European culture began with an act of profanation and plagiarism.

How profoundly different was the Hebrew conception of meaning from the Kemetic and other "non-European" conceptions. It was a conception that promoted the arduous activity of recording in writing the religious laws of its people and thereby gave birth to the idea of the "scriptures." Within the European context "culture" and "law" are reified and, therefore through writing, are deified; religion has greater force, is "truer," because it is codified in writing. Starting with other presuppositions, however, it would seem that it is only as laws become alienated from the human spirit that conformity to them requires that they be put on paper.

The Monotheistic Ideal;
Incipient European Cultural Chauvinism

Our concern here is with "monotheism" as a culturally expressed value. In these terms the counterpart of the "good/bad" dichotomy of European value becomes that of "monotheism/polytheism." For Europeans the one-god idea, like written codification, represents a socio-technological "advance" along the evolutionary spectrum. Judaism proclaims this ideal. It is recognized as a Jewish concept—in spite of Akhnaten—for in Judaism, it becomes hardened ideology. The statement of this ideal expresses the European *utamaroho* dramatically. What follows is Hugh Schonfield's characterization of this "ideal":

> Messianism was a product of the Jewish spirit. It was inspired by the Hebrew reading of the riddle of the creation and the destiny of mankind. Though some of its features did not originate with the Hebrews, they absorbed them and brought them into relationship with a great vision of the ultimate Brotherhood of Man under the rule of the One God and Father of all men. The vision was not simply a cherished ideal; it was associated with a plan for its realisation. According to this plan God had chosen and set apart one nation among the nations of the world, neither numerous nor powerful, to be the recipient of his laws, and by observing them to offer a universal example. The Theocracy of Israel would be the persuasive illustration of a World Theocracy; it would be "a kingdom of priests and a holy nation" witnessing to all nations. Manifestly, according to this view, the redemption of humanity waited upon the attainment by Israel of a state of perfect obedience to the will of God. By so much as Israel failed to meet the Divine requirements, by so much was the peace and well-being of mankind retarded.[8]

This characterization of Hebrew theology is an accurate statement of the European self-image: one type of person—one culture—whose task it is to "save" all people. This vision of a larger world in relation to a special culture (one's own) contains the germ of "universalism," the critical ingredient of European cultural imperialism. Early in Judaism the indication of this theme appears, a theme that we shall follow in this study as it develops both historically and synchronically through the various aspects of European culture. The Judaic statement also laid the groundwork for the secularization of history. By interpreting history as the unfolding of divine law, profane lineal time (historicity) rather than Hantu (sacred time and space) became the sanctioning force.

There is an important connection between the expression of the "monotheistic" ideal and that of Plato's ontology as expressed in several of his dialogues. The humanness and inconsistency of the gods is illogical (*Euthyphro*) and, therefore, immoral. Value must be abstract, universal, unchanging. The Republic is perfect because it is modeled after such an abstraction. It is really not the *content* of the "ideal" so much as its "form" that is significant. The "logical" and ontological "authority" that issues from the "good" or from "God" must be monolithic. It is a more suitable structure, the ideally organized state for the growth and nurture of technology and for a particular kind of ideology. The concept of monotheism provides an ontological justification for the State as an efficient mechanism of assured control. While wars have always been (and will always be, although the rhetoric may become more subtle) for all people "religious" wars, and while religious statements have always been statements of cultural nationalistic ideology, the religious statement of the Hebrews corresponded to a qualitatively different nationalistic conception. Their religion put forth the proposition that all religions that did not espouse the one-god ideal were evolutionarily inferior. The adherents of this religious statement, in effect, declared war on (that is, opposed themselves to) all peoples who did not profess this idea. It is important here to reiterate a distinction that must be kept in mind between Jewish religion and others at this historical juncture.

All religions are by necessity culturally nationalistic in that they profess in some way the specialness if not the moral superiority of those who are "born into" them and, in fact (most importantly), involve an explanation of the sacred origins of the group. But there is a crucial difference between the way in which the European image of its culture represents its members as advanced on an evolutionary spectrum. This ideological thesis demands a vision of themselves in invidious comparison with others and therefore in relation to a larger order. One idea—the sacralization of the group—does not rule out the validity of a plurality of other groups. The other—evolutionary superiority—is a supremacist concept and allows only for a monolithic reality.

For the Jews, those who did not profess the one-god ideal—those who "worshipped images"—were in fact irreligious. It was impious and immoral to worship many gods. Moreover, it was stupid; it was backward. And, therefore, the violent hostility towards all other religions was not only justified; it was morally compelling. And here we find the first concrete statement of what can be called the dichotomy of European chauvinism, the evolution of which we can trace historically and ideologically.

According to the logic of European ideology as manifested in its early stage of Judaic culture, the cultural statement ofgood/bad, of we/they, becomes Jew/Gentile. To be Jewish was to be not only special and "chosen" but also "religious" and therefore culturally superior in an evolutionary sense. A Gentile is non-Jewish: a heathen and pagan, is idolatrous and actually irreligious (has no religion), is ignorant, is culturally inferior in an evolutionary sense. With certain critical amplification, this was later to become the logic that supported European cultural imperialism; and it has been alarmingly consistent, left intact for over two thousand years, an unchanging tradition in a culture that propagandizes itself as the embodiment of "change" and self-criticism.

The Jewish/Gentile dichotomy is the early form of expression on the continuum of the civilized/primitive dichotomy of European cultural chauvinism. Within the framework of this chauvinistic expression the concept of authoritative "scriptures" and the written codification of tradition, the monotheistic ideal and the Jewish/ Gentile dichotomy all combine in unique configuration to reinforce each other in the logic of a belief system that can be identified as the earliest institutionalized manifestation of the European *utamaroho*— seeking to fulfill the *asili* of the culture.

Written codification and its promulgation encourages the linear mode of conception that in turn establishes a "logical" system that produces the thesis of evolution and advance. This thesis, in turn, introduces the deification of the written word; and so the circle continues. Monotheism, which had philosophical (not spiritual) appeal to the European mind and which served best the purposes of social control in a European context, was placed at the valued end of the "evolutionary" spectrum. It is again significant that Europeans have never left that aspect of social organization open-ended as a superficial understanding of *progress ideology* would imply but retain the monolithic image of their very first model.

The monotheistic ideal (and the thesis of its "evolutionary" superiority) then leads to and at the same time is recreated by the dichotomy of European nationalistic ideology. "We" become(s) the group that is "advanced," practices monotheism, deifies writing; "they" become *the rest of the world,* the group that is backward, idolatrous, irreligious, possesses no impressive body of written religious laws, and of course believes in "many gods." No punishment is too severe for this group, and "we" must go to great lengths to ensure that "we" are not contaminated by "their" backwardness. The Judaic statement of this position was a violently defensive one, since the threat from without was, at that point, very real.

> If thy brother, the son of thy mother, or thy son, or thy daughter, or the wife of thy bosom, or thy friend, which is as thine own soul, entice thee secretly, saying, let us go and serve other gods, which thou hast known, thou, nor thy fathers;

> Namely, of the gods of the people which are round and about you nigh unto thee or far off from thee. . .

> Thou shalt not consent unto him, nor harken unto him; neither shall thine eye pity him, neither shalt thou spare, neither shalt thou conceal him:

> But thou shalt surely kill him; thine hand shall be first upon him to put him to death, and afterwards the hand of all the people.

> And thou shalt stone him with stones, that he die; because he hath sought to thrust thee away from the Lord thy God, which brought thee out of Egypt, from the house of bondage.

> — Deuteronomy: 13:6—13:10 (See also 13:12, 13, 15, 16.)

> When the Lord thy God shall bring thee into the land whither thou goest to possess it, and hath cast out many nations before thee, the Hittites, and the Girgashites, and the Amorites, and the Canaanites, and the Persites, and the Hivites, and the Jebusites, seven nations greater and mightier than thou;

> And when the Lord thy God shall deliver them before thee; thou shalt smite them and utterly destroy them; thou shalt make not covenant with them, nor show mercy unto them:

> Neither shalt thou make marriages with them; thy daughter shalt not give unto his son, nor his daughter shalt thou take unto they son.

> Ye shall destroy their altars, and break down their images, and cut down their groves, and burn their graven images with fire.

> For thou *art* an holy people unto the Lord thy God: the Lord thy God hath chosen thee to be a special people unto himself, above all people that *are* upon the face of the earth.

> — Deuteronomy 7:1, 7:6

In the Christian context this statement becomes stronger and more powerfully aggressive (yet at the same time more subtle, less explicit) as opposed to the adamently defensive nature of the Jewish statement, which seeks to protect itself against contamination. All of the necessary ingredients were already present, including the European self-image as "world-savior." Put into the context of European ideology this can be seen as an ideal vehicle for the cultural-imperialistic projection of the European objective, which, in fact, it became later. That is an African-centered interpretation of what in Eurocentric rhetoric is stated as "a vision of the ultimate Brotherhood of Man under the rule of One God and Father of all men."[8] The implication of this "vision" is, indeed, a European theocracy.

The Judeo-Christian Schism

The "Christian" formulation becomes the next identifiable stage in the development of the European *utamaroho* as expressed by institutionalized religion. Christianity owed much to the early Judaic tradition; so much, in fact, that the questions become: What exactly *was* the difference in this "new" religion? In what way was it new? Why did the followers of Jesus consider themselves distinct from, even antagonistic toward, other Jews and vice-versa?

According to European tradition the critical theological differences between the Jews and Jesus are fixed on his claim to be the "Son of God" and, correlatively, the refusal of the Jews to recognize him as the "Son" of their "God." But the ideological issue is lodged in the implications of Jesus' teachings for Jewish nationalism, and the cultural imperialistic implications of Paul's elaboration and interpretation of them. From this perspective the schism and resulting antagonism makes political sense. I do not impose consciously political motives on any of these teachings. I mean rather to point to the political implications of the ideas when put into the context of embryonic European nationalist and cultural behavior patterns. In other words, the point is that some religious statements can be used to support certain political objectives while others cannot.

For the Jews, while their god was projected as the one "true" god for humankind, the emphasis and essential feature of Judaism was not the possibility of world-wide application, but rather the specialness of the Jewish people. According to them it is only the Jews who had been "chosen" to fulfill God's prophecy:

> For thou an holy people unto the Lord thy God: the Lord thy God
> hath chosen thee to be a special people unto himself, above all peo-
> ple that *are* upon the face of the earth.
>
> Deuteronomy: 7:6

But they were to fulfill this prophecy by presenting a normative example to other peoples, *not through conquest.*

The cultural-political implications of Paul's strategy or interpretation of Jesus' teachings were quite different. In Paul's view, converted Gentiles would be assured the same privileges as those
enjoyed by the Jewish believers, and they would also inherit the
reward and promises made to Israel.[9] The Christian organization also
added an increased stratification to the Jewish model through a hierarchy created out of the need for "correct interpretation." This was
not a primarily religious function for the Jews since their doctrine
emphasized the "letter" of the written law.

The critical difference is to be found in Paul's attention to the
Gentiles, a move that was both the cause and the effect of rejection by
the Jewish nationalists. The many Jews who became the first
"Christians" were not, of course, Jewish nationalists. It is in this context and at this point that a distinction began to exist between primarily self-deterministic Jewish nationalism and the more imperialistic
European cultural chauvinism. This is a distinction that has remained
consistent to contemporary times, for while the Jewish interest may
seek power, it is not expansionistic in the sense of seeking converts.

The Judaic formulation was the ideal vehicle for the expressly
limited objective of Jewish cultural solidarity, the solidarity necessary
for the efficient socio-political organization and consolidation of the
efforts of its members. It was the perfect statement of nationalistic
expression to the Jewish people as it encouraged their identification
with the group through an assumed historical (transcending the territorial) experience and destiny, and functioned as a defensive mechanism necessary for their self-determination—a need that was
intensified by their extreme "minority" circumstance.

As the European *utamaroho* began to emerge in the wider context created by an ever-expanding self-image, itself defined in terms
of ever-increasing power, the needs of European nationalistic/chau-
vinistic expression required much more than Judaism provided.
Judaism did indeed promote and encourage several of the rather critical values viewed as necessary for the planted European *asili* but
clearly its nationalistic statement was grossly inadequate for the
expanding European self-image. While it was a statement of political

self-determination and defensive social cohesion, it was not a statement of world imperialistic objectives. The Judaic vision was elitist-
isolationist; the expanded European vision sought the control and
cultural exploitation of other groups. Terrence Penelhum says, "When
Christianity appeared on the scene, it came not merely as one more
religion but rather as an implacable rival to all others. It claimed total
allegiance from all men . . . .[10] Oswald Spengler makes this difference
in political implication clear:

> Even in the first days the question arose which decided the whole
> Destiny of the new revelation. Jesus and his friends were Jews by
> birth, but they did not belong to the land of Judea. Here in
> Jerusalem men looked for the Messiah of their old sacred books, a
> Messiah who was to appear for the "Jewish people," in the old tribal
> sense, and only for them. But all the rest of the Aramaean world
> waited upon the Saviour of the *World*, the Redeemer and Son of
> Man, the figure of all apocalyptic literature, whether written out in
> Jewish, Persian, Chaldean, or Mandean terms. In the one view the
> death and resurrection of Jesus were merely local events; in the
> other they betokened a world-change . . . . In the Judaic view there
> was essentially no need for recruiting—quite the reverse, as it was
> a contradiction to the Messiah-idea. The words "tribe" and "mis-
> sion" are reciprocally exclusive. The members of the Chosen
> People, and in particular the priesthood, had merely to convince
> *themselves* that their longing was now fulfilled. But to the Magian
> nation, based on consensus or community of feeling, what the
> Resurrection conveyed was a full and definitive truth, and consen-
> sus in the matter of this truth gave the *principle of the true nation,*
> which must necessarily expand till it had taken in all older and con-
> ceptually incomplete principles.[Spengler's itallics.][11]

It is the European *utamawazo* (cultural thought structure) that makes
the Christian statement appear to be conceptually more complete.

The significance of Spengler's observation is that while the overwhelming body of the Christian formulation, as taught by Jesus and
interpretively elaborated by Paul, was consistent with and not contradictory to Jewish belief, two critical and related features were
added. These additional features molded the Jewish idea into an ideological statement that supported and justified not only a nascent
European definition of value, but also a new brand of imperialism, an
imperialism that suited the European *utamaroho*. One of those features was the *rhetorically* universalistic and nonexclusive definition
of the group (or "object") that "could be saved"; the other was the
related feature of the mandate to proselytize. Christianity, then,

became the ideal formulation for the unlimited expansion of a culture with a supremacist ideology, and at the same time it provided the ideological tool for the control of the resultant empire through its rhetorical "universalistic" component.

Why did the Jews refuse to accept Jesus as the Messiah they had long awaited? Possibly because they refused to enlarge the cultural-national group with which they identified, and, in part, because they refused to become absorbed in (though always intimately ethno-historically related to) the larger ideological entity that was forming and that was to culminate in Western European culture. One refusal was dictated by the other, and the separation and antagonism between the two groups (Christians and Jews) can be seen as one of political identification and strategy worked out in religious terminology. The question then, as now, is one of allegiance. In so far as the Jewish people refuse to identify with the nationalistic expression and destiny of the larger and dominant group whose territory they share, they constitute a "thorn in the side" of that group and have been, therefore, mistrusted and, what is worse, terrorized. In spite of this victimization, and because of the similarity of value orientation and compatibility of *utamaroho* and *utamawazo* between the Jewish people and the larger Western European group, Jews are not referred to as "pagan" or "primitive" and are not considered to be "evolutionarily inferior" as other victims of Western European oppression have been. They are indeed totally "Western" in this sense. Even Rheinhold Niebuhr recognizes the fact that Christianity was inconsistent with Jewish nationalism, but he fails to observe the new nationalistic statement of Christian ideology, or rather he mistakes its cultural imperialistic expression for a morally superior "universalism."

> The freedom of God over the instruments of his will . . . is asserted according to insights of prophetic universalism, as against the lower level of nationalistic Messianism. It is significant, however, that Christianity does not finally purge itself of the nationalistic particularism until St. Paul asserts the right to preach the gospel to the Gentiles, rejects the validity of Jewish law for Christians, and substitutes the church for the nation as the "Israel of God."[12]

An interesting treatment of the difference between the Jewish and Christian statements is found in Schonfield's *The Passover Plot*. Schonfield is expressly concerned with documenting the evidence for his contention that Jesus, perhaps convinced that he was in fact the Messiah, devoted his short life to arranging his "crucifixion" and subsequent "resurrection," so as to guarantee the fulfillment of the

Jewish prophecy (which itself is from earlier non-Western traditions). Schonfield's avowed stance is one of "objective scholarship." He wants to "shed light" on a subject too long clouded by "religious bias." In his introductory statements he says that his objective is "to be of helpful service" and that of the "patient seeking after truth."[13] But, in fact, Schonfield's perspective is one of both Jewish nationalism (though he probably does not identify himself religiously as a Jew) and Western cultural chauvinism. His argument is that the Christian conception of Jesus as the Son of "God" de-Westernized the Hebrew formulation and was therefore a retrogression from the intellectual "advance" that Judaism had made from the "superstitions" of the "pagans."

> Christianity was still much too close to the paganism over which it had scored a technical victory to be happy with a faith in God as pure spirit. There had never been in the Church a complete conversion from heathenism. We might be living in the second half of the twentieth century, but the Gentile need remained for a human embodiment of deity. God had still to be grasped through a physical kinship with man and his earthly concerns, and there yet lingered the sense of the efficacy of the substitutionary and propitiatory sacrifice of a victim.[13]

We hear an echo of Spengler's analysis but interestingly enough with the reverse position. For Spengler, the Christian idea is "conceptually" more complete, while for Schonfield it is less "pure." Both are using Platonic rules consistent with the European *utamawazo*. They are ideologically committed to the same values. The civilized is represented by the technologically more efficient, the conceptually more abstract, the perceptively less subjective. In this critique of the Christian conception by Schonfield, an "apology" for the Jewish rejection of Jesus as the Messiah is a perfect and concise statement of the European religious ideal, and the correlative of the mode of European religion. Of the Christian image of Jesus he says,

> Such a man could have his god-like moments, but could never be consistently a reflection of the Divine except for those whose notion of deity would permit the gods to share our human frailties . . .

> Far too many Christians do not know God in any other way than through Jesus and their faith in God is imperiled or destroyed. The New Testament is not entirely to be blamed for this. The major fault lies with those who have pandered to the ignorance and superstition of the people in giving them a God created in the image of man.

Yet Jesus and his nation, differently taught, could love and worship God without recourse to incarnation.[14]

Ironically, it is precisely the "mystical" ingredient of the Jesus
legend that gives Christianity its religious appeal, as well as other
aspects that are taken from prior cultural traditions. There is no sense
in which Schonfield's statements above can be called "objective,"
even if it is agreed for the moment that "objectivity" is a valid concept.
His use of the term "pagan" corresponds to that of not only Christian
and Jewish theologians but to "nonreligious" and so-called objective
European social scientists.

There are few terms common in both ordinary and scientific
usage that so blatantly reveal the *utamaroho* (collective personality)
and self-image of Europeans as does "pagan." It is perhaps the epitome of European arrogance and self-delusion that Europeans can
with seriousness describe First World peoples as being "irreligious."
Schonfield points out, disparagingly, that the Church has absorbed
many so-called pagan customs and beliefs.[15] He does not, however,
state the political significance of this fact: that much of Christian
mythology comes from older cultural and religious traditions, which
has aided the Christians in their "conversion" of Africans and other
non-European peoples. This factor served the objectives of Western
European cultural imperialism well, for while people of other cultures
were in part being "converted" to *their own conceptions,* they were at
the same time being absorbed into an organization that controlled
them for the benefit of Europeans.

The Roman Cooptation: Two Imperialistic Ideologies

At the close of the Principate the pagan world presented a great
confusion of religious beliefs and doctrines. But the various pagan
cults were tolerant of one another, for the followers of one god
were ready to acknowledge the divinity of the gods worshipped by
their neighbors. On the contrary, the adherents of Judaism and
Christianity refused to recognize the pagan gods and hence stood
in irreconcilable opposition to the whole pagan world.[16]

Politically, the Roman ideology was the perfect counterpart to
this "religious" formulation, as Arthur Boak's *History of Rome* characterizes it. Just as the Christian projection was that of a benevo-
lence that sought to share enlightenment in the form of the word
with those unfortunate enough to have so far escaped it, so the
Roman nationalistic image was that of a people in possession of "civilization" prepared to bestow its blessings on "barbarians."

Christianity offers salvation to all, providing they "come into the fold," accepting Jesus as the "Son of God," therefore gaining eternal life; the Romans offered citizenship to all, providing, as Aristides says, they possessed "talent," "courage," and "leadership" potential. "Cultural" boundaries did not matter. Both were offers of "civilization" and a supposedly evolutionary superior way of life. These formulations posited a perpetual opposition between those who did not share the ideologies expressed and those who did. Both statements, importantly, contained justifications and directives for the "conversion" and "recruitment" of those outside the cultural group with which they were identified. Perhaps the single most important ingredient shared by these "brother" ideologies (actually two arms of the same ideological weapon) is their vision of the world as the "turf" of a single culture. Any and everyone presently under the ideological and political control of the Christians and Romans was fair game. Never before had ideologies so explicitly stated this worldwide objective. This indeed was the "technical victory" to which Schonfield and Spengler allude. And this unique self-image that projects itself as the proper model for all, we can identify as European. This self-image and its projection are part of a centuries-old process through which Europeans miraculously become the universal paradigm for all humanity.

While it is clear that both the Christian and the Roman formulations could serve as ideological statements of a world imperialistic endeavor, it is also clear that the two could not coexist as competing ideologies. But this did not constitute an irreconcilable opposition. Their synthesis made much political sense. It was represented in the cooptation of the Church by and for the purposes of the State, or one can just as easily reverse this statement. The solution was, indeed, culturally, as well as historically, compelling. The two ideologies, put to the service of one cultural group and espousing compatible values and objectives, worked hand in hand, to command the same allegiances, to conquer the same world.

Constantine's conversion is often characterized by European historians as a "turning point" in European history. Norman Baynes says that Constantine's conversion is hard to explain based on what came before him and that he "diverted the stream of human history."[17] Ethnologically, it was not a "turning point," but the concretization of a tendency—a push in a direction already identifiable in the continuum of Western European development. Constantine's "conversion" was demanded by the European *asili*, the cultural seed. It was a necessary step for the growth and solidification of the Roman

Empire. The religious formulations that had existed previously in the state were not compatible with the socio-political objectives that guided the Roman leadership—they were not compatible with the Western ideal. These prior religious formulations did not share the imperialist vision.

According to Constantine's own account (if we are to use Eusebius as an authority), his conversion was intimately bound up with his immediate military objectives. In A.D. 312 Constantine was one of four competitors left in a bloody struggle for the rule of the Roman Empire. In that year he invaded Italy from Gaul and "gained control over the whole West by his victory over Maxentius at the gates of Rome."[18]

Eusebius says that Constantine had searched in vain for a god capable of assuring the success of his military endeavors. He decided to try his father's god: the Christian god. He prayed to this god, asking for a sign, and one appeared to him,

> he saw with his own eyes the trophy of a cross of light in the heavens, above the sun, and bearing the inscription, "Conquer by This. . ."

> in his sleep the Christ of God appeared to him with the same sign which he had seen in the heavens, and commanded him to make a likeness of that sign which he had seen in the heavens, and to use it as a safeguard in all engagements with his enemies. . . . The emperor constantly made use of this sign of salvation as a safeguard against every adverse and hostile power, and commanded that others similar to it should be carried at the head of all his armies.[19]

This, then, in a very real sense was the first "crusade." In 313 Constantine and Licinius agreed, in the Edict of Milan, to the official recognition of the Christian religion by the state. The agreement with Licinius was for "joint rule," but,

> While Constantine granted ever greater privileges and advantages to the Christians, Licinius gradually reversed his policy of toleration and initiated repressive measures. It became obvious that Constantine aimed to be sole emperor.[20]

Timothy Barne's view of these same issues in his book, *Constantine and Eusebius,* is that:

> It seems natural to conclude that he was converted to Christianity

before the Battle of the Milvian Bridge. But the moment of psychological conviction may have followed, rather than preceded, his own avowal: It perhaps occurred during the battle, at the moment victory became certain. In the ultimate reckoning, however, the precise details of Constantine's conversion matter little. After 28 October 312 the emperor consistently thought of himself as God's servant, entrusted with a divine mission to convert the Roman Empire to Christianity.[21]

This same servant of "god" probably later had Licinius, who was his brother-in-law, killed along with Licinius' nine-year-old son. Evidently this did not conflict with Constantine's "Christianity."

Barnes says that by 324, Constantine was taking every opportunity to "stress the truth of Christianity" because of his "religious sympathies," and he concludes that "an emperor with these convictions could not be expected to tolerate pagan practices which all Christians found morally offensive."[22] Barnes continues, "He established Christianity as the official religion of the Roman Empire. . . . Christians received preference in official appointment. . . .Constantine forbade the erection of cult statues, the consultation of pagan oracles, divination of any sort, and sacrifice to the gods under any circumstances."[22] Not only was Constantine concerned with the spread of Christianity throughout the Empire, but he was equally concerned with ideological unity *among the Christians.* If institutionalized Christianity was to be of political benefit, its leaders must speak with one voice. Theological disputes were of little import in Constantine's view when the unity of the Church was at stake. His role was therefore one of mediation, and he mandated that the bishops settle their differences, calling the first ecumenical council of the Christian Church, the Council of Nicaea, in 325.

Arthur E. R. Boak gives *his* interpretation of Constantine's actions and convictions:

> It is clear that on the eve of the final encounter with Maxentius, he placed both himself and his army under the protection of the Christian's God, and that he was convinced that his victory then and his later success in winning the whole Empire were due to the power and favor of this divinity. From 312 A.D., he looked upon himself as designated by God to rule the Roman World. And in return for this divine recognition, he felt the obligation to promote the cause of Christianity in all possible ways. This meant that Christianity must receive official recognition as state religion; not only that, it must become the only state religion, for Christians could recognize no other gods but One. Thus Constantine saw in

Christianity the religion which could and should provide a spiritual bond among his subjects as well as a moral basis for political loyalty to himself as the elect of God.[23]

It is compelling to add, "and a 'moral' basis for world imperialism." Boak continues.

Having decided to make Christianity the one state religion, he also felt obligated to take the initiative in ensuring the unity of the Christian community itself. . . .Constantine made full use of his autocratic power to develop a totalitarian regime for which the foundations had been laid by earlier emperors.[24]

These accounts and descriptions of Constantine's "conversion" inadvertently (in spite of the intentions of their authors) point to the political expediency and suitability of the marriage of the Roman and orthodox Christian ideologies for the imperialistic ambitions of the Western nation of the fourth century. Constantine's association with the new god—the "European god"—gave him additional support afforded by religious sanction of his political and military power, and the religion he chose had the advantage of itself incorporating a vision of complete worldwide power and control. Eusebius says, "Thus then the God of all, the Supreme Governor of the whole universe, by his own will appointed Constantine, the descendent of so renowned a parent, to be prince and sovereign: so that, while others have been raised to this distinction by the election of their fellowmen, his is the only one to whose elevation no mortal may boast of having contributed."[25] This process, having been put in motion by Constantine, was further solidified by Theodosius, in the Theodosian Code.

In the fifth century, the Senate was thoroughly Christian. As early as 380 A.D. Theodosius had ordered all his subjects to accept the Christian creed formulated at the Council of Nicaea in 325. In 391 he ordered the destruction of the image and temple of Sarapis in Alexandria, a step which sounded the death knell of paganism in the eastern part of the Empire. The following year he unconditionally forbade pagan worship under penalties for treason and sacrilege. Theodosius II continued the vigorous persecution of the pagans. Adherence to pagan beliefs was declared criminal, and in the Theodosian Code laws against pagans are included among the laws regulating civic life."[26]

Constantine had laid the groundwork for the proclamation of

Christianity as the religion of an orthodox Roman State. It was his brilliance to recognize the compatibility, rather than antagonism,
between the political objectives of the Roman State and the Christian
ideology. Many European historians, in fact, begin the Medieval
period of European culture with Constantine's innovation.

Lest the identity of these ideologies remain too abstract or
ambiguously stated let us offer here some very concrete ethnographic data, i.e., Constantine's own statements of his objectives and
interpretation of his "new Christian" mission. Constantine says of
those who did not worship his supreme god with fitting veneration,

> I will destroy and disperse [them] . . . . What can be done by me
> more consonant with my fixed resolve and with the duty of an
> emperor than, having dissipated errors and cut off all unfounded
> opinions, to cause all men to present the omnipotent God, true reli-
> gion, unfeigned concord, and the worship which is his due.[27]

This is taken from a letter written by Constantine to a group of
bishops at the Council of Arles regarding the official policy to be
adopted toward "pagans" and Donatists. The Donatists were a
Christian sect who opposed the alignment of the Church with the
Imperial Government. This position is analogous to the attempt to set
a sailboat on an "upwind" course. For the die had been cast:
"Europeanness" was already set in motion—gaining momentum
rapidly, its successful development (the fulfillment of the *asili*)
demanded the monolithic model and ideological justification that
this alignment offered. Constantine says,

> God sought my service and judged that service fitted to achieve His
> purpose. Starting from Britain God had scattered the evil powers
> that mankind might be recalled to true religion instructed through
> my agency, and that the blessed faith might spread under his guid-
> ing hand. And from the West, believing that this gift had been
> entrusted to myself, I have come to the East which was in sorer
> need of my aid.[28]

Licinius, in the East, who did not claim the Christian god, stood
temporarily in the way of Constantine's unified control. Licinius' persecution of the Christians becomes understandable as a political
necessity in his efforts to prevent Constantine's take over. By the
same token, the realization of Constantine's ambitions were facilitated by his mission in spreading the faith.

I knew that, if in accordance with my prayers I could establish a common agreement amongst all servants of God, then the need of the state would as the fruit of that agreement undergo a change in a consonance with the pious desires of all.[29]

Norman Bayne's interpretation of Constantine's objectives is stated as two separate aims: to overthrow Licinius and thereby "heal the body of the Roman world," and to "unite his subjects in one common religious belief."[30] He even remarks on the "close connection between the fortunes of the state and the unity of the Church," in the mind of Constantine.[31] Yet, this historian of early European development never explicitly interprets Constantine's motives as having been imperialistic. That is because this interpretation of European development does not serve the interests of European nationalism. It is quite clear, even from his own words, that the Christian cause gave Constantine a powerful tool with which to unify Rome under his control and to conquer those not yet within this Empire. For this reason Constantine is adamantly opposed to disunity among the avowed Christians: "Open to me by your unity the road to the East."[29] The recurring theme in his directives to his bishops is unity; for unity was the political necessity of the day. The world could not be made a European hegemony until European culture was itself solidified. Constantine says,

For truly it would be a terrible thing—a very terrible thing—that now when wars are ended and none dares to offer further resistance we should begin to attack each other and thus give excuse for pleasure and for laughter to the pagan world.[32]

One of the internecine disputes within the Church during Constantine's reign had to do with who, in fact, was a Christian; particularly with regard to those who wished to convert. When Arius announced that he had "surrendered" to the Christian god, Athanasius did not want to accept him. Constantine wrote to Athanasius: "Now you know my will: to all those who desire to enter the Church do you provide free entry." This had to be official policy if the cloak of Christianity was to do its job for Western European imperialism. Its counterpart was the offer of Roman citizenship, to which everyone was to aspire, to the "elite" of other cultures. Both were inclusive in that no one was to be excluded from European dominion. Of Roman citizenship, Aristides, writing approximately two centuries before the time of Constantine (ca. A.D. 144 or 156) says:

Dividing into two groups all those in your empire—with this sword I have indicated the entire civilized world—you have everywhere appointed to your citizenship, or even to kinship with you, the better part of the world's talent, courage, and leadership, while the rest you recognize as a league under your hegemony. . . . Neither seas nor intervening continent are bars to citizenship, nor are Asia and Europe divided in their treatment here. In your empire all paths are open to all. No one worthy of rule or trust remains an alien, but a civil community of the World has been established as a Free Republic under one, as into a common civic center, in order to receive each man his due.[33]

The previous quotations, taken from Constantine's own correspondence and statements, are included for the purpose of providing concrete examples of the potentially isomorphic relationship of the Christian and Roman world-imperialistic ideologies and the actual realization of their oneness of purpose through Constantine's policy. The source for these quotations is a lecture given by Baynes in 1930. His objective is to show that Constantine's primary concern was in bringing Christianity to the pagan world. This Baynes argues in opposition to the divergent interpretation that Edward Schwartz presents in *The Emperor Constantine and the Christian Church.* The following is Bayne's interpretation of Schwartz's analysis:

He [Schwartz] has found the Open Sesame to the Understanding of the reign in Constantine's resolution to exploit in his own interest the organization which gave to the Christian Church its corporate strength: through alliance with the Church Constantine sought to attain victory and the sole mastery of the Roman World.[34]

The interpretation of Theodor Brieger (1800) is also a forceful statement of what Baynes terms the "view of purely political motivation." Schwartz is the "modern representative of this standpoint." But Baynes is adamant:

I believe that his conception of the character and aims alike of Constantine and Athanasius is essentially inhuman. This prodigious simplification does scant justice to the complexity of human personality. The view that Constantine adopted in religious diplomacy as his principle of action the Roman maxim "divide et impera" I find impossible to believe.[35]

From an African-centered perspective, on the other hand, I find Schwartz's view of to be the most "human" of interpretations. It is Baynes' explanation, in his own admission, which fails to offer cultural-historical continuity. His reluctance, in this instance, to do what he has supposedly been well trained to do as an historian, forces him to fix on the absolutely irrelevant and moot issue of whether or not Constantine was a "true convert!" It then becomes hard for him to explain Constantine, and so he resorts to the "great personality" theory:

> If the reconstruction of the past "difficulties" are, at times, caused by the interposition in the stream of history of outstanding personalities which resist rationalization and remain unexpected and embarrassing. . . [Constantine was] an erratic block which has diverted the stream of human history.[36]

Again, it is understandable, in ethnological terms, that interpretations of Constantine's religious policies as being politically motivated are unpopular within the tradition of European social theory. The interpretation of which Schwartz's view is representative (though virtually unrecognized) is consistent with the reality of human self-interest within the parochial context of a given culture and ideological setting. By the same token, such an interpretation is diametrically opposed to the "disinterested," "beneficient," and "altruistic" stance of European "universalism" that has been projected as a part of the propaganda of European cultural imperialism since the archaic states of that culture. Baynes' interpretation of Constantine, therefore, provides us with an ethnographic example of European nationalism.

The Threat of Non-Orthodox Christianity

One of the concerns of this chapter is the relationship between religion and national consciousness, i.e., behavior. Nowhere is this relationship better exemplified then in European cultural history. In no culture is the supportive relationship of formalized religion more successfully developed and elaborated. One of the correlates of this view of the relationship between religion and nationalism is that in order to understand the dynamics of a particular religious statement, one must first be aware of the ideological commitment of the people who identify with it, their *utamaroho* and their relationship to other cultures. This is, of course, a radical departure from the usual approach to the study of religion and in direct conflict with Christian theologians. Those who would argue the "revolutionary" political implications of Christianity (see Liberation Theology literature) also imply, rather unconvincingly, that the 2000-year imperialistic quest of Western Europe, then Euro-America, was successfully maintained *in spite of* a religion that spoke for more humanistic goals. That is simply implausible and it does not make sense. It is not contradiction but consistency that has made for Western European imperial success.

Elaine Pagels, in her interpretation of the significance of the developments of early Christianity, supports my view in that she points to the social and political implications of apostolic Christianism, as opposed to those of the Gnostic tradition that the orthodox church condemned, and over which it triumphed (although we must not confuse political triumph with spiritual triumph). Perhaps it would be more fitting to begin with a discussion of the African or Kemetic (ancient Egyptian) origins of Christian mythology and symbolism, though Pagels does not refer to these at all. But since we cannot take the time here for such a discussion, the reader is referred to the works of Gerald Massey (1973), John G. Jackson (1985), Yosef Ben Jochaman (1973), and others. Suffice it to say that the mythology and symbolism surrounding Usir, also known as Asar, and Osiris by the Greeks, introduced the concept of a resurrected savior 3000 years before the advent of Christianity. A study of this tradition also explains why the date of December 25 is used for the birthdate of Jesus, the symbolism of the stable as a place for his birth, the three "wisemen," and so forth.[37]

Clearly, however, there had to have been something "special," something "different" about the formulation of what is now accepted as biblical Christianity, or it would not have been so well suited to the archaic European *utamaroho* as expressed in the Roman State. In Pagel's book, *The Gnostic Gospels,* one of the things that we already know is reaffirmed: Gnosticism was unacceptable to, and considered heresy by, those who were in the process of establishing the orthodox Christian Church. These gospels were "written out" of the religion. Pagels offers us a plausible explanation, one that fits with my understanding of the Western European cultural reality. Gnosticism was not different enough from the Kemetic and other ancient origins. Its *utamaroho* was too close to these. It was neither politically oriented nor materialistic enough. Resurrection was understood symbolically and spiritually—much deeper than unending "physical" existence. Pagels tells us that the Gnostics believed that resurrection was to be experienced spiritually, that one experienced Christ on a spiritual level. "This may occur in dreams, in ecstatic trance, in visions, or in moments of spiritual illumination."[38] Rebirth for the ancients was after all a result of illumination and intense self-knowledge—a heightened spiritual level of development. But contrary to this, orthodoxy that opposed the Gnostic view, was indeed threatened by it, arguing as Tertuillian did, that "as Christ rose bodily from the grave so every believer should anticipate the resurrection of the flesh."[39] Interestingly enough, this is precisely the criticism that Schonfield has of Christianity, when comparing it with Judaism.[40] But in this case the "materialization" of the god-concept serves not to bring it closer to the human, but facilitates its use as the justification for authority. Tertuillian insists that the resurrection of Christ is undeniably physical, material in a very real *earthly* sense. "Tertuillian declares that anyone who denies the resurrection of the the *flesh* is a heretic, not a Christian."[38] The Gnostic emphasis on personal, spiritual growth and development, along with its deemphasis of proselytization made it ill-suited for the imperial quest.

Pagels raises the compelling question: "Why did orthodox tradition adopt the literal view of resurrection?"[38] And I would add: Why were they so threatened by the Gnostic teachings and those of the ancient Kemites? Pagels opens the way to the answers. She tells us that upon his resurrection in the New Testament, Jesus "proves" to his disciples that he is "not a ghost," and "Thomas declares that he will not believe that Jesus had actually risen from the grave unless he personally can see and touch him."[38] But, she continues, other accounts in the New Testament could lead one to the conclusion that some people had experienced visions of Jesus' return. "Paul describes the resurrection as 'a mystery,' the transformation from physical to spiritual existence."[41] The related questions restated: Why did orthodox Christianity insist on the literal, physical interpretation as opposed to a more metaphysical transcendental one, and why did they label other interpretations as heretical?[41] The answer, according to Pagels, is that

> the doctrine of bodily resurrection also serves an essentially *political* function. . . . [Pagel's italics]

> It legitimizes the authority of certain men who claim to exercise leadership over the churches as the successors of the apostle Peter. From the second century, the doctrine [of bodily resurrection] has served to validate the apostolic succession of bishops, the basis of papal authority to this day.[41]

What Pagels argues is that the idea or claim of the resurrection of Jesus provided a source of authority for his earthly successor: Peter. It was crucial that some such claim be possible given the fact that the leader or absolute authority within the movement was gone, and hundreds of people were claiming to interpret his teachings in almost as many different ways. In order for Peter to be the established "rock" or foundation of a structured, institutionalized organization, all other groups had to be discredited. What better way than through his *actual* contact with a *physically* resurrected Jesus, who had explicitly given him authority to begin the institutionalization of his (Jesus') teachings.[42] (See Matthew 16: 13–19.) Given this political necessity for a doctrine of physical resurrection, the Gnostic teachings of a more metaphysical and symbolic concept of resurrection were most threatening to the establishment of the church. Not only did the apostles get authority in this way, but they were the only ones who could confer it on those who succeeded them. Christians in the second century used Luke's account to set the groundwork for establishing specific, restricted chains of command for all future generations of Christians, concludes Pagels.[43] So that present popes must rely on their connection to Peter, who had originally witnessed the physical resurrection of Jesus, for their authority.

But the Gnostics were indeed heretical, because they did not seem to be concerned with establishing an institution that would exercise total control. They insisted that the resurrection "was not a unique event in the past: instead, it symbolized how Christ's presence could be experienced in the present. What mattered was not literal seeing, but spiritual vision."[43] And in this way they continued the tradition of the mystery religions that predated orthodox Christianity, which Constantine, Justinian, Theodosius, and others were so bent on destroying. The emphasis in the Kemetic (ancient Egyptian) and derivative religious forms was on initiation into a process of spiritual development and enlightment. The emphasis within orthodox Christianity was (and is) on the acceptance of a dogma that could be the basis of socio-political structure and control.

These insights of Pagels coincide with my analysis of the function of institutionalized religion in European development. The secular, historical emphasis within Christian doctrine, and this includes the various "non-orthodox" forms that evolved as a result of the "Reformation," is a direct result of the need to claim superiority to other religions, which, in turn imparts cultural and therefore political superiority or control. No Christian will accept an authentically "spiritual" or metaphysical interpretation of Christian teachings. Herein lies the telling contradiction of Christian theology. To be a "Christian" is to insist on a "historical Christ" (in a rigidly secular sense); yet this adjective should contradict the noun it purports to describe. The reason for this strange characteristic of Christianity, as it was interpreted in the development of archaic European civilization has to do with the *utamaroho* that was also becoming standardized, as well as the ideological needs of the new order. The spurious dichotomy between history and mythology would become the handmaiden of the civilized/primitive dichotomy, so essential to Western European cultural nationalism and imperialism. According to European nationalism, other traditions and earlier ones were expressions of mythological beliefs only: Christianity was an expression of historical fact. To this day the most threatening appositional phrase that an avowed Christian can be presented with is "Christian Mythology." To accept its validity is to shake the ground of her/his belief.

The Gnostics, like the Africans and many contemporary non-Christians were concerned with the attainment of spiritual intuition, which would reveal the nature of cosmic reality. According to Pagels, they talked about, "the possibility of encountering the risen Christ in the present."[44] But imagine what that would do to the establishment of the apostolic Church as an institution if people could continue to "witness the resurrection!" The Gnostics claimed to have kept the esoteric aspect of Jesus' teachings, which were necessarily secret and could be revealed only to initiates.[45] This is, of course, how all the ancient African spiritual systems were organized, which still represents the basic structure of spiritual learning and development among Africans who adhere to their own "non-European" conceptions. It would seem reasonable to assume that Jesus himself was an initiate of a derived, albeit adulterated "mystery system" as his teachings can be interpreted as being consistent with these earlier traditions, and it was out of these traditions that Christianity evolved.

Both Pagels and I put emphasis on the institutionalization of Christianity. She says that, "the controversy over resurrection, then, proved critical in shaping the Christian movement into an institutional religion.[46] I share this emphasis because of the critical role of this institution within the matrix of European imperialism, especially in certain stages of European development. Gnosticism could not lead to the subsequent developments—the Roman cooptation, Constantine's "conversion"—that were necessary for the expansion of imperial techno-political control. For, according to Pagels, the Gnostics argued that "only one's own experience offers the ultimate criterion of truth. . . ." She tells us that "they celebrated every form of creative invention as evidence that a person has become spiritually alive. On this theory, the structure of authority can never be fixed into an institutional framework: it must remain spontaneous, charismatic, and open."[46] But that is not how empires are built. It does not suit the European *asili*, and the European imperial quest has been more successful than any other, because it has always been based on the claim of superior culture. In the budding stages of the quest, as the European *utamaroho* took shape, a tightly structured, institutionalized and secularly codified religion was the key to this claim.

> . . . in terms of the social order. . . the orthodox teaching on resurrection had a different effect: it legitimized a hierarchy of persons through whose authority all others must approach God. Gnostic teaching. . . was politically subversive of this order: it claimed to offer to every initiate direct access to God of which the priests and bishops themselves might be ignorant.[47]

Certainly there is no universal or absolute moral imperative that dictates that it is culturally superior to recognize the existence of only one god. Therefore, in the ethnological analysis of European culture, we must look for tendencies within it that would make avowed monotheism desirable. We look to European ideology—more specifically to Rome at the time of its Christianization. A political/ideological interpretation of the significance of the monotheistic ideal, again, makes sense. Pagel's analysis fits: "As the doctrine of Christ's bodily resurrection establishes the initial framework for clerical authority, so the doctrine of the 'one God' confirms, for Orthodox Christians, the emerging institution of the 'one bishop' as monarch ('sole ruler') of the Church."[48] She argues that another aspect of the threat to orthodoxy posed by Gnosticism was their lack of recognition of the Church hierarchy. Valentinus says that the Gnostics "join together as equals, enjoying mutual love, spontaneously helping one another" as opposed to the ordinary Christians, who "wanted to command one another, outrivalling one another in their empty ambition," inflated with "lust for power," "each one imagining that he is superior to the others." While the "lust for power" is the nature of the European *asili*, Pagels tells us that the Gnostics refused to rank themselves "into superior and inferior orders within a hierarchy, and that they followed the principle of strict equality."[49] On the other hand, she says, Tertuillian, advocate of the orthodoxy, considered certain distinctions essential to Church order: namely, those between "newcomers and experienced Christians; between women and men: between a professional clergy and people occupied with secular employment; between readers, deacons, priests, and bishops—and above, between the clergy and the laity."[50]

The Gnostics emphasized spiritual attainment and said they related to a concept of god that was beyond that of the mere image of god to whom the ordinary Christians related. They called this lesser god the "demiurge" and said that this "creator" made false claims to power. In Pagel's explanation of Gnostic thought, achieving *gnosis* involved "coming to recognize the true source of divine power— namely, 'the depth' of all being." But the god of Clement, Irenaeus, and Tertullian claimed, "I am God, and there is no other. . . . I am a jealous God." And to them the concept of a transcendent force reachable through initiation was "heresy" that "encourage(d) insubordination to clerical authority." To Irenaeus the meetings of the Gnostics were "unauthorized." The concept of authority is key. If spiritual growth had been the focus for Irenaeus and others, the Gnostics would not have been threatening. The Church represented a structure of authority, and that structure had to be monolithic. Therefore, in Pagel's words: "If God is One, then there can only be one true church, and only one representative of the God in the community—the Bishop."[51] This "One God" became the basis for the power of "One Emperor" of the "One Civilization" as well. Belief in *him* gave the emperor authority to conquer all nonbelievers in his name. In a sense Gnosticism was anachronistic, while orthodox Christianity was "right on time." Religious formulations that were more spiritual and transcendent, less political and secular in intent, were simply not expedient.

Augustine and Political Conservatism

The strength of the Christian ideological formulation in its function as a tool of European cultural imperialism is twofold: (1) It subtly justifies two kinds of political activity; that is, it appeals to two different layers of the world's population. (2) It unifies the conquerors while simultaneously pacifying the conquered. This, in part, is reflected in the strikingly different tones or "moods" of the Old and New Testaments in terms of their political possibilities for the Roman Empire. The Old Testament is extremely militaristic and aggressive. It is often an unveiled directive: the blatant command that a homogeneous and limited cultural group resist all alien influences through the prohibition of intermarriage and other social intercourse with cultural groups adhering to different ideologies. The task of the New Testament, on the other hand, is much more complicated. What was later interpreted as the directive for aggression is there stated as the desire to spread enlightenment. What developed into the mandate to bring those "who are *not like us* under our domain" is there molded into the rhetoric of "soul-saving," and at the same time, it sells passive acceptance to those "souls." The Christian statement, as an established aspect of European culture, is, after all, a nationalistic ideology (in that it is the expression of the ideology of a particular culture just as any religious statement is), and its function in this regard is to serve the interests of that culture. The docility and lack of aggression of the conquered peoples serves this interest, and so the Christian directive is dual in nature; while it provides a justification for a world-order in the service of a European god, its teachings encourage others to be nonpolitical and discourages their cultural nationalism (identification with their national gods and belief systems).

There is a curious characterization of Jesus as a "revolutionary" in the literature of Liberation Theology and Black Theology. Unfortunately, persecution and unpopularity do not necessarily make ideas revolutionary. The Jewish ideology in its stubborn nationalism could in this sense be considered more revolutionary in the face of Roman policy than that of Jesus and his followers. It would be very difficult to imagine, if we did not consistently put our data into the context of the European *asili*, how any historian or social theorist could identify the so-called "Christian virtues"; i.e., the "Christian ethic" or mode of behavior as being in any way new or innovative at the time of Jesus. The mandate to regard and treat one another as brothers and sisters (i.e., as members of a "family" kin group) had existed probably since the beginnings of human civilization in Africa. The African ideological statement, of this mode of behavior as an ethical imperative is much more philosophically profound than the Christian-European statement of it and, of course, so much more consistent and authentic. It originates in a spiritualistic world-view.[52]

What was "new" about the teachings that purported to have resulted from the activities of Jesus was that they proclaimed that one was to treat members of other cultural groups in this way, and, more importantly, one was to treat one's enemies in this (the same) way—"enemies" being those who were hostile to one's cultural group or one's "family." This directive is, of course, debilitating and castrating to political cultural nationalism and counter to the demands of self-determination. This feature, along with that of the direction of attention towards "another world" in which justice is sought, may certainly combine to form a new statement, but it can hardly be called a politically revolutionary one.

Otto Spengler concerns himself with this political duality of Christian doctrine in the *Decline of the West*. He accuses those in the West who would seek to apply the "brotherhood" and "love" espoused by Jesus to the "unfortunate" and "oppressed" in the society of his day of having in fact misinterpreted Jesus' teachings:

Moralizing is Nineteenth-century Philistinism. To ascribe social purposes to Jesus is blasphemy. His occasional utterances of a social kind, so far as they are authentic and not merely attributed sayings, tend merely to edification. . . . *Religion is, first and last, metaphysic,* otherworldliness, awareness in a world of which the evidence of the senses merely lights the foreground. It is life in and with the super-sensible.[53]

Spengler is arguing that the ostensible teachings of Jesus are irrelevant to European life; i.e., that they were not meant to be used in a way that would act against the self-interest of the ruling Western European elite. He gives examples of passages that in his opinion point to the apolitical (asocial) intent of the Christian teachings. It is the misinterpretaion of these teachings, so as to give them political relevance to the plight of the poor, the oppressed, and the racially despised, that Spengler objects to so vehemently:

"My kingdom is *not* of this world," and only he who can look into the depths that this flash illumines can comprehend the voices that come out of them. It is the Late, city periods that, no longer capable of seeing into the depths, have turned, the remnants of religiousness upon the external world and replaced religion by humanities, and metaphysics by moralization and social ethics.

In Jesus we have the direct opposite. "Give unto Caesar the things that are Caesar's" means: "Fit yourselves to the powers of the fact-world, be patient, suffer, and ask it not whether they are 'just.'" What alone matters is the salvation of the soul, "consider the lilies" means: "Give no heed to riches *and poverty,* for both fetter the soul to cares of this world." "Man cannot serve both God and Mammon"—by Mammon is meant the *whole* of actuality. It is shallow, and it is cowardly, to argue away the grand significance of this demand. Between working for the increase of one's own riches, and working for the social ease of everyone, he would have felt no difference whatever.[53]

It is indeed Spengler's interpretation that is consistent with that of the Roman State, from Constantine onward, and it is this same "potential" within the Christian ideology that has allowed it to be a consistent part of European culture, from that time to the present. But Spengler is needlessly critical. The Christian doctrine has only aided the imperialistic ideal, not hindered its realization. Anyone who has ever, with illusions of altruism, approached the battlefield armed merely with Christian rhetoric did so totally unprepared to do anything but further the objectives of European expansion.

The compatibility of "the Christian way" with the objectives of the Roman State is argued for by St. Augustine in *The City of God.* This was one of the many "apologies" written in defense of Christianity against its non-Christian critics, as well as the Donatists. Through Augustine the political compatibility of Roman and Christian ideology and, therefore, the "counter-revolutionary" role of the followers of Jesus and Paul are clearly demonstrated. Augustine says that all earthly authority is "approved" by and "issues" from God. He quotes from the scriptures:

> Hear therefore, O ye Kings, and understand, for power is given you of the Lord and "Sovereignty from the Highest."
> Wisdom of Solomon vi, 3

> For there is no power, but God; the powers that be ordained of God. Therefore he that resisteth the power, withstandeth the ordinance of God: and they that withstand shall receive to themselves judgement."
> Romans xiii, 1-2

Norman Baynes paraphrases the method of Augustine's argument,

> Because rulers are chosen by divine Providence, the servants of Christ are bidden to tolerate even the worst and most vicious of states, and that they can do by realising that on earth they are but pilgrims, and that their home is not here but in heaven.[54]

We must remember that Augustine's purpose is to convince the Church that the Roman State is its proper earthly vehicle, and, by the same token, to assure the politicians that Christianity was not meant to interfere with the State but, in fact, to complement it. In Baynes' words, "St. Paul had urged obedience to the state upon the ground that the state rewards the good and punishes the evil."[55] In Augustine's view, "God" had helped the Romans, for even though they were vain seekers of earthly glory, according to the relative standard of the earthly state, they were good people. And in rewarding them, "God" had in view a further purpose—that the Romans might on their own level be an example and an inspiration to the Christians.

> These things being so, we do not attribute the power of giving kingdom and empires to any save the true God, who gives the happiness in the kingdom of heaven to the pious alone, but gives kingly power on earth both to the pious and the impious, as it may please Him, whose good pleasure is always just. . .

The same is true in respect of men as well as nations. He who gave power to Marius gave it also to Caius Caesar; He who gave it to Augustus gave it also to Nero; He also who gave it to the most benignant emperors, the Vespasians, father and son, gave it also to the cruel Domitian; and, finally, to avoid the necessity of going over them all, He who gave it to the Christian Constantine gave it also to the apostate Julian, whose gifted mind was deceived by a sacrilegious and detestable curiosity, stimulated by the love of power.[56]

Augustine writes this to Marcellinus:

Let those who say that the doctrine of Christ is incompatible with the State's wellbeing give us an army such as the doctrine of Christ requires soldiers to be, let them give us subjects, such as husbands and wives, such parents and children, such masters and servants, such Kings, such judges, in fine even such tax-payers and tax-gatherers, as the Christian religion has taught that men should be and then let them dare to say that it is adverse to the State's well-being! Nay rather let them no longer hesitate to confess that this doctrine, if it were obeyed, would be the salvation of the State.[57]

It would be difficult to state the compatibility of these two ideologies more clearly than Augustine has. Niebuhr attempts to absolve Augustine of the implications of these writings. But even he cannot pretend to ignore the imperialistic nature of the Church-State alliance in the Middle Ages which Augustine justified, inspired and helped bring to realization.

[Augustine identified] the City of God with the historic church, an identification which was later to be stripped of all its Augustinian reservations to become the instrument of the spiritual pride of a universal church in its conflict with the political pride of an empire. This identification had the merit of introducing a religio-political institution into the world which actually placed a check upon the autonomy of nations; but at the price of developing in that institution dangerous similarities to the old Roman Empire, and of establishing the pope as a kind of spiritualized Caesar."[58]

In Augustine's view it is paganism and the "immoralities of the pagan gods" that society must battle. On these grounds as well he justifies the suppression by the state of non-Christian religious practices. With the Church resides the authority to decide what the "true faith" is, which is the duty of the State to protect and defend. At the same time it behooves Christians to obey laws and pay taxes as long as their faith is not violated. ("Render unto Caesar. . . .") Augustine's

Platonic influence is evidenced in his conception of the Church, reminiscent of Plato's conception of the Republic. The Church represents those who are on their way to the celestial city. According to Baynes, "it is the organ and representative in the world of the eternal city of God."[59] And rigid class hierarchy, human exploitation, even slavery become for Augustine embodiments of "justice" in the "world of becoming" through the concept of sin.[60]

The similarity between the developmental roles of Augustine and Constantine are striking but not ethnologically surprising. To Augustine was left the task of "selling" the idea of the Christian-Roman merger, which Constantine had initiated. Constantine had convinced the non-Christian Romans. Augustine had now to convince the "non-political" Christians. He concerned himself with the unification and solidification of the Christian organization and, therefore, devoted much of his attention to the "clarification" of Church doctrine—especially in terms of its political implications and its suppression of dissidents.

Augustine's battle was with the Donatists and other "heretics" within, and with the Manicheanists (who were basically non-European culturally), for these voices represented the political threat of disunity. His task was that of forging a more dogmatic formulation of Christian teachings; it would be taken up again later by Aquinas. His philosophical influence was that of Plato via the neo-Platonists. His inherited ontological "monism" dictated a theory of being that would admit of only one principle—as opposed to the Manicheanites, who said that there were two ultimate principles: good and evil. Augustine's contribution to the orthodoxy and unity of the Church was consonant with his mission to assure its triumph as a political-ideological force, and he is probably most responsible for its early monolithic nature. Of African birth, he contributed to the development of the European empire, the Church, and European imperialism "Go into all the world and preach the gospel to every creature." [John: 3-16]

The gentile (pagan) of Jewish nationalism became the heathen (pagan) in its broader archaic Western European form under Christian doctrine. Many of the same criteria for this distinction are found in the new expression. The hypothesis of theological evolution is present in the Jewish formulation, based on the implied goal (i.e., superiority) of belief in and commitment to a god as an abstract principle or "pure spirit," and the accumulation of religious precepts documented in written form. In the Christian expression we begin to see an additional emphasis: the concept of "revelation." "Revealed religion" begins to be closely associated with the idea of monotheism and its "progressive" nature. The illusion of the "objective truth" of Christian teachings is heightened. The Jews had no problem; they had been born the "chosen people." Christians had to create a criterion for admittance into the brotherhood, with its rhetorical inclusiveness and its pragmatic exclusivity.

Proselytization and Imperialism: "Saving" and "Ruling"

This concept of revelation is of interest both culturally (politically) and philosophically (metaphysically). Traditionally, anthropologists have regarded revealed religion as a characteristic of the state of "civilization." For Tylor, the related characteristic of belief in retribution was a mark that helped to separate the "civilized" from the "primitive." One should have to *deserve* the good ("after") life. This concept has strange ethnological implications. It cannot be interpreted simply as the Christian view of the "religious" or "extraordinary" experience (Eliade's hierogamy). The traditions of other cultures are filled with, often centered around, the transcendent as a category of human experience. Traditionally, one is born into a religion just as one is born into a culture. One's religion is considered a birthright. Culture is indeed the natural context for religious belief.

Christian ideology radically altered this concept and by so doing fashioned a religious statement that was potentially elitist, "intellectual" as opposed to "spiritual-emotional,"[61] and at the same time universal-imperialistic. One is not born a Christian, one must be baptized by the proper authorities. In some sects Jesus must be first accepted as "The Christ" in the hope that the Christian god will reveal himself to the properly pious. This idea is related to the imperialistic nature of Christianity. It is justifiable (and, in fact, an act of piety) for missionaries to proselytize the Christian religion, because, in their view, those whom they seek to convert have no religion, properly so-called.

It is only because of the political implications and related consequences that it seems so "immoral" to Tylor that there is no punishment-reward system associated with the after-life cosmology of many non-European religions. Unless Christianity is able to offer the blessings of "heaven," rather than the tortures of "hell"; unless Christians are able to convince people from other cultures that these are the alternative fates open to them, and that they (the Christians) have the key, then Europeans lose one of the most persuasive tools they have with which to control other peoples. In the words of Rheinhold Niebhur,

... only in a religion of revelation, whose God reveals Himself to man from beyond himself and from beyond the contrast of vitality and form, can man discover the root of sin to be within himself.[62]

And Mbiti, in his discussion of African religions, says that,

Traditional religions have no missionaries to propagate them, and one individual does not preach his religion to another.... Traditional religions are not universal; they are tribal or national... the propagation of a religion would involve propagating the entire life of the people.[63]

And Jomo Kenyatta says,

In Gikuyu religion there is no provision for official priesthood, nor is there any religious preaching. Converting campaigns are, of course, a thing unknown. This is due to the fact that the religion is interwoven with traditions and social customs of the people. Thus all members of the community are automatically considered to have acquired, during their childhood teachings, all that it is necessary to know about religion and custom. The duty of imparting this knowledge to the children is entrusted to the parents, who are looked upon as the official ministers of both religious ethics and social customs.[64]

All religions promote cultural nationalistic expression, and Christianity is only universal in that European cultural nationalism is characterized by universal or international imperialistic ambition. This theme will recur again and again throughout our study. And its recognition is crucial to an understanding of the uniqueness of the European mind and political effectiveness of European cultural imperialistic ideology in the quest for world power. It is a theme that is masked and subtly expressed in the presentation of European culture. The international character of the European political ambition or objective has been continually and tragically (for its "objects") confused with the spurious universalism of European cultural and ideological identification. In many respects, of course, this is precisely the desired effect of such formulations that become part of the armaments of European imperialism. The proselytization of Christianity has perhaps the greatest culturally immobilizing and demoralizing effect on its "objects."

Since its inception, the Church has participated in and supported the European imperialist enterprise. European culture is no different from other cultures in this respect, since the relationship between religion and nationalism is most certainly a universal cultural fact. No cultural group goes off to war without invoking the names of its national gods, and the reasons for declaring war are usually reformulated on a conscious level in religious terms or most certainly in terms that are consistent with the religiously stated ideology. The nature of this relationship in the European context is only "special" because European imperialism and European nationalism are so unique and intense. The uniqueness and intensity issue from the *asili* of the culture and the *utamaroho* through which it is expressed. But let us briefly trace the nature of the relationship between Christianity and the European imperialist venture.

We have looked at examples taken from the Old Testament which serve as evidence of the way that the religious laws and precepts of the Jews supported and encouraged their militantly nationalistic ideology. This ideology was stated in terms that were to become pivotal in the rhetoric of European cultural imperialism; e.g., the quest for the "universal good of mankind"—a good that, having been realized or at least recognized by Europeans (Jewish, Christian, "civilized," "religious" people), made it incumbent upon them to spread it among and thus "enlighten" (conquer, enslave, control) those less fortunate and "slower" than they ("gentiles," "primitives," "pagans," "heathens"). We have seen how the Christian formulation elaborated and altered the Jewish conception, enlarging it to suit the expanded European *utamaroho* and imperial world ambitions of the European. The Roman State had already conceived of the world-imperialistic objective politically, but Roman religion lagged behind—not yet sophisticated enough to support a world order. We have also seen in what manner the Christian formulation was coopted and used in the Roman pursuit.

My objective is not to argue that the Christian doctrine was consciously formulated for the purposes of European imperialism nor that Constantine was not in fact "a true convert" and came to believe in the Christian god. Speculation on that level is pointless and irrelevant for the purposes of this discussion. The obvious and significant cultural fact is that the Christian and Roman ideologies expressed the same values and political objectives, supported the same activities, and encouraged the same behavior of Europeans toward people of other cultures. The Judaic, Christian, and Roman conceptions constitute separate but culturally related developmental stages in European nationalistic expression. They coalesced in the European cultural *asili*. They meshed to give early definition to the European self-image and *utamaroho*, an *utamaroho* that demanded imperialistic behavior.

The role the Church has played has sometimes been that of the aggressor in a military and political imperialist pursuit. Most often and most successfully, though, it has been the protagonist in the drama of European cultural imperialism. The Church has taken a leading role in cultural aggression, because, of all the facets of European expansion, it has easiest access to non-European peoples and greatest potential for their ideological destruction. Only rarely, and never very effectively nor aggressively, has the Christian Church attempted to act against what it considered to be the excesses of European nationalism and even in these instances, by virtue of its conversionism, the Church still occupies a central position in the European offensive, for as has already been pointed out, European imperialist tendencies may be easily grafted onto Christian ideology.

It remains here to cite only a very few of the instances of the Church's support of the European imperialist venture. During the greater part of the Medieval period, Church and State were barely distinguishable, or more properly speaking, the Church was more powerful than the State, and the term "Christendom" reflected the intimacy of this relationship. The following statement is a characterization of the "Christian holy wars" from a Eurocentric perspective, one of the more obvious varieties of European nationalism.

> During the tenth century, when the Kings of Wessex were winning back the midlands and Northumbria from the heathen Danes, other heroic Kings were saving Christendom from its heathen enemies in the German lands. The Saxon King, Henry the Fowler, drove back the Danes in the north and the fierce Hungarian archers in the east. His grandson, Otto the Great, destroyed a great Hungarian army in 955. These men shared with the men of Wessex the honor of saving Christian Europe. And the defeated heathen were converted to the Christian faith.[65]

Generally, the First Crusade is set in the eleventh century, but the above is obviously a description of an earlier successful "Christian" imperialist campaign. The Crusades were, of course, the primary instrument of Western European expansion during the European Medieval period and at the same time remain an example of the most militaristic and aggressive expressions of the European conquering *utamaroho*. The Church not only condoned these actions in terms such as those in the statement above but was itself the initiator of these campaigns. The following description from William McNeill makes clear the stark reality of the intimate and inextricable relationship between Christian ideology and European expansionism. The religious, military-political, and commercial institutions of the West meshed easily into a united imperialistic endeavor.

The most spectacular early step in the expansion of Europe was the conquest of the eastern Mediterranean coast as a result of the First Crusade (1096–1099). The Crusade was proclaimed by Pope Urban II. . .

The motives which impelled the Crusaders to embark on their venture were mixed. Religious enthusiasm, stirred up by the pope and by numerous preachers, played a decisive part. The aim of the Crusade was to free the Holy Land from Moslem rule, and Crusaders were promised absolution from their sins as a consequence of their service to a religious cause. Other motives, of course, were added to religious ones: the spirit of adventure, the hope of carving out new estates and principalities, the diplomacy of the Byzantine emperors who needed military help against the Turks, and, to some (small) extent, the commercial ambitions of a few Italian towns all contributed to the First Crusade. Yet, when due allowance is made for these subsidiary motives, it still seems safe to regard the First Crusade as a striking example of the power of the Church and of Christian ideals to inspire military and political action.[66]

During this period the Church was the spearhead of European expansion, and historically we can view the Crusades as one of the most important military ventures in the expansion of Europe. The internal politics of the Church was itself to become quite "worldly," creating the ironic and embarrassing situation of the "profanation" of European institutionalized religion. It is only reasonable to conclude that the effects of these cultural tendencies were far-reaching and that they have made themselves felt long afterward in the moral decay of the contemporary West. The period of intrapolitical maneuverings and power plays—extreme and sometimes violent competition for the papacy—was perhaps the height of "religious profanity" within European culture, but its legacy remains.

Christianity, colonialism and cultural imperialism: "Heathen," "Native," and "Primitive."

The next period of the involvement of organized religion in European expansion is that of colonization. The justification for the Church's involvement was always couched in terms of conversion. Many European historians identify conversionist sentiment with something they call "humanitarianism," which, in turn, is identified as the universally altruistic motivation of behavior. Although this may sound contradictory, if understood as a manifestation of European nationalism, such interpretations of "conversionism" become, at least, ethnologically understandable in terms of the cultural *asili*. They represent the hypocritical semantics demanded by the commitment to a view of the culture as superior.

In *The Image of Africa*, Phillip Curtin quotes from proceedings in the British Parliament concerning the question of "aborigines" in 1935-7. The responsibility of the committee dealing with this question was to investigate government policy:

> Native inhabitants or Countries where British Settlements are made, and to the neighboring Tribes, in order to secure to them the due observation of Justice, and the protection of Rights; to promote the spread of Civilization among them; and to lead them to the peaceful and voluntary reception of the Christian religion.[67]

This is an example of what Curtin characterizes as the "humanitarian" concerns of the missionaries for the British Niger Expedition of the 1840s. He identifies "conversionist sentiment" with "Christian humanitarianism":

> [Between 1830 and 1870] The dominant British attitude toward Africa became more conversionist than ever. The Niger Expedition itself was a large-scale public effort to convert barbarians to Western ways. The middle decades of the century represent, indeed, the height of conversionist sentiment.[68]

The missionary interest group argued that "only a previous indoctrination with Christianity and the ways of 'Western Civilization' could prepare them [the Africans] for the impact of European Settlement. Furthermore, in their view, Christianity and civilization were inseparable."[69] "After 1870," says Curtin, "the idea of conversion declined. Humanitarian motives found new manifestations."[68] These examples from Curtin are helpful because they afford us the opportunity of making clear the relationship between what Europeans have termed "humanitarianism" (supposedly characterized by "altruism" and identification with a "universal good") and what I recognize as imperialistic behavior, the epitome, and most visible expression, of European *self*-interest.

The tendency to ignore the political implication of this kind of humanitarianism (so-called) is displayed consistently in Western social theory. In *Race: The History of an Idea in America* Thomas Gossett argues that the idea of the "unity of mankind" is inherent in

Christianity and that it has acted against "racism," which he sees as distinct from and somehow bad as compared with the good intentions of "conversionism."

> Slavery, it has sometimes been argued, was first considered in the colonies as an interim institution designed to convert both Negroes and Indians to Christianity. . . It is interesting, however, that among the colonies of the seventeenth centuries it is the heathenism of the Negroes and Indians, rather than their race, which is emphasized as a basis for their enslavement.[70]

The fine distinction between the connotations of "heathen" and "nigger" may well be interesting to Gossett, but from an African-centered perspective they become one and the same—both denote "objects" of European imperialism. Of the two, the concept of "heathen" is perhaps potentially more debilitating as it is more rapidly adopted by the oppressed herself and incorporated into her own self-image.

There are some few accounts, exceptional and difficult to find, which do not get trapped between Christian ideology and European imperialism. Let us take time to quote from a few of these, which together give a much more accurate picture of the historical relationship between the Christian Church and some of the more base manifestations of European nationalism.

Katherine George entertains a discussion of what she calls "ethnocentricism" as manifested in descriptions by Europeans of Africans written between the sixteenth and nineteenth centuries. To be more precise she is offering evidence of "Eurocentrism"; more accurately we might call it "Western European nationalism," which translates into a "culturalism" and, of course, "white racism." Her research affords us an excellent example of the supportive relationship of Christian ideology to the invidious comparisons fundamental to European cultural nationalism. The image of European peoples that Christianity presents has provided ideological support for the European's view of himself in relation to those who are not within his cultural group. This image is also essential to the Christian argument; it was upon this supposition of the moral and therefore "evolutionary" inferiority of all other people that the proselytizing mission was founded, a mission that provided moral justification for the expansionist mission of Western European imperialism. The author of the following statement was endeavoring to justify the Portugese slave trade:

And so their lot was now quite contrary of what it had been; since before they had lived in perdition of soul and body; of their souls, in that they were pagans, without the clearness and the light of holy faith; and of their bodies, in that they lived like beasts, without any custom of reasonable beings—for they had no knowledge of bread or wine, and they were without the covering of clothes, or the lodgement of houses; and worse than all, through the great ignorance that was in them, in that they had no understanding of good, but only knew how to live in a bestial sloth.[71]

Of the above statement, Katherine George says:

... Christianity did not eliminate older hierarchies based on race, nationality, class or occupational status, but it rather collaborated with such hierarchies and more frequently than not strengthened instead of weakening them—though it did introduce the complicating idea of a possible restatement of human relations in the society of another world. The availability of salvation to all properly indoctrinated souls alike, despite bodily inequalities—we find this gift of Christianity in the previously cited passage. But does it lessen the writer's prejudice? To the contrary. It enables him instead to commend actions (the kidnapping of helpless people) as morally virtuous, actions which to classical observers would have seemed merely expedient.[71]

To Serve The Devil is a two-volume work that documents American behavior and attitude—toward primary peoples. Here, an advocate of Hawaiian colonization writes on the mutually beneficial relationship between the American commercial interests and those of the missionaries in Hawaii:

Christianity civilizes in the broadest sense. Commerce, industry, science and literature all accompany her majestic march to universal dominion. Thus, while it denies the suffiency of commerce alone to transform the savage, it encourages a legitimate commerce and even courts its alliance as one of the most important instrumentalities.[72]

In contradiction to Gossett's analysis, the authors of *To Serve The Devil,* Paul Jacobs et al., comment,

... the destruction of the Indians was written into the first chapter of the successful white colonization in America. The pure ideals of Christianity were easily molded into a racist ideology that matched the economic and social needs of expanding settlers.[73]

The fact is that almost from its inception the continuous venture of European expansion ensued not only with the blessings of the Church but, where necessary, by its decree. In the early fifteenth century Pope Edward IV issued a papal bull "granting to the Crown of Portugal all the countries which the Portuguese should discover from Cape Non to India," to accommodate the "discoveries" of Prince Henry the Navigator, on the African Coast. After Columbus' "discovery," according to William Howitt, "His sponsoring Monarchs, Ferdinand and Isabella, lost no time in applying for a similar grant. Alexander VI, a Spaniard, was equally generous with his predecessor, and accordingly divided the world between the Spaniards and Portuguese."[74] The Pope as earthly representation of Jesus Christ was supposed to have a right of dominion over the entire earth. Alexander VI, an infamous pontiff, was determined to stay in Ferdinand's good graces in order to ensure his own protection and accumulation of wealth. Anxious, therefore, to gratify Ferdinand and Isabella, he granted "full rights" to them to all the countries inhabited by "infidels" that they had discovered or would discover.

As the Pope's dominion was held to be worldwide, he had authority over vast regions he had never even heard of. To prevent this grant to Spain from interfering with lands already "given" to Portugal by a previous bull (issued by Pope Edward IV), he proclaimed that an invisible line existed from pole to pole, one hundred leagues west of the Azores, separating the two territories. Everything to the east of the line of demarcation he bestowed upon the Portuguese; all to the west of it went to the Spaniards. His motivation was supposedly his enthusiasm for the propagation of the Christian faith. In this way the Church divided up the world between two European powers.

The apologists for the Church cite the public emancipation of *two slaves* by Pope Gregory "the Great" as evidence of the Church's official position against slavery. This interpretation is very much out of tune with the historical/political reality. Chapman Cohen, in a work published in 1931, says:

> Not only were there thousands of unfreed slaves in the possession of ecclesiastics even a thousand years after Gregory had published this "death warrant" to servitude, but Gregory in person possessed at least hundreds, and perhaps thousands of slaves whom he did not free. Again, as Pope, he was trustee for the possession of thousands more, chattels of the Roman Church; yet he initiated no general papal movement for the liberation of Church serfs. On the contrary, ecclesiastical laws constantly opposed such a policy. . . .[75]

The English slave trade, like that of other European nations, was launched with the blessings of the Church. It is ironic but not contradictory that the first English slaver was named "Jesus" and that the first two rules Captain John Hawkins imposed on his crew were, to serve God daily, and to love one another. "The piety of the expedition," says Cohen bitingly, "was beyond reproach."[76]

There is no doubt that the Christian community gave its blessings to the slaving venture, participated in it and contributed to its success by embracing it within Western "morality." W. E. B. DuBois brings home this point when he says, in reference to West Africa, "Protestants of England, the Huguenots of France, and the Calvinists of Holland started mortal struggle for Guinea."[77]

Another valuable work, exceptional in European scholarship, is E. D. Morel's *The Black Man's Burden,* written in 1920. Here he comments on and offers a first-hand account of a slave raid by Europeans.

The African was a heathen, and as such fair game for the prowess of the noble Christian Knights who opposed their steel breastplates, tempered swords and cross-bows, to his bare chest and primitive spear. Here is a typical account of one of these predatory forays:

Then might you see mothers forsaking their children and husbands their wives, each striving to escape as best he could. Some drowned themselves in the water, others thought to escape by hiding under their huts; others stowed their children among the sea-weed, where our men found them afterwards, hoping they would escape notice. . . . And at last our Lord God, who giveth a reward for every good deed, willed that for the toil they had undergone in His service they should that day obtain victory over their enemies, as well as a guerdon and a payment for all their labour and expense; for they took captive of those Moors, what with men, women and children, 165, besides those that perished and were killed. And when the battle was over, all praised God for the great mercy He had shown them, in that He had willed to give them such victory, and with so little damage to themselves. They were all very joyful, praising loudly the Lord God for that He deigned to give such help to such a handful of His Christian people. [According to Morel, this comes from Portuguese chronicles.]

Thus did Europe first bring the "glad tidings" to the African. It did not take long to ascertain that the spiritual consolation derived from converting the African to Christianity had its utilitarian counterpart.[78]

The contemporary European imperialistic endeavor, contrary to its projected image, is understood by its perpetrators precisely in the same terms as the Crusades and the subsequent period of colonizing ventures. The following is the text of a prayer for the American Special Forces in South East Asia:

Almighty God, who art the Author of liberty and the Champion of the oppressed, hear our prayer-
We, the men of Special Forces, acknowledge our dependence upon Thee in the preservation of human freedom—
Go with us as we seek to defend the defenseless and to free the enslaved—
May we ever remember that our nation, whose motto is "In God We Trust,"
expects that we shall acquit ourselves with honor, that we may never
bring shame upon our faith, our families, or our fellow men—
Grant us wisdom from Thy mind, courage from Thine heart, strength from Thine arm, and protection by thine hand
—
It is for Thee that we do battle, and to Thee belongs the victor's crown.
For Thine is the Kingdom, and the power and the glory, forever, Amen.[79]

From its inception Christian ideology has traditionally condoned and often mandated violent aggression and brutality on the part of the European. The members of the Special Forces are simply taking direction from the Bible.

Now go and smite Amalek, and utterly destroy all that they have, and spare them not; but slay both man and woman, infant and suckling, ox and sheep, camel and ass...

And when the Lord thy God hath delivered it [the City] into thine hands, thou shalt smite every male thereof with the edge of the sword. But the women and the little ones, and the cattle, and all that is in the city, even all the spoil thereof, thou shalt take unto thyself; and thou shalt eat the spoil of thine enemies which the Lord thy God hath given thee... of the cities of these people which the Lord thy God doth give thee for an inheritance, thou shalt save alive nothing that breatheth.[80]

The European's invocation of his god to aid him in his imperialistic pursuits is consistent with his self-image and his image of those who are not like him. His "religion" itself is an expression of these dialectical images.

Of the historical relationship between Christianity and the enslavement of people of color by Europeans, Cohen says:

> (But) we have another slave system to deal with. This took its rise in Christian times. It was created by Christians, it was continued by Christians, it was in some respects more barbarous than anything the world had yet seen, and its worst features were to be witnessed in countries that were most ostentatious in their parade of Christianity. It is this that provides the final and unanswerable indictment of the Christian Church.[81]

Cohen, in contrast to Curtin, Gossett, Kovel (*White Racism: A Psychohistory*), and others, has correctly assessed the meaning of the Christian ideal of "the brotherhood of man":

> Its brotherhood of man never meant, even in theory, more than a brotherhood of believers, and in practice it did not always mean that. It recognized duties and obligations between members of the same church or sect, but outside these boundaries it applied a different code of ethics. What kind of brotherhood did Christians bestow on Jews and heretics for hundreds of years? Christians in their heyday of power would have looked with amazement on anyone who claimed consideration for either. What kind of brotherly attention did the inhabitants of ancient Mexico and Peru receive from the Christian conquerors? How fared the Redskins of North America, the Maoris of New Zealand, or inhabitants of Africa at the hands of their Christian brothers? In practice nearly always, and in theory often, Christians have shown that their doctrine of brotherhood meant little more than the mere brotherhood of a gang. Within the gang rules must be observed. Outside the gang they might be broken with impunity.[82]

The costly political error of non-Europen converts has been to think that they would ever be included in the European "Christian brotherhood" in the same way they were part of their own cultures.

Chinweizu admonishes us to "recall that European rule was entrenched in Africa by means of a Western Christian culture, a western political power structure, and a colonial economy."[83] The "holy alliance" left a defeated Africa in its wake,

Because white missionaries of Christ working in Buganda clamored that their losing efforts to recruit black souls for the heaven of their white god needed to be protected by white troops, and because the British masters of Egypt were demanding that all of the Nile valley should be placed under British rule, the Imperial British East Africa Company (IBEA) was in 1890 granted authority by England to trade in and administer the territory of the headwaters of the Nile. The invading captains of the IBEA, in their quest for trading monopolies, attacked the sovereignties of the African Kingdoms of the upper Nile.[84]

As we have noted earlier, and Chinweizu agrees, the wide-scale destruction of African sovereignty necessitated the simultaneous destruction of an African consciousness. Here European Christianity had a unique advantage.

To buttress and crown their creation, the founders of the colonial order embarked on a cultural reorganization of Africa. If the African auxiliaries of empire were to be docile and loyal servants, their allegiance to Africa had to be undermined. Total admiration for Europe had to be instilled into them. Besides the technical skills they would need to carry out their practical duties to the employers, they were to be taught Christian values of a servile-making sort. Unquestioning obedience to white men was presented as a cardinal virtue. The retooling of their minds and values was entrusted to the schools. Whether run by missionaries hunting for black converts for their white heavens, or run by colonial bureaucrats, these imperialist schools not only taught reading, writing and arithmetic to their inmates, they also stuffed the heads of their victims with church devotional hymns, filled their psyches with submissive Christian attitudes, and undermined their attachment to the culture of their ancestors. These schools inculcated in their wards a Christian theology and cosmology, and a western individualist ethos that weakened their African identity, destroyed their commitment to an African communalist ethos, and erased their sense of patriotic responsibility to Africa.[85]

The Christians had no compunctions about destroying indigenous religious movements not to their liking. They had done it before in Europe. Their creed was, after all, one of violent proselytization when called for. Chinweizu cites examples in Africa such as the burning of Bwiti chapels in Gabon, where this syncretistic religious movement was seen as a possible nurturing ground for African nationalism. Chinweizu comments that "especially at the beginning of the colonial era, the church was an arm of colonial destruction of African organizations and movements."[86]

These passages reflect the direct and very political relationship between the European Church and European imperialism. It is a relationship between "brothers." Ironically it is the subtle aspects of this relationship that have proven to be much more devastating in the long run to indigenous forms wherever the expansionist West has sought to exercise its control.

The phenomenon of cultural imperialism, if it is to be distinguished from its strictly militaristic, political, and economic components, is that which strikes the "death blow" at a people's ability to resist aggression. There has never been, in the history of the human race, more expert dealers of that blow than Europeans. They alone have realized the full strategic potential of destroying the ideological life of a cultural entity. Christian ideology is an ideally fashioned weapon for the destruction of the self-image and value-system of African and other non-European peoples. With its delusionary rhetoric of "love" and "peace," its debilitating image of the non-white (non-European, "backward," "heathen"), and its false "universality," it has succeeded where guns never could in tearing people from the cultural base necessary for the formulation of an effective self-deterministic ideology. A Christian with a gun in the armed forces is one thing—he might end up with a spear in his back; but a missionary with a Bible and a well-meaning smile who speaks of "eternal love" is wholly different. It takes a great deal of political sophistication to recognize *him* as a potential menace.

> Disease played a major role in killing off the Hawaiians, especially venereal diseases. Measles and cholera swept through the population and alcoholism weakened the islanders so badly that they often succumbed to the common cold. But more important was the psychological sickness that struck the islanders as their culture and religion disappeared. "Nkanaka okuu wale aku no I kau uhane." ("The people dismissed freely their souls and died.")[87]

Christianity and European Paganism:

So as not to ignore a relevant stage of European development, we ask: What is the relationship between European Christianity and European "paganism" (a term that implies the Eurocentric and Christian perspective)? In the attempt to understand the *asili* of European cultural development, this aspect of European religious tradition cannot be overlooked. I have focused on the institutional-ization of religion in the form of the Christian Church because of the way in which it expresses the underlying ideology or mythoform of the culture. But for a moment let us take a brief look at non-Christian Europe.

"Violence and battle were always at hand in the lives of men of the heathen period in northwestern Europe."[88] This statement by H.R. Ellis Davidson allows us to glance at the warrior gods of Northern Europe: Wodan (Odin), Tiwas (Mars), Mercury, Tyr, and Indra of Aryan India. There are others, but the pattern is clear. War, the war-rior, and violence were worshipped among these Indo-European antecedents of the present day Europeans. Odin—a warrior himself—held to be the divine ancestor of the Swedes and most of the Anglo-Saxon kings, rewarded those who served him and who died in battle with weapons, immunity against wounds, and a place in glorious Valhalla, the famous "warrior heaven." The beliefs of these "ancient Northmen" and women were a testimony to the glorification of war. Davidson quotes from Saxo Grammaticus, who in turn quotes a speech of the warrior Biarki,

> War springs from the nobly born; famous pedigrees are the makers of war. For the perilous deeds which chiefs attempt are not to be done by the ventures of common men. . . . No dim and lowly race, no low-born dead, no base souls are Pluto's prey, but he weaves the dooms of the mighty, and fills Phlegthon with noble shapes."[89]

The style of battle was very individualistic, emphasizing single combat. Confidence in one's war god gave psychological advantage akin to "possession."[90] In Davidson's words,

> Throughout the heathen period in northern Europe there was clear need of a god of war. The story of the Germanic peoples and the Vikings is one in which local battles, feuds, invasions, and wars of a national scale are the order of the day. The heroic literature is based on an unsettled society, accustomed to violence and short-ness of life. . . . Clearly men reared in such a world were bound to turn to the god whom they served to protect them in the hour of battle. . . .[91]

The violence in this early European religion did not only express itself in terms of war and the killings of enemies but also through the enactment of bloody ritual sacrifice to the warrior god as well.

In the earlier days of Germanic heathenism the terrible wholesale slaughter of captured forces and criminals implies a belief in a god of battles who demanded that blood should flow in his honour. Blood had to be constantly provided for the mighty deity, or else he would be compelled by his nature to seize on the lives of worshippers.[91]

Among the Heruli, worshippers of Odin (Wodin) practiced a ritual in which human beings were first stabbed and then burned.[92] Such practices were common among the warlike Indo-European tribes.

In spite of variations of detail in the many myths of these tribes, Georges Dumezil finds a consistency in what he calls the underlying "ideological datum" that explains the various myths. This is a crucial point, for it affirms and justifies the methodology and theoretical premise of this study. Dumezil's recognition of a common ideological base shared by Indo-European peoples also argues for a vital relationship of continuity between the consciousness of contemporary Europeans and their forbears of the classical and prehistoric periods. The "ideological datum" of which Dumezil speaks, in his book *The Destiny of The Warrior,* is related to Armstrong's concept of "mythoform." Is there a relationship between the mythoform of "pagan" and Christian Europe?

Dumezil points to the parallels in Roman and Aryan-Indian religions: between Indra and Tullus; Varuna and Mitra; Romulus and Numa. Of the beliefs, he says,

What the Indian and Roman thinkers have maintained in clearest form are: (1) the idea of a necessary victory, a victory in a single combat in which, inspired by the grand master of the warrior function (either king or god) and for his sake, "a third hero triumphs over a triple adversary"—with stain implicit in the exploit, and with a purification of the "third" and of the society which he represents, so that he finds himself to be the specialist, the agent, and the instrument of this purification, a sort of scapegoat after having been a champion; (2) the idea of a victory brought off not by combat but by a surprise which follows upon a betrayal, betrayal and surprise succeeding one another under the pretext and within the context of a solemn agreement of friendship, with the result that the surprise act of revenge includes a disquieting note.[93]

Suppose we use this schema to interpret the crucifixion of Jesus and Judas' betrayal of him? Dumezil speaks of the "collective memory" of the Indo-European and of the moral and political doctrine that constituted their "moral conscience."[94]

But how then can we account for the supposed hiatus between Christian Europe and its pagan origins? Only to Christians does the appearance of "god" in human form explain this evolution. In what terms do Europeans usually express the difference/relationship? They do so always in terms of the dichotomy of European nationalism/chauvinism. Yes, even with regard to their own predecessors/ancestors. Davidson says: "Northern heathenism, that is, the pre-Christian beliefs of the Germanic peoples and the Scandinavians, came to an end in the eleventh century." In the nineth and tenth centuries we know that the Vikings were a great power, but, in Davidson's words, they were "a menace to Christian civilization."[95]

Christianity is associated with "civilization"; non-Christian religion is called "heathen" or "pagan," but very rarely, even in scholarly writing, are these latter terms defined. "Pagan" is, in some cases, simply used to mean "non-Christian," but looking to the dictionary, the ideological uses of these terms become explicit. The term "heathen" has the following uses:

1. an irreligious or unenlightened person; 2. an unconverted individual of a people that do not acknowledge the God of the Bible; one who is neither a Jew, Christian, nor Muslim; pagan; 3. (Formerly) any person neither Christian nor Jewish, esp. a member of the Islamic faith or a polytheistic religion.[96]

For the word "pagan" we find:

1. one of a people or community professing a polytheistic religion as the ancient Romans, Greeks, etc.; 2. a person who is not a Christian, Jew or Muslim; 3. an irreligious or hedonistic person.[97]

The Latin *pagus* means village or rural district, and so "pagan" has the derogatory sense of "peasant" or a person of the countryside. As we, in contemporary parlance, might say "bumpkin" or "hick," indicating one who lacks the "sophistication" of the cities.

"Christian," "heathen," and "pagan," therefore, do not merely represent religious differentiation. They indicate ideological differences, differences in world-view. They are culturalist terms defined from a Eurocentric or Arab nationalist perspective. European Christians consider Jews to be religious, even though they may disagree bitterly with them as to the nature of historical truth. (There is some ambivalence concerning Muslims, who are not considered "heathens," but who once were. They pose a cultural embarrassment since it was Muslim scholarship that "rescued" European civilization from the "dark ages.") Why are the Europeans so hard on their so-called "pagans" and "polytheistic" forbears?

What, in the European context, represents the proper form of a religious statement is intimately involved with their concept of "civilization" or, as Europeans see it, the "civilizing" process. These ideas cannot be understood without reference to the two basic concepts of European ideology: evolution and progress.

One of the reasons that the terms "heathen" and "pagan" hold such reproach and are so derogatory from a Eurocentric perspective is that initially it was the European "past" to which they referred. Nothing requires defeat so much as the past in the logic of the European mythoform. It is the non-European in the contemporary world who becomes associated with the past in the European mind. (The anthropologists studied the "past," which meant non-Euro-Caucasians.) But we must remember that Europeans still practiced what in Christian parlance were "pagan" religions until the eleventh century. This means that these "backward" peoples were actually both within and outside the culture simultaneously. "Heretics" were culturally acceptable (though dangerous). "Pagans" were not. In this critical period of transition there could be no equivocation concerning the correct path toward progress; the shape of the new national culture.

This "paganism" did not die easily. Christians have always been willing to fight bloody battles and wars to "convert" others to their way of thinking, even their own people. Perhaps the threat of those who dared to persist in the religions into which they had been born issued from the fear that Christianity might not triumph as the ideological champion of the "new" European. Imagine the anxiety that this caused for those who were convinced of the necessity of "progress!"

An African-centered perspective forces us to look more closely at this history, this cultural development. We must make sense of it. Using the concept of *asili,* seemingly complex "paranoid" behavior on the part of the European becomes crystal clear and makes "sense," unfolding from the logic of European development. Why should a people who were non-Christians and who were slaughtering Christians become Christians themselves and begin to slaughter their brothers and sisters in order to make them so? What is the connection between this new religion and the ethos of the religions practiced by early and "backward" Europeans?

The concept of *asili* tells us to look for consistency; the consistency for which we search lies within the explanatory and generating principle of European development. Europeans have always been involved in an unrelenting quest for power, political hegemony, expansion, and technical control. As this drive to conquer developed more intensely, the parameters of the conquering self and of the territory (world) to be conquered expanded. Constantine had ingeniously perceived the effectiveness of institutionalized Christianity as a supportive mechanism for the cohesion of the Empire. Later, Christianity would be fashioned as the appropriate vehicle for a much more expanded concept of imperialism, one which required a more refined concept of progress, and more importantly, *a more cohesive, and at the same time, expanded identification of the conquering culture: Europe.*

Davidson says, "Since they themselves [the 'heathens'] had no desire to make converts, they were at a serious disadvantage, and it was only a matter of time before the new religion replaced the old."[98] Whether knowingly or not, she is pointing to a *political* and *ideological* disadvantage. Conversely she hits on the political and ideological advantage enjoyed by Christians. "Pagans" do not seek converts. These "pagan" Europeans may have been "barbarian heathens," conquering others and even expanding their territories, but *they had not used their religions to do so.* The posture of their religions had not been imperialistic. It was not outer-directed. They had not understood the political uses of religion. (Africans and most other non-Europeans still do not. Arabs are the only non-Europeans to have used religion in this way.) Proselytization is inherently imperialistic; perfectly suited to supporting an expansionistic *utamaroho*. Now we can begin to understand in what sense "paganism" was "backward" from a Eurocentric perspective.

There are other dynamics to this phenomenon; other pieces to the puzzle of why Christianity and not paganism. Pagan Indo-European culture was violent, aggressive, xenophobic, and individualistic. Its religion called for the sacrifice of human blood, as did many religions. Is the answer then that Christianity was more suited to the European *utamaroho* because the Europeans became more peaceful, loving, and communalistic? That answer is illogical, for Europe has never been characterized by those values. To the contrary, European Christian behavior is equally xenophobic—in spite of its rhetorical xenophilia—and embraces war and violence in the name of the Christian god. In later periods it envelops the individualistic ethic of capitalist-materialism. And, what is more, it demanded human sacrifice!

But there *is* certainly a difference between European Christianity and European Paganism. The *utamaroho* of Pagan Indo-European culture is the same. The formal structures through which it is expressed are different in much the same way as European peasant culture and archaic European culture are different from the cosmopolitan culture of the European "multinational." It is a question of "sophistication," but not to indicate valued behavior in any universally valid sense. "Sophistication" refers to the hypocrisy that began to develop within the bowels of European culture. It was a matter of pragmatism and efficiency. Christianity was a more refined tool for the selling of European imperialism.

There are certain traits that have made for the success of European civilization in its quest for supreme dominance and control of others. It is a culture based on an ideology of superficial change. This allows its hegemony to expand while being maintained. If what can be called "modal changes" do not occur at strategic historical points, the objective of total domination will fail. The Platonic epistemological mode (*utamawazo*) put archaic European culture on the right track, as it were, towards successful imperialistic expansion by establishing the intellectual confines of that ideology. The aggressive *utamaroho* was already in place. It had to be harnessed for efficient performance. Herein lies the genius of Europe!

What classical Greece had achieved on the intellectual level, classical Rome must achieve politically. "Paganism" didn't fit. It was as simple as that. As the imperialistic goals of these fledgeling Europeans expanded, the various modalities of the cultural structure grew out of sync with one another. If they had not been reshaped, readjusted so as to form a cohesive unit, Europe would have failed— just another culture living peacefully in a culturally pluralistic universe. Unfortunately for the rest of us, it didn't. At least not at this juncture. (Medieval Europe represents a long period of dormancy; a loss of momentum, perhaps even intellectual ambivalence as far as the ideology of progress and change are concerned. But subsequently the culture regrouped itself and catapulted once again on to the road towards world domination through technological advance.) The Protestant revolution and the rise of capitalism represent the necessary creative responses at other such junctures in European history. The cooptation of Christianity was such a response in A.D. 312. Constantine was the shrewd strategist in question. And it worked.

Violence, aggression, and xenophobia could no longer be expressed in the form of European paganism if these nascent Europeans were to further develop their empire. The *utamaroho* was consistent. It still demanded control, aggression, and human sacrifice. But the *vision* was changing: the vision of what was possible and in turn, what was necessary. *A more expanded vision required a more sophisticated technique.* This had been the immutable law of European development.

The European institutionalization of Christianity was something akin to a technological advance. It added the element of proselytization that more suited the objective of imperialistic expansionism within which those objectives could be hidden or camouflaged. Xenophobic, aggressive, and violent tendencies were molded into a more subtle statement that packaged them in a universalistic, peaceful, and moralistic rhetoric. In other words, "barbarian" Indo-European pagan religion became more "modern" in Christian formulation, more suited to the new demands of European "progress," progress clearly referring to ever greater efficiency of the mechanism for total control. European civilization can be understood as nothing more than the most efficient mechanism for that end.

As always, the *utamaroho* remains the same. That is the consistent, unchanging factor. The ideology is informed by the *utamaroho*, but must develop as the vision grows. For the *utamaroho,* is expansionistic; always seeking a larger space in which to be housed, a large "turf" to control. This brings us to a second aspect of the European political genius. *As the vision grows, so must the national consciousness.* This is critical, for the nature of the *utamaroho* requires an expanded definition of the self. We are talking about the growth of political consciousness. This is why cultural and political behavior can only superficially be separated. They are united in ideology. Political behavior on a national level requires the definition of the interest of the nation *vis-à-vis* other nations. The definition of the interest requires a national consciousness. Culture creates that consciousness through its ideological function.

In early European or Indo-European history we witness violent tribes or hordes whose lives were ordered by war. True, they tended to move at various points, on the more peacefully oriented, less aggressive peoples, generally of the south. After this southern invasion, when their *utamaroho* was implanted into the Mediterranean, what then? *They continued to move against each other!* Rome was eventually overtaken by these Germanic peoples. The culture went through periods of uncertain development, instability, and insecurity. Clearly, if the European hegemony was to be achieved this penchant for violent behavior must be turned towards "others." Christianity helped to define who the "others" were in a way that fitted the European progress ideology. Making a Roman, a Briton, a Frank, and so forth into a "European" would not be easy, but it was the order of

the day in terms of the logic of European development. First, orthodox Christianity provided the perfect structure within which the (sublimated) statement of aggression, even human sacrifice, and
imperialistic ideology could be meshed; and lastly, it provided the
perfect structure for the forging of a European consciousness that
could carry out this vision of a European-dominated world.

Christianity achieved the unification of the new European self.
It acted as a unifying element as it housed and solidified the nascent
European *utamaroho,* one inherited from a northern, "heathen" past.
It helped to redefine European nationalism as universal imperialism.
(This is why the Jewish statement was insufficient.) European civilization has been so successful in part because of its ability to outer-
direct hostility, another example of political genius. When this ability
is hindered, the survival of the culture is threatened. The destructive
tendencies within are so intense and so endemic to the culture that
they must continually be redirected. The cooptation of Christianity
represented such a redirection of aggressive energy.

Now the difference and relationship between European paganism and European Christianism can be placed in its proper context.
Pagan religions were aggressive but not expansionist. They did not
have this vision, and they were too separatist to be successfully imperialistic. Christianism took the concept of human blood sacrifice and
raised it to the pinnacle of religiousity by sacralizing it in the symbol
of Jesus; this acted as a sanction against the killing of other
Christians. They then legitimized its actual practice by superficially
(ideologically) dehumanizing non-Christian non-Europeans and then
sacrificing them to their god.

But this change would not take place overnight and, as we have
seen, well into the eleventh century, the more "sophisticated"
Europeans, who had incorporated the vision of European hegemony
and now identified as Europeans, would fight and kill their more
"backward" brothers. First, Celts, Goths, Druids, Teutons, Angles,
Saxons, etc., then finally and fiercely, the Vikings, who would wage
constant battle to protect their national identities, as they defined
them, unwilling to accept this new "European" consciousness, a consciousness that Saint-Simon would still be seeking to solidify in the
early part of the nineteenth century. The identity of this long period
of internecine wars can be understood then, not as the battle of the
enlightened and the "civilized" against the unenlightened barbarians,
but as a stage in the struggle to institute and consolidate a new imperial order.

Patriarchy in the Development of European Religion

Indo-European pagan culture did however contribute characteristics to European Judeo-Christian ideology. Although it is possible to identify practices of male dominance in most societies of the world, patriarchy, as an institutionalized value, as an intrinsic characteristic of *utamaroho* can be associated with Indo-European origins of Western civilization. One of the aspects of cultural development that demonstrates this most clearly is religion.

In the ancient religious traditions of Africa and other parts of the world, we find again and again the predominance of the mother goddess; the valorization of the female principle, the earth symbol. These traditions were well-developed before it was possible to speak of a "Western" or "Western European" peoples. The older, more "Southern" civilizations can be generalized into one cultural or ideological model in contrast to the younger and more aggressive Northern groups comprising what has been called the "Tumuli" civilization, associated culturally with the Indo-European and racially as the Aryans. It is this latter group with which we are concerned as they represent the cultural/racial forbears—the ancestors—of what we now call "Europe." These people came from "the regions North of the Black Sea, between the Carpathians, and the Caucasians," according to Mircea Eliade.[99]

A brief statement of Cheikh Anta Diop's "Two Cradle" theory of the origins of Civilization, will help to initiate our consideration of the theme of patriarchy in European religion. Diop's concern in his book *The Cultural Unity of Black Africa* is with "the Domains of Patriarchy and Matriarchy in Classical Antiquity." For him these types of social order correspond to two contrasting "cradles" of civilization. These two cradles are areas of origin for two different kinds of civilization that reflect two different world-views and corresponding lifestyles. The differences between these two places of origin seem to originate in ecology, according to Diop's explanation.

The environment of the Northern Cradle was harsh, cold, and relatively infertile, lacking in opportunities for agriculture. Adaptation to this environment produced a series of cultural/social characteristics, among them aggressiveness, individualism, the predominance of meat in the diet, and monogamy. There were other characteristics, but they will be discussed more thoroughly, along with a deeper elaboration of Diop's theory in subsequent chapters. It is interesting to note, however, that Diop is arguing against Eurocentric interpretations of Bachofen, Morgan, and Engels concerning the origins of "mother-right" and polygyny.

Our focus here is on religion, and, according to Diop, the nomadic and transcient nature of the lifestyle of the ancient Indo-European had some interesting effects:

In this existence which was reduced to a series of perpetual migrations, the economic role of the woman was reduced to a strict minimum; she was only a burden that the man dragged behind him. Outside her function of child-bearing, her role in nomadic society is nil. It is from these considerations that a new explanation may be sought to account for the lot of the woman in Indo-European society.[100]

This devaluation of the female role was incorporated into their religious practices. Among the nomads, who had no permanent residence, cremation took presidence over burial, and fire, which gave much needed warmth in a land with little direct or close sunlight, was "worshipped." Fire rituals can still be witnessed in some European communities. (See James Frazier's, *The Golden Bough*, New York: Mentor, 1964.) By contrast, according to Diop's theory, in the "Southern Cradle" the earth takes prominence as agricultural activity and fertility abound. The population is more peaceful, secure, and sedentary. Women play a critical part in the economy and in subsistence. The female principle is the foundation of the cosmological conceptions.

Mircea Eliade, in his work *A History of Religious Ideas,* Vol. I, identifies these warlike Aryans as the "Proto Indo-Europeans" and the "Indo-Europeans." These are the people of Diop's "Northern cradle." Eliade identifies them as the initiators of a destructive period of invasions into the Southern regions between 2300 and 1200 years before the Christian Era. This is part of what he calls the process of "Indo-Europeanization," which had an effect on the religious ideas and practices of the areas into which these people expanded. Eliade is concerned with delineating and understanding these effects.

In terms of an African-centered analysis, the process Eliade identified is part of the historically continuous process of European imperialistic expansion. This "Indo-Europeanization" of which Eliade speaks is the earliest expression of the European *utamaroho*. Eliade says,

This characteristic process—migration, conquest of new territories, submission of inhabitants, followed by their assimilation—did not end until the nineteenth century of our era. Such an example of linguistic and cultural expansion is otherwise unknown.[101]

If we accept Eliade's statement as accurate, it would seem that as social scientists and historians, we should be curious as to the reason for the peculiar intensity of this phenomenon. What accounts for this atypical behavior and for its "success?"

According to Eliade, the Tumuli (Kurgan) culture developed between the fifth and third millenia and expanded westward about 4000 B.C.E. They then proceeded to "make their way into Central Europe, the Balkan Peninsula, Transcaucasia, Anatolia, and Northern Iran (ca. 3500–3000 B.C.); in the third millenium they reached northern Europe, the Aegean Zone (Greece and the Coasts of Anatolia), and the Mediterranean." These, he says were the Proto Indo-Europeans. This developing Indo-European culture was influenced by the more developed civilizations of Africa (the "Near East" is a misnomer) and the East.[102] They practiced agriculture, but "preferred to develop a pastoral economy." Eliade's explanation, contrary to Diop's, would imply that there was something other than ecological necessity that determined this predilection for the nomadic lifestyle, but he doesn't say what that factor might be. "Pastoral nomadism, the patriarchal structure of the family, a proclivity for raids, and a military organization designed for conquest are characteristic features of Indo-European societies."[102]

Eliade is interested in determining the relationship between a lifestyle of pastoral nomadism, war, and conquest, on the one hand, and the "emergence of specific religious values," on the other. He makes an attempt to reconstruct themes of a common Indo-European religion. He suggests the idea of celestial sacredness, light and height or elevation; the idea of creativity in its immediate meaning, the idea of sovereignty, the sky-god as supreme father, and that fire kindled by lightning is celestial in origin. "The cult of fire is a characteristic element of the Indo-European religions." Whereas, "Mother Earth as a religious concept is recent among this group." "The Aryans had no cities and knew nothing of writing. . . . Iron began to be used only about 1050 B.C."[103]

Rosemary Ruether goes even further in her analysis and identifies patriarchal tendencies in European religion with monotheism:

> It is possible that the social origins of male monotheism lie in nomadic herding societies. These cultures lacked the female gardening role and tended to image God as the Sky-Father. Nomadic religions were characterized by exclusivism and an aggressive, hostile relationship to the agricultural people of the land and their religion.[104]

While her analysis echoes those of Diop and Eliade in many ways, in neither of the other two theories do we see this connection between what for us are critical and characteristic aspects of European Christianity: patriarchy and monotheism. Clearly, monotheism is related to the monarch and monolith, to forms of power. Who is the monarch? Certainly the European answer would be that the monarch must be male.

In Ruether's view:

> Male monotheism becomes the vehicle of a psychocultural revolution of the male ruling class in its relationship to surrounding reality. Whereas ancient myth had seen the Gods and Goddesses as within the matrix of one physical-spiritual reality, male monotheism begins to split reality into a dualism of transcendent spirit (mind, ego) and inferior and dependent physical nature.[105]

Ruether points to one of the characteristics of the European *utamawazo* (which we discussed in Chap. 1): the tendency to "split" reality into valued and devalued categories, which are dictated by an *utamaroho* that must relate to phenomena as either the superior self or inferior other, so as to justify conquest and control.

> The male is seen essentially as the image of the male transcendent ego or God, woman is seen as the image of the lower, material nature. . . . Gender becomes a primary symbol for the dualism of transcendence and immanence, spirit, matter.[105]

Elaine Pagels also picks up the theme of the patriarchal nature of European Orthodox Christianity, but she correctly includes Judaism and Islam in her description. These three religious traditions are conspicious in their lack of positive female symbolism, whereas most of the world's religions "abound in female symbolism."[106] But what about the early Christian tradition? According to Pagels, the Gnostics combined the female and male principles in their image of the divine. Valentinus "suggests that the divine can be imagined as a dyad; consisting, in part, of the Ineffable, the Depth, the Primal Farther; and, in the other, of Grace, Silence, the womb and Mother of All."[107]

In the African view, we would speak of the harmonious interaction of the complementary Divine Feminine and Masculine. This idea of complementarity, so noticeably absent in the European worldview, was still present to some degree in the Gnostic (African-influenced, early Christian, pre-political) conception of deity. Pagels tells us that some Gnostics said that the Divine was "masculo-feminine—

the great male-female power;" others said that the divine had no gender; and a third group held that it was *either,* depending on which attribute you wished to emphasize.[108] Some Gnostics, she says, described their god as Mother, Father, and Son. This would resemble the African conception of Wsir (Osiris), Ast (Isis), and Heru (Horus). Feminine powers, for the Gnostics, were associated with thought, intelligence, and foresight.[109] Pagels refers to material from the "secret" gospels, revelations, and mystical teachings that, she says, are replete with feminine and sexual metaphor, and the valorization of female aspects of creation and godliness.

But the process of censorship by the self-acclaimed representatives of Jesus on earth then took place, and

> Every one of the secret texts which gnostic groups revered was omitted from the canonical collection, and branded as heretical by those who called themselves orthodox Christians. By the time the process of sorting the various writings ended—probably as late as the year 200—virtually all the feminine imagery for God had disappeared from the orthodox Christian tradition.[110]

The acceptance and sacralization of the feminine went hand in hand with greater involvement of women in the gnostic movement when compared with the orthodox church and more prominent positions of women in the organization. The orthodox leaders were outraged. Pagels quotes Tertullian: "These heretical women—how audacious they are! They have no modesty; they are bold enough to teach, to engage in argument, to enact exorcisms, to undertake cures, and, it may be, even to baptize!" Irenaeus chastises Marcus, a Gnostic, who "invited women to act as priests in celebrating the eucharist with him." (Marcus) "hands cups to women to offer up the eucharist prayer, and to pronounce the words of consecration." Tertullian speaks for the orthodox view, "It is not permitted for a woman to speak in the church, nor is it permitted for her to teach, nor to baptize, nor to offer [the eucharist], nor to claim for herself a share in any *masculine* function—not to mention any priestly office."[111]

Pagels says that "from the year 200 we have no evidence for women taking prophetic priestly and episcopal roles among orthodox churches."[112] From Judaism and Jewish values the Church inherited much of its patriarchal character, and though Paul recognized women as deacons and fellow workers, he "argues from his own—traditionally Jewish—conception of a monistic, masculine God for a divinely ordained hierarchy of social subordination: as God has authority over Christ, he declares, citing Genesis 2-3, so man has authority over women."[112] In I Corinthians 11:7-9, "a man . . . is the image and glory of God; but woman is the glory of man. For man was not made from woman, but woman from man. Neither was man created for woman, but woman for man."

Pagels contrasts the position of women in Egypt, Greece, and Rome, where women enjoyed many rights with men or were in the process of being given more rights, with "women of the Jewish communities [who] were excluded from actively participating in public worship, education, in social and political life outside of the family."[113] (Actually, the position of women in Kemet was far superior to that of women in either Greece *or* Rome. So much so that travellers from these areas were appalled. See B. Lesko, *The Remarkable Women of Ancient Egypt,* 1987.) But the scriptures were to say:

> Let a woman learn in silence with all submissiveness. I permit no woman to teach or to have authority over men; she is to keep silent.

> I Timothy 2:11-12

The Apostolic Church decided that no woman was to become a priest, and the orthodox view of women was as having come into being for man's fulfillment. This puts Christians in a bind. Clearly this concept of fulfillment is not spiritual, therefore women are created solely for the purpose of their sexuality; the same sexuality that is damned. It is women who are inherently evil and all of humanity who are caught in a hopeless contradiction. Why were women "created" in the first place? Pagels says,

> By the late Second Century, the orthodox community came to accept the domination of men over women as the divinely ordained order, not only for social and family life, but also for the Christian Churches.[114]

This period of formulation was of tremendous historical significance, and was impressively successful from the perspective of consistency and adherence to dogma. The history of the Church is proof that monolith makes for ideological control. In 1977, Pope Paul VI, Bishop of Rome, declared that a woman could not be a priest "because our Lord was a man."[115]

What we are observing throughout this study is the process of "Europeanization," a continuance of what Eliade has called "Indo-Europeanization." The mindset, the *utamawazo*, the *utamaroho*, the behavioral tendencies that this racial-cultural stock possessed was continually creating and refining modes through which to express themselves. We are not surprised to see the connections between early Indo-European religion, social organization, and conquest, namely, seminal classical Greek thought, as expressed in Plato's writings, and the Orthodox church of the second century. They are all part of one ideological tradition; each influencing and helping to determine the next historical cultural form; a link in the chain that would become "Western civilization." More specifically, the devaluation of women is adumbrated in classical Greek thought, where it is explicitly elaborated in philosophic discourse by Plato and Aristotle. They paved the way, along with Jewish social values, for a patriarchal church. What may have happened in Greek society especially is that men attempted to incorporate the female principle within themselves, thereby relegating the woman to a merely physically different being who had little of value to contribute to the construction and maintenance of the State. In this way, men, who were the valued form of being, were not forced to look outside of themselves for wholeness, or so they led themselves to believe. In her book *Centaurs and Amazons,* Page duBois discusses this process of devaluation through an examination of the *Timaeus:*

> The philosopher maintains his closeness to the divine, moving upward in the scale of beings, while men who fail in the effort of philosophy are punished by becoming women in their second lives. No woman can be a philosopher. She must wait until after death, when her soul might be reincarnated in the body of a man.[116]

And again, of the *Timaeus,*

> The male sex is assimilated to the divine part of the soul; men, like that divine soul, must be protected from the miasma, the pollution represented by women. That worse part of the soul, likened to women, is superior to the worse of the body, which is like an animal. She says, "women were associated with the body, which was inferior to the mind; thus they, like the body, served the soul, the head, the philosopher, the male."[117]

And from the *Republic,* she quotes: " . . . all those creatures generated as men who proved themselves cowardly (*deiloi*) and spent their lives in wrong doing were transformed, at their second incarnation, into women."[118] The fathers of the Church were merely continuing and further elaborating a tradition that reflected a particular view of reality, a view that had already surfaced in Indo-European culture and classical Greek thought.

The Religion and Rationality Syndrome

One of the consequences of the specious universalization of the Christian statement was that it—together with its adoption of the Platonic mode—launched the European into a fruitlessly unreasonable and senseless enterprise. In the words of E. L. Allen, "Socrates' greatest achievement to many is his insistence on the use of reason to decide moral questions."[119] Yet, while this may very well be one the most significant legacies of Platonic thought, it may also be the most misguiding, given the Platonic understanding of the nature of "reason." It is here that we can clearly recognize the definitive function/role of the European *utamawazo*. It shapes the consciousness and limits the possibilities of conceptual experience. The European identification of religion with rationality is a demonstration of this tendency, ultimately originating in the need to control. The European interpretation of this "use of reason" was bound to the attempt to remove the religious experience from its natural cultural base, and thereby was confronted with the task of "finding" (which in this case means "creating") the proper religious statement. Given the predominant perceptual mode of European thought, Europeans were destined to search within the confines of the abstract and the rationalistic.

Even Rheinhold Niehbuhr recognizes the dilemma posed by the attempt to approach and justify the religious by way of the rationalistic. And he is forced to attest to the Church's perennial susceptibility to this mistake:

> . . . obviously a view which depends upon an ultra-rational presupposition is immediately endangered when rationally explicated; for reason which seeks to bring all things into terms of rational coherence is tempted to make one known thing the principle of explanation and to derive all other things from it. Its most natural inclination is to make itself that ultimate principle, and thus in effect to declare itself God. Christian psychology and philosophy have never completely freed themselves from this fault, which explains why naturalists plausibly though erroneously regard Christian faith as the very fountain source of idealism.[120]

What Niebuhr does not want to admit is that Christian philosophy is plagued by this particular conception, because that conception is itself characteristic of the whole of European philosophy.

The Europeans had trapped themselves by assuming that religious truth consisted of nothing more than the philosophical systems of their own creation and therefore religious activity for them

seemed properly to be contained in their own "philosophical investigations." They had already established the criterion of "true" religion to fit into this framework when they declared that monotheism
and revelation were more consistent, universal, and therefore "rational" religious conceptions than were polytheistic ones. But the religious statements that they themselves made became increasingly
unsatisfying; for obvious reasons, these conceptions did nothing to
fulfill them spiritually. Some examples from the ongoing European
theological discussion will help to clarify the point.

Terence Penelhum has devoted an entire work to the subject of
Religion and Rationality. The pursuit to "rationalize" religion in this
way is a proper one in his opinion. His book is something of an historical survey of the many attempts of Europeans to "prove" that
their god exists. The work offers excellent ethnographic material as
it demonstrates in broad historical spectrum the peculiar flavor of
European thought and the uniqueness of European theology.

Natural Theology represented the elaboration and refinement of
a fusion of principles that had taken place when Plato identified the
"true" with the "good." (In Kemetic [ancient Egyptian] thought, for
instance, philosophy, theology and science were never separate.
Their integration becomes only problematical because of the reification of the "Platonic Abstraction," which tends to reduce thought to
a limited rationalism.) What does the attempted "fusion" do when
rationalistically defined? The following passage is taken from the
work of Aquinas:

> Now, since we have proved that God is the source of being to some
> things, we must further show that everything besides Himself is
> from Him.

> For whatever belongs to a thing otherwise than as such, belongs to
> it through some cause, as *white* to a man: because that which has
> no cause is something first and immediate, wherefore it must needs
> belong to the thing essentially and as such. Now it is impossible for
> any one thing to belong to two and to both of them as such. For that
> which is said of a thing as such, does not go beyond that thing: for
> instance to have three angles equal to two right angles does not go
> beyond a triangle. Accordingly if something belongs to two things,
> it will not belong to both as such: wherefore it is impossible for any
> one thing to be predicated of two so as to be said of neither by rea-
> son of a cause, but it is necessary that either the one be the cause
> of the other,—for instance fire is the cause of heat in a mixed body,
> and yet each is called *hot;*—or else some third thing must be the
> cause of both, for instance fire is the cause of candles giving light.

Now *being* is said of everything that is. Wherefore it is impossible
that there be two things neither of which has a cause of its being
through a cause, or else the one must be the cause of being to the
other. Hence everything that, in any ways whatever, is, must needs
be from that to which nothing is a cause of being. Now we have
proved above [He refers to Bk I, Ch. xiii where he says "there must
needs be a first mover separate and altogether, immovable, and
this is God," p. 31] that God is this being to which nothing is a cause
of being. Therefore from Him is everything that, in any way whatever, is. If however it be said that *being* is not a unequivocal predi-
cate, the above conclusion follows none the less. For it is not said
of many equivocally, but analogically; and thus it is necessary to be
brought back to one thing.[121]

Only within the context of the European *utamawazo* and *utamaroho* would such a statement be recognizable as having anything
remotely resembling religion or spirituality as its subject matter. The
need to "prove" the existence of the spiritually true is a European
need. The inability to distinguish between the "logic" of the mathematical syllogism (proposition) and "reasonableness" or "truth"; and
the inability to recognize the limitation of pure logical analysis points
to a European conceptual weakness. One is tempted to view Aquinas'
statement as the product of a strange dementia, but if it is, it is a
dementia determined by the European *asili*, the ideological, cultural
seed. It is characteristic of the European *utamawazo*, as discussed in
Chap. 1, and becomes intelligible, if not totally "understandable," as
one comes to know the European *utamaroho*. For when rationalism
becomes sanctified, then, of course, formal theology must become
rational, to be deemed suitable for superior minds. And, after all, that
is what European culture is all about.

Here is another curious specimen of similar genre taken from
Leibniz' writing in the *Principles of Nature and of Grace, Founded on
Reason:*

It follows from the supreme perfection of God that producing the universe He chose the best possible plan, containing the greatest order;
the best arranged situation, place, and time; the greatest effect produced by the simplest means; the most power, the most knowledge,
the most happiness and goodness in created things of which the universe admitted. For as all possible things have a claim to existence
in the understanding of God in proportion to their perfections, the
result of all these claims must be the most perfect actual world
which is possible. Otherwise it would not be possible to explain why
things happened as they have rather than otherwise.[122]

Again, the lack of sophistication or depth of spiritual insight is striking here—areas so impressively developed in African, and other First World-descendant philosophical systems. There is much in Leibniz that bears the stamp of Plato, while Aquinas is obviously much more in the debt of Aristotle and his "self-moving mover." But like Aquinas and Leibniz, Plato and Aristotle represent only slightly different manifestations of the same ethnological traditions and tendencies: All fit the *asili* and so were embraced.

In the introduction to his work *Primitive Religion,* Robert Lowie says that Leibniz' conceptions "belong to a different compartment" from that of "religion" and that, "In Leibniz religious flavor is singularly absent because his abstract propositions leave the *religious* consciousness cold."[123] His term "compartment" is well chosen for it implies at least a conceptual differentiation between the nature of spiritual and scientific activities. This is a differentiation necessitated by the European definition of science and the accompanying materialization of the universe. The problem is how one develops spiritual conceptions that can be applicable to a world that one has already effectively (or affectively) materialized. The solution is unavoidable: Reduce spirit to matter; the essence to its manifestation.

Most European theological and philosophical discussions make the same "compartment" or, to use Gilbert Ryle's term, "category mistake." For the European mind, operating outside of the rationalistic sphere means a loss of control. It necessitates the recognition of a power greater than itself, and such a possibility is contradictory to the European *utamaroho.* And so Europeans are faced with a dilemma, for religion has by definition to do with the awareness of the supernatural; i.e., a power that transcends the *mortal* self. Yet it is immanent within the *immortal* being/spirit. It is a dilemma never escaped in European theology, and Europeans end up with an image of the all-powerful or supreme being as "the most rational mind"—which is of course their image of themselves. Having inherited religious insights from older traditions, they were bound to misinterpret them.

It is the appearance of rationality that was added—a characteristic that only they needed. This characteristic exhibited in the statements from Leibniz were long before adumbrated in Platonic thought—symptoms that became more and more acute as the European tradition grew older and more hardened. The "coldness" of Aquinas and Leibniz reflect the coldness of a culture unequipped to provide its members with either spiritual perceptiveness or a related moral base. The "strength" of European culture lies in its fanatical commitment to the technical-scientific. Its weakness lies in the ill-fated attempt to derive meaningful value from a mythology of the "eternal truths of a universal logic," the absoluteness of the rational mode.

Much of William James' *The Varieties of Religious Experience* bears on the problem of "religion and rationality" in that he is concerned with the way in which the religious experience is presented to human beings. Instead of making the mistake of assuming that it must properly occur within the confines of rationalism, James perceptively observes the relationship of the emotional to religious conviction. In the passage below, he is discussing the convincingness of certain "feelings of reality":

> They are as convincing to those who have them as direct sensible experiences can be, and they are, as a rule, much more convincing than results established by mere logic ever are . . . you cannot help regarding them as genuine perceptions of truth, as revelations of a kind of reality which no adverse argument, however unanswerable by you in words, can expel from your belief. The opinion opposed to mysticism in philosophy is sometimes spoken of as *rationalism*. Rationalism insists that all our beliefs ought ultimately to find for themselves articulate grounds. Such grounds, for rationalism, must consist of . . . (1) definitely statable abstract principles; (2) definite inferences logically drawn. Vague impressions of something indefinable have no place in the rationalistic system.

And further:

> If you have intuitions at all, they come from a deeper level of your nature than the loquacious level which rationalism inhabits. Your whole subconscious life, your impulses, your faiths, your needs, your divinations, have prepared the promises, of which your consciousness now feels the weight of the result; and something in you absolutely *knows* that that result must be truer than any logic-chopping rationalistic talk, however clever, that may contradict it. This inferiority of the rationalistic level in founding belief is just as manifest when rationalism argues for religion as when against it.[124]

For this reason all of Schonfield's labors of documentation "proving" what he calls the "Passover Plot," and his attempted logical rigor, should not be able to convince a Christian that Christ was not the "Son of God" (or "Son of Man"), since faith belongs to the sphere of myth rather than to the category of secular history, which is merely temporal.[125] The matter becomes further complicated, however, in the European context, because the Christian claim is precisely that of possessing "historical truth."

James makes the distinction between what he calls "existential judgment" and "propositions of value" or "spiritual judgement." In his association of value with the spiritual, James is atypical; and so is his recognition of the fact that these two areas of judgment "proceed from the diverse intellectual preoccupations."[126] He is rejecting the European *utamawazo*—battling the logic of the European *asili*. And so he himself is rejected by the cultural traditions (and not included in the required reading of Philosophy 101, 102, or 103).

In terms of the European *utamawazo* religions became associated with belief (nonvalue), while philosophy was associated with knowledge (value). Therefore the task of the theologian was to give European religion the shape of European philosophy, so as to enhance its value. First, the European *utamawazo* artificially separated spirit from matter (known), then it devalued spirit (unknown) and attempted to redefine it in terms of material reality. The ancient Africans had done the reverse; for them all meaningful reality was rooted in the spiritual.

The rationalistic approach to religion is the counterpart of the European conviction that values are "discovered" intellectually rather than created via cultural activity. This ideological tendency has its historical and epistemological origins in Platonic thought and finds its development and interpretation in Aristotle and the Scholastics. This "syndrome" perhaps points more dramatically to the spiritual failure of European religious formulations than any other single aspect.

The Techno-Social Order

Though Judeo-Christian thought is always heralded as being tremendously influential in the development of the European tradition, it is not as often made clear in what ways this influence made itself felt. It is certainly obvious that the avowed belief in "universal brotherhood" and "peace" were not incorporated into European ideology; that this espoused Christian morality has not had a formulative influence on the European ethic is quite clear. To an extent it is again a question of the compatibility of ideological perspective and cultural tendencies. Christianity was, in the early stages of European development, conducive to the growth of technology. A religious statement that was not compatible with European development in this respect would not have been successful in the European context.

As with Judaism, Christianity functioned to support and promote the recording of tradition in written form as a valued activity. Doctrine was made authoritative by putting oral tradition into written form. Writing in this way acted as a sanction in the developing culture, and at the same time facilitated state organization.

The growth of Christianity in the early history of European culture was also associated with the cities in the same way that the European chauvinistic expression associated European culture with "city-life."[127]

The European ideological frame of reference seemed to house comfortably both the institutionalization of the Christian formulation and the growth of European technological society. It is a question of not only compatibility but, in the European context, one of necessity. There are most definitely religious formulations that are not conducive to the growth of technology as it occurred in the West.

The growth of cities, the use of writing as a preferred mode, and the general emphasis on technology as a social goal all go hand in hand with an assumption of and belief in the "idea of progress" in which the continued intensification of these social facts constitute absolute value. The Judeo-Christian formulation is based on precisely the same concept. Within this tradition "religion" is seen almost as a technological advance, and, therefore, is aided by and aids the growth of the technical order. Christianity, then, is in this sense, as well as others, quite "worldly" or "secular." It is the advantage of the "world religions," according to traditional European social theory, that they enable man to "discover" future time and, therefore, to achieve a higher stage of cultural development. These analyses do not raise the question of the conceptually limiting effects of a strictly one dimensional concept of time in combination with a progress ideology; a combination that implies the creation of a hypothetical future. European religion must deal with what is a European problem, the deeply ingrained assumption of an unknown and limitless future.

This conception of time and of an oppressive future functions culturally to direct the activities of a people toward the creation of an ever-increasing rationalized technical order. In so far as Christian ideology is predicated on lineal and not cyclical or repetitive conceptions, it supported this kind of development and was, therefore, an important aspect of early European development. For while the accelerated growth of the technical collossus may have been many centuries away, the ideological germs were already incubating, laying the groundwork for a more mature Westernization.

It is compelling here to diverge briefly, to mention the seemingly anomalous case of Islam, which has several of the same ideological features as Judaism and Christianity. Islam provides a model for social organization that promotes some of the characteristics associated with European culture: patriarchy, the monotheistic ideal, an emphasis on the accumulation of literature and institutionalized learning as opposed to traditional education. While Europe was going through the embarrassment of her "blind age," the Islamic culture was preserving and developing the tradition of scholarship that Europe had associated with her own history. Why, then, isn't Islam considered a "Western" religion? Or is it? It is never considered to be such in the textbooks in which Europeans define themselves. Europeans did not, of course, choose to follow Muhammad.

But, again, using the index of cultural chauvinism and ethnic identity, the case of Islam and its relationship to the Judeo-Christian experience becomes quite clear. The Islamic religion politically supported a statement of Arab nationalism and conquest, while the Jewish and Christian religions are statements of Jewish and Western European nationalism, respectively. Just as the Jewish religious statement was not meant for non-Jews, so the Christian religious statement was never meant to be and cannot tolerate an interpretation that encourages the self-determination or military solidification, defense, or aggression of any "non-Western," "non-European" peoples. The critical distinction between Islam and Christianity is racial-cultural, not theological-ideological. The vicious, prolonged, and bloody crusades constituted a series of racial-cultural ("ethnic") wars, "color wars." It is grossly inaccurate and misleading for them to be referred to as "religious wars" without reference to ethnicity, race, or cultural identification, as is usually done.

One of the most important connections between Christianity and technology since the colonial period is that missionary Christianism paves the way for capitalism and the European-centered market economy. This form of Christianization in areas such as Africa was an ideological preparation for acquiescence to the mechanisms of exploitation represented by colonialism. The colonies were needed for the economic growth and development of Europe, which meant that the indigenous population had to be convinced that they had been born to serve their European masters and, further, would benefit from such servitude. What better way to make this argument than by selling them on the superiority of Christianity, which could save them from the fate of being irreligious, sinful, backward, and black? Once convinced of this, the colonized begin to assimilate attitudes that help to prepare them to fit into European-style technological organization, because these attitudes are implicit in European Christianity.

One mark of the new mindset is the concept of time. For the African ordinary time is punctuated by sacred time, and time is valued according to what the community experiences. Therefore, we can speak qualitatively of different "times," because they are experienced differently. Christianization repudiates this concept as it demeans African culture and substitutes a secularized concept of uniform lineal time, suiting the more mechanized order, which the European colonizers and neocolonialists need to establish.

In his book *Breast of the Earth,* Kofi Awoonor has an excellent discussion of Christianity's role in this regard and tells us that "The school was the most important instrument of missionary work in Africa."[128] It was the key to the process that would strip Africans of their culture so that they could become part of the technical order; albeit at the lowest level. The school always took African children away from their elders and caused them to be ashamed of the very things that could have been a source of political strength and resistance to colonial rule.

The new technology of exploitation required that the African become an imitation of the European.[129] It required a total transformation that embodied new standards of success and social status.[130] Christianity, of course, meant "civilization." To be civilized was to become as much like the European as possible. Awoonor tells us that, "The converts were also encouraged to acquire European material culture . . . . The superiority of the European way of life was rigorously inculcated."[129] This included living in the townships that the missionaries established, in opposition to the very villages in which the African extended kin lived.

The missionary school discouraged the use of African languages. "Christian conversion meant cultural change," a change essential to the donning of the cultural clothing of European technology. "Christ was a white man; the saints were white; and the missionaries were white . . . . Continuously the African was told he was cursed in his adherence to the ways of his fathers, and because he was black-skinned, the implications were not lost to him. . . . The fundamental erosion of the African's confidence in himself began with the first Christian convert."[131]

One of the most important ways that missionary education prepared Africans for capitalism and the European techno-social order was by destroying the integrity of lineage organization that formed the basis of the traditional communal structure. Christianity stressed individual salvation and the "Judeo-Christian material culture," as Awoonor phrases it, and it denounced all communal forms such as polygyny, the traditional educational system, and especially, economic communalism; i.e., the communal ownership and distribution of resources. Individualism was an implicit value of missionary Christianism as it revealed itself among those colonized by the Europeans.

The "civilized African" behaved and dressed and spoke like a European. He had been educated in European schools that began with the mission school and was therefore trained to uphold European values and to perpetuate European control: The purpose of any educational system is to perpetuate the society that it creates. The "*non-evolue*" or "uncivilized" African was an "unsaved," "uneducated" primitive and non-Christian and therefore "a usable chattel for mines and farms—" so thought the Europeans and their "civilized" Africans.[132] Missionary Christianism stripped colonized, "non-Europeans" of everything. In this psychologically insecure state they could then be immersed in the ideology of the technical order. And so many Africans themselves will speak of the "blessings" of Christianity, because they are sold on the "ideology of progress" to which its European adherents subscribe.

It is not only in terms of the specific technological tendencies manifested in the Christian lifestyle that the essence of this relationship lies (e.g., deification of writing, literacy, the growth of cities, etc.). The compatibility of the Christian doctrine and the development of technology in the West is found at a deeper and more critical level. Christian ideology is teleological, providing a conceptual model peculiar to the European *utamawazo*; both are based on and peculiar to a particular image of the human. The Christian-European interpretation of the human is of a being who derives meaning from his ability to move toward a universal goal—both "progressive" and "rational." It is this and not the "not-of-this-world," "do-unto-others" idea that operates as the motivating factor in Christian ideology; "other-worldliness" goes against the grain of technological "advance." The ideal, of course, is an abstraction; it implies unending movement itself. It is in some crucial way associated with the creation of power that is in turn associated with efficiency. Both power and efficiency are identified with the control of nature and people and the belief that it is the natural and proper destiny of humans to negate nature and/or the "primary" condition.

Rheinhold Niebuhr proudly declares, "The idea of progress is possible only upon the ground of a Christian culture."[133] Niebuhr intends here to point to a "positive," and culturally desirable, attribute of that ideology. He is not questioning the universal validity of the concept. Niebuhr never really repudiates the idea in terms of its ideological thrust; he merely nibbles a bit at the edges.

As noted in Chap. 1, Lynn White has pointed to specific periods in European development, and has presented an impressive case for the supportive relationship between European technology and European religion. "Modern science," which White identifies with European culture, is predicated on certain assumptions about the nature of the human and our relationship to the environment. Christian ideology supports these assumptions. In White's view, "Our [European] technological and our scientific movements got their start, acquired their character, and achieved world dominance in the Middle Ages."[134] The unique style in which these activities have been carried out in the West required particular ontological conceptions, conceptions that, White says are "religious" in origin. In his view, the ideas about nature, our relationship to it, and our destiny, which crystallized in Medieval Christian theology, were the dominant contributor to the ideological ascendancy of science and technology in the West, an ascendancy that accounts for the present Western European "ecological crisis," since the technical order is essentially exploitative of the natural order.

But we can look to an even earlier period for the origins of the development. Judeo-Christian thought in the company of Platonic epistemology initiated the desacralization of nature that would allow for a dehumanized techno-social order and the materialist, mechanized conception of the universe on which European science depends. This desacralized cosmos was an early conception within the Hebrew tradition. Mircea Eliade says,

> Cosmic religiousity continued the most elementary dialectic of the sacred, especially the belief that the divine is incarnated, or manifests itself, in cosmic objects and rhythms. Such a belief was denounced by the adherents of Yahweh as the worst possible idolatry, and this ever since the Israelites' entrance into Palestine . . . . The prophets finally succeeded in emptying nature of any divine presence.[135]

This amounted to an attack on nature as an integral part of our human existence; an attitude that went hand in hand with the Hebrew submergence of the power of women. The Divine Feminine is associated with the fecundity of the earth and the centrality of the cyclical order and the workings of nature in our lives. The feminine, in other traditions, was symbolic of the force of nature, which is generative of all life. If the divine is identified with the fecundity of the Earth and with nature, then, as Rosemary Ruether points out, the tendency in Judeo-Christian thought to desacralize nature would go hand in hand with the need to devalue the feminine and, therefore, to masculinize the conception of a god.[136] Ruether points out that in Genesis I, God commands Adam to "Fill the earth and subdue it and have dominion over it."[137]

This masculinization in the Hebrew conception of "god" is linked to the need to believe that being can be mechanically, technically "created." And while this early Hebrew society may be distant in time from the technical colossus that we now experience, the view of reality on which this colossus was constructed was being put in place in the early Judaic statement. Two divergent world-views emerged: (1) the more ancient, in which nature was associated with meaningful experience; and (2) the Platonic, Judeo-Christian world-view, in which meaningful being was a human-controlled, "denatured" reality.

In his book *The Sacred and the Profane,* Mircea Eliade gives us a phenomenological view of the sacred and of the religious that directly contradicts this Judeo-Christian desacralization of nature. "For religious man, nature is never only "natural"; it is always fraught with a religious value." The gods "manifest(ed) the different modalities of the sacred in the very structure of the world and cosmic phenomena."[138] He says that to the religious person, the universe presents itself as a divine creation, as cosmos. "The cosmic rhythms manifest order, harmony, permanence, fecundity." Nature always expresses something that transcends it. It is "supernature," not nature.[139] We "become aware of the sacred because it shows itself as something wholly different from the profane . . . the manifestation of a reality that does not belong to our world." But this reality can be felt within objects that are part of the profane world.[140] Eliade then says something very revealing about culture:

> The modern Occidental experiences a certain uneasiness before many manifestations of the sacred. He finds it difficult to accept the fact that, for many human beings, the sacred can be manifested in stones or trees, for example.[140]

The sacred African tree, the sacred ancestral sculpture—(what Jews, Christians, and Muslims call "idols") are not merely *Kintu* (objects), they are "hierophanies."[141] Is the Christian cross an idol? Was Jesus an idol? Perhaps the true idols are the dollar bills in Euro-American society—literally "concretized" in one-hundred-story buildings. This is true idolatry: worship of the object.

Eliade says, "the wholly desacralized cosmos is a recent discovery in the history of the human spirit. . . desacralization pervades the entire experience of the nonreligious man of modern societies and . . . in consequence, he finds it increasingly difficult to rediscover the existential dimensions of religious man in archaic societies."[142] If we substitute "European" for "modern" and "non-European" for "archaic," we have a formulation that leads towards a meaningful critique of European culture.

Lynn White traces the development of the ontological conceptions inherent in European religion, on which depends the European commitment to create an artificial, technically controlled environment. The Judeo-Christian world-view introduced an all-powerful "God" who created "man;" but, says White, it is "man" who "named all the animals, thus establishing his dominance over them."

> God planned all of this explicitly for man's benefit and rule: no item in the physical creation had any purpose save to serve man's purposes. And, although man's body is made of clay, he is not simply part of nature: he is made in God's image. . . . Christianity is the most anthropomorphic religion the world has seen. . . . Man shares in great measure, God's transcendence of nature. Christianity. . . not only established a dualism of man and nature but also insisted that it is God's will that man exploit nature for his proper ends. . . . By destroying pagan animism, Christianity made it possible to exploit nature in a mood of indifference to the feelings of natural objects. . . . The spirits *in* natural objects, which formerly had protected nature from man, evaporated. Man's effective monopoly on spirit in this world was confirmed, and the old inhibitions to the exploitation of nature crumbled.[143]

By the thirteenth century natural theology in the Latin West was "becoming the effort to understand God's mind by discovering how his creation operates."[143] In this way, "modern Western science was cast in the matrix of Christian theology. The dynamism of religious devotion, shaped by the Judeo-Christian dogma of creation, gave it impetus."[144] Because European ecological conceptions are implicit in the development of the technical order, "Christian" attitudes can be seen to have been its prerequisites. White says,

> We are superior to nature, contemptuous of it, willing to use it for our slightest whim. . . . To a Christian a tree can be no more than a physical fact. The whole concept of the Sacred Grove is alien to Christianity and to the ethos of the West. For nearly two millenia Christian missionaries have been chopping down Sacred groves, which are idolatrous because they assume spirit in nature.[144]

I have said earlier that religion is the sacralization of ideology. The technical order is the rationalization of nature. It was a process hinted at long ago in European commitment. This commitment required moral sanction, and what was formally recognized as religion in the West, in turn, had to be compatible with this commitment, or it would have taken another form. In other words, the religious formulation cannot change without commitment changing, and vice-versa. As White says, "the present increasing disruption of the global environment is the product of a dynamic technology and science. . . their growth cannot be understood historically apart from distinctive attitudes toward nature which are deeply grounded in Christian dogma."[145] European science and technology are, then, ideologically dependent on this Christian arrogance toward nature.

> Our daily habits of action are dominated by an implicit faith in perpetual progress. . . rooted in and indefensible apart from Judeo-Christian teleology. . . .We can continue today to live, as we have lived for about 1700 years, very largely in a context of Christian axioms.[146]

Christian ideology has played a supportive cultural role in the uniqueness of Western European techno-social development at certain formulative periods in this cultural/historical process.

The Record Versus the "Apology"

The cultural/historical record of the European experience clarifies the interdependent relationship between the institutionalization of European Christianity and the European imperialistic endeavor, as well as the compatibility of Christian ideology with European cultural nationalism.

The efforts of Reinhold Niebuhr to salvage Christianity and cleanse it of this historical record are perhaps the most impressive of any Christian apologist, but in our view his failure is nonetheless evident. His discussion is helpful to us, as it is in his attempts to extricate the essence of Christianity from the history and character of the European imperial order that he touches on some of the most significant issues raised in our discussion.

One of these issues is that of the so-called universality of the Church. For Niebuhr, the historical evils of the West issue from "collective egotism," "cultural particularism," or "nationalism"; while the "universalism" of the Church is a tendency toward the good that can save us from these "evils." However, he is forced to admit that "the Church, as well as the state, can become the vehicle of collective egotism."[147] Imperialists and slavers that they were, Popes Paul III, Paul IV, Pius V, Gregory, et al., in Niebuhr's view, were only embarrassing exceptions to the pattern. Certainly from an African-centered perspective, we cannot view them as such, for, as Cohen and others have pointed out, there were far too many of them, and if the "real" Christians had no part in the creation of the European empire and are not responsible for the inequities perpetuated by it, then one is forced to ask, where are they, and where have they been? If in fact they exist at all, surely they have not been part of the European "experience." And if the only "real" Christians are outside of Europe, then are they Christians? In other words, the question is raised as to whether the non-European values and ideas claimed by Christians like Niebuhr, who would exonerate Christianity from its militaristic and culturally aggressive aspects, can be identified with the European tradition at all!

"Christianity" is a configuration of values, attitudes and behaviors that are inseparable from the history of Europe.[148] Unhappily for non-European people, "real" European Christians do exist and have existed in large enough numbers to have successfully imposed their own brand of European cultural nationalism wherever they have ventured, inevitably backed with the armed might of the West.

Niebuhr employs what is perhaps the most ideologically affective tool and manifestation of European cultural imperialism in his use of the concept of "universalism." The subtle, but critical, issue raised by his claims is a philosophical-ideological one. It lies partially in the implicit value dichotomy he makes between nationalism and universalism. Nationalism in his view is "bad" and represents negative particularism in which the self (ego) is the source of motivation, sentiment, and behavior; while universalism is its positive opposite and represents the ability to identify with the universal good of all people, i.e., takes an abstraction called "humanity" as its inspirational source.

First, I challenge this formulation on the grounds that it, itself, is not a "universal" statement, though its value for the European lies in the fact it has all the earmarks of such. It is a moot question as to whether any such "universalism" is desirable even if it were possible. Nationalistic, i.e., (self) group identification, is positive because it is humanly feasible and originates in the concrete circumstance of cultural definition. Hope for humankind lies in the possibilities for fashioning nationalistic ideologies that are not definitionally predicated on the destruction of other cultural groups. European nationalism and above all its Christianism are therefore "negative" from this viewpoint. Second, even if the ability to identify with others is accepted as a normative goal, it is neither Christian thought nor European ideology that makes such identification possible. The European concept of self is an isolating one, and the Christian concept of spiritual enlightenment is individualistic, as opposed to being group or community oriented. Christianity is a European "nationalistic" (i.e., cultural imperialistic) statement in opposition to the "non-European" nationalists it wishes to conquer.

In other words, from the African-centered perspective, it is not nationalism (cultural particularism) that is negative, but the content that a particular nationalist ideology is given that makes it a threat to the survival of others. In this regard, it is clearly European nationalism, of which Christianity is an example, that has been most destructive of the peaceful coexistence of divergent cultural groupings. The projection of so-called "universalism" as an assumed goal of human behavior is not desirable or culturally meaningful, but it allows Europeans to thereby project European particularism as something other than it is. The claim to "universality," whether made by a Christian apologist, a social theorist, or a military leader, is merely a packaging device. The "struggle of the Christian religion against the pride and self-will of nations"[147] that Niebuhr wants to see does not exist, but by giving voice to this supposed "struggle" the impression is conveyed of the moral superiority of Christianity based on the implied invidious comparison between a nonexistent, abstract "universalism," "the embodiment of the good," and cultural nationalism, "the expression of evil." The real question becomes, Why has the European made so much of this claim of universalism? (See Chap. 10 of this work.)

Niebuhr criticizes the universalism of the "classical" philosophers of ancient Greece as being merely "the extension of their particular viewpoint," like that of "a modern communist" who "is a universalist in his hope that communism may become the basis of a world civilization."[149] But Christian "universalism" has precisely the same concrete implications in its existential acting out, and is of the same vintage. The *difference* that is so important to Niebuhr is only in its semantical/philosophical expression, and merely facilitates the extension of a particular viewpoint—namely, that of Christianity.

It is facilitated in that it can more thoroughly extend itself over a wider and more diverse arena of cultures. Europeans simply discovered the political value of not verbally identifying "god and nation"; that is not to say that this identification ceased to exist. Most other cultures have had no political ambitions that required such rhetoric, and when they have, they were certainly not as successful or as "well-equipped" to carry them out. They therefore speak of "a god" in necessary relationship to "their nation" or culture. Niebuhr makes much of this terminological difference in Chap. 8, Vol. I, of *The Nature and Destiny of Man*. But to delete the article "a" from its usual position before "god" and to write it always with a capital "G" merely gives a quasireligious statement, like that of European Christianism, greater imperialistic potential. In one case a religious statement is openly identified with the cultural entity that is its source, and in the other, it is formulated to be put at the service of a cultural entity in its world imperialistic pursuits.

Niebuhr cannot avoid the imperialistic uses of Christianity, but his perspective obliges him to explain European imperialism as ultimately inconsistent with Christian teachings: "prophetic religion, " he says, "had its very inception in a conflict with national self-deification."[150] However, it appears that the European Christian definition ("universalistic," absolutist, and monistic) is reinforced by the international ambitions of the European nation, the cultural supremism of the European ideology, and the expansionism of the European *utamaroho*. Far from "struggling" against "collective pride," I have argued that Christianity was ideally fashioned to express European "collective pride" (nationalism). This explanation, among other ethnologically satisfying characteristics, has the advantage of being consistent with the history of the Christian Church, while Niebuhr and other Christian apologists are hopelessly involved in the impossible task of explaining away millions of "unreal" Christians and centuries of characteristically "un-Chrisitianlike" behavior of the Christian world.

Conclusion: Religion and Power

The strength of institutionalized religion in the European experience is also its weakness. Morality in a secular society proports to be intellectual. In European culture its models are rational. It is despiritualized. Early in the developing European tradition, the advantage of a religious statement that rhetorically sanctioned its political objectives was discovered. But the result, as well as the cause, was a spiritual deficit in the culture. The Christian emphasis on a heavenly afterlife does not alleviate European anxiety concerning death, primarily because it is a remote abstraction rather than a lived belief and does not address itself to the spiritual isolation of individuals—which is the real basis of their anxiety. This anxiety is the price paid for the cognitive structure of European culture (the *utamawazo*), and the Christ image in this context is merely or triumphantly, depending on one's view point, symbolic of the illusion of "progress," a constant striving for that which cannot be achieved. Perhaps this image of a resurrected savior, born in African metaphor, but intensified and reified in European mythology, unconsciously represents, as well, the "humanity" that was indeed sacrificed for European success.

But no other civilization has been as successfully imperialistic. No other has used its institutionalized religion as pragmatically in the support of its imperialistic objectives. The spiritual deficit does not appear to count for much, if one is impressed by world dominance. The *asili* demands power and is itself powerful. The modality and dogma of European religion have been mandated by the *asili*, which they, in turn, reinforce.

In African religion and in many other primary religious formulations, it is the spiritual-emotional needs of the people within the culture that are served. At the same time the values of the culture are sanctioned, and the mechanisms for its continuance are sacralized. Spiritual/philosophical conceptions such as ancestor communion, which help to explain the universe as a spiritual whole in which all life and being are periodically regenerated, give the African an emotional security and confidence that the European lacks. But such conceptions did not prepare the African, nor her Native American or Oceanic counterparts to deal politically with the aggression of the European. These conceptions have not been used successfully in the defense of culture. Non-European religions were not fashioned for worldwide acceptance nor for international propaganda. There is no superficial, merely rhetorical, component of these religions. Ethnologically, both European and "non-European" religions serve the ideological needs of the cultures in question as defined by their members. The radical difference between them issues from the differences in these two sets of ideology: One is based on the pursuit of world dominance; the others seek to use the forces of the universe to ensure a harmonious existence. The two types of ideology involve two different conceptions of power. Europeans are culturally nurtured with a keen political sense that is simultaneously defensive and aggressive. The *utamaroho* comes with an awareness of "others." It is therefore intensely political.

What begins to emerge in these first two chapters is a pattern in which, at critical points in the development of European culture, when its ascendancy appears to have been threatened because of ambivalence, confusion, or a malfunctioning of the "machine," masterful adjustments had been made that brought new clarity of purpose, a reconsolidation of energies, retrieving focus so that the machine would once again be efficient. These adjustments were sometimes in the form of what I have called "modal changes," sometimes creations of political genius, fanatically devoted to the objective of total control.

We have, to some degree, traced the intimate relationship between religion and *utamaroho* in European development from its Indo-European pagan origins, through its initial nationalistic statement in Judaism, its Roman cooptation by Constantine, and the battle against the apolitical interpretations of the Gnostics, the Donatists, and others. At another critical point Augustine sells the idea of the merger of Church and State, and Europe is well on its way to the creation of a national consciousness with a religious statement supportive of its imperialistic ambitions. At each juncture a monolithic doctrine was required, and it was created. The threat of dissension and disunity were dealt with. Threats would continue, but the mechanisms were in place with which to destroy them or keep them in check: The three "great" inquisitions (initiated by Pope Gregory IX, 1231; Pope Sixtus IV, 1478; Pope Paul III, 1542) merely represented some of the more infamous and blatantly sadistic methods of such control.

The objective of this study is to identify and understand the *asili* of European development. A history of Europe would disclose other junctures, set backs, and personalities who were instrumental in the creation of the empire. The fall of Rome is a setback because the focus is deflected as the "Europeans" become disunified, perceiving themselves as Germanic and Asian "tribes." Clovis the Frank (481) becomes a Christian and unifies the Franks. Charles Martel reunites the Merovingian Kingdom, establishing the Carolingian line. In the 600s, Charlemagne increases the size of the Frankish Kingdom, again spreads Christianity, and together with the Pope in the year 800 declares himself the Emperor of the New Holy Roman Empire.

The process continued through the Norman Conquest (1066) and beyond. During this early period, throughout the Middle Ages, Christianity was used to forge and solidify a European consciousness. Later, in the Renaissance and into the modern period, both the physical and social sciences would be used in the same way, the Church no longer occupying a central position in this process. The establishment of a scientific ideology and the various disciplines of the European Academy through which to promote it, takes over there. Institutionalized religion, so essential to the construction of the imperial order and the creation of a European consciousness in the early stages of European development, will become almost obsolete, taking a back seat to Science: the new religion.

We have seen that religion, as associated with European culture, is shaped by *utamawazo* and *asili,* which shape the culture itself. That, of course, is what we would expect. The concept of *asili* tells us that it is possible to identify the seed/germ of the culture, which is at once its explanatory and generating principle. Once we understand that germinating core, all aspects of the culture fall into place. Institutionalized religion in the European experience poses confrontational dichotomies for the purposes of proselytization and dominance. It is absolutist, offering an abstraction as the proper object of religious devotion. It struggles to present a rationalistic proof of the existence of its deity. The literal mode becomes religiously authoritative. Lineal conception, which valorizes secular, historical time, becomes a validating mechanism for religious superiority. In the process of the unfolding of this religious tradition it desacralizes nature, denies the vision of a cosmos to its adherents, thereby alienating nature and paving the way for the technical order.

The focus in this chapter has been on the institution of religion as it related to early European cultural and political imperialism. The normative intracultural ethic is not to be found in this earlier Christian statement. It is not until its reformulation in Protestantism that European institutionalized religion becomes to some extent a verbal reflection of the European way of life. In Protestantism it becomes a functioning directive of internal behavior; that is, *within* the culture. This issue will surface in Chap. 7.

In the chapters that follow we turn our attention to the mechanisms of value-definition and look at the images provided by the cultural mythoform that act to support the pattern of behavior towards non-European peoples. I attempt to paint the portrait of an *utamaroho* that has already begun to emerge from the previous discussion of religion and ideology in early European development and from the themes of the European *utamawazo.*

. . . That our left eye should be set to see against its twin, not with it—surely that is part of the white destroyers' two thousand seasons of triumph against us? That the sight of the eye should be unconnected, cut off from the mind's embracing consciousness; that the ear's hearing should be blocked off from the larger knowledge of the mind, that the nose's smelling and the tongue's tasting should be pushed apart from the mind's whole consciousness—what is that but death's whiteness in delirious triumph?. . . the walls of whiteness built to separate sense from sense. . .
— Ayi Kwei Armah

Chapter 3

Aesthetic: The Power of Symbols

The Meaning of "Aesthetic"

There are two uses of the term "aesthetic" that will have relevance in this discussion corresponding to its usages in European culture. First, we want to identify the European conception of beauty, in the sense of the forms, images, and experiences that evoke positive emotional responses from those who have been enculturated in the tradition. This sense of the European aesthetic is closely related to value; that is, its themes are "expressions" of European value. This is the aesthetic that reaches to every layer of the culture. The values and images involved are not limited to the ordinary person, although they are more consciously expressed in the media that addresses itself to the "nonintellectual"—and to the popular art forms. But this should not confuse the issue, because (perhaps unconsciously or at least nonverbally) this aesthetic affects the "intellectual" as well.

Because of the peculiar nature of European culture, we have to include another meaning of the term "aesthetic." In characteristic European fashion there is not only the experience of the beautiful, but there is the "objectification" of that experience as well. In keeping with the *asili* of the culture, it follows that there must be a "science" based on this objectification. So that our discussion must touch on aesthetics or Western European philosophical thought about the nature of the beautiful and its apprehension, insofar as it is relevant to our overall objective.

These two senses of "the European aesthetic" interest us at various points. Consistent with the dynamics of European culture, this "scientific" or "philosophical" aesthetic seeks to influence and control the emotional experience of what Europeans consider beautiful; while, on the other hand, the philosophic aesthetics takes its shape, its form, and its style from those habits of mental organization that are "emotionally" appealing to the European mind: the *utamawazo*.

The mode of "rationalism" itself forms an important part of the European aesthetic. It is not possible to understand this *utamawazo*, nor the construct of the culture, unless it is realized that its standards of thought, behavior, and social institutions are all touched by this predilection for rationalistic forms. Max Weber discusses "rationality" in Western art forms:

> The rational use of the Gothic vault as a means of distributing pressure and of roofing spaces of all forms, and above all as the constructive principle of great monumental buildings and the foundation of a *style* extending to sculpture and painting, such as that created by our Middle Ages, does not occur elsewhere. The technical basis of our architecture came from the Orient. But the Orient lacked that solution of the problem of the dome and that type of classic rationalization of all art—in painting by the rational utilization of lines and spatial perspective—which the Renaissance created for us."[1]

A discussion of the experience of the beautiful in the context of European culture illuminates this point well. On a conscious level the attempt is made to separate this experience and raise it "above" its effectively emotional aspect. That presents special problems as even the European philosopher is forced to recognize that the person must react initially to what she considers to be beautiful with her senses and with her feelings; i.e., that one apprehends beauty initially as sensation. Therefore philosophers in the European tradition found themselves in the position of intellectualizing; that is, making "conscious," in a technical sense, even the emotional aspect of the perception, apprehension—the experience of "beauty."

Again, as with the attempt to merge rationalism and religion, the results are very strange. One consequence has been "aesthetics" or the "science" of the aesthetically valid: a rationalistic discussion of the rules by which the experience of the beautiful takes place, of what properly constitutes "beauty" in a "logical" sense. Of course, this discussion purports to have universal significance. European philosophers never claim to describe their own aesthetic experiences (and in truth one doubts that they could possibly be), but they do claim to prescribe the proper rules for determining "the beautiful" and to describe the nature of "true" aesthetic experience. They are setting the "standards" for judgement and criticism. But none of these discussions is satisfying to anyone other than European philosophers. One questions their motives and the reason the subject occupies the attention and energy that it does. The answer is that this speculative/philosophic activity functions in its own way to reinforce and validate the cultural *asili* and to strengthen the national consciousness; the collective self-image as superior to others, a universal standard for humanity.

A reading of Kant's "analytic of the beautiful," in the *Critique of Judgement,* gives one the impression that the things he is trying so desperately to define, to verbalize, to "enclose within the word," as Steiner says (cited in Chap. 1), do not lend themselves to the forms of thought he employs, and moreover, that aesthetic experience itself is in no way connected to this discussion and certainly not aided by it.

> The beautiful is that which pleases universally without (requiring) a concept. If we wish to explain what a purpose is according to its transcendental determinations. . . [We say that] the purpose is the object of a concept, in so far as the concept is regarded as the cause of the object (the real ground of its possibility); and the causality of a concept in respect of its object is its purposiveness (form finalis). . . the tone of mind which is self-maintaining and of speculative universal validity is subordinated to the way of thinking which can be maintained only by painful resolve, but is of objective universal validity.[2]

These are only a few statements from a lengthy and incredibly abstruse treatise, but they are exemplary of the work. One wonders if the work itself is necessary for Kant to come to conclusions that appear intuitively obvious.

There can be no objective rule of taste which shall determine, by means of concepts, what is beautiful. For every judgement from this source is aesthetical; i.e. the feeling of the subject, and not a concept of the object, is its determining ground. To seek for a principle of taste which shall furnish, by means of definite concepts, a universal criterion of the beautiful, is fruitless trouble, because what is sought is impossible and self-contradictory.[3]

Then why this effort? Why does what Europe considers to be one of its greatest minds concern himself with an "analytic of the beautiful?" There appears to be no ultimate purpose other than that this exercise itself gives to a segment of society a strange kind of pleasure. The analytical and the "rational" are so valued that they become a part of the emotional experience of pleasure among a select group of people. There is no doubt that the undergraduate who is required to read the *Critique of Judgement* gets no pleasure from the experience and in fact may regard it as punishment; but the power of the sanctions in the culture should not be underestimated, for if the student pursues philosophy until the end of her college career and into graduate school, she will no doubt begin to consider the *Critique* a "work of art" and be convinced therefore of the pleasure it should convey, at least to "understand" it (if not to read it).

The Tyranny of Rationalism

This attempt on the part of Europeans to reflect on the nature of beauty spills over into their experienced culture, and a further consequence is the intellectualization of the artistic experience. In European culture "art" becomes the domain of the intellectual elite, because it is they (in the tradition of Plato's *Symposium* and Aristotle's *Poetics*) who determine the criteria of its perfection; it is they who say what its attributes should and should not be. The ordinary participant in the culture does not have access to, nor is he considered capable of enjoying, "true" art. What he does enjoy is not considered to be "art"; nor is it "beautiful." Again we return to Platonic definitions and find the precedent for a rationalistic aesthetic. For "beauty," as well as the "good," is identified with the "true." All are apprehended by the same method. The position relegated to the emotional experience is a low one. It is "reason" that triumphs.

As the result Europeans are taught to approach the aesthetic experience through analysis. They objectify the experience; they tear it apart; they verbalize it, incessantly, and teach and are taught that in this way they come to understand the experience more—to better appreciate it. Yet for most people it is the sensually immediate and not the intellectually mediated that gives pleasure, that evokes emotional response. The intensification of this tendency leads to the actual replacement of the authentic emotional sensitivity with an artificial intellectual aesthetic; and people lose the ability to respond emotionally and to create that to which others can, indeed, respond. This is a consequence of the cultural value and *utamawazo* that splits human faculties into the "rational" and "emotional," and then dictates that the emotional be controlled, "weeded" out, ignored if possible—its existence being recognized only because the European begrudgingly acknowledges that the "human" is afterall part "animal."

But very different philosophical premises inform the art forms of other cultures and the ideas about the aesthetics they generate. The awakening of the human spirit in emotional communion with the sacred, however that may be defined, is its primary goal. There are several authors worth mentioning whose comparisons help to elucidate some of the characteristic features of the European aesthetic experience.

Willie Abraham says of the Akan art form:

> . . . they expressed their philosophico-religious ideas through art, through the timeless, immemorial, silent, and elemental power so characteristic of African traditional art. Indeed this is the main reason why it was not lifelike in a representational sense. Forms had to be distorted. In art there was a moral-philosophical preoccupation which led it to portray forces of the world, and to portray a force it was essential that it should not be treated like something assimilated, and consequently like something overcome, as the rendering of it in life-like figures would have been.[4]

In the African view of the human, the emotional-spiritual and the rational-material are inextricably bound together, and if anything, it is a human being's spirituality that defines her as human, providing the context within which she is able to create art as well as technology. Such a view leads to a very different emphasis in artistic expression. The emotional identification with, and participation in, the art form by the person and the community are primary values that help to determine its shape. In this way the form itself becomes less of an "object." In European culture the tendency and emphasis are much the opposite. While artists may still attempt to evoke certain isolated emotional responses from their audiences, these responses theoretically have very little "cultural" or "moral" significance, and the entire experience from the creation of the *objet d'art* to its presentation is much more "individualized." The artist creates out of his own particular response to his environment, and his work is appreciated by separate and distinct "individuals," who reach into their distinct experiences for whatever identification they can find.

As Abraham says, this is the mark of a "secular art." What the culture as a whole does for the individuals involved is to suggest that they "objectify" their experience, isolate the "object," and approach it analytically. That is really the only preparation they are given by their cultural experience. And so the circle of people who participate in this exchange for pleasure (who derive pleasure from it) is very small. The aesthetic sense of the rest is aroused by that which is not "art," and they have no "taste," or so their culture says. Abraham's distinction between "secular" and sacred or "moral art" is very significant, and the European has always approached the art of other cultures as though it were meant to be as "amoral" as his own. Abraham says,

> When critics like Gombrich say that the African artists were incapable of realistic presentation, they quite miss the point of African art. If they seek life-like representation, they should turn to secular art, the art which was produced for decorative purposes or the purposes of records, rather than moral art, the art whose inspiration is the intuition of a world force.[4]

Awoonor says that African art expresses the relationship between humans and the Creator. It expresses our will and wishes to the Creator; is "an assertation of (our) own temporality as a *living* being, and more importantly, an articulate statement of that spirituality through a cyclic order within (our) cosmos."[5] Art (carvings) at shrines are instruments that affirm the divine link between us and our Creator.[6]

In earlier European development artistic expression is also intimately bound to religious understanding. This interrelationship reaches its height in the medieval period, though theorists debate as to the degree of secular humanism and religiousity in Renaissance art. In earlier periods there is even a strong communal aspect to musical creations. But with the advent of scientism, that is, the triumph of scientific-rationalism, initiated by Bacon and others, the assault on the remaining vestiges of the sacred and the communal begins. What is emphasized in this discussion are the tendencies in the European aesthetic experience that began to emerge with Abelard and expanded throughout the Renaissance, reaching dominance by the Enlightenment. (DaVinci's misgivings about the separation from and ascendence of science over its spiritual grounding did not have the cultural backing to resist the ideological momentum of the European *asili.*) European art, already heavily rationalistic, was to become secular, individualized, and elitist.

The more intellectual, individualized, and individual art became in the West, the more technical it became. The artist regarded his work as an object to be made technically perfect. That is, his ideas of perfection were much more influenced by the concept of technical and mechanical perfection than in other cultures, and this is primarily the way in which the European artist is presently shaped by his culture; these are the models with which he is presented and he perceives them "rationalistically."

Sorokin says that as European art searches for diversity and ever-increasing variety, it loses "all harmony, unity and balance," which become "submerged in an ocean of incoherency and chaos." These trends, he continues, lead to an emphasis on the technical means of production rather than the art itself. These tools become increasingly complicated ends in themselves.[7]

In his view, European art becomes increasingly "a commodity manufactured for the market" tending toward the vulgar. We should point out that the interesting contradiction in European culture is that its art may be commercially inspired ("the artist must live, after all"), geared to consumption, inspired by the desire for recognition, and at the same time remain an elitist form; that is, essentially separated from the people, because the art, like the culture, creates (controls) the people, rather than the reverse. According to Sorokin, in the artist's tendency to disregard religious and moral values, the art itself

> comes to be more and more divorced from truly cultural values and turns into an empty art known euphemistically as "art for art's sake," at once amoral, nonreligious, and nonsocial, and often *antimoral, antireligious,* and *antisocial.*[8]

This "amorality" is directly connected to the "nonsocial" character of European art. It is symptomatic of the character of the culture and can be traced from Platonic misconception, as evidenced in Havelock's work in praise of Platonic epistemology. In Havelock's view it was a "discovery" and an "advance" when the Greeks were "able" to conceive of the individual psyche as the seat of rationally determined moral judgements. But there can be no such thing as a morality lodged primarily by or initiated in the "individual." "Reason," if it is to be distinguished from emotion and feeling, is sorely insufficient to dictate "human" moral behavior. The source of human morality must necessarily be in the interaction of human beings. It must be communal, which, more than "social," implies a joining of persons. This basic fact of human existence is of primary importance in other cultures and informs their modes of organization. The lack of authentic community, i.e., the substitution of the social for the communal, accounts for much of the atrophied development of the West. Art that is noncommunal cannot be moral, and a rationally, individually conceived "ethic" is humanly, even personally, inadequate.

Daiseti Suzuki makes some observations on the comparison of European and Buddhist symbolism that help to further delineate the nature of the European aesthetic. He presents a *haiku* by an eighteenth century Japanese poet, Basho, and discusses its poetic and philosophical significance. The *haiku* form contrasts dramatically with European verbal art forms, because of its extreme simplicity and directness of intent.

> Oh! Old Pond!
> A frog leaps in,
> The water's sound!

Of this *haiku* Suzuki says the following,

> Basho was no other than the frog when he heard the sound of the water caused by its leaping. The leaping, the sound, the frog, and the pond and Basho were all in one and one in all. There was an absolute totality; that is, an absolute identity, or to use Buddhist terminology a perfect state of emptiness (i.e. *Sunyata*) or suchness (i.e. Tathata).[9]

This sense of identity is most difficult for those nurtured in European culture to comprehend, because the culture dictates the necessity for experience to be continually mediated through concepts, through "the word," and it must be analytically absorbed. And so, it is difficult to imagine how Kant's "Analytic" or Aristotle's *Poetics* could relate to the *haiku*, for just as the mode of *haiku* reflects the principles of Buddhist philosophy, the understanding and approach of these philosophers reflects the nature of the European *utamawazo*. It follows, then, that the European idea of "symbol" is not adequate to explain Buddhist symbolism. Suzuki continues,

> ...do we call "the old pond" or the water's sound or the leaping frog a symbol for ultimate reality? In Buddhist philosophy there is nothing behind the old pond, because it is complete in itself and does not point to anything behind or beyond or outside itself. The old

pond (or the water or the frog) itself is reality. . . .

Buddhist symbolism would. . .declare that everything is symbolic, it carries meaning with it, it has values of its own, it exists by its own right pointing to no reality other than itself.[10]

But lineal, causal, purposive thought presupposes a relation between "objects," and a reality that is "other than" and "outside of," them. Since this is characteristic of European ontology, it effects European art. Wade Nobles characterizes the African "symbolic method" as involving a "transformation-synchronistic-analogic modality," while the contemporary European cultural understanding of "symbol" is as a "representational-sequential-analytical" mode.[11]

Suzuki describes the feeling of exaltation that comes from identification with the pond and simultaneously with the universe itself. But in the European experience, exaltation is achieved from feelings of "control over" a passive object-and separation from it. For this reason, there is no precedent in the European tradition for identification with other people; that is, the culture does not support such identification. Suzuki points out that like *haiku,* which fixes on the immediate rather than the mediated experience,

Zen Buddhism avoids generalization and abstraction. . . . To Buddhists, being is meaning. Being and meaning are one and not separate; the separation or bifurcation comes from intellection, and intellection distorts the suchness of things.[12]

The habit of analysis does not make room for this kind of apprehension, and the predominance of the analytic mode in the European experience has all but eliminated the sensitivity to immediately perceivable beauty and its definition. It is the European conviction that an experience of art must be difficult; that profundity is only comprehended through intellectual struggle.

Willie Abraham says,

The amount of get up, preparation and education which the modern European mind requires to resuscitate its sense of *rapport* with the beautiful and the sublime, the arid technicalities of his sophistication is artificial sensitivity. It is only when sensitivity is natural that it is immediate, effortless, picturesque, non-nostalgic, and intuitive. The sophisticated sensitivity must tear apart what it contemplates. It is analytic inquisitive, carving-knife sensitivity.[13]

This analytical mental habit results in a culturally problematical aesthetic. The creation of a reflective, scientific aesthetic—superficial and nonauthentic from the point of view of the human/emotional— establishes a quasiseparation between an elitist art form and a "popular" one. But also a division is made—of which the members of the culture themselves are not aware—between a consciously imitated or normative aesthetic, operating most successfully among the intellectualist minority, and a most often unconscious aesthetic common to Europeans in general. The latter is, in my view, the more properly speaking "European aesthetic" in the sense that it embodies the European standards of beauty and the feelings, styles, modes in which the members of the culture participate pleasurably.

The dichotomy between these two senses is culturally unproductive and stultifying, and brings us to another effect of this symptomatic distinction; the factors that work to promote a lack of creativity and sterility in European art. These are cultural factors that the creative European artist must overcome. Art divorced from spirituality is culturally debilitating. Secular art is not natural, but artificial, and the European artist is under immense pressure to perform an all but impossible task: She must create an object of beauty for a passive audience whose aesthetic sense must be aroused, yet an audience with whom she has shared nothing but the unaesthetic experience of European culture—a culture that has excelled in its ability to separate her from the very people to whom she must present her work. She shares nothing that would serve as an experiential base through which she and her audience can communicate emotion. Armstrong says, "The individual consciousness must define itself in the only way it can, which is to say in opposition to all others."[14] This is the result of an epistemology (*utamawazo*) that isolates the knowing self as a definition of "superior" evolved human consciousness. What the artist and the other members of the culture *do* share, however, is commitment to the affirmation of the superiority of their culture *vis-à-vis* other cultures. On an unconscious level the European artist validates these feelings, satisfies these needs.

On a conscious level European audiences must constantly speculate about the artists' source of inspiration and guess at her intention; her "message." "What is she trying to say?" is the question heard at a New York art gallery. The artist is conceived of as a person who, out of his own unique and individual experience and agony, joy and suffering, seeks to express himself to moral and cultural strangers. It is no wonder that in the West, art appears to have no place in life; it seems to be carried on as an adjunctive activity as though it does not affect the vast majority of Europeans. It does however: Subliminally, it effects the European national consciousness. There is a sense in which "art" could cease to exist, and the average European would only become aware of its demise if it were chronicled in the newspapers. There is another sense in which European art serves as the scaffolding of the nationalistic psyche. Aziza Gibson Hunter calls it "the invisible clothing of the West."[15] This elite art and popular art have different, but related, purposes.

But art has a radically different significance in non-European cultures, where it is most often intimately bound with the sacralized pattern and existence of the total lifeways of the group. Because of this critical difference, the confrontation between the European and non-European art is a phenomenon of culture shock. The European is either blinded by his cultural chauvinism to the parochial nature of his own aesthetic sense, and so cannot appreciate the profundity of non-European forms; or, the European artist, his creativity strangled by a dying culture, is forced to draw inspiration outside of that culture from these same non-European forms. Robert Goldwater says,

> As artists who felt their own native traditions weakened and increasingly meaningless who were convinced that the necessary renewal could not come about by continuing, but only beginning again—by a rebirth; as artists who wished to cast off Western devotion to appearances and to devote themselves to realities; as artists who wanted to strip away the surface in order to reveal the essentials, they turned to the primitive. The primitive could set them an example, could show them how to start anew. Because it was itself an art of power and conviction it would aid them to create their own meaningful art.[16]

Goldwater, of course, is careful to say that he is not using the term "primitive" in a pejorative sense, and that in this use it connotes something that the European artists considered to be positive. The term is most often essentially valuative, however, because it usually connotes a kind of temporal "incongruity," from a Eurocentric perspective. What Goldwater does not say is that the European artists, impressed with African and other non-European forms, used them as a new source of energy for the validation of their own cultural chauvinism. Like the Greeks, they stole, and then used what they stole to convince others of their superiority.

An Aesthetic of Control

Perhaps there is no better form of artistic expression than that of music to demonstrate the peculiar dynamics of the European aesthetic. The European mind responded to music in precisely the same way as it responded to every kind of phenomenon with which it was presented. Music was analyzed, dissected, "studied" and translated into the language of mathematics. It was written down, and then it could be "read" as one would read a mathematical equation. And true to the pattern of European development, the intellectuals who created this new music were successful in introducing it into the culture as a whole because the culture itself was predisposed to value such an approach. With writing comes control, and with control, for Europeans, comes power. This is the nature of the *utamaroho*. This obviously is far more aesthetically pleasing to them than the creativity and spontaneity that results from the interaction between human emotion and the medium of music. In the West, an artist of African descent who has somehow miraculously inherited the genius of her culture, via her "ancestral memory," and plays without ever having studied the tools of the European, is an embarrassment. It is like European science being confronted by the astronomical knowledge of the Dogon people. It exists, but it shouldn't!

Centuries of tradition of the mathematization and rationalization of music have caused the European to forget its origin and how it is produced naturally—as opposed to synthetically (the mere imitation and description of music). Europeans created neither the first music nor the first musical instruments; they found them and made them objects of study. Because there was only one way in which they could understand this music with which they were confronted, they analyzed it, looking for "laws" of harmony, and melodic relationships, yet unable to hear / feel / comprehend the cosmic manifestation of sound. (Even in the Middle Ages, music was the study of harmonics and proportion and, as such, was related to mathematics; (in an academic-technical, not a cosmic-metaphysical sense); Augustine's *De Musica* was the standard textbook.) The Europeans then created a facscimile and style in which they excelled; i.e., a style that expressed all the power and control of the European aesthetic and value. They created the symphony—a technical and organizational masterpiece, the epitome of specialization in performance.

Their inventiveness, their uniqueness, their *utamaroho* expressed itself primarily within their "classical" dimension; the other expressions of music in European culture are primarily borrowed forms, adaptations, and imitations. The accomplishment of the symphony should not have caused Europeans to forget the origins of musical expression nor the plethora of differing styles more creative and spontaneous, which had demonstrated a greater elemental genius than the symphonic form, with its emphasis on structure. With this in mind the existence of the African musician who plays "by ear" is only a "wonder" in that it is perhaps one of the suprarational "facts" of human existence.

Again, it is the technical aspect of the craft that is emphasized in the European tradition, and as the technical order intensifies, its musical instruments become more and more mechanical, electronic, synthetic, and unnatural. Those who play them become better and better technicians, but their compositions would be just as mechanical, synthetic, and uninspiring as the instruments on which they were played if it were not for the utilization of the musical creativity and awareness of the African experience. In America innovation in music, dance, and language is influenced by African culture through the contribution of the Africans who live there. This influence is in turn exported to the larger European community. European culture can prepare an individual for the technical mastery of European musical instruments and machines, and is able to train a small minority to perform the music it has created—commonly referred to as "classical," "long-hair," or "good" music, commonly referred to among Africans in America as "dead" music. But European culture must rely on the creativity inspired by the African musical and expressive genius for the music and dance that most of its members enjoy. This circumstance is directly related to the nature and ideology of the culture and to the radical differences between the two *utamarohos*.

In Ortiz Walton's comparison of the African and Western aesthetics in music, he points to some of the trends in Western cultural history that account for the predominant mode of European music. He says that written music cannot be considered improvisation. We see that in the European's attempt to plan and predict, he has lost the opportunity to develop the art of improvisation and spontaneity on which a vibrant and creative musical expression depends. European music, says Walton, "became highly rationalized with the Greeks." (It will be remembered that Plato associates music with a despiritualized mathematics; both should be an important aspect of the education of the Guardians, because they help to encourage and develop the "proper mental habits.") Later the Church further "rationalized" music in its attempt to control its content. He says that a system of notation began in the West with the Greek idea of *ethoi,* "which has been added onto in the following centuries, casting western music into a rigid, unalterable, fixed phenomenon."[17] Walton adds that the makers of European instruments reflected the European predilection for rationalization in

> . . . a new technology of tempered instruments. . . . Valveless horns resembling their African prototypes, and keyless woodwind instruments, were replaced by the highly rationalized and mechanical keys and valves. It is difficult to comprehend these developments in the West except as a passion for the rational. . . .
>
> The order of the auditory world had now been transformed into a visual, mechanical, and predictive phenomenon. Now all a player had to do was look at the music and put the finger a certain place and out would come the sound that had been conceived long before in somebody's head.[18]

Max Weber talks about "rationality" in the development of Western, European music:

> rational harmonious music, both counterpoint and harmony, formation of the tone material on the basis of three triads with the harmonic third; our chromatics and enharmonics, not interpreted in terms of space, but, since the Renaissance, of harmony; our orchestra, with its string quartet as a nucleus, and the organization of ensembles of wind instruments; our bass accompaniment; our system of notation, which has made possible the composition and production of modern musical works, and thus their very survival, as a means to all these, our fundamental instruments, the organ, piano, violin, etc.; all those things are known only in the Occident, although programme music, tone poetry, alteration of tones and chromatics, have existed in various musical traditions as a means of expression.[19]

Though Weber uses this principle of rationality to make claim to the "superiority" and "universality" of Western forms, he, according to Walton, indicates, as well, his own ambivalence towards the ultimate effect of the obsessive rationalism of Western culture:

> Weber concluded that only in Western music is the drive toward rationalism a predominant concern. And his findings resulted in what became, for him, a central question: Why does efficiency of means in relation to ends (Weber's definition of rationalism) result in a spirit of "disenchantment with life"—a state of being where life (or death) has no meaning.[20]

While in the West the tendency was for this "written," controlled music to become elitist and for a passive audience to be "confronted" with a performance, in Africa the cultural priorities and values demanded a communal musical form in which there was no real separation between "performer" and "audience": a participatory experience for everyone involved. Walton says,

> Contrasted with the music-for-the-elite philosophy prevalent in the West, African music retained its functional and collective characteristics. The element of improvisation was developed rather than abandoned, and it found its way into Black music in this country. Similarly, the unifying element of audience participation was also retained.[21]

There were most certainly forms of European music designed for communal participation (sometimes hundreds of singing voices walking through the European countryside), at earlier stages in European development. But the *asili* was such that this form would soon be eclipsed by those that suited an *utamaroho* craving power and an *utamawazo* constructing mechanisms of control. Communal and participatory music/art forms would be discouraged until they all but disappeared, since they did not reflect the ideological matrix/thrust of the culture. They were not "European" enough.

The emphasis on communal participation in African music gave rise to antiphony or the "call-response," "question-answer" form that has carried over into the musical creations of Africans in the Americas, as Walton points out. Whereas control, technical precision, and theoretical complexities are valued in European classical music, rhythm and tonal variation are primary concerns in African music, and the symphony therefore has limited aesthetic potential to the African ear.* What few have understood, however, is that the African predilection for rhythm in its various complexities is not happenstance, but is intimately bound to African melanated bio-chemistry and to the cosmic nature of the African world-view.[22]

It is only through contrast with other art forms that the peculiarity and uniqueness of the European aesthetic is made clear. This suggestion of contrast is compelling in an ethnology of the culture, in the attempt to counteract successful European nationalism that projects European ideology in the form of universals, as opposed to European choice and particularism. The development of a "science" of aesthetics in the West only helps to confuse the issue, and in the

---

* This point is made by Joseph Okpaku in *New African Literature,* Vol. I, ed. Okpaku, New York: Thomas Crowell, Apollo Edition, 1970, p. 18.

main it has been the particularly European brand of cultural nationalism that allowed European critics to "evaluate" African and other
forms of non-European art. Joseph Okpaku offers us a prime example
of the inevitable Eurocentricism that results from this presumptive
posture. He quotes from Jones-Quartey, who is commenting on an
event in which an African audience found a Western tragedy amusing. Jones-Quartey says that Africans have a "misconception of meaning," and

> that drama of any genre is pure entertainment (to Africans) and
> nothing else. But, secondly, and at a deeper level still, it is also pos-
> sible that Africans are unwilling to isolate, or incapable of isolating,
> the one element of death or disaster from their trivial concept of
> existence as consisting of the dead, the living, and the unborn and
> treating this element separately or differently.[23]

Indeed, the "misconceptions" of self-appointed European critics
of non-European aesthetic conceptions are, unfortunately, not usually
so obvious as the above example. The writer's characterization of the
African conception of death as "trivial" would be simply amusing if
such judgements were not so successfully supported by the apparatus of European imperialism.

In his article "Afro-American Ritual Drama," Carlton Molette
makes some perceptive observations on the European aesthetic by
way of comparison. Molette points out that mimesis or imitation and
mimicry are aesthetically pleasing to the African, while the European
observer will often complain of what he calls "monotony." Plato's
attitude toward "mimesis" is that it is an aspect of that natural human
weakness that must be expelled from the official media of the State.
For the European the "maintenance of reality" is crucial, while in
African ritualism the form "is of much greater importance." As with
the musical experience, the European audience is passive, while the
African objective is total participation of the group. All of these factors, says Molette, are operative in the African-American church service, which he identifies as "ritual drama." "The tradition. . . .aims at
creating. . . an illusion of reality of time, place and character other
than the actual one."[24] African ritual drama creates the "eternal
moment" that transcends ordinary time, joining the categories of time
and place (*hantu*) into a single boundless, experience of spiritual communion: the ultimate meaningful reality.[25]

And the lack of subjective identification that characterizes the
European *utamawazo*, which Havelock applauds, can be seen as being
dysfunctional to artistic expression and appreciation, as it prevents

or limits the emotional involvement of the audience. The following comment of Molette reinforces our observations concerning the rationalistic conception of the human inherited from Plato and Christian theology:

> The Afro-American aesthetic does not operate on the characteris- •
> tically Euro-American assumption that all human behavior is either
> rationally motivated, resulting in elevated behavior, or emotionally
> motivated, resulting in base behavior. The Afro-American aesthetic
> places a very high value upon emotionally motivated behavior; or
> another term that might be used to describe it, I think more accu-
> rately, would be spiritually motivated behavior.[24]

Molette is accurate in his use of the term "spiritual" here, because it is this understanding of spirituality that is lacking and/or ignored in the European aesthetic and mythoform, especially in the last two hundred years. This is due not only to the rationalistic conception of the human psyche or "soul" but also to the confused European conception of "art-for-art's sake"—an idea predicated on the assumption that there is value in separating the function of art from the life-blood of the group. Molette counters this with an outline of the purposes of Afro-American ritual drama. "One of these purposes is to celebrate the affirmation of a sense of community, a feeling of togetherness. . . based upon the assumption that *we who are gathered here to participate in this event are and belong together.*" (Molette's italics.) This he says is frequently emphasized through physical contact, like holding hands. Euro-American forms, on the other hand, emphasize the individual, his uniqueness and differentness. The individual, then, is constantly aware of himself as "individualized" (Diamond's term) and cannot easily perceive the group (which, therefore, often becomes "non-existent" for him). He perceives himself as an "observer," distinct from that which he observes. But "a purpose of Black ritual drama is to create a total spiritual involvement" in the event. "Another purpose of Black ritual drama is to serve some functional, useful purpose. . .a funeral ritual is supposed to have a certain specific useful future effect upon the soul of the deceased brother or sister."[26]

This brings us again to the critical question of the cultural significance of European art. European art forms have an avowed purpose. Their goal is to represent a "universal," "abstract," and "eternal truth" (European truth). They are not designed to create an immediate cultural effect; and they are most definitely not inspired by a conception of oneness or communal feeling of the group. For, we are told, the European artist creates "art for art's sake." She is able to break out of the socio-cultural limitations and definitions of the creative experience and therefore produces art that has no other purpose than that of expressing the artist's own individual ego. This, we are told, is "progress," just as Havelock regards the Greek conception of "knowledge" as a "discovery" leading to intellectual "advance."

But this formulation is both intellectually and emotionally unimpressive. It is meaningless, incomprehensible, and confusing. Is it any wonder that elite art produced under the guidance of such a philosophy fails to reach the major portion of the culture, often has no cultural significance other than material power and tends toward spiritual demise? The "fine arts" in the West tend to become merely intellectual exercises. "Art for art's sake" is peculiarly European and should be rejected as a critical standard in other cultures. Yet this very peculiar misconception has been one of the main tools used by Europeans in their criticism of non-European art. Sometimes surrounded by the terminology of a contradictory and superficially restrictive "universalism," it becomes difficult to realize the severity of European distortion and self-deception. In regard to "the idea of art," René Wassing, in the book *African Art* says: "Fundamentally it is a European idea developed in the mental climate of European philosophy and applied to the expression of European culture."[27]

Universalism, so called by the European, is actually very particular, and these statements serve as evidence of the nature of the peculiar European *utamaroho*. Evidently, it never occurs to Wassing that he is talking about the *European* "idea of art" or that that idea used in the context of African art might be extremely misleading, to say the least. What are the indications that an idea of art exists in a culture? Its verbal documentation; its systematization; its translation into European philosophical terminology; its "objectification" or the attempt to isolate it from other aspects of culture, in the European habit, as with what is regarded by them as "religion?" This is a manifestation of the same ethos, displayed by Placide Tempels, who wishes to "teach" the Africans their own concept of being. It would be so much more helpful if "objective," "open-minded" would-be culturalists like Wassing would put more effort into an explication of their own conceptions. (A few years ago I had occasion to attend a Haitian Art exhibit, at which the guest speaker [a European "expert" on Haitian Art] informed us that he was delighted to see this display, because when he first started going to Haiti, "there was no such thing as Haitian Art"; that he had in fact brought the idea to the Haitians.)

Of Africans and their art, Wassing says:

It must. . . be remembered that the artist did not consciously set out to create a work of art. They considered a piece a success if it ful-filled the task set, a task which was primarily functional. Whatever function a piece might have—economic, magical or religious—the aesthetic principle never became an end in itself, in the manner of "art for art's sake." Aesthetic appreciation and criticism of the mate-rial culture of Africa is a western invention founded on a discovery made not long before, the development of which runs parallel with the developing concept of art in western history.[27]

It is in statements about other cultures that Europeans reveal themselves most and the limitations of their own forms of thought. Wassing's statement says a bit about African culture, while it inad-vertently reveals much about the difficulties inherent in the European concept of art. Artistic creation tends to become identified with tech-nical awareness. There is no doubt that the traditional African artist has set out to carve the most powerful ancestral stool or ceremonial mask that will best capture the nature of the spirit it is to express. His goal is both aesthetic and functional, and because the experience of beauty is intimately bound up with the manipulation of force or com-munication with the sacred, or gift-exchange, it is not less valid. Indeed, this is a more existentially real and spiritual understanding of "beauty." If he were not writing for a European audience, Wassing would have to be prepared to defend a conception of beauty that is divorced from life; *that* is what is problematical. But he, in charac-teristic European fashion, has confused the abstraction with the expe-rience. And it is easy for him first to be misled and then to mislead; because, in European logic, first Europeans invent a concept, method, or "creed," then treat it as a "discovery" about the nature of the uni-verse—something everyone should know and utilize. The idea of "art for art's sake" is not only a European aberration with little relevance outside of the European context, but it is of limited value within the culture itself and may indeed be symptomatic of a lack of creativity, spirituality, and vitality in much of European art.

Traditionally, the European discussion is not of "the European aesthetic" but of "Aesthetics," and the discussants claim to be delin-eating the necessary rules and dynamics of a universal "science" of the beautiful. While Kant can say, on the one hand, that it is fruitless to seek a "universal criterion of the beautiful," he can, at the same time, devote seemingly boundless intellectual energy to a "pure judge-ment" and "analytic of the Beautiful." But such philosophical and ana-lytical discussions are always concerned with the consciously, intellectualistic "aesthetic" of the European. The generally unconscious or less conscious, nonintellectual aesthetic definitions and the images that appeal emotionally to the Europeans rarely surface in their academically oriented discussions of "Aesthetics."

To get at these aspects of the contemporary European aesthetic one must look at what comes out of Hollywood, Madison Avenue, children's picture books, magazines, imagery in ordinary language usage, and "fairy tales"—media that abound with cultural symbols (religious paintings, novels, comic books, and the like), the symbols of "popular art" and of educational materials, and what is left of a European religious cosmology. If we take the "European aesthetic" to include that which is pleasing to Europeans, then we would have to include certain "feelings" with regard to other people, as well as certain forms of thought.

The European receives pleasure from a feeling of control over other people; this feeling is extended to the most "ordinary" participant in the culture through her identification with the European hegemony. Power is aesthetically experienced in the ability to manipulate others, and this desire has been culturally sustained and generated perhaps since the "Indo-European" experience. It is so deeply a part of the European aesthetic that even those who consider themselves to be free of the excesses and distortions of European chauvinism, critics of American foreign policy for instance, are not prepared to face the consequences of a dramatic depreciation in European power.

The Western aesthetic is, in this sense, tied to the European *utamaroho* (need for supremacy) and European ethic. And the European's image of himself as the "adventurer-discoverer" who continually seeks new lands, peoples, and resources to conquer—all of this is emotionally pleasing to him. Similarly, as both William James and Arthur Lovejoy have pointed out, rationalism, the mode of abstraction, and the "idea of progress" and "evolutionism" are all aesthetically and emotionally satisfying to the European mind. They seem to fit. They are harmonious with the Western conceptions of the universe and are dictated by the *asili* of the culture.

European art is oppositional, developed through what Armstrong calls "a dialectic of polarities." In his view, European art, therefore, can be understood as a series of competitions based on contrasts. "There are those arts which compete for gravity, those that compete with emptiness, and those that compete with silence."[28] Here again is the *asili* of the culture revealing itself; the seed/germ that while unfolding dictates the style of each modality. Each contributing to ensure the over-all organization of a culture dictated by a single-set of objectives, working to satisfy the insatiable *utamaroho*.

Through separation the self is isolated, opposed to "other," and placed into a competitive relationship. The one who controls most wins. It pays to be aggressive.

"White," "Good," and "Beautiful"

The "whiteness" of the European aesthetic may be consciously ignored by the European intellectual, but nevertheless it permeates the culture and reaches her as well. Jesus, the symbol of perfection for the European Christian, is reinterpreted as white and often with blond hair, and similarly every symbol of purity is white, all innocence is blond youth hence the expression "fair-haired boy." Even the ideal (but unattainable) sex object is blond. In simplistic depictions, villains are dark haired, mustached, unshaven, and wear black. And, of course, the other physical attributes associated with the Caucasian race are part of the European aesthetic. These images are all visible on any Saturday morning cartoon feast offered by American television. In *The Passing of the Great Race,* Madison Grant supports this observation:

> . . . in Celtic legend as in the Graeco-Roman and medieval romances, prince and princess are always fair, a fact rather indicating that the mass of the people were brunet [sic] at the time when the legends were taking shape. In fact, "fair" is a synonym for beauty.

> The Gods of Olympus were almost all described as blond, and it would be difficult to imagine a Greek artist painting a brunet [sic] Venus. In Church pictures all angels are blond, while the denizens of the lower regions revel in deep brunetness. "Non Angli sed angeli," remarked Pope Gregory when he first saw Saxon children exposed for sale in the Roman slave-mart.

> In depicting the crucifixion no artist hesitates to make the two thieves brunet [sic] in contrast to the blond Savior. This is something more than a convention, as such quasi-authentic traditions as we have of our Lord strongly suggest Nordic, possibly Greek, physical and moral attributes.[29]

But Grant's view only emphasizes the fact that mythical reality is so much more important than secular history, since Jesus would have to have been a mutant to be blond and blue-eyed, given his place of origin.

The European media demonstrates this aspect of the European aesthetic well, but it is in the literature of avowed white nationalism that the aesthetic is blatantly expressed. Within the geographical confines of "new Europe" it has been the person of African descent who has done most to expose this aspect of the European aesthetic, as she came to recognize it as a tool that had kept her psychologically and ideologically locked into the role of pawn for the European *utamaroho;* if white was "right" and good, then she must be wrong and very, very bad.

Addison Gayle, Jr. traces the genesis of the idea of white as "good" and of black as its opposite in European literature. These are the value symbols of European culture. With Plato, says Gayle, comes the imagery of the dark cave of ignorance as opposed to the "light" of knowledge. The lower (bad) as opposed to the upper (good) regions. Christian symbolism intensified this imagery, and in it, whiteness as value becomes expressly stated. Chaucer, Petrarch, and other writers of the Middle Ages "established their dichotomies as a result of the influence of Neo-Platonism and Christianity."[30] Gayle writes about the white (beautiful, good)/black (ugly, bad) dichotomy of the English "morality plays." White, in the syntax of the European aesthetic, also represents the universal, while black is parochial. And of course European Christianity tells us that white represents purity, while blackness is sin. The "dark ages" are Europe's "unproductive" years. "Dark period" refers to the melancholia of Gothic novels, Gayle tells us, and in the eighteenth century English novel the symbolism became directly translated into racial and cultural terminology. Gayle writes:

> *Robinson Crusoe* was published at a historically significant time. In the year 1719, the English had all but completed their colonization of Africa. The slave trade in America was on its way to becoming a booming industry; in Africa, Black people were enslaved mentally as well as physically by such strange bedfellows as criminals, businessmen, and Christians. In the social and political spheres, a rationale was needed and help came from the artist—in this case, the novelist—in the form of *Robinson Crusoe*. In the novel, Defoe brings together both Christian and Platonic symbolism, sharpening the dichotomy between light and dark on the one hand, while on the other establishing a criterion for the inferiority of Black people as opposed to the superiority of white.

> One needed only compare Crusoe with Friday to validate both of these statements. Crusoe is majestic, wise, white and a colonialist; Friday is savage, ignorant, black and a colonial. Therefore, Crusoe the colonialist has a double task. On the one hand he must transform the island (Africa—unproductive, barren, dead) into a little England (prosperous, life-giving, fertile), and he must recreate Friday in his own image, thus bringing him as close to being an

Englishman as possible. At the end of the novel, Crusoe has accomplished both undertakings; the island is a replica of "mother England"; and Friday has been transformed into a white man, now capable of immigrating to the lands of the gods.[31]

It would be difficult to exaggerate the degree to which the aesthetic Gayle describes here permeates the culture. A continual pressure exerts itself upon the psyche of a "nonwhite" person living within the ubiquitous confines of the West to "remold," "refashion," "paint," "refine" herself in conformity with this European aesthetical image of what a human being should be. The pressures begin at birth and outlive the person, often breaking her spirit long before her physical demise. This aspect of the European aesthetic is a deadly weapon at the service of the need to dominate and destroy. So deep is the wound it inflicts that in Senegal, West Africa, women, some of the most beautiful in the world, burn and disfigure their rich, smooth, melanic, ebony skin with lye in the attempt to make it white. Since the *Maafa,*[32] it is only very recently, particularly within the African community in North America, that an alternative and more culturally valid aesthetic has been presented to "non-Western," "nonwhite" peoples to emulate and to value.

Gayle refers to the work of Hinton Helper, a European-American chauvinist writing in 1867, who contributed explicitly to the establishment and support of the "white aesthetic" in America. In Gayle's opinion, Helper's work was influential in presenting "the cultural and social symbols of inferiority under which Blacks have labored."

> Helper intended, as he states frankly in his preface, "to write the negro out of America." In the headings of the two major chapters of the book, the whole symbolic apparatus of the white aesthetic handed down from Plato to America is graphically revealed: the heading of one chapter reads: "White: A Thing of Life, Health, and Beauty."

> Under the first heading, Helper argues that the color black "has always been associated with the sinister things such as mourning, the devil, the darkness of night." Under the second, "White has always been associated with the light of day, divine transfiguration, the beneficent moon and stars. . . the fair complexion of romantic ladies, the costumes of Romans and angels, and the white of the American flag so beautifully combined with blue and red without ever a touch of the black that has been for the flag of pirates."[33]

Joel Kovel sums it up this way, "THE WEST IS A WHITE CIVILIZA-

TION; no other civilization has made that claim. White emblemizes purity, but purity implies a purification, a removing of impurities. . . it is upon this symbol of whiteness that the psychohistory of our racism rests."[34]

These comments present a view of the usually "unconscious" or "nonreflective" sense of the European aesthetic; that which in some senses would be referred to as the affective European idea of beauty. The theme of "whiteness" as a value in European cultural history will occur repeatedly as we discuss further aspects of the European *utamaroho*.

We have suggested that, in addition to the quality of whiteness and the mental habits of rationalism, the experience and ideas of "power," "control," and manipulation are aesthetically pleasing to the Europeans in a way that does not affect the *utamaroho* of others. These are apparently the uncontrollable aspects of the European cultural aesthetic. The desire to relate to other people in this way is insatiable for Europeans. They can never have enough power; they can never control enough objects. The pleasure derived from power and control determines their behavior to an inordinate degree, and it is expressed in their fantasies via the movie industry and various other media.

Giovanni Gentile observes precisely this element of the European aesthetic, but, as is usually the case with Europeans, he conveniently universalizes the particular through the concept of "modernity." Yet the spurious universalistic ideas that Gentile presents need not be emulated by other cultures.

> The most striking difference between ancient and modern times [is that] the reality that now begins to attract men's minds, and to arouse their main interest, is no longer the reality which they find in the world but that which they create within it. Man begins to feel a power capable of confronting and opposing nature; his independence and creative energy are asserted though not yet proved. Man's power and virtue are seen as capable of winning over fortune and all those events on which he has no control and which constitute his nature. This human energy is most evident and most striking in art and literature, in which man fancies an inner world of his own where he can enclose himself and reign as absolute master.[35]

The Myth of a Universal Aesthetic

The European philosophical statement of aesthetics acts to support European cultural imperialism and control of other cultures in a crucial yet dangerously subtle manner. A primary criterion for the aesthetic value of art, according to European philosophy, is its "universalism." Asante warns African poets and writers, "Universal is another of those words that has been used to hold the enemy in our brains." The "Afrocentric base" is classified as "narrow" or parochial, while the "Eurocentric base is considered universal."[36]

This concept of "universalism" is an ideological statement of such wide and devastating political-cultural ramifications that it warrants continual discussion in the process of delineating the critical expressions of European cultural imperialism. It is a theme found in every aspect of European nationalism. It is cultural commitment disguised.

We have seen how both the claim to universality and the projection of universality as a value to be emulated by other cultures have functioned historically to facilitate the proselytization and imposition of Christianity. Universalism has also been projected as a criterion of worth in art to effectively force non-European artists to reject their own well-springs of cultural creativity. Gayle uses the word "strangulation," and it is a good one. Joseph Okpaku offers an example of the more obvious brand of European nationalism in aesthetic criticism form Jones-Quartey, but at this stage in the game that kind of Eurocentricism no longer presents a "clear and present danger" to the African artist. What does continue to threaten her expression of the uniqueness of her culture, however, are the ideas of the "enlightened" philosophers who, in their struggle to move beyond the uglier aspects of their own culture, posit the virtues of a "universal humanity" towards which every artist should direct her efforts—the negation of culture. Though this conception may tend to strangle African and "non-European" artists, they find it almost impossible to argue against, because it is emotionally and symbolically connected to the Christian "brotherhood of man"—the "we are all one" rhetoric. In the moralistic climate of the European rhetorical ethic, the rejection of this proposition is made to appear evil, and yet the proposition is itself a most unnatural and therefore immoral one; it is quite "moral" to hate one's enemies. Much the same thing is accomplished with the European proposition of the universal normative in the aesthetic experience. Universality as a normative goal becomes difficult to reject intellectually, given the presuppositions of European thought. That is why the road towards intellectual decolonization begins with a precarious obstacle path and escape from the maze of European mythoform.

Aristotle says that poetic statements are "of the nature. . . of universals" and that by a universal statement he means "one as to which

such or such a kind of man will probably or necessarily say or do."[37]
This problem of the European normative statement of "universality"
in art may stem partially from an attempt to achieve transcendence.
But this is a serious misapprehension, for transcendence and universality are not in the same categories. The transcendent is a very
special kind of human experience, while universality is only a semantical "fact" in the syntax of European thought. Gentile presents us
with an excellent example of this sort of European philosophical
statement. Seemingly apolitical and acultural, it lays the theoretical
groundwork for a damaging conception of the purposes of art. Of
these "diverse minds," he says,

> Each of them has his life and his world, his ideals and his passions,
> but all feel at bottom of their souls one common need which they
> cannot satisfy unless they strip off these particular passions and
> ideas and lay bare that human soul which is one and the same in
> all of them and which perceives and creates beauty. The true
> human soul is one, and it is capable of preserving its unity through
> different nations, races, and ages, however indelibly every work of
> art may bear the imprint of its age and birthplace, that is, the ideas
> and passions which contributed to shape the life of its creator. It is
> true that, behind all apparent human differences, there lives in each
> man that one free soul, by virtue of which all men have, deeply
> within themselves, a common humanity.[38]

The European intellectual is so well conditioned and has so successfully conditioned others that what Gentile says here has the
sound of "goodness itself." The question is, what does it mean? What
effect does it have on the artist and her art? Gentile might be, as so
many European philosophers have been, unaware of the intercultural
(i.e., political) implications of his statement, but that does not make
it any the less harmful; to the contrary, it becomes more effective and
more delibitating, because the reader and artist make the mistake of
being influenced by what they *suppose* Gentile's intention to be. They
are misled by his apparent "false-consciousness." Politically, of
course, and for our purposes, his "intention" is irrelevant.

Robert Armstrong criticizes traditional anthropology in that
anthropologists bring "structures" and tools in the attempt to understand alien cultures that do not "fit" them. These tools, therefore,
cannot explain the cultures under scrutiny. But they *do*, however,
"fit" the anthropologist's mind. One such tool, he says, is the idea of
a universal concept of "the beautiful." When this "universal" cannot
be found in the objects of study, anthropologists contribute its

absence to a lack of understanding, vagueness, or sorcery on the part of the informants.[39] But Armstrong needs to look more closely at the purpose of the anthropologist's "study" to understand better the function of the "universal." Anthropology itself is an expansion of the European *utamaroho* and satisfies the need to perceive oneself as being superior. The universal, then, allows the European to judge other cultures: all repetitions of a familiar theme.

Again, it is only very recently that, from a critical perspective of European culture, some African and other non-European artists and critiques have begun to question the validity of this concept of universality. One must not get lost in the emotional quality of particular semantics. What matters is the use of a conception: what it does; how it helps; what comprises its concrete implications. From an African-centered perspective, we ask, Is it good for African people?[40] Or is it merely an abstraction used to endorse a particular value or viewpoint? The problem is always that the nature of the "universal" must be defined and delineated, and it is always the European who is designated to this task. Joseph Okpaku hits the mark when he says,

> There is no universal aesthetic, and if there were it would be most undesirable. The greatest value of art lies in the very fact that there are at least as many different and sometimes conflicting forms as there are different cultures. This is the basis of the wealth and richness of art. For full enjoyment of art, it is not necessary that all art be reduced to a single form (the Western form) in order to make it easily comprehensible and acceptable to the Western audience and to all those who have acquired its taste (by "proper education"), but rather that the would-be connoisseur make an effort to learn to appreciate different art forms.[41]

Johari Amini pierces through to the political essence of the European concept of "universal art." Unfortunately, we rarely find artists who have the critical ability to view European values in terms of European objectives as opposed to the "scientific" and "objective" truths they are presented to be. Because of the prominence of this theme in European cultural imperialism, and its pernicious effect on other peoples, Amini's perceptive and succinct analysis is invaluable. The statement below follows a passage in which she has been discussing the way in which European cultural definitions act to culturally control "non-Europeans":

> For a closer examination of the interaction here, we can take the terms "universal art" and "protest literature," which are used as explicit definitions by the European literary establishment and are

labels to imply an opposition in purpose and intent, and a distinction in the level of creative ability, and aesthetic value. The use of these labels, definitions, however, is definitely expedient for anyone who has the power to define the existence of and maintain dominance over large masses of people. . . .

. . ."universalism" is a highly functional definition used by Europeans who attempt to impose their cultural values on others. The concept of "universalism" is invalid: there is no art, of any people, which emanates from a basis common to all cultures. Even European art, which makes claims to "universality," cannot address itself with any degree of relevance to peoples of other cultural backgrounds. But in the claim of "universality," racism is projected; since European art is "universal," all humans can relate to it; and by the same token, if Africans, Asians, Latin Americans, or any other indigenous non-European peoples are unable to relate to it, then they are "culturally deprived" (of European cultural values), the further implication being that they are, in addition, less than human.[42]

Addison Gayle, in turn, demonstrates the way in which the theme of universalism in the statement of the European philosophical aesthetic acts to (culturally) debilitate the African and African-American, as they struggle to become what Europeans say they should be: mythological "universal" people. Referring to Robinson Crusoe, Gayle says:

From such mystical artifacts has the literature and criticism of the Western world sprung; based upon such narrow prejudices as those of DeFoe, the art of Black people throughout the world has been described as parochial and inferior. Friday was parochial and inferior until, having denounced his own culture, he assimilated another. Once this was done, symbolically, Friday underwent a change. To deal with him after the conversion was to deal with him in terms of a character who had been civilized and therefore had moved beyond racial parochialism.[43]

Universalism is a European myth used to oppress non-European artists. If there is something in an artistic creation that appeals aesthetically to people in cultures other than that which produced the artist, all well and good. But that is not a criterion of its value, nor should it be a concern of the artist. It is nonessential and peripheral. The political uses of universalistic rhetoric are exposed by African-centered analysis.

The Connecting Thread: Aesthetic, *Utamawazo,* and *Utamaroho*

By using the concept of *asili* to explore the European aesthetic, we arrive at a distinction between "elite" and "popular" art. Though somewhat different in function, these two layers of art in the European experience issue from the same mythoform, the same ideological base. The elite art functions mainly to support the *utamawazo* as it is and in turn acts to standardize and reinforce the cognitive modality that, in terms of European ideology, is understood as being superior. The elite art addresses the intellectual consciousness of European experience. It helps to establish, along with the Academy, science and all European speculative endeavors, the standards by which the "true" is judged: For as Keats has told us, for the European, "truth is beauty and beauty truth." The genesis of this aspect of the European aesthetic is the tale of the reinterpretation of an ancient "pre-Western" conception of truth. It is a story that demonstrates the essence of *utamaroho*, and the way in which *utamawazo* dictates cultural response. A divergent *utamaroho* demands a radically different interpretation and elaboration of the original idea.

To understand the European *utamawazo,* as always we return to Plato. Both he and Pythagoras (who seems to have influenced Plato greatly) traveled widely and studied in various "mystery schools," most notably those in Kemet (ancient "Egypt"), which were held in highest esteem. The teachings in these schools were considered esoteric and were not to be written down or taught to the uninitiated. Pythagoras, after having been initiated into the mathematical knowledge of the African priests/scholars, returned to Samos somewhere between 540 and 530 B.C.E., and taught the new philosophy he had learned. The ideas were so alien and threatening to the integrity of the culture that he was forced to leave; a familiar pattern, as similar fates befell Socrates, Plato, and Aristotle. Pythagoras then went to Maga Graecia and established a secret fraternity or "mystery school" of his own. It involved three degrees of enlightenment, as do most mystery traditions, where mathematical knowledge represented the highest level of understanding. For Pythagoras, "number" embodied the fundamental nature of the universe. Plato was initiated into the Pythagorean brotherhood and its secret doctrine concerning mathematical knowledge. The Crotoniate League, the political aspect of the Pythagorean Brotherhood, influenced Plato's idea of the "ideal state" ruled by an elite of philosophers.[44]

In the more ancient conceptions, from which Plato and Pythagoras had learned, the universe was a cosmos, a harmoniously ordered whole. Since all phenomena were connected by a universal life-force, which made a unity of being, the "truth" of the macrocosm was reflected in the reality of the microcosm. This is still the cosmic vision of African peoples.[45] But when the Platonic mentality confronted the African esoteric, spiritualistic conception, it was rendered intellectualist, cerebral, exoteric, and ideological. The harmoniously ordered whole was understood to be reflected in the proportions of the perfect human body and in the perfect work of art.[46] Plato arrived at a concept of absolute beauty; the archetypical "idea" of "beauty."

Among the ancients the construction of a dodecahedron represented the "divine proportion" of the Golden Section. But the science of the cosmos, which later came to be known as alchemy, used mathematics, not only in a concretely physical way (in the construction of pyramids, obelisks, and so forth), but more significantly as a metaphorical expression and symbolic language that allowed the knowing person to participate in eternal truths.

For Plato and those whom he influenced, mathematical, geometrical proportions became the standard of "beauty." The order had been reversed. Spirit was no longer primary, creating symmetry and proportion in the natural sphere, but symmetry and proportion were now used to impose a standard of beauty on the natural and on human conceptions. For Plato the geometrical form became a measure of perfection; indeed beauty was identified with perfection and so with truth. Matila Ghyka traces from their Platonic origins Western conceptions of art and methods of composition. "Number is knowledge itself," this quoted from Plato (in the *Timaeus*). Ghyka says that this maxim was "to become the main tool of western artistic composition, that is, the concept of proportion."[47] The proportional mean or "harmonizing link between two magnitudes based on the principle of analogy influenced Gothic and Renaissance architecture." Ghyka quotes Vituvius, a Platonist: "Symmetry resides in the correlation by measurement between the various elements of the plan, and between each of those elements and the whole."[48]

Plato is credited with initiating the search for "absolute beauty," free of earthly contamination. This conception is discussed in the *Symposium,* where the more ethereal aspects of his concept are developed: This is beauty "uncreated" and "imperishable," "true beauty," "divine beauty," "pure and clear and unalloyed," "not clogged with the pollutions of mortality and all the colours and vanities of human life."[49]

The other aspect of the concept is as a measurable, physical reality; in the *Philebus,* Socrates says,

> I do not mean by beauty of form such beauty as that of animals or
> pictures, which the many would suppose to be my meaning; but,
> ... understand me to mean straight lines and curves, the plane or
> solid figures which are formed out of them by turning-lathes and
> rulers and measures of angles; for these I affirm to be not only rel-
> atively beautiful, like other things, but they are eternally and
> absolutely beautiful. . . ."[50]

Augustine demonstrates the Platonic influence: "Reason, turning to
the domain of sight, that is, to the earth and sky, noticed that in the
world it is beauty that pleases the sight; in beauty, figures; in figures
measures; in measures, numbers.[51] Precisely! Europeans approach
the beautiful (which is after all an *experience*) with their reason. And
"reason" has been given a rationalistic definition, which implies control: mechanical relationship rather than organic interaction. This
issues from the nature of the *asili* of the culture.

Ghyka traces this peculiarly developed European conception of
beauty through European music and architecture, so that "eurythmy"
or the principle of "symphonic composition" along with the "conscious use of proportion" can be identified as the "dominant characteristic of western art."[52] We see it in European dance, where, as
Kariamu Asante tells us, ballet is valued because of its classical
nature, relying heavily on "symmetrical, proportional, and profile-
oriented form".[53] European ballet is control in the sense of the restriction and precise extension of muscles, according to an exact
preconceived and prescribed form. But the African dancer gains mastery paradoxically by developing the ability to allow his/her body to
express the perceived/felt universal life force within: that which we
know as *rhythm*.

The European aesthetic set in the ideological context of
European culture oppresses, distorts, and strangles the African spirit.
The European aesthetic wedded to a materialist conception of perfect
mathematical proportion, defines the African as excessive. Her spirit
is "too much"; she is too emotional, too dark; her nose is too broad.
And as the African attempts to conform to the restrictions of
European ballet she is constantly reminded that the buttocks are too
rounded, too shapely, too pronounced! Can there be a clearer, more
convincing example of the ideological uses of the European aesthetic?
For decades little African girls have been taught to hate their natural
selves as they studied a dance form created to express the European
utamaroho and to simultaneously discredit the aesthetic viability of
not only other cultures but of other human forms! Straighten your
hair so that it can be pulled up into a bun (even if it is not long

enough). "Tuck your behind under, so that the profile of your body is as straight as possible!" Ballet is "universal"; other forms are "ethnic" and therefore "culturally based." So continues the myth of the European aesthetic. The Greek conception of beauty still effects whites (European Caucasians) and tyrannizes blacks (Africans), who judge their physical appearance in relation to how closely they approximate the blond Adonis and Venus. African culture itself (and this is certainly true of other non-European cultures) offends the European aesthetic. It is too human.

An aesthetic that strives after a model of perfection; that perfection represented by proper proportion to be determined by precision of measurement and mathematical relationship of line and space—such is the inherited classical European aesthetic. As an expression of the European *utamawazo* this aesthetic became rationalistic, and controlling, representing a striving toward perfection, associated with whiteness the lack of color (which is seen as excessive), and it experiences pleasure in power (*utamaroho*), not "power to," which is energy; but "power over," which is destruction. So that even as the European aesthetic relates to other aesthetics, it incorporates and reinterprets, and then discards them. But the cultures that created these ideas can never be totally discarded because they are a much-needed source of creativity.

The nascent European mentality—a literal, superficial, controlling mentality—mistook metaphor for reality, reducing spiritual complexity to technical mathematical formula. And this was the birth of the "elite" art—art that could be used ideologically to support a perfect state order, which would in turn oppress the nonelite and colonize the "cultural other." Elite art in contemporary Europe reinforces European ontological and epistemological conceptions, which as we have seen, take on ideological significance in the development of the culture and its stance *vis-à-vis* other cultures. In this way the elite aesthetic conception supports European nationalism and European cultural imperialism.

This brings us to the forms of popular art. An obvious interpretation of the function of art on this level would be to give pleasure to the European (European-American) masses. Such a view misses the mark. That is only a part of the reality, because it doesn't employ the concept of *asili*. An African-centered perspective allows us to understand the ideological and political uses of this art. In Chap. 2 we saw that European Christianity played an essential role in the development of a European national consciousness from the Roman period through the Middle Ages. Science began to take over during the

Renaissance, and then capitalism and industrialization joined in forming an edifice of European identity. In contemporary Euro-America
popular art directs itself to the subconscious life of the ordinary participants in an effort to reinforce their identification and loyalty as
"Americans," "Europeans," "Caucasians." Popular art affirms the
forms of the national consciousness. This function of popular art has
become heightened and more overt recently because of the perceived
crisis in American nationalism (patriotism) and the attendant psychical insecurity believed to be brought about by the reality of
Japanese "success."

While elite art presents and reaffirms *utamawazo* (the cultural
cognitive style), popular art services *utamaroho* (the affective life-
force of the culture). Of course, European *utamawazo* and *utamaroho*
are intimately connected in a symbiotic relationship, feeding on each
other. It would be wrong to think of them as disparate phenomena.
The generalized cognitive modality *(utamawazo)* takes a particular
form because of the nature of the cultural personality; the shared
characteristic spirit of the people *(utamaroho)*. *Utamaroho* and aesthetic spring from the same bedrock of cultural reality. Both have to
do with "feelings"—that which would be psychological on the personal level. *Utamaroho* is the source of cultural aesthetic, in the sense
of a kind of "pleasure principle."

The peculiar nature of European culture is that its "success" is
totally dependent on the maintenance of its unique *utamaroho*. The
utamaroho—power-seeking, expansionistic, spiritually deficient,
needing control—is the driving force beneath the mechanisms and
behavior patterns that contribute to the definition of the culture. This
utamaroho is the energy-source that keeps the culture going. Popular
art is used to present the ikons that tap the energy of the *utamaroho*.
It is in this sense that art in the culture is not peripheral, but is an
essential part of its sustaining ideological matrix, touching the lives
of its members on a deep level.

An image is an ikon when it becomes a forceful presentation of
the national/cultural idea. It is a sensory presence defined by the collective vision and self-image. An ikon is a powerful image that causes
one to feel and internalize a culture. (The most effective mechanism
that performs this function in African culture is ritual drama.) The
art/design is used to present the ikon to the individual psyche. The
ikon has the special ability to forge individual psyches into a collective psyche. In this way a national consciousness is created, affirmed,
and/or strengthened. This is an on-going process. But it is a process
of which the ordinary participant in European/European-American

culture is unaware. Often the ikons are camouflaged; in this way they are better able to effect the individual psyche on a subliminal level. Presently, it is possible to witness many obvious presentations, such as eagles, flags, the national colors on cars, Jeans, school uniforms, boxes of cereal, and toys. And of course there are pronounced ikons such as the cross (crucifix). These are ikons that promote a Euro-American national consciousness; there are other, more subtle ones, that relate to the broader European consciousness. Advertising media uses these ikons, such as blond-haired women with straight aquiline noses. There are also verbal ikons that abound in European and European-American popular culture, so that we continually hear the juxtaposition of terms like "civilized" and "terrorist," or terms like "future," "tomorrow," "newest" to indicate value. These are what Aziza Gibson-Hunter refers to as "literal-ikons."[54] We are usually unaware of the ways that popular art welds the collective psyche into a national consciousness of identity.

One of the most prevalent expressions/uses of popular art as it collectivizes the individual European psyche is in design. If studied from an African-centered perspective, we see that design is a powerful and ubiquitous influence in our lives. The cars we drive; the furniture on which we sit, sleep, or eat; the appliances that we use; even the colors and fabrics with which we decorate our homes—all employ the European aesthetic of line, dimension, and space. Oftentimes, objects themselves become ikons. The television is a Euro-American ikon. Popular art acts aesthetically; that is, it conditions the cultural psyche to respond with pleasure to the ikons that represent the national identity. Aesthetic is above all, in this sense, an emotional mechanism.

This aesthetic is used ideologically. Ingeniously, it gives different signals to different segments of the population. Ikons like the American flag, for instance, or even a Greek statue, engender feelings of pride in a person of European descent, as he identifies with what he understands to be a superior cultural tradition. It is easy (cultural) for him to feel this because of his ancestral memory and the various mechanisms, institutions, textbooks, theories, games, movies, videos, teachers, and forms *ad infinitum* that surround him, all reinforcing the idea of his cultural superiority, all making use of the ikons.

But the very same ikon reaches the individual psyche of a person of African descent, creating and reinforcing feelings of inferiority, dependency, and humiliation. As the person of African descent internalizes the image of the ikon into her individual feeling self, she actually "desires" her relationship of dependency, seeking to consume (buy) as many products as possible that incorporate the ikon. The internalization of the ikon-image causes her to want to be controlled by what she perceives to be the superior culture. And so she adorns herself and her home (personal space) with European ikons, giving them total access to her consciousness.

The person of non-European background becomes a victim of the European ikon that acts on her as a powerful weapon of control. The reason for this is that European ikons only act to collectivize or unite the European psyche: The psyche that is linked to the European ancestral memory. But for the non-European it has the opposite effect. It takes what it finds of an African or other non-European collective conscious and splits it up; individualizes it, so that it can be placed at the service of the European nationalist cause. The solution is not as difficult as we might think. To break the control of the European ikon we have simply to respond with our collective conscious will.[55] An African consciousness either automatically rejects European ikons as displeasing or acts as a filter screening for that which reinforces African being. Through this process, they are robbed of their ideological power and are no longer ikons. This ability is promoted through the use and creation of African ikons that tap the energy of the African ancestral memory. But in Euro-America the popular aesthetic is supported by the elite aesthetic (art) that makes non-European ikons appear to represent ignorance, imperfection, backwardness; all that which lacks value.

The reason the city is the valued mode of social organization in European ideology is not only because of its supposed efficiency for the technical order. In the European urbanized setting, the mechanized and visual media have the greatest access to the human mind/soul. The city is media! The myth of sophistication is that in the city one becomes a "free-thinker," liberated from the control of small-town morality. In point of fact there is no corner of the city that allows us the privacy of our own thoughts. By shaping human experience the city-system shapes people. *That* is its value. The plethora of media (of which the educational system is a part) creates our environment and therefore, in a very real sense, creates us.[56] The ikons of the "state order," the "national order," of a European-dominated "world order"; the ikons of European tradition, of Caucasian, Indo-European racial memory and pride; the ikons of European expansionism and imperialism—these ikons are constantly invading the subconscious and conscious of those who live in the metropole. Our visual and auditory images are continuously mediated through the acoutrements of "city life." The city is media-filled; it is made of media. What better way to control sentiments, commitments that become behavior patterns and goals, than by effecting consciousness and affective responses? The Euro-American city creates and mediates images. That is its purpose and perhaps the most important purpose of the popular art form. (This art form also functions as a safety valve to express fears and ambivalence about the national/cultural self. This point will be discussed further in the following chapter.) Graffiti represents the production of images not controlled by the state order. It is therefore "despicable," a "defacement of property." But the advertisements that steal our sight, that crowd our vision, that fill the air which transmits sound are not considered "defacements," because they contribute to the control of the image; to the creation of the ikon.

By using the concept of *asili* we see that the European aesthetic is part of the consistent development of the cultural seed/germ. The *utamaroho* is political in nature. It is defensive/aggressive, always intent on separating self from other; the other that is perceived hostily. The uses of art and the character of the aesthetic, therefore, take on an intensely ideological and political definition. Both the elite and popular art forms are essential in the creation and reinforcement of the Euro-Caucasian self-image and, dialectically, of the European image of the "cultural-other." Consideration of the cultural function of the European aesthetic leads us first to a discussion of these two images (Part II) and then to a discussion of their relationship to European culturally patterned behavior (Part III).

PART TWO

IMAGE AND NATIONAL CONSCIOUSNESS

*Here indeed was the white man in action . . . the
godlike, the white man descended among the black
people to do magical wonders. The white man was
a god, among mere men, a beloved father, god
among infant-men.*

— *Ayi Kwei Armah,* The Healers, *p. 201*

Chapter 4

Self-Image

The bard of a modern Imperialism has sung of the White Man's burden.

The notes strike the granite surface of racial pride and fling back echoes which reverberate through the corridors of history, exultant, stirring the blood with memories of heroic adventure, deeds of desperate daring, ploughing of unknown seas, vistas of mysterious continents, perils affronted and overcome, obstacles triumphantly surmounted.

But mingled with these anthems to national elation another sound is borne to us, the white peoples of the earth, along the trackless byways of the past, in melancholy cadence. We should prefer to close our ears to its haunting refrain, stifle its appeal in the clashing melodies of rapturous self-esteem. We cannot. And, today, we tear and rend ourselves, we who have torn and rent the weaker folk in our imperial stride, it gathers volume and insistence.[1]

The European's view of himself reveals the nature of the European *utamaroho* and is dialectically related to his view of others. It is because of the nature of this *utamaroho* that one of the most accurate indices of the European self-image is their image of others. This discussion is comprised of two overlapping and interrelated sec-

tions: the first (Chap. 4) emphasizes European descriptions and feelings about self ("positive"); the second (Chap. 5) emphasizes the
complementary descriptions and images of others ("negative") that
serve to reinforce the former, i.e., through the dialectics of value
dichotomy. From the general behavior, literature, and other cultural
expressions of Europeans, there emerges a consistent autobio-
graphical statement of how they envision themselves and what they
"want to be" in relation to others. By isolating the components of this
self-image, we have found that the European "cultural ego" is composed of elements traceable to the early and formulative stages of
European culture; traits that matured and developed simultaneously
with the culture itself. The isolatable features are interrelated and
each functions to support the other, combining to form a cohesive
"ego," which uses the conflict/tension, resulting from an inherent
deficiency as a continuous source of energy. What emerges in this discussion is the culturally visible self-image that functions meaning-
fully to support European normative, sanctioned behavior.

The term "cultural ego" is used by Joel Kovel; it is a useful concept for this study. Kovel says,

> The ego we are discussing is not that of an individual...but rather
> the egos of a mass of personalities as they present themselves in a
> historical situation. Let us call it a Cultural Ego....[2]

> The sense of self and the sense of identity are reflections of the
> synthetic work of the ego. All the elements presented to the indi-
> vidual by his drives, his past development and the needs of the
> environment in which he finds himself, must be fused together into
> a coherent self-image and sense of identity.[3]

Europeans responded with enthusiasm to the initial Platonic
directive by adopting the self-image of "rational man." What is it that
the abstraction "man" ought properly to be in the European view?
And how do they view themselves? The culture is "successful"
because it convinces them that these two answers are synonymous.
The two are identified with one another, and the universalistic
abstraction collapses into the particular, concrete European self-
image. European philosophic discourse deals with the specific, the
images, standards, desires, and goals of the Europeans. But it
employs a universalistic semantics. It is essential that we learn to
recognize expressions of European value and self-image when they
appear. In the language of the European tradition, terms such as
"man," "mankind," "humanity" connote "European" and conjure up

self-images in the mind of the European. (For "the rest of us," these terms, defined Eurocentrically, present images of what we think we should be but cannot become, no matter how hard we strive. And that can be attributed to the success of European cultural imperialism.)

"Rational Man"

The implications of "rationality" for the European mind are crucial. The essential characteristics associated with this concept, within the European world-view, are control and consequently power—the theme that reverberates endlessly in the ethnological unfolding of the culture, echoed in every statement of value. The "rational man," in European terms, is above all the person who is in control of his passions. He makes decisions—choices based on reason—the proper and invulnerable guide. Being in control of himself puts him in a better position to manipulate and control others—those who are irrational or at least less rational. He has power over others by virtue of his rationalism. Through the institutionalization and abstraction of this "rational" decision-making process—of which science is constituted—he believes that he can even control his destiny. He plans, predicts, and creates his future; activities usually associated with a "god."

When Plato described "justice" as the triumph of "reason" over "passion" in human beings, he was laying out a blue print for what he wanted the "men" of the Republic to become—even in terms of breeding. When the philosophers of the Enlightenment called for the planning of society according to the "laws of reason," they were announcing their own entrance onto the stage of "history" as its undisputed vanguard. They were the "rational men" who had been mandated to determine these laws. They and their progeny would fashion a social order as only rational men could.

The contemporary "critical" version of this position, which unfortunately many disenchanted African scholars look to for direction instead of developing their own African-centered analyses, is that of Jurgen Habermas. In the 1980s Habermas calls for a "rationalized lifeworld"[4] that will lead to rationality in the "conduct of life." While he professes to be avoiding the universalization of an "occidental understanding of the world,"[5] he claims to have achieved a universally applicable definition of rational behavior, which includes having "good reasons" for actions; more specifically, reasons that are cognitively "correct" or "successful," and morally and practically "reliable" and "insightful."[4] There is obviously no escaping judgement, value, and world-view; for what frame of reference is to be used in the definition of these terms? Habermas, like Plato, talks about an "objective universe." He has succeeded in updating (contemporizing) the European *utamaroho* that expresses itself in the desire to be "rational man," as he himself, strives to posit a "world-historical process of rationalization of world-views."[6]

Habermas' quest is to clean up the European act by separating the mythological from the rational in the European world-view, but in so doing his thinking is structured comfortably by the European *utamawazo* that understands "truth" and "rightness" as universals, rationally superior to cultural values that are "local" and "specific."[7] Habermas' ideal is the "rational man" par excellence, who, as such, will be able to claim moral superiority. The circle completes itself; the modality is unchanged.

The European image of the "non-European," the African, or their own antithesis reinforces these observations. Recognizable in it are all those things that they repudiate—that which they do not want to be. In their view, people of other cultures are basically irrational. Therefore, these people do not choose; they do not make decisions. They have no control over their destinies. This is what Europeans want the case to be, and consequently they proceed to act in such a way as to bring that condition into being. Just as they struggle to become what they want to be, and in struggling, succeed, they must be the ones "who control" (i.e., they represent rational man). Europeans devote their cultural lifetime to becoming what to others is not necessarily desirable. Accordingly, the benefits of "rationality" must be shared—that is "progress." It is "irrationality" that must be stamped out—subdued; that too is "progress." Rationalization (efficient order) becomes rationality (control of the emotional). This combination is an essential ingredient of the European self-image —although such rationality might very possibly be considered the height (or depth) of the unreasonable in other cultures.

The self-image that we are reconstructing is all part of the mythology with which Europeans equip themselves. By the term "mythology" I do not mean to comment on the truth or falsity of these images; such terms have no relevance to "mythology" as I use it. I am referring to a composite of beliefs, the very language of which is culturally determined. It is the setting forth in symbolic matrix an expression of the culturally operable definition of the "true." It makes little sense to discuss whether Europeans are "rational"; what matters is what they conceive "rational" to mean, that they identify themselves with this conception, and that this identification guides their behavior. It may well be that this "rationality" to which Europeans aspire

and view themselves as possessing is not recognizable as a normative goal for other people.

This view of rationality is part of a related series of characteristics or attributes with which Europeans associate themselves. In their
collective self-image they are the "critical man." Havelock writes in
praise of the emergence in Greek culture of what he calls a "self-conscious critical intelligence." This is contrasted with the inadequacy
of the poetic media of pre-Platonic Greece, which was predicated on
"uncritical acceptance," "self-identification, and self-surrender." He
describes the Homeric Greek as having been under a "hypnotic spell."
Havelock is, in effect, offering the Europeans' view of themselves
("critical") and their view of non-Europeans ("noncritical"). And, as
with the idea of rational man, critical implies "control over." For the
European mind, it implies an agent who acts on things, people, information; while the noncritical being is passive, in a trance, to be manipulated by events, objects, emotions, and by critical man. For Havelock
the "surrender" of noncritical man is "accomplished through the lavish employment of emotions."[8] Again, a relationship of power is
implied and underlies the European's conception of himself as "critical, rational man."

The idea of "critical man" is in turn related to the concept of
"objectivity," as we have seen in Chap. 1. This is one of the most significant components of the European mythoform. Europeans are "critical" and "reflective" because they believe that they can separate
themselves from their emotions and from the "objects" they seek to
"know." Havelock says,

> Thus the autonomous subject who no longer recalls and feels, but
> knows, can now be confronted with a thousand abstracted laws,
> principles, topics, and formulas which become the objects of his
> knowledge.[9]

And because Europeans are able to separate themselves from the
object, it is assumed that they can be objective. This association of
critique with the European notion of objectivity has had very unfortunate consequences, for in actuality, a critical perspective towards
one set of assumptions can only be informed by the commitment to
another, at least when these assumptions are epistemological. There
is no such thing as true human objectivity, just as it is not possible
for a person to separate one "part" of herself from another.

But according to European mythology, they are indeed in possession of an objectivity that places them, as it were, way ahead of
the pack. For while others flounder in a sea of emotion (i.e., cultural

commitment) that colors and clouds their vision, Europeans are able to rise above this attachment (identification). With rationality and objectivity comes "universality." Europeans are closest to being "universal" because, by being rational, they are best able to choose and design the proper social and intellectual forms for all people. They are what it is hoped others will become, however remote that possibility may be. By being objective their vision and interpretation can be international in scope and have universal significance, as opposed to being parochial and culturally bound. The myth continues.

All of these normative themes affect the European intellectual aesthetic, just as they affect European behavior. These are the characteristics, the attributes for which a participant in the culture strives, and, at the same time, they combine to form an important part of the ontological construct that governs the *utamawazo*. Criticism and analysis are considered important parts of the European aesthetic experience. In this view, other cultures barely possess "art," in part because they cannot "critically" assess it.

The European as "Male"

The feminist critique of European society has its roots in the bowels of the European tradition.[10] The patriarchal nature of early Indo-European religion (see Chap. 2) indicates more than a desire of men to dominate women. It also results from the association of "maleness" with superiority and "femaleness" with inferiority. Perhaps the earliest European definition of "self" and "other" was as male and female. In reaction to a more than 4000-year-old tradition of male control European feminists organize for an end to female oppression. Some see the base of their movement in the equality of men and women, which they translate as "sameness." From an African-centered perspective this position is incorrect. Others have developed a "feminist ideology," much of which uses the tenets of an African world-view as its foundation within the category of what Ruether calls "reform feminism,"[11] although they do not identify it as such. The question looms: Why was it the male in the Indo-European experience who sought separation and dominance rather than the female? Or did the female share the same ambitions but simply lost out because of disparity in physical strength? Susan Brownmiller seems to be saying that male domination is related to anatomical characteristics that allowed the human male to rape the human female.[12] Engels offers a materialist analysis that links male dominance to the origin of private property. These explanations are not culture-specific. The concept of *asili* demands that we be above all culture-specific.

In our analysis male domination has a specific history in European culture and is linked to the other cultural forms in a uniquely "European" manner. This phenomenon should not be understood as a universal, because while it may have similar appearances in different cultures, the degree of intensity varies as does the relationship to the *asili* of the culture. Perhaps the answer to the question that looms is that separation and dominance are themselves part of a "male" or "patriarchal" approach to reality, and that this approach became associated for the European with maleness of gender. Indeed, I have argued that separation, opposition, and dominance are characteristic of the European *utamawazo* and mythoform. This imparts what Eric Neumann would call a "patriarchal consciousness" to the culture. This consciousness is directed toward control, distance, and analysis or splitting, and it tends to be threatened by the matriarchal nature of consciousness. Neumann says, "A fundamental development has been to expand the domain of patriarchal consciousness and to draw to it everything that could possibly be added.[13] The patriarchal nature of European culture in this deep sense as part of its *asili* explains many aspects of its development; for instance, why the tradition embraced Freudian theory, but relegated Jungian thought to its lunatic fringes.

In other cultures where we find patterns of female oppression, these patterns do not have the same ideological positioning in the culture as they do in the European tradition and therefore are not as strong. They co-exist in tension with matriarchal philosophies, often matrilineal descent systems, traditions of female leadership, and strong patterns of cooperation and associations among females.[14] The literature and ideology of European feminism reaches towards these cultures for intellectual inspiration and the creation of a new feminine self, or it attempts to compete with the patriarchal nature of the European tradition by denying the female and seeking to dominate the male.

But the analytical mode is not limited to the male gender, and men do not necessarily lack spirituality. It is the culture that tends to create the dominance of the patriarchal consciousness in both genders, i.e., in all who participate therein. What is to be learned from African and other non-European philosophies is the principle of appositional complementarity.[15] It is not a question of which gender dominates nor of whether everyone can become "male" (that is, take the dominant position), rather it is a question of whether our view of existence dictates the necessary cooperation of "female" and "male" principles for the success and continuance of the whole.

Plato was very clear on this question, but he was simply developing the Indo-European *asili* in its intellectual, ideological form. Not only were males superior, but they were superior in ways that demanded their control of women. They were more rational, critical, and intelligent, more capable of grasping higher truths. Only men could be philosophers. In fact, women were not even qualified to be their lovers.[16] But if we accept for the moment a Jungian analysis, the characteristics for which the Europeans breed were indeed "male": coldness, control, oppositional thought. Even females who succeed in these terms are incomplete, as the culture is in a continual state of disequilibrium because of "lopsided" development,[17] since its *asili* is not based on the principle of complementary or wholeness, but rather on dominance and destruction.

The European has no choice other than being "male" in terms of positive self-image. It is not accidental that the term for a male person "man," becomes the term in European languages for all human beings. This issues from the initial European self/other distinction, where male is "self" and "female" is other. Michael Bradley says, "Caucasoid sexes have never really got used to each other, never really completely trusted each other."[18] This, he says, is because of the extreme sexual dimorphism necessitated by Neanderthal development as an adaptation to the glacial environment. Caucasoids, he argues, descend from Neanderthals. Bradley assumes that males are more territorially assertive, and as the category of time was approached "territorially" by Neanderthals, men feared women as the bearers of children who would subsequently supplant them.[18] We will return to Bradley's analysis in a later chapter. What is already apparent, however, is that it has many holes, but it does point to the recognition that male/female relationships and differences are problematical for Europeans, and that this is somehow related to the extreme aggressiveness of the culture.

"Scientific Man"

The European is "scientific man." To them this implies the essence of universality, objectivity, and the ability to be critical and rational. "Scientific man" does not connote to the European mind, simply the person who is engaged in scientific activity. To them the term indicates a state of mind and of being: a way of looking at the world. As science takes on a magical quality in European culture, so the use of its methodology can impart value to the individual. Scientific man is "he" who approaches the universe with a particular attitude. The attitude of science is a vehicle by which the world is consumed. Science for the European is synonymous with "knowledge," and this "knowledge" is the representation of power. Scientific knowledge is the ability to control, manipulate, and predict the movements of people and other "objects." Indeed, Europeans view themselves as this "scientific man" who manipulates the world around "him."

The Problem of the "Mad Scientist"

According to the European self-image, "scientific man" is in a desirable position, for he is above all logical—remote and detached. But this is not quite the same thing as being "a scientist." A scientist, in terms of the European image, is one who envelops himself in science. He is totally immersed in the laboratory and wears special "glasses" that allow him to see nothing but his work—the "objects" on which he experiments. This image has a special place in the European cultural ego. Such "scientists" are relegated to a very small portion of the collective personality, but on an unconscious level this personality is identified with a characteristic tendency of the entire culture. It is a part of the self that Europeans perceive themselves to be; yet they neither want to become nor to identify with it.

In this sense, it is not part of the European self-image as a "positive" self-concept. It is the only aspect of their culture towards which they express ambivalence and possible fear. A major vehicle for the expression of this fear is the "horror" movie. The recurrent theme of the "mad scientist" in the European nightmare fantasy is an expression of the fear and recognition that somehow it is the European *asili* that produces such madness in every "European." The madness of this characterization is not the emotional confusion of an overly sensitive human being who refuses to accommodate to the inhumanity of contemporary life (quite the opposite), nor is it of a weakened and depressed individual. It is nothing caused by ordinary human frailty. It is a culturally induced madness caused by the very absence of humanity.

In the typical plot one finds the same person. He (always male) is committed only to his experiments and will not stop them, no matter what danger they imply to the community. What excites him are the implications of his being able to control and manipulate some part of nature that has previously been untouched, perhaps something sacred. This he insists is "science" and "progress." As he is typically depicted, this man cannot love, has no friends, becomes deaf to the admonitions of those around him. He loses the ability even to understand what they are saying. He is a fanatic in the fullest sense of the term. This is Dr. Frankenstein (depicted in 1920, 1932, and 1941 films),

Dr. Jekyll and all the others not sufficiently infamous to be known by name, but always there. *The Deadly Mantis* (1957); *Dr. Cyclops* (1940); *The Island of Dr. Moreau* (1977); *The Thing* (1951); *Alien* (1979, the more modern vintage)—the theme does not "go out of style" but continues to provide material for the European/American science fiction "thriller."

An intensive ethnological study of such films alone would no doubt provide valuable insights into the nature of the European psyche. But unfortunately all "mad scientists" are not as bizarre as these films depict them. There are those who have had deep cultural/philosophical commitments. There is a certain "madness" even in the fanaticism and unidirection of men like Plato, Aristotle, Augustine, and Aquinas. All of the most ideologically influential people in European development had this fanatical dedication either to total systematization or to visions of what the world should be and a determination to make it that way—monolithic and consistently European. This appears to be the only aspect of the European self-image that may be perceived as negative-undesirable. They want to be rational, critical, objective, universal, and scientific; but they are not certain that they want to be "the scientist." They sense somehow that in this cold rationalism they will lose control. The nightmare of the self they envision, therefore, is that they have completely lost their humanity and have become monstrous (for it is the mad scientist who is the "monster" in these monster movies). The reality of the nightmare is that the nature of European culture is such that this monster can and does gain the power to endanger the lives of those not only in his culture but throughout the world.

"Civilized Man"

The terms "modern" and "civilized" are also those with which Europeans describe themselves. They represent the epitome of value on the scale of "progress"; their own interpretation and description of value and the abstraction to which the human endeavor is most properly committed. If this is kept in mind, it becomes easier to recognize instances in which Europeans are describing themselves, even as they struggle, and usually succeed, to make it appear that they are doing otherwise. This is the most common manifestation of European cultural nationalism/imperialism.

Most certainly historian Harry Elmer Barnes would claim that he is being "objective" in the statement which follows:

From the intellectual standpoint, then, a man is a modern if he thinks in a logical fashion and acquires his information through the inductive methods of observation and experimentation. Insofar as he believes in supernatural causation, thinks illogically, and does not rely upon scientifically ascertained facts, his thinking is of a primitive cast, whether he be a graduate of a leading American university in the second third of the twentieth century or an illiterate bushman.[19]

In terms of a European scientific rhetoric, the last phrase is proof of the universal validity and objectivity of his statement. To Barnes it is the indication that *he* is not displaying Eurocentricism. As long as his remarks apply "universally," they are "scientific" and "rational," not "emotional" or "political." The fact is, of course, that the phrase in question does nothing to change the nationalistic impact of the statement. The positive image in his mind is undoubtedly that of the graduate of a leading university who is striving with all his might to think in a "logical fashion," while representing the antithesis of the "illiterate bushman." Barnes continues,

So powerful is the mystical or religious aspect of the preliterate mind that in many respects civilization advances only in the degree to which man frees himself from the spell of the supernatural, puts away his animism, taboos, fetishes, totems—as a growing child puts away its toys—and relies upon his intellect and observations to interpret the varying manifestations of nature and the activities of his own psyche.[20]

Here one should read, "Only as we weed out African (non-European) religion and philosophy do we succeed in spreading our culture, for we Europeans rely on our intelligence, rather than mysticism, and are, therefore, adult, mature, and in control of our destiny."

William Schockley says that black people are genetically less intelligent than whites; how different is that from the implications of Barnes' statement? Schockley loses effectiveness, is even shouted down by college students and not allowed to speak, because he uses the terms of "race." Barnes' work, on the other hand, is considered solid, respectable material for teaching a course on the History of Western Civilization, a basic required course for most undergraduates in Europe and Euro-America. In using "universalistic" and "objective" terms—the terms of disinterest—Barnes succeeds in proselytizing the European world-view where Schockley fails. Perhaps it is Barnes who is more of a nationalist. In an examination of the dynamics and nature of European culture, it is imperative that we compare the function of the term "civilized" with the idea of "whiteness." They function in the same way: But one clouds European commitment, while the other avows it. Those who are critical would be much less upset by the theories of Schockley, Jensen, and others if they simply viewed them as statements of the European self-image and valued characteristics expressed in the terms of the European *utamawazo*. In other words, these Europeans must be understood to be talking about themselves and their culture; and therefore providing valuable material if one is concerned with examining European mental and emotional life.

These characteristics to which Europeans aspire and to which they attach themselves all have to do with their desire for power and the way in which they interpret power. Power comes from control—the ability to "objectify," manipulate, and predict. And these intellectual manifestations of power have their counterpart in the European self-portrait, in the image of their behavior in the international political arena. MacDougall quotes Lord MacCaulay as boasting that the history of England "is emphatically the history of progress." The English people "have become the greatest and most highly civilized people that ever the world saw."[21] This was reiterated by a multitude of European nationalists throughout the nineteenth century.

"The Conqueror": Expansionism in the European *Utamaroho*

In a speech urging President McKinley to keep the Philippines, Albert J. Beveridge said of United States control,

> It means opportunity for all the glorious young manhood of the republic—the most virile, ambitious, impatient, militant manhood the world has ever seen. It means that the resources and the commerce of these immensely rich dominions will be increased as much as American energy is greater than Spanish sloth; for Americans henceforth will monopolize those resources and that commerce.[22]

The exercise of this power, which Europeans attribute to themselves and which they continuously seek, is manifested in the ability—no, the mandate—to conquer everything they find. Their assessment of themselves includes their birthright to conquer, not only that with which they happen to come in contact, but that which they seek—new lands, nature, people. This activity of "conquering" is sanctioned by the European *utamaroho* that provides a kind of moral justification for it. This characteristic can be traced from the early Indo-European heritage of the culture. The conquering *uta-maroho* houses the intrinsic aggressive tendencies. The culture itself redirects these tendencies as "progressive energy." Destructiveness becomes reconstruction of the world in the conquering self-image. This characteristic helps to determine the Europeans' behavior towards other peoples. The quoted passage from Beveridge (written in the 1890s) expresses the same conviction and self-concept as the speeches of Ronald Reagan in 1988, those of Richard Nixon in 1974, those of Bush in 1990, those of the Catholic popes during the Crusades, and those of the Roman orators in the Archaic "West." The history of Western Europe abounds with such examples. The consistency and power of this *utamaroho* is formidable, having been symbolically expressed at least 2500 years ago in the Persian (Iranian) myth of Yima, reputedly the first leader of the Aryan people, who was personally appointed by Ahura Mazda, the god of "light" and "goodness," to "rule the world."[23]

The following are excerpts from a speech delivered in Rome in the second century. It is praise offered by Aristides, a professional orator, for Rome, "the eternal city." It is evidence of the Roman *uta-maroho:* of how they saw themselves, and of those characteristics of which they were most proud. Mikhail Rostovtzeff has said that this speech is one of the most important sources of information on the political ideas and mentality of the age of Antonines.

> . . . if one looks at the whole empire and reflects how small a fraction rules the whole world, he may be amazed at the city, but when he has beheld the city herself and the boundaries of the city, he can no longer be amazed that the entire civilized world is ruled by one so great. (Section 9)

> Your possession is equal to what the sun can pass, and the sun passes over your land. Neither the Chelidonean nor the Cyanean promontories limit your empire, nor does the distance from which a horseman can reach the sea in one day, nor do you reign within fixed boundaries, nor does another dictate to what point your control reaches; but the sea like a girdle lies extended, at once in the middle of the civilized world and of your hegemony. (Section 10)

> . . . the present empire has been extended to boundaries of no mean distance, to such, in fact that one cannot even measure the area within them. On the contrary, for one who begins a journey westward from the point where at that period the empire of the Persian found its limit, the rest is far more than the entirety of his domain,

and there are no sections which you have omitted, neither city nor tribe nor harbor nor district, except possibly some that you condemned as worthless. The Red Sea and the Cataracts of the Nile and Lake Maeotis, which formerly were said to lie on the boundaries of the earth, are like the courtyard walls to the house which is this city of yours. On the other hand, you have explored the Ocean. Some flowed around the earth; they thought that poets had invented the name and had introduced it into literature for the sake of entertainment. But you have explored it so thoroughly that not even the island therein has escaped you. (Sections 23, 24)[24]

What is it that causes Aristides and his Roman audience to feel self-pride? That only a small fraction of the world's men rule the rest; that this fraction is the "best," the "most talented," the "smartest"; and that the rest are their "subjects"—whom they rule with perfection. Their empire stretches as far as they can conceive; empire connotes "all in my power." What is associated with them is the entire "civilized" world; i.e., "everything of value in the world." What is left is only of value in that it can be used by them. These are the dreams, ambitions, and images that comprise the European *utamaroho*. The same today as they were when Aristides made this speech.

This self-image as the conqueror of all imagined is manifested in the desire to spread themselves over all they see (the Sun never set on the British Empire); in this way what they control becomes an extension of themselves. The European self-image becomes translated into fanatical expansionism—insatiable and limitless. They continually seek new lands, people, objects to conquer and in so doing to expand their cultural ego symbolically—until everything relates to their image (either mirrors it or is its reverse). It is not accidental that the European speaks of "conquering space." This expansionist *utamaroho* has been consistently a part of the cultural ego and self-image from Roman times to contemporary American life, compelling them to consume the universe.

In Joel Kovel's words,

The West became intoxicated with the idea of distant space, which was represented in the dream of a New World (and today, a new universe) to be conquered.

Here was the nuclear synthesis of man and his world that could become extended into infinity.

The immense landscape, stretching endlessly onward and drawing Americans to its receding horizons, itself became symbolic nutrient.

It became represented inwardly as the idea of spaciousness, an expansiveness of personal style; an accompanying inner sense of blankness that was to fuse with the whiteness of the settler's skin into the conception of a self both pure and unbounded, a self that has the right, the necessity and the manifest destiny to dominate the continent and the darker peoples upon it. A self grew in this symbolic soil that could abstractly split apart its universe as readily as it cleaved the unstructured land.[25]

"World Savior"

Only the West developed theistic, providential religion . . . the belief that God works actively in history to perfect the world . . . Westerners were forced to take social change and history seriously, and they found it natural to envisage themselves as agents of Providence striving to perfect temporal society.[26]

Consistent with the self-image as "world conqueror" is the European self-proclaimed mandate to save the world. This image is found rather explicitly in European religious formulations and, therefore, in the earlier stages of European development. Though Judaism did not seek to include the world in its nationalistic statement, it did contain a statement of the obligation to humankind of providing the proper example that would therefore be the world's salvation. Thus begins the imperative of the European *utamaroho*—the "voice" that tells the European that he is somehow "special," that he has superior qualities and knowledge that oblige him to shoulder the burden of guiding those less fortunate than he (the rest of the world). The Christian statement is the epitome of this image, and, indeed, presented a "world savior" to the world. This aspect of the European *utamaroho* implies the idea of European superiority; it does not imply altruism, as it has been misunderstood to do. Europeans are themselves the "Christ," who would save the world and whose qualities are superior enough to enable them to stand as a model for all of us to emulate.

The expression of this aspect of the European *utamaroho* in the form of Christian ideology made it more acceptable and subtle—more effective among those who were to be "saved." The implications of superiority, and of the self-image of world savior, are as much a part of missionary activity as it is of the *utamaroho* expressed in Kipling's concept of "the white man's burden." Phillip Curtin says, "The conversionist sentiment of the mid-century [nineteenth] and trusteeship at the end were two ways of assessing the proper goals for non-western peoples."[27] The arrogance and presumption in the European self-image in relation to the rest of the world are evidenced in the expansionist expeditions they have undertaken. Whether in the early or contemporary stages of their developing empire, Europeans, at best, have related with paternalism to the rest of the world. Curtin says,

> In that great age of imperialism racism became dominant in European thought. Few believed that any "lower race" could actually reach the heights of Western achievement. Their salvation would be achieved in some other way; but meanwhile they were entitled, in their inferiority, to the paternal protection of a Western power. The idea of trusteeship gradually replaced that of conversion.[28]

Joel Kovel offers his own psycho-cultural interpretation of this "savior" image and its implications for the European's political relationship to others. Kovel says,

> When the Marine officer described the American obliteration of a city in Vietnam by explaining that, "We had to destroy the City in order to save it," was he not expressing in the succinct form given by such an extreme situation, the pure, nuclear fantasy underlying Western history—to save and destroy, include and extrude?[29]

The point he makes is that Western "saving" has meant a "making over," possession, and destruction, until what the world needs most is to be saved from the insatiable appetite and egotism of the European.

The European *utamaroho* allows people to experience an intense ideology of cultural and racial supremacy as "beneficence" and "altruism." This, in essence, is the message to be gleaned from an examination of the European self-image. Europeans do not merely commit atrocities against other peoples and then rationalize them in nationalistic expression; they seem to believe that they have the *right* and the *obligation* to "think" and "act"—to make moral decisions—for other peoples and therefore to commit such atrocities. As we have seen in Chap. 1, the European *utamawazo* allows them to "believe" this. The European *utamaroho* is a unique ethnological phenomenon and accounts for the intensity of European/Euro-American cultural behavior.

Yehoshua Arieli says,

> This Protestant nationalism adopted peculiar racial theories. The legitimation of the right to conquest and the theory of manifest destiny, wherever preached by Americans, accepted to a certain

degree the idea of the superiority of the Anglo-American "race" as a progressive force which would impose liberty on all mankind. The New England concept of the nature of the American mission blended universalism and nationalism in an ideology which accounted for its own achievements by a theory of race and yet believed that its patterns of life could be imposed on others. The Anglo-American race had the duty of transmitting the pattern of life it had developed to the whole world in order to promote pure Christianity. The expansion of the American nation was the means by which Providence furthered the cause of religion and the spread of pure faith.[30]

Arieli, quoting from Horace Bushnell in *Christian Nurture,* offers these examples:

"Any people that is physiologically advanced . . . is sure to live down and finally live out its inferior (sic). Nothing can save the inferior race but a ready and pliant assimilation. . . . What if it should be God's plan to people the world with better and finer material. Certain it is . . . (his plan) that there is a tremendous overbearing surge of power in the Christian nations, which . . . will inevitably submerge and bury. . .(the less capable) forever."

"The Anglo-Saxon and Anglo-American, of all modern races, possess the strongest national character and the one best fitted for universal domination, and that, too, not a dominion of despotism but one which makes its subjects free citizens . . . In them . . . the impulse towards freedom and the sense of law and order are inseparably united, both rest on a moral basis."[30]

This is precisely the same sentiment, mood, and conviction that Aristides expressed in behalf of the Romans. The Roman self-image as "world conqueror" and "savior" issues from an ego that does not confine itself to the limitations of a culture, a nation, or even a continent, but from an ego that views its boundaries as ultrauniversal. This is the counterpart of the intellectual self-image of the European as "universal man." He is "universal" in his freedom from emotional attachment and objectivity, by virtue of his scientific approach and use of "logic"; he, therefore, has the right to spread himself universally in order to "enlighten" the world.

Aristides says,

To Rome, you who are "great greatly" distributed your citizenship. It was not because you stood off and refused to give a share in it to any of the others that you made your citizenship an object of wonder. On the contrary, you sought its expansion to be the label, not of membership in a city, but of some common nationality, and this not just one among all, but one balancing all the rest. For the categories into which you now divide the world are not Hellenes and Barbarians, and it is not absurd, the distinction which you made, because you show them a citizenry more numerous, so to speak, than the entire Hellenistic race. The division which you substituted is one into Romans and non-Romans.[31]

And so, indeed, the world became divided into "European" and "non-European," the valued and the nonvalued, the worthy and the unworthy.

Europeans, above all, see themselves as the "grand organizers," the forgers of order from chaos. They do not recognize the order that they find in nature and in other cultures, and so they impose their own wherever they go. (He is not "religious" man in the phenomenological sense that Eliade uses this term, and therefore for him the world does not present itself as "cosmos"—only chaos that he must reshape into a manmade, desacralized, wholly rational "order."[32] Land and people (and even space) are not conquered until they are so ordered; Christianity is, above all, an "ordering" of the individual. And it is the military in European culture that represents the epitome of this kind of order. Aristides says again,

> In respect to military science, furthermore, you have made all men look like children. . . . Like a spinning of thread which is continuously drawn from many filaments into fewer and fewer strands, the many individuals of your forces are always drawn together into fewer and fewer formations; and so they reach their complete integration throughout those who are at each point placed in command, one over others, each others over others still, and so on. Does this not rise above Man's power of organization?[33]

Below Philip Curtin describes the British Niger Expedition. It exemplifies the mood, presumption, and *utamaroho* we are describing, the peculiar European self-image:

> The government expedition sailed in April 1841 in a mood of high hope. Every care was taken. The steamers were especially constructed and placed under the command of experienced naval officers. They were also to sign anti-slave trade treaties with the African authorities and establish one or more trading posts, plus a "model farm" on land purchased from the Africans at the juncture of the Niger and Benue. The government supplied the ships. The African Civilization Society supplied the scientific staff. The Church

Missionary Society sent representation, organized as a private firm, took responsibility for the model farm.[34]

The assumption underlying this endeavor is that the European has the right and the duty to sail into alien lands; no lands are in fact "alien" to them. The Niger Expedition was nothing more than an invasion (fortunately for the Africans, in this instance anyway, it failed). But to those who participated in it, it was a "mission of mercy." For Europeans there are no lands that belong to others. All land and space (air and water) belong to them. And as they bring "order," they bring "peace." Aristides says again of Rome's accomplishments:

> ... before your empire there had been confusion everywhere and things were taking a random course, but when you assumed the presidency, confusion and strife ceased, and universal order entered as a brilliant light over the private and public affairs of man, laws appeared and altars of gods received man's confidence ... now a clear and universal freedom from all fear has been granted both to the world and to those who live in it.[35]

And so the European becomes the world's peace-maker. It becomes their mission to bring "peace" and "freedom" to all by the imposition of their order. *Pax Romanus* is the "Roman world order," just as the American objective of peace means as much United States control as possible. In a speech delivered on April 4, 1973, Nixon said, "only America has the power to build peace." The *utamaroho* that inspired this statement is precisely the same as that to which Aristides responds in his paean to Rome in the second century. These men represent the same cultural tradition and are both nationalistic proponents of that tradition.

Race and National Identity

The creation of a national consciousness has been a crucial component of European success, because of the preeminence of political definition in the nature of the European *utamaroho*. Consciousness presupposes identity. The question of national identity is essential. No group of people have realized this more than European historians.

What Platonic thought, Christianity, and science have done for the unification of Europe is complemented by what Europe's historians have contributed to the mythology of the racial and national origins of European peoples. Hugh MacDougall begins his book *Racial Myth in English History* by saying: "Myths of origin enable people to locate themselves in time and space." This is true for most cultures, but an oversimplification in the case of the European experience, as MacDougall's book demonstrates. Myths of origin for Europeans have functioned most significantly to justify and to inspire imperialistic behavior toward non-European peoples.

The European national self-image had to fit and support the European *utamaroho* and ideology. Its construction was part of a long slow process, seemingly disparate at times, as each European nationality immersed itself within the limited parameters of its own narrowly defined boundaries. But even this competitive process fed into the building of a larger European national consciousness and the self-image on which it depended. European cultural history, understood from the perspective of the *asili* concept, reveals the centrality of myth and myth-making to political success (in this case imperialism). What surfaces as central in the European experience in this regard is the myth of national/racial origin. And even in competing myths of the German, French, English, Italian, and Spanish, we can identify certain common themes that eventually jelled into and emerged as a monolithic and powerful "preferred" European self-image.

In his book *The Aryan Myth,* Leon Poliakov focuses on what he calls in one passage, "Germanomania."[36] In this way he describes what is perhaps the most common myth of national origin among Europeans: "Aryan" descent. At first even the obsession with German origins was colored by an attachment to biblical mythology, and all European nations claimed that their people descended from Japheth. Even Martin Luther as late as the early sixteenth century said that the German people descended from Ashkenaz, who was the first born of Gomer, who was the first born of Japheth and Noe, who came directly from Adam.[37] Such claims were common throughout European history.

Martin Luther, celebrated for his inspiration of religious reformation, was above all a German nationalist rebelling against the control of Latin Christendom. He compared the Pope to the anti-Christ and gave voice to national feelings of the German people, who felt exploited by Rome. Poliakov points out that the Protestant Reformation can also be understood, in part, as a German reaction to the Italian Papacy.[38] If Orthodox Christianity, having served its purpose in the creation of the myth of European superiority, was now perceived as interfering with the realization of the German national self, then it had to step aside. Centuries later Adolf Hitler would follow in the same tradition, as German self-image conflicted with the practical matter of European unity. In European development it was essential that the people, especially those in leadership, possess an image of themselves that would enable them to galvanize their energies in the fulfillment of an envisioned destiny. Papal control conflicted with German self-image.

In Spain, Russia, and England as well, the desire to be associated with a German heritage was compelling. This association became a conviction that helped to inspire Europeans to seek power over others. Poliakov says that early in European history Gothic descent was understood to be superior. "The Christian princes of medieval Spain, inspired by the conviction that they were Goths, made every effort to behave like the offspring of a conquering race."[39] The European *utamaroho* demanded identification with the conquering mode. "The old tendency in Spain was to over-value Germanic blood and to give preference to descent from Magog over the indigenous posterity of Tubal.[40] The earlier claims to descent from biblical characters were later replaced by racial and nationalistic ideologies. "During the Renaissance the influence of antiquity began to rival that of the sacred scriptures."[41]

In the following passage from the prologue to the Salic Law, written in the eighth century, the French drew a self-portrait, calling themselves "Franks" because of the prestige in which German origins were held: "illustrious race, founded by God Himself, strong in arms, steadfast in alliance, wise in counsel, of singular beauty and fairness, noble and sound in body, daring, swift and awesome, converted to the Catholic faith. . . ."[42] From the onset "fairness" or "whiteness" was part of the European self-image. This perhaps is part of the reason for the obsession with Germanic origins.

The European *utamaroho* very early on demanded the creation of a nationalist myth of superiority. The myth would inspire the people to what they perceived to be "greatness." The early Roman self-image had suffered in comparison with what they considered to be a superior Greek cultural heritage, and in the second century before the Christian Era, they sought to connect themselves with this heritage by claiming descent from the Trojans though Aeneaes, the mythical founder of Troy.[43] Centuries later the English would attempt to do the same thing. The French wanted to be "Franks," because they were convinced, as were other Europeans, of the superiority of ancient "Germanic virtues." Montesquieu wrote that the German ancestors of the French enjoyed a tradition of liberty and independence, an ingredient of the European self-image that was to become hardened into the ideological substructure of the civilization. The German "forebears" of the French were honorable, courageous, and proud; "they hanged their traitors and they drowned their cowards."[44] Poliakov says that Montesquieu argued that English Parliamentary institutions were of this ancient Germanic origin and that the French should emulate their example.[45]

It would seem that the European mentality, since its inception in the Indo-European hordes of the North, caused them to fear strangers and therefore to react to their fear with aggressiveness.[46] A warlike disposition was necessary, or else one could not enjoy "liberty." This is the theme that surfaces again and again in the self-image of the European who identified with a defensiveness and distrust of others that translated into aggressive destruction/consumption of all that was "other": the "love of liberty" and the mandate to "lead" others in "freedom."

An African-centered interpretation of European cultural history, using the analytical tool of the *asili* concept, demonstrates the centrality of racialist thought, of racial myth in European ideology. The concept of racial superiority is inextricably entwined in the matrix of the European mythoform. Racialist thought has even been systemic to European development. It complements capitalistic, exploitative, aggressive behavior; but is not caused by this behavior. Racism is endemic to European chauvinism, a consistent factor of European history. It is based on the nature of the *utamaroho,* i.e., threatened by difference, essentially materialistic and aggressive. It is the European *utamaroho* that creates the system of capitalism, which in turn complements the national consciousness, an ingredient of which white nationalism consists. We see this pattern again and again in the historical/ethnological record.

The development of England as a national entity exemplifies the special role of racial thought in the creation of a national identity in the European experience. The history of England is the history of the European self-image, forcing itself into the consciousness of humanity. It also demonstrates the indispensable role of the historian in the process and answers the question of why it was so important to first create the European myth of a secular "objective" and "scientific" history. Cultural myth had to be understood as historical "fact." (This is the problem that underlies most biblical interpretation.)

In eleventh- and twelfth-century England, the political problem was that of bringing Britons, Anglo-Saxons, and Normans together into a single nation; that is, of getting these groups to identify as one nationality. In 1136, Geoffrey of Monmouth completed his history of the groups in question. His "history" created the Arthurian legend that connected them all to Trojan myth. Hugh MacDougall, in this regard, says that Geoffrey's "history," "as, a work of creative imagination was a superb achievement."[47] It provided the mythological framework and justification for a nation based on a royal monarchy in which the king had absolute authority. This authority was supported by a mythology that praised the legendary achievements of past kings, but as the power of the royalty began to give way to the demands of the newly developing commercial interests, a new economic structure, and the parliamentary form that accompanied these changes, the legend of King Arthur was no longer politically useful.[48] Trojan origins gave way in inspirational power to Germanic origins. The English self-image was evolving. MacDougall says,

> Anglo-Saxonism, born in the sixteenth century in response to a need to demonstrate an historical continuity for the national church and nourished in the seventeenth century in debates over racial supremacy, finally triumphed and became the dominant myth that fixed the national imagination.[48]

Basically Anglo-Saxonism held that the English people descended from German Angles, Saxons, and Jutes, and while this myth of racial origin may not have become dominant until the sixteenth century, it was prefigured much earlier in the work of Bede, "the father of English history," writing in 731. that the English had been elected by God to establish political hegemony.[49] This supposed superiority came more and more to be associated with alleged German origins. This myth, according to MacDougall, alternately referred to as "Anglo-Saxonism," "Teutonism," or "Gothicism," had four postulates:

1. Germanic peoples are of unmixed origins, having a universal civilizing mission and are superior to all others.

2. The English are of Germanic origin; Their history beginning with the landing of Hengist and Horsa at Ebbsfield, Kent in 449.

3. English political and religious institutions are the freest in the world. This is a legacy of German ancestors.

4. The English represent the genius of German heritage to a greater degree than any of the other descendants and therefore carry a special responsibility of leadership in the world.[50]

This Germanic heritage was to be extolled by countless historians, literati, and political leaders of almost every European nationality. English racial and national myth began to be linked more and more with that of Germany, which saw itself as having been maligned and neglected in order to facilitate domination by a Latin Church hierarchy. This reasoning must have had tremendous appeal for the English, who, under the leadership of Henry VIII, sought religious independence from Rome. English nationalism created an English church, and it is interesting that while Henry rejected Latin authority, he did not reject Christianity itself, because of its deep association with the definition of "civilization."

Martin Luther said for the Germans what Anglicanism was saying for the English, "I thank God that I am able to hear and find my God in the German Language, whom [sic] neither I nor you would ever find in Latin or Greek or Hebrew."[51] The Germanic consciousness of England was further encouraged by the fact that London became a place of refuge for German Protestants fleeing persecution. "Out of the Renaissance and the Reformation a myth developed of an original Germanic people with roots reaching back to Adam, possessing a language and culture richer than and independent from any other."[52]

William Camden (1551-1663) was, according to MacDougall, the first Englishman to treat the history of the Anglo-Saxons in a serious and detailed manner. He said that he was motivated by "a common love for our country and the glory of the English name," and that he was intent on emphasizing the Germanic origins of "English Saxons."[53] According to Camden, England owed its language and greatness to the historical victories of the Germans. These Germans were the triumphant Franks and Burgundians in France; the Heruli, West Goths, Vandals, and Lombards in Italy; the Suevians and Vandals in Spain; and the English-Saxons in England. The Greatness of the Saxons was expressed by Camden as: "This warlike, victorious, stiff, stout, and vigorous nation."[53] This is further evidence of the function of social science, in this case history, in the service of the national myth and imperial ambition. It is also evidence of the self-image of the European as warlord.

In order to convincingly argue for Germanic origins of the English people and their culture, Norman influence had to be minimized. MacDougall describes Richard Verstegen's *Restitution of Decayed Intelligence* (1605) as a "Panegyric to Germanic descent of the English" and says that it was "the first comprehensive presentation in English of a theory of national origin based on a belief in the racial superiority of the Germanic people."[54]

The ability of a nation or a nationality to mobilize itself for resistance against oppression, or for imperial aggression, cannot exist in

a vacuum. It is of necessity linked to a peoples' definition of themselves, and such self-definition must locate itself in time and space.
The rootedness that results is a product of the national myth.
Successful political action is linked to positive self-image. A concerted
military campaign is strengthened to the degree that the people in
question identify as a single entity with a common source and a common destiny. Belief in special origins will inspire special behavior.
Europe has understood this better than others and long before other
cultural groups felt the need to act politically. For the most part the
African and other non-European political sense has suffered under
humanistic priorities. As people of African descent and others assert
their definitions of self in an effort to create a national consciousness, European academia belittles these efforts as juvenile and unnecessary. Can it be that they do this (1) because their own myths of
national origin have long ago been constructed and have served their
purposes well and (2) because they are well aware of the motiva-
tional power of such myths?

The English, in reality a people with very little to be proud of,
whose own history began as a result of colonization by others, self-
consciously turned a heritage of mediocrity into one that inspired
imperial success the likes of which had never been seen. They then
denied the process to others and pretended that it had never
occurred among them, extolling the virtues of "objectivity" and scientific historicism! But scrutiny of English history paints a very different picture.

As the English rising commercial class fought to establish a parliament that would take power from one group and place it into the
hands of another, they argued that such an institution owed its genesis to Saxon Germany. English law was said to have originated there
as well. The argument was for the limitation of the power of the
Crown. People like John Toland (1701) and Catherine MaCaulay
(1763) argued in favor of a tradition of "freedom" that demanded that
they be freed from the yolk of royal power.

Herein lies an aspect of the European self-image that has been
consistently expressed in European nationalism, so that we have no
difficulty in identifying it in contemporary Euro-America. The Aryan
(Sanskrit: Arya, "noble") Saxons were a "freedom-loving" people. This
is perhaps the most significant aspect of the national/racial myth.
Supposedly, German people loved their freedom and had never
allowed themselves to be conquered. The English, of all descendants
of the Germanic peoples, had the responsibility of carrying on the heritage of "freedom" and the obligation of sharing it with others through

their rule. This theme was to be echoed again and again throughout the history of European and Euro-American chauvinism. Ancient Germany was held to have been inhabited by a people who loved liberty, and the English sought to associate their political and social institutions with the "freedom" of these forebears. In a speech delivered in 1832, Baron Henry Bulwer said, "It was in the free forests of Germany that the light of our purer religion first arose."[55] In his famous work *The Decline and Fall of the Roman Empire,* Edward Gibbon held that the "puny" Romans had been rescued by the "fierce giants of the North, their German invaders."[56] The implication is that these "fierce giants" brought freedom, no matter how violent the deliverance of the Romans. Even Kant placed the highest value on this notion of "freedom" and said that in order to be moral one had to be "free."[57]

According to MacDougall, Sharon Turner (*History of the Anglo-Saxon,* 1805) wrote that although the Germanic tribes were barbarian, they had a "love of individual independence and a high sense of political liberty" and that these characteristics were "the source of our [England's] greatest improvements in legislature, society, knowledge and general comfort."[58] Turner characterized the "nomadic mind" as being especially well suited to the creation of free social institutions. It is fascinating how historians are able to take what they usually judge as a culturally debilitating factor—nomadism—and turn it into a strength in order to serve the national myth.

"The nomadic mind is a mind of great energy and sagacity, in the pursuits and necessities peculiar to that state, and has devised many principles of laws, governments, customs, and institutions, which have been superior to others that the earlier civilized have established."[58] Turner adds that among Germanic tribes the Saxons were "superior to others in energy, strength, and warlike fortitude," and that the Anglican Church found its rudimentary beginnings in Saxony.[59]

The French had also used a myth of national origin to support the struggle of the rising bourgeoisie against the royal power of the Crown: a struggle that the protagonists viewed in terms of "freedom" against "tyranny." Diderot, an encyclopedist, connected this need for "freedom" with the Frankish legacy:

> Three kinds of nobles existed at the beginning of the monarchy: those descended from the Gaulish chivalry who followed the profession of arms; others who derived from the Roman magistrature and who combined the exercise of arms with the administration of justice, civil government or finance; and the third were the Frank,

all dedicated to the practice of arms, who were exempt from all personal servitudes and taxes. For this they were called *Franks,* as opposed to the rest of the population which consisted almost entirely of serfs. This franchise was understood as the hallmark of nobility itself so that *Frank, Freeman* or *Nobleman* were normally synonymous expressions.[60]

The self-image, which Euro-America has inherited from its European ancestors, of the conqueror who "frees," is accompanied by a value that becomes part of European ideology. This "freedom" is defined in terms of individualism and the license to "achieve" no matter what the cost to others. This peculiarly capitalist "morality" is the hand-maiden of American imperialism. But European-Americans are following a long-established tradition in this pattern of cultural/political behavior. Charles Kingsley writing in the mid-nine-teenth century said that the English were Teutons with a universal mission: "The welfare of the Teutonic race is the welfare of the world."[61] And, of course, they had been chosen by "God." The American president Woodrow Wilson would make the world "safe" for "democracy." Richard Nixon and Ronald Reagan created police-men. The concept of being self-appointed leaders of the world, which obligates people of European descent to "free" others, is part of the logic of a self-image linked in mythology to the ancient hordes of the German forests, reinterpreted as a "freedom-loving" race. It is out of this cultural tradition that the concepts of "freedom," "liberty," and "free enterprise," "the pursuit" of "whatever"—associated with the Western world and Western value—were born.

Verstegen, writing in 1605, had said that these ancient Germans were great because: (1) no other people had inhabited Germany; (2) they had not mixed with any other racial group; and (3) they had never been subdued by any other group.[54] While James Ronde, writ-ing in 1865, said that "the ignorant and selfish may be and are justly compelled for their own advantage to obey a rule which rescues them from their natural weakness . . . and those who cannot prescribe a law to themselves, if they desire to be free must be content to accept direction from others."[62] These two sets of ideas, coupled together, produced the self-image that matched the power *utamaroho,* the ide-ology of expansionism, and the *utamawazo* of control.

But there was to be yet another ingredient to the overwhelm-ingly successful self-portrait. The ideology of "progress" was the *coup de grace* of the conquering cultural ego. "The nineteenth century was England's century." So says MacDougall. What made such success possible? It was a combination of cultural factors, all ideologically consistent. Nothing was better suited to this ideology than the vision of European progress. Its optimism, arrogance, and freedom from the fetters of common human morality, which ordinarily prevents other peoples from wanton theft, rape, and wholesale murder. The nineteenth century was "England's century," because there was nothing that the English would not do—there were no holds barred for the English nation—no place they would not go in the service of greed and in fulfillment of this insatiable *utamaroho*. The ideology of progress justified every possible act that could be committed in this service. Progress was a path that had to be followed by "civilizing" human beings, and the English were the leaders whose destiny it was to take everyone towards this abstract goal. A powerful self-image![63]

In MacDougall's view;

> As a directive force moving Western society to an ever higher form of civilization, the notion of progress was accepted as axiomatic by most major thinkers. Conceived by men of the Enlightenment as a secular substitute for the ancient belief in divine providential rule, it dominated European thought by the end of the French Revolution. In association with neo-nationalism and industrialism, it provided the dynamism which led to western world hegemony.[64]

He says that Kant supported this self-image with a theory of history as being the unfolding of meaning and truth and as serving the purposes of morality. This theory leads to the interpretation of history as justifying all actions of its European "lords": industrialists, capitalists, imperialists alike. This was the "age of progress." MacDougall points out that "Hegel led the way in identifying the process of universal history with Germanic political thought and culture. He asserted that the final stage of history was reached with the development of Christian Europe and specifically with the manifestation in his own time of the Germanic spirit."[65] "The German spirit is the spirit of the new world." (Hegel quoted in MacDougall, p. 90.)

MacDougall reminds us that no other profession served the cause of the progress ideology and Anglo-Saxonism more than that of the historian. But that is because it is the historian who bears the responsibility for the construction of the myth of national origin on which a national identity and successful image rests. Within the European cultural tradition it is in the progress ideology that "history" takes on meaning. The ideology of progress is distinctively European, because it is based on the European *utamaroho,* generating an effectively aggressive self-image. (See Chap. 9.)

Underlying all of these themes of Saxonism, "freedom," and

:"progress" is the concept of "race," as defined in the context of white nationalism. MacDougall quotes from Charles Wentworth Dilke (b. 1866): "The gradual extinction of the inferior races is not only a law of nature, but a blessing to mankind."[66] The Aryans were seen to be the parents of Western European culture. The great mission had been assigned to three superior Aryan groups: the Greeks, Romans, and Teutons. Each in its turn were "to be rulers and teachers of the world." This was according to Edward Freeman in his *History of the Norman Conquest* (1876).[67] Victorian England had descended in an unbroken line form Teutonic Germany, so went the myth of racial and national origin. "Elitist racial theories stressing Nordic superiority received further confirmation from the new sciences of ethnology and anthropology." Beginning in the eighteenth century Linnaeus, Comte de Buffon, and Blumenbach classified human beings on the basis of biological differences.[68] Phrenology involved the measuring of skulls, which was supposed to be an indication of intellectual ability.

It was inevitable that the myth of national origin, the question of national identity, and the positive self-image of European peoples should be ultimately expressed in white nationalist terms. As Europe became more unified in terms of a cohesive national consciousness, the categories of racial distinction would of course become broader with competition between European nationalities giving way to a statement of racial identification that tended to unite them—the myth of Aryan descent always reigning supreme. As the British Empire spread to exploit more melanated people who could in no way claim Germanic heritage, the lines of "race" became more clearly attached to the broad cultural/historical lines that separated Europe from the rest of the world. The European self-image has always been based on the implicit perception of cultural/racial difference. The *utamaroho* thrives on this difference. Because of the nature of this *utamaroho,* the dialectical complement of the positive European self-image is a negative image of others.

Media and Self-Image

Kovel says that mass media and advertising "hold the main force of the cultural superego,"[69] and most certainly the themes isolated above are blatantly expressed in the European, Euro-American media. The movie industry has had an obvious nationalist propagandistic character; a function that it has performed expertly. There is nothing comparable in any other culture, in terms of effect. The line between the projected image and the truly operative self-image is very thin, if it is to be drawn at all, and there is no doubt that Euro-American-made films reveal the European *utamaroho*. Movies that depict the "virtuous" pioneer family defending itself against the "vicious" and irrationally "hostile" Native Americans function to justify the actions of the European-Americans and their behavior towards the indigenous population. But it is also the case that these pioneers must, in fact, have thought of themselves as the virtuous, adventurous souls they are depicted to be. Surely they believed it their "manifest destiny" to "brave the wilds of untamed lands" and that by building their homesteads, and thereby bringing family life and "civilization" to the "wilds," they were being the most moral of beings. It is equally certain that they could not understand the intransigent hostility of the "Indians"—after all, were they not making great sacrifices to bring their inherited talent for "civilization" to these ingrates?! This image had to be assimilated into the Western European self-image. It had been adumbrated in the earliest manifestations of Westernness. The movies that project this are consistent with the European self-image as "they who create order from chaos," and "they who conquer the unconquerable."

The British films that are the counterpart of the British imperial ethos portray the East Indian and African nationalists as "irresponsible elements" who seek to bring suffering, violence, and disorder to their people—for their own personal gain or, at best, for misdirected political reasons. The British officer and his forces, on the other hand, represent the interest of the natives and bring rationality, peace, and, above all, stability with their rule. Again, this is, of course, European nationalistic propaganda, but it is also consistent with the operative European self-image as "world peace-maker," "world organizer," and "world superior." The white man's burden concept is not merely propaganda, it is an internalized self-portrait that functions normatively. This helps us to understand the European-American reaction to the airing of the *The Africans* series on Public Television (November 1986). Major films, documentaries, and other media productions that do not serve to propagandize the preferred self-image of the European are resented and seen as "biased."

The location of European films is often an indication of that aspect of the European self-image the film is projecting. When the story takes place on foreign soil, the film becomes an opportunity for the expression of the European self-image in relation to the image of others. The lands of other peoples often provide exotic settings and backgrounds for the "love affairs" and political and economic intrigues of the European protagonists. ("Their love set the Dark Continent aflame!") The reason that this setting is so common in European (American) films is that it has become a meaningful aspect of the European *utamaroho*. The world exists as a playground—a backdrop—for sport and play, for the adventures of the European. (The movie *Out of Africa* is a contemporary example.) Peoples of other cultures are actually experienced as "props," supportive to the main (important) action of the script. These exotic settings are excellent for such purposes; a sexually stimulating "native" dancer at a strategic moment in a love affair—the romantic atmosphere of an "unspoiled" (not yet "civilized") terrain—help to excite the "sophisticated" and sated imagination of the European audience. Sometimes a "native" girl helps to comprise part of the "unspoiled" resource to be enjoyed; at others, the European gets involved with the native surroundings to the extent that he becomes a temporary "god" or "chief." All of this points to the very real belief and assumption of Europeans that the lands of other people provide an environment in which they are to act out their fantasies.

In advertising, this use of and relationship to other cultures is a dominant theme. Not only the terrain but the indigenous peoples themselves are no more than "ornaments" used to enhance the appeal of the European who is being depicted. There is no more accurate expression of the European *utamaroho* than a fashion ad with an "exotic" setting or an airline commercial in which the world is represented as one vast resort area to which Europeans can escape from the "seriousness" of their "important" work. Pan American Airlines attests to all the places it has "opened up" to the West: "*We* can take you anywhere in this world *we've opened.*" Delta Airlines talks about "*Our* Caribbean" and the various other places that "belong" to them. These phrases express the European's conviction and assumption that he owns the world, or at least that it is potentially his. The task becomes simply a matter of transforming it—bit by bit—into their kind of world, into what is familiar and comfortable for them. The airlines, hotels, travel agencies, businesses make sure that this happens. They want to be able to assure the European-American and European that they are working to make yet another area, part of the "Western world" (and therefore of the "civilized" world).

Of course, the implications of this process are that these areas become more and more *un*comfortable for the indigenous populations that inhabit them as the original inhabitants become less and less welcomed by the invaders. Only in very controlled roles are they welcomed—as waiters, bellhops, and the like—which helps to reinforce the European self-image. It is characteristic of the European *utamaroho* that the plague of European-American "adventure-tourists" are most attracted to places that have been least contaminated by themselves. But the groundwork must have been laid by the "advance men" to assure them that the European stamp has been put there; that they are indeed protected against "non-European disorder" and hostility. The European/European-American desire historically (as potent now as at any time in western history) is to "save" and destroy (Kovel); to "discover" and take over; to "open up" and move in.

William Golding's book, and the film based on it, *Lord of the Flies* is an excellent source for the study of expression of the European *utamaroho* in European literature. It contains quite explicit statements of the European self-image in relation to the European image of others. The polar dichotomies of the book mirror those of Western European nationalism: order (law) versus chaos; the ubiquitous good versus evil; "the chief" and Piggy (who represent civilization) versus Jack and "the hunters" (who represent the primitive). An underlying current throughout the plot is the battle of "knowledge" against the abyss of "superstition."

The story revolves around a group of very young English boys (probably from six to twelve years old), who are marooned on an uninhabited island without adults during a crisis caused by nuclear warfare. The most intelligent and well-mannered boys (the "good guys"), led by Ralph, "the chief," devise a plan for decision-making and the maintenance of order and assurance of survival. Opposing them are "the hunters." These are the "primitives," the bad guys, the not very intelligent ones. They are led by Jack, who is divisive, "regressive," and destructive. He threatens the "civilized" order of the group by going off by himself and inducing others to join his "tribe." The bad guys are utterly irresponsible; they play with fire, they grunt more often than they talk, and they partake in "ritual" (not the ordered, culturally constructive ritual that we know of in African societies), in which they run around wildly, killing the good guys and shouting, "Kill the beast." The "beast" is a mythical being in which the "hunters" believe; a belief they foster and use as a justification for killing the good guys. In the film the hunters are made to look like the European image of non-Europeans. They give the impression of having darker skins, they paint their faces, they scream and yell and make noises like animals and supposedly like "primitive" peoples. Piggy (who is chubby) is the brainy intellectual whom Jack despises from the outset, and at one point Piggy says to Jack, "Are you going to be a pack of savages or sensible like Ralph?"

And therein lies the theme of the story, which is that of the continual regression of the boys in the absence of adult (European) supervision. The hunters kill Piggy, but before they can get to Ralph the boys are rescued by adults. In European terms, the boys have culturally moved "backward" thousands of years in one and a half hours of film time. This is an expression of one of the European's greatest fears. Perhaps the worst fate that could befall Europeans is that they lose their "civilization" (superiority) and become reduced to what they view the "non-Europeans" to be. The dichotomies that are presented are not those that accurately indicate the distinctiveness of European-derived culture or even the difference between traditional cultures and secular societies. The images presented are almost the reverse of these distinctions. African and other primary societies are characterized as being "disordered," "uncontrolled," and "immoral"; European society supposedly symbolized the movement away from this into order, morality, and responsibility—where the individual can feel safe!

The 1954 Hollywood film *The Naked Jungle* is a prototype of the media's interpretation of "the saga of Western man," in which he is depicted as "conquering new lands" and "taming the wilds." Whether the setting is Africa, India, the Pacific Islands, or South America, the story is ethnologically the same.

Charleton Heston is a "strong," "rugged," "fearless" Euro-American plantation owner in South America. He is also very, very proud. He tells his newly arrived girl friend, "I came here when I was nineteen and started with just twenty acres. I built all of this with my own hands, I hewed it out. There was *nothing* when I came here." But he warns her, lest she make the mistake of thinking that everything is like the paradise he has built. "Civilization is only as far as my land goes, after that you are in the jungle, where no man has a name. In the jungle man is reduced to an animal and the only law is survival."

At one point they meet a native "friend." The hero explains to the woman that his friend "is more civilized than the others [because] he has Mayan blood." At another point they view a "cruel" indigenous ritual in which a man is being killed for taking another man's wife. The white woman is horrified at such "immorality" and protests that it should be stopped.

The movie gives the impression of being one long, very authoritative command from Charleton Heston, the undisputed "boss" of everything and everyone, punctuated by the sound of gun shots that issue from the pistol he carries constantly, the cold rationality of which is the supreme symbol of white power in the picture.

The plot reaches its high point when Heston comes up against the "soldier ants." These are ants that "think" and travel in such immense numbers that they can decimate the side of a mountain. They hold most of South America in terror. Everyone on the plantation wants to flee, but not Heston, whose image is nothing short of that of a white god. He says that he will stay and fight! His friend, the South American police officer, thinks he is crazy. He says to Heston, "If you won't think of yourself at least think of your men [all indigenous]." Whereupon Heston replies (in the voice of Moses handing down the Ten Commandments): "I *am* thinking of them. Fifteen years ago they were savages. I took them out of the jungle. If I leave they'll go back, and civilization will go with them."

Next comes the inevitable scene in which he confronts the "witch doctor" (who also thinks that Heston is crazy). With good reason, the "witch doctor" is trying to convince the indigenous people to get out as fast as they can. But Heston, the white god, tells them to "be brave like his white woman." He is victorious, for the men decide to stay, and the "witch doctor" slinks away, looking cowardly and weak. Once again non-European cultural tradition is defeated.

The remainder of the film is concerned with Heston's death-defying, heroic battle with the soldier ants, a battle that he, of course, wins. And so Europeans are again successful; but then they deserve to be. They are strong" and "brave," "intelligent" and "good." They are above all "unselfish" in their efforts to bring "civilization" to an unfortunate "backward" land. The money and power they receive from their plantations do not contradict the altruism of their motives, for, after all, this adventuresome, expansionistic spirit should properly be rewarded.

In an excellent (and excruciatingly rare) satiric treatment of the conquering *utamaroho* of the European, the British comic film *Carry on Cleo* lampoons not only the Romans and their incessant military expeditions, but all the Hollywood films that glorify this age of Western imperialism as well. In the film, during one conquering campaign, Antony says to Julius Caesar, "You *know*, Julie, I don't think these people *want* to be conquered," and Caesar answers, "I *know* what you mean—*apathetic!* . . . They won't even use the nice new roads I built them."

Kipling's message to his European brothers is that "Yours is the Earth and Everything that's in it." There is no doubt that many of the aspects of the European *utamaroho* and self-image are extremely "positive" in the sense that, in terms of their own interpretation of their nationalistic interest, their *utamaroho* gives them the confidence, self-assurance, and optimism necessary to support their objectives. The self-image is functional. This is the function of a national-istic ideology. But the definition of European nationalism (which becomes expansionism) and the European cultural ego are so extreme and so massive that "positive self-image" in the context of European culture becomes monstrous presumption and arrogance. It is predicated on the degradation and demeaning of other peoples, on the support and persistence of a negative image of "others," and on a lack of respect for their legitimate self-deterministic expression. It is European culture that cannot allow or coexist with "difference," yet paradoxically thrives on it.

The European Self-Image in the Literature of White Nationalism

The literature of white nationalism is significant here not because it expresses an erratic or bizzare element in European cul-ture, but on the contrary, because the same themes are recognizable in it as those found in European philosophical discourse, in the lit-erature of European social science, in European aesthetic expres-sion, and in the Western media—wherever Europeans (explicitly or implicitly) give testament to their collective self-image.

The various manifestations of the European self-image reveal an *utamaroho* that is consistent with that of white nationalism. The descriptive term "racism," if not inaccurate, is certainly misleading. It takes attention away from the very special nature of white nationalism, usually with the political objective of debunking any form of cultural nationalism—thereby ignoring the possibilities of nationalist ideolo-gies. What is ethnologically significant is how the European-Caucasian spokesmen define their nationalism and the characteristics they iden-tify as "European," "good," or "white."

William Hepworth Dixon writes in praise of European man, the conqueror:

The tale of a hundred years of white progress is a Marvelous History . . . The European races are spreading over every conti-nent, and mastering the isles and inlets of every sea. . .

Russia . . . has carried her arms into Finland, Crim, Tartary, The Caucasus and the Monhammedan, Khanales, extending the White empire on the Caspian and the Euxine . . . Vaster still have been the marches and the conquests of Great Britain . . . Hardly less strik-ing than the progress of Russia and England has been that of the United States. . .

China has been standing still, while England, Russia and America have been conquering, planting, and annexing lands. . .

The surface of the earth is passing into Anglo-Saxon hands.[70]

In the writings of Joseph Arthur Gobineau, it becomes clear how important the concept of "civilization" is to the white nationalist position and therefore why the Western European discipline of anthropology has been historically linked so closely to its arguments, for it is this discipline that has contributed most to the European nationalistic definition and use of the term "civilization." Gobineau says,

> I am continually speaking of "civilization," and cannot help doing so; for it is only by the existence in some measure or the complete absence, of this attribute, that I can gauge the relative merits of the different races.[71]

After describing the "negro" and "yellow" races, Gobineau offers the following description of the white race. Interwoven in this statement are European ideals, the themes of European nationalism, and the attributes claimed by the European self-image.

> We come now to the white peoples. These are gifted with reflective energy, or rather with an energetic intelligence. They have a feeling for utility, but in a sense far wider and higher, more courageous and ideal, than the yellow races; a perseverance that takes account of obstacles and ultimately finds a means of overcoming them; a greater physical power, an extraordinary instinct for order, not merely as a guarantee of peace and tranquility, but as an indispensable means of self-preservation. At the same time, they have remarkable, even extreme love of liberty, and are openly hostile to the formalism under which the Chinese are glad to vegetate, as well as the strict despotism which is the only way of governing the Negro. . .

> The immense superiority of the white peoples in the whole field of the intellect is balanced by an inferiority in the intensity of their sensations. In the world of the senses, the white man is far less gifted than the others, and so is less tempted and less absorbed by considerations of the body, although in physical structure he is far the most vigorous.[72]

Wayne MacLeod, who refers to himself as a "racialist," makes the following significant observation,

Although many peoples have considered themselves superior to their neighbors—the Japanese, the Jews, even some African tribes—it has been the typical white variety of Caucasian with whom the self-centered notions of race supremacy have been associated.[73]

It is very important, as MacLeod observes, to recognize the fact that ethnic or cultural nationalism does not necessarily imply theories of ethnic or cultural supremacy. There is a "natural" tendency for cultural groups to believe that their ways are somehow better or more desirable than the ways of other groups, for after all, these are the implications of cultural commitment. It does not follow, however, that they must impose that culture on others or that they must be supreme or rulers among them.

For MacLeod, European peoples are "rulers of conquered peoples and creators of civilization. . . . The tendency of people resembling north Europeans to spread and conquer is one of their historical characteristics."[74]

MacLeod explains that historically it has been the Aryan race that has transmitted the phenomenon of (and therefore the "capacity" to generate) "civilization" from generation to generation. The concept of "civilization" is again paramount in this statement of white nationalism. MacLeod's concern is that it will be destroyed if the race is allowed to die out. (It should be remembered as well that "purity" and control of racial inheritance was an important aspect of Plato's strategy.)

Below MacLeod recites those characteristics of Western European cultural tradition of which he is most proud; those things, in his conception, the European has given to the world. (The cultural traits that Weber lists in his introduction to *The Protestant Ethic and the Spirit of Capitalism* as "Western" are very similar.)

Knowledge and observation based on mathematics, the systematic forms of thought of Roman Law, the methods of experiment and the laboratory, rational chemistry and science, spacial perspective in painting, printed literature, the Press, the State with a written constitution, the concept of the citizen, free labor, the orchestra with sonatas and symphonies—were all unknown to the world before the emergence of the Occident, not to mention the strides in invention and discovery, transport improvements, electrical communication, etc., promoted by the same racial type, that is "like unto itself only."[75]

For MacLeod the superior types of temperament that will produce "progressive standards" are characterized by "pensive, nervous, forceful dispositions"; as opposed to those who are "easy man-nered," "lacking aggressiveness," and "given to animated extrover-sion." "Intellect," says MacLeod, "is analytical, it dissects, divides." And translated into the language of international political ambition, all of this says that a United Empire of the Western World will be the "ultimate expression of our civilization. . . . This is our natural des-tiny."[76]

These are the images provided by Lothrop Stoddard in *The Rising Tide of Color:*

> The man who . . . opened his atlas to a political map of the world [in 1914] . . . probably got one fundamental impression: the over-whelming preponderance of the white race in the ordering of the world's affairs. Judged by accepted canons of statecraft, the white man towered as the indisputable master of the planet. For from Europe's teeming motherhive the imperious Sons of Japhet had swarmed for centuries to plant laws, their customs, and their bat-tle-flags at the uttermost ends of earth. Two whole continents, North America and Australia, had been made virtually as white in blood as the European motherland; two other continents, South America and Africa, had been extensively colonized by white stocks; while even huge Asia has seen its empty north marsh, Siberia, pre-empted for the white man's abode. Even where white populations had not locked themselves to the soil few regions of the earth had escaped the white man's imperial sway, and vast areas inhabited by uncounted myriads of dusky folk obeyed the white man's will.[77]

Stoddard speaks of the "White Nationalist Commitment," and if the heavily racialist rhetoric is not allowed to get in the way, we can see that the political history of Europe in Africa up to and including the present is accurately described in his statements.

> Fortunately the white man has every reason for keeping a firm hold on Africa. Not only are its central tropics prime sources of raw materials and foodstuffs which white direction can alone develop, but to north and south the white man has struck deep roots into the soil. Both extremities of the continent are "white man's country," where strong white peoples should ultimately arise. Two of the chief white powers, Britain and France, are pledged to the hill in this racial task and will spare no effort to safeguard the heritage of their pioneering children. . . . In short, the real danger to white control of Africa lies not in brown attack or black revolt, but in possible white weakness through chronic discord within the white world itself.[78]

In 1920, Lothrop Stoddard was calling for the unity of white peoples in the cause of Western European nationalism. Today, the United States, the European Economic Community, the former Soviet Union and South Africa are displaying that unity for that cause, in spite of the fact that they may find it convenient to use slightly different rhetoric from that of Stoddard.

Stoddard describes what he calls "The White Flood"; i.e., the worldwide expansion of the white race during the four centuries between 1500 and 1900, "the most prodigious phenomenon in all recorded history."[79] (Recorded by the "prodigious phenomenon" itself!) Since Roman times, he says, the race had been diminishing for various reasons including the Black Death and reluctance to "multiply."[80]

> But after the great discoveries [Columbus, 1492 and Da Gama, 1494], the white man could flank his old opponents. Whole new worlds peopled by primitive races were unmasked, where the white man's weapons made victory certain, and whence he could draw stores of wealth to quicken his home life and initiate a progress that would soon place him immeasurably above his once-dreaded assailants.

> And the white proved worthy of his opportunity. His inherent racial aptitudes had been stimulated by his past. The hard conditions of Medieval life had disciplined him to adversity and had weeded him by natural selection . . . the northern nations — even more vigorous and audacious (than Portugal and Spain) — instantly sprang to the fore and carried forward the proud oriflame of white expansion and world domination.[81]

It was Stoddard's hope that "the whites would universally form a governing caste, directing by virtue of higher intelligence and more resolute will, and exploiting natural resources to the incalculable profit of the whole white race."[82] His hopes have been realized.[83]

But Stoddard was writing in 1920. Is it still possible to find overt expressions of extreme white nationalism? The answer is, of course, yes. In fact we have an instance in which the sentiments of white nationalism are openly used to determine the governmental policies of a powerful, albeit illegally constituted, state in Africa. The following statements were made by P.W. Botha, President of the Republic of South Africa, in 1985,

> My beloved White Afrikaaners, Greetings to all of you brothers and sisters in the name of our holy blood. . .

Pretoria had been made by the white mind for the white man. . . .
We are superior people. . . . The Republic of South Africa . . . has not
been created by wishful thinking. We have created it at the expense
of intelligence, sweat and blood. . .

Intellectually we are superior to the Blacks; that has been proven
beyond any reasonable doubt over the years. . .

Isn't it plausible (therefore) that the White man is created to rule
the Black man?[84]

The themes of the European *utamaroho* are what is significant
in this sampling of white nationalist literature: the European "man"
the conqueror, world savior, bearer of order, and most importantly,
of "civilization," superior and therefore magnanimous in his effort to
impose on them the benefits of his knowledge and talents. It doesn't
matter for African peoples (for the "rest of us") whether Europeans
say that their blessed state of "civilization" is transmitted "racially"
(physically) or culturally; this is ultimately a very fine distinction.
The consequences of blatant "racialist" theory may be even less damaging culturally, as they could "logically" lead to a noninterference,
separation-type policy. On the other hand, ethnologically, the
European *utamaroho* is a subtle admixture of race, culture, and the
ideological conceptions of "civilization" and "progress." The white
nationalist statements are the statements of the liberal European
nationalist with the addition of a racialist rhetoric; a rhetoric that
has been abandoned by contemporary European intelligentsia. This
latter group is accustomed to hiding its nationalism in a barrage of
so-called universalistic terminology and methodology. Which is the
more formidable enemy?

For this reason, if for no other, African and other non-Europeans
must not allow themselves to be frightened by the word "race"; and
the lesson to be learned is that "white man" really does "speak with
forked tongue."

These various aspects of the European *utamaroho* combine to
form a self-image that externally supports European imperialistic
behavior and internally or intraculturally supports extreme rationality, fanatical scientism, a superficial and analytic aesthetic, and a
severe lack of spirituality. Imperialism is supported by the scientists
who construct theories by which the world is consumed; by intellectuals and academicians who use this "knowledge" as power; by
missionaries (modern-day "crusaders") who seek only to impose
their "peace" on the world (so they "altruistically" offer "citizenship"

in their empire). All of these types of individuals have the mentality of the "world savior"—the counterpart of the "world conqueror." The European "humanitarian" shares many of these features as well. He often has the same image of himself in relation to others, as has the European imperialist. Both believe that they are in possession of an "absolute truth" that they would share with the world—like it or not! European-style rationalism ends up in European hegemony, no matter how you cut it. The paternalism of the liberal or the scientific humanist is still an expression of the European *utamaroho* as it implies European superiority. "Humanitarianism" becomes in this interpretation the sharing of that superiority. The intellectual-liberals may have the same self-image as the avowed white nationalists and European cultural imperialists; they use the term "modern" instead of one that is more obviously culture-bound, more blatantly nationalistic. The problem is not the intention these people may have, but to recognize that the ideology that underlies their scientific disciplines is a product of the same cultural/historical development as that of white nationalism.

Again the concept of *asili* surfaces as our most valuable tool in this critique. It demands that we place these various expressions and characteristics of "Europeanness" into one meaningful reality: i.e., the only reality that explains them as parts of a cultural/ideological whole. The *asili* of the culture dictates an obsession with power as control. This can be sought through knowledge ("science") and/or physical assault (military imperialism) and/or cultural imperialism ("progressivism"-Christianity) or the extremely effective combination of all three. The self-image that justifies these aggressive behaviors, and the national consciousness that demands them, are mandated by the epistemology that separates the universe into "self" and "other" and then makes an object of the other. It matters little whether the object is called "pagan," "colonial subject," "underdeveloped," or "black"—she is still "non-European." It matters little whether the self is avowedly identified as "civilized" scientist, Christian, "savior," "modern," or "white"; the conquering self is always European. The concept of *asili* makes it apparent that the *utamawazo* creates a consistent self-image. Both *utamaroho* and self-image are prefigured in the cultural germ (*asili*) and thereby carried in the "cultural genes."

The native is declared insensible to ethics; he represents not only the absence of values, but also the negation of values. He is, ... the enemy of values, ... the absolute evil. He is the corrosive element, destroying all that comes near him; he is the deforming element, disfiguring all that has to do with beauty of morality; he is the depository of maleficent powers, the unconscious and irretrievable instrument of blind forces . . . . All values, in fact, are irrevocably poisoned and diseased as soon as they are allowed in contact with the colonised race. The customs of the colonised people, their traditions, their myths — above all, their myths — are the very sign of that poverty of spirit and of their constitutional depravity.

— *Franz Fanon,* The Wretched of the Earth

Chapter 5

Image of Others

The Complement of the European Self-Image

The persistence of the European *utamaroho* is inherently dependent on the image that Europeans have created of their "opposites." The image of others, the dialectical antithesis of the European self-image, helps to define it. The European image of others is a composite of all those things that represent lack of value; i.e., "negative" human characteristics, within the dictates of European ideology. It is the opposite of this negative image that they "breed for," that their culture strives to produce. The European self-image is a "positive" one in terms of normative European behavior; it is functional in terms of European goals. It does its job well. A negative conception of "other" is the basis upon which Europeans build their image of other peoples; i.e., the conceptual construct is provided by the nature of their culture, and Europeans create vivid images with which to fill it. The *utamaroho* is such that they could not survive (as European) without this image of an opposite upon whom they can "act out" all those things that help to maintain their "positive" self-image. This is important when people talk about "good" and "bad." If, in terms of their own belief-system, they had to treat everyone as themselves, they could not survive as "European." This is precisely why a "universal brotherhood-of-man" philosophy can only be ethnologically interpreted as having a rhetorical function when it is stated within European culture, since it is ideologically alien to and incompatible with the value-thrust and definitions of that culture. It does not fit the *asili*. The culture itself *needs* "nonbrothers"; it needs those who can be treated totally as objects, as "other."

One of the strongest supportive mechanisms in and influences on the development of the European image of others—certainly in the early stages—has been Christian thought. This is a facet that sharply brings home the hypocrisy of the identification of Christianity with the ideals of universal "brotherhood." The Christian view of the "non-European" is generally as "savage" in need of "the word," abandoned to the sins and evils of an ungodly existence, ignorant of the true principles of morality. A missionary, writing in 1838, describes the Hawaiians this way;

> This people have much idle time on their hands, which we feel anxious to have employed to some valuable end. It is a most difficult task to teach industry to an idle people. But it is necessary to the promotion of their Christian character. An idle, improvident Christian is a contradiction in terms. And such have ever been the lazy habits of this people that they cannot improve on themselves without the influence and example of those who are willing to persevere in teaching and encouraging them to work. A little labor will suffice to provide a supply of food for their own consumption and, besides this, the wants of nature's children are few. . . . Their time must therefore be spent in indolence or, what is worse, in exposure to corrupting influences to which their fondness for each other's society peculiarly leads them. To this influence our churches will continue to be exposed until some means of employment can be devised which shall tend to raise them from their poverty and degradation.[1]

A strong contender with Christianity for the development, maintenance, and proselytization of this image is the anthropological discipline, a discipline that fell naturally to this task since its subject matter was to be "whatever was not European." As the anthropologist defined "primitive" or "savage," she/he defined the "opposite" of "European." In these descriptions the European self-image was implied. They were essential to the idea of "civilization," a term by which Europeans denoted themselves and the values of their culture. The "primitive" was noncritical, nonrational, nonscientific, uncontrolled, immoral, irreligious, and, most of all, incapable of creating "civilization." She was, therefore, in need of "saving" and of "civilizing."

Anthropologists sometimes used these very terms to describe Africans and other "non-Europeans," but more often they provided the materials and the theories that, in terms of the European *utamawazo,* supported such an image. Evolutionism in ethnological theory relates the European *utamawazo* (culturally structured thought), to European behavior towards others, and to the European *utamaroho* (vital principle). The primitive/civilized dichotomy has been used by and large to project and substantiate the theory of cultural evolution that, in turn, supports the European *utamaroho.* Use of this dichotomy to provide meaningful alternatives has been neither characteristic of the culture nor ideologically supported by it, and such an interpretation certainly never contributed to what can be generalized as "the European image of others." Without doubt the thrust of the anthropologist's contribution to the European image of others has been to characterize others as culturally negative, i.e., as lacking "civilization" ("high" culture) and as representing "early stages" in their own development. Anthropologists have helped posit a kind of "child to adult" relationship between Europeans and other people. This theme can be found in the thought of almost any Western social theorist and is often quite explicit, where "primitive" (the non-European) is likened to "child" of European culture and her culture to the very early "childhood" of European "civilization."

This is a very significant aspect of the European view of others. It is implied in Edward Tylor's definition of "the primitive":

> . . . the early condition of man . . . can be regarded as a primitive condition . . . this hypothetical primitive condition corresponds in a considerable degree to that of modern savage tribes, who, in spite of their difference and distance, have in common certain elements of civilization which seem remains of an early state of the human race at large . . . the main tendency of culture from primeval up to modern times has been from savagery towards civilization."[2]

Freud's *Totem and Taboo* is one of the most notorious theoretical works in this regard, but it is not atypical; its basic assumptions are those of most Europeans who consider themselves to be liberal and "objective," even as they use others to theorize about their own psychological and cultural development, one that is supposedly natural to all humans. Implicit even in enlightened anthropological theory is the invidiously comparative image of Europeans with people of other cultures, which manifests itself as unconvincing apologia for the "failure" of those who did not "develop civilization."[3]

Harry Elmer Barnes offers the following characterization of "the primitive":

Practically speaking, the primitive mentality is dominated by comparative ignorance, and by a type of attitude we call superstitious, from which the civilized and educated man of today is relatively emancipated. Primitive man also lacks the mental discipline which comes from some training in logic. Consequently, his imagination is more or less unrestrained. He creates and believes in a great number of mythologies. He tries to control nature by magic—that is, by incantations, prayers, rituals, and festivals. Such intellectual advances as civilized man has made have been achieved mainly through release from such naivete.[4]

These are the statements in which one finds the European self-image and their image of others. These images are to be found in what they call "the intellectual histories of Mankind" and the "histories of Western civilization." They need not, and most often will not, say "me" and "him" or "we" and "they" but will use terms far more damaging to their "objects." We are concerned with the relationship between European descriptions of others and their descriptions of "self."

Why "the Other" Is Black ("Non-white")

Gobineau, articulating white nationalism, describes first Africans, then Asians:

The negroid variety is the lowest, and stands at the foot of the ladder. The animal character, that appears in the shape of the pelvis, is stamped on the Negro from birth, and foreshadows his destiny. His intellect will always move within a very narrow circle. If his mental faculties are dull or even non-existent, he often has an intensity of desire, and so of will, which may be called terrible. Many of his senses, especially taste and smell, are developed to an extent unknown to the other two races.

The very strength of his sensations is the most striking proof of his inferiority. All food is good in his eyes, nothing disgusts or repels him. What he desires is to eat, to eat furiously, and to excess; no carrion is too revolting to be swallowed by him. It is the same with odours; his inordinate desires are satisfied with all, however coarse or even horrible. To these qualities may be added an instability and capriciousness of feeling, that cannot be tied down to any single object, and which, so far as he is concerned, do away with all distinctions of good and evil. . . . Finally, he is equally careless of his own life and that of others: he kills willingly, for the sake of killing; and this human sacrifice, in whom it is so easy to arouse emotion, shows, in face of suffering, either a monstrous indifference or a cowardice that seeks a voluntary refuge in death. . .

The yellow race is the exact opposite of this type. The skull points forward, not backward. The forehead is wide and bony, often high and projecting. . . . There is a further proneness to obesity. . . . The yellow man has little physical energy, and is inclined to apathy. . . . His desires are feeble, and his will-power rather obstinate than violent. . . . He tends to mediocrity in everything. . . . He does not dream or theorize; he invents little, but can appreciate and take over what is useful to him. . . . The yellow races are thus clearly superior to the black. Every founder of a civilization would wish the backbone of society, his middle class, to consist of such men. But no civilized society could be created by them; they could not supply its nerve force, or set in motion the springs of beauty and action.[5]

If we compare Gobineau's first description with his characterization of the "white" race (see Chap. 4 of this work), it becomes clear that one is the antithesis of the other. In Lothrop Stoddard's view, another avowed white nationalist, African's are also the "lowest" on the human scale and the true converse of the European:

. . . the brown and yellow peoples have contributed greatly to the civilization of the world and have profoundly influenced human progress. The negro, on the contrary, has contributed virtually nothing. Left to himself, he remained a savage, and in the past his only quickening has been where brown men have imposed their ideas and altered his blood. The Originating powers of the European and the Asiatic are not in him.[6]

The black race has never shown real constructive power. It has never built up a native civilization. Such progress as certain negro groups have made has been due to external pressure and has never long outlived that pressure's removal, for the negro, when left to himself, as in Haiti and Liberia, rapidly reverts to his ancestral ways. The negro is a facile, even eager imitator; but there he stops. He adopts; but he does not adapt, assimilate, and give forth creatively again. . . . None of the black races, whether negro or Australian, have shown within historic times the capacity to develop civilization. They have never passed the boundaries of their own habitats as Conquerors, and never exercised the smallest influence over peoples not black. They have never founded as stone city, have never built a ship, have never produced a literature, have never suggested a creed. . . . There seems to be no reason for this except race.[7]

"Whiteness" is central to the European self-image, just as their image of others necessarily involves "blackness" or "nonwhiteness," as it is put negatively in European terms. This aspect of the European aesthetic helps to define the content of European cultural nationalism, and white supremism, in this way, becomes identifiable as one of its most significant characteristics. Statements such as those by Gobineau and Stoddard demand cultural explanation, that is, an explanation in terms of the *asili*. No ethnology of European culture can with honesty ignore the significance of color in the mind of the European.

Joel Kovel uses Freudian analysis to argue that because European-Americans are "white," they were able to discover the "power" implied in the use of anal fantasies on a cultural level; the white/black dichotomy of "purity" and "dirt."[8] But, in disagreement, we could use terms of the same analysis to argue that European development has been prematurely frozen in a stage of psychological infancy (anal stage), which people of other cultures outgrow as children. Moving beyond Freud, however, in repudiation of European social theory, generally, we can understand Europeans culturally as *yurugu*, the incomplete and forever immature being.

While in Kovel's view, Africans (blacks) represent "dirt" that is despised universally by human beings on a repressed, subconscious level, two other theorists, Frances Welsing and Richard King, also psychiatrists, have quite different explanations. In their views this reaction is not common to all peoples. They understand European hatred of blackness and of human color generally to be peculiar to them. They argue that the phenomenon is very much culture-specific. Both Welsing and King focus on the absence of melanin as a key to the etiology of white nationalism. In Welsing's view the European value of whiteness is a defense mechanism growing out of a sense of inadequacy as Europeans become aware of their extreme minority status in the world. This realization caused a psychological response. Through a process of reaction-formation they have changed a desired characteristic (blackness, color) into a devalued one, and in reverse, whiteness (or the lack of color), then, could be valued. They then created and have sustained a system in which the minority controls the majority (the "system of white supremacy"). This process, in Welsing's view, explains the substance of European civilization.

Richard King argues that for the Caucasian (Africans who became "demelanated" [my term], as a result of their physical survival during the last glacial period in Eurasia), blackness is traumatic. It is associated with the loss of their culture and spiritual consciousness caused by a decreased functioning of the pineal gland which secretes melatonin (a consciousness altering hormone) and by their isolation from African ancestors. He argues that Caucasians reacted to this loss with fear of what had become inaccessible (unknown); then they turned that which they feared into that which they hated. Blackness became evil in this process, and dialectically, whiteness (the known) came to represent good or value.

These theories and others of European white racist behavior will be discussed more fully in Chap. 8. In this instance we are focusing on the significance of blackness in the negative European image of others. The pivotal dichotomy of blackness and whiteness in European symbiology are, of course, linked to that development. It is visible in the mythology, as far as we can tell, from the beginning of their cultural experience. Merlin Stone in her work on racism, calls attention to the *Zend-Avesta* (ca. 600 B.C.E.), the religious literature of the Aryans that is attributed to Zoroaster. Stone suggests that the mythology found therein expresses the beliefs inherited from a much more archaic oral tradition. It revolves around the great and continuous battle between two gods and their respective followers. Ahriman is dark and evil, and those who follow him are a dark "race of demons." Ahura Mazda is the god of light and goodness; his followers are the foes of evil.[9]

Vulindlela Wobogo reminds us that the caste system in India finds its origins in the Aryan invasion of that civilization in about 1700 B.C.E. Wobogo argues that all racist theory can be traced to European origins. In support of this view he uses Cheikh Anta Diop's Northern Cradle theory of Indo-European cultural development. (Diop's theory is discussed in Chaps. 2 and 8 of this study.) Wobogo refers, as well, to an essay by Mlalaskera and Jagatilleke entitled "Buddhism and the Race Question," which discusses the ideas of early Buddhist religious teachers. According to these ideas the human race is broken down into six species, the characteristics of which are immutable, determining abilities and status. This is the origin of the caste system. Each "species" is designated by a color: "To the Black species belonged the butchers, towlers, hunters, fishermen, dacoit, and executioners and all those who adopt a cruel mode of living." (See Mlalaskera and Jagatilleke.[10]) They were the lowest caste of darkest complexion. The caste system that evolved has made those of Dravidian origins, the earliest rulers of India, the outcasts or "untouchables," whose shadows must not even touch a person of a higher caste. The Dravidians are black, indeed as black as any human beings on earth. Varna, which means "skin color," is the word that designates "caste."

Here we see the Aryan image of others as black, repulsive, and lowly. While the "pure white" species, the highest group, according to the religious teachings of these Aryans, were the perfect saints (Aryan self-image).[10] The ideas of reincarnation and Karma helped to explain that this saintly condition was not due to anything that the members of this group had done or achieved, but rather to their natural state of birth (ascribed), just as the black group was lowly and evil by birth and could never hope to change.

The Cress Theory has some more immediately relevant implications that relate to our survey of white nationalist literature. There is a theme that continually arises in the theories of white supremism that seems to support Welsing's observations. Europeans express a fear of being "outnumbered," and where this circumstance does not already exist, they appear to anticipate the probability of a change in the ratio between them and the black people ("nonwhites") who are proximate to them. As Welsing says, the sheer fact of the composition of the world's people would be enough to fill Europeans with this anxiety—given their perception of the world as a basically hostile "other" that must be controlled. But Europeans have themselves created forced environments in which their minority status is intensified.

The nature of the European *utamaroho* both defines others as competitors and enemies, and, at the same time, compels Europeans to leave "home" (where they are at least surrounded by those who look and act like them) and to move into alien lands in which they are the "strangers." Colonial situations and slave plantations are cases in point. The European's sense of power is exhilarated by the fact that they are among a very few whites who control many dark-skinned "natives." Yet imagine, as well, the deep underlying fear—the recurring nightmare—that some day these "natural underlings" will "get together" and overcome them by sheer numbers, or kill them in their sleep. Consider the only partially repressed emotional dynamics of a white person in "Rhodesia" who lived with the fear that any moment it would become Zimbabwe and that she will be destroyed in the process. In South Africa the ratio of whites to Africans is necessarily a political issue, and whites are openly encouraged to procreate. In America intellectuals allow themselves to rationalize their fears by identifying ecological sanity with contraception, but it is black population growth that inevitably frightens white America.

The thrust of any eugenicist theory is the elimination of "nonwhite" peoples and the proliferation of whites; for in the process of making European culture what these architects want it to be, they also make it "whiter." Eugenic "improvement" of the "white race" presupposes indirectly the destruction and exclusion of other peoples. Madison Grant's argument is representative:

> Under existing conditions the most practical and hopeful method of race improvement is through the elimination of the least desirable elements in the nation by depriving them of the power to contribute to future generations. . . . In mankind it would not be a matter of great difficulty to secure a general consensus of public opinion as to the least desirable, let us say, ten per cent of the community. When this unemployed human residuum has been eliminated together with the great mass of crime, poverty, alcoholism and feeblemindedness associated therewith it would be easy to consider the advisability of further restricting the perpetuation of the then remaining least valuable types. By this method mankind might ultimately become sufficiently intelligent to choose deliberately the most vital and intellectual strains to carry the race.[11]

Again it is possible to interpret this theme as being "ethnological" in terms of European ideology; i.e., issuing from the *asili* of the culture. It is consistent with and reminiscent of the Platonic social ideal. Lothrop Stoddard expresses precisely the concerns upon which Frances Welsing bases her theory:

> The whites are . . . the slowest breeders, and they will undoubtedly become slower still, since section after section of the white race is revealing that lowered birthrate which in France has reached the extreme of a stationary population.[12]

Stoddard refers, on the other hand, to the "extreme fecundity" of the "negro" and labels him as the "quickest of breeders." "In ethnic crossings, the negro strikingly displays his potency, for black blood, once entering human stock, seems never really bred out again."[13] Stoddard's entire work, *The Rising Tide of Colour,* one of the most significant in white nationalist theory, is, in fact, based on the theme of the imminent danger of Africans and other people of color overturning their common enemy, the white man.

For a contemporary expression of this European fear of being out-numbered and an ethnographic example of the Western European view of others, we offer the following statements from P.W. Botha, taken from a speech delivered in 1985, addressed to his "beloved White Afrikaaners":

Priority number one, we should not, by all means allow anymore increases of the Black population lest we be choked very soon. [He advocates the use of] Chemical weapons . . . to combat any further population increases [and] fertility destroyers.

I am also sending a special request to all Afrikaaner mothers to double their birth rate . . . we should engage higher gear to make sure that Black men are separated from their women and fines be imposed upon married wives who bear illegitimate children.

[He refers to Africans/blacks as] greedy savages who are after our blood. . . . We cannot simply stand and watch all the laurels we have created being plundered by these barbaric and lazy kaffirs. . .

It is our strong conviction (therefore) that the Black is the raw material for the white man. So Brothers and Sisters, let us join hands together to fight against this Black devil. . .

By now everyone of us has seen it practically that the blacks cannot rule themselves. Give them guns and they will kill each other. They are good in nothing else but making noise, dancing, marrying many wives and indulging in sex. . . . Let us all accept that the Black man is the symbol of poverty, mental inferiority, laziness and emotional incompetence.

. . . Our experts should work day and night to set the Black man against his fellow man. His inferior sense of morals can be exploited beautifully. And here is a creature that lacks foresight. . . . The average Black does not plan his life beyond a year. . . .[14]

Botha's white nationalism is obvious. It is of the vintage that now embarrasses the typical white liberal American. Botha has nothing to hide. He is what Kovel might call a "dominative" racist: direct and obsessive. The white American liberal is an "aversive" racist, who, consciously or not, participates in a "metaracist" society and therefore cannot escape its inherent institutional racism.[15] The rhetoric of the dominative and the aversive racist may vary, but the underlying sentiment and ultimate result are the same.

Let us take, for instance, the argument of Ben J. Wattenberg as expressed in his book *The Birth Dearth.*[16] The book is subtitled: *What happens when people in free countries don't have enough babies?* Wattenberg does not *say,* as Botha does, that he is concerned lest Africans and other people of color eclipse whites in the world, in fact, he denies that race is an issue. His only stated concern with this "sensitive issue," as he calls it, is that according to some projections, by the year 2080, the American majority white European stock of 80 percent (1986) will have dropped to 60 percent and will still be declining.[17] And while America, in his view, is not "essentially a racist or bigoted country, anti-black or anti-Asian, anti-Hispanic or anti-Islamic," given present patterns of fertility and immigration certain doubts about the future arise. These "doubts," according to Wattenberg, are not those of racists, "only of those wondering whither we are headed and fearing that where we are going is not where we want to go." He refers us to a book written by Colorado Governor Richard Lamm and Gary Imhoff entitled: *The Immigration Time Bomb: the Fragmenting of America.* The book addresses the issue of increased numbers of nonwhite "third-world" immigrants, while the numbers of Europeans immigrating diminishes.[18] Wattenberg's answer to this "problem" is quite simple. To white, middle-class Americans he says start reproducing yourself! To the Afrikaaner mother Botha says double your birth rate!

Botha says that black people are "barbaric." Wattenberg says that the "less-developed" countries of the world need "the West" for models of wealth, freedom, technology, "free markets," and "democratic modern values."[19] The implications are the same. If left alone Africans and other "nonwestern" peoples will not "progress." But for Wattenberg, the issues are those of culture, progress, and ideology—not race—or so he claims.

What is the problem in this so-called nonracist view? In this "Western world" there will be no growth by the early twenty-first century (Wattenberg calls this "the birth dearth"), then there will be shrinkage. He asks what this will mean for the world? His answer is that the decline in the birthrate in Western nations may eventually take a "heavy economic, geopolitical, personal and social toll."[20] Wattenberg is concerned with the good of us all! He says, "relying on their technological and organizational superiority, the industrial democracies could protect their position and perhaps even enhance the growth of democratic values elsewhere."[21] How magnanimous! Wattenberg argues that with a decline in population the "Western world" cannot share these benefits with those less fortunate, nor can it bestow its leadership. The issue is ideological and cultural after all. Those who threaten the power of "democracy" just happen to be black.

Wattenberg compares the projected birthrates of the "industrial democracies" with those of the "less developed countries plus the Soviet bloc" from 1950 to 2100.[22] Lest there be any question as to who the "industrial democracies" are, they are listed: Canada, U.S., Australia, Belgium, Denmark, Finland, France, West Germany, Iceland, U.K., Italy, Luxemborg, Netherlands, Norway, Spain, Sweden, Switzerland, and Japan. (In another listing Wattenberg includes Israel.) With the exception of Japan, all of these nations are white dominated and/or white majority nations. They may have different names, but they are merely "provinces" of a single white European hegemony. Japan sticks in the craw of the European cultural nationalist, included in the list because of technological superiority. But then the Japanese projected fertility rate is also slow, with a median age for the year 2025 projected to be forty-four.[23] So they are not a numerical threat.

Wattenberg states his fear, "the Third World will be growing larger both absolutely and relatively, in decades to come." He then asks, "Could Third World culture become dominant? Could it erode our culture?"[24] It makes little difference whether he is considered a culturalist or a racist. From an African-centered perspective, we *are* our culture. To deprecate one is to demean the other. To fear African culture is to fear Africans. Wattenberg makes this fear explicit. In effect, he is saying that if there are more of them, their culture will contaminate us. If there are fewer of us, there will be less of our culture, and therefore we will have less power.[19] But, says, Wattenberg, "This view should not be seen simply as Western chauvinism," because the West has so much to give to the world.[25] Here we see the dialectic of self-image and image of other as it functions to fulfill the cultural *asili* and to express the *utamaroho*. The European is the "savior," the "civilizer"; therefore the "non-European" must be the sinful "savage." Botha's bigotry is expressed through Wattenberg's blatant paternalism. For Wattenberg "the West" is the "first world," offering hope of freedom to people in communist countries.[26] Therefore, the most serious world problem is the "decline of the West," because the culture bearers, middle and upperclass white Europeans and European descendants have such a low fertility rate as to cause a "birth dearth" among their population.

Wattenberg has presented the quintessential statement of contemporary liberal white nationalism, in which the image of Europeans and the culture that they bear is "remarkable, potent, productive, humane, beneficent"—"the last best hope of mankind."[27] The image of others that he projects is as being "less-developed (therefore lazy, indolent, poor), less *able* to develop (therefore incompetent, lacking culture, self-indulgent), dependent on white Western European leadership (therefore nonprogressive, unfit for self-rule, unable to plan for the future), fertile and threatening to the American way of life. The final analysis is that the white nationalist, whether of the Gobineau, Stoddard, Botha or Wattenberg variety, is petrified of black fertility, because it threatens white dominance. This anxiety is consistent with the European *asili, utamawazo,* and *utamaroho.*

Slavery, Its Aftermath, and the Image of Others

The relationship between European enslavement of other peoples and the European image of others is one of interdependence; they feed on each other. As with all characteristic European behavior, the enslavement of other peoples is dependent on the nature of the European *utamaroho.* By this I mean that it is not wholly accurate to say that images proffered of African peoples served the purpose of justifying or rationalizing slavery if by this it is meant to imply that the fact of slavery was prior to the image. Although the defenders of slavery were very dependent on negative images for their arguments, it must be realized that such behavior on the part of Europeans could never have been initiated nor sustained had it not, from the outset, been consistent with the European *utamaroho.* And the image of Africans that accompanied the slave trade existed long before it was initiated, and still survives.

James Pope-Hennessy argues against those who hold that initially slavery had nothing to do with white nationalism. Proponents of this position point to a few isolated examples of Englishmen being enslaved by Portuguese slave-traders, in other words, to anomalous situations. Pope-Hennessy, on the other hand, makes clear the essential difference between a European's view of other Europeans and his image of Africans.

> Undoubtedly they suffered torments, but they never came to be looked on, as were Negro slaves and their descendants, as chattel property—as, that is to say, an automatically inferior form of humanity, a kind of two-legged domestic animal.[28]

(Plato was not opposed to slavery, only to the enslavement of other Greeks.)

Arguments used to support European enslavement of African

peoples are significant here, because of the image of Africans upon which the arguments depend. This image, though presented unabashedly and in terms that are now embarrassing to the European intellectual, is consistent with and dialectically related to the self-image expressed in the statement quoted from Harry Elmer Barne's work. (See Chap. 4 of this work.) The presuppositions on which Barnes' statements rests, lead ethnologically to the slaver's conclusions. (See Barnes earlier quote in this chapter.) Here are two examples of the white slaver's image of others:

> The social, moral, and political, as well as the physical history of the negro race, bears strong testimony against them; it furnishes the most undeniable proof of their mental inferiority. In no age or condition has the real negro shown a capacity to throw off the chains of barbarism and brutality that have long bound down the nations of that race: or to rise above the common cloud of darkness that still broods over them.[29]

> As to the black race, we have already drifted into a condition which seriously suggests the limitation of the political rights heretofore, perhaps mistakenly, granted them, the inauguration of a humane national policy which by co-operative action of the nation and the southern states, shall recognize that the blacks are a race of children, requiring guidance, industrial training, and the development of self-control, and other measures designed to reduce the danger of that race complication, formerly sectional, but now rapidly becoming national.[30]

The images are consistent with those presented by the European nationalists whom we considered in Chap. 4 and by most of Western European anthropology; they act to support the characteristic European self-image. Yet the attempt is made to dismiss the images (and slavery as well) as being inconsistent, "out of character," not "in tune" with the main thrust of development or with the overall European world-view. The images and behavior with which they correspond cannot be "disowned" by Europeans until the nature of the European *utamaroho* has changed and that would require a different *asili,* a new culture. (A qualitatively different culture cannot be created by the same people.) It is because the *utamaroho,* which serves as the basis for these kinds of images of others, is still characteristic of European culture that it is possible for Europeans to behave in a systematically aggressive and antagonistic manner towards "non-European" peoples.

"Ancient cultures," says Wayne MacLeod, "needed the toiling

masses, whether aboriginal or imported, for menial tasks of life, thereby freeing conquering man for higher thoughts and deeds."[31] "Non-European" man is "nonman." The apprehension of "the other" "nonhuman" is natural to the culture that defines "humanness" in terms of its own ambitions, its own "rationalism." There is no question of morality involved here, since "slaves," quite simply, do not enter into the European system of ethics. The "slave," like the machine, is simply a tool or a prop used by Europeans to enact the "history" that they perceive to be their "destiny." MacLeod says,

> Although Germanic Man is the last of the conquering races, he no longer needs the institution of slavery for cultural advancement; machines have taken over slave functions. It is no coincidence that the most slave-mastering race in the past is also the one that today seeks to promote its technical possessions.[31]

But did the nature of the European *utamaroho* and the image of others on which it depends change with the demise of slavery? To the contrary, Europeans/European-Americans continued to consider it their obligation to rationally organize the world, and a white South African regime represents to them that rational order.

Merlin Stone understands racism as a process that initiates in an economic aspect (motivated by greed), then rationalized in cultural terms ("cultural racism"). This results in what she describes as "stages" of racism in which land, resources, and labor are stolen from one group by another, and the supportive state of cultural racism in which beliefs about the racial or ethnic group under attack are propagandized by the conquerors. Stone assiduously avoids the obvious in the presentation of her theory: that this pattern of behavior is characteristic of Europeans. Yet the bulk of her "evidence" of racism is taken from the Aryan experience.

Stone's "cultural racism" clearly involves our "image of others." She says that the theft of land is supported by the assertion that the victims are "innately immoral, even innately evil, e.g., demons, cannibals, head hunters, savages, bloodthirsty, merciless, sadistic, vicious, child killers, rapists, heathens, in league with the devil, criminal, devious, sly, sexually perverse, dishonest, cunning, etc."[32] In this stage, the moral inferiority of the "cultural other" (my term) is the issue. She goes on to say that the purpose of cultural racism is to incite unprovoked aggression and the extreme violence characteristic of the first state of economic racism. (But these images are not contrived, they are part of the unfolding of the *asili*.) According to Stone, this stage of "cultural racism" lasts until the "others" are subdued; their land is now in the conqueror's name.

In the next stage of economic racism, overt violence is not as necessary. The supportive form of "cultural racism" in this stage is one in which the objects of aggression are said to be "innately mentally inferior, e.g., less able to learn, less inventive, less creative, less motivated towards cultural accomplishments, at a lower level of human mental development, etc.[33] These assertions are then institutionalized, which forces their internalization on those who have been enslaved or conquered.

This is the function of the European image of others: (1) to support the European self-image and (2) to be imposed on the "cultural others" in such a way that they indeed become that which they have been "imaged" to be. One becomes a "slave" when one thinks as a "slave." Thus a reality is constructed. The most effective weapon against this imposed image is a strong national consciousness: Liberation is a question of consciousness.

Media and the Image of Others

In the aftermath of slavery, during "Reconstruction" in the United States (the late 1800s and early 1900s), the image of the African suffered under a systematic assault of visual propaganda, at the hands of American whites. Now that slavery, as an institution, had ended, the attempt to dehumanize Africans on the part of the European would have to be continued using other methods. It was important to the system of white supremacy that (1) white people continually reinforce their European consciousness at the expense of the African image, i.e., through our degradation, and (2) that the Africans continued to act like "slaves" of a new sort and indeed become what Europeans portrayed them to be. The objective of the European was thwarted to the degree that an African consciousness was sustained among people of African descent that allowed them to reject the European-created image of them.

It was during this period that a Euro-American controlled media began its long career as one of the most effective weapons used to ensure the exploitation and dependency of people of African descent. Black faces were used to sell everything from tooth paste to pancakes. Distorted images appeared on boxes and tubes, and even on vaudeville stages, to make white people laugh. But the media had really done its job well when black people laughed too, and in 1987 when black people had "arrived" and could therefore collect these vintage products of a racist media as "black memorabilia."

The "faces" which appeared, distorted carefully chosen characteristics of the African physiognomy: the color of the skin, the texture of the hair, the contours of the lips and the nose. Images brought attention to features that contrasted most with European features. The *asili* of European culture demanded this kind of image-making and destruction for the enhancement of the European self-image. If they were to believe themselves physically beautiful, what they considered to be their opposite must be projected as grotesque. That which had been positively expressed in the African aesthetic, i.e., braided hair, dark skin, and full features, were now made to appear ridiculous. The intricate African braiding patterns became braids standing straight up in an artificially stiff manner with ribbons tied around their ends. Very dark smooth African skin became a shiny plasticlike black, with accentuated rolling eyes and an enlarged, open red-lipped mouth. These images, of course, had the double effect of heightening European self-esteem (which must have been unusually vulnerable to require such extreme reinforcement), while at the same time devastating African self-esteem, as Africans replaced an African aesthetic with a European aesthetic.

Then Hollywood took over the image-making business, and not only could black people in America be lampooned in this way but also Africans on the continent. The result was that both Europeans and Africans rejected what was visually African. Because Hollywood (the film industry) reigned supreme in the creation and reinforcement of the European self-image, it also had to be the most devastating weapon in the destruction of the self-image of "non-European" peoples, since that is the flip-side of the coin. Seen another way, the films were tools with which to create a negative image of others. From African safaris to Bob Hope comedies, with white Cleopatras and crazed "Indians" in between, a motley array of blatant stupidity screamed, attacked, giggled, and shuffled itself across the screen, representing "non-European" peoples in European consciousness. In fact, the image created in the Hollywood modality is a cartoonesque exaggeration of the characteristics already conjured by the European psyche out of the depths of its cultural *utamawazo* (collective cognitive structure) and *utamaroho* (collective emotional tone). What had been added was the audio-visual negative image-making: First, the Amoses and Andys and the Beulahs; and now the Nells (to replace Hattie McDaniel), the new clowns like George Jefferson (to replace Steppin' Fetchit), and the Arnold Wilson/Webster perennial puerility syndrome of anti-African nationalist sentiment—all struck their blows for the European self-image. Music video's vie with these other forms of media in the production of the grotesque—the European image of others.

There is yet another, new genre of the expression of the European image of others. The "comedy" in which, as sophisticated movie goers of the 1980s, we laugh at contrived situations created by the interaction of "modern," "civilized" European culture with "backward," "primitive" isolated culture. Beneath the laughter is an image of Africans that dialectically supports the positive European self-image. In *The Gods Must Be Crazy,* naïve Khoi-Khoi in the Kalihari Desert become disoriented as they discover a Coca-Cola bottle. Aspects of their culture are mercilessly held up for ridicule as they attempt to understand the object's "meaning." The film is justified by liberals—black and white alike—who maintain that it is making a statement about the "purity" of African culture in contrast to the corrupt European culture. Somehow this subtle point gets drowned in a sea of laughter directed at the image of Africans that the film offers. Similarly, in the movie *Airplane,* a white woman organizes a Tupperware party for the "native" African women, and a white man attempts to teach the African men basketball. This is all in fun, so we are told. But this kind of racial humor is for us out of place in a world still very much controlled by the system of white supremacy. From an African-centered perspective, using the concept of *asili,* the objective of such films becomes clear. They are about the business of creating and sustaining images of others for the European that reinforce their perception of themselves as superiors relating to inferior beings.

Exigencies of the European *Utamaroho*

The functionally "successful" self-image of the European is dependent on a negative image of others and on the hypothesis of the existence of inferior beings. This is not a universal dynamic of culture nor, therefore, of human nature. The natural pride and commitment to self-definition in other cultures is not predicated on, not dependent on the existence of other people among whom these "cultural selves" must be supreme. European world supremacy is part of the definition of European ideology and helps to determine the character of the European image of others. In this world-view the universe is there to be conquered. It is "just" (i.e., "rational") that inferiors should be conquered by superior beings. In this way European self-definition and self-fulfillment became dependent on a "negative" image of others (in terms of European value) and a correspondingly dehumanizing concept of others. We might say that European culture begins its development, as a distinctive cultural entity, with the aggregation of peoples, the character of whose *utamaroho* is predicated on the image of a world in opposition to themselves and on the projection of themselves into that world as conquerors and as supreme beings. We can identify "Westernness" as that definition of self and world that naturally views "self" in a power relationship to "other" (the rest of the world). In this view the *asili,* or seed of "Westernness," is the power relationship and was planted very early in the Indo-European experience. As a result, it is in the nature of the European *utamaroho* that it cannot be sustained by a merely intracultural ethic or the idea of a self-contained environment that generates the principle of harmony and mutual respect. It is European culture that is dependent on the existence of other cultures. Perhaps the habit of relating to the rest of the world on the basis of an unending striving for power has spilled over and infested the internal fabric of the society itself. Circularly, the need to relate to "others" in this way can be explained by the functional need to mitigate internally destructive behavior.

Viewed a different way, the process begins with the embryonic European (Indo-European) self, which fears all difference. This fear is then translated into an epistemological paradigm by the archaic European (Greek) where the self/other opposition becomes paramount. Then in Medieval and Renaissance Europe the perceived self is expanded, so that the continuance of the culture may be assured (the *asili* fulfilled), otherwise it would self-destruct. Therefore, aggression against "cultural others" becomes a necessity.

With this understanding the image of others becomes a "rational" or "logical" expression of the *utamawazo;* i.e., interrelated to and interdependent with its other dominant themes and principles. When Thomas Jefferson said, "Blacks, whether originally a distinct race, or made distinct by time and circumstances, are inferior to the whites in the endowment of body and mind,"[34] he was simply manifesting the need of the European *utamaroho* for an inferior object. The extremity of the image that was offered reflects the intensity of the need for supremacy and power. It should not surprise us, therefore, that it was the scientists, the philosophers, the "enlightened" people of European culture who contributed most to the negative image of others. Given their privileged ideological status in the culture, the images that they offered became normative. This function was not inconsistent with their rationalistic commitments. It is only now in the contemporary West that it has become "irrational," i.e., dysfunctional, explicitly or overtly expressing a negative image of people of other cultures. In the contemporary West, the mode of hypocrisy and political rhetoric is the "order of the day." Indeed, it was the theoreticians of Western European culture who defined Africans as either "not quite human" or "just barely human" for the culture as a whole. Who was better qualified to make these pronouncements, since "humanness" was associated by means of the European *utamawazo* with "rationality" and the ability to create European culture (civilization).

All of the following statements are consistent with the definitions of the *utamawazo* as outlined in Chap. 1 and are therefore "logical," given the nature of the *asili* and the values of the culture.

> At some future period, not very distant as measured by centuries, the civilized races of man will almost certainly exterminate and replace, the savage races throughout the world. At the same time the anthropomorphous apes . . . will no doubt be exterminated. The break will then be rendered wider, for it will intervene between man in some more civilized state . . . than the Caucasian, and some ape as low as a baboon, instead of as at present between the negro or Australian and the gorilla.
>
> Charles Darwin[35]

> If their understanding is not of a different nature from ours, it is at least greatly inferior. They are not capable of any great application or association of ideas, and seemed formed neither for the advantages nor the abuses of philosophy.
>
> Voltaire (concerning Africans)[36]

> There never was a civilized nation of any other complexion than white, nor even any individual eminent either in action or speculation. No ingenious manufacturer among them, no arts, no sciences. . . . Such a uniform and constant difference could not happen, in so many countries and ages, if nature had not made an original distinction betwixt these breeds of men.
>
> David Hume[37]

> . . . incapable of contemplating any objective entity such as God or Law. . . . Nothing remotely human is to be found in their [the Negroes'] character. Extensive reports by missionaries confirm this and Mohammedanism seems to be the only thing which can, in some measure, bring them nearer to a civilized condition.
>
> Georg Hegel[38]

> I will say then, that I am not or ever have been in favor of bringing about in any way, the social and political equality, of the white and black races. That I am not, nor ever have been, in favor of making voters or jurors of Negroes, not of qualifying them to hold office, nor to intermarry with white people and I will say in addition to this, that there is a physical difference between the white and black races, which will ever forbid the two races living together on terms of social and political equality. And as much as they cannot so live,

while they do remain together, there must be a position of Superior and Inferior, and I as much as any other man, am in favor of having the Superior position assigned to the White Race.

Abraham Lincoln (1858)

Our assailants are numerous, and it is indispensible that we should meet the assault with vigor and activity. Nothing is wanting but manly discussion to convince our own people at least, that in continuing to command the services of the slaves, they violate no law divine or human, and that in the faithful discharge of their reciprocal obligations lies their duty.

Edgar Allen Poe (*Southern Literary Messenger*, 1836)

It is vain to deny that they [Blacks] are an inferior race—very far inferior to the European variety. They have learned in slavery all that they know in civilization. When first brought from the country of their origin they were naked savages and where they have been left to their own devices or escaped the control of the white race they have lapsed, to a greater or less degree into barbarism.

Andrew Johnson (1867)

Why increase the sons of Africa, by planting them in America, where we have so fair an opportunity, by excluding blacks and tawnys, of increasing the lovely white and red?

Benjamin Franklin
(*Observations Concerning the Increase of Mankind*, 1753)

It will be seen that when we classify Mankind by colour, the only one of the primary races, given by this classification, which has not made a creative contribution to any of our twenty-one civilizations is the Black Race. (Vol I, p. 233)

... within the first six thousand years, the Black Race has not helped to create any civilization. (Vol. I, p. 238)

Arnold Toynbee[39]

The Negro is a child, and with children nothing can be done without the use of authority. We must, therefore, so arrange the circumstances of our daily life that my authority can find expression. With regard to the Negroes, then, I have coined the formula: "I am your brother, it is true, but your elder brother."

Albert Schweitzer (*On the Edge of Primeval Forest*, 1961)

Nature has color-coded groups of individuals so that statistically reliable predictions of their adaptability for intellectually rewarding and effective lives can easily be made and profitably be used by the pragmatic man in the street.

        William B. Shockley (Nobel Laureate for Physics, 1956)

It is now entirely clear to me that, as his cranial structure and hair type prove, Lassalle is descended from the Negroes who joined Moses' flight from Egypt. That is, assuming his mother, or his paternal grandmother, did not cross with a nigger. Now this union of Jewry and Germanism with the negro-like basic substance must necessarily result in a remarkable product. The officiousness of the fellow is also nigger-like.

        Karl Marx (Letter to Friedrich Engels, 1862)

The old antislavery school says that women must stay back, that they must wait until male Negroes are voters. But we say, if you will not give the whole loaf of justice to an entire people, give it to the most intelligent first. If intelligence, justice, and morality are to be placed in the government, then let the question of "white" women be brought up first and that of the Negro last.

        Susan B. Anthony (Reply to Frederick Douglass, 1869)

Of Kant's interpretation of the "Great Chain of Being," Arthur Lovejoy says, "Kant concludes . . . [that] the higher beings of these other spheres must view a Newton as we view a Hottentot or an ape."[40] Lovejoy says that Soame Jenyns held that

> while the psychological difference between the highest animals and the lowest men is scarcely appreciable between either of these and the most highly endowed of civilized mankind the gradations are many and the distance wide.[41]

In Jenyn's own words, "From this lowest degree in the brutal Hottentot reason with the assistance of learning and science, advances through the various stages of human understanding, which rise above each other till in a Bacon or a Newton it attains the summit."[41]

    According to Lovejoy, Fenelon says that it is in the natural order of things that men be provided with "ferocious animals" to kill, "so that men might be relieved of the necessity of killing one another."[42] Ethnicity and cultural differentiation enter European ideology in precisely this same form, and they dictate the discrepancy between the European's behavior towards other Europeans and his behavior towards "non-Europeans" or those whom he perceives as "animals" and therefore of less value than himself. This theme is consistent—from Plato to Saint-Simon, from Constantine to Lothrop Stoddard. It is generated by an image of self and of others, the "logic" of which is that the existence of Africans and people of color helps to assure the "constructive" solidarity of Western Europeans. As long as they have "nonwhite" peoples to conquer (like having animals to kill), to subjugate, enslave, colonize, and exploit (morally acceptable behavior), it will lessen the chances of their attempting to do so within the Western European community (immoral behavior). This is not to say that European intracultural behavior is typically "loving," "kind," or "considerate" according to these definitions within other cultures, but the culture sanctions behavior towards "others" that is of a totally different and more dehumanizing character than is acceptable behavior towards each other. If the Jews had not been able to convince the Western world hegemony that they were part of the European family, German behavior toward them would not have touched the "conscience" of that hegemony with force. The European slave trade and contemporary European complicity in the illicit white South African regime bring home the point very sharply. This pattern of European cultural behavior will be discussed more fully in Chaps. 7 and 8.

Documentation of the European image of Africans and other peoples of color is not difficult to come by. And it becomes clear in the "records" that we are considered to be the "cultural other" or outsider by the European. The authors of *To Serve the Devil*[43] present vivid examples of this image and have made a commendable contribution to its easily accessible documentation. In this way they have made it more difficult for those who would attempt to disregard this aspect of the American character. George Stocking's *Race, Culture and Evolution* (1968), while not as voluminous in its documentation, is a greater cultural/historical indictment, as it reaches further into the depths of the Western European intellectual tradition. Rather than attempting to duplicate these works, let us move on to further implications of the European image of others.

The European Response to the "Non-European" *Utamaroho*

Other cultural philosophies encourage radically different behavior patterns than that of European culture. The initial encounter between Europeans and "non-European" peoples inevitably emphasizes these differences. Even as Europeans come face to face with human beings whose behavior would seem to conflict with the image necessitated by European ideology, they are able automatically to turn these "virtues" into attributes that correspond with a negative definition. In this way positive images and impressions become "put downs" or derogatory appraisals. This reaction is overwhelmingly consistent and is to be found in the journals of European "explorers."

Columbus describes his meeting with those he called "Indians":

Anything they have if it be asked for they never say no, but rather invite the person to accept it, and show so much lovingness as though they would give their hearts.[44]

Captain Cook describes the behavior of the Hawaiians:

These people merited our best commendations, in this commercial intercourse, never once attempting to cheat us, either ashore, or along-side the ships. Some of them . . . betrayed a thievish disposition; or rather, they thought that they had a right to everything they could lay their hands upon; but they soon laid aside a conduct, which, we convinced them, they could not persevere in with immunity. . .

The civilities of this society were not, however, confined to mere ceremony and parade. Our party on shore received from them, every day, a constant supply of hogs and vegetables, more than sufficient for our subsistence; and several canoes loaded with provisions were sent to the ships with the same punctuality. No return was ever demanded, or even hinted at in the most distant manner. Their presents were made with a regularity, more like the discharge of a religious duty, than the effect of mere liberality; and when we enquired at whose charge all this munificence was displayed, we were told, it was at the expense of a great man . . . the chief of priests, and grandfather to Kaireckeca, who was at that time absent attending the king of the island. . . .[45]

He reacts and interprets the tradition of gift-exchange and gift-giving in a characteristic manner; i.e., out of his own cultural priorities and in terms of the concept of "private property" and the sanctity of material possessions. He sees no contradiction in describing the Hawaiians as "thievish" and generous at the same time.

They seem to be blest with a frank, cheerful disposition. . . . They seem to live very sociably in their intercourse with one another; and, except for the propensity to thieving, which seems innate in most of the people we have visited in this ocean, they were exceedingly friendly to us. And it does their sensibility no little credit, without flattering ourselves, that when they saw the various articles of our European manufacture, they could not help expressing their surprise, by a mixture of joy and concern, that seemed to apply the case, as a lesson of humility to themselves; and, on all occasions, they have appeared deeply impressed with a consciousness of their own inferiority.[46]

In the telling of these encounters, the Europeans are forced to interpret the experience in terms of European meaning and definition. They therefore express their image of others and in this way reaffirm their self-image. Thereby, the descriptions become part of European mythology; they become part of the cultural storehouse that affirms European meaning and valuation. This is how the image of others is to be understood; i.e., in terms of its relationship to the *asili*.

Cook's consciousness is informed by the nature of his own culture and knowledge of his own motivations, just as the people he meets find it difficult to understand a cultural being so different from themselves. These encounters invariably point to the operative value-systems and behavior patterns generated by each culture. Europeans come filled with arrogance and motivated by a lust for power and the desire to possess whatever they find. Often as not this "mood" is described in their literature as "the spirit of adventure," which is related to their "enterprising nature," terms that are "positive" for them. Because their motives are to usurp, to exploit, and to bring what they find within their dominion, they necessarily come with the distrust and antagonism with which one approaches a potential enemy. This has always cooperated to their strategical advantage. Their culture provides them with a "natural" political astuteness and cunning. They are perpetually competitive and well equipped to deal in power play. On the other hand, the "natives" whom Europeans meet most often greet them with open hearts, "smiles," gifts, and trust. They commit political suicide! Their culture has not "bred" them for the necessary hatred and disdain conducive to an exploitative, imperialistic, or effectively defensive nature. Ayi Kwei Armah writes:

A ruinous openness we had,
For those who came as beggars
Turned to snakes after feeding.
The suspicious among us had pronounced fears
Incomprehensible to our spirit then,
Words generosity failed to understand.

"These are makers of carrion,"
The wary ones said,
"Do not shelter them.

See their eyes, their noses.
Such are the beaks
Of all the desert's predatory birds."

We laughed at the fearful ones,
Gave the askers shelter
And watched them unsuspicious,
watched them turn in the fecundity of our way,
Turn into the force that pushed us
Till the proper flowing of all our people,
The way itself,
Became a lonely memory
For abandoned minds.[47]

What characteristics do Africans and others display? And what would these characteristics indicate about our ethical systems, our world-view? We, people of other cultures, all too often make the mistake of attempting to treat this European, who comes to take our land and who looks so different from us as a brother or a sister! Africans and other non-European peoples invariably seek to include him in our system of gift-exchange, offering him love and peace. In other words, the purely rhetorical precepts of behavior propagandized as the "Christian virtues" are actually the models of behavior natural to other cultures and older traditions than that of the European. And Europeans naturally display behavior patterns that are in direct contradiction to what they have labeled as "Christian virtues"; i.e., virtues that are actually African/non-European values and standards of behavior, which their own culture does not generate, support, motivate, nor sanction. People of other cultures often must be taught to mistrust their enemy; those who would destroy them. Europeans instinctively "hate," or rather, do not love those outside their culture, who are, *a priori*, "enemies." Cheikh Anta Diop says,

> What I find remarkable is that in the individual attitude of Blacks towards other races there's a difference of approach. Blacks are not racists. Blacks are not afraid of ethnic contacts. Whites are. I think that much of racism stems from that fear. Is it an inherited trait of the nomadic life of the primitive Aryan? I don't know. Is it a biological or other type of instinct? I don't know that either. What is quite evident, however, is that xenophobia is definitely an entrenched trait of European cultures from way back. I think even European scholars would agree with me on this. In fact, as it turns out, one of the weaknesses of Black Civilization, particularly during medieval times, was the openness, the cosmopolitanism of these societies.

The medieval Black kingdoms were open to peoples of all horizons. And today, one of the basic weaknesses of African societies is that they still maintain this inherited cosmopolitan trait. Nationalism in Africa emerged as a purely defensive reflex. Narrow nationalism, xenophobia, exclusion of foreigners, has never been a policy of African cultures. We always find it associated with Indo-European cultures.[48]

What is the reaction of a European when he is greeted by one who offers trust and friendship? First of all, he regards such people as charmingly "childlike" (as puerile, really), because in his culture, where such behavior is not valued, only very young children, not yet properly socialized, would behave in such a manner. Second, as Cook says, such behavior is an indication to a European that the people in question "recognize their own inferiority." In other words, it is culturally impossible for him to view this automatic and natural trust of strangers as a positive, valued characteristic (in contradistinction to his "Christian" propaganda). He sees it, instead, merely as a sign of "weakness" and lack of self-esteem. This reaction is a key to the European *utamaroho* and to the European view of human nature. The xenophilia of what Diop terms as "Southern Cradle" civilization (Africa) is exploited by the xenophobia of "Northern Cradle" civilization (Europe).

It is a recognition of the "naturalness" and consistency of this view of the human and the behavior that accompanies it that must inform more realistic and effective self-deterministic ideologies for Africans and other primary peoples. But the vast majority of the world's peoples are still unable to absorb the fact of European *group* behavior. This raises, among other things, the question of whether those other cultures are able to prepare their members for the possibility of the sort of deceit and destructiveness of which the European is capable. It is part of the evil genius of the Europeans to feed on this political "naïveté," as it were, among First World peoples by presenting them with their own "weakness" (i.e., the ability to love) in the guise of a "new" and superior religion. This "new" religious statement is held up to them as a standard of behavior, interpreted as the command to "love one's enemies." The "enemy" who presents it is much too politically astute to be affected by his own rhetoric. It is because of this aspect of the African *utamaroho* that Christianity was such a successful tool for European political expansion. (This issue is taken up in Chap. 6.)

Unencumbered by the deceitful stance of most would-be conquerors, Wayne MacLeod testifies to honest rather than rhetorical

European value:

> Many consider amiability, rather than pervasiveness, to be the cri-
> terion of racial calibre; but amiability has no bearing on the essence
> and decadence of civilization.

> There is not a single instance where history has rewarded people
> of wealth, prestige and power because they were well liked, it has
> invariably been the aggressive nations that have been the promot-
> ers of society.[49]

Image and Value-Definitions

Johari Amini fixes on the cultural-political dynamic of value-
definition. She refers to the "dialectic of definition" that helps us to
recognize the dialectical relationship between the European self-
image and their image of others; for as Amini says, by defining something its opposite is also defined.[50]

The political implications of cultural imperialism become
astoundingly clear: "Functioning with someone else's definitions is
dangerous to the self-image, the self-concept."[51] Europeans are successful in their efforts to economically and politically control others,
because culturally they are able to force us to assimilate their definition of our inferiority into our own self-image, while at the same time
gaining support for their image of themselves as superior—again the
dialectic. As Amini says, the European definition of "good" functions
destructively for the African and other "non-European" peoples who
accept it. "It functions constructively for the European by projecting
and reinforcing his own positive self-image, and establishing a functional cultural norm which has wide political/social/economic benefits."[51] Terms such as master/slave; man/boy are initiated by the
Europeans from their frame of reference and function to serve their
purposes, in opposition to those of the communities on which they
are imposed. Here again we see the value of the myth of "universalism" for what enables Europeans to impose their definitions so successfully is, in part, their ability to convince their political objects that
they are not European definitions and do not serve European interests, but that they are *universally* valid definitions, which serve the
benefit of "humankind." The myth of "universalism" is always the
coup de grace in the pursuit of European cultural imperialism; and
inevitably European "definitions" are translated into "universalistic"
terms. This aspect of European ideology will be discussed more fully
in Chap. 10 of this study.

The European *utamaroho,* then, is created and supported by the dialectical relationship of self-image to image of others:

Europeans are rational	**Others are irrational**
"critical"	*"noncritical"*
"scientific"	*"superstitious," "magical"*
"logical"	*"illogical"*
"civilized," "advanced"	*"uncivilized," "primitive"*
"modern"	*"backward"*
"lawful," "orderly"	*"unlawful," "unruly"*
"responsible," "adult"	*"childlike"*
"universal"	*"parochial"*
"energetic"	*"lazy"*
"active"	*"passive"*
"enterprising"	*"apathetic"*
"creative"	*"imitative"*
white	*black, colored*

These images and concepts of European value definition then become translated into the power relationship that is demanded by the *utamaroho* and *asili* of the culture:

Europeans are	**Others are**
world savior	*objects to be controlled*
conqueror	*and manipulated*
organizer	
peace-maker	

The relationship between the European aesthetic, self-image, and image of others are not only dialectical, but part of a circular and unending process of value-definition. These aspects of the European *utamaroho* continually interrelate in a way that is supportive to one another. European philosophy of aesthetics is connected to European epistemological definitions (*utamawazo*) of a rationalistic universe and a rationalistic view of the human: The European sees himself as this "rational" being who is, most properly speaking, "man." The aesthetic is supportive to the self-image; it generates the value of "whiteness" and rationalism. The ego requires that the person views herself/himself in opposition to other persons; it requires a ceaseless pursuit of power for its emotional satisfaction. Power is interpreted or defined in terms of control over objects (people, nature, material objects). Control is achieved through rationalism, abstraction, analysis, "objectification," and the subjugation of nature; all this with the aid of "science." In the realm of human relationships, control is achieved through imperialistic structures, i.e., subjugation and exploitation of other cultures. These cultures are made up of people who, in the European definition, are considered as objects. In the rhetoric of European cultural imperialism this becomes "saving" the world, and "ordering" it by a superior rational European "man," for the benefit of an inferior irrational "non-European" being. Europeans sometimes even convince themselves of their own magnanimity and altruism in their willingness to bear the awesome responsibility of ruling the world: But, if not me, who else?—and what would become of us all? The dichotomies charted here are essential to the logic of Western European cultural nationalism.

James Baldwin describes the European image of others in this way;

> In the case of the Negro . . . his shameful history was carried quite literally, on his brow. Shameful; for he was heathen as well as black and would never have discovered the healing blood of Christ had we not braved the jungles to bring him these glad tidings. Shameful; for, since our role as missionary had not been wholly disinterested, it was necessary to recall the shame from which we had delivered him in order more easily to escape our own. As he accepted the alabaster of Christ and the bloody cross—in the bearing of which he would find his redemption . . . he must, henceforth, accept that image we then gave him of himself: having no other and standing, moreover, in danger of death should he fail to accept the dazzling light thus brought into such darkness.[52]

Baldwin hints at the relationship of our previous discussion to what follows. In the subsequent discussion we are concerned with the patterns of behavior encouraged by the European self-image and the European image of others; and with the characteristics of European behavior *within* the culture as it is dialectically related to the nature of the European *utamaroho*. These relationships and cultural patterns are dictated by the *asili* of the culture, which like a blue print establishes its developmental priorities. The *asili* is a template containing the logos of the culture. In this sense it implies ethnological consistency. *Utamawazo, utamaroho,* behavior, and image cannot be inconsistent with one another. They must be compatible, working together to forge a successful ideological construct. The concept of *asili* helps us to understand this ethnological fact of European culture and to clear away the brush of rhetoric (Chap. 6) that too often blocks our view.

PART THREE

BEHAVIOR
AND ETHICS

In us has been the need to spend life. . . cutting through deceiving superficialities to reach again the essential truths the destroyers must hide from spirits if their white road is to prevail;...
— Ayi Kwei Armah

Dishonest words are the food of rotten spirits.
— Ayi Kwei Armah

Chapter 6

Rhetoric and Behavior

Watergate is no mere accident of history. It is the natural consequence of a government faced with the problem of trying to preserve the facade of democracy before its citizens while waging imperialist war abroad, plundering the public treasury at home, and supporting reaction wherever it can be found. To maintain the myth of American righteousness, the government has no other recourse except to lie. Indeed, lying becomes the central political behavior of the state.[1]
William Strickland

What's in a Lie?

The Iranian Deal: United States sale of arms to Iran in exchange for the release of American hostages.

November 13, 1986:   Reagan says that charges that his administration had swapped arms for hostages are "utterly false."

November 16, 1986:   Reagan removes Vice Admiral John M.
                       Poindexter from the office of National Security
                       Advisor, for his role in the Iranian Arms Deal.

Background: The United States stands to gain from the con-
                       tinuation of the war between Iran and Iraq,
                       which retards progressive forces in Iran. The
                       goal of the United States has been to keep
                       either side from winning a decisive victory.
                       This is called "neutrality" on the part of the
                       United States by the American propaganda
                       machine. Actually the United States ships
                       arms to which ever side appears to be losing.
                       Documents of the Heritage Foundation "an
                       influential political strategist for the Reagan
                       Administration," make this position clear. In
                       "Mandate II" published in 1985, the foundation
                       says that the U.S. should maintain a public
                       posture of "Strict political neutrality" in the
                       Iranian-Iraqi war, but "quietly give military
                       help to whichever side is losing. . . The U.S.
                       interest continues to be that neither side wins.
                       In the long term, good relations with Iran
                       remain far more important. With a population
                       of 45 million and borders on the Soviet Union
                       and the Persian Gulf, Iran undeniably is a
                       strategic prize."[2]

January, 1991:   The United States invades the Persian Gulf.
                       President George Bush declares war on the
                       Iraqi Government for the purposes of "liber-
                       ating" Kuwait.

Hypocrisy as a Way of Life

Within the nature of European culture there exists a statement
of value or of "moral" behavior that has no meaning for the members
of that culture. I call this the "rhetorical ethic"; it is of great importance for the understanding of the dynamics of the culture. The concepts of traditional European anthropology are inadequate to explain
the phenomenon to which I am referring here, as it has no counterpart in the types of cultures to which anthropologists have generally
directed their attention in the past. But with the concept of *asili*,

which facilitates an ideological approach to the study of culture, the rhetorical ethic becomes visible; even compelling. It fits the logic of the European *asili*, assisting the culture in the achievement and maintenance of power. Without this interpretation certain manifestations within the verbal iconography of the culture appear to be inconsistent with its underlying ideological thrust. And that simply would not make sense. Let us see how the mechanism of the rhetorical ethic works.

The related distinction used traditionally in anthropology is stated in terms of "ideal culture" and "actual behavior" and is said to be characteristic of all cultures, thereby helping to confuse the issue of the uniqueness and problematical nature of European culture. The conventional distinction is illustrated in the following manner by the authors of a recently published anthropology textbook.

> For example, an idealized belief, long cherished in America, is that all doctors are selfless, friendly people who chose medicine as their profession because they felt themselves "called" to serve humanity, and who have little interest in either the money or the prestige of their position. Of course, many physicians do not measure up to this ideal. Nevertheless, the continued success of television programs that portray the average American M.D. as a paragon of virtue indicates how deeply rooted in our collective psyche the ideal of the noble physician is.[3]

This is a common misconception that has led to a mistaken view and superficial understanding of the nature of European (Euro-American) society. To refer to the images offered above as "ideal" is a misuse or at least a misleading use of the term "ideal." The projection and success of the image of the committed, altruistic doctor do not indicate that it is a "deeply rooted" ideal in the American psyche. It is rather an indication of the fact that this is how Americans want to appear to others, most often to non-European peoples—their "objects." In this case it is the way that the doctor wants to appear to his patients, or "objects," because this appearance works to his advantage. On the other hand, an image that projects him as a potential exploiter can lead to the possibility of malpractice suits and to the institutionalization of socialized medicine—neither of which is lucrative for him.

An "ideal" should be understood to be something that functions normatively and something that is emulated; that which has meaning for those who share it. It is the European experience that encourages the confounding of meaning and commitment with mere verbal expression. (It was within the incipient European experience that "rhetoric" came to be regarded as art.) In African culture words have power. The European mind is a political one and for this reason constantly aware of the political effect of words and images as they are used for the purposes of manipulation. By "political" I mean to indicate an ego that consistently experiences people as others; as representatives of interests defined differently and, therefore, as conflicting with this "ego." The individual is concerned, therefore, with the way in which his verbal expression and the image he projects can influence the behavior of those to whom he relates, be they patients (would-be consumers), neocolonial subjects, an opposing candidate for office, or an African selfdeterminist/nationalist. This is what is "deeply rooted" in the American mind—the psychology of "public relations," "salesmanship," and political strategy. It is in the Euro-American vernacular that the word "image" is used so frequently. To be concerned with one's image as opposed to one's self is a European characteristic.

To be aware of the strategical advantage of appearing to be altruistic when one is operating out of self-interest does not mean that altruism is a meaningful "ideal" in terms of one's value-system. It is, instead, an outgrowth of the propaganda that the Europeans have fed "non-European" peoples since they first sought to conquer them. Because they exported ("sold") this altruistic image so successfully, they have had to project themselves as adhering to this "ideal"; similarly, the projection of themselves or their motives in this way has been essential to the successful imposition of this "ethic" on others. The basic principle to be kept in mind in order to understand this dynamic of European culture is that the major contributing factor to the success of European nationalism has been its projection as disinterested internationalism.

The use of "ideal" in the passage quoted above is simply an inadequate concept for the ethnological analysis of European culture. Hoebel, in an earlier textbook, offers his version, which is similarly inadequate: "*Ideal Culture* consists of a people's verbally expressed standards and behavior." The examples that these anthropologists offer from other cultures to explicate the distinction between "ideal" and "actual" in no way represent the phenomenon in Western culture under consideration.[4]

Hoebel describes "normative postulates or values" as "deeplying assumptions about whether things or acts are good and to be sought after, or bad and to be rejected."[5] This is precisely what the "rhetorical ethic" is not. Hoebel's definition can be used to get at the converse of the phenomenon I wish to describe. A "rhetorical ethic" is not a "deep-lying assumption." It is a superficial verbal expression that is not intended for assimilation by the members of the culture that produced it. The "rhetorical ethic," a European phenomenon, has been neglected in conventional ethnological theory, which has consistently offered concepts devoid of political significance. Anthropologists talk about the gap in all cultures between thought and deed, between ideas and actions. The gap to which I am referring, however, is between verbal expression and belief or commitment; between what people say and what they do. Nowhere other than in European culture do words mean so little as indices of belief. It is this characteristic that is of concern here and this characteristic for which the concepts of traditional anthropology are inadequate to explain.

As a cultural trait it has, however, been described by others, particularly those who have been made victims of European cunning. Below an indigenous American describes European behavior:

> They would make slaves of us if they could; but as they cannot, they kill us. There is no faith to be placed in their words.
>
> They will say to an Indian, "My friend; my brother!" They will take him by the hand and, at the same moment destroy him. . . . Remember that this day I warned you to beware of such friends as these. I know the Long-Knives. They are not to be trusted.[6]

It is an inherent characteristic of the culture that it prepares members of the culture to be able to act like friends toward those they regard as enemies; to be able to convince others that they have come to help when they, in fact, have come to destroy the others and their culture. That some may "believe" that they are actually doing good only makes them more dangerous, for they have swallowed their own rhetoric—perhaps a convenient self-delusion. Hypocritical behavior is sanctioned and rewarded in European culture. The rhetorical ethic helps to sanction it. European culture cannot be understood in terms of the dynamics of other cultures alone. It is a culture that breeds hypocrisy—in which hypocrisy is a supportive theme—a standard of behavior. Its hypocritical nature is linked to the Platonic abstraction, to objectification, to the compartmentalization of the person and the denial of the emotional self. Below Havelock characteristically understands the case:

> Another thing noticeable about them ["pre-Platonic" Greeks] in this period is their capacity for direct action and sincere action and for

direct and sincere expression of motive and desire. They almost
entirely lack those slight hypocrisies without which our civilization does not seem to work.[7]

The distinction and definitions that can lead to a better understanding of the Europeans and their culture can only come from a perspective that is not one of European chauvinism; for it is the method
of European chauvinism or cultural nationalism to conceal European
interest. As I use it, "value" is only meaningful value; it is that which
motivates behavior and is the origin of human commitment. Value
determines what is imitated and preserved, what is selected for and
encouraged. "Avowed values" on the other hand, which are merely
professed, which find expression only verbally, which are not indicative of behavior, belong to what I have called the "rhetorical ethic."
The European rhetorical ethic is precisely that—purely rhetorical—
and, as such, has its own origins as a creation for export; i.e., for the
political, intercultural activity of the European. It is designed to create an image that will prevent others from successfully anticipating
European behavior, and its objective is to encourage nonstrategic
(i.e., naive, rather than successful) political behavior on the part of
others. (This is the same as "nonpolitical" behavior.) It is designed to
sell, to dupe, to promote European nationalistic objectives. It "packages" European cultural imperialism in a wrapping that makes it
appear more attractive, less harmful. None of these features represents what can culturally be referred to as an "ideal" in any sense. The
rhetorical ethic is, therefore, not dysfunctional in European culture.
It does not generate nor reflect conflict in European ideology or belief-
system; but it is, rather, necessary to the maintenance and projection
of the *utamaroho*.and performs a vital function in sustaining European
cultural nationalism in the pursuit of its international objectives.

The rhetorical ethic is made possible by the fact that hypocrisy
as a mode of behavior is a valued theme in European life; the same
hypocritical behavior that its presence sanctions. Again, "value"
refers to that which is encouraged and approved in a culture.
European culture is constructed in such a way that successful survival within it discourages honesty and directness and encourages
dishonesty and deceit—the ability to appear to be something other
than what one is; to hide one's "self," one's motives and intent. People
who are duped by others and relate to a projected image are considered fools or "country bumpkins." Hypocrisy in this way becomes
not a negative personality trait, not immoral or abnormal behavior,
but it is both expected and cultivated. It is considered to be a crucial
ingredient of "sophistication," a European goal. European intracul-

tural, political behavior is based on hypocrisy—as are business relations, the advertising media, and most other areas of public, and social interaction. It is merely a manifestation of this theme when Americans claim that politicians are basically honest. The claim itself is hypocritical, and the public expects it to be so. We all know that the objective of commercial advertising is to convince us to buy products so that manufacturers can make large profits, but the slogans attempt to persuade us that the product is beneficial to our well being, as though the producer has our welfare at heart. This hypocrisy touches the lives of every member of the culture in their dealings with one another, and yet it originates in part in the nature of their intercultural relationships. It is a part of the mechanism of European expansionism. All of these factors must go into the understanding of the rhetorical ethic and not an overly simplistic distinction between "ideal" and "actual" culture; perhaps a relevant distinction with regard to other cultures that create and are created by very different "cultural personalities." Let us look more closely at this "ethic" and see how it has functioned historically.

The Rhetorical Function of the "Christian Ethic"

The idea inherent here is crucial for it implies an unfolding of the *asili*. What I have argued earlier and wish to reiterate and develop further in this discussion is that what is invariably referred to as the "conflict" between Christian "values" and European imperialistic and aggressive behavior has indeed never represented conflict but is to be understood in terms of the intent of Christian ideology. As I said, all religious statements are likely to be shaped in time so as to be consistent with the nationalistic objectives of the cultures within which they were created. Religious statements provide ideological, spiritual, and emotional support for the maintenance of cultural entities and help to define, simultaneously as they reflect, the definition of the collective personality of the individuals within them. European culture is, in this respect, no different from any other. What varies from culture to culture is its ideological content; its *asili*. The character and definition of its "nationalism," the religious statement and the cultural *utamawazo* necessarily share the same characteristics. This is true whether the culture is basically "traditional" and "sacred," in which case the two are barely distinct, or if it is "secular," where religion becomes separated and institutionalized. In either case, the religious statement of a particular culture must by definition be consistent with the values of that culture, as both religion and value are determined by the *asili*. It is the function of any "official religion" to give ideological support to the culture as a whole. Once established and formalized, all religious ideologies are, in this sense, "nationalistic" ideologies. In spite of the elements in the Christian formulation that can be traced to Africa (Kemet), Christian ideology is essentially a creation of the European *asili* and can only be understood as a statement that supports the values of that culture.

European cultural commitment is unique among "nationalist" ideologies and in fact becomes internationalist in expression. Its primary objective is the worldwide expansion of European culture and the resultant control of other peoples. The Christian formulation, when hardened into ideology, developed as consistent and not in conflict with this objective. As European nationalism and the European *utamaroho* were both dependent on and directed toward "others" (people, places, cultures) to be controlled—to have power over—so the Christian statement was a mandate for archaic Europe (Roman) control, and propaganda was addressed to the objects of that control as well. No matter how subtly and ingeniously this function was performed, the fact remains that what is usually referred to as the "Christian ethic" ("universal love, brotherhood and peace," "the meek shall inherit the earth," "turn the other cheek," "love thine enemy"), once officially recognized by the State, was not designed for the assimilation or moral guidance of the Europeans. (What is referred to as the "Protestant ethic" is another case to be discussed in relation to European behavior in Chap. 7.) There is something wrong with a cultural/historical analysis that maintains that a culture as successfully sustained and as persistent as that of Europe could have been created, have survived, developed, and intensified to such mammoth proportions under the continual handicap of a religious statement that basically contradicted and conflicted with that growth and the form that it took! This is where the contradiction lies, and this ethnological contradiction alone should have given rise to other explanations of the "Christian ethic" in its European context. The *asili* concept demands an ideologically consistent explanation of cultural phenomena.

To recapitulate briefly: The Christian statement said that religion should be "universal," thereby discrediting other religions that were obviously and avowedly culture-bound. It claimed, in fact, to be the properly "universalistic" religion; giving European conquerors the moral justification they needed to turn their politically aggressive actions into seemingly altruistic ones. (See Chap. 2) But what is most important here is that the Christian ideology pronounced as virtuous those very modes of behavior that immobilize a culture politically, render its members susceptible to European control, and less able to resist: The pursuit of "peace," the "love" of one's enemy (which concretely implies the betrayal of oneself), the "brotherhood of man"—an abstraction that concretely manifests itself as the denial of one's culture and therefore one's ideology and commitment. All of these elements combined to form the ideal psycho/cultural counterpart to political subjugation. And it succeeded in doing the job that it was culturally designed to do. It did not affect the overwhelming historical pattern of European behavior, which is characterized by antithetical tendencies to those mentioned above. The growth of the empire was not impeded by passivity and love; rather it thrived on the intensely aggressive and hostile behavior that the *asili* of the culture encouraged. European theorists have invariably failed to interpret correctly this function of the "Christian ethic" in its European context—a failure that has been endemic to Western social theory whether representative of the right or the left—whether avowedly nationalistic or "critical."

Joel Kovel says, "Within the original Christian world-view, there was no way to rationalize or include the strivings for greed and domination that persisted within civilization."[8] Constantine apparently recognized the value of Christian ideology for Western European expansion and had no difficulty using it without refashioning the "original" Christian formulation. (If by "original" we are referring to its archaic European manifestation and not its earlier African origins.) A "use" that Kovel, himself inadvertently describes:

> Christianity spread over the West and created a community out of what had been barbarian splinters. It did this through the power of a concrete institution, the Catholic Church. It was the Church's immediate influence that held aloft the subliminatory ideal of Christ and, through that ideal, gave Europeans a scaffold of identification with which to bind themselves into a unified civilization.[9]

Kovel says that Christianity turned "away form the world" and that it "could only curse from a distance," thereby introducing "a split into the cultural universe." This "turning away" can be interpreted as being "written in" to the definition of an early adumbration of the two-sided nature of the European ethic. It is not the European's "cultural universe" that is split; that remains consistent and intact precisely because of the distinction between the standards of intracultural behavior and the standards of behavior towards others; between his words and his deeds; between the "rhetorical ethic" and the ethic that in fact guides European behavior. As a result of their *utamawazo* and the nature of their intercultural objectives, Europeans have developed an entire semantical system designed for export—for the purposes of nationalistic propaganda—for appearance—for "others," e.g., like advertising.

The fact that some individuals may have begun to incorporate the image that has been projected of them, does not alter the cultural significance of that image. Their behavior is anomalous. The fact remains that the "Christian ethic" never informed or reflected characteristic European behavior. The behavior pattern it suggests never corresponded with the European cultural self-image. That is the ethnological point. It always represented an image that Europeans found to be politically expedient in terms of their expansionist and exploitative objectives with regard to other people. And this relationship to the nature of the culture is not a new one; to the contrary, it is an aspect of the cultural affinity between the developing archaic Western empire and the Christian formulation—a reason for the early cooptation of the latter.

If this seems unreasonable in terms of the behavior and psychodynamics of most peoples, it must be continually kept in mind that the European *utamaroho* is unique and must be understood in terms of itself and its own peculiar dynamics—the *asili* of the culture. In this theoretical context the "split" becomes ethnologically explainable. It is culturally designed to serve the imperialistic pursuit of a culture whose dominant cohesive ideology is based on a power drive, or, in Nietzschean terms, "The will to power." To ensure success, it was necessary to have a hypocritical element; an "avowed," professed ethic that masked the European's true intent; to describe "arrogance" as "humility." Raw aggressiveness towards other people would have been resisted by them much more successfully without the use of the "rhetorical ethic." With it, Europeans could elicit the cooperation of those within the cultures they sought to conquer. To view European imperialism as beneficient "universalism" and "altruism" also helps to enlist the aid of those individuals within European culture who need to view themselves as "world saviors"; they can encourage the imperialistic pursuit in the form of European paternalism. But this is not the primary function of the "rhetorical ethic"; it is primarily designed for export.

Kovel says that as a result of the "split," the "West became faced with an increasing gap between its superego ideal and its ego practice."[8] Not only do these so-called ideals fail to represent the European's "superego" or any other part of his psyche, but it becomes questionable whether the commandment to "love" all people, including one's enemies, could ever represent a culturally viable goal.

Since its early history, the "corruption" of the Church has been the concern of the "good" Christians. These are the individuals born into European culture who never understood Christianity in its European interpretation. The fact is that the overwhelming majority of Europeans automatically—not necessarily reflectively, but "naturally"—"understand" how to use this ethic because of their mutual participation in a common *utamaroho*; the ideology and collective personality that they share. The isolated instances of those who do not identify with this *utamaroho* (energy source) properly or totally and those who become confused by the "rhetorical ethic" have encouraged the illusion that it represents "conflict" in European ideology. Kierkegaard represents the epitome of the individual who seems to be searching desperately in the culture for something that it was never meant to contain. He does not understand the *asili*. Kierkegaard's accusation is that the "Christianity of the New Testament" no longer exists, but in my view it has never "existed," certainly not as a European cultural possibility. Ironically, it is within other cultures that some of the espoused "Christian" values exist, insofar as they are humanly meaningful and concretely realizable. It is outside of the West that peace, compassion, spirituality, the lack of aggression, and intercultural tolerance are more likely to be found, since it is here that cultural philosophies are found to support such behavior. Kierkegaard's "attack" is representative of the awareness of European hypocrisy, without the recognition of its ethno/historical significance. He says,

> We are what is called a "Christian" nation—but in such a sense that not a single one of us is in the character of the Christianity of the New Testament. . . Christendom is . . . the betrayal of Christianity. . . .

He adds that "Christendom" has done "away with Christianity by a false way of spreading it, making Christians of everybody and giving this activity the appearance of zeal for the spreading of the doctrine."[10] He is in the position in which anyone would find themselves were they to expect European social interaction to be determined by an altruistic, humble, or, simply, honestly verbalized ethic.

Spengler's conception of the "Christian ethic" is much more accurate, and his very different perspective brings him closer to a more realistic assessment of the significance of the Christian teachings in the context of European ideology:

My kingdom is not of this world . . . A ruler who wishes to improve religion in the direction of political, practical purposes is a fool. A sociologist-preacher who tries to bring truth, righteousness, peace, and forgiveness into the world, of actuality is a fool also. No faith yet has altered the world, and no fact can ever rebut a faith. There is no bridge between directional Time and timeless Eternity, between the *course* of history and the *existence* of a divine world-order. *This is the final meaning of the moment in which Jesus and Pilate confronted one another.* In the one world, the historical, the Roman caused the Galilean to be crucified—that was his Destiny. In the other world, Rome was cast for perdition and the Cross became the pledge of Redemption—that was the "will of God."

Religion is metaphysic and nothing else. . . and this metaphysic is not the metaphysic of knowledge, argument, proof (which is merely philosophy or learnedness), but *lived and experienced* metaphysic—that is, the unthinkable as a certainty, the supernatural as a fact, life as existence in a world that is non-actual, but true. . . . To ascribe social purposes to Jesus is a blasphemy. . . . His teaching was proclamation, nothing but the proclamation of those Last Things with whose images he was constantly filled, the dawn of the New Age, the advent of heavenly envoys, the last judgement, a new heaven and a new earth. [Italics added][11]

Spengler goes against the Judeo-Christian teleological concept of secular history, but otherwise his observations are informed by a characteristically European consciousness. They have a certain accuracy. In the Christian formulation, in its European interpretation, there is no authentic "communion" between the human and the divine. This is rarely achieved, and so results in the "split" that Kovel talks about. This is not true of all religious formulations, however. In African thought, for instance, this meeting is achieved through the apprehension of the world as spirit and the philosophical conception of ancestor communion that it allows, as well as other cultural mechanisms such as ritual drama. The presence of sacred time and space are felt and evidenced in the ordinary existence of the people.

Spengler, in opposition to Kierkegaard, interprets the meaning of Christian teachings in a way that is workable for the European *uta-maroho*. In this interpretation Jesus' life was not meant to be emulated by those who would survive on this earth, especially as it has been transformed by the Europeans. And, in opposition to Kovel, he implies that Christianity did not "turn away from the world" after the fact but was initially conceived as "otherworldly," as remote and detached. Spengler's concern is with those whose misconceptions would cause them to attempt to bring these "abstractions" into the "world of reality"; he is concerned lest those who do not understand the "true" nature (i.e., function in terms of the European *asili*) of the Christian teachings begin to convince the Europeans that they must behave according to the "rhetorical ethic," and this would mean changing the culture. But Luther and Calvin succeeded, in effect, in fashioning a new ethical statement, which was more in accord with the internal dynamics of the culture. The doctrines that they developed supported the competitive, individualistic, aggressive, rationalistic, nonspiritual, and detached behavior necessary for survival within the culture. There was no longer a question of emulating the New Testament portrait of Jesus.

Ayn Rand, like Spengler, is concerned that what she calls the "humanitarians" are "in power," in fact, that their "antiscientific" influence has been felt throughout history. She is worried that they will defeat capitalism. "Capitalism," she says "never had a moral base in this country. . . . There is a fundamental contradiction between capitalism and altruistic morality—capitalism demands the pursuit of one's own interests."[12] This last point is absolutely correct and has deep cultural and historical significance. The historically exploitative, aggressive, cupacious, and selfish nature of European culture is the antithesis of the professed Christian virtues of "brotherhood," "meekness," "humility," generosity and altruism. But somewhere along the line Rand has missed something vitally important. The very traits of capitalism and European culture that she values are perpetuated not hampered by the claims of dishonest "humanitarians." The Rockefellers do all they can to create a "humanitarian" image of themselves for public consumption. All of the most successful capitalists (therefore successful Europeans) are also Europe's (Euro-America's) greatest humanitarians. It is precisely those characteristics that Ayn Rand considers virtuous that have survived in European culture. This should be an indication that capitalism most certainly does have a strong moral base in the United States and that there is no functioning, normative "altruistic morality" in European-derived culture. She has been the victim of the rhetoric of her own culture; rhetoric not meant for her consumption.

Nietzsche is plagued by a similar concern in the "Anti-Christ". It is difficult to understand why Nietzsche does not see that he is fighting an enemy that does not exist. He is concerned that the "Christian ethic" will retard the development and survival of the "superman."[13] He accurately describes the debilitating effect of Christianity but does not say that it has had this effect on "non-European" peoples in their dealing with the West. Nietzsche says that it tends to "weaken," and he is right. But it "weakens" other cultures, while strengthening European power.

> Christianity is called the religion of sympathy. . .

> Sympathy stands in antithesis to the tonic passions which elevate the energy of the feeling of life: it operates depressively. One loses force by sympathising.[14]

And this is precisely the effect which Christianity has invariably had on those who would oppose European control; i.e., teaching them to sympathize with their enemies. Nietzsche makes the point that Jesus "dying for others" is the epitome of the negative political image—an amazingly astute observation. But he fails to make the connection between Europe's overwhelming political success and its complete rejection of this image. Nietzsche's fears are unfounded; the rhetorical ethic does not effect the European.

What is interesting in the thoughts of Spengler, Nietzsche, and even Rand is the lack of hypocrisy that I am considering here as a theme in European culture. They apparently reject the European rhetorical ethic; that is, they refuse to make the "Christian ethic" a part of their own "rhetoric." Often theorists of the "right" in the West are more honest in their denial of the professed values of the "Christian ethic" than are European liberals in their verbal support. All too often this is the only distinguishing feature between them.

The Rhetorical Ethic in Operation

Very few European theorists have fixed on the political use and function of the rhetorical ethic. Below Chapman Cohen succinctly describes the imperialistic use of the Christian statement—a use that points to the hypocritical nature of the "love-peace-brotherhood" rhetoric:

> The conquering white professes the Christian religion. . . in nearly every case his conquest is advanced under cover of giving to the coloured peoples a purer religion and a higher civilisation.[15]

But more often in Western social theory, the rhetorical ethic has been mistakenly used to characterize European behavior and values. The following statement is from Robin Williams, whose ostensible stance is one of uncommitted, that is, "objective" sociological analysis of contemporary American society.

The proverbial generosity of American people toward other societies facing mass disaster—for example, earthquakes, floods, fire,
famine—has elements of exaggeration and myth; but it does index
a real and persistent theme broadly based on religious or quasi-reli-
gious ideas of brotherhood, even though it has often been overrid-
den by dividing interests and competing values. The enormous
range of relatively disinterested humanitarian activities in
America—the commonplace United Fund, the "service club" activities, the public welfare agencies, the numerous private philan-
thropies, and so on—stand in striking contrast to the treatment
meted out to "the poor" and the "sturdy beggars" in many other
parts of Western society within the past two centuries.[16]

Williams attributes the existence of this kind of behavior to a
commitment to the abstractions of "brotherhood" and "humanitarianism." This is to completely misunderstand the nature of the culture.
Care packages and the welfare system support European Americans
in the maintenance of their image of superiority. They are manifestations of paternalism towards others, not of "brotherhood" nor of
disinterest. This "brotherhood" never prompted the American government to leave foreign countries, and it never dictated that
Europeans relinquish their hold on resources they had stolen. True
"brotherhood" rests on the identification with others as oneself, as
one's kin; Europeans could never respond to nonEuropeans in this
way. Indeed it would be "unnatural" for any culture to do so, but it is
especially contradictory in the context of the European *utamaroho,*
where self-definition depends on the existence of "others" considered to be inferior, incapable, and unworthy. Philanthropic "giving"
reinforces the European self-image as "superior," not as "brother."

Williams continues with his description of the values of
American society:

Humanitarian Mores
We shall use the term "humanitarianism" to refer to another important value cluster in American society, meaning by it emphasis upon
any type of disinterested concern and helpfulness, including personal kindliness, aid and comfort, spontaneous aid in mass disas-
ters, as well as the more important personal patterns of organized
philanthropy. Do these things represent important values in
America?

It is easy to amass contrary evidence. We could site the expulsion
and extermination of the Indians, slavery, the sweatshop pattern of
industry, and a long catalog of child labor, lynching, vigilantes, and
social callousness in many forms. Probably few peoples have so

copiously documented and analyzed what they themselves consider to be the "bad" aspects of their history—a revealing fact in
itself, for it was broadly the same culture that produced the behavior and then pronounced it undesirable or wrong. Even so, the evi-
dences of humanitarian values meet all our tests for a major value.
For one thing it is striking that failure to follow the standards of concern and helpfulness have not been defended as legitimate in themselves; they have been interpreted as *deviance from* a criterion that
is not basically challenged or "justified" in terms of other, allegedly
more vital values. Certain patterns of mutual helpfulness and generosity were already apparent in colonial America, despite the stern
theology and stringently disciplined individualism, and have persisted to an important extent down to the present time.[17]

While the avowed European chauvinist openly sings her praises
of the Western way, Williams "tests" his euphemistic descriptions
against criteria that he has established. He is right; it is most certainly "revealing" that only Europeans study, document, and label as
"bad," aspects of their own history—their own behavior—that have
been called into question internationally. What it reveals, however,
is that it is in the nature of the culture that its participants can "say"
one thing and "feel" another; that words do not indicate commitment;
that hypocrisy is a behavioral standard; and that this kind of verbal
denouncing and superficial analysis, in fact, allows for the persistence of those very aspects that have been pronounced as "bad."
Williams is, at the very least, naïve in his belief that verbal condem-
nation of exploitative and imperialistic behavior implies that
American culture emphasizes "disinterested concern for others."
Again, it is often the avowed European chauvinist who offers more
accurate descriptions of European behavior. Wayne MacLeod makes
the following observation about Western European culture:

> Although "Christianity" preaches the values of peacefulness and
> kindly purposes, Europe has adhered to these virtues with diffi-
> culty, and has preferred a war-like history. The 20th century "Nazi"
> movement, that encouraged vigor and activity, is an example of an
> ideology more suited to the north-European temperament.[18]

White supremacy is characteristic of European culture—not
exceptional or aberrant. And Nazism is the manifestation of the
extreme possibilities of these tendencies when the control-mecha-
nisms of the culture fail; that is, when the destructive tendencies are
unleashed among Europeans. Robin Williams, on the other hand,
struggles to demonstrate the "logical" inconsistency of "racial deter-

minism" with Western ideals.[19] The strategy is simple. By verbally dis-
avowing white nationalism (the practice of white supremacy)
Europeans (European Americans) are thereby able to avoid dealing
with it. They cannot confront it, because intuitively they know what
they would never admit; that it is an inherent part of their cultural
heritage. They are committed to their culture and therefore, indirectly, to white nationalism. To eradicate white supremist ideology
from the institutionalization of the culture would imply radically
changing themselves and what it means to be "European": It would
imply a different *asili*—a different bio-cultural being.

The European cultural imperialistic creation, projection, and
use of the theme "universalism" as a normative standard of human
behavior and commitment are a primary concern of this study.
Yehoshua Arieli gets at it partially in his discussion of Protestant
nationalism, which I have cited in Chap. 4.[20]

Compare Arieli's statement with the following one from Robin
Williams on the same issue:

> This sense of satisfaction incorporates supposedly universal val-
> ues. A purely tribal patriotism conceives of its culture as having a
> unique destiny and does not think of extending its values to the rest
> of mankind. But American nationalism, like the religions that have
> contributed so heavily to the culture, involves the idea that ele-
> ments of the American way of life should be widely adopted else-
> where. This secular counterpart of the missionary spirit is both an
> index of the strength of nationalistic feeling and a potent source of
> misunderstanding and resentment in international affairs. In peace
> as well as in war, many citizens have believed that the United States
> must have a mission as a crusader for righteousness. Other peoples
> have not always regarded the matter in that light.[21]

It is tempting to dismiss Williams' statements as being obviously
inaccurate and superficial. But using the *asili* approach, these statements become very significant as ethnographic data, since they exem-
plify the manifestations of western European cultural chauvinism that
have been most difficult to combat. These manifestations have most
effectively inhibited the accurate cultural/political interpretation and
characterization of that which is European. "Analyses" such as that of
Williams attest to the fact that contrary to their "self-image" and to the
"advances" that the Platonists were convinced they were making, the
European is no more critical (in the Platonic use of that term) than any
other cultural being; in fact their culture contains a mechanism for systematic deception that is not found in other cultures.

"Ethical Theory" and the Rhetorical Ethic

It has been part of the posture of the moral philosophers of European culture to disavow cultural commitment, yet their work has contributed significantly to the survival and intensification of the rhetorical ethic—the hypocrisy and the deception that constitute a vital and definitive part of the content of European cultural imperialism—and, therefore, to nationalistic objectives.

To begin with the Platonic-influenced *utamawazo* provides the theoretical basis for a conceptual ethics; an ethical system, the themes of which are considered to be *valid,* as long as they are consistent in terms of the logic of that system. What is "ethical" becomes what is "rational" and "logical." The most "ethical" statement is the purest abstraction. As Havelock correctly observes, the individual "thinking" psyche becomes the seat of morality and the individual's ability to act ethically is based on his ability to think "rationally"; i.e., "abstractly." The result, again, is "talk." The European idea is that words divorced from action, feeling, commitment, from human involvement can themselves be relevant to (and properly inform) human interaction—as long as they are part of a consistent syntax; an approved semantical system. This pursuit itself is an exercise in self-deception. Primary cultures are characterized by an "existential ethic" (Stanley Diamond) that is based on and refers to actual behavior. European culture gives rise to semantical systems and instead of being concerned with the inconsistency between "word" and "deed" (which could conceivably be the determinant of ethical behavior), the moral philosophers are merely concerned with verbal and what they call "logical" inconsistency. One result of this characteristic of the culture is a tendency to make philosophers the most irrelevant of people and to effectively divorce their work from any decision-making capacity or role that in any way influences the ethical behavior of European peoples. What this tradition has done instead is to support the culture in its ability to use words without meaning, and to support Europeans in their quest to deceive others and themselves as well. The body of literature known as "ethical theory" has to a large degree been conducive to the growth of moral hypocrisy in European culture.

It is the "liberal" academic tradition in contemporary European/European American culture that uses the rhetorical ethic best to support the objectives of European chauvinism. Ingeniously these theorists use the semantical systems of the moral philosophers, the "brotherhood" rhetoric of the Christian statement and empty abstractions like "humanitarianism" and "universalistic ethics" as evidence of the ideological commitments of the Europeans and therefore as indices of the nature of European culture. They are "critical," because they say that the imperialistic behavior of the European has represented a conflicting theme or "negative" tendency in European development. The result of their theories, however, is that they succeed in making the European responsible for everything—the "good" as well as the "bad"—and in the end the good far outweighs the bad and will, of course, triumph along with "reason."

Norman F. Cantor provides an excellent example of the subtle chauvinism of the European liberal academician in his work on Western culture. He says,

> The new ethos of the late 1960's sought to restore to their central place in Western culture the religious, mystical, compassionate, imaginative, and altruistic ideals that had been tarnished or ignored by industrialism and secularism, by the mechanism and bureaucracy of modern life.[22]

> The new ethos had indigenous roots in some of the central currents of the Western tradition—in Christian mysticism, in the Enlightenment's vision of a happy and peaceful world, in Romanticism's yearning of the union of self and nature and for the union of all individuals in the Absolute Spirit, in anarchism's faith in the spontaneous association of men in a harmonious community when freed from the brutality and oppression of the state, in Nietzsche's life-affirming ethic and Freud's revelation of the primacy of erotic impulses, and in the existential philosophy of Camus, Sartre, and Jaspers.[23]

The trick is to "claim" ideas that have failed to influence the definition of the culture: because they do not fit in with the *asili*. In this way, any critique of European ideology informed by a vision of the human that could only have been created either by a rejection of European value or in a culture qualitatively different from European culture itself becomes a "Western" product. And this argument (if "argued" at all) is made on the basis of values that were, for the European, never more than rhetoric! "Christian mysticism" becomes "Western," and the "Enlightenment's vision of a happy world" is not tarnished by the fact that this world was to be defined in terms of and controlled by European "progress."

Cantor's characterization of "Western liberalism" is a perfect statement of what I have called the "rhetorical ethic." In the statement that follows, taken from the concluding paragraphs of his three-volume work on European cultural history, Cantor claims, for the culture, its most severe critics. Movements that would seek the destruction of what the West has meant are characterized as expressions of Western humanism and of Western ideals. This excerpt is evidence of the characteristic of European cultural nationalism that we are here delineating. This particular example is all the more significant because it represents a fairly recently published text, used to explain and interpret to the European-American college student, the nature and meaning of Western-European history:

> It is a pernicious misreading of history to identify Western civilization with the racism, imperialism, and capitalism of the late nineteenth century. Even in their heyday, these attitudes and institutions were only one side of the Western world view and way of life. The destiny of Western civilization immeasurably transcends the mistakes of one era. The West has had its confusion, horror, and misery, its moments when anti-human doctrine have seemed on the verge of carrying all before them. But it is the glory of Western civilization that it has never stood still and has never neglected for long the quest for institutions that can contribute to the realization of human freedom. Soon its best minds have recalled the highest ideals of the classical and Christian traditions; they have inspired their contemporaries with the vision of a great age of beginning anew, of the establishment of God's kingdom on earth or a secular equivalent in their own time.[22]

Cantor concludes his panegyric with the assurance that the "great upheavals of the 1960's were collectively only manifestations of the age-old western tradition by which Western 'civilization' periodically 'renews itself.'" In this way he debunks the need for revolution; and in fact "claims" the revolutionaries, who, he says, will inevitably and happily be overshadowed by the "rationalists and moderates,"

> who have restructured the institutions of the past and redirected the ideas of the present. The result has never been perfect justice or absolute truth but sufficient justice and enough truth to satisfy the anxieties of the contemporary era while reestablishing the social peace and political order that the progress of civilization requires.[22]

And so ends Cantor's historical study of the "genesis and destiny" of Western culture. With its greatest minds as the custodians of "civilization"—not just "European civilization." My interpretation of that history is quite different, as it is informed by an African-centered perspective and methodology. Cantor is concerned lest the students of the "new ethos" would "shatter" and irrevocably separate from what has historically been Western European culture. Our conclusion is that the European tradition *must* be "shattered" if a truly "new ethos" is to replace the old. This means a new utamaroho to fulfill a different *asili*. But then centered in African interest I understand European culture to be identified with anti-Africanism, the imperialistic pursuit, and with a denial of the human spirit; whereas Cantor finds this identification "pernicious" and makes the claim that the "liberation of the human spirit" has been a "central current" in the Western tradition. Ultimately Cantor's objectives are chauvinistic. He is concerned with influencing students in such a way that they will act to maintain the "peace" and "order" necessary for the continuance of the European conception of "progress," i.e., the persistence of European power.

The Ethnological Significance of the Rhetorical Ethic

The rhetorical ethic has its origins in the *asili* of the culture and the objective of imperialism and is therefore directed toward European political "objects" in an effort to disguise Europe's imperialistic intent and to politically disarm those whom Europeans would control. But it has also effected one segment of the European population. Through continual efforts to deceive others by means of the construction of an elaborate rhetorical systems, a small proportion of the culture has no doubt succeeded in deceiving itself. This is precisely the same dynamic that often occurs within the European entertainment milieu. A bizarre image of a performer is projected by the media and her public relations machine in order to "make" her and to sustain her as a "star." Though the image is radically different from her true nature, she becomes a victim of her own propaganda and of the power of the media and begins to believe that she is what she sees on the screen, etc. The example is appropriate because it allows us to see that even this kind of selfdeception must be carefully distinguished from a functional ideal or value. The confusion of her public-relations image with herself does not imply that the image is her ideal in the sense of what she wants to be; it usually implies very much the opposite.

This kind of cultural confusion can also have another effect. As Amos Wilson has reworked Paulo Friere's concept of "false consciousness" (*Pedagogy of the Oppressed*), it becomes useful here. The European who takes the rhetorical ethic seriously does so out of a "false consciousness" that prevents him from perceiving his own group interest as defined by his culture. The result is dangerous for people of African descent and other non-Europeans who mistakenly take the resultant anomalous behavior for a possible "rule." A European acting out of a "false consciousness" debilitates the "objects" of European oppression by lessening their ability to "see straight" or to correctly analyze European behavior based on an understanding of the *asili* of the culture. A European who is deceived about who he is merely succeeds in deceiving non-Europeans. A European who understands the nature of her culture, but does not share the *utamaroho* of her culture (a highly improbable circumstance, since it contradicts the *asili*), must act to change the culture's *utamaroho*, to get rid of its "carriers": That is her only recourse, if she is honest.

The nature of the rhetorical ethic is further complicated by the fact that what are projected as cultural ideals are mere verbal abstractions without human content. No culture could be informed by such things as "universal altruism," or the abstract "love of mankind." The philosophies of many primary cultures might imply a more sympathetic relationship to all peoples, but even here "universal" identification cannot be a primary or immediate goal. The abstract terms of the rhetorical ethic, even if conceivable, do not necessarily generate moral behavior. "Loving mankind" is not existentially translatable into respect for other people, and "international peace" is perfectly compatible with "world rule," as it has inevitably been interpreted in the West.

The confused liberal becomes the most dangerous European chauvinist of all. His wearing of "two hats" does more to maintain the European system than the work of those who are recognized as chauvinists. If a missionary sincerely believes that he has come to help Africans, then this can only be regarded as a dangerous form of delusion. The politically wise attitude of his victims would be to regard him exactly as they would any other would-be conqueror. Unfortunately for them, in the past, First World peoples who have understood the implications of European missionizing, whether of the "secular" or the "religious" variety, have expended great energy in the attempt to convince the missionary of the real cultural/political effect of his work. This is a hopeless cause. Such efforts only involve them in the endless rhetorical abyss of European culture, instead of in active self-defense. The point here is that although the rhetorical ethic may sometimes represent instances of self-deception within European culture itself, this does not alter the fact of its function and effectiveness with regard to Western imperialism. The only way to help First World peoples is to accurately represent the nature of European culture and the motives of European behavior. The decision as to what changes are to be made in our cultures are ours, and must be initiated by us.

Frances Welsing has said:

> People of color have not understood where white people were coming from, from day one. Right now Black people keep assuming that what they feel about other people, white people also feel. Non white people all over the world are baffled by how easily white people move into hypocrisy and deceit. We just have not been able to fathom it. If you are operating on one logic system and you encounter somebody who is coming from a completely different logic system, you may not be able to figure it out, especially if they are really fine in their methodology of deceit.[24]

Welsing's statement hits the mark. It helps to drive home the point that dishonesty, hypocrisy, and the "moral lie" are inherent in and functional to the cohesion of European-derived culture. The normalcy of these behavioral characteristics sanctions and defines the rhetorical nature of the "Christian ethic," which is, therefore, not actually in conflict with dominant European/Euro-American behavior. It is impossible to understand the behavior of the European until this is recognized, just as it is impossible to understand European behavior on the basis of the ethical dynamics of other cultures and other people. It is clear that this characteristic of the culture cannot be reduced to the traditional anthropological distinction between "ideal" and actualized values. Such distinctions merely obstruct the understanding of the nature of European culture. Listed below are the characteristics of the rhetorical ethic that distinguish it from anything that could be called a cultural ideal:

1. It is a statement that is in no way normative for the European; i.e., it is not a guide for behavior.
2. It is directed toward, i.e., meant to affect, people outside of European societies – those who are the intended political victims.
3. Its purpose is to facilitate Western European imperialism by
   - immobilizing nationalistic resistance movements of other peoples and
   - making European dominance appear to be the result of disinterested and altruistic motivation.

There is *nothing* in the European belief-system that supports action on behalf of others. It is absurd to describe "altruism" as a "major value" or "central current" in European ideology, as Williams and Cantor have done. Rather, the claim to ideals of "altruism" and "universal brotherhood of man" must be recognized in terms of their crucial propagandistic value. There is no more politically cunning and self-interested being than the European.

It may well be that European culture is the the only culture that must have a rhetorical ethic in addition to the ethic that actually influences behavior. Only the European *utamaroho* seems to require a vision of itself in opposition to "other"; that is, where this vision becomes the fundamental and definitional aspect of *utamaroho*. This awareness of "other" does not originate in an abstract conception of "humanity," but rather in the European fear of difference and the need to feel superior. Indeed, the abstraction, if anything, can be understood as having been conceived to clothe the nakedness of the European power drive. It is dictated by the *asili* of European culture that the European should have "two faces" and a "forked tongue." He must lie.

In European culture the "moral lie" is epistemologically reinforced by the methodology of "objectification" and ontologically by a conception of the human that seeks always to invalidate emotional responses. This makes possible, without ideological conflict, the creation of a rhetorical ethic for purely political purposes. What has been referred to throughout Western European history as the "Christian ethic" has little meaning for the European. It does not represent conflict in the European commitment but must be explained in terms of the overwhelming consistency and cohesion of the culture: the *asili*. The rhetorical ethic is, therefore, because of the peculiar nature of European culture, in which deceit and hypocrisy become normal, functional to the European conative striving for world supremacy.

The concept of *asili* brings the rhetorical ethic sharply into focus. As the ideological core of the culture, it provides us with a frame of reference—an authentic context within which to interpret the conventional rhetoric used by Europeans to describe their attitudes towards others. Since the *asili* tells us that each significant trait, each dominant mode of the culture, must fit accordingly to the "logic" of its germinating template, we understand that the rhetorical ethic could not be a functioning ideal, a determinant of behavior, for that would cause a malfunctioning of the machine. It would motivate inconsistent behavior and ideological confusion on the part of the members of the culture. Such inconsistency would cause the culture (machine) to become dysfunctional in relationship to its objective (purpose). The rhetorical ethic only makes sense if it is indeed merely rhetorical; it "fits" the *asili*. At the same time the *asili* of the culture "demands" a rhetorical ethic because of its need for hypocrisy to render its raw aggression more effective. It is needed for successful "P.R." The concept of *asili*, when applied to European culture, tells us that if the rhetorical ethic were indeed to become an operative determinant of behavior, the culture in its imperialistic, mechanistic drive would be destroyed. Ultimately, its nucleic source would become incoherent. The culture would cease to exist in its prototypical form. It would die or become something else. But the reverse has been the case. The European tradition has been overwhelmingly successful in perpetuating itself. Destruction of its *asili* must be effected from without.

The rhetorical ethic plays a crucial role in the maintenance of the European utamaroho and the support of Western European cultural imperialism. It is the primary factor in a successful proselytization of the culture through the creation of a false image of the European. And yet because of its subtly manipulative methodology and inherently deceptive technique, it has, for the most part, gone undetected as an expression of European cultural nationalism. With a proper understanding of the functioning of the rhetorical ethic in European culture, it becomes easier to understand the patterns of European intracultural (Chap. 7) and intercultural behavior (Chap. 8).

*. . . in these surroundings dominated by the walls of
whiteness built . . . to cut faculty from faculty, pull
member from member and drive person against
person. . .*
— Ayi Kwei Armah

Chapter 7

Intracultural Behavior

The Question of Norms

What are the "values" or standards that guide the behavior of
Europeans within their culture; that is, their behavior towards other
Europeans? "Ethic," here, indicates the beliefs that are implied by (1)
the way in which they treat the other members of their culture, (2)
the goals towards which they strive, and (3) the methods by which
they attempt to reach them. These cultural conceptions of what is
"ethical" are handed to Europeans (European Americans) by the tradition they share with others in their culture, and their acceptance
of these conceptions implies a system of "morality" to which
Europeans adhere. We can, then, look at European culture as a determinant of patterned behavior.

In his study *American Society*, Robin Williams' characterization
of his own concern coincides with my objective in this chapter. He
says that he is attempting to describe "culture as a normative structure."[1] "Values," he says, "concern standards of desirability" (which
relate the European aesthetic and self-image to the European ethic);
"they are couched in terms of good or bad, beautiful or ugly, pleas-
ant or unpleasant, appropriate or inappropriate." Norms "are rules of
conduct" that "specify what should and should not be done." The
"normative aspects of culture" combine to form a "set of guidelines
by which people regulate their own behavior and that of their fellows."[2] So that "values" and "norms" as they are used here can only
be supported or positively "sanctioned" within the culture in such a

way that behavior that conforms to them is "rewarded"—meets with "success" and "approval"—while behavior that contradicts them is "punished"—results in "failure" and is "put-down" by one's "fellows" or is simply not rewarded in any way, i.e., is not recognized as "valued" behavior.

What Williams refers to as "institutional norms" are precisely those aspects of concern here. "For a whole group or society, probably the best index to an institutional norm is the occurrence of severe penalties for violation." Institutional norms are

1. widely known, accepted, and applied;
2. based on revered sources;
3. widely enforced by strong sanctions continuously applied;
4. internalized in individual personalities;
5. objects of consistent and prevalent conformity.[3]

One final point that I would emphasize in focusing this discussion is that Williams is correct when he says that a characteristic of the normative aspect of culture: "It is inferred from *observation* of *behavior*."[4] [Italics added.]

The terms I have alluded to above are germane and basic to any ethnological discussion, and there is nothing objectionable about the way in which Williams here defines and describes them. Yet the values of American society, as he ascertains them, do not to any appreciable degree correspond to the behavior of its members. And in this respect Williams' work fits into the pattern of Eurocentric descriptions of European society, which fix on what I have called the "rhetorical ethic" of the culture rather than its "normative structure." This chapter is concerned with ascertaining the values that, *in fact*, determine European behavior. I am not interested in duplicating the plethora of sociological descriptions of various European (Euro-American) institutions, but rather in emphasizing the shared beliefs, values and conceptions that provide the ideological foundation of these institutions. There is no other culture in the world that devotes so much energy to its own "analysis"; yet it is difficult to find a work that contributes to the understanding of the underlying nature of the culture.

We seek to demonstrate the relationship between European rationalism, "objectification," and "abstractification," and such European conceptions as those of "self" or "ego," "individuality," and "freedom," which in turn help to regulate the way in which Europeans are treated and behave within their culture. This approach emphasizes the ethos of capitalism, for instance, not as an isolated or determining system, but as an ontologically and "ethically" consistent statement of "morality" within the *asili*/logos of European development. My emphasis is, then, more on the ideological implications of European behavior than on the ethnographic description of that behavior. As with any ethnology we are looking for a pattern and characteristic behavior; as the concept of culture implies generalization, so we generalize. It does not make ethnological sense to accept idiosyncratic or incongruent behavior as the expression of "European culture." Instead we would expect this discussion to indicate a "type of person" the culture has produced and is likely to produce; how he behaves and how he believes he should live. We seek the "collective personality": the *utamaroho*. My objective, then, is the isolation of the ideas that motivate and guide European behavior and the understanding of the relationship of these ideas or themes to the total picture.

We can discuss the areas of European intracultural behavior and European behavior towards "others" separately. This approach reflects the belief that there is a significant distinction between these two aspects of European behavior, and that, while they are dialectically related, European conceptions about them generate two distinct "ethical" systems. This, again, is central, because the distinction between "self" and "other," and that between the "cultural self" (the group) and those outside the culture, is nowhere as significant as it is for the expression of the European *utamaroho*. The assumption of the existence of people who do not participate in the culture is essential to the European *utamaroho* and plays a definitive role in determining the rules of conduct both within and outside of the culture. For this reason Chap. 8 follows with a discussion of the "rules" and conceptions that govern the behavior of Europeans towards "outsiders" or the "cultural other."

"Individuality," "Freedom," and "Self"

While Euro-American and European are not isomorphic, it is in contemporary American culture that the dominant theme of Western European development reaches greatest intensification. The concept of "individuality" and "freedom" and their interpretations in contemporary American society are an appropriate starting point because they are so prominent in the European's own conception of the value and superiority of his culture. In his mind they are traceable to his Indo-European origins. Moreover, these concepts are of interest because of their relationship to the European *utamawazo*. In addition we are ultimately concerned with European nationalism and its effect on "non-European" peoples in the context of cultural imperialism. The unquestioning acceptance and attempted assimilation of the European concept of "individuality" and the related concept of "individual freedom" has continually misguided and weakened First World struggles for self-determination. Their noncritical acceptance has delayed the victory. Where these movements have been strong there has always been a rejection of this aspect of Western European ideology, along with other related aspects, and alternative conceptions of "freedom" and of the person's relationship to the group have supplanted the character of European conceptions. Therefore, a critical exploration of these related concepts is helpful in a comparison of European, African, and other cultural ideologies, and it will also bring us closer to an ethnological understanding of the unique character of European intracultural behavior. How does this behavior relate to the *asili*? How does it make ideological sense?

The Euro-American idea of freedom is inextricably bound to the Western European conception of "self." As Durkheim has said, the value of the individual personality is a "cult" of European culture.[5]

Williams says that the Western concept of individual freedom

> sets a high value on the unique development of each individual personality and is correspondingly adverse to invasion of individual integrity; to be a person is to be independent, responsible, and self-respecting, and thereby to be worthy of concern and respect in one's own right. To be a person, in this sense, is to be an autonomous and responsible agent, not merely a reflection of external pressures, and to have an internal center of gravity, a set of standards, and a conviction of personal worth.
>
> The "value of individual personality" as impressionistically conceived represents an extremely complex cluster of more specific desirable states or conditions, such as uniqueness, self-direction, autonomy of choice, self-regulation, emotional independence, spontaneity, privacy, respect for other persons, defense of self, and many others."[6]

His discussion is not very helpful since he does not explore the concept that he refers to as "the value of the individual," but he is right in saying that the concept comes from "the deepest levels of its [American society's] unconscious presuppositions" and that the "value complex" associated with it "is embedded in the central affective-cognitive structure of the personalities of the culture."[6] With this let us turn to a deeper consideration of the cognitive and related behavioral implications of this concept.

In the European tradition it is customary to place, as Williams does, the philosophical origins of the American concept of individual freedom in seventeenth century European thought, but the work of John Locke and others merely provided a verbal crystallization and formal presentation of conceptions already implicit in the cognitive structures of European culture; and even earlier, in the *asili*/seed. Williams talks about the "autonomous" self and, again, of "moral autonomy"; but we have seen this before—in Plato and in Eric Havelock's discussion of Platonic epistemological conceptions. (See Chap. I). The Platonic mode, and its methodology based on the assumption of the "thinking-self" that exists separately and distinctly from the objects it encounters, enabled Europeans to construct a rationalistic science. It also provided a cognitive habit that would house the contemporary European concept and value of "individualism." Indeed, as Havelock argues, in Plato's day there may have been only an inconsequential number of people "capable" (an indication of Havelock's perspective) of conceiving in this way, but the layers thickened and grew until it became characteristic of the "culture-bearers" and the "ordinary" people of the culture. Now Europeans are almost "born" with a concept of themselves as housing a distinct psyche necessarily isolated from all "others" and as being responsible only to themselves. This conception is inculcated at a very early age. What followed from this Platonic conception was the concept of a rationalistic ethic, which, along with secularization, provided the basis for an individualistic conception (or misconception) of human happiness. If all of these related epistemological premises were valid, then it followed that the individual herself had to determine what was in her interest, i.e., what made her happy. Self-interest in this way becomes paramount, and "freedom" is then the ability to pursue this interest.

Havelock stresses the importance of the ability to separate self from other: The lack of identification with other was in Plato's conception the primary rational act. This idea is reinforced throughout the culture, and so it is that the idea of "identification with," love of, and sympathy or empathetic understanding for others goes against the grain of the European tradition; it is in epistemological, ideological, political, and spiritual contradiction. A morality based on "altruism" is inconceivable in the European context. In the West the self is primary, and survival depends on the cultivation of self-centeredness. One must be "allowed" to be properly selfish; and that is what it means to be "free."

In a series of essays, Dorothy Lee explores the concepts of freedom and individuality in the West and raises the question of the meaning of these concepts, in juxtaposition with conceptions of other cultures. As with other discussions of Lee's, these help us to go beyond the taken-for-granted aspect of European value and to see really what it does mean in the actual living situation for an American to say that he has "a conviction of personal worth," as Robin Williams does, or that in American society "freedom" is a "major value."[7]

The first important observation to be made is that this concept as Lee points out, is peculiar to European society. It is a concept rarely present in other societies. Williams equates "freedom" with "a wide range of moral autonomy in decision-making" and contrasts it with "simple group conformity." But an African-centered perspective helps us to recognize that (1) the kind of "freedom" that Williams describes may be meaningless or undesirable to people whose concepts of personal worth and human value are radically different and/or that (2) "freedom," as an abstract concept, may itself lack value as a human or cultural goal. In other words, in America "freedom" is a household word that children are raised on ("I can so; it's a free country!"), but it may well be that within the context of a harmonious communal grouping that does, in fact, protect and nurture the growth of the person, this "freedom" is merely the description of something negative.

As discussed earlier (see Chap. 4), this idea of "freedom" that emerges in the European cultural psyche, has been handed down through the various states of the development of the European collective consciousness. The origins of this mythoform—love of freedom and liberty—are traditionally traced to the forest of Germany where the Saxons reigned, supposedly never having allowed themselves to be conquered. The "fierce individualism" and "love of freedom" of the early Germans was to have been inherited by their European descendants, further developed by the English who developed parliamentary government based on this ethos of "freedom" and passed it to the American colonials, who have established the ultimate citadel of "liberty" with a "democratic" constitution that safe-guards the right to "individual freedom"; a social order that values "individuality" almost as much as material gain. They, in fact, have developed to its greatest intensity an economic system in which the goal of unlimited gain is linked to this concept of individual freedom and liberty, with a minimum of government ("group") interference: the Government's main purpose being to ensure the protection of private property.

In an effort to get at "the idea of freedom which is peculiar to American society," Dorothy Lee observed the areas in which

"Americans still expressed a sense of freedom in their linguistic usage."[8] She found that "free" usually indicated a lack of constraint or obligation; i.e., "freedom from entanglement" in regard to interpersonal relationships. She found that oddly enough the idea of "freedom," as in "free" objects—tickets, for instance, meant that they were desirable but had no value. One saves money when something is "free" in this sense, but because it does not cost money, it is, therefore, not itself valuable. Then there is the idea of freedom as in "free time," where free means "uncommitted." Again Lee found that such "free time" was not itself valuable, that is, it became so only when it was "filled" and in accordance with how it was filled. It is somehow wrong to have too much "free time." "One has to go on and give an explanation or a justification for such freedom, so as to endow it with a validity which is certainly not self-evident." The person who has "nothing that he has to do" is suspect and lacks value; "conversely, I hear people speaking proudly of all they have to do, whether they are referring to committed time, or to what they do during their 'free time.'" (The Protestant ethic, of course, regulates European behavior in this way so that "work" is active and positive, and to be free from work is to be somehow immoral.) Lee concludes that "free," as in free time, is, therefore, a negative condition; "free" refers to emptiness and must be "filled":

> Our free time is "leisure" time, potentially passive and empty—and subject to boredom, unless we plan it carefully and fill it with activities. In fact, we have now a number of professions whose function is to provide means and aid to people for the filling of empty time. And an increasing leisure is viewed with apprehension by many of our leaders.[9]

So what becomes even clearer as a result of this discussion is that it is not simply the idea of "freedom" (per se) that is valued in contemporary European society but a very specific kind of freedom associated almost totally with the unique European concept of validity and necessity of the autonomous individual. "Freedom," as an attribute of space or time, has no worth so long as it remains in that state. "Space is empty and to be occupied with matter; time is empty and to be filled with activity." Whereas often in other cultures, "free space and time have being and integrity." In evidence of this, Lee goes on to cite examples from other cultures in which "The experience of silence; of the space between and within is meaningful." She speaks of such Japanese perceptions that "persists in spite of the adoption of western culture and science." In non-European cultures,

Lee continues, "free time, through being recognized as valid existence, can and does contain value." Whereas, "In our own culture it is perceived as the unallocated, the unscheduled, the nothing; and it cannot contain value, as it contains no being." In addition to the fact that they contain no value, "empty spaces" are indeed "uncomfortable" to the European, and he "experiences silence" as either embarrassing or frightening.

This "negative" freedom, Lee sees as being related to the European concept of self and as helping to define positive freedom or freedom as value. The situation loses significance "with increasing emphasis on the individual, on the self as a focus." The individual is not interested in "what can be done," but rather in "what I can do." Therefore the positive idea of "freedom" is "expressed as capacity in the person."[10] And here it is possible to see how the concepts of "self" and of "freedom" relate to the conative striving that is the life-blood of European life and with the epistemological tools and definitions that determine European cognition. All of these aspects are consistent and are dictated by the *asili* of Western European culture: they help to construct the European *utamawazo* and express the *utamaroho*.

The concept of freedom that Lee describes here in its "positive" implications, i.e., as value, has to do with the "ability" (lack of constraining forces) to do. This "freedom" is the existential prerequisite to individual power, and that is its significance for understanding the European mind and European cultural behavior. "Power," as a European concept, is the ability to control and to manipulate; control of the self—in order to control and manipulate objects external to the self. One must be a "free agent"—free in the interest of self. This also implies "freedom" from moral or ethical considerations. This concept of power is synonymous with the European *utamaroho*; it is the most basic motivating force in the culture, touching every aspect of belief and behavior. Within European societies, that is between European peoples, the individual is the seat of this power, just as he is the seat of the "freedom" that makes it possible. He is free to "wheel and deal"; i.e., to maneuver, operate, procure, achieve (etc.) for self. Interculturally, the entire culture bands together expertly in group effort to ensure its power over other cultures.

It is this same power that is achieved through the illusion of objectification. As discussed in Chap. 1, it was only by separating the self from the object of knowledge that, as defined by the Platonic mode, one could "know." "Knowledge," then, is itself power to control. Havelock's descriptions of the "Homeric" or "pre-Platonic"

Greek were all in terms of the lack or absence of power and control. "Identification with" indicates "passivity" and "manipulation by" – a willessness because the self is not separated from the other. The Homeric man was not a "free agent"; he had no power (knowledge). It is this all-important need to distinguish self from other (cognitively, emotionally, and politically) and its relationship to the quest for power on which the European *utamaroho* depends, that gives direction to European cultural nationalism (the primary behavioral manifestation of which is European imperialism.) The dynamics of this ideology are linked to the separation of self, the related definition of ego as an isolate, and the resultant desire to control that which remains (alien) when the ego is abstracted. In this frame of reference to be "other than" is to be "opposed to"; and so all "other" is potential enemy and must be controlled (made powerless). (In terms of African ontological formulations, on the other hand, the "person" has her own "power" or "force" by virtue of being a part of the cosmological whole.)

Dorothy Lee puts it this way: "The definition of the self in our own cultures rests on our laws of contradiction. The self cannot be both self and not self, both self and other; the self excludes the other."[11] Norman Brown makes a similar observation when he says that Freud was "misled by his own metaphysical bias toward dualism"[12] and that "one can see Freud's thought inhibited by a conception of self and other as mutually exclusive alternatives."[13] In this respect, Freud's thought is simply manifesting characteristics of the European *utamawazo*, an *utamawazo* besieged by irreconcilable dichotomies such as "subject/object," "self/other," which become the terms of European value distinctions like "knowledge/opinion," "reason/emotion," etc.

Paul Goodman has described this tendency in relation to European psychoanalytic theory as "neurotic dichotomies . . . some of which are prejudices of psychotherapy itself."[14] Goodman discusses the nature of some of these "splits" that plague European thought:

> "Body and "Mind": this split is still popularly current, although among the best physicians the psychosomatic unity is taken for granted. We shall show that it is the exercise of a habitual and finally unaware deliberatedness in the face of chronic emergency, especially the threat to organic functioning, that has made this crippling division inevitable and almost indemic, resulting in the joylessness and gracelessness of culture.

"Self" and "External World": this division is an article of faith uniformly throughout modern western science. It goes along with the previous split, but perhaps with more emphasis on threats of a political and inter-personal nature. Unfortunately those who in the history of recent philosophy have shown the absurdity of this division have mostly themselves been infected with either a kind of mentalism or materialism.

"Emotional" (subjective) and "Real" (objective): this split is again a general scientific article of faith, unitarily involved with the preceding. It is the result of the avoidance of contact and involvement and the deliberate isolation of the sensoric and motoric functions from each other. (The recent history of statistical sociology is a study in these avoidances raised to a fine art.) We shall try to show that the real is intrinsically an involvement or "engagement."[15]

The *raison d'etre* for these "splits" is to be found in the basic goal of European behavior. The idea of separation is necessary for the sensation of control, i.e., of European power. It must be experienced as "control of" and "control over." One part controls the other; "I control you." Where entities are merged or conceived as unity there can be no question of "control over" or of "power" in the European sense.

This conception of the self and the ontology that generates it do not exhaust the possibilites of human meaning or of conceptual models. Lee says that it is possible to have a system that is not based on a law of contradiction. Among the Wintu, she says, "The individual is particularized transiently, but is not set in opposition."[16] Lee prefaces her comments on the Wintu conception of self by saying that this conception probably no longer exists. But it is possible to find examples from cultures that remain dynamic survival systems, and it is necessary for a viable critique of European culture that we do not become locked into a continual comparison of European forms with those that it has destroyed (or made obsolete); often such comparisons encourage the impression of the inevitability of the Europeanization of the world—no matter how negatively one may claim to view this process.

Vernon Dixon tells us that the African objective is "the use of forces in nature to restore a more harmonious relationship between man and the universe."[17] Human beings and the phenomenal world are interdependent. "The phenomenal world becomes personalized."[18] In Dixon's comparison of the African and European worldviews, he discusses the respective concepts of self that emerge from these two philosophies. In the European view, he says, the self is in a state of perpetual battle with "an external, impersonal system." The self battles even with nature since "nature does not have his [the self's] interest at heart." Dixon explains that this conception results in a separation of the European self *from itself* predicated on the assumption or perception of two distinct realities: the "thinking being" and the being that experiences ("phenomenal man"). "The individual becomes the center of social space. There is no conception of the group as a whole except as a collection of individuals. We are because I am; and since I am, therefore we are."[19] Or, more importantly, "I am, therefore *it* is."

According to Carlton Molette's description of African-American ritual drama, its cultural "success" rests on the ability of those participating to share spiritual selves—so to speak—as does so much of African ritual.[20] The Haiku described by Suzuki depends on an understanding and identification that transcends the Western European definition and limitation of self; a limitation that is rarely surmounted. There are many such examples from the artistic experiences of majority cultures. As our discussion of the European aesthetic revealed, European art suffers from this concept of self as isolated and in antagonistic relationship to other.

Lee continues with her explanation of the European concept of self:

> In our own culture, we are clear as to the boundaries of the self. In our commonly held unreflective view, the self is a distinct unit, something we can name and define. We know what is the self and what is not the self; and the distinction between the two is always the same . . . . Our own linguistic usage through the years reveals a conception of an increasingly assertive, active and even aggressive self; as well as of an increasingly delimited self.[16]

This juxtaposition extends even to characterizations of interpersonal romantic "attachments" where one would expect identification to be paramount. Lee says:

> Not only do we think of ourselves as actors here, but we phrase this "activity" as directed at a distinct order. When I say: I like him, I cast my statement into the subject-to-object-affected mold; I imply that I have done something to him. Actually, he may be totally ignorant of my liking and unaffected; only I myself am certainly and directly affected by it.[21]

We are repeatedly brought back to the "revolution" that Plato worked so diligently to bring about. Though, as Eric Havelock argues, in his time his fight was all "up hill" and very much in opposition to the traditional epistemological mode, Plato's successors were ultimately overwhelmingly successful in shaping the Western concept of self that presupposed its isolation as the prerequisite to objectification. In this analysis his success is explainable by the intimate relationship of his ideas to the ideological principles already present in the germinating *asili* of the culture. According to Lee,

> Over the years, the English language has followed an analytic and isolating trend and it is possible that in linguistic reference there has been an increasing separation of the self from the encompassing situation.[21]

What is also revealed in the language of the European is that "freedom" of the self to control implies "freedom" to possess what is not self. Lee continues,

> Our language implies not only that the self is narrowly delimited, but that it is also in control. *My* is the pronoun which we call possessive; whose distinguishing characteristic, we are told, is that of possession or ownership; and possession in our culture means control: mine, to do with as I wish. And *My* is a word frequently used.[21]

In the international arena, as we have seen, the European cultural ego expresses itself in the need to possess everything, and the reverse struggle against Western domination is that of other people and majority cultures merely to "possess" and "define" themselves. The European American/European use of the first person possessive is indeed a significant point in an analysis of the culture. When one observes children in European society, the words "my" and "mine" seem to be said earliest and most often in their interactions with each other. The "our" and "ours," which are significant in communal societies, also signify possession. But Lee is correct, the difference is in the relationship to the idea and experience of control. The communal "our" takes the locus of control away from the "individual" (the "person" must consult others who share possession). At the same time it forces responsibility on the person to organize the community in order to gain control (influence) which can only be exercised through communal participation. This kind of control is not enough to satisfy the needs of the European *utamaroho*, which is shaped by an *asili* that demands power for its integrity.

Lee reminds us of the splitting of the European self that makes possible the sensation of a controlling and active "reason," rather than the perception of a controlled and passive "emotion." Her comments further demonstrate the relationship between the concept of the human generated by the European *utamawazo,* and the concept of self held by ordinary participants in the culture: One is self-conscious and speculative; the other is assumed. But they are both part of the same whole. Lee says,

> When it comes to the non-physical aspects, we note a reflection of the dualism of mind, and matter and the hierarchy which is a corollary of this. "Passions" are considered lower: I *fall* in love, I *fall* into a passion or a rage. I delve into my unconscious, which is implicitly underneath: but I analyze my conscious, where I do not need to excavate, since it is on my level. I lose and recover my consciousness or my reason; I never *fall* into consciousness or reason. Neither do I control my will; I exercise it. The self is most nearly identified with consciousness—spell mastery and control. So here, too, we find the implication that the self is in control of the other.[22]

Lee makes some additional observations about the relationship of the self to that which the self experiences (Dixon's separation of "man from phenomenal man").[23] Here again, we see the tyranny of Aristotelian logic and epistemology over the European mind and the consistently limiting effect of its absolutism on conceptual possibilities.

> Linguistic analysis further shows us a different relationship between the self and reality in general from that which is basic to our own culture. The Wintu never asserts the truth as absolute, as we do when we say *it is.*[24]

According to Lee, the Wintu say, "I-think-it-to-be-bread" or something with similar implications rather than "It is bread."

> The statement is made about the other, the bread, but with the implication that its validity is limited by the specified experience of the speaker . . . . For us, that which we sense or know according to man-made rules of logic, is; and that which is beyond my apprehension, beyond my sensing or cognition, is fiction, that is, it is not. The self is the measure of all things . . . . Art and metaphysics and religious experience are barely tolerated on the fringes of our culture . . . Mysticism is defined negatively as loss of self; and no one in ecstasy is taken seriously, until he comes to his senses. Only when the self is logically and cognitively in control, is experience valid, and except in the arts and religion only that which is ultimately open to such experience is true.[24]

What is tolerated is the attempt to mold art, metaphysics and religion into the shape of the "logically" controlled, thereby robbing these aspects of culture of their worth.

The universe for the minority European is centered in the self. This is radically different from world majority ontological systems. Is it any wonder, then, that the corresponding European concept of freedom would be lodged in the individual, isolated self as well? This implies, to the European, that the individual has particular value in the culture. But when the culture is examined, it becomes clear that in the quest for the all-important self, much is sacrificed. Europeans are accustomed to viewing other cultures from the heights of invidious comparison to their own in which traditional classical African and other majority cultures represent the depths of constraint and lack of respect for "individuality." Yet the priorities of European ideology result in a kind of suppression of the human spirit unknown elsewhere.

Among the Hopi, Lee found that "Every individual, young and old, is charged with responsibility for the welfare of the social unit."[25] This supports Diamond, who says that in traditional society the average individual participates to a greater extent than does the ordinary individual in European society. The result of this is that the person has a significance that she lacks in European culture. Her importance is qualitatively different. There is not simply a verbal commitment to "valuing the individual." She means more to the group; her value is given content.[26]

Again, what happens is that the *asili* of the culture demands the creation of both conceptual and phenomenal (experiential) realities that will work to maintain its wholeness and consistency. Since the foundation or germinating seed of the culture puts in motion an insatiable power drive, conceptions and definitions must be created that facilitate the will-to-power. Power becomes defined/experienced as control over other. This, in turn, necessitates the splitting of self from other, as we have seen. What results is the concept of the individual ("not divisible"); the smallest unit of the social group. This atom of the human universe is invented by the European as the seat of rational thought, the seat of moral action, the locus of power (since power must be an intensely narcissistic experience). Is it any wonder that cooperation between such entities is problematical? Clearly the concept of the "individual" is uniquely European, as is the resultant ideology of individualism and the economic system of capitalism that accompanies it. An "individual" can never truly experience the "weness" of things; an "individual" can never experience phenomenal reality as an extension of self, only as a negation of self. What is socially problematical is a communal impossibility. There is no counterpart to the European "individual" in African civilization. It is simply impractical; it does not suit the *asili* of African culture and therefore does not exist (except as destructive /"evil"). The concept of "the person" in African thought extends to encompass the entire universe. But then the objective is not personal control or power. The social objective is the experience of "we." The African limitation is difficulty in defining the political "they." The European political advantage is that every experience is defined politically, based on the identification of the threatening "other." This intense politicization begins with "Indo-European" or archaic European xenophobia, perhaps functioning to offset their minority status in the world.

European culture creates a being who thrives on competition and, therefore, on individual and distinct achievement. Because there is not a natural regard for personal worth born from and supported by the culture—because a person's existence as a member of the group does not in itself mean much—the individual strives to be "better than," to stand apart from others in his craving for recognition. This serves to reinforce his separate awareness and to further decrease his ability to identify with others. He, least of all, can define his good or his goals in terms of universal harmony. It should be even clearer now that there is no supportive mechanism or precedent for an "altruistic" ethic or spirit of "universal brotherhood." The only thing that binds members of the culture together in the final analysis—that binds them into a unified cultural whole—is the common goal of the suppression, exploitation, and control of the rest of the world; the environment, the earth and its people; that which is other than the cultural self. It is a union of like-minded people, who have cooperated in the creation of a technological giant—or monster.

In Lee's description of the Hopi, we see the possibility of an alternative definition of normative behavior:

> It is not only the physical act, or overt behavior, which is effective according to the Hopi view. Thought and will and intent are at least as effective; so that it is not enough for the individual to act peacefully; he must also feel nonaggressive, think harmonious thoughts, and be imbued with a singleness of purpose. It is his duty to be happy, for the sake of the group, and a mind in conflict and full of anxiety brings disruption, ill-being, to the social unit and, at a time of prayer and ceremony, to the entire universe.[27]

European society is, on the other hand, characteristically composed of anxious, aggressive, and always potentially conflicting individuals. The units within it are held together by the mechanisms of Weberian-defined "rationality" (efficient organization); mechanisms that control competition and ameliorate conflict only by delimiting the individual. The European conception of being tends to eliminate the need to consider the thoughts and spiritual states of persons, since in that dimension they are considered "powerless." It is part of the mythology that the European is motivated by strong "inner" convictions and a high degree of self-respect (Williams); while people in traditional cultures are more like "non-thinking automatons," whose spirits are ruled by their cultures. But it is often in majority cultures that one finds impressively strong standards of behavior and personal commitment to ethical behavior. Identification with group well-being should not be confused with lack of personal conviction or inability to make ethical decisions. These are all the characterizations implicit in Williams' earlier statement of the Euro-American "value of individuality." They are the same terms of Havelock's characterization of the "pre-Platonic" Greek.

In the African world-view the European dichotomy of opposition between the "individual" and the group collapses, and, instead, the person and the community are defined in terms of each other. They are interdependent, merging beings who together form the meaningful reality. The person is nothing (spiritually dead) outside of the context of the community because of the emotional, spiritual, and physical necessity for interaction with other human beings: This is necessary for the realization of humanness. The community is created by the spiritual communion or joining of persons. Its proper functioning and perpetuation is dependent on healthy, whole, committed, happy persons. That is why healing rituals have a communal aspect and why the morally evil is represented by a person who attempts to function autonomously (the "individual"), causing harm to others and creating distrust (the sorcerer). The power of such anticommunal thought must be neutralized if the community is to be able to keep its members (persons) healthy. Thus the African world-view leads to a very different concept of personal happiness. Just as the aim of the Hopi ceremonial "is the well-being of the universal whole."[28]

It becomes ever more imperative that we understand the full implications of the existence of a minority culture in our midst; a culture that has no formal or institutional reflection of the universal order, especially since this culture is by nature expansionistic. This is a culture based on the belief that the only reality is that which human beings create through manipulation of matter. It is based on a series of destructive acts that disorder and deplete, but do not harmonize or replenish. It may have taken centuries to reach the point of obvious breakdown that the workings of European culture now exhibit, but the seeds of destruction were always there in the *asili* that generated an initial ontology that attempted to eliminate the spiritual from human consciousness. As long as the European believes the autonomous individual can be the basis of his own happiness, or that the "individual psyche," as Havelock puts it, is the seat of moral conviction and that rationalism can be a source of morality, so then will his culture continue toward moral disintegration and his spirit continue to wither. The process started long ago, but the worst is yet to come. It is precisely the "autonomous individual" in Western European society who is its weakness. There are no longer guidelines for him to follow, and he has no tradition within his historical awareness from which to create them.

What happens in the contemporary West is that the individual feels overwhelmed by the institutions that surround her and powerless to affect the whole (the group, the social entity).[29] As she grows older she begins to feel more and more that she is interchangeable and so loses a sense of her own worth. This is the fate of the vast majority who do not achieve recognition beyond the crowd by extreme competitiveness, aggression, and selfishness. Joel Kovel says,

> What we have thought to be an increase in our individual power and freedom granted by modern progress, is in reality a much more ambiguous and complex process. To a large extent, people have been freed by handing over to culture their autonomy, for which they are repaid with material bounty and the freedom from manual toil. These are substantial boons, but for the mass of men, they are obtained at enormous cost. For, along with the diminution of self-autonomy, occurs the complementary growth of culture and its magical machines. As the self becomes dedifferentiated, society takes over the process of history, becoming both more articulated and more controlled . . . . We are talking, of course, of that unique modern phenomenon, totalitarianism, which we have already seen in this century in particularly horrid, and perhaps premature, forms, but which seems to be given existence simply by the natural unfolding of the logos of Western civilization.[30]

This last phrase hints of the *asili* concept, which focuses on inherent ideological tendencies. Paradoxically, as Kovel accurately identifies the pattern of ever-increasing institutional and state control in European development, he does not seem to recognize the idea of "self-autonomy," the loss of which he laments, as the culprit. He seems to have confused "self-autonomy" with "personal integrity." They are not synonymous, for "self-autonomy" is the converse of community. In the oppressive and repressive state order that the European *asili* generates, the self does indeed become more spiritually separate, thereby resulting in a collection of alienated selves. It is spiritual joining that creates "community," and it is community, not autonomy, that has the power to defeat the totalitarian order.

For Lee, "Respect for individual integrity, for what we call human dignity, has long been a tenet in American culture."[31] But what does this mean? And Williams in his sociological description of American society does not raise the question of what actually happens to the individual in that society but appears to merely accept the "tenet." We can, however, provide a basis from which such questions may be asked and a basis for a deeper understanding of the cultural meaning of this supposed European value as well as the cognitive structure that underlies it.

Stanley Diamond's discussion in *The Search for the Primitive* helps, by offering another view of what becomes of the individual in European society. Redfield, he says, described "ideological individualism" as being a reflection of "individualization," which "denotes the increasingly mechanical separation of persons from each other, as a result of the replacement of primitive organic ties by civil, collective connections." Diamond touches on one of the most revealing illnesses of contemporary Euro-American society: what he calls the "pathological loneliness" of the individual. This loneliness is symptomatic of the spiritual failing of the culture, the result of an ontology that conceives of the self as autonomous. This ontology leads to severe "personal isolation." Diamond says that the Western technical order tends to produce "standards" and "modal" types "rather than natural varieties of persons" in spite of (or perhaps because of) the "ideology of individualism." "The individual is always in danger of dissolving into the function or the status."[32] He continues,

> In the name of individualism, civilization manufactures stereotypes
> . . . such stereotyping usually leads to a culturally formed stupidity, a stupidity of the job itself, which grows to encompass the person, feeding on itself as both a defense against experience and the result of being deprived.[33]

Yet the belief that European society produces and is protective of some special freedom that is the lifeblood of the individual runs very deep in the American psyche. In undergraduate, introductory anthropology courses the instructor's descriptions of majority cultures are invariably met with the exclamation, "But they have absolutely no individual freedom. It must be horrible." And yet Jomo Kenyatta can say, "The African is conditioned by the cultural and social institutions of centuries, to a freedom of which Europe has little conception . . . . "[34] Contrary to ideology, group awareness and personal significance are not contradictory. As Diamond observes,

> Anyone who has ever witnessed a ceremonial African dance will certainly agree that the individual's sense of personal power and worth is immeasurably heightened by the communal nature of the event.[35]

He makes the critical distinction between the idea of "community" and that of "collectivity." And it is a significant one for the understanding of the failure of European culture in terms of what it does not offer its members. "Community," he says, can no longer be found in modern Western society, which is, instead, based on "collectives" that are "functional to specialized ends, and they generate a sense of being imposed from without. They are objectively perceived, objectifying, and estranging structures." The mob, according to Diamond, is the converse of the "organic group"; it is a "collectivity of detached individuals."[35] "The image of the mob is part of our image of the city." The word "community" itself implies the idea of a spiritual basis for joining with others; as in "communion."

It is interesting here to take note of the two connotations of the European term "jungle," related only via the logic of European chauvinism. One of these is that of an area of land, dense and thick with vegetation, which has not been inhabited or cultivated. The other is that of a grouping of "detached individuals," each one willing to commit any amount of violence to another to ensure her/his own survival. This image carries with it that of pervasive fear that comes with the complete loss of communal and, therefore, moral order; when one is continually aware of the possibility of being attacked from anywhere, at any time. The image is that of the Euro-American city. The true "jungle," in this second connotation, are the "New Yorks." : The concrete structures that are truly opposites of the first definition of "jungle." That is where this extreme deterioration prevails, as opposed to those areas least touched by European culture. Europeans have finally made their own conceptual invention—the complete lack of moral order—a reality. And this is the final outcome of the "ideology of individualism."

It remains for us to see what kind of intracultural ethic supports and is in turn generated by this isolating concept of self.

The "Protestant Ethic" and European Behavior

Most social historians would agree that Protestantism was the religion of the merchant emerging from medieval feudalistic society. Weber describes what he calls the bearers of sixteenth-century Western culture as he relates the "Protestant ethic" to the "spirit of capitalism," in his attempt to demonstrate

> the influence of certain religious ideas on the development of an economic spirit, or the *ethos* of an economic system. In this case we are dealing with the connection of the spirit of modern economic life with the rational ethics of ascetic Protestantism.[36]

But Lewis Mumford takes exception to the overwhelming concurrence with Weber's conclusions. In *The Condition of Man*, he says,

> Max Weber's thesis, that Protestantism played a prime part in the conception and development of Capitalism, has become current during the last generation. In view of the patent facts of history, this belief is as strange as it is indefensible: for it assumes that modern Capitalism did not take form until the sixteenth century; whereas it existed as a mutation at least three centuries earlier and by the fourteenth century it pervaded Italy: a country where Protestantism has never been able to gain hold.

> Capitalism was, in fact, the great heresy of the Middle Ages: the chief challenge to the ideal claims of Christianity . . . . There is no doubt . . . . that theological capitalism made its appearance far in advance of any protestant doctrine in either religion or economics.[37]

Mumford fixes on the issue of whether or not Protestantism was prior to capitalism and on the initial relationship of the two ideologies, which in his view was antagonistic.[38] Mumford is most probably right, the seeds of capitalism did not wait for the soil of Protestantism to be planted.

But clearly the strength of Weber's observation is correct. Protestantism, itself, obviously had to have its "origins" in the Church, yet this historical fact does not make the differences between its doctrines (role) and that of the Apostolic Church any the less real. Ethnologically, the indisputable fact is that no matter how much earlier than the sixteenth century the seeds of capitalism and

Protestantism may have been sown, nor what form they may have taken in these early stages, ultimately their development converged to reinforce one another and to form a culturally and ideologically congruent system that was to strengthen the tendencies of Western European development. Both cohere in the European *asili*. Capitalism could not have survived without a supportive ethical statement within the culture; a statement that sanctioned the intracultural behavior it dictated. Protestantism, and not the so-called "Christian ethic" (rhetorical), provided that sanction. Mumford himself sees ultimate correlations.

> Thrift, foresight, parsimony, order, punctuality, perseverance, sacrifice: out of these austere protestant virtues a new kind of economy was created, and within it, a new kind of personality proceeded to function. At one end of classic capitalism stands Jacob Fugger II: at the other end, John D. Rockefeller I.[39]

> The Protestant sought to curb the capitalist spirit and in the end he deepened its channels: he challenged the political rule of the despot and brought into business enterprise the ruthless ego that has hitherto dominated only the machinery of state.[40]

Joel Kovel's assessment of the significance of Weber's theory appears to be more to the point:

> He was actually looking for an example of the organicity of culture—how, in this case, the "spirit," that is the psychology, of capitalist activity, was decisively influenced by the new style of religious activity devised by Calvin, and by Luther before him. Religion has been, up to recent times, the source of our cultural worldview. A world-view must be presented as a set of normative controls, which must in turn be equilibrated with the superego structures of the individuals within culture. Thus the decisive change in the development of the capitalist spirit was the granting by Protestantism of a stern inner conscience to direct productive activity rationally.

And Kovel credits Weber with having presented the "definitive description" of "the new class whose rationalized activity so transformed the globe."[41]

Our task here is not to recapitulate Weber's observations nor the plethora of related theories that have emerged as a result of his work, but to point to a new dynamic that Protestantism and the Reformation brought to European culture. I have termed the values traditionally associated with the early Christian ethic as "rhetorical" in function because they are not characteristically reflected in European behavior. The rhetorical ethic is primarily for purposes of export. Internally, it serves the purpose of conscience-salvaging for those who need it, but it is directed outwardly (to a large degree); toward the "cultural-other." To be properly understood, it should come under the heading of "public" or "international relations" and belongs to the arena of international politics. The functions of the early Church in this regard left the culture without a set of normative controls, for contrary to what Kovel says, religion was not the source of the European worldview, but rather a systematically supportive statement of European ideology. Prior to the Protestant statement what tended to give direction to European behavior was (1) the common desire to rule the world and, (2) the shared commitment to build a technological colossus. There was no formal intracultural ethic provided by an institutionalized religious statement. There were only the informal normative directives of what would later become "scientism" and the order imposed by the European interpretation of the rational. (That is what is found in Plato's *Republic.*)

What Protestantism did for the Christian statement was to make it relevant to the inner dynamics of European culture. For the first time in the development of the West there was a correlation between a formal religious statement and the actual valued behavior of the European. The Protestant ethic was in this sense a moral or normative statement (a statement of ideal behavior), but it was only with great difficulty a spiritual statement. It was not primarily informed by, nor did it address itself to, spirituality. It was therefore consistent with the "spirit," the *utamaroho* or life-force of the West. In other cultures formal religion may be the source of worldview, but in European culture, what is referred to as formal religion has always served the politico-economic interests dictated by an ideology informed by a nonspiritual base.

The Cultural Role of the Early Church

The discussion in Chap. 2 deals only with the Apostolic Church, which for what has been the major portion of Western European history was its predominant formal religious statement. But the Church in its reformed model—in the form of Protestantism after the sixteenth century—related to the matrix of the culture in a way that was significantly different. A partial restatement here of some of our earlier conclusions will help to elucidate this difference.

The objective of the early Christian statement was not to be a normative statement of European personal or "individual" behavior. The European did not emulate Jesus "The Christ"; such behavior would have been, as it was for him, suicidal in the context of European culture. The Christian statement, instead, functioned to sanction European imperialistic expansion by giving moral status to the European concepts of "universalism" and evolutionism-progressivism. The Church in this way performed a vital function in the creation of the Western European empire. Because of this objective its "ethic" was directed not toward the European, which would have been in direct contradiction to the imperialistic objective and to the *utamaroho*, but to "cultural other," and did indeed complement the imperialistic objective. Most of the imagery, cosmology and mythology of the Bible has ancient African origins and is easily recognizable as the product of other cultures.[42]

The maintenance of these aspects greatly facilitated the imperialistic objective as it made the early Christian statement emotionally appealing and familiar to those whom the European wished to conquer, and First World peoples were offered images created out of a spiritual context with which they could identify. Catholicism absorbed just enough of the characteristics of the culture it invaded so as to ensure the loyal participation of its converts. It is the Catholic Church that represents the early Christian mission—to complement the political mission of the West—that of empire building. It is in "Catholic" countries and communities that the celebrations and rituals of African peoples reach the heights of bacchanal (e.g., during the week preceding Ash Wednesday). It is the Church in its early form that has been most "tolerant" of majority world culture, because a primary objective was political control of First World peoples, and political control within Europe; not the moral guidance of Europeans.

A void existed; there was no normative religious statement intraculturally. There was no religious statement with respect to the standards of behavior of one European towards another. It is not that such values did not exist. Values that did, in fact, regulate internal European behavior (i.e., behavior *within* European culture) did not come from and were not supported by what was recognized as "religion" in the culture, i.e., prior to the Reformation. What directed the behavior of Europeans towards their "brothers" and "sisters" (other Europeans) was a secular statement and a concurrence of material values and directives. (Attempts at reformulation within the Church prior to the Reformation were, for the most part, either unsuccessful or of minor consequence, in terms of its relationship to the dominant ideology of the culture.)

Because of the cultural imperialistic function of the Church, its "other-directedness" in this sense, it has always been markedly paternalistic. Its function was to encourage dependency, not to provide moral strength, strong will, or independence in the individuals to whom it was addressed. Obviously, for the purposes of cultural and political control of First World peoples, individual initiative and self-reliance are not desirable traits to encourage. Again, the early Christian Church was ideal for European expansion, but not for building strength in the European in terms of European values and ideals. It could not aid in the regulation of the behavior of the members of Western society in accordance with an aggressive and strong individualistic and self-reliant politico-economic system. An outgrowth of the imperialist concerns of the Church was that within European culture it has fostered dependency and a kind of moral weakness (see the film, *The Rosary Murders* 1989), because it offered no concrete ethical statement applicable to the culture. All that was left was a residual of the paternalistic attitude with which "cultural others" were addressed. In simple terms, it was excellent for the purposes of subjugation, but not for the creation of the aggressive individual; not for self-determination, nor for the budding capitalist. It was the objective of Western European imperialism that accounted for the leniency and paternalism of the Catholic Church.

A further related characteristic of the early Church that contrasts with the role of Protestantism was its unifying function. From the time of its earliest cooptation by the Roman Government, the Church functioned to unify the Western European Empire—again, to facilitate its imperialistic-expansionistic objective. (When it began to fail in this regard, also, it began to lose significance.) This function, along with other imperatives of the European *utamawazo*, gave rise to the need for ultra consistency and the quest for doctrinaire systematization. The work of Augustine and others contributed to the dogmatism and rigidity of the Church and later the Inquisition fanatically attempted to weed out remaining dissension. This aspect of the nature of the Church was, then, attributable to its intense political purpose. Since the time of the early Church and subsequent to the Reformation and the growth of "non-Catholic" religious formulations in the West, the political unification of Western Europe has never been provided by formal religion (i.e. the formally religious statement of the culture has never been the vehicle of unification since that time). It remains now for us to see how, in fact, the function of formal religion shifted with the advent of Protestantism.

Reformation: the New Role of the Church

The essence of the change brought about by the Reformation, within the context of this discussion, is that Protestantism represented not a statement fashioned for the missionizing of First World peoples, but an inward turning of Western European religion. For the first time in European development formal religion addressed itself not primarily to imperial expansion but to the regulation of behavior among peoples *within* European culture. This is not to say that Protestantism did not support the colonialist and missionizing venture. It most certainly did and does. The point here is that its primary function at the time of the Reformation, in terms of European development, was to provide a normative statement for the behavior of the individual within the culture. Moreover, in so doing, it emphasized the individual self as the axis and regulating force of the ethic it put forth.

This was an ethic, therefore, totally consistent with the values of the West and supportive of the capitalistic venture that was to play such a vital role in the political unification of Western European culture and the further development of national consciousness. It is a gross error for Ayn Rand and others of her persuasion to lament the so-called contradictions between "Christian altruism" and the ethics of capitalism, for in keeping with the organicity of European culture— the *asili*—the capitalist ethic received the sanctions necessary for its success from this new religious statement, as well as from the European *utamawazo* and ideology.

What was needed for the growth of the modern Western European capitalist empire was a kind of person who could be depended upon to behave in accordance with a particular code. Protestantism directed itself toward the civil order, rather than the world order, and toward the inner person. It is in this context that the ideas of Luther and, later, of Calvin supported one another. Luther's emphasis laid the groundwork for Calvin's political thrust. Mumford makes the following comments on Luther's ideas:

> Safety and freedom were not to be found only in the inner world: not that of the monastery, where authority also threatened, but within the citadel of the private self, outside the range of tyrannical fathers and tongued lightning.[43]

Here again he points to the extreme inwardness and self-reliance that Luther's ideas expressed:

> Luther's doctrine of faith lent itself to exploitation by far darker

powers than those this doctrine opposed: the very fact that the private world of the believer became sacred for him, prevented him from acknowledging the criterion of sanity—the congruence of private conviction with the historic experience and the common sense of other men.[44]

This is Kovel's description of this newly emphasized self:

A materialized world without intrinsic value is acted upon by a self freed from that world by an inward turning. Superego at last moves inward to rationalize gain and production decisively, and so becomes the lord of history.[45]

According to Mumford, then, Calvin applied this doctrine of self to the maintenance of a special kind of civil order. He "fortified the Augustinian doctrine of predestination" and "laid the foundations for civil liberty and self-government: the City of Man."

. . . the civil order devoted itself to the systematic establishment of the moral order . . . . A sin was a crime against the State: a crime was a sin against the Church.[46]

Mumford touches on the critical point I am making—that Protestantism represented a new direction of attention of the formal religious body toward the inner dynamics of Western European society. But he does not seem to understand the real significance of this new direction possibly because he is mistaken about the nature of early Christianity.

Calvinism was a real attempt to render unto God the things which are Caesar's: a return to that classic republicanism in which civic virtue counted high in the human scale: a return to Christian principles in realms from which it had been progressively banished: a re-union of eternal doctrine and daily deed.[47]

Here I think Mumford is wrong. He speaks of "return" and "reunion" as though there had not been an inherent separation between these two realms in the very nature of Christian ideology as it was initiated. It is Spengler who seems to interpret the "intention" of early Christianity correctly, that is, in the European interpretation. In its adoption by the West, it was never meant to apply to the concrete existence of the daily life of the European. Protestantism was not a return, but a true reformation for new purposes.

The intent of Protestantism was to mold a particular kind of person. This person was suited to the growth of capitalism and the development of modern Western society. He was an extreme individualist (which, of course, had precedents in the earliest traditions of the European *utamawazo* (culturally structured thought) only the emphasis was new). He was extremely self-reliant. He was the prototype of the "good" and successful businessman. Mumford says, "the Protestant personality was businesslike even when there was no business in hand."[48] Calvin openly sanctioned the ethics of business; a sanction that was absolutely necessary. If a modern capitalistic state was to develop and prosper, a belief in the morality and sacredness of personal property and the fulfillment of contracts was essential. (We are only now beginning to witness the implications for the capitalist system and the Western empire when such an ethic is not accepted; not in the advent of Russian socialism, but in the coming of the "sky-jacker" and other forms of so-called "terrorism." "Terror" to the West because the West loses control.)

In direct contrast to the Catholic posture, the Protestant attitude towards adherents to the faith was one of severity and the presentation of exacting standards and goals of behavior that the individual was expected to maintain independently; without the aid of a church which forgave all and possibly served as a crutch for the morally weak. The Protestant ethic implied a diametrically opposed philosophy from that of the Catholic confessional. In support of this point Mumford says,

> So long as the sinner did not cut himself off from God by Heresy, the Catholic Church was lenient to him. But Calvin's government practices no such indulgence: its aim was to reduce temptation and to root out sin.

> By the seventeenth century Protestantism had created an ideal ego: that which comes down to us in the image of the Puritan. The dominant traits of this character were austerity and perseverance, a narrowing of the circle of human interests and an immense concentration of the will . . .

> The Protestant shut himself off from the sensual expansion and the erotic dilation of the baroque order: and the avenues of sense were now carefully guarded, sometimes completely shut. Not only did images and figures disappear from his architecture, but even figured patterns, which the silk manufacturers of the period had learned to manufacture in their sumptuous brocades, disappeared from personal adornment. Grave atire and somber colors became the distinguishable marks of the Reformation.[49]

Catholicism has been historically successful in its vigorous mis-sionizing efforts among majority peoples, while Protestant missions have never been comparable in this endeavor. (The later "success" of the non-Catholic church among First World peoples—African Aladura, Puerto Rican Pentacostal, African-Caribbean Shango Baptist, African-American Baptist Church—is ironically bought at the price of the total denial of reformation Protestantism.) Again, the purposes and objectives of these two religious statements were different. Catholicism, representing the early Christian Church in its imperial-istic role, would never have been successful in gaining First World converts if it had approached them with the harshness of the puritan ethic. And what is more important, such an approach would have defeated the purpose of European imperialism; it would have been the attempt to promote an ideology of self-sufficiency, independence, and defensive strength among African peoples (much as the Nation of Islam does).

The Protestant statement, on the other hand, directed inwardly toward its own people, sought precisely to build such an individual. Asceticism and sterility, the negation of the humanness and warmth of other cultures, were interpreted as positive characteristics. Therefore, whereas Catholicism found a valuable tool in the mainte-nance and incorporation of majority cultural forms, Protestantism diligently rid itself of all sensuality, emotional and artistic vitality, and expansive ritual. Protestantism flatly rejected everything it con-sidered non-European and in the process helped greatly to harden in European culture the sterile and the "abstract," the nonhuman ten-dencies already recognizable in its development dictated by the *asili*. Mumford says,

> Not merely were the images of the Catholic Church rejected: all images became suspect as superstitious idols, too easily wor-shipped for their own sake . . . to dance, to attend theaters, to wit-ness public spectacles, to participate in carnivals, and above all to gamble at dice or at cards all lay outside the pale of his [the Protestant's] daily practice; when he was not actively engaged in business he turned to the sermon, the tract, the newspaper: the world of black and white.[48]

In Protestantism aesthetic imagery became more European.

Constantine, Augustine, Aquinas, and those they influenced con-tributed to the monument of political and doctrinal systematization that is Catholicism. They left the legacy of a monolithic, and above all, unified politico-religious statement; the perfect vehicle for early

Western expansion. Mumford laments the fact that Protestantism did not make the same contribution to European development. Again, this fact must be understood in terms of its function within European culture and its role and historical "timing" in European development. Protestantism was not meant to unify the European empire. This purpose was being fulfilled by secular aspects of European ideology and culture. Its purpose was to aid in the regulation of the behavior of individuals within the culture in order that that behavior be predictable and correspond to the controlling institutions and goals of the West. Protestantism, says Mumford, has an "inherent tendency toward fission," because "revelation" and not "reason' is thought to be the appropriate means by which to interpret the Bible. There was, therefore, in its early days a continual growth of antagonistic groups and the creation of ever new sects based on differing interpretations of the Bible. But Mumford does not seem to understand that these "sects" only represented political decentralization. They were merely variations on a theme, all of which, no matter how bizarre their interpretations (from extreme Ascetism to snake handling), served the purpose of providing strict moral statements for the guidance of behavior within European culture and the necessary building of a strong superego in the individual.

> Thus individualism turned into mere atomism. And the final flower of Protestant teaching was a willful denial of the need for unity: each man lived in a private world, described by a system of private science, edified by a private religion, governed by a private code, subject to no law but his own conscience, obedient to no impulse but that of his own private will. That was indeed the Utopia of the irresponsible bourgeousie: it erected specious moral foundations for the utmost caprice.[50]

Mumford's observations here point perhaps to a much later effect of Protestant individualism in combination with the European *utamawazo*, but within the *asili* of European development, and in terms of the needs of sixteenth century, it is not capriciousness nor irresponsibility that Protestantism fostered, but consistent and predictable behavior, oriented toward the goals of individual "achievement" and based on a mechanism of control internal to the individual, as opposed to being predominantly external as it had been under the early church.

Mumford is looking for something in Protestantism that is historically "out of place" in the context of European development, and that is most probably because of his own commitment to a spurious

"universalism" that is neither politically desirable nor culturally feasible. It is pointless to evaluate Protestantism, Catholicism, capitalism, or any other ideological-institutional development within
Western European culture from the vantage point of an abstractly
conceived human goal of "universalism"—a consistent thread to be
found throughout Mumford's works. These European institutions can
be understood only in terms of the specific objectives and commitments of European ideology. No European cultural form has been
created out of the need or desire to unify "man." The early church
never had this as its objective, unless European world expansion is
interpreted to be in the interest of all peoples, clearly a Eurocentric
interpretation. It is incumbent on the cultural historian to look at
Protestantism in terms of the needs of the specific developmental
period in which it flourished; that is, if she hopes to understand its
significance.

Catholicism, in its authoritarianism and concern for imperial
expansion, control, and unification gave no attention to the building
of the individual European superego. It could not do both, and therefore left a void in terms of an internal European ethical statement
and normative guide for behavior. Protestantism, on the other hand,
focused on the individual within European culture and did indeed
provide a model that the individual could internalize and that he was
led to believe could lead to "success" within the European value-system and the new institutions that were taking form. This was in opposition to his reliance in the past on a systematized abstract theology
that he was not expected to understand and on the performance of
external ritual. It is Protestantism, and not early Christianity (and
certainly not all religion), that is the "opiate of the masses" in that it
is designed to give the working classes the experience of a kind of
pseudo-success within the European system through the adherence
to strict rules of personal conduct; a "success" that is calculated to
compensate for the improbable success of the real capitalist, which
obviously is only accessible to a chosen few. Protestantism could
not simultaneously fulfill the function of unifying the West; moreover,
it was not called upon to do so. Scientism, then industrialism and
progressivism would do the job. Historically Catholicism has furiously weeded out heresy in its ranks. From this perspective the
Inquisition makes "ethnological sense"; if we use the concept of *asili*,
since the needs of Europe were at that time the solidification of an ideologically monolithic world organization. But Protestantism could
survive an "inherent tendency toward fission" and still perform its
function in European culture. It directed its attention toward the indi-

vidual psyche. If that was properly controlled, there would be no need for the paternalistic control of the unified Catholic hierarchy.

Protestantism and the European Ego

There are other features of Protestantism that help to explain its place in the formation of these more mature stages of European development. As Mumford points out, Protestantism did much to promote literacy in the West. Literacy became more wide-spread to a great degree because of the emphasis put on individual salvation with the aid of familiarity with and interpretation of the Bible.[48]

Protestantism, in its emphasis on the private "inner sanctums" of the individual-being reinforced and was consistent with the development of the European concept of individualism and the value of individual freedom and autonomy. This emphasis and value were encouraged by the already existing European conceptions of the human psyche—a legacy from archaic Europe. While it is true that this conception of "freedom" led ultimately to the tendencies of moral decay in the twentieth century West, Mumford exaggerates and is mistaken about its more immediate implications.

> Seeking personal freedom to avoid the vices of an arbitrary ecclesiastical authority, the Protestant finally became an advocate of freedom in order to establish an equally arbitrary authority of his own. If he lacked the outward power of a despot, he tended toward negative despotism: nonconformity—ultimately nihilism.[51]

The immorality of the West (the sacrifice of the human spirit in the name of power) is not at all the same as nihilism (inherently unsuccessful, since it does not seek to build): Again Mumford views the cultural implications of Protestantism in such extreme terms because of his "universalistic" ideology.

It should be understood that Protestantism further heightened the momentum of Western European development in its commitment to a mechanical model and its alliance with the "machine." Mumford, like Friedrich Juenger (See Chap. 1), points to the coincidence of the watchmaking "capital" (Geneva) with the initial focal point of Calvinism. He says,

> The machine became thus a double-headed symbol: it stood for both despotic authority and for the power that challenged that authority: it stood for them and it united them. The bourgeoisie became the new Elect; and the proletariat, even so down to the mere infant hardly out of the cradle, were obviously those predes-

tined to damnation. Thus the Calvinist concentration on the will, delivering into the world generation after generation of moral athletes with bunchy spiritual muscles and proud ones, nevertheless throttles the full human personality; and the City of Man was once more undermined by the very engines of power that the Calvinists themselves so ingeniously, so inventively, helped to install in its catacombs.[52]

The attempt to understand the cultural significance of Protestantism points to an important characteristic of European culture that can be easily misinterpreted. The Protestant ethic cannot be understood merely in terms of the nature and function of formal religions in primary cultural settings. Like religious statements in primary cultures, it both provided and reinforced the culturally accepted behavior models and was in this sense a statement of "morality," but unlike more spiritualistic religious statements. It was in fact with the help of Protestantism and capitalism that the final deathblows to spiritual awareness were dealt to the Western European consciousness. Spirituality had never informed the direction of European development nor the character of European culture; (it is not contained in the *asili*) but now it was thoroughly exorcised.

For the sake of clarity, we should reiterate what is meant by "spirituality," rather than assuming its definition. We mean to imply a particular vision of a universal reality in which a given order underlies organic interrelationship of all beings within the resultant cosmos. This order, which is both perceived and is, at the same time, a matter of faith, is of a metaphysical-essentialist nature. It is on this ultimate, primordial level that meaning is derived, which then helps to explain material (physical) reality. Perhaps the most significant characteristic of this concept of spirituality is its transcendent nature. While one functions pragmatically within a profane reality, that "reality" is never thought to be the essence of meaning. In spiritual conceptions there is always a striving for the experience of a deeper reality that joins all being. Learning is the movement from superficial difference to essential sameness (Na'im Akbar). This "sameness" is spirit; beyond and ontologically prior to matter. It is the basis for human value. One's spirituality involves the attempt to live and structure one's life on a national, communal, and personal level in accordance with universal spiritual principles. It allows for the apprehension of spirit (energy) in matter (form).

Let's look at an example of contemporary European intracultural behavior, which perhaps concretely demonstrates what is meant by the lack of a spiritual base in the culture. In March and April of 1987, a controversial court case emerged in the headlines and newscasts involving the custody of an infant, who became known as "Baby M." The case brought attention to a new practice called "surrogate mothering," in which a woman leases her womb to a couple who cannot have a child. For a price, in this case $10,000, she allows herself to be artificially impregnated with the man's sperm, carries the fetus for nine months and gives birth to a baby, who then "belongs" to the man and his wife. In the case of "Baby M," the person referred to as the "surrogate mother," who actually gave birth to the baby, changed her mind and wanted to keep the baby, claiming that it was rightfully hers.

A situation such as this is inconceivable from the perspective of a spiritualistic world-view. Everyone involved is reacting in a materialistic manner to a profoundly spiritual event. And they have to resolve it legally! The natural mother is called "surrogate" because she has "sold" the rights to her body; she has "contracted" the function of her womb. Something she spiritually cannot do; that could only be conceived of in the context of the European world-view, which objectifies all reality. The body (womb) of the natural mother is regarded as though it were a mechanical incubator on a hospital ward. Yet the body (womb) is inextricably and interdependently joined to a human spirit, soul, and emotional being. There may be no other phenomenon that effects a woman's emotional being more intensely than the act of carrying a child and giving birth. Only Europeans would attempt to void the birth process of its spiritual meaning—and treat another human being as a "womb" and biological process only. In this instance, the most sacred occurrence, in terms of the African world-view, becomes a business deal in which not only a woman's womb but the baby to whom she gives birth is a commodity: The ultimate profanation. Spiritual depth and maturity is also lacking in the childless couple who, instead of adopting a child, must desacralize a sacred phenomenon by "acting out" their extreme and narcissistic egotism.

Centuries earlier in European development, Protestantism was laying the groundwork for such an intensely nonspiritual approach to reality. Protestantism was practical, mechanical, and materialistic. It was in this sense "secular" (or "profane" in the sense of Mircea Eliade's distinction).[53] As Mumford has indicated, its concern was the concrete European "City of Man." Protestantism was about the business of aggressive life and material survival. Moral personal conduct and behavior were a prerequisite to civil order, but the essence of the human spirit was not the source of this morality, rather it was being destroyed by it. Protestantism with its emphasis on the Western conceived ego helped to destroy the self. Kovel says,

> Through the expedient of abstraction, most forcefully expressed in Calvinist theology, a God-symbol arose to justify individual suffering by turning it to economic use in the compulsions of work without pleasure and gain without joy.[54]

Clearly this describes a nonspiritual ethic or morality; a phenomenon that is totally European, and one that should be understood as such. Modern bourgeois man, says Kovel, "who began his development propped up by the Protestant faith, succeeds in pushing God aside even as he worships Him."[55]

The implications of "anality" in the psychoanalytic description of personality structure are diametrically opposed to what I mean by "spirituality." It is the result of the denial of the human spirit. Kovel identifies the Protestant ethic and its development with the anal personality. In his view it was a "natural" outgrowth of the anal Western personality. This interpretation is the basis of his theory of European imperialism and "white racism." He takes this explanation to its extreme in his characterization of Luther. (Norman Brown has made the same point.[56])

> His personality was to a considerable extent elaborated upon anal fantasies. Two of his personality traits, stubbornness and defiance, were of decisive aid to him in his rebellion against papal authority . . . the turning point in modern Western history, [was when] Luther's idea of the power of individual faith, struck him in a flash of inspiration while he sat upon the privy, and that this genius was not loath to stress the importance of this in applying fecal symbolism to all evil parts of the universe, and especially to the Devil, God's black antagonist.[57]

Luther's personality is generalized and becomes that of the successful (and unsuccessful but ardent supporter of the system), aggressive European. "Similar character configurations [have] aided countless other westerners in their stubborn and defiant efforts to impose a new world culture upon other civilizations." Below Kovel isolates the characteristics that describe the behavior of the European, sanctioned and directed by the Protestant ethic:

> . . . control, stubbornness, defiance, orderliness, cleanliness, punctuality and thrift—these complicated traits which have character-

ized the West more than any other civilization—devolve into anal fantasies and the resolution of their logical incompatibility is achieved through an unconscious symbolic root in infantile fantasies about excretion.[57]

Kovel is not the only one who has hinted at a relationship between European anal development and European aggression. The film, *Cradle of Humanity*, made by a team of European psychologists for UNESCO, documents a study that they conducted of the relationship between mothers and infants in West Africa. They concluded that the closeness of this relationship encourages precocious mental and physical development in very early childhood. In the course of the film some comparisons are made with European childrearing practices and attitudes. One point of comparison concerned toilet-training, a very problematical transition in the development of the European in which the child experiences rejection and separation from the parent and from the self; it results in a kind of traumatization in which fear and confusion becomes hostility and imposed order (pleasure associated with control?). The European child is made to sit alone on an alien, cold object and cannot "rejoin the group" in a sense until he is "cleansed." Since the mother/parent is not sure of the exact time of the need to excrete, this very young child often sits for long periods alone or with a book or leaves only to be "placed in isolation" again, (sometimes as a punishment).

As the film reveals, the traditional African practice is startingly different. The mother and child, who are almost literally never physically separated, develop a special way of communicating that has deep spiritual (even psychological) significance. The child uses this special language to indicate to her mother when she wants to relieve herself. The mother then takes the child from her back, where she is carried, and sitting on the ground with her legs stretched out in front of her, she positions the child so that she (the child) is sitting on her (the mother's) legs facing her mother. The mother's legs are spaced so that the child excretes on the ground. If for some reason the child does not relieve herself, the mother makes a "shushing" sound that somehow encourages the child to do so. The result of this is an extremely different kind of experience from that which children raised in European societies undergo. One is a natural process depending on spiritual connection between the closest of human beings. The other is a frighteningly artificial procedure that interjects sterile material objects into an organic process and succeeds in alienating human beings from one another as it imposes order on human life by denying human spirituality.

This pattern of denial in European infancy is consistent as babies are separated from their mothers at very early ages (at birth in hospitals), and made to sleep in separate beds and rooms or to relate to strangers for long periods during the day. This again is in stark contrast to traditional African practice in which the mother carries the baby everywhere on her back even sleeping with her at night. She breast feeds the child on demand and refrains from sexual relations with her husband until the child is weaned. In European culture the baby must compete with the husband for the attention and affection of the mother. The film implies that the European child develops the need to aggressively seek attention, since that attention is not readily accessible. Aggression becomes the normal pattern of behavior, since that is the way to achieve what is necessary. What kind of adult develops from a lonely baby? Perhaps what Freud regarded as universal human aggression, arising out of the trauma and conflicts of the anal phase and infant individuation, are merely projections on his part of a European syndrome that begins to intensify with Protestant reformist thought and behavior.

What began to be referred to as the "Protestant ethic" also resembled ideologically in several striking ways the cultural characteristics of early Judaism. As I have said earlier, the Judaic statement was fashioned for the creation and survival of a strong, self-sufficient, and isolated cultural group. Its primary objectives were not those of world expansion. It possessed an inner-directed ideology; strongly nationalistic in the self-deterministic sense. In Judaism is found a rational, political and material base (with the exception of the Qabbala), as opposed to a spiritual supernatural one. In Protestantism there is the same emphasis on self-improvement and self-reliance that has historically characterized the Jewish population. And it reflects a corresponding period in which Europe addressed itself to its internal structures and to the kind of person who would be appropriate to and supportive of the perceived cultural mission.

Without sacrificing the momentum of its expansionism, Western culture used the new religious formulation to build a culture that was assured of survival and an individual who was loyal to its objectives. Mumford, again, hits on this contrast between Protestantism and Catholicism, but shows no understanding of the cultural-political significance of early "universalistic" Christianity. He speaks of the effort of the sixteenth-century West "to achieve cultural self-sufficiency: a perverse rebound from the Universal Church . . . Luther . . . associated internationalism with corruption and isolationism with purity."[58]

And from this perspective, Mumford recognizes a relationship between Protestantism and Judaism:

> Under the protestant [sic] passion for individual salvation, the common man lifted himself up by heroic mental efforts: he read and mastered the history, the laws, the ethics, and the poetry of one of the greatest cultures the world has ever known: that of the Jews.[59]

Earlier, he says, "Calvinism was Christianity reinvigorated by the morality of the Jewish prophets and the political and educational traditions of the Jewish synagogue."[47] In the formulative stages of Western culture it was precisely the isolationism and self deterministic emphasis of Judaism that rendered it inappropriate for the expanded European ego and the newly conceived European world imperialistic objective. The Christian statement of the ancient West incorporated many of the cultural and ideological characteristics of Judaism, while adding to it the universalism and proselytizing mandate necessary to sanction the building of a world empire. Mumford says of a much later period in Western European history that "Hitler's religion of power, with himself for God, was an effort to overthrow what was left of the universal and the human: an effort to turn the world as a whole into the German fatherland."[58] What he does not recognize is that all "universalistic" statements and ideologies throughout the history of Europe have been variations on the common theme of turning the world into a European empire. Christianity was the first such statement in formally religious terms, while Judaism was politically inadequate, because at that stage of European development it was too early for an inner-directed, isolationist, and self-deterministic religious statement. The first order of business was to conquer the world; to expand "the self." By the sixteenth century the European had gained his foothold on the world; now he was ready to direct some of his attention to the inner dynamics of his culture and to the ethical control of the individuals within it. If such an "ethic" had not come forth the insatiable European *utamaroho* would have directed itself toward itself as well, destroying the European empire from within. It was time for Protestantism and the return to a more Judaic-like emphasis on the self and on the cultural entity; i.e., now that the "European consciousness" was assured and the cultural self was defined in expanded terms.

Mumford calls Protestantism the "gospel of self-sufficiency and self-determination."[60] It is interesting that these are precisely the goals of contemporary revolutionary and anti-imperialistic movements of Africans and other majority peoples. Indeed, the nationalism of such peoples is defined in terms of self-definition and ideologies of independence. China's strength was not to be found primarily in the adoption of an "international" political strategy, or even its socialism—most certainly a viable tool for the implementation of a nonexploitative ideology—but in its "nationalism," the ideological emphasis on self-reliance. The Western imperialistic objective obviously needs subjects (i.e., political "objects") and is successful only to the degree that there exist "colonials" who lack confidence in their ability to survive alone. This is why the European attitude towards majority peoples is always characterized by paternalism. Ultimately, Africa does not need "handouts" from the World Bank and the International Monetary Fund; Africa needs Europeans to leave its natural resources alone. The objective has always been to prohibit independence: psychological, political, and ideological. Africans and other world-majority peoples, who are convinced that they need the capital of the West to survive, will by definition be eternally dependent and, therefore, "colonial."

The Protestant ethic also sought to create inner strength, aggressiveness (defensiveness), and self-reliance, but its presentation of "self" was an inhibitive and negative force rather than a creative one for the European. The Protestant formulation dictates both an isolated definition of the individual self and at the same time, an inordinate control of the natural inclination of that self. It creates, thereby, a frustrated personality that characteristically suffers from a lack of emotional fulfillment.

The emphasis on self and ethnicity found in First World self-determinism is based on the awareness of a shared spiritual source, and a nonindividualistic concept of freedom; i.e., a communally-based "freedom" and goal of well-being. The aggressive and defensive energies evoked are directed outward toward the European oppressor and his control—that which seeks to destroy the "cultural self." This emphasis on self is, therefore, not based on a separation of self from other as the European *utamawazo* dictates, but rather on a discovery of the importance of self through identification with the cultural whole—a discovery that is not possible in the absence of such identification. It is a spiritually based awareness of self that implies and relies on communion with that which is more than self. The expansion of the self is, therefore, a spiritual phenomenon, not materially based as in the minority European case. In this way it incorporates the wisdom of traditional, First World ideologies. Compare the following statement by William Strickland on African self-determinism with the ideology of Protestantism:

> Blacks must build a new politics, with a new social vision—a poli-
> tics of true revolution, which is always and finally, a politics of self-
> reliance. Our future task is self-evident, it is self-development,
> building anew like our fallen brother Amilcar Cabral, even as we
> fight. Developing in the midst of depression, developing under
> siege. Developing without resources, except human resources.[61]

This is the only revolutionary possibility for a colonized people.
The self-reliance and self-denial of the Protestant ethic, on the other
hand, helps to maintain the existing order; and the self is taught to
be dependent on material capital and material resources.

Luther's emphasis on moral virtue as the proper performance
of one's task or "calling," no matter how menial, foreshadows a critical regulative role that Protestantism was to play. The European *utamaroho* is one of extreme arrogance and ambitions of power. This
expression is constructive (in terms of the European objective) as
long as it is directed outward. Protestantism allowed for identification
of the individual with the European/Euro-American imperialist objective, at the same time encouraging an attitude of acceptance and
humility among the less powerful within the culture with regard to
their inferior status. The Protestant ethic has been most successful
in this respect, as it is still one of the most impenetrable strengths of
the European empire that its "inferior" members can identify as
"superiors" of the world and, therefore, contribute loyally to the
European cause. As the culture became divided into capitalist and
wage-earner, Protestantism helped to assure that those exploited
within the culture would be not only content with their lot but would
feel that they were providing a vital function in a larger "order of
things." The "good" Protestant supported the system; in so doing he
was "answering his calling": opiate of the masses.

Themes in Interpersonal Interaction: Survival, Competition, Control

We are attempting to give definition to the "ethic" that guides
European (Euro-American) interpersonal, intracultural behavior.
Protestantism was a partial formal statement of this ethic at a particular stage in European development. Capitalism, which it complemented, is a dominant source of the intracultural ethic in the modern
West. Both of these directives of behavior, however, were born out
of and supported by tendencies in an ideological statement, visible
in the earlier European experience and further complemented by
other European institutions (academic, social, and political).
Ethnologically, therefore, it is not surprising that they are totally con-

sistent and compatible with the rationalism and materialism that became ever more pervasive in the course of European development. This is because the germs of both the Protestant ethic and capitalism are contained within the *asili* of the culture. They emerged as part of its "natural unfolding."

Interpersonal behavior among European (European-American) peoples is competitive, aggressive, exploitative, and based on a European-defined "survivalism"; one made necessary by the nature of the culture itself. This behavior is, therefore, characterized by hostility and defensiveness. The European "personality" is above all a product of a conception of self that isolates the individual. He is alone and vulnerable, surrounded by other alone, vulnerable and therefore defensive personalities. Once past the level of the primary ideological substratum of the culture, which tends to bind European individuals together, there is no identification between him and other individuals within the culture. Beyond this there is no commonality. He defines himself as their "opposite," and his interest as "opposed to" or "in conflict with" theirs. "Meaning," at the level of secondary or derived values, is determined by the needs of survival among hostile beings. The culture into which the individual is born provides him with an individualistic and isolating concept of self, while it fails to provide him with a spiritual base of emotional inspiration and support. With these givens he has no choice but to go about the business of surviving as best he can. He is, indeed, in a "jungle." An initially defensive posture soon becomes aggressively offensive behavior. The individual perceives that the best way to assure his own survival is to disarm others; to "beat" them, to "win," to "get ahead," to usurp the objects of value before they do, to control them. He must do all of these things before they are done to him (that becomes the Golden Rule).

To make matters worse, the culture thrives on violence, and it is becoming more intense. The popular media is a laboratory for the study of the European American need for violence. Eli Sagan places the origin of the theme of violence in Homeric Greece; surely we can trace it further back into the source of European culture. Sagan says, "Culturally we are children of Greece"; How could he possibly arrive at that conclusion? It might be said that Europe is the cultural child of Greece, but it is absurdly Eurocentric to say that the rest of the world's people are.

At any rate, Sagan does look specifically at early Greek culture and finds that "faith in the efficacy of violence was a central belief in the Greek value system," and that "violence was not merely one of the many important factors, nor was it an incidental expression of the culture."[62] Instead, in his analysis, "the characteristic form of immorality and aggression—a primary ambivalence—in Greek culture was a commitment to sadistic violence, a love of killing . . . "[63]

Sagan uses psychoanalytic theory and the examination of Homeric literature, primarily the *Iliad,* on which to base his argument. Sagan reaches a different conclusion from that which, according to Freud, is implied by the Oedipus complex. Sagan refers to the "complex" as the "womb of antiquity,"[64] then uses this explanation of the development of the psyche to explain Greek ambivalence towards violence and the need to enact it excessively. The Oedipus complex is male-centered. So was Greek society. (So, of course, is Freudian theory for that matter.) Sagan, therefore, feels justified in examining this cultural process from a male perspective.

The Oedipus complex involves sexual feelings towards the mother and competitive feelings towards the father. Aggressively, the male child, according to Freud, wishes to replace (kill) the father. At the same time he fears him. In Freud's view, since the child's sexuality becomes focused in his genitals, he both wishes to castrate his father and fears being castrated by him. In fact, the Oedipus complex resolves itself in fear of castration. It is at this point that Sagan disagrees with Freud. He argues that such fear would permanently immobilize the boy, never allowing him to become a man. Instead the "healthy" response is for the boy to be able to "imagine" himself "having" his mother and becoming or "incorporating" his father, i.e., taking over his role. "Incorporating his father" means that his father's moral authority moves within the boy; admonishing, punishing, making demands. Indeed this "father within" becomes the conscience or the "superego."[65] According to Sagan, this imagining allows the child to mature. If the child is never able to imagine the fulfillment of his desires, they will continually return, never allowing him to become an adult, preventing him from developing an inner moral conscience, i.e., the "superego."

According to Freud, the "feminine" attitude develops in a boy when he reacts passively to the Oedipus complex, wanting to take the place of the mother and become the love object of the father. The castration complex has this effect.[66] Sagan argues that the greater a boy's capacity to imagine the fulfillment of his Oedipal desires, the more "masculine" will be his stance; "the less will be his passive stance toward his father and towards all men in authority."[66] He reasons, therefore, that there is a connection between Greek male homosexuality and the fear of Oedipal aggression.[67]

Myths allow people to imagine what they cannot do, Sagan continues. Oedipus kills his father and marries his mother; Zeus over-
throws his father, Uranos. In Sagan's view, these myths have a
healthy, psychocultural function. But Homer's consistent message is
that rebellion against authority leads to disaster. Sagan says that the
Greeks considered offenses against the father as the greatest sin;
hubris. This is clearly a reinforcement of the patriarchal world-view.
For Sagan, Achilles' violent behavior when he fails in his rebellion
against Agamemnon is like the tantrum of a little boy, which threatens to take the culture "back" to a state of barbarism.[68]

Finally Sagan attempts to use all of this as a foundation on which
to build an explanation of the "prevalence of graphic sadism" in the
Iliad. He asks the same question about contemporary European
American society;

> Why do well-dressed middle-class couples go to movie houses to
> witness graphic scenes of machine-gun bullets perforating the
> body of some unfortunate victim, or a group of small boys pour-
> ing gasoline on the body of a derelict before setting him afire?
> Why has our culture returned to the detached eyeball and the
> inward guts? It is reasonable to make the assumption that the
> escalation of graphic sadism in the popular arts of our society
> indicates that we are going through a cultural situation similar to
> that faced by Homeric society.[69]

He concludes that excessive violence in the life and popular culture of these two related societies is caused by "a conflict within the
value system of the culture." For Sagan the "conscience" of ancient
Greece, as with that of contemporary Euro-America, is "in advance"
of the behavior of its people. The society refuses to implement the
moral goals that it has set for itself. "The promptings of the superego
demand a new order of sublimation of aggression . . . . The ego
becomes more violent in order to protect itself against the demands
of conscience."[69] "When those in a culture will not do what conscience demands, the tension rises," and people respond to the tension by running from the conflict. Oedipus ran from his parents only
to run directly into them; "the culture flees from the problem into the
heart of the problem." The conflict originates with problems concerning legitimate aggression, says Sagan. The escape from the problem results in a popular culture concerned with violence.[69] "The
vicarious, fanciful brutality of the movies serves the purpose of making all violence unreal. The real violence in our society, directed at
real people goes unnoticed."[70] The sadism of the *Iliad,* in Sagan's

view, indicates that the culture was not at ease with its conscience.

Sagan's explanation is interesting, even helpful, but it is based on an incorrect assumption. European/European American culture has no "conscience" in the sense that majority peoples would use that term. It does have "moral" codes or norms concerning behavior towards those whom it recognizes as "human," but that is not a "conscience," it is a "superego" that functions to protect the machine; i.e., to protect the culture from itself. Conscience originates in ideas about what is right and wrong, which in turn are related to the ideological core of the culture. The ideology of European-derived societies is that anything goes in the service of power.

Sagan is correct: There is a basic conflict, but the conflict issues from the extreme individualistic and materialistic world-view of the culture. These terms are so strong that they act in opposition to the needs, even of a European social order—of a European consciousness. That is the only conflict within the European *asili*: Individual consciousness versus European consciousness. It is difficult for Europeans to treat other Europeans nonaggressively. That is the source of "moral," behavioral tension. The superego, to borrow Freud's term, of the culture then instructs its members to direct unacceptable violent aggression toward "noncultural" beings *outside* the culture; "communists," "gooks," "niggers," etc. On this level the conflict is resolved. Such violence, like the movies, is not experienced as violence, nor is the violence that is directed at Africans in America. Sagan is a victim of the rhetorical ethic. His explanation gives this "ethic" a function that it does not have. It blurs his vision, so that he can say of the United States, "we have an ideal of love, a moral vision."[71] But we, who have been victimized, know that to be a lie.

The Western ethic is the epitome of selfishness. Contrary to the verbal expression of the rhetorical ethic, it is not considered immoral in the West to act in one's own interest at the expense of the well-being of others; rather, selfishness, competitiveness, exploitation of others are necessary for survival, dictated by the ideology of the culture, indicating, therefore, "moral" (acceptable, encouraged) behavior patterns. These characteristics represent moral behavior in the context of European (Euro-American) culture in that they are sanctioned by every aspect of the culture, and the individual within it is conditioned to manifest them. The successful "culture-bearers" of Europe (as Weber puts it) possess these characteristics. The truly "Western man" is the most competitive and aggressive person. While the least successful person in the culture, who in no way determines what the West becomes, is characterized by humility and love, i.e., identification with and consequent respect for those around her, resulting in nonaggressiveness (internal peace). This person is trampled upon in and by European culture. She is considered "worthless." What is more, she is "unethical" in that she attempts to defy the normative behavior sanctioned by the culture as a whole.

A person such as this must "possess" a radically different conception of self than that which European ideology proffers and that which the members of the culture are inculcated. Is it, then, any wonder that such a person is rare in European derived societies? For as Kovel says, "culture is organized into sets of symbols which are congruent with the structure of the personalities within it."[72] The personality described by the early Christian or rhetorical ethical statement is indeed incongruent with European culture. That person contradicts the *asili* and functions from a different *utamaroho*. Can such a person exist?

A self that must be distinct in order to know becomes emotionally a self that perceives value in terms of itself in isolation. This is not the natural context for the creation of human value—which is normally created out of shared emotional commitment. The values of the European individual are, therefore, necessarily material. They are not true "human" values. Such a self is alone, afraid, defensive, and aggressive. Acquisitiveness, fanatical accumulation, and mutual exploitation are merely the logical and rational outgrowths of such a perception of reality. Because of the conception of self—the values of a European-defined "individuality" and "freedom"—that the culture generates, the personality strives for a security not provided by his culture, in an arena from which it can never come. Material accumulation becomes the tool of an assurance against the hostilities and attacks of others. The individual becomes obsessed with the negative and threatening possibilities of the future—with accident and with death. He lives in a culture diseased with thanatophobia and one that provides him with insurances "against" every kind of physical or material possibility imaginable, yet knowing that no amount of financial gain can redeem his soul. He is truly Faustian man—but he did not choose to be so. The "choice" is already implicit in the *asili* of the culture: the bio-cultural, ideological core.

European culture, then, fails in the primary function of a cultural construct, i.e., to provide the human being with the emotional security brought by spiritual communion. This sense of security, which the European fails to achieve, in majority cultures is created out of the spirituality of human interrelatedness and a concept of shared human value; an arena that transcends the material. European culture is a culture with a nonspiritual ideological base. This essential and defining characteristic has allowed it to become the most materially successful culture, the most aggressively political culture, the most scientifically rational culture, and the most psychopathological culture the world has ever known.

It is at the same time the only culture that provides little or no source of spiritual or emotional well-being for its members. It carries little tradition of insight into the human spirit and virtually no knowledge of the human soul. It is atrophied toward nonhuman realities. European culture presents the individual it produces with only the alternatives of materialism, scientism, and rationalism, when what she needs is the inner peace that comes with communion (merging) with others, the sense of oneness, and emotional identification with other people. What she needs is "love." As Kovel says, "the current state of our culture is inadequate to meet the full human need of its people."[73] Using the concepts suggested by Alexis Kagame, and interpreted by Janheinz Jahn, European culture, as an oppressive *Kuntu* (structured modality) destroys the *Muntuness* (human beingness) of its participants, because it is based on the valoration of *Kintu* (material objects).[74]

The characteristics we have discussed are basically those that determine European interpersonal behavior. The institutions and forms of the culture can be understood as structured sets of rules that are based on these given norms and that act to regulate the behavior of individuals so that a support system for its intercultural behavior is maintained. In other words, what accounts for the survival of the culture as a cohesive whole is its ideological objective of the control and subjugation of all other peoples and the related commitment to technological and material superiority. A friend of mine points out that Europeans would indeed destroy each other if they did not have "others" to destroy. By the same token, the integrative function of the culture could not have survived so long the disintegrative tendencies of an individualistic ethic had it not been for the outwardly directed imperialistic objective and quest for world supremacy. That quest is definitive to the European *utamaroho* and the emotional satisfaction (itself a negation of spirit) with which members of European culture identify.

Because of the spiritual void in European culture and its ideological individualism, capitalism was able to gain hold and to flourish; in turn it supported these themes. And because of the success of capitalism in the West the concepts of individual freedom and possession were reinforced, while any attempt to discover human spirituality was discouraged. The essence of the human spirit is inseparable from communalism. The ethos of capitalism presupposes and thrives on "moral" individualism and autonomy—the denial of human spirituality.

The themes that I have been pointing to recur in other descriptions of European culture, not only in the more critical analyses, but they are also recognizable in the noncritical, chauvinistic descriptions. The juxtaposition of the analyses of Joel Kovel and Robin Williams helps to demonstrate how similar traits of Western society are made to appear both from a critical and a noncritical perspective.

From the perspective of a critical understanding of the European concept of self it is possible to understand better the ideology of individualism and the related assumed value of human freedom as it is interpreted in European culture. The ideal of "democracy," a by-word of American nationalism, is seen as the translation of the European concept of self into a particularly European statement of value, instead of a universally valid human goal. Robin Williams' description of the theme or value of democracy is couched in terms that attempt to cloud the issue of its uniqueness to the culture; but even in these terms it is clear that the values expressed do not have universal significance. In fact, Western "democracy" is necessary to assuage the fear and distrust that individuals have of each other.

> Major themes in the gradual crystallization of the main democratic creed thus included equality of certain formal rights and formal equality of opportunity, a faith in the rule of impersonal law, optimistic rationalism, and ethical individualism . . . the theme of democracy was, concretely, an agreement upon *procedure* in distributing power and in settling conflicts. Liberal democracy, American model, arose in reaction to an epoch in which the great threats to security and freedom were seen in strong, autocratic, central government. The new system was devised in such a way as to limit and check centralized governmental power and to establish an ordered pattern for agreeing to disagree. Such a pluralistic view of social power was clear and explicit on questions of procedure, although it left the common ends of the society largely undefined.[75]

The European brand of democracy—a counterpart to the European concept of freedom—is related to the desire to control and exert power over others, which motivates so much of European behavior. Democracy is envisioned as the system that guarantees the "freedom" of the individual to do what she must on behalf of her own self-interest, which in turn she interprets as the control of others. This power drive accounts for the fanaticism that characterizes

European behavior, as well as the institutions that guide and regulate it. There are no compromises in the structures of European culture; they are not tempered by considerations other than the "profane," materialistic ones upon which they are based. Once the human spirit had been devalued as a determinant and inspiration of culture, the character of the culture itself began to move further and further in the direction of the denial of that spirit. Once "rationality" (in the Weberian sense) had become synonymous with European value, the forms of European culture became rational in excess. The culture is given to extremes and encourages intensely unidirectional activity on the part of its participants. The balance is lost. The sense of power, then, becomes not just sometimes desirable or pleasurable, or the objective of just a few, but is an uncontrollable and predominant directive of behavior. Theodore Roszak describes European behavior this way:

> The original sin to which science was born: *hubris*—at last becomes pandemic. "We have now," the head of a prominent think-tank announces, "or know how to acquire the technical capability to do very nearly anything we want . . . if not now or in five years or ten years, then certainly in 25 or 50 in 100."
>
> "And ye shall be as gods . . . ."
>
> Our presidents still take oaths upon bibles; our astronauts read us scripture from outer space. But the mark of the beast is upon the appetites and aspirations that most govern our collective conduct: demonic imbalance—endless distraction by unholy infinities of desire: to produce and devour without limit, to build big, kill big, control big. Anything goes—but where anything goes, nothing counts. No natural standard gives discipline. Mephisto's strategy with Faust: to make absence of restraint matter more than presence of purpose; to make liberation nihilism's bait. Until at last, even the man in the street takes the unthinkable in stride, perhaps tries his own hand at a Faustian turn or two. Was not Buchenwald administered by bank clerks—by *good* bank clerks, responsible employees with clean fingernails? And My Lai massacred by last year's high school basketball stars: nice boys, "not at all like that . . . really?"[76]

This is the result of the desacralization of the universe via the European *utamawazo* and the arrogance that accompanies it.

Williams' characterization of this obsessiveness is noteworthy. He correctly relates it to European cosmological and ontological conceptions, but then disguises the whole mood or character of this essential trait by translating it into the positive euphemistic terms of European jargon. Fanaticism becomes "single-mindedness." His description has the earmarks of European chauvinistic expression. Williams says,

> In its most explicit and highly elaborated forms, this theme involves a sharp separation of man from nature on the one hand, and of the human from the divine on the other. In this view, however, man is the child of God, or carries a divine spark or divine mandate. Set over against the world, he is above all "lesser creatures." He has a special charter to occupy the earth and to "have dominion over" both inanimate nature and other living things. Cut off from the omnipotent and omniscience attributed to the active source of creation, he strives to attain infinite powers—immortality, perfect goodness, total control. Actual personal commitment to this Faustian or Promethean world view would define a *doing* orientation to life. And the tangible expression of such a will to *do* and to master must be concentratred purposiveness in task-like activity. Such activity necessarily would tend to have a highly selective "single-minded" quality.[77]

The ethnological significance of capitalism is, of course, that it is a system of ethics that regulates the behavior of individuals in definite directions and in accord with a consistent image of the human being and of his proper relation to others. It is the statement, and creation of specific values and ideals of behavior. Mumford gives his view of the "morality" of capitalism, and his discussion points to the way in which capitalism reinforces the inherent European tendency toward excess, toward extremity and fanaticism. It is a system of unlimited accumulation that gives the illusion and in many senses the reality of ever-increasing power. Mumford stresses the "newness" of the capitalistic ethic (as does Weber), but I would emphasize the sense in which it encouraged and provides another vehicle for the expression of the insatiable European "will-to-power" that was already recognizable, both as potential and actuality, in the early European *utamaroho*. In other words, the *asili* (cultural seed), once planted, demanded an *utamaroho* (energy-force) for its fulfillment, which came to be expressed in the ideology of capitalism.

Capitalism gave a new and intense form to the characteristics that already set European culture apart from other cultures of the world. Kovel outlines the ideological opposition between European capitalism and the traditional, non-European system of gift-giving. The ultimate achievement of the capitalist system was the completion of a process that began when the abstraction of money came into use to replace objects of value. Value itself in capitalism becomes defined in terms of the accumulation of money; i.e., the representation of power over one's fellows. In this system the "will-to-power" becomes institutionally sanctioned.

Majority cultures—that is First World or primary cultures—reflect an inherent concept of self in which the person identifies her well-being with that of others in her community. This is, of course, not to say that selfishness and conflicts of interest do not exist. It is to say, however, that the epistemological conceptions support identification rather than separation, and the *utamaroho* (life-force; collective personality) is much less aggressive and more dependent on caring communal relationships. Therefore the mechanisms that support communalism are well developed.

The success of capitalism required an ever greater separation of the self from the communal interest and from other individuals. Capitalism, then, is thoroughly and completely Western in that it is based on the European *utamawazo* and conception of self—which it generates. And it is only within the context of capitalism as an economic system that the peculiar European concept of "individual freedom" takes on meaning.[78]

One of the most valuable aspects of Kovel's work is the way in which he interrelates the character of European institutions with European forms of thought, a primary objective of our study. He says:

By abstracting and quantifying everything within reach, the ambit of the market could be widened to include the whole world. Things abstracted can be given a number, and numbers can be equated with each other; hence the magical value of material things could be widely spread to elements of the world that had never previously been held in much regard. The whole world became materialized in consequence of this abstraction. The basic mental process of the West had borne its strange fruit. And it was a potent operation, for now all the energy that had been directed toward the simple acquisition of wealth could be directed toward the *generation* of wealth. With this new mystique, the process of gaining could be continuous. Production entered the world through this reduction of everything to its abstract quality, and through the union of these abstractions into rationalized relationships. What was rationalized, however, was the pure desire to gain lifeless, pleasureless, and abstracted matter.[79]

Capitalism provided an ideological structure in which the European could give full vent to his desire for power. Its value was that it was limitless—offering goals that were infinite. It accelerated the despiritualization of the world of Europeans as it "materialized" it for them. The mode of abstraction on which the capitalist enterprise depends—itself the denial of the existential meaning of humanness—was already there, a theme that had appeared with the beginnings of Western development: the unfolding of its *asili*.

In concrete terms, the patterns characteristic of European intracultural behavior and sanctioned by the capitalist system were those dictated by a hostile relationship. In Western European society each individual considers his interest as defined distinctly from and in opposition to that of everyone else. Human associations are often only political and strategical compromises. They are transient in nature and serve some specific end. "Natural" and timeless human groupings (e.g., the family et al.) tend toward disintegration, while the political machine gets stronger. Success in capitalism is aided by mistrust of others; greater gain is made possible by hypocrisy and deceit, by emotional control and detachment. The successful businessman is competitive, aggressive, acquisitive, and exploitative. No single object symbolizes European value as powerfully as does the abstraction that is money; so the system that controls and generates it becomes the dominant aspect of the culture.

Materialism, the ideological denial of spirituality and its significance, is supported by capitalism but is rooted in the very beginnings of the European rationalistic drive towards technological development,which perhaps originates in the mutant beginnings of the caucasian, in the struggle for survival in the caves of Europe (Diop) and in the initial ontological conceptions of the European. The human being's purpose is to control nature. Nature is matter; the amount of matter (material objects) one controls (possesses) indicates the amount of power (value) one has. Again, Robin Williams' characterization of this theme in European life attempts to mitigate the extent and effect of this malaise on the culture.

> Of course, a kind of "materialism" may emerge in a society, even though it is not initially a primary criterion of desirability—in the sense that sheer availability of creature comforts and the incessant advertising used to sell them creates a social pressure to concentrate effort and attention upon them. It is in this derivative way that an economy of affluence may drain away energy and commitment from values that stand higher in the nominal hierarchy of preferences.[80]

Williams "explains away" the lack of spiritual values in American life as though it were not intimately tied up with the dominant tendencies of the European cultural tradition; as though materialism were not in fact a characteristic of European ideology. He does not use the concept of *asili* and therefore never reaches the ideological core.

Willie Abraham presents a very different view of the matter. His view comes closer to the ideological significance of "materialism" in the culture. Abraham says "that synthesis of man which makes him out to be an economic animal is accompanied by a culture which has marked tropisms towards consumption and materialism."[81] In his view, "materialism" even affects Western social theory: "Social research in European . . . has had an intransient materialist basis; this is because the European mind is materialist."[82] Perhaps this accounts for Williams' inability to recognize the true ideological significance of materialism in American life.

Abraham discusses culture in terms of what he calls its three "facets": the material, which includes property systems and technology; the institutional; and that concerned with value. Material culture, he says, tends to have a corrosive effect on the value aspect of culture. In Africa the value aspect is dominant and emphasizes what he calls the "integrative function of culture." He warns that Africans must avoid the "excesses which have been associated with a lopsided expansion of material culture in Europe."[83] It is this process of the culture to which the materialism in contemporary European American life is linked.

In concrete terms once again, European behavior is characterized by the overt striving for material possessions, which symbolize value. The desired possession of these objects acts to motivate the individual in the culture in a way that nonmaterial objectives do not. Material gain is a more powerful factor in determining behavior than achievements such as spiritual fulfillment and love. What is both ironic and tragic for Europeans is that their ultimate (nonrational) concern is indeed with spiritual fulfillment, but they have been deluded by the presuppositions of their cultural tradition into looking for it in the "wrong places." They have been taught to erroneously and superficially "resolve" the basic conflict between the will-to-power and the will-to-love into a fanatical and inordinately destructive will-to-power. In this warped vision to have power means that love is not necessary. And, of course, it is precisely love that they need and actually seek. The cycle is endless, and they are placed on a treadmill, striving for what they can never achieve – for completion of self: *Yurugu*. And the only thing that does "progress" in a lineal direction, and does not resolve, is the destruction of the human spirit caused by this ideology. As Kovel says,

> We see an ever-accelerating system of striving and craving, which fills itself up with material pleasures that evaporate inside the abstracted self . . . . Abstraction and splitting gain power without awareness, and so serve the needs of repression. But they also diminish the self, and progressively cut it off externally from what is done to the world.[84]

Williams talks about the value of "efficiency" and "practicality" in Western culture.[85] This theme, which is such a strong determinant of individual behavior and an important criterion by which value and appreciation are judged, is related to the ideology of evolutionism and to the idea of progress. This ideological commitment extends beyond intracultural behavior to affect attitudes of Europeans towards other cultures that do not share their emphasis on "material culture." "Efficiency" is a nonhuman value; it is a statement of the means-ends relationship characteristic of Weberian "rationality." This kind of "rationality" gives shape to every institution in European culture, as they are rationally organized towards technological and material ends; not human goals.

We are presented by Williams with a noncritical, nonsynthetical characterization of the place of science and rationalism in European American culture. His euphemistic comments are representative of the kinds of works that have helped to lock the European mind into the prison of "scientism."

> Very broadly, emphasis upon science in America has reflected the values of the rationalistic-individualistic tradition. Science is disciplined, rational, functional, active; it requires systematic diligence and honesty; it is congruent with the "means" emphasis of the culture—the focus of interest upon pragmatism and efficiency and the tendency to minimize absolutes and ultimates. The applications of science profusely regard the strivings for self-externalizing mastery of the environment. We think it fair to say that science is at root fully compatible with a culture orientation that attempts to deny frustration and refuses to accept the idea of a fundamentally unreasonable and capricious world.[86]

(Note: The reader should compare the comments above with those of Arthur O. Lovejoy and William James cited in Chapter 1, "Supremacy of the Absolute, the Abstract, and the Analytical")

Epistemology and Behavior

The European American's conception of self as separate from others, and therefore in opposition to others, is an extension of the European ontological conception of the human being as being against or in opposition to nature. In isolating himself from nature he succeeds in constructing the illusion of a despiritualized world of which he has complete control, because he can control and manipulate the material within it with his science and technology. In isolating himself from others he robs himself of a source of emotional definition and security that comes with communal identification. However, within himself he isolates that part of himself that he considers "proper" to him (because he associates it with control and power) from that which is "improper" (because it represents "passivity" and therefore weakness). He trains himself to eliminate emotion and to replace it with "reason," thereby achieving the illusion of superiority to those who are part of Nature and whose source of power is spirit. This consistent theme and process in the culture determines the possibilities of European behavior, both toward "non-Europeans" (others) and toward one another.

Beginning with the "Platonic abstraction," the abstract mode came ever more to dominate and shape the cognitive world of the European. Havelock lauds this "revolution"—after all, it enabled the European to perform great intellectual feats. But what is culturally significant are the far-reaching, negative effects of this mental habit on European behavior and the interrelation of this penchant for abstraction with the characteristics of the European cultural personality. Much of Kovel's psycho-cultural theory of the nature of European culture is concerned with the activity of "abstractification," and he links the European quest for the pure with the Western anal personality. European culture functions consistently to remove the concrete, the emotional, and the existential from the individual's consciousness and thereby from her experienced reality. An abstraction is devoid of all human and emotional possibility; it defies genuine emotional identification.[87]

"Abstractification," therefore, as Kovel points out, adds to the dehumanization and despiritualization of the culture. Individuals within it can avoid the concrete and existential implications of events through the various mechanisms of abstraction, and a by-product of this artificially created atmosphere is that it becomes more and more devoid of meaning. It is ironically and tragically the case that the "modern self," (not "modern" in African terms) that Kovel describes has its cultural origins in what Havelock calls the "Platonic mode" and an epistemology based on the mechanism of "objectification." "Moral autonomy" (a term used by Havelock) is a contradiction in terms outside of European discourse. It generates the communally destructive, competitive, and aggressive ethic of "morality" that reaches its height in the West. A rationalistic ethic, accompanied by an isolating concept of self, is, in the context of majority cultural philosophies, diametrically opposed to that which is moral, as "morality"—the proper attitude and behavior toward others—is based on love or identification, which necessitates a "joining with other." This "union" is a spiritual rather than a rationalistic phenomenon and cannot be achieved by an act of "reason" (conceived as abstracted from "emotion"). It is a repudiation of the idea of "objectification."

Kovel says that the result of the "abstracted self" is an "inner world, which is filled synthetically. . . ."[88] As one becomes more involved in the exploration of European forms, the "organicity" of the culture (as Kovel puts it) becomes more and more apparent. In our terms it is the unfolding of the *asili* that is revealed. The nature of the aesthetic is influenced by the European conception of the self and the materialist and rationalistic substratum of the culture. The behavior and responses that characterize the individual in European society are causally related to the epistemological conceptions and ideological choices on which her culture is based; just as is the case in any culture. The symptomatic and severe loneliness characteristic of Europeans is an effect of the lack of communal function of their culture. Europeans are bound to each other by virtue of a shared *utamaroho* of power, domination, world supremacy, and expansion. The inner cultural dynamics of aggressiveness, competition, and mutual distrust are all separating, not binding. The outer-directed drives bind them into a tremendously efficient machine of aggression. The culture is supremely successful in this regard. European culture is not based on a vision of the essentially human. It does not serve human needs because it is not "designed" to do so.

In Kovel's view of European thought, "If something in the world can be made clean and pure, and if it can be made cold and nonsensuous as well, then it will meet the criterion of goodness. What is good in the world is identified with what is good in the person—not his body, but his mind."[89] Abstractions are "clean and pure," and they are also "cold and non-sensuous"; and so is a rationally constructed society; it becomes more so the more rationally constructed it becomes. As Kovel continues with his characterization of Western life, the relationship between what we have described as the European *utamawazo* (Chap. 1) and European cultural behavior become more apparent.

> One overriding quality determines what is good and bad within the analyzed world: purity. And within the entire spectrum of reality, one aspect of knowledge fulfills this quality: *abstraction*. An abstract idea is a purified idea, freed from annoyingly concrete and sensuous particulars. Words themselves are abstractions. The non-sensuous senses, sight and hearing, are the mediators of abstract activity. Smell, taste and touch are concrete, syncretic, incapable of making the fine distinctions necessary to sort out what is abstract from what is sensuous. Abstraction means distance from immediate experience, the substitution of a relatively remote symbol for a given sensuous reality. Sight and hearing are thus those senses which best fulfill the possibility of a remote relationship to the world. Western civilization began its expansion with the discovery of perspective, and the perfection of remote, visually organized, abstracted activities—whether in navigation or in the development of firearms that could kill from a distance.[90]

European culture began its history as a uniquely definable entity not with the "discovery" of this kind of perspective, but when it became the dominant cognitive mechanism and began to invalidate other systems of cognition. Eventually it became, in fact, normative in function, determining value and significance. It was indeed "perspective" (or what the Dogon in Africa call "word from the side," *Benne so*) that was lost, as the European excluded the possibility of other epistemological methodologies, and therefore a wide variety of experiences. Objectification became an ideological formulation, one which (in combination with the "unbalanced" European *utamaroho*) had many unfortunate effects. Kovel is also limited in his understanding of the significance of "hearing"/"sound." He does not make the important distinction between the audio and the visual. European culture actually has a tendancy to reject the ear (receiving) in favor of the eye (controlling). That is why the written word is more highly valued than the spoken word.

A scientific ideology was unavoidably attractive to the European mind. What they called "scientific truth"—a truth stripped of its human implications—could be imparted and absorbed coldly and rationally ("scientifically"). The extension of the scientific method in every aspect of human contemplation and experience was dictated by the European fear of the spiritual-emotional, which does not lend itself readily to manipulation and control. Objectification and the scientific method give the illusion of the kind of control and power that the European *utamaroho* requires. In the circular relationship of cultural phenomena, scientific-rationalism comes to shape European behavior even as it is shaped by it. The success of the culture comes from the fact that power is the ability to shape reality (Amos Wilson). Therefore the illusion of control becomes a reality—where it appears to be most significant: politically and materially.

Kovel says that the "central activity" of Western culture is the "creation, production, abstractification and rational acquisition of property, and the joyless passion which seeks ever more avidly that which recedes into remoteness through the process of seeking."[91] Through the activity of "abstractification," Kovel links capitalism, scientism, rationalism, "white racism," and the European imperialistic drive. In his study, Kovel demonstrates via the terms of common everyday experience in contemporary American life how the method of "abstractification" affects the lives and perception of participants in American society.

It is the theorists who have moved beyond the impressiveness of the overwhelming material success of European rationalism, whose works are most helpful in sorting out the myriad implications and effects that such "rationalism" has had on the totality of the European experience. European rationalistic ideology has "created" a particular kind of person who can be expected to behave in certain characteristic ways. If the uniqueness to the culture is not understood, the positive possibilities of other cultures will get lost and, whether consciously or not, this is a thoroughly Eurocentric objective. For this reason, we assume the particularity of the European form and therefore the need to explain its development, not as the result of some "universal" process, but by understanding its *asili*—a unique combination of factors that in circular relationship generate the personalities and ideological commitments that form the influencing matrix.

This explanation is all the more compelling since Europeans represent an extreme minority culture. It is the realization that Europe is in fact a culture in which imperial domination of others does indeed become a "comprehensive world-view" that is important. This is unique in the world and the characteristics (themes) of European culture—its "rationalism," violence, and lack of spirituality—are not merely isolated pathologies; rather these characteristics are linked to each other in a developmental matrix (*asili*) that is itself "pathological" in the context of human societies. It is this recognition that is to Kovel's credit. He uses a Freudian model:

> We have noted that power has accrued to the West through the yoking of energy and reason within one cultural ego. Other cultures had the energy, still others had the control, and some even combined

the two; but no culture carried the combination to such extremes. The very passion expressed by the western drive to power is representative, on a cultural level, of the tapping of deep infantile desires. This culture, at once the most advanced, is also the most infantile . . . . The deeper one returns into infancy, the more profound and limitless becomes desire.[91]

In the descriptions of Robin Williams, it is impossible to recognize the pathology of European culture, so that Eurocentric works such as his perpetuate this pathology and contribute to its global expansion. He helps to erect a battery of seemingly "morally neutral" statements that inhibit the understanding of the culture ideologically. But his work *American Society*, is not an anomaly. I have used it as cultural data because it is characteristic of the portrait of the West that has been collectively painted by the more respected Western social theorists—who write from a Eurocentric perspective.

European "Self" and the Problem of Love

There are several cultural factors that combine and complement each other in such a way as to successfully reinforce and direct a particular style of behavior in the participants of European culture. It is inaccurate to say that one of these is "primary" or generative in the chain that eventually makes up the European configuration of cultural traits. What is generative is the *asili* itself, the germ/logos of the culture. Joel Kovel, whose commitments are to psychoanalytic explanation, appears to lodge the etiology of European behavior in an inordinate elaboration of the "anal fantasy." (See Chap. 8 for a more thorough discussion.) However, it is not so important whether or not one can rigorously "prove" that a particular theory of behavioral causality is accurate, but rather that the approach used allows one to isolate and to link the characteristic features of European behavior to the matrix of European culture. We have attempted an explanation of European behavioral characteristics that lays them before us in such a way that their interconnectedness is felt and the ethnological inevitability of the European style of behavior is demonstrated.

In this discussion we have focused on the European conception of self. Of the importance of the "conception of self" generated by a culture in determining or influencing the behavior of its members. A. Irving Hallowell has said,

. . . self-identification and culturally constituted notions of the nature of the self are essential to the operation of all human societies and . . . a functional corollary is the cognitive orientation of the self to a world of objects other than self. Since the nature of these objects is likewise culturally constituted, a unified phenomenal field of thought, values, and action which is integral with the kind of world view that characterizes a society is provided for its members. The behavioral environment of the self thus becomes structured in terms of a diversified world of objects other than the self.[92]

Therefore our discussion of European behavior is grounded in the earlier discussion of the European *utamawazo* (Chap. 1).

The following comments by Norman O. Brown on "the self and other," further illustrate the way in which the European conception of self influences European cultural behavior. In discussing Freud's views Brown says,

Close examination of Freud's own premises and arguments suggests that there is only one loving relationship to objects in the world, a relation of being-one-with-the-world which, though closer to Freud's narcissistic relation (identification), is also at the root of his other category of possessive love (object-choice).[93]

Of the human experience of "love," he says: "If love seeks only identification with objects in the world, then possessiveness is not an essential feature of love."[93] He continues: "The aim of Eros is union with objects outside the self; and at the same time Eros is fundamentally narcissistic, self-loving." He speaks of "the expansion of the self," and of "unifying our body with other bodies in the world." Brown, then, as European theorists invariably do, proceeds to "universalize" what is essentially European psychology.[94]

While the conception of love as the desire and ability to merge or unite with "other" may be accurate, "expansion" of the self is not the same as unification of self and other. And this is crucial to understanding the problems that beset, not "humankind," but the European specifically. If the ability to love is predicated on the capacity of identifying "self" with "other," then it is clear from this discussion that European culture does not provide a basis for the love-experience; instead it imposes an *utamawazo* that inhibits (devalues) identification and emotional participation and an ethic that complements and is consistent with this cognitive structure. We have come full circle to Plato. For him "knowing" was more important than "loving," and "to know" meant knowing as "object," something separate and distinct from self. Europeans, perhaps, do not love themselves and have no basis from which to love "others." Norman Brown says,

Freud's later writings attribute to the human ego a basic tendency to "reconcile," 'synthesize," "unify," the dualisms and conflicts with which the human being is beset; Abraham sets the goal of achieving a "post-ambivalent" stage: Ferenczi calls for a "fresh instinctual fusion." But the possibility of post-ambivalent instinctual refusion must remain hypothetical until we have examined the cause of the ambivalence and the nature of Eros' antagonist.[95]

The European mind struggles to find rational means to synthesis, but it is the genius of African and majority cultures that their *utamawazo*(s) implicitly "reconcile" dichotomies that for the European are inevitably irreconcilable. Through the spiritualistic modalities of ritual and ancestor communion, through the sacralization of life, they achieve what rationalistic theories cannot offer. It is by employing the modes of participation and identification, by conceiving of the self as properly joined with other, indeed as defined in terms of other, and by valuing emotional response that unity and harmony are achieved. Ambivalence and ambiguity only become frightening and culturally destructive in the European context, which cannot deal with paradox. Majority cultures contain sophisticated mechanisms that turn these dimensions of human experience into yet another means of uniting people spiritually.

I have said that the underlying principle that explains and unites the various aspects of European life and behavior is the need to control; this is directly related to and easily explains the European problem with loving. While "control" represents value, "love" does not. In terms of the European conception of human emotion they are opposites. In this view one loves to the extent that one gives up control of one's emotions; one controls oneself by not allowing oneself to love. The experience of control is predicated on the rigid separation and distinction between self and other; love is the experiencing of self as being merged with other. A lack of control is repugnant to the European sense of self; conceived only as properly distinct from other.

But this is not a universal conception of love. It is romanticized (unrealistic), and it issues out of the inadequacy of the European self. The African concept of love, while more pervasive (that is, it includes mutually respectful and reciprocal relationships of many kinds), is supported by the structures within the culture and is at the same time not obsessive. We do not risk the loss of self in love relationships because love is the natural state of being: offered before birth, guaranteed by the kin-base natures of the culture, and therefore taken for granted. It is not anxiety-producing. It is natural. Michael Bradley says that the European conception of romantic love is necessary to overcome the intense hostility between genders among the Caucasians. He refers to this as the "truce of love."[96]

Ironically, obsession with ego results in the loss of self through a loss of meaningful contact with others. Fanatical self-autonomy becomes painful alienation. In 1988 the chronic loneliness and alienation reached new heights as people in America began to spend money to talk to strangers on the telephone. Forced into the isolation of their homes they "communicate" with others who, from their own cells of self-imposed "privacy" cry out for human contact. Phone numbers are now advertised on television that intensely isolated individuals can call in order to "meet" people, hear other human voices (in an effort to affirm their own human existence), make "confessions," attempt to communicate in a world that has obviously robbed them of the natural sources of human interaction and warmth that we of majority cultures take for granted. (In this view anonymous sexual encounters in the parks of America's cities, become cultural—not individual—pathology.) Somehow the symbolism of these machines (television and telephone) which mechanize communication as substitutes for organic human interpersonal interrelationship, is the penultimate statement of the failure (and "success") of Europe.

This alienating condition is not universal. "Objectification," the determinant of the isolating European conception of self, is dominant only within the European *utamawazo* and in European ideology. It does not have the same influence on other cultural ideologies. And the quest for a truly revolutionary society must be to assign and limit the epistemological method of objectification to its proper place on the list of cultural priorities. While the conceptual modes of other cultures may encourage "identification with other," those of European culture are based on the separation of the self.

The Western European (Euro-American) State is Plato's Republic. It depends on "objectification" and abstraction. It is an ongoing attempt to create the perfectly rational; it is both theory and method. It is an ideal based on mistaken conceptions of the "rationalized human" and of "moral autonomy," and on the costly error of identification of the good with the scientifically provable. All moral (human) problems are considered to be solved (inherently) in the structure of the State, so there is no basis for a system of morality in the Republic. Morality presupposes human interaction. It also presupposes ambiguity and fallibility. The issue of morality arises from the need for meaning, from emotional response to other human beings, and from regard for them in relation to self. One continually seeks to answer the ethical questions of "acting" in the correct manner. To be immoral is not to be concerned with this question. The question of human morality requires a spiritual base. The Republic eliminates spirit, emotion and identification with other, and, therefore, it eliminates human meaning. European (Euro-American) culture, at the other end of the chronological spectrum, ends up deficient in moral sensibility; i.e., without a guide for human conduct.

The "love" that Plato talks about is without human meaning. It is an abstract, philosophical, "ideal." In the *Symposium*, male homosexual love between a philosopher (mentor) and a "youth" (student) is the closest human relationship to ideal "love," since it most approximates the love of "truth" (*Symposium*: 184). Love is of the "beautiful" and the "good." (*Symposium*:206). And Diotima tells Socrates that the mysteries of love involve moving from the concrete to the abstract, from the particular to the universal and finally to the realm of "Forms":

> being not like a servant in love with beauty of one youth or man or institution, himself a slave mean and narrow-minded, but drawing towards and contemplating the vast sea of beauty, he will create many fair and noble thoughts and notions in boundless love of wisdom; until on that shore he grows and waxes strong, and at last the vision is revealed to him of a single science, which is science of beauty everywhere."[97]

Ordinary love is problematical in European culture. What this means is that in order for an individual who has been socialized in the European tradition to act with love, she must overcome her traditions (which are powerful). She must overcome the ontological-epistemological presuppositions with which she has been inculcated and the constraints of social institutions that surround her. She will then risk being "unsuccessful" (as success in European culture depends on competitiveness and aggression, not love) and she will find herself surrounded by individuals who cannot (dare not) return her love.

When love *is* translated into the terms of human phenomenal reality for the European, its interpretation issues from a bedrock of chronic illness, fear, and aggression. These inherited ancestral emotions (experiences) generate an obsessive-possessiveness; a clinging smothering, narcissistic, and compulsively unrealistic "romantic" conception of what love should be.

Edward T. Hall, a psychologist and anthropologist, talks about the "identification-syndrome" in relationship to loving. He uses the term "identification" not in the positive sense of joining with other, but in the sense of the "projection" of the self that one does not like onto another human "object." This syndrome comes about as a result of an earlier process of "dissociation" in which the person has unconsciously dissociated (but not changed/resolved) behavior from herself that her parents or other significant adults find to be objectionable. Hall outlines Sullivan's psychological conceptualization. The "bad" behavior continues but is dissociated from the self so that the self can be respected.[98] What happens subsequently is that the person will "identify" with someone (often her daughter) who has the traits with which she does not want to identify herself. She then has negative and problematic feelings about the person, as she does about the aspects of her own personality that she does not like and has repressed.[98] Hall takes this concept beyond personal identification and says that it operates on a cultural level as well. Suppose Europeans are carrying around the baggage of centuries of antihuman behavior, of a pathological *utamaroho*. For Hall this syndrome has a direct bearing on the ability to love,

> The paradoxical part of the identification syndrome is that until it has been resolved there can be no friendship and no love—only hate. Until we can allow others to be themselves, and ourselves to be free, it is impossible to truly love another human being; neurotic and dependent love is perhaps possible, but not genuine love, which can be generated only in the self.[100]

Again what is evident is a description of European pathology, originating from a deep sense of inadequacy; an unhappiness with self, therefore the inability to give love as a healthy, energizing force.

European behavior, then, is not even "ideally" characterized by the love relationship, but by separateness, alienation, hostility, competitiveness and aggression. The culture is an overwhelmingly efficient machine, designed to consume the universe. The behavioral pattern that this "machine" has generated has, as its primary concern, the continued efficiency of the machine. If the "human" were coterminus with the "material," then European culture would, indeed, be the most successful of human constructs. But human beings are not machines, and the culture is, instead, rapidly losing its efficiency (rationality), even in terms of its own rational ends. Watergate and the "Iranian Contra Deal" are evidence of its "mechanical" breakdown and of the inability of the machine to regenerate itself. Purely and simply, a thoroughly materialist culture must eventually fail in its ability to motivate an operable ethic. It runs out of steam. In European culture there is no residual spiritual base that survives to give inspiration when the human spirit has become bored with the possibilities of materialism. Material values can only be temporary; they can never be "ultimate." Love, spirit, empathy have all but escaped Europeans, and their behavior is ethnologically explainable in the context of this cultural "deficiency."

Intracultural vs. Intercultural

It is important to recognize the difference between the "other" within European culture and the "cultural other" in terms of the behavior of European: The discussion of European religion (Chap. 2) demonstrates the important function of the "we/they" dichotomy for European ideology. The cultural other is the "nonhuman" or the "not properly human." European anthropologists have all too often described majority cultural conceptions of people outside of their culture in these terms, but it is the behavior of Europeans that is most characterized by the dehumanization of those outside their culture. It is the ideological conceptual basis of European imperialistic behavior that the "cultural-other" be conceived of as "nonhuman." This conception is mandated by the *asili*, which seeks power.

On the other hand, however negatively and aggressively Europeans may behave toward those within their culture, they are considered to be "cultural brothers," and this has very significant consequences for behavior towards them. Each person within the culture is given space to do what she can to protect herself and to stay out of the way of the other. That is really what "individual freedom" means in the European context. Other Europeans are not "fodder" to be used, their land cannot be stolen, they cannot be enslaved, they need not be missionized. If you are a participant in a European culture, they have the same rights that you have. They have the right to be your "enemy," that is, to treat you with suspicion and aggression; they have "selves." Those outside of the culture do not have that right: they are not "selves" in the European sense. The Protestant ethic and the Capitalistic ethic are meant to encompass European behavior toward European individuals. Quite clearly, non-Europeans who live in European societies are treated as "cultural others." (For example, the entire community of Africans in America: the Scottsboro boys (1931); the victims of the Tuskegee Syphillis Experiment (1932–1972); Michael Stewart (1983); Eleanor Bumpers (1984); Michael Griffith (1986); Edmond Perry (1986); Ashanti Bartlett (1987). We know the list of atrocities is far greater than this.)

Ideally and historically, the existence of the European imperialistic endeavor allows limits to be placed on the aggression of intracultural European behavior. European culture is an arena in which separate selves agree to compete without destroying the system and agree to cooperate in the destruction and consumption of other systems (e.g. cultures). One of the signs of the breakdown of the European system is that more and more Europeans begin to treat each other as they have heretofore only "ethically" treated the "cultural other." That is what alarmed the American public as they watched the Watergate hearings. As William Strickland says,

> The administration simply began employing at home the politics of immorality used to build the American Empire abroad. Certainly it was no big step from subverting elections in Vietnam to subverting them in New Hampshire, Florida and Wisconsin. In the end, then, Black and Third World exploitation, inside and outside America, provided the essential experience out of which the White House, covertly but systematically, scuttled the last vestige of American democracy (even in its whites-only manifestations).[101]

Majority peoples, who are also African/black and colored peoples, are considered to be qualitatively different from Europeans and are, therefore, treated differently. It is the "cultural other" or outsider who becomes the complete or total object. Other Europeans are not totally objectified if only because of the limits placed on their destruction. It is European cultural nationalism that provides the distinction between the European's behavior toward "others" and his behavior toward other Europeans. In order for the *asili* to remain in tact this distinction is of primary importance. The *asili* is complemented by an *utamaroho* (energy source) that is by nature aggressive: The endless quest for power over other. There must be an "other" to subdue; at the same time, there must be an "other" on which to displace the inherent aggression of the *utamaroho*, if there is to be a successful cultural self. The distinction between self and other is the fundamental distinction of the European *asili*, and it generates two distinctly different, while related, "ethics" and behavior patterns.

Whereever there is life, even if it be only a possibil-
ity, the harbingers of death must go to destroy it.
See the footsteps they have left over all the world.
Wherever they have been they have destroyed
along their road, taking, taking, taking.
                                              — Ayi Kwei Armah

Chapter 8

Behavior Toward Others

Asili as Matrix

The European conception of and attitude toward those outside of the culture together comprise one of the most significant and definitive characteristics of European culture. It is the way in which the European treats those outside of his culture, which is most indicative of the nature of the culture itself. And to understand the nature of European imperialism we must understand the cultural conceptions that provide the ideological support for this kind of behavior; the belief-system that makes it possible and that reinforces it.

We will not document the horrors that have amassed over approximately twenty centuries of European imperialism. There are such works to which the reader will be referred (e.g., the U.S. Congressional Record contains an impressive listing of acts of "intervention" by the United States from only 1798 to1845, which alone are enough to stagger the imagination; imagine what could be compiled since the start of the Roman Empire!), and while there is a need for many more works of this nature, the number of additional ones appears to grow steadily. For an excellent historical record of European aggression, written from the vantage of an African-centered perspective, see Chinweizu's *The West and the Rest of Us*. Chinweizu's work can stand alone as a most damaging indictment of European behavior towards others.

It is not enough, however, to document the phenomenon of

European imperialism. What is imperative is the attempt to offer an explanation that ethnologically relates it to the culture that has produced it: To explain it in terms of the ideological core of the culture, the *asili*. Eurocentric theorists and historians list the atrocity stories as though they were merely pathological acts of an otherwise healthy culture. And too often, the fact of European imperialism is presented in the liberal tradition, as a destructive tendency in European culture, that can be effectively counterbalanced by the "humanitarian" aspects of its ideology. ("All we have to do is get rid of the bad guys.")[1]

The interpretation offered here leads to quite different conclusions. The concept of *asili* helps us to demonstrate the way in which the imperialistic-expansionist and exploitative drive is inherent and, therefore, "natural" in the context of European culture: It is logically generated by the *asili* of the culture. This activity and endeavor is not in any way peripheral to the main thrust of the culture; it is not merely an aspect among many, unrelated characteristics. It is, instead, a central theme in European behavior with origins in the core of European ideology. White nationalism and aggression, both cultural and economic, are endemic to European culture: embedded in its ideological matrix. To reverse the tendency of which European imperialism is a manifestation would be to radically change the basis, the essential nature of the culture itself. In other words, we would be dealing with a different *asili*, which in turn would generate a different *utamawazo* and *utamaroho*.

Kovel raises these questions concerning the pattern of European behavior:

> What kinds of conceptions of the world are needed for this, and what styles of actions must be engendered in the inhabitants of the West to make them so driven and so controlled?
>
> . . . Let us look at the crucial aspects of our culture for an answer.[2]

It is the answer to these questions with which we are concerned in this chapter.

The Concept of the "Cultural Other"

A crucial aspect of European culture for the understanding of its imperialistic posture is what I term the European conception of the "cultural other." This conception helps to make European behavior towards others possible. It is closely related to the European image of others, but is not quite the same. I mean to imply that it is more a conceptual construct—a mental category—that becomes the "proper" receptacle for what would otherwise be considered unsupportable, unsanctioned behavior. The European image of others, of course, reinforces this concept and ensures its continuance as a part of the European world-view. The concept of the cultural other further enables the continued existence of the extremely negative image of others that is a dialectically *necessary* part of the European self-image. Let us look, therefore, at this conception and the style of behavior that it implies.

The cultural other is a creation of European culture, constructed, in part, to answer the needs of the European *utamaroho*. The *utamaroho* is expansionistic. This, as a cultural characteristic, is itself very important to understand. The ego seeks to infinitely expand itself. This kind of self expansion should not be confused with the desire to "give of oneself"—to "merge self with other" or to "become one with the world." All of these are identified with the spiritual experience of love. Expansionism is the psychological, emotional and ideological opposite of these. Expansionism is the projection and imposition of the cultural ego onto the world. (It is possible to interpret all manifestations of "universalism" in this way.) It is the expression of arrogance, greed, and an obsession to consume all that is distinguished from self. In this setting, "discovered" phenomena automatically become areas *to conquer*—to be made *ours*. European expansionism is the delimitation and redefinition of the world in terms of the European self; as opposed to the "losing of self" in the world or in the "other," which is the obliteration of the isolating boundaries of self.

In European ideology the cultural other is like the land—territory or space into which Europeans expand themselves. The cultural other is there for Europeans to define, to "make over." That is why they can describe their new awareness of objects, peoples, and territories as *their* "discovery." This idea is coherent for them because according to their world-view it is their role to impart definition to the world. People of other cultural traditions and "persuasions" are part of the world to be defined; it is a European world. And in this sense, the conception of the cultural other is that of the nonhuman. It is Europeans who define "humanness" in terms of their own self-image and with such intensity that the ethic and rules of behavior that apply to those who are like them do not apply to those who are not. The cultural other is, therefore, the person (object) who can be treated in any manner—with an unlimited degree of hostility and brutality, as is evident when one reviews the history of the European's relations to peoples of other cultures. It is only nonaggressive and nonexploitative behavior towards the cultural other that is negatively sanctioned in European culture.

The thrust of my argument is that (1) the ethic that guides the behavior of Europeans *within* their culture is quantitatively and qualitatively different from that which is acceptable and sanctioned behavior toward those outside of the culture; and that (2) the characteristic behavior of Europeans toward those outside their culture is made culturally possible (i.e., the culture can support and sustain it) by the existence within European ideology of the conception of the cultural other. This conception, along with the *utamaroho* that supports it, makes possible a degree of aggression and successful imperialistic behavior unique in human history.

European Versus "Non-European"

When I refer to the "intracultural" behavior of Europeans, I do not mean to indicate merely their behavior within the geographical or territorial confines of nations considered to be European. I refer rather to the way in which one European is expected to behave towards another. This excludes many people who are colonized within European nations (such as the United States, part of the European diaspora) and includes Europeans living within the territorial boundaries of non-European nations. Though the European's behavior is characteristically aggressive and competitive, there are limitations placed on the "acting out" of that aggression within his culture, as there are acts that the culture does not sanction intraculturally. Europeans are not supported culturally in the murder of other Europeans. It is not allowed; it is difficult to get away with. War among Western European nations is regretted and avoided in a way that war between a European nation and a non-European nation could never be. European intracultural behavior is characterized by a lack of trust as a basis for love, as discussed in the previous chapter. Aggressiveness and hostility on the part of the individual makes emotional life precarious within the culture. It is obvious that the culture could not survive as a viable entity if there were not some "safety-valve" for this aggression. This cultural need creates the cultural other, whose existence makes possible, on a cultural level, the absorption of dysfunctional internal aggression. Put simply: If the cultural other did not exist, Europeans would destroy each other.

One of the dynamics in the historical development of the West is that as the culture matured—as it developed—its ideology "progressively" adjusted itself so that the limitations on treatment of

Europeans became more circumscribed with respect to certain extreme forms of political relationships. More precisely, the tendency that can be recognized is that first slavery, then serfdom of Europeans by Europeans became negatively sanctioned within the culture, and in general it became increasingly less acceptable to hold extreme overt political power over other European nations. This, of course, was Hitler's greatest crime in terms of the European ethic; the methods by which he sought to control the Western world were obsolete—were no longer sanctioned. The European reaction to first British and then United States world ascendency is very different. It is within this cultural-ideological process of the redefinition and maturation of Western European political nationalism that the call for European unity became audible and the negative image of others and the concept of the cultural other became intensified. In 1814 Saint-Simon called for a "European Confederation."

> All undertakings of common advantage to the European community will be directed by the great parliament; thus, for instance, it will link the Danube to the Rhine by canals, the Rhine to the Baltic, etc. Without external activity, there is no internal tranquility. The surest means of maintaining peace in Confederation will be to keep it constantly occupied beyond its own borders, and engaged without pause in great internal enterprises. To colonize the world with the European race, superior to every other human race; to make the world accessible and habitable like Europe—such is the sort of enterprise by which the European parliament should continually keep Europe active and healthy.[3]

There is a subtle but important point to be made in this connection. While it has been pointed out that what Eurocentricists call the "civilization process" (we would call it "Europeanization") is actually one of ever increasingly repressive structures within European culture, at the same time the concept of *asili* points to the simultaneous tendency to obliterate the severely brutal and exploitative relationships that become reserved for intercultural behavior. It is for this reason that a description of the European's behavior towards the cultural other helps to explain his intracultural behavior. The nature of the culture is, indeed, intrinsically repressive, and yet its survival and successful functioning depend on contract agreement, cooperation, and the cultural identification among its members. European ideology cannot condone the destruction of its own members; that is, in terms of its own definition of destruction. The conception of the cultural other, therefore, becomes that which can be destroyed or, more practically speaking, that upon which culturally destructive behavior can be unleashed. The difference is that while the culture may be repressive for its participants, *they* do not think it repressive—it represents that which they value; while the cultural other is treated as they (Europeans) would not wish to be treated themselves and as they would not be comfortable in treating each other. This is why a class analysis is insufficient in the explanation of European socio-political behavior. As Saint-Simon indicates above, anything can be done to those outside the culture if it helps to keep the European community "healthy."

As the slogans of European "revolutions" became those of "the rights of man" and "liberte, egalite, fraternite," European behavior towards majority peoples became more and more extreme in its exploitativeness and its brutality. Africans and other majority peoples became more and more excluded from the category of "man." Here again it is possible to witness an "ingenious" creation of the *asili* of the culture. The "logic" of European (Euro-American) ideology leads to the continual intensification of the power drive, or acquisitiveness and greed, and of the need to consume and destroy, to oppress and exploit: the nature of the *utamaroho*. While the eighteenth-century "humanists" were ensuring that these behavioral characteristics would not be used to disrupt the coherence of European culture, they accepted an image of those outside the culture that made such peoples the logical, justifiable, and ethically acceptable objects of that behavior. In Kovel's view, this definitional and behavioral process continued and intensified until its more recent form, "the deinstitutionalization of Africa allowed the West to discharge upon it whatever was forbidden and dark, while that of America led to the creation of a new, white, institutional order."[4]

The ravages of European imperialism must not be viewed merely as evidence of the indiscriminately applied abuses of European behavior but of the patterned character of that behavior towards people who are not European. What allows Europeans to act as they do is the nature of their world-view, a crucial aspect of which is a definition of other peoples as essentially nonhuman.

W. E. B. Dubois recognized the difference in behavior:

There was no Nazi atrocity—concentration camps, wholesale maiming and murder, defilement of women or ghastly blasphemy of childhood—which the Christian civilization of Europe had not long been practicing against colored folk in all parts of the world in the name of and for the defense of a Superior Race born to rule the world.[5]

Alphonso Pinckney makes the connection between the conception of the cultural other and European behavior towards others:

> The American soldiers involved in the Mylai massacre were motivated to commit such acts, at least in part, by deeply rooted prejudices against the Vietnamese people. Had they seen these people as human beings it is doubtful that they could simply have annihilated them. They were "dirty gooks," and some of them were suspected of being "commie"; the combination reduced them to a status less than that of human beings.[6]

How do Europeans decide who, in fact, is the cultural other? This, of course, has been "decided" for them. The tradition they inherit is partially an historical process in which this definition has taken place—hardened and matured. Then, as Johari Amini says, "Interpretation and perception usually take place unconsciously, as products of socialization."[7] And since in cultural settings the "dialectic of definition" takes place whereby in defining "good" we hereby define "bad," the cultural other (negative) is the dialectical opposite of those with whom the European identifies (positive). This should not be confused with emotional identification; there are certainly precious few individuals, even within their own culture, with whom the Europeans "identify." Here we are discussing cultural identification as it relates to value-definition and behavior. In this sense, Europeans "identify with" those with whom they share a common "self-image." The issue here is one of a cultural-political phenomenon. In the view of the Europeans, other Europeans share with them those characteristics and roles that we have isolated in the discussion of their collective self-image. (See Chap. 4). They share the position of being among the "superiors" of the world. In fact, they share the world with each other in a way that is restricted to others (all the more peculiar since they represent such a small minority of the world). The price they pay for this cultural identification is that they must treat each other in a "special" way.

They know that other Europeans are committed to the same ideology to which they are committed. This ideology is ontologically and epistemologically delineated and expressed through the *utamawazo* in the ways that have been discussed. But it also includes the commitment to the supremacy of the European cultural group, as well as to the continual development of a rationalized technology. The ideological description of those with whom Europeans identify culturally involves the commitment to the values we have been describing and the cultural description involves the related styles of behavior. If "racial" terms are used, they identify with those who are "white" (Caucasian). Together, these characteristics form a national and cultural ethnicity—a concept that combines the cultural-ideological and physical groupings of people. In the dialectical process of the European definition of value of individuals, "whiteness" has been central, overriding even the measure of successful performance within the Western European value-system. A "white" individual can be a failure and still be a part of the cultural group—that is, still "European" and, therefore, treated specially. While a black person or an individual of color, no matter how successfully acculturated, is still an outsider. This is the way of the European tribe.

Even so, it is a mistake to focus on the issue of skin-color when examining European behavior toward others; that is, it is a mistake to isolate this aspect of European ideology as somehow logically prior to its other aspects. It should be viewed as one related theme, among many expressions of the European *utamawazo*. Isolation of and undo emphasis on "color" as an ideological theme in European ideology has in the past and still continues to invariably lead "liberal" theorists into the trap of attempting to argue that physical traits are not related to cultural-ideological ones and are, therefore, irrelevant. Franz Boas argued that neither race nor genetics cause cultural "inferiority" (Eurocentrically defined). Acceptance of this position encouraged self-hatred and self-denial among Africans. ("I really am the same as they are.") That position is politically inept and itself concerned with the irrelevant. What is pathological, and historically and politically significant, is the European's *treatment of* and *behavior towards* African/black and other colored peoples, not the fact that they have linked color with culture. Their very existence argues for this link. What should be of concern politically to Africans and people of color is the recognition of European systematic behavior towards them. The rhetoric or "logic" with which they support this behavior is, in terms of political strategy, beside the point. We cannot allow their arguments to distract us from our mission.

It is another testament to the political genius of Europeans (who lack color) that they have been able for centuries to engage the energies of First world peoples in polemics that focus on the rhetoric of their scientism and "logic." The issue is not whether or not majority peoples are different. We most certainly are! And there are many other kinds of differences among the world's peoples as well. The crucial issue is what the difference implies for behavior within a particular ideological system. In European ideology, Africans and other more melanated people automatically become cultural others. The way that Kovel poses the question points to a different emphasis from that of Boas and his followers—the "liberals."

> How have the meaningful presentation of the world and the meaningful styles of historical action become harmonized with the themes of white and black in the culture of the West, so as to permit the generation of power by the nations of the West, most particularly the United States.[8]

Our concerns in this chapter are with the character of European behavior and the conceptions that determine that behavior. As such, what has been called "race" is an important ingredient in the conception of the cultural other and is undeniably a cultural reality—made so by twenty centuries of European concepts in action if nothing else. It helps to avoid the term "racism" by talking instead about the character of European white nationalism, if only because in the contemporary Eurocentric discourse there is a tendency to lump together all forms of cultural nationalism under "racism." It is an ethnological error to equate European nationalism with other nationalisms and to ignore the qualitative differences in their character. And racism is not attitude alone, but the power to control the lives of those who are despised. If we are politically astute, we are not concerned with European feelings about us (we do not need them to like us); we are only concerned with their power to oppress us. But this confusion is presently in vogue because it furthers the objectives of the more sophisticated European cultural imperialists who wish to thwart ideological independence and self-definition among majority peoples.

Let us return in the dialectic of definition to the "bad" or negative side of the coin. The cultural other for the European belongs to a different ethnic persuasion, has a different racial origin. She is not "white"; she is committed to goals different from those of the West; she is unsuccessful in terms of European values (her style of behavior is different); and she was born into a different cultural tradition. She, therefore, shares a different cultural heritage. The significant fact in terms of understanding European culture is what all of these perceived factors imply behaviorally.

The "Cultural Other" and European "Law"

The authors of *To Serve the Devil* offer a statement published in the *San Francisco Argonaut* in 1902 defending U.S. Army action in the Philippine Islands. It is a response to criticism of American soldiers in their treatment of the Filipino insurgents, and as such it is a good

ethnographic example of the way in which the European definition of
the cultural other determines the European's behavior towards others. Its additional value lies in the character of its frankness in departure from the European tradition of rhetorical hypocrisy. After stating
the American objective and presenting the American image of the
Filipinos, the statement continues,

> Doubtless, many of the excellent gentlemen in Congress would
> repudiate these sentiments as brutal. But we are only saying what
> they are doing. We believe in stripping all hypocritical verbiage
> from national declarations, and telling the truth simply and boldly.
> We repeat—the American people, after thought and deliberation,
> have shown their wishes. THEY DO NOT WANT THE FILIPINOS.
> THEY WANT THE PHILIPPINES. [Their capitalization][9]

The authors are speaking for all wars waged by the European
minority against all majority peoples throughout the history of the
European diaspora.

The statement touches on a recurrent theme in the patterned
behavior of the Europeans toward the cultural other; the usurping of
our land and resources. Among Europeans governed by the capitalistic ethic, there is nothing that approaches the sacred more than the
rights of property and contract. The successful capitalist can do anything to rob the poor of whatever meagre resources they have, but
as long as what he does is "legal"—as long as he fulfills his contract
with the wage-earner or consumer—his actions are considered ethical. Similarly, European social institutions may take from Europeans
their initiative and creativity, their energy and spirit, but the system
will protect their right to their material possessions; for this is their
"property." Whatever they have, in this sense, is theirs to do with as
they please. That is the meaning of the right to ownership in the West;
indeed, in capitalist countries that is the meaning of "freedom."

An "ethical" implication of the European concept of the cultural
other is that there are those who have no right to such property;
they especially have no right to own land. A correlative of this is that
these cultural others are not truly human—not really people; therefore, they can no more "own" land than the wild animals that inhabit
it, and, therefore, cannot be "stolen" from. To take land from the cultural other is not to steal. As the authors of the statement quoted
above indicate, another by-product of this concept is the idea that
Europeans (European-Americans) "know how" to use land and
resources. The cultural other is not capable of doing so and has no
idea of their proper uses; Europeans, therefore, have the right and the

duty to expropriate the land and resources and to make use of them. This is, then, the ideological source of the contemporary typology of nations as either "developed" or "underdeveloped." The natural environment is there for "something to be done with it." Europeans know what to do with it and, therefore, have rights to everything occupied by people who are not of European descent—for that is the same as being "unoccupied," and anything "unoccupied" belongs to the European.

Kenyatta's discussion of land tenure in *Facing Mt. Kenya* offers a good comparison of Gikuyu and European attitudes and values. In their colonial penetration of Kenya, Europeans conveniently misconceived the "big tracts of lands used for other purposes than cultivation and which were equally important to the community"[10] as being "underdeveloped"—a term that means "that which can and should be taken over by Europeans" in the language of European ideology. At the same time, the Gikuyu have a category of relationship to the land termed *Mohoi,* meaning "one who acquires cultivation rights on the *ng'ondo* or lands of another man or family unit, on a friendly basis without any payment for the use of the land."[11] This idea would be a violation of the European concept of self, of individual freedom; and a person who allowed her land to be used in this way would be considered a fool. Yet the Gikuyu had a concept of themselves and of those outside their culture that allowed them to treat Europeans as *Mohoi;* "this generosity of giving temporary cultivation or building rights to strangers was extended to the Europeans when they arrived in the Gikuyu land."[12] Needless to say, such behavior is considered evidence of weakness and stupidity by the Europeans who use it to further their own objectives.

The colonial pattern was repeated again and again wherever Europeans "discovered" the cultural other. The land was taken, the people were encarcerated, a colonial "government" was established to import the morality and institutions of the Western Europeans and to regulate their behavior among themselves. The government would make available to Europeans those lands that could best be cultivated; each "settler" receiving a large track of land, the idea being that he deserved to be "rewarded" for his pioneering spirit and his willingness to "settle" "untamed" lands (e.g., lands previously inhabited by the cultural other). His "European presence" gave colonial governments the excuse to "protect" him.

This behavioral pattern is consistent with the European's image of himself as the world "organizer"; i.e., the initiator of "order." The cultural other, however, would be placed in reserved areas or reservations that were invariably overcrowded and that represented the poorest agricultural possibilities. Land ownership and property rights are jealously protected among Europeans, but there is no comparison with the spiritual and ideological violation that is committed against majority peoples when they are forcibly removed from the land of their ancestors. But it is pointless to dwell on this fact in a discussion of European behavior towards others, because it in no way affects the behavior of Europeans; nor does it reach their "moral" consciousness. It is, therefore, irrelevant in the attempt to understand European behavior and ideology.

Another purpose of the establishment of the colonial government is to give the illusion of a kind of legality, propriety or ethical presence that does not exist. There is no European concept of "legality" that extends to non-European peoples. It is the traditional political strategy of the European to create the impression that such exists, thereby disarming the cultural other whom they exploit, as well as those within their culture who purport to be concerned with the wellbeing of the exploited peoples. If this aspect of European behavior could be understood by peoples of majority cultures, it would be to their distinct political advantage. It is perhaps more significant than any other single behavioral characteristic. There simply are no guiding rules of conduct, no limitations, no inhibitions in the European's relationship with the cultural other. Therefore, the first and most important political achievement for us is to recognize that we are ultimately and inevitably, in the European's world-view cultural others. Next, the implications of this concept for European behavior must be understood; it then becomes easy to anticipate their behavior in the intercultural arena. If those who have been objects of European aggression begin to understand the cultural context of that aggression—the *asili*, or germinating core of the culture that explains it— they will be much more successful in counteracting it.

In interviews with Japanese Americans who had experienced the second world war in the United States, statement after statement attested to the fact that "relocation" was passively accepted in many instances because not until they were actually in the camps did the Japanese believe that the American government would go through with what they had threatened. When asked why, the invariable reply was "because it was unconstitutional for them to treat Americans in this way." These Japanese victims of the European concept of the cultural other had failed to make the distinction that Europeans themselves make—the critical chauvinistic distinction between European and non-European, Western and non-Western, white and nonwhite.

The chimera of legality that inevitably accompanies the most brutal and immoral acts of European imperialistic expansion is difficult for those from different cultural traditions to understand. Again it can be understood only as it relates to the complex, atypical character of the European system of values. Dishonesty and hypocrisy in dealing with the cultural other is the norm for European behavior. This behavior is not negatively sanctioned within the culture. Indeed, it is expressly for such interactions that the rhetorical ethic exists. This style of behavior is so strange from the point of view of other cultures that their participants find it difficult to believe that deceit and fraud are to be expected—that it represents the rule and not the exception—in the European's behavior toward them.

As a prelude to his sadistically brutal behavior towards Africans in Central Africa, Leopold of Belgium formed the International African Association, avowedly to be concerned with the well-being of the indigenous African population. In a conference held in West Africa in 1884, the European powers "gave" to this organization lands in Central Africa. Chapman Cohen says,

> The Conference gave what didn't belong to it to an Association that had no claim to what it received. In August, 1885, Leopold notified the signatories that his Association would henceforth be known as the "Congo Free State," and that he himself was monarch of the domain.[13]

Having thus "legally" and in a "civilized" manner usurped land that did not belong to him, he then proceeded to brutalize its inhabitants. This behavior fits the pattern of European behavior toward the cultural other. Leopold "civilized" the Africans by chopping off their hands. The "enlightened" Europeans (the Rockefellers, Morgans, and Guggenheims) thought such behavior uncalled for; they simply entrenched themselves in the Congo vowing not to leave until the last drop of natural wealth was gone. They are still there. The following is a report from an American missionary on events in the Congo:

> It is blood-curdling to see them returning with hands of the slain, and to find the hands of young children amongst the bigger ones evidencing their bravery. . . . The rubber from this district has cost hundreds of lives, and the scenes I have witnessed, while unable to help the oppressed have been almost enough to make me wish I were dead. . . . The rubber traffic is steeped in blood, and if the natives were to rise and sweep every white person on the Upper Congo into eternity, there would still be left a fearful balance to their credit.[14]

A part of that pattern is that the stealing of land must be accompanied by "treaties" and "agreements" between the European and the "native," which are meaningless in terms of the European ethic and invalid or immoral in terms of the traditional concepts of land tenure. The ancestral lands cannot be "signed" away. "Everywhere we have the same story: obtaining 'concessions' from native chiefs under misleading pretexts, of childish bribes, or deliberate fraud."[15] For Europeans, breaking such "treaties" is, of course, also the rule and is in no way punishable or disapproved of by European society. What deserves attention is the apparent need that Europeans have to "legalize" everything; in fact their concept of legality itself bears scrutiny. It is this spurious cultural institution that victimizes those people unfortunate enough to get in the way of Europe's imperial stride. Such victims unfortunately confuse the concept with "mortality"; but the ideas of legality and morality have little relationship in European ideology. "Legality" has to do with behavioral consistency and order and is secularly sanctioned.

But why do Europeans go to the trouble of creating the appearance of legality in their dealings with majority peoples? Why not simply steal and exploit without the charade? The answer is (1) that this "acting out" constitutes a strategical tool that politically disarms the victims of European expansion, and (2) it plays an important part in the maintenance and support of the European self-image. The importance of this self-image must not be underestimated. One of the deepest beliefs of the Europeans is in the related notions of "civilization," "progress," and the "evolutionary" superiority of their culture. The concept of "codified law" is a definitive ingredient of that of civilization; for with civilization, according to European ideology, comes order and legality assures "lasting order"—not moral conduct but consistent and predictable conduct. So that the "civilized" way—the European way—is to bring laws, however forcibly, and the structures of European culture ("civilization") to those whom one treats immorally and for whom one has no respect. Along with "development," this justifies expansionism—for after all, Europeans bring "law and order" to people who must have previously lived quite "disorderly" lives (or so they believe). "Good" law is written law and therefore truly legal; unwritten law is not really law; it is "bad" and backward. How many times have the victims of European hypocrisy been duped into trying to deal with those laws rather than with the true nature of the European ethic?

The story begins with the Romans who blessed the world with their laws—even now thought to be their greatest achievement. Who were the barbarians? Those who defied and ignored the laws—who lived according to other patterns. Who are the barbarians now? The skyjackers, kidnappers, and other "terrorists" (revolutionaries). We are told by the European press that their acts are "uncivilized," and indeed, their behavior poses a threat to European ideology. By refusing to relate to Western order, these individuals and armies disarm Europeans. They succeed in robbing them of a potent tool for psychological and ideological enslavement.

To Reagan, Quaddafy is a "mad dog," who supports acts of "terrorism" against the "free world" (European, Euro-American interests). Therefore Reagan could intentionally provoke Libya into a defensive attack by invading the Gulf of Sidra, twelve miles within Libya's coast line. Then "in retaliation," he could indiscriminately bomb the Libyan city of Tripoli, perhaps in an effort to assassinate Quaddafy. Reagan's act is called "defending civilization," while Quaddafy is accused of supporting acts of "terrorism." But those who are called terrorists by Europeans are people who have refused to accept the semantics of European ideology and the rules of European culture. In the view of these revolutionaries, Europeans are "war criminals," on trial for centuries of systematic exploitation, rape, and murder perpetrated against various majority peoples. Those whom the Europeans label "terrorists" understand that we are fools if we accept the war-mongers rules of war. If, indeed, we wish to destroy their power to defeat us, we must deny them the right to judge us and our behavior. Who is Reagan to define moral or even political terms for the world?

It is always a matter of "the entire civilized community being shocked by these barbaric acts." It is the "barbarian" now, as in Ancient Rome, who is the true "revolutionary"; if only in the sense that he poses the greatest threat to the European order. Those few who have come to understand the principles of the European's attitudes and behavior towards the cultural other are considered to be paranoid, hateful, extreme, and violent by the rest who still relate to the European façade. Since European "laws" never work for the cultural other anyway, the best thing for non-Europeans to do is to ignore them. That was one of the lessons of the Mississippi experience that black people, learned at the Democratic National Convention in 1964, much to the embarrassment of the Democratic Party: that its rules for the election of delegates were not meant to include Mississippi; that the whites of that state would be upheld in their attempt to exclude blacks, because to do otherwise would, indeed, upset the "order" of the convention. The separation of morality and "law," the phenomenon of mass hypocrisy; the separation of emotional commitment from action are all encouraged by the European tradition in the use of words without meaning. To be "civilized" is to be able to hide one's true motives, and "civilization" is the appearance of a moral order that does not exist. If these things are understood then it is more easily realized that to be a cultural other implies that there are no laws that govern or inhibit the European's behavior towards you.

Where this becomes immediately apparent is in the European's overt behavior; in their expressions of violence and brutality. However inadvertently, the freedom rides and sit-ins demonstrated that there was no "conscience" to be reached in white America sensitive to physical brutality being enacted upon African people—in spite of the intended objective of appealing to that hypothetical "conscience." If the nature of European ideology had been properly understood, this strategic error could never have been made. But, again, perhaps it was a timely error, though it is difficult to imagine any gain worth those lost lives or the physical and emotional brutality suffered by a young and naïvely idealistic community. The "gain," if any, is to be reckoned in the removal of the hypocritical veneer and disarming image that America had presented to the world. America's behavior towards people of African descent during the Southern Movement revealed an ugly slice of the European ethic that was not meant to be shown. African descendants had, of course, long endured such brutality; but they had been "invisible," i.e., "hidden" within a conceptual construct that did not allow them to be seen as human. This revelation helped a few more victims of European brutality and exploitation to understand the implications of the European concept of the "cultural other." Those few were accordingly able to radically alter their political strategy for the attainment of the self-determination that they sought.

Political Violence: Seek and Destroy

Violence and physical and emotional brutality are part of the Western way of life—a fact well demonstrated in Alphonso Pinckney's *The American Way of Violence* (1972). This characteristic of the culture, along with several others (e.g., the capitalistic ethic, aggressiveness, competitiveness, the isolating concept of self) is a potential threat to the survival and unity of the cultural whole. Clearly, it is not in the interests of European nationalism to allow such destructiveness to be unleashed upon the very people on whose survival the culture depends. This tendency is therefore curbed within the culture, and European ideology (the values that are presented to the individual) inhibits or limits the violence and brutality with which one European can treat another. The concept of the cultural other contributes to the survival of European culture, i.e., to its internal cohesion, acting to maintain the integrity of its *asili*.

The bombing of Japan was culturally supportable because the Japanese were considered to be cultural others. The massacres in Vietnam; the torture during the Algerian Revolution; the treatment of Africans in South Africa; Leopold's mutilations in the Congo; the treatment first of the indigenous population and then of kidnapped Africans in America—all of these phenomena involved the interaction of Europeans with the cultural other. The pattern presented by the history of European behavior towards majority peoples must be ethnologically interpreted as evidence of a concept of us as those who may be treated with any amount of violence and brutality. The pattern indicates that acts of brutality committed against majority peoples are not ethically condemned in European culture—there is no ideological basis from which to do so. These cultural-historical facts must be taken as evidence of the existence of the European concept of the cultural other; a concept generated by the *asili* of European culture.

The European is capable of decimating whole populations of cultural others. Actions taken on behalf of the European imperialist enterprise attest to the fact that, according to the "logic" of European ideology, cultural others can be destroyed with impunity—without inhibitive emotional reaction among those who kill or from within the culture as a whole. Cohen describes the situation in the Congo under Leopold:

> Whole districts were depopulated. Of eight villages with a population of over 3,000, only ten persons were left. Of another district the population dropped in fifteen years from 50,000 to 5,000. The Bolangi tribe, formerly numbering 40,000, sank to 8,000. King Leopold, it is calculated, netted a profit of between three and five million sterling, and could call to God to witness the purity to his motives and his desire to promote civilization.[16]

On August 6, 1945 at 8:15 a.m., Paul Tippin, acting for the American people, dropped an atomic bomb on Hiroshima, Japan. The bomb was known to be more devastating than any previously developed. Approximately one minute after dropping it, Tippin could feel the effects of tremors in his plane flying about 30,000 feet above, and when he looked down a short while later all that he could see that was left of the city was a kind of "black debris." He had been anxious during those first few seconds before the bomb exploded. "Maybe it won't work," he thought. But with satisfaction and relief he sent a message back to his superiors in the United States; "Results better than expected." Back home President Truman and Secretary of State Byrnes were quite pleased. Tippin reported a "routine" flight back; he even let his subordinate take the controls and went to the back of the plane to "get some sleep." On the ground 70,000 people had been killed; 70,000 more were injured; radiation sickness would kill approximately 1,000 more in the years to come. The President of the United States called it "the greatest thing in history."[17]

German reparations and Jewish statehood, after the atrocities of World War II, illustrate the difference between the European intracultural ethic and European behavior toward others. German treatment of the Jews during Hitler's rule was effectively condemned by the Western world as no other act of mass brutality committed by a Western European nation has ever been. Yet, it would appear from the record that it wasn't because this brutality exceeded any other ever committed against a cultural group. Unfortunately the history of European imperialism has much worse tales to tell. It was effectively condemned by the West because of the identity of the victims in terms of the cultural definitions of the European. The victims, in this case, were ultimately considered to be Europeans and therefore not cultural others. The Germans had made a mistake. The Boers in South Africa; the Americans in North America, Japan, Vietnam; etc., the Spanish in South America, the British in China, India, Africa, the Caribbean Islands; the Christian Church during the Crusades—the list could go on and on—but *none* of these actions by Europeans could ever be forcefully or seriously condemned by the Western world, for in each instance the perpetrators had chosen the "ethnically proper" victims—non-European, nonwhite, nonwestern peoples. Ian Smith was responsible for the murder of 30,000 Africans in Rhodesia, but he was never charged with "war crimes." Africans must do that themselves.

On the southern tip of the African continent, a settler population of 4.5 million Europeans controls a land area of 472,359 square miles, which they identify as "The Republic of South Africa." This European minority holds 21 million Africans (and 3 million others of mixed Indian background) hostage in their indigenous homeland. The Africans cannot vote, cannot buy or sell land; they cannot live where they choose, move around at will, nor work where they wish. They cannot be elected to public office nor be members of parliament; they, therefore, have no political power and no control over their lives. Africans are 72 percent of the population and are relegated to

13 percent of the land, called "Bantustans." Eighty-seven percent of the land is reserved for Europeans, who comprise only 16 percent of the population. Africans earn 29.4 percent of the nation's wages and can expect an average income of 330 rands per annum. Europeans earn 58.7 percent of the nation's wages and can expect an annual income of 1300 rands. All public education is racially segregated and based on a philosophy of what might be called "racial pragmatism," to put it euphemistically. Prime Minister Verwoerd, then Minister of Native Affairs, put it this way in 1953:

> Education must train and teach people in accordance with their opportunities in life, according to the sphere in which they live . . . . The Bantu must be guided to serve his own community in all respects. There is no place for him in the European community above the level of certain forms of labor. Within his own community, however, all doors are open. For that reason it is of no avail for him to receive a training which has as its aim absorption in the European community while he cannot and will not be absorbed there.[18]

During the 1982–83 school year the government spent $1,323 for the education of each European student for the year. For Africans the figure was $178 per student.[18] In 1982 only 2 percent of African students went past high school; the figure for Europeans was 15 percent. (*South African Perspectives*, January 1984.) The teacher-student ratio is 1:18.9 for Europeans and 1:40.7 for Africans.

In the area of health, there was one doctor for every 330 Europeans and one doctor for every 19,000 Africans. There was a child mortality rate of 14 percent, and a life expectancy of 67 for the Europeans, with a child mortality rate of 60 percent and a life expectancy of 55 for Africans.[19] In 1983 it was estimated that 2.9 million black children suffered from malnutrition.

This political situation is under constant attack from the African community and has been, in varying degrees, since the coming of the Europeans in 1652. Because of the escalation of organized African resistance in recent years, the white government has intensified "legal" repression. In 1982 the Terrorism Act, the Unlawful Organization Act, and the General Laws Amendment Act were consolidated under the Internal Security Act. This act allows:

- indefinite incommunicado detention without charge or trial;
- outlawing of any organization alleged to be threatening to public safety or order;
- prohibition of the printing, publication or dissemination of any

periodical or any other publication
- prohibition of any gathering or meeting;
- random police searches;
- curtailment of travel rights of any person, and restriction of rights of communication, association and participation in any activity ("banning").

In order to control their movements, to inhibit their ability to organize, to control their labor, and for purposes of surveillance— Africans 16 years of age and over are required to be fingerprinted and to carry a pass-book at all times. The book contains a record of their Bantustan identification, of their employment, permits to enter white areas, and a record of taxes and family status.

South Africa had, until recently, the highest per capita prison population in the world.(According to *South African Perspectives,* by 1991, it was second, after the United States.) For every 100,000 of the population 440 people were jailed. Forty percent of the prisoners in jail have been convicted of pass law violations, which only Africans can commit. In 1980, of 130 people hanged, only one was white. In 1960, 69 people were gunned down by the police for expressing their opposition to the regime in a nonviolent demonstration.

The international European community makes this reality possible. They need South Africa's mineral and human resources to make up for the deficiencies of their own natural and human resources. The major investors in South Africa are: Great Britain, the United States, West Germany, Switzerland, France, Israel, and Japan (which in many ways has become an "honorary European" nation in terms of its materialist and technological priorities). The largest investor is Great Britain, with closest historical ties to the area. The United States, which has inherited Europe's imperial crown from Britain, is the second largest investor, accounting for 20 percent of all direct foreign investment in South Africa. In 1982 more than 350 U.S. companies had subsidiaries in South Africa. Major American corporate investments in South Africa include Mobil Oil ($426 million); Caltex i.e., Standard Oil, Texico ($334 million); SOHIO ($345 million); the list continues. As of June 1983, loans from U.S. Banks to South Africa totalled $3.88 billion.[20] These companies are supported by European-American society. New York State alone has invested over $6 billion in companies doing business in South Africa.[21] The United States seeks to "free" people from communist rule, but it supports the infamous white regime in South Africa. The victims are cultural others and the booty is irresistible.

The nation of Grenada is situated on a tiny island in the

Caribbean, north of Venezuela on the South American continent. Its population is approximately twice the size of Staten Island, New York—110,000 people. On Tuesday, October 25, 1983, the United States Government, representing a nation with a population of 220 million people, situated on the continent of North America, with probably the most powerful military organization in the world, invaded this tiny country with a minimum of 6000 U.S. marines, paratroopers, and the 82nd Airbourne Division troops. Ronald Reagan, the president of the United States, authorized an illegal and unconstitutional act that totally violated Grenada's national sovereignty.

> The U.S. invasion included the use of fire bombers, gas bombs, and military might of the type used in Vietnam. Grenadian and international solidarity workers defending the island, its homes and worksites from the invaders, were brutally murdered, injured, and imprisoned with no regard for international law.[22]

How did the United States justify such an act of imperialistic aggression, against a tiny country that could in no way be perceived as a threat to them? The Grenadian people were committed to a socialist form of government; therefore they became the "enemy" of the United States. It was up to the European Americans to "save" the people of Grenada from themselves, so to speak; to save them from communist dictatorship and Cuban rule. The Cubans were building an airfield in Grenada that was to be used as a base for Soviet military machinery, or so the story went. Following the assassination of Maurice Bishop, the popular Grenadian Head of State, Eugenia Charles, Prime Minister of the Dominican Republic; Tom Adams, the Prime Minister of Barbados; and Edward Seaga of Jamaica—all pro-U.S. governments—"invited" the United States to rid the Caribbean of the clear and present danger which they said Grenadian instability posed. The United States claimed that it was obligated to help in the restoration of stability. In addition, Reagan claimed that they had to protect U.S. citizens living in Grenada, a large number of whom were medical students at a Grenadian medical school.

And so the United States did all that it could to destroy the Grenadian Revolution; a revolution that was the attempt of a people of African descent to determine their own destiny. Their success would have tarnished the self-image of Euro-America, while providing a beacon of light for 30 million Africans colonized within the United States. Reagan simply had heard the call of European manifest destiny, and acted in accord with the principles of the Monroe Doctrine. This action, so horrendous, was quite logical to Reagan and fits neatly within the dictates of the *asili* of the culture. Such is the face of European political violence against cultural others.

In 1981 Ronald Reagan was faced with the problem of the psychological ill-effects caused by the United State's defeat in Vietnam. He had to prove to the world and to the American people that the United States was still more powerful than the Soviet Union. At the same time the enemy—communism—was not just far away in Southeast Asia but threatening close at hand, in South and Central America. The Marxist-Leninists would not rest until all of Central America was under communist rule. They would eventually get to the borders of the United States, not satisfied until the entire planet was under communist control. So goes the line of U.S. militarism, its own obsession justified by the alleged obsession of others. What is so bad about communism? The question might be asked in a more intellectually free environment. The answer predictably is that communism denies people "freedom to choose." It is not usually added that socialism denies American capitalists access to the material resources that they need, but do not own; indeed, the spread of socialism limits capitalist control. The immediate issue is not whether we agree or disagree with this view, but what kinds of Euro-American behavior towards others is justified by the so-called communist threat.

Their villages under attack, the people of Nicaragua are not phenotipically European. Their hair is dark and their skins are much darker than that of European Americans. They look very much like the original inhabitants of the Americas, from whom many of them are descended. (Europeans have already decimated such a population.) They are a poor, humble people. But they have earned the amnity of a powerful cultural/racial enemy.

The Sandonista government came into power in Nicaragua in July 1979. It proclaimed revolutionary goals, which automatically placed it in opposition to the United States. But Nicaragua insisted that they would relate to the United States on terms of full sovereignty and that their right to make their own decisions should be respected. Yet they had to have known that the United States would attack the Nicaraguan Revolution.

In 1981 the Nicaraguan government began supporting the revolutionary movement in El Salvador by sending arms. Reagan pounced on the opportunity to begin to restore America's image as the overseer of the world. On May 9, 1981 Ronald Reagan signed a secret directive stating that because Nicaragua was a threat to El Salvador, and to the United States; he was authorizing the Central Intelligence

Agency to organize rebel groups against the Sandonista Government. The United States threatened to stop its aid to Nicaragua if the government did not stop its arms shipments. Nicaragua agreed to stop, but aid was cut nonetheless.

In November 1981 Reagan issued another secret directive to the CIA to develop a paramilitary force whose objective would be to remove the Sandonista government from power. That was the covert objective; the overt objective was to stop the arms flow between Nicaragua and El Salvador. The military force was made up of South Americans, not European Americans, and they were dubbed counter-revolutionaries or "Contras." Among themselves their purpose was clear; get rid of the Sandonistas.

In reaction, the Nicaraguan Government declared a state of emergency, removing villagers from their homes, allegedly brutalizing the Mosquito Indians, who had been helping the Contras. By the summer of 1982 the extremely violent nature of this act of political violence orchestrated by the United States was clear. The Contras targeted villagers, killing babies, attacking schools, health clinics, and farm cooperatives. The CIA calls this "low intensity warfare." It surpasses even conventional strategies in violence and demonstrates an unbelievable tolerance and ability for systematic inhuman brutality. Incredible, if we did not hear it explicitly described, explained in detail and supported by European American military leaders. But such systematic brutality is demanded by European nationalism. European culture becomes the quintessence of means-ends rationalization.

There followed a move within Congress to cut off funds to the Contras, as the realities of yet another "undeclared war" became known to the American public. The CIA was put in the position of justifying their actions to the American people. Edgar Chamorro, a former Contra leader, is shown in films lying to the American press about his lack of contact with the CIA, as the Agency instructed him to do. He said that he had not been given orders by them. Congress responded by authorizing more money. The Boland Amendment authorized this money "as long as it would not be used to destabilize the Nicaraguan Government." Everyone knew that this was the precise intent. The question was put to Reagan: "Why the fiction? Why not openly support the 7000 Contras?" Reagan answered: "Because we want to keep on obeying the laws of this country." Question: "Doesn't the U.S. want the Government of Nicaragua changed?" Answer: "No, because that would be against the law." In May of 1987, the fiction was no longer necessary, and there was evidence of similar involvement in Guatemala.

The "low intensity warfare" waged by the Contras under the direction of the CIA, financed by the American Government was intensified. "Low intensity warfare" means that the targets are intentionally civilian. The intent is to cause extreme suffering among the people in order to make them unhappy with the present government. In an interview on the television program *Frontline* the question was put to Lieutenant General William Nutting: "What does this war accomplish?" He answered: "It engages the Sandonista armed forces; it alerts the populace, and hopefully results in uprisings." Question: "How long will it take?" Answer: "Maybe five or ten years. It is evolutionary." The advantage of this undeclared war when compared to the one lost by the U.S. in Vietnam is that white people are not being killed. In April of 1987, $105 million in additional funds were authorized for the Contras.

Chamorro, the ex-Contra leader, realized that he had been used in a process of intentional self-deception. In his words, he had been "in the midst of insanity. You called someone a communist so that you could kill him."[23]

The situation of U.S. involvement in Nicaragua demonstrates the cold remoteness with which European-Caucasians can plan and execute not only the destruction of non-European people, but somehow what seems worse, how they can slowly torture people, mentally and physically, over a long period of time—all the while attempting to convince themselves that they do this in order to "free" those under torture. Any amount of violence can be tolerated toward the cultural other without conflict. A pattern emerges. The rhetoric of European ideology is always to say the opposite of the truth: We enslave you to free you. Is there any wonder that the Nicaraguan national anthem includes the phrase, "Yankees, the enemies of mankind!"

What was the attitude of European Americans to the Contra scandal? The Contra hearings were called by the U.S. Congress in order to ascertain what, if any, illegal or unauthorized acts had been committed by United States officials with regard to the Iranian arms deal. In the record-breaking heat of July 1987, the American public sat glued to their television sets. The Contra Hearings even topped the day-time soaps.

To what degree was the President of the United States involved in the Iranian arms deal, in which the United States had sold arms to Iran, freed some hostages in the process, and used the profits to finance the Contras in Nicaragua, all without Congressional approval? The President at first denied that the U.S. had sold arms to Iran; then said that if the U.S. had sold them, he hadn't known about it, or that if he had known about it, he couldn't remember! These were the words of the President of the most powerful nation in the world!

In the hearings Oliver North testified that not only had such a deal "gone down" in which he had participated, but that he had done so with the approval of his superiors, and that he had prepared erroneous documents to "mislead Congress" so that a hearing would never take place again. He said that he had also promised three heads of state in Central America support for their counter-revolutionary activity, and that the United States Government had promised him "discretion."

The people of Nicaragua were never the issue in the Contra hearings. Congressmen appeared either to be "hurt" because they had not been trusted with the secrets of a covert action or appalled that government officials would take it upon themselves to make such important policy decisions without consulting the President. Honesty and integrity were certainly not displayed during the hearings, so that no one seemed to know who was telling the truth, if it was being told at all. But no one seemed to question the morality of such "covert actions." Admiral John Poindexter, who was given credit for having authorized the deal, said that he purposefully hadn't asked or told the President in the event that there would be hearings. It was okay though, because he "knew that the President would have approved."

The entire scenario would have been pitifully comic if it were not for the fact that while top U.S. Government officials exposed their lack of integrity to the world, the Nicaraguan people were being slaughtered by American-paid mercenaries, tortured and denied their right to self-determination in the process. No one cared, because they were only cultural others.

Johari Amini demonstrates the way in which the system of European values operates to define people as "bad" or "subhuman" and is therefore able to *absorb* any amount of violent acts committed against them. Her explanation reiterates the behavioral implications of the European distinction between themselves and the cultural other. She correctly assesses the significance of the facts that (1) it was only the Japanese-Americans, and not Italian- or German-Americans who were "relocated" during World War II; and that (2) the atomic bomb was used on the Japanese. Johari Amini says,

> In 1945, after the European Allies had defeated the Europeans in Germany and Italy through methods of conventional warfare, they proceeded to defeat the Asians in Japan by destroying the cities of Hiroshima and Nagasaki with atomic bombs—nuclear weapons

which had been developed in time for use on Berlin and Munich, or on Rome and Naples. But they were not used in Europe. They were used in Asia instead. And why? Because underneath of all the discussion and furor about the differences between fascism and democracy, the European Allies' war against Europeans in Germany and Italy was, at worst, a tribal warfare and not designed for *their* genocide. The situation in Asia was quite different, on the other hand. The Allies' war against Asians in Japan represented one more stepping-stone in the decimation of Asiatic populations by Europeans. By way of rationale, the Asians in Japan did not have needs, interests, goals, or backgrounds similar to the European Allies, whereas the Europeans in Germany and Italy did; therefore it would not have been "right" or "good" or "positive" for Europeans to use nuclear weapons in fighting their tribal wars in Europe, but it was indeed "right" and "good" and "positive" and even "just" to use nuclear weapons to destroy Asians in Japan. The act of the bombing was *legitimized* by the European definition of "Japanese" ("Yellow Jap," "Tojo the Jap," slant-eyed, snake-like, vicious in characterization). [Amini's italics.]

That these actions taken against the Asians in Japan were, and remain, highly consistent with European working definitions of "right," "good," and "just," as well as European values generally (particularly religious values), is made obvious upon examination of the prayer that was offered on behalf of the men who were flying the bombers. The prayer was, of course, made to God in the hope that this bombing would cause the war to end soon so there would be peace on earth, that the bombers would go and return in safety because they were in His care just as all of them were in His care, and was prayed "in the name of Jesus Christ" . . . [these themes] did not then, and do not now, contradict each other within the European framework of values.[24]

In this last paragraph Amini describes the "rhetorical ethic" in operation. The concept of *asili* allows us to properly assess the significance of the verbalized Christian ethic in conjunction with the pattern of behavior towards others. The concept similarly allows us to identify interpretations of European group behavior that are consistent with the essential core, or nature of the culture. It leads us, at the same time, to an analysis that explains the dominant modes of European thought and behavior as being part of a consistent and united ideological whole. The concept of the cultural other places the behavior that Amini describes squarely within the confines of that sanctioned by the European ethic; as she says, such behavior is consistent with European "working definitions."

Cultural Violence: Destroying the Will

The capacity of one cultural group to commit acts of physical brutality and destruction against another is proportionate to the place of power (i.e., control over "other") in its ideology and the degree to which its image and conception of those outside the culture lack the characteristics of "humanness." European culture has an enormous capacity for the perpetration of physical violence against other cultures; it's integrity is neither threatened nor disrupted by such occurrences.

The physical body may be critical to the maintenance of human existence, but the *quality* of that existence depends very much on our mental and spiritual condition. First World cultures tend to be spiritually oriented, and therefore cultural violence (ideological and psychological) is at least as damaging to their humanity as is physical violence. It would be difficult to say which does the most harm. Indeed, they cannot be separated.

Here again, the European is the master. The West initially set out to conquer the world with the might of its Roman armies, but the lesson they soon learned was that building an empire was not a matter of military superiority alone; it was necessary to impose culture as well—and so the Romans "civilized" (did cultural violence) as they went. And in the centuries to come Christianity became the tool that dealt the deathblow to the objects of European imperialism. How much easier it was to control a culture once the coherence of its ideology had been destroyed; and wasn't this, after all, the way to really take it over, to possess it? Again, it was the cultural other who was the only fair game for cultural imperialism. Only her forms of social organization, her religion, her material culture, her art forms, were "inferior." They could, therefore, be destroyed with impunity. The destruction of the ideological structures of Africans and other majority peoples was far more costly to them than even incarceration; for without these they had no rationale for defense; neither a reason for living, nor one for dying. Awoonor analyzes the process well:

> By far the most powerful of European cultural contact and change in Africa has been the Christian Church. . . missionary work began in Africa as a sporadic attempt . . . to extend the gospel to the "unfortunate" heathens [but] the metropolitan political machinery . . . became its closest defender, ally, and ultimate beneficiary.

> The Christian Church in Africa refused to accept the legitimacy of the African's religious position. He was accused of being a pagan, a devil worshipper; Satan was said to have employed his agency to

erase every vestige of religious impression from the African's mind, leaving him without a single ray to guide him away from the dark and dread futurity.[25]

The attack was cultural, aimed at the spirit and self-esteem of the African, entities that had been held firmly in tact by a cohesive communal organization. Christianity appealed to the outcasts in order to subvert the solidarity and integrity of the society. It was individualistic, not communalistic like African spiritual conceptions. One sought personal and individual salvation through piety and belief in Christ. "The school was the most important instrument of Christian missionary work in Africa."[26] Children entered missionary schools only to cut ties with their families and with their traditional rituals and rites of passage; i.e., those institutions that had given Africans such a deep sense of security and identity. Africans were forced to change their names in order to become good Christians—docile, humble and obedient.

Speaking African languages was discouraged, while imitating Europe was encouraged; including Europe's material culture.

> This situation led to the development of a sense of insecurity and inferiority in Africans, marked by a simple process of the loss of identity and of independence in the most traumatic manner.... For this group [the Europeans], the bulk of the Africans represented a despicable lower level of creatures, with obnoxious religious and social habits who must not be tolerated around the precincts of decent homes.[27]

Soon the "educated" Africans would be taught to think these things about their own people. They could then be used to "lead." Africans were considered to be "half child, half devil." But "Christ was a white man; the saints were white; the missionaries were white."[28]

Clearly, it has been the evil political genius of the West, since the beginnings of European imperialism, to concentrate its efforts on the cultural and therefore ideological destruction of the people it conquered. The instances of European military control in which its victims continued to deny European cultural superiority are not imperialist successes. Here Europeans have not been able to truly impose and "expand" themselves. It is for this reason that Vietnam is the most bitter failure of European imperialism to date. And yet a people who have been ideologically conquered rarely require the threat of arms to be kept in control. Carter G. Woodson tells us:

If you control a man's thinking you do not have to worry about his actions. When you determine what a man shall think you do not have to concern yourself about what he will do. If you make a man feel that he is inferior, you do not have to compel him to accept an inferior status, for he will seek it himself. If you make a man think that he is justly an outcast, you do not have to order him to the back door. He will go without being told; and if there is no back door, his very nature will demand one.[29]

It is the nature of European behavior toward the cultural other to enact cultural violence against her in the attempt to destroy her spiritual as well and material culture. E. D. Morel says that the destructive effects of the "scientifically applied" evils of western exploitation are "permanent":

> . . . in its permanence resides its fatal consequences. It kills not the body merely, but the soul. It breaks the spirit. It attacks the African at every turn, from every point of vantage. It wrecks his polity, uproots him from the land, invades his family life, destroys his natural pursuits and occupations, claims his whole time, enslaves him in his own home.[30]

It is the consistent objective of Europeans in their behavior toward the cultural other to destroy culture and thereby to destroy dignity. Whether the vehicle is a chain put on her ankle, a Bible placed in her hand, or a "pacification" or "development" program, the objective is always the same, and physical violence is just one (not necessarily the most devastating or destructive) aspect of this endeavor.

The cultural other represents that which is negative in the European definition of value; it is the symbol of nonvalue. Yet Europeans have consistently acted to place themselves into a position of proximity with the peoples whom they despise—whom they consider unworthy. Only in terms of the dynamics of the European *utamaroho* does this behavior make sense.

The principles of capitalism, and the greed that it unleashes, certainly contribute to the European quest for "relationship" with the cultural other and results in what appears often to be contradictory behavior in which the sentiments of a staunch, white nationalism seemingly conflict with the interests of economic exploitation. From the point of view of Wayne McLeod (who describes himself as a "racialist"): "Avaricious Capitalism becomes evident as an enemy to the Culture-bearing strata of Western Society when it recruits labor of the darker races, endangering the livelihood of the White."[31] This would appear to be the "logical" position given the premises of white nationalist ideology. And if it had been taken consistently, once the indigenous population had been exterminated, American society would have been homogeneously white, Western European—or maybe the first comers would never have left Europe in the first place. But the patterned behavior of Europeans points to the presence of other dynamics that lie beneath the surface of common white nationalist propaganda. White nationalism is, after all, white supremism and, therefore, requires two variables—a superior and an inferior.

After the discovery of gold in California in 1848, the Chinese were brought to America in increasingly larger numbers to provide cheap labor. By 1852, 20,000 Chinese had entered the United States. They had been transported under the worst possible conditions—kidnapped and duped. With the settling in of the immigrant population, the anti-Chinese mood of America heightened, initiating decades of violence and atrocities committed against them in the 1870s. It was when Chinese labor was no longer greedily consumed that Americans became more concerned with the limitation and prohibition of Chinese immigration.[32] Just as with the behavior of the European-American population toward the Africans, whom they imported during the slave trade, these episodes display the familiar pattern in European treatment of peoples of other cultures. Europeans import majority peoples to do their dirty work and simultaneously deprecate them and rave about the negative effect they are having on their culture. They then legislate to change, control, and superficially segregate these cultural others. How such people came to be there in the first place never appears to be a fact of consideration (it is not as though they had "invaded" the West), and unfortunately for them, there is almost never a concerted effort to return them to their homelands. It was the greed and hypocrisy of the white southerner that placed him in the position of having to be proximate to Africans. As MacLeod inadvertently points out, a consistent position of white nationalism should have prevented African slavery in the first place.

Scrawled across an advertisement written in Spanish on a New York City bus are the words, "This is America. Speak English!" But obviously the best way to keep America "English speaking," European, and white is to bar entry to peoples of other cultures and colors; neither to use them nor to "annex" (colonize) their countries. At the same time immigration policies will be more open to people of European descent, while they allow enough darker peoples to immigrate (legally and illegally) to provide the type of labor that whites will not do. Distained work is for distained people. Even many "illegal aliens" can hope to remain in the United States because they will be used as twentieth-century "slaves."

What kind of person allows someone from a despised race/culture to nurse and raise her children and to live in her house? The peculiar perversions of the European *utamaroho* are dramatically enacted in the Sembene Ousman film *Black Girl*. In this film a young Senegalese woman is hired by a French couple to provide them with a symbol of superiority—a requisite for success in European ideology. She cannot endure the cultural violence that her condition inflicts; liberating herself by committing suicide (the sacrifice of physical existence). In this way her spirit can return to her people.

The East Side, and now the Upper West Side of Manhattan parades such symbols daily as women of African descent are to be seen transporting small white children on and off the buses of Lexington Avenue or walking them in strollers. What irony! Are these children being sacrificed for the sake of white supremacy—or is it an even more complex phenomenon in which a maternal superiority is associated with the race of the original mother? Whatever the answer, it is for us, the essence of exploitation.

But in the "logic" of European ideology the importation of despised peoples is not contradictory, rather the action and the sentiment complement each other within the complex and unique construct that is the European *utamaroho*. That is why capitalist behavior and white nationalism do not conflict and why it takes more than the factor of the capitalist ethic to explain the European's need for the presence of the cultural other. (Kovel talks about "ambivalence" towards feces.) This historical pattern in the behavior of the European, in so far as it is motivated by the desired presence of peoples of other cultures, is ethnologically understood by the recognition of two related factors. First, as stated earlier, the nature of the culture *requires* the cultural other as the "proper" object of its destructiveness in order to mitigate these negative effects within the culture itself. (Other cultures can survive in isolation; European culture, by its very nature, cannot.) And second, there is the need of the cultural ego to feel assured of its superiority. The presence of the cultural other and her successful dehumanization is, for Europeans, the necessary demonstration of European supremacy. This constant reaffirmation is essential.

The determining factor in the European's behavior towards those outside her culture is the driving power theme that dominates her ideology. It underlies their fanatical rationalism, their lack of spirituality, their obsession with the material and the technical, and their imperialistic expansionism. The cultural other becomes the object of the most extreme manifestations of this power drive and a necessary component of the European world-view. This helps us to understand why the object of cultural violence or cultural aggression is never the transformation of the cultural other *into* a European. (This is why the Ghanaian with a British accent is an object of ridicule for the European.) The *utamaroho* does not demand the creation of more Europeans. It needs, instead, the cultural other to fulfill the role of "object." Cultural destruction is, therefore, achieved by convincing people of other cultures that they are in fact destined or created to be controlled by Europeans. Or, what is equally harmful, convincing them that they can become European (an ethnological racial impossibility). The latter is the ideological basis for the creation of the African elite that Chinweizu (1978) and Awoonor (1975) discuss as primary banes of African self-determination. Cultural destruction is successful when majority peoples accept the definitions of themselves given them within the terms of European ideology. Chinweizu vividly describes the "civilizing" process as he experienced it, i.e., a process of "miseducation":

> It was a miseducation process which, by encouraging me to glorify all things European, and by teaching me a low esteem for and negative attitudes towards things African, sought to cultivate in me that kind of inferiority complex which drives a perfectly fine right foot to strive to mutilate itself into a left foot. It was a miseducation full of gaps and misleading pictures: it sought thereby to indoctrinate me with the colonizers' ideology; it sought to structure my eyes to see the world in the imperialist ways of seeing the world; it sought to internalize in my consciousness the values of the colonizers.... [33]

The motivating factor underlying European cultural aggression appears to be the power drive, which is fully acted out on the cultural other. This is often quite literally and dramatically the case; it is not merely a subtle implication of their cultural behavior. In 1816 a community of Africans, who had escaped from white slavers and who were living a quite peaceful, constructive, and culturally coherent existence in Florida, were attacked by a unit under the command of General Gaines of the United States Army; they were subsequently slaughtered.[34]

In 1945 the U.S. Government was capable of destroying two Japanese cities; wreaking unprecedented destruction and pain in a single act of violence with the objective of displaying its newly acquired power to the world. The Japanese people were regarded as mice in a scientist's laboratory or as mannequins in a store window.

Genocidal Behavior: "Wipe Them Out!"

This land is ours, not through murder, not through theft, not by way of violence or any other trickery. This has always been our land. Here we began. Here we will continue even after the thousand season's scattering and the thousand seasons' groping, through the white death sometimes openly, often covertly, seductively now, brutally at other times, changes means but always seeks one end: our extermination.

— Armah

With a knowledge of the nature of European culture (its *asili*), and being aware of history, the African-centered person similarly understands that the European (European-American) is capable of doing *anything* to destroy people of African descent (or any other majority people), as long as it is perceived to be in the European interest. The concept of the cultural other eliminates the question of morality. That is its function. Since whatever moral issues are raised pertain to the European only, the discussion is "in house."

Two circumstances come to mind that can be interpreted as part of an ongoing attempt to destroy African people, both on the continent and in the Diaspora. One is the infamous Tuskegee Experiment (1932-1972); the other is the current existence and spread of the AIDS virus.

For forty years the United States Government via its Public Health Service (PHS) conducted a study of the effects of untreated syphilis on African men in Macon County, Alabama. Referred to as "The Tuskegee Study," after the name of the county seat and the famous educational institute founded by Booker T. Washington, the experiment involved 399 African men with syphilis and 201 African men free of the disease, who were used as "controls." This "experiment" is documented in a book entitled Bad Blood, written by James H. Jones.

A variety of tests and medical examinations were performed on the men during scores of visits by PHS physicians over the years, but the basic procedures called for periodic blood testing and routine autopsies to supplement the information that was obtained through clinical examinations.[35]

The men with Syphilis were chosen because they were in the last or "tertiary" stage of the disease. The scientists wanted to learn about the serious complications that occurred during the final phase. The study established that the men with Syphilis died more quickly than those who did not have it. This conclusion hardly seems worth the effort. But since the objective was simply to observe the devastating effects of Syphilis, coldly, "rationally" and "scientifically,"—from the point of view of the Europeans—the study was deemed a "success."

The physicians involved, in the service of the United States Government, can be charged with antihuman, genocidal behavior, behavior that makes hypocritical nonsense of the Hippocratic oath. James Jones comments: "The Tuskegee Experiment had nothing to do with treatment." No new drugs were developed or tested! No old drugs were evaluated! "It was a non-therapeutic experiment."[36] In other words, diseased patients were diagnosed by physicians and then *not treated* so that their condition could deteriorate, leading, in most cases, to untimely death.

If there is any doubt as to the severe nature of the disease under discussion, let us take the time to describe it briefly. Syphilis has been divided into three states of progression: primary, secondary, and tertiary. The details of these stages were known to European medical science in 1932. The primary stage lasts from ten to sixty days and involves a chancre ulcer. The secondary stage begins within six weeks to six months with a rash and often skin eruptions. Other complications are the aching of bones and joints, circulatory disturbances, fever, indigestion, and headaches. Skin lesions may develop, causing hair to drop from the scalp. "The greatest proliferation and most widespread distribution of the infectious spirochetes throughout the body occurs in secondary syphilis."[37] The tertiary or final stage is the most severe and most significant for an understanding of this grotesque human experiment. In the tertiary state a person develops gummy or rubbery tumors, lesions. and tumors that coalesce on the skin forming large ulcers covered with a crust consisting of several layers of dried exuded matter. They produce deterioration of the bone, sometimes eating away the bone. The liver may also be affected. Syphilis also attacks the cardiovascular and central nervous systems, and patients often die of problems related to this condition.

> The tumors may attack the walls of the heart or the blood vessels. When the aorta is involved, the walls become weakened, scar tissue forms over the lesion, the artery dilates, and the valves of the heart no longer open and close properly and begin to leak. The stretching of the vessel walls may produce an aneurysm, a balloonlike bulge in the aorta. If the bulge bursts, and sooner or later most do, the result is sudden death.[38]

Neurosyphilis effects the brain. The most common form is pare-sis, which is a softening of the brain that causes progressive paraly-sis and mental disorder. Syphilis also can effect the spinal cord, the optic nerve (causing blindness), or a cranial nerve (causing deaf-ness).[39]

What is described above is what the physicians were able to coldly observe in the name of "science." In Jones' book, there is tes-timony from patients to the effect that they did not know that they had syphilis but were told vaguely that they had "bad blood." And, what is worse, that they were given the impression (some for over thirty years) that they were being treated for whatever condition they had. On the other hand, officials at the Center for Disease Control in Atlanta told reporters in 1972 that participants had been informed that they had syphilis and were given the opportunity to withdraw from the program and receive treatment. But this was contradicted by a physician who had been involved in the experiment in 1932. He said that neither the attending interns nor the subjects knew what the study involved. Why would anyone who knew that they were seri-ously ill remain in a program that denied them treatment when they could leave and get treatment elsewhere?

The implications of the Tuskegee Experiment are staggering but only if one does not understand the nature (*asili*) of European culture and the character of European ideology. Black men were asked to allow themselves to be tested for "bad blood." If chosen, either because they tested positive or as a part of the "control" group, they were to come periodically to the clinics for observation. They were under the impression that they were coming for treatment. Why did they respond at all? They were mostly poor and were given incentives such as free physical examinations, free rides to and from the clinics, hot meals on examination days, and free treatment for minor ail-ments.[40] They were also "befriended" by a negro nurse, Nurse Rivers, whom they trusted and who served as a liason between whites and their black objects of study. She made the men feel that they were part of an exclusive social club and burial society that guaranteed their relatives $50.00 for their funerals.[41] Eunice Rivers was perhaps the most victimized of all: transformed into an enemy of her people.

The participants were denied treatment from the beginning of the project, and in 1940 when penicillin was in use, they were denied that drug as well. Care was taken to prevent them from getting treat-ment elsewhere if they had been identified for the study. Unsuspecting physicians who coincidentally diagnosed their condi-tion would be told, in effect, "hands off."

After twenty-five years in the experiment the participants were given "certificates." What images allowed such hypocritical, antihuman behavior? Europeans were saying to themselves: Let a group of black men die and suffer from syphilis without treatment so that we can observe its effects. Fortunately black people are available—the cultural other.

In 1972 when the experiment was finally publicized, newsman Harry Reasoner reported that human beings had been used "as laboratory animals in a long and inefficient study of how long it takes syphilis to kill someone."[41] But these men of African descent were not considered "human beings." "Human beingness" is not merely a scientific classification; it denotes a spiritual empathetic relationship.

The cleverness and deceit of Europeans as as cultural group is systematic and effective. Syphilis, a notorious disease resulting from sexual license and nonhygienic practices of a morally decadent European society, was introduced to indigenous peoples all over the world during European colonial penetration and its aftermath, in some cases decimating whole populations. Then centuries later the disease becomes associated with the victims of European contamination, while Europeans admonish each other against contact with cultural others, lest *they* be contaminated by the disease that originated *among them*.

"From our knowledge of the negro we should be inclined to the opinion that a chance for an education or even its acquisition does not materially influence his well known sexual promiscuity," wrote Dr. Louis Wender."[42] Another fifty years will find an unsyphilitic negro a freak," said Dr. Bruce McVey.[42] This pernicious association of people of African descent with sexual promiscuity established the atmosphere in which the Tuskegee Experiment could be tolerated. There was another critical ingredient to the image: ignorance. "Ignorance and uncleanliness have ever gone hand in hand with disease. . . ."[43] Low moral standards were said to be in the "very nature" of black people.[44] Ignorance and sexual promiscuity—the double barrel leveled at Africans in America—set us up to be deserving guinea pigs; even worse, objects of genocide.

It is a moot question as to whether the European physicians failed to treat the Africans because they wanted to observe them dying or because they wanted to kill them. From an African-centered perspective, it is the same thing. (And what about all of the people who could have been and were infected by the men with syphilis who didn't know that they had it? Perhaps this was also part of the "experiment.")

Knowing what we do of the European cultural *asili*, of the perverse nature of the European *utamaroho*, and of the implications of the European concept of the cultural other, we can even conjecture that they would be capable of injecting people of African descent with the syphilis spirochetes if only for the same reasons that they ostensibly conducted the "experiment." Certainly the Nazi doctors did this, and germ warfare is now used as a matter of course.[45]

In the last two decades of the twentieth century, the most discussed and thought-about disease, without doubt, will be Acquired Immune Deficiency Syndrome (AIDS). Contrary to the projections of the medical establishment and the U.S. Government, confusion is generated by and is reflective of the confusion of the European-American and European scientists. If one keeps abreast of the information released by various agencies and experts, the pattern of contradiction, conflicting "findings," and vagueness becomes obvious. The message is clear. They simply do not know what they are talking about. The public is told repeatedly: "There is no proven case in which AIDS has been transmitted by casual contact. Objects touched or handled by people with AIDS are not contaminated and need not be feared; the only possible exceptions are objects which might be contaminated with blood—especially razors, toothbrushes, tweezers." "Don't worry, HTLV-III is an extremely fragile virus." Yet at the same time we are told that it is "lenti" or "slow" with an incubation period of seven years. Statements abound such as "there is no evidence that. . ." and "there is only a small risk that. . . ." and "it is not thought that. . . ." This phraseology is not in the least reassuring. In May 1987, three nurses contracted AIDS supposedly from "accidents" in which they touched contaminated blood samples. The point is that AIDS kills and that there is no known cure. With an incubation period of seven years (Dr. Strecker doubles this figure) a person could be infected without knowing it or without others knowing it. This certainly limits the exact knowledge that medical science has of the disease. Therefore most lay people, and justifiably so, are not willing to take chances with speculation—scientific or not.

AIDS has been associated with the male homosexual community in the United States, which is by and large of European descent but includes men of African and other non-European backgrounds. In 1985, 70-75 percent of the people with AIDS were homosexual or bisexual men; 17 percent were intravenous drug abusers. Hemophiliacs and other blood transfusion recipients are also at high risk, for obvious reasons. The retrovirus HTLV-III or AIDS-causing virus is said to be present in the body fluids (blood, semen, saliva) of people who are infected. The virus is transmitted through exchange of bodily fluids.

What does all of this mean from an African-centered perspective, and how is it related to European behavior towards others? Suddenly Africa emerged as the "probable" birthplace of the AIDS virus. "Experts" on talk shows focusing on AIDS would briefly make statements to this effect, and then quickly move on to another point, never giving evidence to support such a conclusion. Homosexuality is not associated with African civilization since African cultural values place priority on female-male conjugal relationship as the basis of the "extended" family and for the procreation of children. Yet the experts get around this: AIDS in Africa is a heterosexual disease, and the virus has a slightly different chemical composition. They begin to talk about the Green Monkey as somehow being associated with the contracting of AIDS. In the minds of the American public were conjured pictures of bizarre practices in which Africans had sex with monkeys. Later it was "clarified" that STLV-III (S for "Simian") was carried by monkeys, but that they did not die from it and that Africans could have gotten it from eating the monkeys or being bitten by them.

As of August 5, 1987, the World Health Organization (WHO) figures for known AIDS cases worldwide were 54,661 overall; 38,160 in the United States, and only 4,714 in Africa. That is one reality. But on ABC's *Nightline* a very different reality was created for the American public. On Wednesday night, May 13, 1987 (when the figures for Africa were even less) Ted Koppel, (with Dr. Milton Silverman, Renee Sabatier and George Strait) assaulted the international African community. The gun barrels had been reloaded. The parallels with the Tuskegee Experiment were striking in terms of the associations, arguments, and images that were presented. To a mind trained to recognize patterns of European cultural/political behavior towards others, the game plan was clear. People of African descent were being set up as objects of "justified" genocidal behavior by people of European descent. Our minds were being prepared to accept the self-fulfilling prophecy that by 1992 5½ million people would be infected in the motherland, and that men, women, and children of African descent in the United States would be the largest group at risk.

The program began with a visual focus on people suffering and dying from AIDS in Africa (at least we were told that the disease in question was AIDS). Mothers were shown wasting away with their children around them. Projections were made of rapid growth in the number of AIDS cases in Africa by the year 2000. The number of people already infected with the AIDS virus was estimated to be 10 million! The picture was one of disaster. Why did the future look so bleak for Africa? The "experts" said because of "cultural differences," "lack of communication" (lack of television sets), "sexual practices," polygamy, and the fact that Africans "like to have children." The premise was that the spread of AIDS could be controlled by "better public understanding."

The association was clearly made between AIDS and sexual promiscuity. The inference was that African culture in general and the practice of polygamy in particular condoned sexual promiscuity, as well as undisciplined behavior with regard to sexual relations. It does not matter that polygamy (polygyny) is not the predominant form of marriage in Africa, nor that it involves a controlled situation of sexual relations. It does not matter that the African value system placed on having children does not raise the degree of sexual promiscuity; Africans also value stable family situations that provide cultural and emotional support for children. It does not matter that traditional African culture is an extremely disciplined (compared with contemporary American society), morally ordered, kin-based and spiritually-based construct. None of these realities that abound in anthropological descriptions were made visible. Instead a white woman was shown teaching a coeducational group of 15-year-old Africans how to use condoms. It does not matter that both homosexual and heterosexual prostitution were introduced by Europeans into Africa or that moral discipline breaks down with "Europeanization."

The conclusion reached was that since it would be difficult (for all of the reasons listed above) for European "experts" to communicate with the afflicted Africans so that their "behavior" could be modified through an "understanding of the problem," AIDS could be expected to spread at an alarming rate throughout Africa. AIDS means death. We must remember that as we listen to those arguments. According to the program, women with AIDS were not told that they had AIDS, in this case supposedly for their own protection, which hardly sounds like a program of "education." The "protection" program is another interesting parallel with the Tuskegee Experiment. In their capacity as "saviors" they are now experimenting with Africans who are "desperate." Dr. Daniel Zagury, a French physician, has been experimenting in Zaire. The program portrayed his experiment as being highly secret but most probably involving the injection of purified AIDS virus into human beings in order to stimulate the immune system! Could that be done to Europeans? The answer is "no," only to the "cultural other!"

That was the prognosis for Africa (with actually only about 4,714 known AIDS cases with forty-three countries reporting). By 1992 there were reportedly 5½ million people infected in Africa. What about the outlook for the United States (with about 38,160 known AIDS cases)? According to Silverman we can actually be optimistic about the future of AIDS in the United States. Why? Because in America people can be educated, they can be reached through the media (two or three televisions in every home), and their behavior can be modified. How does he know? Because the male homosexual community in the United States has already, according to Silverman and Sabatier, responded to education about the disease and demonstrated that it is possible to consciously change sexual practices through an understanding of the implications of AIDS. Americans have cause for hope! But does that include all of those who live within its boundaries?

Ted Koppel raised the question: "You talk about polygamy in Africa, but there is casual sex in the United States. . ." (Note the incorrect association between polygamy and casual sex.) Silverman never answered Koppel's implied question. But what he *did* say parallels the position taken by the medical establishment as far back as 1913 with regard to black people.[44] Silverman said, "I didn't say we wouldn't have some problems. There are the inner city youths; the minorities; the blacks and Hispanics who must come to grips with what we are saying, and the drug addicts." The message is clear—just as it was in 1932 when the Tuskegee Experiment was initiated. Control comes with "education" and change. European-American male homosexuals can be "educated." Blacks and Latinos cannot. AIDS among male homosexuals will be contained. AIDS among blacks and Latinos will spread. Magically, everything is reversed. The percentage of known AIDS cases is highest among male homosexuals, but in the future we can expect it to be highest among blacks and Latinos across the board. If AIDS is associated with sexual promiscuity, undisciplined behavior, "cultural difference" (different from what?), and ignorance, then what does this imply about Blacks and Latinos. People of African descent are being set up as the victims who victimize themselves; who because of their own inadequacies can expect to be ravaged by a killer disease.

In 1913, according to James Jones (1986), the American Social Hygiene Association took the position that "social hygiene for whites rested on the assumption that attitudinal changes could produce behavioral changes. A single standard of high moral behavior could be produced by molding sexual attitudes through moral education. For blacks, however, a change in their nature seemed to be required."[46] This supported their position of neglect with regard to the African community. Later it allowed the United States Government to watch black people die of syphilis and to allow it to be spread. In the 1980s the stage was set for AIDS to be understood as an African disease that spreads amidst "sexual promiscuity," ignorance, and drug abuse. With this understanding the scenario of the suffering and death of our people will appear to "make sense," no matter how much it may be lamented. The latest word from the "experts" is that Africans have a blood factor GPC that makes them more susceptible. This can be said even though initially AIDS among Europeans outnumbered AIDS among Africans by 10 to 1. Now the ratio is much closer. Already the AIDS "disinformation" is being used to discriminate against Africans. In an article entitled: "AIDS: Racist Myths, Hard Facts," correspondent David Dickson says the following:

> Some have complained bitterly that the suspicion that Africans have a higher chance of carrying the virus than populations of other continents is already used as a covert form of racist discrimination. For example, in many countries African students complain that they are being made the target of restrictions and health requirement that are not being imposed on other nationals.[47] On April 20, 1990, 100,000 African-Haitians demonstrated in New York City, protesting the fact that they were not being allowed to donate blood to their relatives.[47]

The *asili* concept tells us to look within the logic of the European *utamawazo* and *utamaroho* in order to understand, predict and interpret European behavior. AIDS is a mystery. That is clear. Let us suppose that it is a human-made virus. Suppose that it is primarily a product of biochemical warfare, secondarily spread through sexual and other contact. Dr. Frances Cress Welsing puts forth this hypothesis, which she says is as good as any until it has been proven to be wrong. Is there any supporting evidence? In Dr. Welsing's view:

> Indeed, a number of aware black people have systematically raised the question as to whether or not this new virus was "man-made" and possibly manufactured at a facility such as the center at Ft. Derrick, Maryland or other such centers in the western world that are involved in the research on and the production of chemical and biological warfare weapons.

She continues,

> The Tuskegee experiments were conducted by the United States Government, namely, the United States Public Health Administration

and the Center for Disease Control in Atlanta, Georgia. It was even then verbalized that allowing the spread of syphilis could be a method used to destroy the black population.

Thus, aware black people do not find it at all inconceivable that persons with the same mind-set and psychological orientation would not go further and develop a deadly disease that could be spread via the venereal route and then introduce this disease into black and other "undesirable" population groups. . . again for the purpose of a systematic depopulation agenda.[48]

The Vervet Monkey disease is referred to in *A Survey of Chemical and Biological Warfare* (1969) as a disease created by European scientists to be used to kill the enemies of Europe and Euro-America. It is unrelated to any other organism known and impervious to any known antibiotics. Handling of blood and tissues can cause infection. Infection causes death in some cases and it can be transmitted venereally. The Vervet Monkey and the African Green Monkey are of the same genus. Vervet Monkey disease is similar to the African Green Monkey disease found in East and Southern Africa. There is 95 percent nucleotide homology between STLVI (Simian) and HTLVI (human). This is evidence that the two are related and not for spontaneous mutation. Yet SLTIII and HTLVIII have only 75 percent neucleotide homology, a development which would not be expected under the normal process of evolution. This argues for intentional human manipulation. The other evidence is what we know of the capacity of Europeans to destroy those whom they consider to be cultural others. The African continent is rich with resources needed by Europe, but they do not need large numbers of African people. In fact, many Europeans believe that their problems would be solved if we were to disappear from the face of the Earth. Understanding the nature of the European *asili* as it works out in the *utamawazo* and the *utamaroho*, it is possible to develop an interpretation of AIDS that makes sense. Dr. Robert Strecker and Dr. William Douglass (along with Dr. Frances Cress Welsing) are convinced that AIDS is a human-made retrovirus. For a thorough explanation of their theory and the evidence with which they support it, the reader is referred to *The Strecker Memorandum* (a video-tape) and "Who Murdered Africa," an article by Douglass.[49] We will only mention a few of the facts and suppositions here, which impact on the question of the attempted genocide of Africans and other majority peoples.

Both Strecker and Douglass suggest that the World Health Organization is the culprit in a deadly crime that has inadvertently been perpetrated against the human race: An experiment that has gotten out of hand, to put it mildly. According to both men, without intervention, the continued existence of the human race may be in question.

> WHO [World Health Organization] is reported to have written in their bulletin that, An attempt should be made to see if viruses can in fact exert selective effects on immune function. The possibility should be looked into that the immune response to the virus itself may be impaired if the infecting virus damages, more or less selectively, the cell responding to the virus.[50]

AIDS does just that. It destroys the T-Cell system of infected human beings. Dr. Strecker claims that the AIDS virus resembles Bovine virus in cattle and the Vesna virus in sheep. He does not believe that it is related to the Green Monkey. According to Strecker, if the Bovine and Vesna viruses are crossed, AIDS is the result. Experiments have, for a long time, taken place in which animal viruses are grown in human tissue.

If the WHO had been successful in creating the virus that they have evidently "called for," how would they test it, and how would they use it? Clearly, knowing what we do about white supremacy in European nationalistic ideology, the guinea pigs would not be Europeans, and if they were, they would be "expendable" Europeans. In the "numbers game" it is very important to understand that people who prefer to have sexual relations with their own gender are likely to produce very few offspring, if any. Therefore AIDS would most likely be introduced in African populations, their descendants, other majority peoples, and European homosexuals.

It is reported that a front page article in *The Times* of London (May 11, 1987) makes the connection between centers established by the WHO, ostensibly to vaccinate people against smallpox and the locations (dates and places) in which AIDS first broke out. They are the same: Africa, Haiti, Brazil, Japan. In addition, 15,000 Haitians were working in Africa during the vaccination project and participated in it. As for the male homosexual community, the connection was made via the injection of homosexual men with Hepititus B Vaccine in a "program" in New York in 1978 and in San Franscico in 1980. The Hepititus B Vaccine-Study limited itself to "males between the ages of 20 and 40, who were not monogamous."[51]

AIDS can live outside of the body. An AIDS virus can be carried by a mosquito. These are claims for which Strecker makes rather convincing arguments. If what Strecker and Douglass say is true, "safe sex" will not prevent AIDS. All the "education" in the world will not prevent or control an AIDS epidemic. An AIDS vaccine can never be "discovered" because AIDS changes. It is estimated that there are 9000^4 possible kinds of AIDS viruses. It appears to spontaneously mutate and recombine.

To develop smallpox vaccine, scabs are taken from cattle infected with the disease. The Bovine virus could have been in the vaccines used in Africa and other areas in 1971 for people innoculated in the WHO project. It could have been accidental. If so, what a costly error! It could also have been intentional, since the creation of such a deadly disease is consistent with the rationale for biochemical warfare and with European megalomania.* There is also a theory that AIDS was introduced in a Polio Vaccine. (See *Rolling Stone,* Mar. 19, 1992.) The only mistake made by the "mad" European scientists this time may have been losing control of the disease. It therefore threatens to destroy those who it was intended to serve. But ultimately, such are the implications of the European *asili.*

Dr. Barbara Justice, a New York surgeon of African descent, believes: (1) The AIDS virus has been adapted to Melanin and is related to the experiment in 1951 with the death of a Diasporic African patient, Henrietta Lass, in which European scientists were able to grow viruses outside of the body in her cells after she had died: (2) The purpose of AIDS is to "clean out" the European gene pool, i.e., to eliminate "undesirables," Africans, and homosexuals; as well as to finally capture the continent of Africa by destroying its present, indigenous population.[52] She refers us to the work of Jack Felder and Alan Cantwell, Jr.[53]

In 1989 African scientists in Kenya, after years of research, developed a possible cure for AIDS based on Interferons. Its success attracted pharmaceutical companies, and together they are now manufacturing a product known as Kemron. In July 1990, an international conference was held in Kenya at KEMRI (the Kenya Medical Research Institute) to announce what they said was a tremendous breakthrough. According to Dr. D. Koech and Dr. A. Obel, writing in the *East African Medical Journal,*

> One hundred and ninety nine symptomatic and 5 asymptomatic patients seropositive for the human immunodeficiency virus type 1 (HIV-1) were treated with KEMRON, a natural human interferon alpha (nHIFa) stabilized in a complex polysachariche carrier. Treatment was given for at least 10 weeks at a daily oral dose of

* For documentation of actual experiments, see *Clouds of Secrecy,* Leonard A. Cole, Savage Md: Little, Adams Quality Paperback, 1990.

approximately 2.0 IU of nHIFa per kg body weight. Karnofsky performance score increased from an average of 60.5 on entry into the study to 100 by the 10th week after treatment. Similarly, common clinical complaints associated with HIV-l infection rapidly reduced per patient from an average of 3.8 to 0.05 and 0 by week 8 and 10 of treatment. Eighteen of the patients serodeconverted by both ELISA and western blot assays during the study period. These observations suggest that KEMRON used as recommended is beneficial in HIV-l seropositive individuals.[54]

   While this was obviously an event of enormous universal significance, no European-American media personnel attended the conference.
   This fact demonstrates the relationship between the European genocidal enterprise against African people, white and Western nationalism, and the European self-image and image of others, which we have discussed in Chap. 4 and 5. The idea of African scientists discovering a cure for a disease that threatens to destroy the world's human population is such an anathema to a "positive," "functional" European self-image, that the Kenyans cannot be given credit, nor could pictures appear of the African scientists in the Euro-American media. We must remember that these are, according to Europeans, the same people who were too ignorant and "backward" to understand the nature of the disease.The United States media did not report KEMRON until it felt comfortable discussing the "controversy" in which it was "embroiled." At the same time Kemron is being discredited, European scientists are working with Interferons in the hope of implementing an AIDS cure, and a Euro-American physician from Texas is claiming to have created it. So that African people, still lose, for the manufacture, distribution, and "ownership" of KEMRON is denied us.
   Perhaps we are faced with the same situation as with the syphilis experiment. Perhaps in both cases we were "given" this disease by Europeans as a genocidal act. Our destruction is then justified to the world by our supposed lack of humanity. *The New York Times*, in May of 1987, printed an article that discussed the alarming rate of population growth in Africa and the equally alarming decline in population growth for whites. Dr. Welsing and white racists themselves have told us that Europeans are afraid of the implications of minority status. Now the United States Government is talking about mandatory blood tests (Reagan: May 31, 1987 speech). What intelligent African would trust such a program? If AIDS does not destroy us, it can certainly be used to control us. The rule is to always reverse European

statements in order to ascertain the truth, and to *always* interpret their actions and statements politically. When they discuss cures for our diseases, we know that they may already be in the process of causing our annihilation by giving us another disease they have created.

There is, of course, another facet of the European genocidal assault on the health of First World and majority peoples. Toxic waste is dumped where we live! According to Donovan Marks:

- Although socio-economic status plays an important role in the location of commercial hazardous waste facilities, race is the leading factor.
- Three out of the five largest commerical hazardous waste landfills in the United States are located in mostly Black or Hispanic communities; these landfills account for 40 percent of the nation's estimated landfill space.
- Three out of five Black and Hispanic Americans live in communities with one or more uncontrolled toxic waste sites.
- 60 percent of the total Black population (15 million) live in communities with one or more uncontrolled toxic waste sites.
- Cities with large Black populations like St Louis, Houston, Cleveland, Chicago, Atlanta, and Memphis have the largest numbers of uncontrolled toxic waste sites.
- Los Angeles has more Hispanics living in communities with uncontrolled toxic waste sites than any other metropolitan area in the U.S. The higher the concentration of Hispanics in an area of the city, the higher the concentration of uncontrolled waste in the same area.
- About half of all Asian/Pacific Islanders and Native Americans live in communities with uncontrolled waste sites.

First World countries are considered garbage dumps by Europeans. We are, afterall, for them the cultural other ("garbage").

- NIGERIA: Between August 1987 and May 1988, almost 4,000 tons of toxic wastes were dumped in Koko, Nigeria. As a result, the people of this small port town have seen a corresponding increase in the number of cholera patients and premature births.
- GUINEA (Conakry): In February 1988, a shipment of garbage and incinerator ash from Philadelphia, which had been previously rejected by Panama and Haiti, was dumped on Kassa Island, a short distance off-shore from the capital, Conakry. Reportedly, it "caused trees on the island to turn brown and die."
- SOUTH AFRICA: The segregated townships and rural homelands in which Africans are forced to live under the system of apartheid

are targets for both international and South African government dumping. American Cyanamid exports 100 tons of mercury wastes each year to Thor Chemicals in Cato Ridge, South Africa. The mercury has contaminated the nearby marshes and Mngeweni River, which flows down into the Valley of a Thousand Hills where the local population uses the water for drinking, cooking, and washing.

- HAITI: In October 1987, the Haitian government issued an import permit for fertilizer to the Khian Sea. The ship's cargo, however, consisted of 13,476 tons of toxic municipal incinerator ash from Philadelphia.[55]

There are many more examples of this pattern of behavior, including punitive measures taken by the European Economic Community and other such European nationalistic organizations when we refuse to be used as garbage pails for European waste. The Environment Community Development and Race Project, directed by Dana A. Alston is supporting a resistance movement.

Theories of Euro-Caucasian Behavior: The Question of Cause

"The power of one man or group of men over others—in our case, of white men over black—is the single most salient thread of history,"[56] and slavery, Kovel asserts is, "the most extreme version of the western symbolic matrix."[57] Kovel does not realize it, but it takes the European world view to understand history as being based on power relationships; such an understanding issues from a confrontational *utamawazo* that insists on definitions of dominance and submission. Nonetheless his comments bring us to the question of the relationship of what is commonly called "racism" to the power drive in European culture. That these two phenomena are related is clear, but the nature of that relationship is not as easily understood.

In Kovel's view the problem of "racism" is "part of the problem of western culture" and "the record of history is basically of the successions of that power. All the complexities of culture are harmonics about this basic theme."[58] What happened to the thousands of years before Europeans had any power to speak of, indeed, before there was a "Europe" at all?

It is because the dynamics of race and ethnicity are so intimately related to the European power drive that I prefer to particularize the European commitment to "white nationalism" or "white supremism" as a dominant component of Western European nationalism. White supremism can never be reduced to the mere definition of peoples and cultures in terms of race. Race or group consciousness, which might logically result in the desire to remain separate and distinct, is qualitatively different from an ideology that requires the physical presence and dehumanization of other peoples for the "acting out" of a power relationship in which the actor has supreme control over those peoples. The conative striving for power as motivating factor here becomes the crucial element.

Let us broaden the terms. The power drive is placed in the formulative and originating process of European culture. The cultural other becomes a creation of that power drive as valued behavior. "Race" (the concept that ambiguously links culture with the gene pool and color) is then one of the determining factors in a cultural identification and, therefore, a definitive component in the European conception of the cultural other.

The value of any theory of white supremism, from an African-centered perspective, lies in its ability to lay bare the dynamics and centricity of the power relationship in European ideology and behavior. Whether it is the "anal personality" theory of Joel Kovel, the "genetic inferiority-complex" theory of Frances Welsing, the Northern Cradle theory of Cheikh Anta Diop, the psychopathic racial personality theory of Bobby Wright, or the historical analyses of W.E.B. DuBois and earlier Pan-Africanists—in each case their value lies in the fact that they place white supremism squarely within the matrix of European ideology and biocultural development. They particularize what they call "white racism" within the spectrum of patterns of behavior based on the idea of race. The significant and indisputable ethnological fact in this regard is that the European conceives of the desirable power relationship in terms of his (white) supremacy over the (black or "colored") cultural other. Whatever its etiology the cultural fact is that the self-image and concept of the European includes "whiteness," while the "cultural other" is its dialectical opposite. Welsing points out, as does Johari Amini, that the European gives to people of other cultures "categories which are dysfunctional" for them.[59]

The present study seeks to explain the pattern of European cultural (group) behavior in terms of the nature of the culture itself. We have demonstrated European behavior towards others (exploitative and destructive imperialism) and attitude towards others (disdain, xenophobia) to be connected within the *asili* or logos of the culture, both to each other and to other patterns within the culture, and our objective is to understand that essential nature (*asili*).

But we have not gone outside of the culture—that is, in a logical sense—to look for an external cause of its peculiar nature. We have sought to identify and understand its *asili*, but not to theorize as to what could have caused such a strange *asili*; what could have caused such an atypical, fanatical "seed" to have been planted in the first place.

Perhaps that question can never be answered satisfactorily, but there are those who have tried. And it is a question that begs to be asked. Why is it that Europeans, who are "white" (a small minority of the world), should exhibit this inordinate power drive that becomes the basis of their culture, which they seek to exercise over those who are not white, or stated positively, those who "have color" (the vast majority)? Why is it that this culture created by European Caucasians appears to be singular among the world's cultures? Why is European culture different in ways that all other cultures are the same? It has a materialistic world-view, whereas other cultural world-views are more spiritualistic in nature. It is individualistic, whereas other cultures have communalistic social structures.

Weber implies that the difference is intellectual. The intelligence of these European Caucasians (whom he calls "western") allowed them to create more "universal" forms. And of course the entire history of European civilization (culture in time) is one of such interpretations. When a racial term is used we have called such interpretations "racist." But this term obfuscates more than it clarifies, because of the moralistic undertones that accompany its use. It never seems to have occurred to any European theorist that the problem was not association of white skin with greater intelligence, rather it was with equating European culture with intelligence, value, or superiority.

We must simply ask the question head on: Can it be an accident that the only people who have built an entire culture based on the dominance of others are also the only ones who are Caucasian? It doesn't matter if it is argued that some few Caucasians do not participate in this system of world-wide dominance. The generalized question begs to be asked.

Bobby Wright, an African psychologist, says simply that the collective behavior of Europeans "reflects an underlying biologically transmitted proclivity with roots deep in evolutionary history."[60] He says that the pattern of behavior that we have been describing is symptomatic of the "psychopathic personality," who, while usually functioning well in (European) society,

- is of average or above average "intelligence,"[61]
- is unable to experience guilt,
- has no feeling of insecurity,

- is unable to accept blame or to learn from experience,
- is sexually inadequate and has difficulty forming close personal relationships,
- appears to be honest and human, but has only selfish motivations,[62]
- has almost no ethical development,
- has almost total disregard for appropriate patterns of behavior,
- consistently ignores concepts of right and wrong,
- and rejects constituted authority.

Wright's boldly African-centered posture placed him in the vanguard (the Ankobia), ideologically and intellectually, among people with an African consciousness in the early 1970s. His concerns were the same as those of the present work: that we understand the nature of European behavior so that we might be in a better position to achieve African self-determination. His untimely death in 1982 was a great loss to the African victory, but his work has propelled us forward.

Psychiatrist, Frances Cress Welsing, also says "No;" it is not coincidental that only Caucasians have based their culture on "dominance." Welsing reasons that the European drive for superiority and supremacy is pathological and that generally such "neurotic" behavior is founded on a deep sense of inadequacy. She further observes that "whites" or Euro-Caucasians represent a small minority of the world's population. What allows her to place all other peoples into the one category is the fact of melanin, which she associates with the "ability to produce color." She says that "white" indicates "the very absence of the ability to produce color."[63] She then defines "whiteness" as a "genetic inadequacy." The fact that the vast majority of the world's people do have some skin pigmentation, she says, suggests that the state of color is normal and that the opposite is abnormal. Her argument follows that European Caucasians reacted to this reality psychologically (as they came in contact with, and observed people of color), with a sense of inadequacy and inferiority, which in turn caused defensive reactions of hostility and aggression towards people with "color potential." The hostility and aggression is greatest towards people of African descent, who have "the greatest color potential." They are, therefore, most envied and feared.[64]

This response led to a primary repression of feelings of inadequacy that in turn led to a series of "defensive mechanisms," the most important of which was a "reaction formation" response:

> . . . whose aim it was to convert (at the psychological level) something that was desired and envied (skin color) but which was wholly

unattainable, into something that is discredited and despised.[65]

Whites "then set about the long drawn out task of evolving a social, political and economic structure with all attendant institutions, to give Blacks and other "non-whites" the appearance of being inferior human beings."[66]

Welsing says that "white supremacy culture degrades the act of sex and the process of self-reproduction because the whiteness, reflective of the inability to produce color, is deeply despised."[67] This would identify self-alienation as the cause of comparative European infertility. She says that hate and lack of respect outwardly manifested towards other groups is reflective of a deep self-hate and lack of self-respect on the part of European Caucasians. This aspect of her explanation certainly appeals to our common sense.

The thrust towards superiority over peoples of color, the drive towards materialism, acquisition and accumulation, the drive towards a technological culture and the drive towards power, all of which are cornerstones of the universal white supremacy culture, are viewed in terms of the color-confrontation thesis as responses to the core psychological sense of inadequacy.[68]

Welsing argues that European Caucasians are so "vulnerable" to their minority status in the world that they fictionalize the "minority" status of the true majority and project themselves as the world's majority. (Indeed, that is the impression one gets after studying "world history" from a Eurocentric perspective; or being steered towards agencies whose titles begin with the word "minority," if one is African). European Caucasians are also concerned with the birthrate of people of color and with their own comparative lack of fertility. We have seen evidence of that concern in Botha's remarks (Chap. 4).

The collective pattern of behavior resulting in the present "system of white supremacy" is, in Welsing's analysis, "the only effective and functional racism existent in the world today."[69] She says that this system is presently one of the dominating forces determining character development and personality formation and that her "theory of color confrontation" gives people of color a rational basis for understanding collective white behavior. She reasons that European Caucasians are successful in their attempt to dominate the majority of the world's people because the majority's experiences did not prepare them to understand patterns of behavior based on color deficiency and numerical inadequacy.[70] But we must bear in mind that European behavior is pathological, i.e., not to be understood as the "natural" reaction to "color deficiency." After all it is not the lack of melanin that is a "disease," but rather the behavior and *utamaroho* that, in Welsing's view, result from that deficiency. Still Welsing's theory "works" for the most part. It is a bold and refreshing description of a syndrome of cultural pathology.

Joel Kovel's theory of "white racism" is more complex, less straight forward. We will simplify it, offering as much clarity as possible, for the purpose of comparison. Kovel, also a psychiatrist, relies heavily on Freudian analysis of personality development. Freud's analysis is based on supposedly "universal" phases of psycho-biological development, said to take place in infancy and early childhood. The dynamics of these phases issue from two basic drives or instincts, again said to be universally human: These drives are sexuality (eros) and aggression and are biological givens. They have an organizing influence on mental development through a process that can be reduced to sequential phases; oral, anal, phallic and oedipal, the latter two usually being described as one; or else the oedipal phase understood as a kind of culmination or "condensation" of the first three.

The heart of the matter, in Kovel's analysis, has to do with the facts that (1) in order to deal with potentially painful conflicts that arise through these phases in infant and childhood development, in which the child's personality is structured and individuation occurs, fantasies structured around symbols are created; and (2) culture both uses these symbols that are created by its members, and provides them for the members, again, on a socially structured level, through the development of the superego which relates directly to cultural norms. In short, Kovel's theory of white racism revolves around the use of infantile symbolic fantasy.

The most important phases for an understanding of his theory appear to be the anal, phallic, and oedipal. The anal is most important of all, since it is in this phase that ideas about excrement are formed. The body is "split" into good (property to be incorporated and possessed) and bad (all that is "dirty" and to be expelled). While the child is being taught to control the elimination process, he (Freudians always refer to males) begins the process of "individuation," the awareness of himself as being separate from his mother.

This process, necessary for normal human development, is painful. The child is conflicted and angry. And so we are introduced to what appears to the a chronic "conflict" between the two drives/instincts endemic to human life: that between eros (the desire to join with other) and aggression (the desire to control and act upon that which is separate from the self). "Anality is the form of drive behavior which predominates during that time when a child is painfully detaching himself from his mother and establishing himself as a separate person."[71] Excrement becomes symbolically associated with ambivalence towards separation from the mother and establishment of autonomy. What is defined as "dirt" or bad becomes the object of anger because of the separation. (But what about cultures in which dirt is "sacred earth" and even feces is associated with fertility? Whom did Freud observe?)

According to Kovel, the love of possessions becomes the substitute for the love from which the child is separating. But aggression is necessary for individuation, and yet aggression towards those whom we love must be repressed. Repression "causes" the development of the unconscious, into which many infantile fantasies are pushed; it is also a necessary by-product of these complex and involved processes. In the phallic/oedipal phase eros becomes associated with the parent of the opposite sex, which is culturally unacceptable. Somehow the male fears castration as the punishment for the incestuous desires, since his sexuality is now focused in his genitals, and he secretly wishes to remove his father's genitals. The child resolves this "complex" by establishing the superego, which "tames his instinctual drives in the interests of cultural pursuits."[72] We have seen a slightly different version of this scenario in the theory of Eli Sagan (Chap. 7).

The Freudian concept of the id appears to be the most threatening to functional social life, since it is described as a "sea" of repressed striving, cut off from reality, unable to act on the world. It is unconscious. The ego, which seems to be the "personality" (in ordinary language), appears to mediate between the unsocialized id and the supersocialized superego; one representing raw instinctive humanity, the other their cultural control. The ego is responsible for activity and performance. In Kovel's view, "A historical group of any potency must structure its culture so as to maximize this kind of ego development among its individuals."[73] But Kovel is not clear as to what he means by "potency." It could be translated as "power," or "aggression." Then he would be stating the assumptions of European ideology.

Now we can move towards a more specifically directed discussion of European culture and the behavior and attitude towards others that it generates—often referred to as "racism." Culture, says

Kovel, is parallel to personality. Infantile aggression is translated into cultural terms, and culture must provide us a "nuclear representation of what men need in order to lift themselves out of the impossible situation of their infantile conflicts."[74] Culture provides meaningful symbols that are "congruent with the personalities of the people within the society."[75] What is important will "endure and matter," influencing other aspects of the culture and remaining part of human consciousness.[76] "Culture provides a worldly scaffolding on which men can erect their inner conflicts."[74] Kovel says that in this way culture helps to give autonomy to the person and a "measure of peace" to his ego. "In this way culture accumulates infantile fantasies through history." The mind gets to know culture through the infantile experience of the body.

All of this allows Kovel to conclude that racist belief is based on fantasy. Racism is a specific historical situation "in which some elemental aspects of human experience are turned toward the classification (and oppression) of people with different ethnic traits." He argues that race fantasies are only secondarily related to racial realities; that they are "actually generated in the universal human setting of childhood, and used by the culture to handle its historical problems."[77] These fantasies are "remnants" of infantile wishes and products of developing human drives and forms of thought. We must remember that during the anal phase "dirt" (bad; to be avoided) becomes the focal point of anger at separation from the mother, while "the Oedipus complex provides the fantasy substratum for the entire historical progression of patriarchal power."[78] The superego that emerges directs aggression back into the self, thereby achieving inner control.

> By adjusting his superego to the set of cultural controls a person adapts and becomes "normal." If he is a white American, it is likely that he will then find an outlet for some of his infantile fantasies about dirt, property, power and sexuality, in his culture's racism."[78]

And further,

> The historical power we study as part of the problem of racism is in some way derived along with race symbols and fantasies—"along with" and not "from" for power is not derived from racism any more than racism is derived directly from power: both the mental attitudes necessary for power within our culture, and those that underly our variant of racism, are generated from common ground. ... I hope to show that the power of which I write stems from a view of the universe that takes the symbols of *whiteness* and *blackness*

with a deadly seriousness, spreads them out to the whole of human activity, and from that point, onto the many-hued skins of men, thereby reducing them to categories of race.[79]

We have come all this way and still the question looms: Why Europeans? Why should *they* be so power-hungry, aggressive, and "racist?" What accounts for their difference? Kovel talks around the issue throughout his book. But his treatment frustrates our desires to account for the peculiar nature of European culture. After all, according to Freud and Kovel, we all experience the same phases of mental/biological development. Is Kovel's argument that the phases are actually cultural phases as well and that European culture some- how experienced a distorted or unresolved anal phase of develop- ment? No, that is not what he says. What follows is the closest he comes to a causal explanation:

A lightly-hued people—aided perhaps by fantasies from their skin color—came to dominate the entire world, and in the process defined themselves as white. The process that generated this white power also generated the fear and dread of black.[80]

Here we have the reverse of Welsing's analysis. In Kovel's view "whiteness" initially represented something desirable to Europeans, and "blackness" represented something negative. No inferiority com- plex here. Kovel goes on to ask the question: How has the West used the themes of black and white to generate power? His answer: All people always have been afraid of darkness. (Quite an assumption to make. We will see that darkness can have a very different connotation indeed!) But "what has distinguished the West from other cultures is that these elementary issues, without their infantile core, have taken on fantastic elaboration: They have been used systematically and organically in the generation of power. No other culture has so drawn upon these primitive beliefs to superordinate itself to others."[80]

Kovel's conclusion with regard to the cause of Europe's strange behavior is certainly disappointing. It seems that on the one hand Europeans became racist because they happened to be white (or almost) and therefore to "fit" infantile symbolic elaboration con- cerning the feces and "good" and "bad" body in the right way—a way that places them in a position to achieve power over the rest of the world, which was darker ("bad" body). Other groups could not make the same use of this "universal" fantasy since they were darker. At the same time the purity that is for them (Europeans) symbolized by their whiteness leads to rationalism. They have combined a "pure form of thought" (*utamawazo*) with an endless source of energy (*uta-maroho*) a "restless zeal" or "fanaticism."[81] First, Europeans split "reason" and "energy"; then, they combined them as part of an inexorable momentum. The result is that "the western genius," which yields pride in whiteness, pulls together these divergent styles into one cultural entity; and Europeans are therefore intensely driven and intensely controlled at the same time.[82] For Kovel this is a "gift" that succeeds in achieving wealth, technological skill, social organization, as well as power. And it is based on racist belief or at least the cultural elaboration of the symbols of black and white that are created during infantile fantasizing.

And so we have a fascinating—if not totally satisfying—explanation of European behavior. Kovel suggests a cause for racist behavior and a reason for the achievement of power but neither a cause nor a reason for the inordinate desire for power over others. He seems to assume that all human groups *desire* power but that the "genius" of the "West" is to have discovered the best way of achieving it, or put another way, to have been fortunately endowed with white skin! From an African-centered perspective, this explanation is not acceptable since it embraces the values that are supposedly under criticism.

This brings us directly to the limitations of Kovel's analysis. He has universalized the particular! It is ironic, but not surprising, for this is a typically European mistake/weapon. This penchant for universalizing is a characteristic of European ideology (discussed in Chap. 10). Kovel leads us towards a piercing indictment of European culture in terms of the depth to which its racialist ideology reaches. Indeed, he is arguing that the success of the culture depends on the symbols of white racism. But the pessimism with which his book concludes is a result of his having dug a hole from which it is impossible to escape. Why should Europeans want to yield power? If their racism, aggression, and materialism assure their power, then these forms of behavior must be maintained.

Kovel, just as the theorist on which he depends so heavily, has perhaps brilliantly described the workings of the European mind; but it is precisely because he relies unquestioningly on Freudian analysis, that he cannot step outside of European assumptions. Freudian theory assumes the European world-view. It is based on conceptions dictated by the European *utamawazo*. Whatever brilliance of analysis contributed to this theory, it had to be formulated in terms of European conceptions of reality. The Freudian model is therefore materialistic and mechanistic. It begins and ends in biological determinism; a despirited biology at that.

On what grounds does Kovel universalize a split between body and spirit? How many First World or majority cultures were studied before it was agreed that all human beings go through the phases of mental organization and psychological development as described by Freud? The very definition of racism is limited if one's conceptualization remains within the European frame of reference. To those of us who are African, Freud's distinctions between "primitive" peoples and "modern civilized man" are offensive.[83] In these distinctions the only value of African and other majority cultures is that they afford Europeans an opportunity for studying their own neurotic ambivalences. In *Totem and Taboo*, Freud says that he will focus on "the most backward and miserable savages, the aborigines of Australia," because of their relationship to "prehistoric man." He appears to use "primitive" and "prehistoric" imprecisely, sometimes linking them together. Nevertheless, according to Freud there are contemporaries of Europeans who resemble "prehistorics":

> Such is our view of those who we describe as savages or half-savages; and their mental life must have a peculiar interest for us if we are right in seeing in it a well-preserved picture of an early stage of our own development.

> If that supposition is correct, a comparison between the psychology of primitive peoples, as it is taught by social anthropology, and the psychology of neurotics, as it has been revealed by psychoanalysis, will be bound to show numerous points of agreement and will throw new light upon familiar facts in both sciences.[84]

Such presumption! Do Europeans become mentally healthier as they "evolve?" This is the theorist upon whose assumptions Kovel bases his theory of white racism! Freud, who admittedly relies on the descriptions of First World peoples by Europeans, arrogantly uses the theories he, a European, has developed to analyze "non-European" peoples. He fits the *asili* of European culture. Kovel is caught in the same trap. It is the trap of the cultural behavior that he describes. Ultimately Kovel fails to place Europe in the world. He isolates the culture in a cocoon of Freudian theory, then (falsely) extends the threads of the cocoon that prevents him from understanding its peculiar nature in totality. To understand the peculiarity of the European means to understand other people, i.e., the rest of humanity; and the assumption of the European world-view precludes that understanding by its very nature.

The importance of Kovel's analysis is: (1) that it connects white racism to capitalist aggression; (2) that it leads to the conclusion that since white racism generates power, Europeans will never cease to be racist; and, most impressively and significantly when critqued from an African-centered perspective, (3) that European attitudes and cultural behavior towards other racial/cultural groups are linked ethnologically or psycho-culturally to rationalism or to what Kovel calls "pure thought."

In our terms it lodges white racialist ideology comfortably within the European *utamawazo*, while the European *utamaroho* dictates white racist behavior. It is important to understand that "rationalism" does not mean "reasonableness" in terms of African and other majority conceptual systems. European rationalism, again, so clearly elaborated in Platonic thought, is predicated on the separation of reason and emotion, with "the will" being placed at the service of the now isolated, uncontaminated "reason."

It was Plato who postulated the "Forms," which represented a higher sphere of existence, untainted by the vulnerability and fallability of ordinary human perception, a cognition that was unable to guarantee its conclusions. European logic becomes the guarantor. The "forms" are pure. The pursuit of this mental purity is rationalism. As a human cultural attitude it sacrifices much. Rather than leading to the perfect morality, as Plato would have us believe, it leads to systematic racist behavior and the construction of institutions that yield power. In this sense the most "rational" Europeans (the Harvard professors?) become the most effective supporters of the superstructure that guarantees European (minority) power over non-Europeans (the majority): i.e., white racism. (What does this imply about an *African* Harvard professor?)

The limitation of Kovel's analysis is that it cannot help us to look critically at the European world-view, because he uses its assumptions. He, therefore, cannot explain the source of the fanatical European power drive. In my view, the inordinate power drive is lodged within the formulative and originating process of the culture; this is the *asili*. It becomes visible only from the vantage point of an other-than-European world-view. Its visibility is aided by an African-centered perspective.

For Welsing, "white" represents the absence of melanin or the absence of the ability to produce color. This "absence," as well as the fact that most of the world's people possess "color potential," creates feelings of inferiority on the part of Europeans, "white people." For Kovel, white (which he says is scientifically the sum of all colors) becomes the symbol of the absence of color and therefore represents purity. It is therefore the root of the feeling of superiority. Both theorists use psychoanalytical models: Welsing, the language of "reaction-formation"; Kovel, the language of infantile anal fantasy. An advantage of Welsing's theory is that it is not based on a universalization of the European experience or European particularity. While Kovel's theory leads to the conclusion that basically all cultures (all people) are potentially "white racist" and driven to have power over others if they had the opportunity or the "genius" or the "whiteness."

Both Welsing and Kovel recognize that white racism is a form of behavior that is systematic. This is important, since it helps us to understand that Europeans have constructed a system of institutions which depend on and encourage a particular pattern of behavior towards "people of color"; i.e., a form of behavior that has been called "racist." The style of behavior is, therefore, lodged comfortably within the matrix of European culture—not a blight to be removed by cosmetic surgery.

Michael Bradley offers another fascinating theory of European racism in his book, *Iceman Inheritance*. Certainly more convoluted than Kovel's, and perhaps even more complex, Bradley's theory is troubled with contradictions but, nonetheless, brings some significant peculiarities of European culture to the surface.

> A uniquely aggressive creature shivered beside his cave fire during the icy Wurm, a uniquely alienated creature, a creature uniquely conscious of physical differences among people . . . and distrustful of those differences.[85]

Here we have Bradley's theory of the strange story of Western civilization and of the origin of its extreme aggression, violent behavior, and propensity for sexism and racism. Bradley begins his book with the statement: "This book is racist." He never elaborates on the statement. But from the analysis offered in his book, it can be interpreted to mean either (1) that since European Caucasians are "naturally" racist because of their genetic inheritance and since he is a European Caucasian, what he writes is necessarily racist, or (2) that the terms that he uses deal with racialist categories and conceptions, linking cultural and behavioral traits to biological and evolutionary factors (circumstances).

Simply outlined, Bradley's argument is that:

1. Contemporary European Caucasians have evolved specifically from the European Neanderthal and have therefore inherited cultural proclivities that developed as a result of the necessities of Neanderthal adaptation during the glacial period (Wurm I), which

effected Europe "the cradle of the Caucasoid race."[86]

2. These Neanderthals were also the first humans to "discover time" or put differently, since for Bradley this "discovery" is the mark of "humanness," they are, strictly speaking, the first "humans." It is important for Bradley that Neanderthal's passed over the "threshold" of humanness while surviving the ice age.

3. Since, according to Bradley, animals are naturally aggressive with regard to territory (especially males), these first humans extended their animal aggression to the new territory of time, i.e., "the Chronos complex," therefore developing a competitive/aggressive relationship to their past, which they must "outdistance" (progress), and to the future, which they must limit. The future, represented by their offspring, threatens to "usurp their territory of time." Therefore, they are, to say the least, ambivalent about reproducing their own kind. This last point fits Welsing's theory, who says that European sexual ambivalence comes from a lack of self-esteem, since they cannot produce color. For Bradley this ambivalence results in "psychosexual conflicts." He assumes that aggression towards the past and the future is a "normal" or "natural" human response. (Wright, Welsing, and Bradley all appear to agree on the characteristic of sexual conflict.)

4. Because of the demands of physical adaptation caused by the extremely harsh, frigid environment during Wurm I, "nature's sexual adaptations conflicted in large measure with Neanderthal glacial adaptations."[87] Nature, says Bradley, works against human temporal territorial approach-avoidance" so that human beings will procreate. Nature does this through sexual adaptations that tempt males and females to engage in sexual intercourse. But in the case of Neanderthal evolution it was also necessary to combat the extreme cold. Neanderthals had to be extremely hairy, heavy, and squat. The male genitalia could not be large or else it would be more vulnerable to the cold. At the same time, says Bradley, nature compensated to a degree by making the female breasts extremely large in the Neanderthal. (Don't they get cold?) The female pelvic area also had to be quite large in order to allow passage of the head of the Neanderthal infant, which he says was "huge."[88] Bradley uses the "Venus figures" to substantiate his claim as to the appearance of the Neanderthal female.[89] But Cheikh Anta Diop uses these same figures as evidence of the presence of African Grimaldy humans in Eurasia. He also brings attention to recent finds of Neanderthal in Africa and cautions that all of the facts aren't in with regard to its place of origin.[90]

5. The exigencies of Neanderthal survival resulted in extreme sexual dimorphism. Males and females looked so different, says Bradley, that he is "inclined to believe that. . .each tended to regard the other as something of a distinct species."[87] Caucasoid sexes, whom he links to Neanderthal (while contradictorally denying them generic continuity), "have never really got used to each other, never really completely trusted each other."[91] A high degree of sexual dimorphism heightened the aggression surrounding sexual encounters given the "temporal territorial behavior." The result is xenophobia, or fear of difference.

6. The dominance of patriarchy and sexism in European culture Bradley explains by drawing an analogy with the tendency of male animals tend to be more territorially aggressive. And therefore as this aggressive behavior extends to temporality, males approach the act of sex with a greater degree of anger and frustration than females.[91] Bradley says that while this is normal to all human males it would be more extreme with the increased sexual dimorphism resulting from Neanderthal development.

Using the approach outlined, Bradley attempts to explain European Caucasian aggression, violent behavior, racism, xenophobia, sexual ambivalence, comparative infertility, alienation, and sexism. In Bradley's view, religion results from the need to communicate with the past, while writing develops because of a need to communicate with the future. The priests and intellectuals, more aware of "time," are more sexually ambivalent, less sexually active, and therefore less fertile. The "average" Caucasoids imitate these "men." Therefore aggression, which would be displaced in sexual activity, is instead directed in violence against other people. The few occasions where males and females do join must be enveloped in the illusion of romantic love—a "truce" made necessary by the severity of European xenophobia and aggression.

Yet, after all this, Bradley says that Caucasoid aggression is not innate, not "racial," and not immutable. Instead, he concludes that western civilization can avoid aggression through sexual-sensual activity, as did ancient "Egyptian" and Chinese civilization. Since, for Bradley, patterns of European behavior towards others is caused by an inordinate degree of undisplaced aggression,

If we are going to borrow something of the world-view from these [Egyptian and Chinese] civilizations in order to combat our own anti-man and anti-nature psychology, then we have an obligation to borrow something of everything from these cultures. We have this obligation because we do not know which of their cultural and racial traits prevented them from making our mistakes.[92]

Perhaps the most unique aspect of Bradley's argument is his conclusion that European values and behavior towards others may be causally tied to European sexual-sensual life. For Bradley, the sexual-sensual is the key to combatting the "anti-human-mono-culture" that is Western civilization. And yet his explanation is not of the Freudian mold; in fact it would seem to contradict Freud's slavish commitment to supposed universal phases of psycho-intellectual development; a model that paints Europeans as normal rather than pathological.

Bradley's theory is creative and speculative. He is accurate in his identification of European pathology, but unfortunately, like Kovel, he assumes certain European conceptions of reality. "Time," so important a part of his theory, is lineal time. It is not a "discovery" but the invention of a materialist understanding. Ironically, Bradley reveals his own ignorance of the spiritualistic and cosmological world-views to which he says Europeans need expose themselves. The African philosophical conception of ancestor communion transcends lineal time and allows people to avoid the limitations of their mortal and finite existences. Africans exist, through cosmic and sacred time, both in the past and the future, as they experience the present. In fact, the distinctions between past, present, and future disappear since the conception is not lineal, but cyclical, spiraling. Having children becomes an honor of participating symbolically in the primordial act of creation. It is a spiritual necessity, a cultural obligation, since birth represents the continuance of the group, and of the "self," our own immortality. Our ancestors and origins are repeated in sacred symbols through which we unite with them, not compete with them.

Such ignorance leads Bradley to a misunderstanding of religion or at least of spiritual concepts. He correctly says that all religions have a concept of time beyond birth and death.[93] But because he again perceives through European eyes, he understands religion as "a symptom that man has claimed a territory which is larger than a single life." His language is the language of the European. For us the religious sense would be the recognition that *we* are indeed "claimed" by a universe that extends beyond the finiteness of our single, physical selves. This is where the concept of the soul comes in; a concept that Bradley never mentions. Our spirituality is the recognition of spiritual connectedness, beyond lineal, ordinary, profane time. This recognition energizes our humanity, influences our priorities, and prevents the alienation that Europeans experience.

If we accept Bradley's definition of humaness (the discovery of lineal time), a by-product of superior intelligence, and his explanation of the "religious" conceptions that human temporal aggresssion necessitates, then Europeans contradictorily emerge as the most intelligent and religious of human groups, since in his view, their direct evolutionary ancestors "discovered time," and therefore Caucasians are the most temporally aggressive of all.

But if we say instead that the natural evolution of sapienism was not with aggression, but with the articulation of consciousness and the creation of culture that limited aggressive and violent behavior, then a very different picture emerges. In this view, the aggression of the European Caucasian becomes even more of an anomaly, and the key to the humanity of African, and other majority civilizations is due to more than their sexual-sensual life; rather it is due to a deeper, more profound cultural existence of which the sexual-sensual is only a part.

Bradley tries and successfully recognizes a connection between biology and psycho-cultural development, though perhaps not their correct connection—and in a different manner from Welsing and Kovel. He understands some of the failings of the culture and styles of thought of Europeans, such as their inability to deal with paradox and inconsistency, which for them represent irreconcilable contradiction.[94] And he understands European technology and "progress" as "future-limiting," "present-identity assertions" that function to enhance the power of the present.[95] But he misses the point in attempting to lodge all of the ills of European cultural behavior in the "ugly" "precociousness" of the Neanderthal.

Cheikh Anta Diop, in the process of refuting Engles, Bachofen, Morgan and others on the origin and significance of "matriarchy" and matrilineality, elaborates a theory of the origins of the European world-view and the pattern of collective behavior that it generates. We have already introduced his ideas in our discussion of European religion (Chap. 2); now it only remains to highlight some of the relevant aspects of his approach.

In explanation of European behavior, Diop, like Bradley, makes much of the nature of the environment in which the Indo-European or Aryan has developed. He refers to this area as the "Northern Cradle of Civilization." But unlike Bradley he does not focus on supposed psycho-biological evolutionary development of early pre-Caucasoids. Instead he concentrates on a much later period (ca. 18,000 B.C.E.) when cultures were beginning to be formed. He posits two "Cradles of Civilization," Northern (Aryan) and Southern (African), which because of their vastly different geographical environments, generated two very different world-views and therefore two very different life-styles and modes of behavior.

These different environments created different "collective personalities." Again the harshness of the environmental conditions of Eurasia comes into play, but this time it is at a later period, subsequent to the ice age, when the Eurasian steppes and forest areas of Northern Europe had been formed. Diop's focus on cultural evolution, rather than physical evolution begins here. These conditions did not allow for the agriculturally sedentary, peaceful life of the Southern Cradle. They forced these early Aryans into a nomadic existence in which women and children were regarded as liabilities, since in the absence of agriculture, their contribution to material survival was extremely limited. The lack of agriculture and of other survival resources severely limited the opportunities for cooperation as a model for social organization; instead these meager resources encouraged a competitive, aggressive attitude toward one's neighbor, i.e., a fierce individualistic battle over the little that existed.

> The ferocity of nature in the Eurasian steppes, the barrenness of those regions, the overall circumstances of material conditions, were to create instincts necessary for survival in such an environment. . . . Here, nature left no illusions of kindliness. . .he must learn to rely on himself alone. . . he would conjure up deities maleficent and cruel, jealous and spiteful. . . . .All the peoples of the area whether white or yellow, were instinctively to love conquest because of a desire to escape from hostile surroundings. . . they had to leave it or succumb, try to conquer a place in the sun in a more clement nature.[96]

Survival in these circumstances rested more on the ability to view others with suspicion than as potential allies. As they encountered people who looked different, they reacted xenophobically and treated others first with suspicion, then aggression. This behavioral mode evolved as a way of life. Diop goes so far as to associate the comparatively larger amount of meat in the Indo-European diet (compared with that of the "Southern Cradle") with their aggressive nature.

Diop's treatment of European patriarchal social structure is interesting. Devalued as functional social beings, women, he says, became viewed with disdain. In fact, the dowries offered by the women's parents became the inducement for men to take wives. The pursuant subjugation of women created guilt in the culture, which, according to Diop, responded with the tragedy of Oedipus; that is, the tragic perspective. This certainly is a very different interpretation of the significance of this infamous tragedy from that of Freud, Kovel and Sagan. The world-view of this Northern Cradle is characteristically pessimistic and guilt-ridden, giving birth to such concepts as original sin.[97] Diop appears to be an environmentalist.

> An ideal of war, violence, crime and conquests, inherited from nomadic life, with, as a consequence, a feeling of guilt and of original sin, which causes pessimistic religious or metaphysical systems to be built, is the special attitude of this [Northern] "Cradle."[98]

Diop may very well be correct in emphasizing the questions of resources and their deficiency as a major influence on the shape of culture and behavior. There are few facts clearer when viewing the contemporary relationship between Europe and its diaspora and the rest of the world than of resource control. Europe, itself an environment with very meagre natural resources, is dependent on the resources of the world's First People for its survival. Europeans, who have almost nothing, have empowered themselves through systematic aggressive behavior (genocide, colonialism, imperialism, slavery), by which they have appropriated the resources of others. If they ceased to have access to those resources, they would be at the mercy of the majority.

Wobogo says that for Diop, European behavior toward other racial/cultural groups is a result of the early experience of the Northern Cradle, since a people's collective personality is determined in their first intense experience as a group, much as a child's personality is determined in its first, formulative years. The personality type persists even when conditions and geographical locations change.[99] This theory is compatible with the concept of *asili*, the cultural seed. The theorists discussed are speculating as to how the seed is planted.

For Welsing, European behavior issues from their minority status and lack of melanin, not primarily from their lack of natural resources. The ideas of Richard King, who like Kovel and Welsing is a trained psychiatrist, brings the issue of melanin back into focus, but in a startling and intellectually radical manner. More than anyone else, it is King above all who turns European symbolism on its head; discarding the European conceptual framework, he explains European behavior using an African understanding of reality; i.e., the African world-view.

As with the other theorists, we cannot hope to do justice to King's theory in a few paragraphs. It is even more difficult in his case because that involves the introduction of a non-European set of assumptions about the nature of the universe, which even we Africans are not accustomed to viewing in a reflective manner. But we will try to introduce his ideas if only to demonstrate the way in which they radically oppose those that issue from the European conceptual mode.

Since our framework is not limited to Europe, but encompasses the human universe, we must begin thousands of years before Europe or Europeans existed. And we must begin with an African definition of science as spiritually based and holistic. For his authority King returns to the source: the symbols and sacred texts of ancient Africa—Kemet (Egypt). Here he finds evidence of the scientific study of human consciousness. King's theory fixes on the pineal gland, which, though ignored by Western medicine, he says was known to these ancient Africans as "the eye of Heru," placed in the middle of the forehead, indicating the *substantia Nigra*, or black substance of the middle brain. This, he says, they knew to be the key to "inner vision," or the door to the collective unconscious, perhaps closest to what we now call "intuition." According to King, a process that takes place in the pineal gland in the brain releases chemicals that allow human beings to learn from their ancestors.[100] Already the concept of and attitude toward time that Bradley assumes is negated in this view. And Freud's perspective is reversed. We learn from these ancient people, because they knew more than we know now; they were more in touch with their humanity. We do not study them as "children" or "neurotics," as Freud implies.

According to Webster's dictionary, the pineal gland resembles a pine cone in shape and unknown function, being present in the brain of all vertebrates having a cranium; it is believed to be vestigial. But for Richard King, the pineal is not only quite functional but the key to biological and conscious life itself. How does this relate to European behavior?

The pineal gland secretes melatonin, which activates the pituitary to release M.S.H. (Melanocyte Stimulating Hormone). It is in the melanocytes that melanin (Fr. Greek *melas*="Black") is produced . Melanin is somewhat analogous to chlorophyll in plants. While chlorophyll allows photosynthesis to occur, or the transference of the sun's energy into food, melanin in animals takes the sun's energy and makes it useful energy for the body. While the growth of plants is directed toward physical sunlight, King contends that the growth of human beings is directed toward higher states of consciousness. This would imply that somehow melanin is related to highly developed states of consciousness, or "spiritual light." "The human form," he says, is attracted toward meaning.[101]

We are familiar with melanin in relation to the pigmentation of the skin. But we are not taught about the relationship between the skin and the brain. The ectoderm or outer layer of the skin is where melanin is produced in the pre-fetus. In the core of the brain are found twelve *black* nuclei, or melanated centers. This outer layer of the blastula (the pre-fetuus) invaginates to form the spinal column, the end of which balloons out, becoming the brain. The twelfth of these "centers," and therefore the "highest," is the *locus coeruleus*.[102] King says that they are related to spirituality and consciousness and also allow human beings access to the world of dreams, thereby learning from ancestral experiences. In animals other than humans, fewer of these "centers" will be pigmented, therefore their degree of "conciousness" is affected.

Melatonin is released from the pineal gland during darkness periodically between 11 p.m. and 7 a.m. It induces sleep and increases the amount of melanin production. In King's terms, it "unlocks the door to the unconscious." At the same time heat and sunlight cause melanocytes to produce melanin so that internally melanin production is regulated by light and dark (hormonal secretion) and externally by heat. Pineal melatonin induces puberty, while, King maintains, melatonin is also related to fertility. (Certainly world population figures and relative fertility rates bear out this contention.)

In addition, it seems that melanin is essential to the life process. The primary and fundamental atom in all biological systems is carbon, which is black. All organic matter comes from a carbon atom. Melanin in the early blastula develops into the spinal cord,[103] the central nervous system, a significant part of the brain, as well as parts of skin, retina of the eyes (the lack of melanin severely impairs vision), the hair, and the ears. The cerebral spinal fluid made in the brain that helps to regulate various glands in the body contains melanin. The chemistry of melanin is that melanocytes contain tyrosine, an amino acid, and an enzyme tyrosinase. Melanin is made when tyrosinase and oxygen cause tyrosine to convert to DOPA, a "precursor amine" that changes to melanin.[104] The lack of tyrosinase results in the genetic disease known as albinism, which has a deleterious effect on the eyesight. Melanin in the retina protects the sensitive eye from the ultraviolet rays of the sun, just as it protects the skin. It also allows for the perception of colors. DOPA is thought to be related to creative thinking and to changes in states of consciousness by the regulation of melanin production.

King argues that blackness or carbon is life and is therefore divine. He says that ancient Africans understood this, and called themselves by various names meaning "black," such as "Kemites" (people of the black earth), from which the Greeks developed the word "chemistry" (and the Arabs "alchemy"). Recognizing the special significance of their blackness, which far transcended the color of the skin, according to King, these ancient scientists studied the workings of their own minds, which they understood as being identified with their entire bodies. (So much for the mind/body split so basic to European thought.) This is what Frankfort describes negatively as cosmic thought. According to King, the ancient Africans studied themselves until they came to understand the relationship of "blackness" to spirituality and inner vision; the higher levels of understanding on which synthesis occurs. For them "Blackness" represented the divine. In his series of works entitled, *The Black Dot*, King supports this contention with an impressive array of references to ancient Kemetic texts and symbolic images and to a host of other theorists and historians.[105] What did these early, advanced scientists discover?

> These original titans found that all life came from a black seed, all life was rooted in blackness, all things possessed a memory of their collective ancestors. Blackness, the universal solvent of all was seen as the one reality from which spun the threads of the loom of life. All colors, all vibratory energies, were but a shade of black; black was the color of the night sky, primeval ocean of outer space, birthplace and womb of the planets, stars and galaxies of the universe; black holes were found at the center of our own galaxy and countless other galaxies; black was the color of carbon, the key atom found in all living matter of our world; carbon atoms linked together to form black melanin, the first chemical that could capture light and reproduce itself, the chemical key to life; and the brain itself was found to be centered around black neuromelanin. Inner vision, intuition, creative genius, and spiritual illumination were all found to be dependent upon pineal gland blood bourne chemical messengers that controlled skin color and opened the hidden door to the darkness of the collective unconscious mind, allowing the ancient priest-scientist to visualize knowledge from the timeless collective unconscious memory banks of the mind. Indeed, the Black Dot was found to be the hidden doorway to universal knowledge of the past, present, and future.[106]

But what happens to Kovel's theory of blackness; the "blackness" that is associated with the darkness of which all human beings are afraid; and the "dirt" about which they fantasize as they learn to control the excretion of their bowels? For King, blackness is life itself and, as such, is understood as divinity; the sacred force of creation. But we are taught that it is evil. How did that come to be? And is it connected, as Welsing would argue, to a reaction on the part of Europeans to their human condition, their history? Perhaps this leads to an explanation of Euro-Caucasian behavior.

In explanation, King turns, as Bradley does, to human evolution and the process through which the earth was populated; in particular, Northern Europe during the glacial period. The evolutionary parents of all human groups were African with very dark skin pigmentation. Human life began in the equatorial zones of tropical Africa. While direct sun seems to have been a creative force, its rays can also be quite harmful to the skin. In this instance, dark skin is an advantage. As early hominids became more *sapien* and less hairy, their skin became darker as the melanocytes produced extra melanin that blocked the ultraviolet rays of the sun, protecting these First People from their harmful effects. But between 50,000 and 30,000 years ago one of several migrations out of Africa into Europe occurred.[107] In the colder climate, where the sun rays were directed at an angle and therefore not as intense, dark skin was no longer necessary. It was, in fact, in this situation, a disadvantage. The sun's rays are needed for the photosynthesis of vitamin D, which allows the calcium in food to be used by the body. In low sunlight highly melanated skin acted to prevent the body from converting vitamin Dl and D2 to its active form of D3 and D4.[108] As a result these early African immigrants into Europe developed soft bones or rickets characterized by curvature of the bones. The cold climate made it worse, since thick animal furs had to be worn, which further blocked the sun. As a result over a period of 20,000 years, the skin color of these "Africans" lightened as they became "Caucasians" through selection (of mutants); more physically adapted/suited to their new environment. Those with darker skin had less chance for survival. With less melanin greater amounts of the energy from the scarce sunlight could be absorbed. Later they began to get vitamin D from other sources such as fish oils.

Even from the little that we now know about melanin, we can assume that there were other side effects as well, for melanin does not only effect the skin. In King's view, with less melanin we could expect an over-all lower level of nervous system integration, less activity of the pineal gland, and therefore greater instance of pineal calcification.[109] This, in turn, might limit access to right-brain functions associated with the pineal gland (see Chap. 1); e.g., the development of intuitiveness, holistic, or "global" thinking, the ability to synthesize mentally, and the ability to comprehend spiritual truths.[110] The comparative lack of melanin in the melanocytes (for all human beings must produce melanin contrary to Welsing's implications) would render them less capable of understanding their emotional life. In King's view, this, in combination with the demands of harsh environmental conditions caused the intensification of left-brain functions, which are cause and effect oriented, and it cut off the unconscious as a source of knowledge. This would account for a materialist world-view, the emphasis on technology, and an inability to get beyond lineal concepts. It would also account for intensely destructive behaviors on a cultural level stemming from the need for control, power, and aggressiveness. For King, melanin and the pineal gland are the keys to a deeper spiritual consciousness on which level human beings can integrate their understanding/knowledge to reach metaphysical truths that unlock the doors of the dark unconscious, bringing with it an emotional, and psychological sense of security: a oneness with self, an inner peace.

These immigrants, whom King comes to regard as "European-Africans,"* because they were cut off from this inner and deeper reality, developed a fear of it. They had been traumatized by their ice-age experience. To a severe degree, they developed what King calls "post-traumatic stress syndrome."[111] The fear of their unconscious, ancestral selves manifested as a fear of others (c.f. Diop's xenophobia). Edward Hall says that others are experienced as the uncontrollable part of ourselves.[112] This would make sense if we particularize it as being true of Europeans. The others in this case, were/are more deeply pigmented, depending on the areas of the world from which they migrated in Africa. Ultimately for King, Africans—their "mothers," "parents," their source—become the most feared "other." They feared that which they were incapable of knowing, which came to represent to them the sensation of a loss of control, of chaos, and disorder. For spiritual reality becomes overwhelming if one loses one's connection to it. Simultaneously, it could be argued, the need to control became a pathological need. It gave birth to a cultural style, a world-view, a civilization, and a pattern of bizarre behavior towards others. Once set in motion this pattern of behavior (*utamaroho*)

---

* This is a misleading term, to say the least, since the evolution of these "Europeans" had to have involved the selection of mutant, nonmelanated forms. They could hardly be considered "Africans" or identified with our original human status.

would be culturally inherited (*asili*) by subsequent generations.

King's theory explains why blackness came to represent evil and why the "dark side" became threatening. Blackness indeed was the spiritual, metaphysical realm to which Europeans had little if any access. The "dark side" of things was the inner vision of the unconscious that opened the door to communication with ancestral symbols and wisdom.[113] His theory would also help to explain the patriarchal nature of European culture, since for C. G. Jung, the matriarchal principle is the key to this primary, spiritual consciousness. The matriarchal principle also represents the African womb. European fear of the knowledge of their own origins would, in addition, account for the reason they work so hard to make it appear that everything of value began with them; a complete reversal of reality, since they know that they and their culture are comparatively young. This accounts for the "progress" theory in which the true place of human origins (Africa) represent a universal state of ignorance (darkness).

King says that towards the end of Freud's life his desk was covered with Kemetic (Egyptian) figurines of Aset (Isis), Heru (Horus), and WSIR (Osiris), God of the underworld or unconscious life.[114] Freud published *Moses and Monotheism* one year before he died. In it he argued that Judaism had ancient Egyptian origins. One wonders what he might have been moving toward. How can Freud be credited with the "discovery" of the unconscious when the unconscious life had been so important to people for millenia before his existence? Jung, in his autobiography, talks about his own anxiety when experiencing *dejà vu* as he went into Africa. He said he felt as though he had been there 5000 years before. (see *Memories, Dreams, Reflections*).[115] Freud is correct. There is much to be learned about European neuroses from the study of First World cultures. We learn of a cultural pathology of the abandoned "child" who developed first in isolation, then in anger at the "parent" (elder) whom he could no longer understand and therefore feared. That is what we can learn, as we use an ancient world-view as a frame of reference. King's theory is most consistent with the obvious lack of spirituality in European culture. A pattern of collective behavior, a world-view that, while not caused by "white skin" in a simplistically physical sense, may be related to the cultural/historical/spiritual experience of an isolated breeding population that initially suffered the relatively sudden and severe loss of melanin at an evolutionarily significant point in their development as a group, physically and culturally. Thereby the *asili* was implanted in the cultural genes.

According to Kobi Kazembe Kalongi Kambon (Joseph Baldwin), white supremacy is a "delusional construction of reality." In his brilliant and creative extension of Welsing's and Wright's ideas, he concludes that white supremacy is the synthesis of a process through which the European "relates" or, in a sense, does not relate, to the rest of the world. Kambon says that "in the first instance," i.e., on the first "occasion of Europeanness," the coming into being of the European takes place as a realization of extreme "differentness": a recognition of being "outside of Nature."

He agrees with Welsing: The relative lack of concentration of melanin in Europeans is an abnormality. Because of this unnatural state the European had to make enormous psychological adjustments to survive. Rather than being in tune with nature, as is the case in normal human development, the European experiences adaptation as a struggle. Nature is therefore perceived as being antagonistic. This antagonistic relationship with nature (the creative and nourishing force of the universe), in Kambon's view, causes a tremendous sense of alienation. The sense of being "other," "not natural," "apart from," of being born as "disordered" caused overwhelming fear, anxiety, and insecurity. This psychological state, in turn, results in perennial suspicion and distrust of the environment. The embryonic European was forced, therefore, to take a vigilant posture; i.e., an aggressive and defensive position with regard to the rest of the world (which was indeed "nature" itself). He existed in an ontological condition defined by a sense of "otherness." He had to reconstruct reality in order to survive reality. Being outside of the natural order, the European, indeed, made *himself* "the order." Nature, then, became the object, and alienation from nature was reconstructed by them as being natural. This perception served to defend their uniquely alienated consciousness: the phenomenal gap. Their psychological defensiveness resulted in psychopathology; a fabricated reality in which the value of the European "white" self is exaggerated. Their creed, says Kambon becomes: I am perfect. In a reality that reverses reality, "Nature (Blackness, Africaness, color) is imperfect." Kambon seems to be saying that Europeans have not only remained severely damaged psychologically, but all of their cultural behavior can be understood as a defense of this condition.[116]

All of the theories presented offer pieces of the puzzle; offering various reasons why Europeans should so consistently behave in such a strangely aggressive and violent manner towards those who look and act differently; indeed, that they should have constructed an entire civilization around the oppression and exploitation of majority peoples. One of the most significant facts about these theories is that they are offered at all. What is in keeping with the European cultural *asili* is that the ideology of its academia, its political liberals, dictates the terms for such discussion. The issue of the peculiar nature of European behavior is so threatening to the integrity of the culture, as it now exists, that they cannot allow this question to be asked; at least not in the proper form.

If we call European behavior towards others "racism"—and such behavior appears to be characteristic of a culture created by Caucasians, who represent a small minority of the world's people, then obviously our intelligence forces the question—why? What is the connection? Yet in Euro-American social and academic institutions that question is never addressed in the ways we have seen it addressed in the above discussion. Rather a new area of discourse is created called "race relations," which implies first of all that all "races" are equally involved in the "problem" of conflict. In addition, the concern is very pragmatic, quite materialistic in fact. "How can we minimize conflict in the work place or other social situations by understanding our 'differences' and attitudes towards one another?" "Differences" apply to all of those groups that may be brought into contact in an urban situation; Africans, Asians, Latinos, Europeans, etc. In other words, even the reactions of "non-Europeans" to white racism become part of the "problem," with the eventual result taking the focus away from the real problem—the European. Anyone who enters this discussion with honesty—i.e., placing Europeans firmly in the spotlight where they belong, focusing on their behavior towards others as the pathology that has set the syndrome in motion—that person, by some ingenious double-think reversal (the familiar pattern of European ideology) is called "a racist!" But we know what the reality is and it is not so much a question, in this instance, of which theorist is "right," but of their courage and ability to ask the right question. It matters little, after all, if the discussion is uncomfortable for Europeans. Certainly we Africans are mandated by ancestral charter to seek answers to the question of European difference.

European Ideology and the Concept of the Cultural Other

We live in a world so polluted with the effects of European ideology and styles of thought that it may appear to be the case that a "positive" self-image within the context of one cultural philosophy necessarily implies a "negative" image of others; that to define the members of one's own culture as "human" means that others must be "nonhuman"; that for those with whom one identifies culturally to represent "good," those in other cultures must be "bad." But this is not a universal phenomenon. It describes the particular dialectic of European ideology and the needs of the *utamaroho* because of the historical reality of European imperialism (the pattern of their behavior toward others), has become a necessary political dialectic in the self-deterministic objectives of majority peoples. Because all cultures without exception have been forcibly placed into a power relationship with European culture, an effective affirmation of their own nationalistic commitments must necessarily be a negation or denial of Europeans insofar as they (Europeans) are the proponents and agents of European ideology. But these ideologies do not inherently imply the dehumanization of the European, while European ideology does inherently imply the reverse, i.e., the dehumanization of those who are not human beings. For this reason, it is the explanation of the interrelationship of European ideology, the European philosophical tradition and European values that is most helpful in the attempt to understand the pattern of European behavior towards others. The documentation of the more blatant acts of European imperialism alone is necessarily of limited consequence.

It is in the nature of the culture to allow for the verbal "disapproval" of the most dramatic instances of European abuse of others; since such disapproval has no existential consequences. Its rhetorical, hypocritical, and abstract style make it possible for the culture that produces such behavior to simultaneously disown it. The massacres, the bombings, the mutilations, and the enslavement of others are singled out as the isolated and horrendous acts of an overzealous or evil militarist, colonialist, imperialist, or slaver. In this way the society's academia, its political liberals, its clergy, and its social theoreticians disassociate themselves from these patterns and absolve their guilt. But such behavior, in terms of the European world-view, is on firm ideological ground and can only be superficially and ineffectively criticized by those whose own ideological commitments are to progressivism, evolutionism, scientism. These assumptions and thought patterns have the same cultural origins as those of King Leopold and Harry Truman; moreover, they are consistent with one another. The theorists who share these Western European traditions make political decisions based on the same premises as the "commanders in chief" and the colonialist adventurers (or they make no decisions at all, which is the same thing).

European intellectual traditions and the imperialistic behavioral patterns of Europeans issue from a common ideological ground. They are dictated by the *utamaroho*, they are explained by the *utamawazo*, and they cohere in the *asili*. It is symbolic of this relationship that the name of Cecil Rhodes can represent simultaneously the essence of European colonial-expansionism and one of the most valued intellectual traditions of the West; they are simply different manifestations of the same *utamaroho*. Yet the "Western way" is deceptive, because it is in the nature of the culture that a contemporary "Rhodes Scholar" can separate herself from the history of "Rhodesia." The concept of *asili* shows us, however, that this quasiseparation is not ethnologically (ideologically) sound. The relationship between the concept of the cultural other and European cognitive structures is adumbrated in our earlier discussion of the European *utamawazo* (Chap. 1).

By providing the conceptual and valuative constructs within which European behavioral patterns and thought are formulated, the philosophers, scientists, theologians, and social theorists become the idealogues of the culture. The "isms" of European thought are all based on an image of the cultural other that in turn regulates the behavior of Europeans towards majority peoples. It will help to look carefully at the dominant themes of European thought (*utamawazo*) in the context of European imperialist ideology (*utamaroho* and behavior).

In Chap. 2 we attempted to clarify the relationship of Christian ideology to European imperialism and pointed to the way in which Christian thought has contributed to European nationalism by intensifying the "we/they" dichotomy on which it depends and by providing corresponding images of Europeans and majority peoples that mandate the unlimited expansion of Western European political control. The essence of the Judeo-Christian tradition is its assumption of theological and moral evolution leading to the superior and humanly proper conception of "one God" (or "pure spirit"); the ultimate abstraction. The Christian mandate to impose this conception on other peoples represents the epitome of the European *utamaroho*. Essential to this proselytizing mission is an invidious comparison in which the non-European (or as Chinweizu put it in 1978, "the rest of us") comes out not only "the loser," but is dehumanized as well. The "pagan," "heathen," "idolater," or "polytheist" have no religion in terms of European definition, yet these are all terms used to describe our spiritual conceptions. We are cultural others; we are morally inferior; we are less than human. Therefore, whatever is done to us with the objective of making us "more human," (e.g., giving us religion) is justifiable.

Christian ideology provides moralistic and universalistic terms of disparagement for the peoples who are objects of Western imperialism, as well as moral justification for their subjugation and exploitation. Katherine George provides an example of the Christian image of the cultural other (see Chap. 2). What she demonstrates is the way in which Christian ideology enables Europeans to behave as they do towards people of other cultures. She speaks of "Christianity's influence upon the civilized view of the primitive." European ideology provides the conception of the cultural other that supports the varied manifestations of European imperialistic behavior. This conception, in partnership with other aspects of the European *utamaroho*, is one that encourages a particular attitude toward peoples outside the culture; an attitude of paternalism and superiority that mandates the quest to control and manipulate them, and one that encourages rather than inhibits their destruction, abuse, and exploitation. Christian thought was a major contributor to this conception and its attendant attitude, particularly in the formulative periods of European development and during the major periods of European expansion.

The Judeo-Christian tradition interlocks with other aspects of European ideology that have played similar roles in terms of the definitions of European cultural nationalism. From the frame of reference of "progressivism-evolutionism," which, it must be understood, is not easily distinguishable from Christian thought, the "pagan" becomes not only nonreligious but *pre*-religious. She becomes "backward" and "ignorant." She lacks the intellectual acumen to develop (reach) "civilization" (European culture). She becomes "primitive," which, as Ashley Montagu has pointed out translates into "backward," "retrogressive," "arrested," "retarded,"[117] in evolutionistic terms. The "primitive" man is not really in a human state but is at best representative of an evolutionarily earlier stage of the European.

Charles A. Beard, in his introduction to J. B. Bury's *Idea of Progress*, says: "This conception of a continuous progress in the evolution of life, resulting in the appearance of uncivilized anthropos, helped to reinforce and increase a belief in the conception of the history of Civilized Anthropos as itself also a continuous progressive development."[118] The European becomes, in this view, "mankind," since at any given time he represents the highest and therefore proper level that man has reached. Marvin Harris says, "We cannot appreciate the strength of the conviction among the evolutionists of the period of 1860–1890 that contemporary primitives could provide valid information about the ancient condition of humanity."[119] These premises can be used subtly, with respect to contemporary European behavior, to support European control via "modernization" and "development" programs or in their extreme interpretations to support the enslavement or genocide of "the rest of us."

In combination, then, progressivism and evolutionism transform people of other cultures into "savages," while the proponents of these theories themselves become "civilized" and therefore responsible for the guidance (control) of those who are not. It is European evolutionism that places the cultural other under the microscope. When she becomes a savage in the mind of the European the assumption is not only that she is a "wild beast," but that she is an object to be studied as well, since she and her culture represent the earliest stages of the European's ("mankind's") existence. The cultural other has exactly the same value as a Neanderthal skull. The assumptions and mood of a scientistic perspective make the above combination of ideas coherent for Europeans. They cohere in the *asili* of the culture. The following clipping appeared in a New York African newspaper in the early 1900s:

> Ota Benga, the African pygmy, is to stay at the Zoological Park a few days longer. This was decided at a conference between Director Hornaday and the committee of Baptist clergy men appointed by the Colored Baptist Minister's Conference, to save Benga from appearing on exhibition in a monkey cage, and if possible, also to get the custody of him. The length of time he is still to remain an inmate of the primate house in the park is dependent on Dr. Verner's return from North Carolina. As soon as he returns he, Director Hornaday and the Rev. Hames II Gordon, the Chairman of the Committee, will have another conference. The clergymen will then try through Mr. Gordon to get possession of Benga, so that they may send him to Lynchburg, Va. to be educated. . . . Director Hornaday . . . is not willing to give him into the hands of the clergy men without an agreement that he will be delivered to Dr. Verner again when he wants him.
>
> *New York Age,* September 20, 1906

It is scientism that makes universalistic schemes compelling. It gives credence to a value-system that defines European culture as a universally beneficial and evolutionarily inevitable stage of human existence: other cultures represent various stages of development toward that culture. What scientism adds to the concept of the cultural other depicted thus far is that of passivity. The true objects of contemplation, according to scientistic epistemology, are, by definition, completely passive. They are inactive as though frozen in time.

This is the impressive power of the reflective thinker: His act of thinking about an object alone gives him the ability to render it motionless—powerless. It must "sit still" for his circumspection; i.e., his theoretical consumption. The cultural other becomes the total "object" of European thought. She is the most fitting object of study. She is otherwise meaningless.

The "isms" of European ideology combine into one idea system that cloaks the sentiments of European cultural imperialism in a syntactical maze of universalistic terminology and logic. Each component of the system is dependent on a conception of the cultural other as the embodiment of the negation of value; for each provides the ideological function of supporting the European self-image as the universal "agent of change," the "doer," the personification of intelligence, and the "inheritor of the earth."

What follows is an equation of European collective behavior towards the "Cultural Other":

European *Ideology*	+	European *Self-Image*	=	Cultural Other *Image as*	∴	Cultural Other *Must be*
Christianity		Religious, Moral, cultural being.		Heathen, Non-religious, Immoral.		Saved
Idea of Progress		Progressive, Modern, cultural being.		Backward		Developed, Advanced.
Evolutionism		Civilized Cultural being.		Primitive		Civilized
Scientism		Scientist, Knower.		Object		Studied, Known, Controlled.
White Supremacy		White racial being, Pure, human.		Black, dirty, Non-human.		Avoided, Pitied, Enslaved, Destroyed.

It must be understood that the ideas of "saving," "advancing," "developing," "civilizing," or "studying" do not indicate an identification with the cultural other, or a desire to make her into a European. They all translate into the idea of "control." They symbolize, primarily and essentially, a power relationship in which Europeans are supreme. Each ideological component contributes to the support of European imperialism and expansionism, because each ideologically supports the objective of power over others and attempts to transform European choices into inevitably and humanly desirable universals. The difference between the militarists and the missionary is only one of *modus operandi*; the blows of one are more physically apparent; those of the other leave battered souls and cultures in their wake.

Each ideological component contributes to the creation of an image of those who are different from the Europeans, which generates a conception that encourages the style of behavior that has characterized the European's relationship to majority peoples. This conception is that of the cultural other; i.e., a being who is justifiably the object of missionizing, or of scientific consumption and manipulation, or of mass brutality. In either case, the cultural other is "grist for the mill"; she is material to be used; she is expendable. This web of interlocking ideological systems is the vehicle by which meaning is injected into European life. What they accomplish is the devaluation of people outside the culture. The essential characteristic of the conception of the cultural other, however, is not merely that she is worth less than a European—but that she is worth *nothing*. The cultural other is a being who lacks meaning, whose existence has no human significance in terms of the European *utamawazo*. The cultural other has significance *only* syntactically as a concept that assures Europeans of value in their own terms; therefore as a concept on which the *utamaroho* thrives and as a concrete object on which Europeans existentially act out their most destructive instincts.

Utamawazo and Imperialism

What is the relationship between the way in which Europeans conceive of the world and the way in which they relate to majority peoples? Put another way: What is the relationship between the dominant modes of European thought and the dominant modes of behavior towards others? What kind of behavior does the *utamawazo* encourage? Joel Kovel asks a similar question and feels justified in linking what he calls "abstractification" to Western "cultural aggression" and "white racism." An effective critique of European cultural behavior must address itself to the belief-system that generates that behavior.

The conceptual realities presented by the European *utamawazo* (ontology/epistemology) combine to promote a mental attitude and outlook that make imperialistic-expansionistic behavior possible and preferred (normative). The Platonic and Christian conception of nature is as sensate disorder, hostile to intelligence (order). Value resides in the "rational," again associated with order. The irrational represents nonvalue. "Man" (the human is properly male) is intelligence and nature, reason and emotion. "His" properly human function is to control the emotional (nature) within "himself" with the aid of "his" rational faculties and "his" will. "His" role in the universe is to use "his" intelligence to give order to (to make proper use of) nature. This involves struggle and conquest, since nature is hostile to rational order. "Man" subdues nature. These ontological conceptions, when placed at the service of the European *utamaroho*, are translated into the concrete terms that become the "working definitions" of European political ("intercultural") behavior.

In the State that Plato constructs, it is the role of the most "intelligent" and "rational" individuals to control those within the State who are "less rational," more emotional, and, therefore, less human. And, indeed, the formulative process in the development of European culture involves the successful ascendance of a particular definition of "intelligence"; the weeding out from positions of power and influence those committed to other ontological/epistemological systems. As this constellation of characteristics and values becomes solidified into a well-defined cultural entity, there is a simultaneous process in which the desire to order and control becomes directed more and more *outside* the culture that is defining itself in relation to the universe. (It is this above all, that makes for European success.) The object of European intelligence (order, power, control) becomes they who are not European, i.e., the cultural other. For nothing represents irrationality so much as a world-view, an *utamawazo*, an ideological system that is not European. The cultural other, then, in terms of the European *utamawazo*, becomes part of nature, to be ordered, controlled, used, and destroyed at the will of the European. In the "Chain of Being" the cultural other is ontologically mere "uncivilized anthropos"; not easily distinguishable from other nonhuman animals. Robin Williams' statement (see Chap. 7 "Themes in Interpersonal Interaction) can now be interpreted properly in terms of the European *utamaroho*. The Europeans see themselves as "man" who is "set over against the world," and the cultural other, a "lesser creature(s)," falls among "inanimate nature and other living things," which they are to "have dominion over." It is the European, "acting out" this *utamaroho*, who sees himself as having a "special charter to occupy the earth."[120] The cultural other is excluded from this category.

Christianism, progressivism and evolutionism, which have ideologically contributed to the dehumanization (devaluation) of the cultural other, are for the European mind logically supported by an *utamawazo* characterized by a lineal conception of time and motion. It "makes sense" that cultures and peoples must relate "lineally" if they are conceived to relate at all, and it is a simple conceptual step to turn the line vertically into the hierarchy of progressivism. The normative Platonic abstraction provides the epistemological support for the universalism so essential to the presuppositions of the ideas of progress and of unilinear evolution. There is no truth but immutable, nonrelative truth. There is no good but universal good. To be in possession of truth is to know what is universally good for humankind. Everything must come to be, or at least be judged in terms of, what "we" are. The European *utamawazo* provides the conceptual framework in which these "isms" become acceptable.

It is the epistemological tool of "objectification" that perhaps has the most critical implications for the nature of European culture and behavior towards others. The mind is trained to objectify. The person believes that by disengaging herself from the phenomenon she wishes to understand, she comes to "know" it; it becomes an object of her knowledge. She therefore attempts fo transform all phonenema into either total "matter" or pure mathematical symbol. She despiritualizes it. But let us suppose that Plato was essentially mistaken; a good mathematician but a weak humanist (social theorist). If human intelligence is not limited to rationality as defined in terms of order and control (power), but rather is revealed in spirituality that may include but certainly transcends rational order, then the European *utamawazo* does not equip Europeans to deal successfully with the "human" in themselves or with other human beings. Instead, it enables them to objectify their experiences with and behavior towards, other people. The more remote such people are from their own culture (from Europe), the more they become "objects" only, for the greater is the European's ability to eliminate emotional reaction to his interaction with them. The cultural other is at the end of the spectrum; she becomes the total object. The outrages of European imperialistic behavior are culturally "possible" because their object is the cultural other with whom Europeans feel no emotional identification.

In Kovel's interpretation, European culture is "packaged" or presented to its members as a series of abstractions, and because they characteristically do not allow themselves to deal with concrete phenomena in terms of their existential implications they are able to behave and live as they do.[121] In terms of European behavior towards the cultural other, then, the abstractions in which it is packaged are "progress" versus "backwardness," "Christian civilization" versus "the heathen barbarians"; rather than the concrete realities of brutality, aggression, and exploitation.

The point is that the epistemological and ontological presuppositions and imperialistic behavior "agree." They both issue from an *asili* that demands power/control. The *utamawazo* creates a mental fortress that sanctions European behavior towards those outside the culture. The *utamaroho* encourages and motivates such behavior. To be effectively critical of European imperialistic behavior we must reject the verbally rhetorical and hypocritical character of the culture. This implies a serious exploration of the behavioral implications (i.e. concrete and existential) of the particular uses of ontological and epistemological assumptions that one tacitly accepts by "successful" participation in European society. To the extent that these assumptions result in the ability to regard human beings as objects—whether they be "scientific," "military," or "religious" objects—imperialistic behavior will not be effectively discouraged or prohibited. It is the essential nature of the *asili* of European culture that must be destroyed if that indeed is the objective. Europeaness must be rejected.

Conclusion: The Logic of Supremacy and Destruction

The relationship between European intracultural behavior and European behavior towards others is that the lack of love (sympathetic relationship) for each other requires an "other" to absorb aggression and to allow a bond of identification to form between the members of the culture. Therefore, while power and racialism may play a part in the collective behavior of other cultural groups, only Europeans are racist by nature and because of their culture. This is so because (1) they are the only people whose cultural *asili* is energized by the drive for power, (2) because racism can be defined as systematic behavior resulting from xenophobia, in combination with the concrete circumstances of power, and (3) finally because only the European *utamaroho* is insufficient, in itself, therefore demanding a cultural/racial "other" to relate to. This combination makes "racism" endemic to European culture and defines the goal of white supremacy, European power over others, as the supreme goal of the culture. That is the statement that no other culture can make.

African and other majority peoples are not passive victims of

European aggression. And we do not intend to give that impression. History is as much the history of our forms of resistance as it is of the power of Europe, to say nothing of the long period of history before Europe came into existence as a cultural entity. But the focus in this discussion is not on "other than Europeans"; it is on Europeans themselves. This is not to say that Europeans have not been effected by the "rest of us." In fact, part of their success issues from their ability to use that influence to further dominate those from which it comes. We are concerned here, however, with the specific relationship between European behavior and the European *utamawazo* (culturally structured thought system). In that regard European conceptions of others become important. We are at present only secondarily concerned with the reactions of other peoples to European behavior; these reactions have only been infrequently discussed when they helped to clarify some aspect of European behavior or ideology. My ultimate concern is to favorably influence the rest of us in our capacity to realize self-determination, i.e., to eliminate Europe as an impediment to our progress and as the cause of our destruction. I believe that scrutiny of European culture will lead us in that direction.

As Johari Amini says, it is our "working definitions" that "are at the foundation of the ways in which we live."[122] The European conception of the cultural other is such a definition. Clearly all cultures define its members as "different" from those outside; that is part of what "culture" means. And this difference is a meaningful one; i.e., the members of one's culture have priority, are more important, emotionally closer than those of other cultures because of the things they share, just as the members of a family mean more to us than those who are not included in the family. It is indeed part of the function of cultural definition to define a group in this way. It follows, then, that for any group there are the definitions of "we" and "they"; "self" and "other." And for any group these definitions should carry with them behavioral implications; "they" are not treated the same as "we," if only because "they" do not have priority—"we" come first. Even though this may appear to be "logical," it is not, given the *asili* of African culture in which nonmembers are often given the same privileges as members. Diop has remarked on this xenophilic African tendency.

The European "we/they" dichotomy has implications that it does not have within the philosophies of other cultures, and the "outsider," as defined by other cultures, is *qualitatively* different from the conception of the cultural other. The European conception of the cultural other is a unique product of European ideology designed to answer the particular needs of the *utamaroho* that houses an inordinate power drive. The outsider as defined by other cultures does not have the features of the cultural other. A cultural other could not be conceived of in these other ontological/epistemological systems. In majority cultures inanimate objects have more meaning (significance) than do cultural others for Europeans.

The cultural other is not the same as the traditional enemy. She does not have the status of an enemy. She is less than an enemy. The concept implies the ultimate in dehumanization—in devaluation. European behavior towards others is so extreme in part because their conception of the cultural other is so negative. Atrocities are no longer atrocities if their objects are invisible. They *become* atrocities only because those on whom they are perpetrated have some meaning.

The cultural other is significant only insofar as its existence (creation) is necessary for the maintenance of the European self-image and *utamaroho*, and provides for the survival of European culture. It is the essential nature (*asili*) of the culture that is revealed in the conception of the cultural other. It is this conception that services the needs of European conative strivings for power, supremacy, and control; all of which are basically destructive to the necessarily integrative function of culture. By creating the cultural other as the proper object of these strivings, Europeans ingeniously use the power drive to keep their culture intact. The result is a culture whose primary rationale is universal supremacy. The culture has survived as a coherent entity because (as stated before) the European's intracultural behavior has been effectively held in check by an ethic that differentiated between the European other and the cultural other. The tendencies of European behavior mandated by the *asili* are so inherently destructive that the cultural other is needed for their uninhibited "acting out."

There is no other *utamaroho* or self-concept that demands a cultural other. There are "enemies," even "barbarians"—but not a cultural other. It is actually a deep-rooted European need. The *asili* demands it. The attitude is unique among cultural groups; it helps to explain a style of behavior that is also unique. Imperialism is not unique to Europe; neither is power. But both the extremity of imperialism and the intensity of power enacted and possessed by European culture are unique—to the great misfortune of the rest of us. Europeans are not the most powerful people in the world because they are the smartest, as they would have us believe. The actualization of power is a function of the need for power as dictated by the *utamaroho* of the culture; its energizing mechanisms. Europeans need power as no other people do. The culture is so successful at gaining power because there is nothing within the culture that effectively conflicts with the achievement of power. What this description of their behavior has shown us is that "anything goes." The "power need" is compounded by and related to the lack of a spiritual substratum on which to base a viable morality. Europeans in a very real sense have no spiritual community. This is a malaise inherent in the formulating (*asili*) and definition of the culture, only now overtly manifesting itself in such a way that it becomes apparent to a tiny portion of its own participants. The pattern of European behavior towards others is inseparable from the European *utamawazo* and therefore the intellectual life of the culture. This pattern of violence, aggression, and destruction is not an aberration. Our study demonstrates that the *asili* mandates all three, and unless the collective cognitive and affective definitions change, that behavior will continue. And these definitions cannot change because of the nature of the European himself. All are part of a coherent ideological whole.

"Ideology" is, of course, implied throughout this discussion, but the final section of this study concentrates explicitly on European ideology and explores the critical themes in all European ideological statements. These are the themes that the concept of *asili* has brought forth. They have emerged from a discussion of European culture, using an approach that looks for consistency and coherence. It is ideology above all that forms the *asili* or explanatory principle of the culture. The ideological substratum unites the various aspects and modes of the culture. The workings of the culture become crystallized as the relationships between *utamawazo* (cognitive structure), *utamaroho* (affective style), behavior, and ideology are made clear.

PART FOUR

IDEOLOGY

"People headed after the setting sun, in that direction even the possibility of regeneration is dead. There the devotees of death take life, consume it, exhaust every living thing. Then they move on, forever seeking new boundaries."
— Ayi Kwei Armah

Chapter 9

Progress as Ideology

Whose "Progress?"

The "idea of progress" as it is euphemistically referred to by Europeans provides an essential dynamic of the main thrust of European ideology. The idea is a fundamental aspect of the European philosophy of life, providing moral justification for the technical order and giving supposed direction to the strivings of individuals within the society. An exploration of the nature of this concept in terms of its profound cultural/ideological implications reveals that its effects have been powerful, though most often subtle, and have spread to other cultures. The idea of progress has been a potent tool in European hands. It has contributed to the formation of the social organization by providing the ideological substratum out of which the oppressive technical order was created. This technical order in which the European is imprisoned leads inevitably to the current ecological imbalance, thereby linking the European condition ethnologically (ideologically) to the "idea of progress."

Approaching this discussion armed with the concept of *asili* will allow us to discover the ideological connections that exist between the *utamawazo* (thought) and the uniqueness of the European technical order. Even the most critical of contemporary works generally identify the intensity of the technological mania with something called "modernity." This merely reveals the progress philosophy to be a part of their perspectives. The advantage of the *asili* concept is that it forces us to be specific, i.e., to demonstrate the relationship between European ideology and the European technical order, thereby particularizing it as a cultural phenomenon. Just as "progress" as an abstraction is a European ontological concept and ideological belief, so the oppressive technical order created within the context of the Western European cultural-historical process is the product of European priorities, the European *utamawazo*, and the European *utamaroho*. The philosophical problem is that of what exactly "modernity" can mean outside of the context of the idea of progress.

The Anatomy of "Progress"

In the setting of European culture, the parochial nature and ideological significance of the idea of progress is difficult to discuss. Like "lineality" in the *utamawazo*, it is more than a conceptual tool in that it becomes part of the meaning of existence for members of the culture. In the classroom, the attempt to present the idea as being culturally bound is met with blank stares. "What do you mean? *Everyone* wants to make progress!" Moreover, because the idea combines European ontological presuppositions and value in such intricate combination and is so deeply embedded in them, finding the right way to present it, so that its ethnological implications for European behavior, attitude, and value become evident, is not an easy task.

The critical conceptual leap is that by which action directed toward a concrete objective becomes confused with change that is merely reflexive, i.e., in which the object is change itself. The "progress" toward which Europeans perceive themselves to be "moving" is neither concrete nor reachable— a spurious goal indeed. Why then has the idea such attraction for the European mind—a mind that is at once rationalistic *and* empirical, a mind that seems to say, "Show me?" The answer lies in the fact that this ingenious invention—"progress" born out of the European *utamaroho*— is ideally fashioned to encourage the growth of the technical order while justifying cultural and political imperialism.

We have said that Europeans are expansionistic. To Europeans, the universe represents actual physical space into which they can impose themselves. Their movement in this respect is never from place to place (they are no longer nomads); it is not *displacement*, but extension. They expand and extend their possessions, never relinquishing territory they have claimed. They never migrate, but always conquer and consume. By this process they themselves become "bigger." The idea of progress allows for this same kind of movement and extension. Conceptually, "progressive" motion consumes all of the past within it, and "progress" is not merely "different from," it is "more than." The idea is, in this way, essentially expansionistic.

As Charles A. Beard says, "It contains within itself the germs of indefinite expansion."[1] What it implies is that there is no fixed limit to change, no limit beyond which the expansion of "our" thrust cannot go. That is how they think. "We" (Europeans) are morally obliged to continually move/change/expand "ourselves"; that is the nature of "progress." For the European it is the abstractness of the idea that makes it fit to be "ideal." Interestingly enough this is precisely the nature of Plato's ideal state; it can only be approximated by humans. The commitment to imitate it necessarily entails endless and infinite effort and therefore assures a certain style of behavior. Both Arthur Lovejoy and J. B. Bury argue that Plato's conception is antithetical to the idea of progress in that it involves a commitment to an absolute order already conceived. As a reason for the failure of the Greeks to "discover" the idea of progress, Bury suggests:

> They believed in the ideal of an absolute order in society, from which, when it is once established, any deviation must be for the worse. Aristotle, considering the subject from a practical point of view, laid down that changes in an established social order are undesirable, and should be as few and slight as possible.[2]

But, as Theodore Roszak points out in his introduction to *Sources*,[3] the establishment becomes the agent of change ("the more it changes the more it stays the same"); in fact it changes *in order* to remain the same. Admittedly change is much more the order of the contemporary West than of Ancient Greece, but Plato's "absolute" can still be interpreted to ideologically support a certain kind of change, in a particular direction, within a determined and well-defined form. The idea of progress does precisely the same thing. What it limits is the *kind* of change that can take place. Ecological sanity, for instance, is not "progress." Bury, himself, says that Greek thought foreshadowed the idea of progress.

The idea should not be considered as a "theory of history" in a limited sense. It is a misunderstanding of the concept to think that it necessarily indicates optimism; for it never presents a clear view of the future. The infinite future, once it has been postulated, becomes irrelevant. It is the subtlety of this phenonemon (idea) that contributes to its distinctiveness. It is a mood—not one of optimism—but one of arrogance, superiority, power, and exploitation. These need not be synonymous with optimism. It is common for one committed to "the Western way" to express concern over where "it" is all leading, and yet to be convinced of his obligation to "take it" there; to bestow the leadership of his culture upon those "less fortunates" who do not know the way.

The idea of progress is a directive of European behavior, a determinant of attitude, a device by which the European judges and imposes those judgements on others. Europeans who "ennoble" the "native" do so from the pinnacles of a state of progress that they believe it is incumbent upon "man" to achieve. It is the European counterpart to what is meant by "tradition" when it is said that tradition functions normatively in "traditional" societies. It is the idea of progress that helps to guarantee that European commitments and values will not change but will always remain within the same modality.

The "idea" is more a methodological commitment than a theory of history. It is a process; an operational mode. Its referent is "rationalism"—*not* a euphoric or glorious state of perfection in the future (only for Marx does it seem to have this connotation). In fact, its viability contradicts the possibility of such a state. Its mood is much closer to a "survival of the fittest" aura. It is concerned with the evolving, not with the end product. Progress is always there to be made, because its index is wherever you are at a given time. There is always "progress" to be made—always a proper way to attack a problem "rationally." Rather than the presumption of a perfect state to be ultimately reached, it rests on the presumption of ceaseless "problems"—always tension; it presupposes disharmony, disequilibrium, imbalance. It is possible to interpret Plato's *Republic* in this way; i.e., a paramount guide to activity, in an endless approach to unattainable perfection. An ideal which, like the dynamic of Zeno's paradox, allows for an infinite degree of approximation without the possibility of duplication. It is the solving of the problem in the most "rational" way that *is progress*. That is the thrust of the idea—*intra*culturally. Its outward thrust (i.e., in relation to other cultures) is to make the "rational" way (the European way) best.

E. O. Bassett says that, in Plato's view, "society executes an infinite progression. . . .The end of progress is progress; the aim is but a directing principle. . . .Since the social as well as the universal aim is maximum orderliness, progress must be perpetual."[4] But Lovejoy and Boas argue that "the Romantic idea of endless progress for progress' sake is alien to Plato's thought."[5] Karl Popper agrees:

> Plato's sense of drift had expressed itself in his theory that all change, at least in certain cosmic periods, must be for the worse; all change is degeneration. Aristotle's theory admits of changes which are improvements; this change may be progress. Plato had taught that all development starts from the original, the perfect Form or Idea, so that the developing thing must lose its perfection in the degree in which its similarity to the original decreases.[6]

The trick is that the perfect form exists *only* as "idea." If one's interpretation of Plato emphasizes the concrete social and cultural implications of his theories for human organization, then it becomes clear that all actual development in the sensate "world of becoming" may properly start from a conceptualized perfection, but certainly not with the "perfect state." Actual movement is, therefore, not away from, but toward the "ideal." If the Ideal could be actualized, then, once this had occurred, all change would, indeed, be for the worse. But such, for Plato, is a contradiction in terms.

Joel Kovel says that the "practical genius" of Protestantism and of the West in general "was to discover that the more remote a desired goal, the more passionately a man would seek it."[7] I would insert European before the generic term "man." This is one of the cultural/behavioral functions of the Christ image, in its *European* interpretation, in relation to a diety conceived as "pure spirit." He is the "human" who is not human. The more than "human being" who only incidentally, and very briefly, took human form. This image calls for the emulation of that which is "superhuman" and therefore unrealizable by humans. As Kovel says, "All that 'counted' was Movement, striving for an endless goal that became ever more remote precisely through the process of striving."[8] One never reaches "progress"; one makes "progress," and in the European view, there is always more of it to be made. This supports the ego that must extend its domain indefinitely; the *utamaroho* that manifests an insatiable "will-to-power." It developed out of the *asili* that demanded it.

We have said that the European self-image requires an "inferior" to which it relates as "superior." The idea of progress helps to explain to Europeans in what way they are superior. They believe, and are able to make others believe, that since they represent the most "progressive" force at any given moment, they are most human, therefore best; others in the world represent varying degrees of inferiority. This characteristic of the European *utamaroho* is already observable in archaic Europe. In comparing the Romans with other peoples, Aristides claimed not only that they are greater than their contemporaries but that they are greater than anything which preceded them. "Hence the inferiority of those who lived in former times appears because the past is so much surpassed, not only in the element at the head of the empire, but also in cases where identical groups have been ruled by others and by you [Rome]."[9]

While a particular kind of "improvement" may be essential to the idea of progress, ethnologically, in terms of the European *utamaroho*, an equally significant aspect of the idea is the assumption that the present is properly better than and superior to the past. The way the idea is put firmly into the service of European cultural imperialism is that the superior "present" becomes something more than merely what is occurring (or exists) now. What is "progressive" or "modern" is the proper form or model for what *ought* to exist in the present. Therefore, existent forms that do not conform to the "progressive" (modern or European) model are not part of the "present"—they are "outdated" and "backward." In this way, the culture, in the vernacular of European cultural nationalism, is made to be superior not only to what precedes it—as does its own past—but also to coexistent "unprogressive" cultures. In other words, the idea of progress provides a scale on which to weigh and by which to compare people via their cultures (their group creations).

The European *utamaroho* requires a self-image of not merely superiority but supremacy, and the "idea of progress" makes Europeans supreme among humans. It is superiority placed into the dimension of lineal time and then the logic of lineal time placed into a timeless dimension. Without the idea and this conceptual sleight of hand, cultures would merely be different; European culture would merely be intensely and obsessively rational; with the assumption of the idea of progress Europe becomes "better." In the ways indicated, then, the idea of progress supports the expansionism and supremism inherent in the European *utamaroho*.

J. B. Bury's description of this idea firmly supports the point being made. He discusses the way in which certain ideas prevalent in and before the Middle Ages set the stage for and were conducive to the emergence of the idea of progress, even though the ascendency of the idea could not be complete until the "idea of Providence," which characterized the Middle Ages, lost hold. Bury demonstrates how the idea of progress supports the European *utamaroho*; the way it functions in a similar manner to the rhetorical Christian ethic; and its compatibility with European imperialist ideology. Using an interpretation based on the concept of *asili*, his observations provide evidence of the meaning and uses of "universalism" and the objective of a "world order" in the context of European cultural imperialism. (See Chap. 10.) For Bury the conception of the "whole inhabited world as unity and totality," like the "imperial theory of Rome," are themselves signs of progress and essential ingredients of what later crystallized as the "idea of progress." Using the concept of *asili*, and an African-centered perspective, they are signs of something else.

If we use the concept of *asili* to interpret the "ecumenical idea" that Bury discusses, we will understand that it marks the development of an important aspect of the European *utamaroho*. With Alexander this *utamaroho* gains recognition in the political philosophy of European nationalism. Remember always that "nationalism" in this sense connotes the commitment to a particular cultural definition and ideology, not necessarily the isolation or limitation of group defintion. In this way, European particularism becomes expressed as cultural imperialist/expansionism, because of the nature of the culture's *asili*. The "Ecumene" is the European empire. Plato had already provided the design for the European state, but the vision of this state as world empire would come later.

The Inevitability of "Progress"

The idea of progress is a "philosophy of change" and as such tends to support any innovation, anything new. Wherever this force leads is by definition "good"; whereas in the context of other world-views what could be defined as "progressive" activity depends on a concretized goal. The idea of progress transforms what is merely change into directed movement. Participants in European culture perceive change in this way. Continually influenced by the images of technology, they are provided with directive signposts and the standard that gives order to otherwise directionless motion. Technology provides the model of efficiency, a model that more perfectly than any imaginable concurs with the "philosophy of change"—for, in the European view, there is no end to efficiency either. No matter how effectively a machine may perform, its function can always be made more effective, thereby creating a new and better machine. Progress is in this way "proven," and Europeans can be said to "advance" as technology "advances." It does not matter that there is nothing towards which they advance. Their innovations all seem to contribute to greater order in their society—at least a certain kind of order. The rationalization of their culture (in the Weberian sense) gives them the impression that they have organized their lives more efficiently. This kind of organization is proof of "progress," just as their machines are. Taken together, this means that they are smart and getting smarter— the best and getting better. To the European self progress is obviously more than an idea.

When technology dominates in this way, it is the "inexorable drive"[10] for power and control characterizing the European *utamaroho* that is ideally complemented; but Europeans understand their nature to be the nature of all human beings, and therefore they project this attitude onto the world, i.e., dominating it.

The idea of progress had an irresistible attraction for Europeans; it was, after all, created out of their own sentiment, their *utamaroho*. It corresponded to their *utamawazo* and comprised part of the conquering mood. But it was technological efficiency that "clinched it"— that provided tangible evidence of material gain and accomplishment. Technological success gave Europeans the illusion of an objectively ("universally") valid criterion by which to judge their progress. If power over others is the ultimate and ever-present goal, and clearly technological superiority brings this kind of power, then the progress ideology that assumes lineality (change) must certainly be right. The African cyclical view of sacred time is characterized by Beard as "the belief in the vicious cycle" and has certainly led to "powerlessness" (or so goes the European argument).

The themes of European culture and ideology complement one another and converge in this way until "progress" becomes a cultural fact imbedded in the *asili*. The more particularized and hardened it becomes in the European experience, the more housed this fact must be in the language of "universalism." Europeans are not like "the rest of us"; their goals and ideals do not seem to work for them unless they can be conceived as universal goals. The idea of progress is nothing if it is not projected as having universal significance, otherwise it does not work. It must be an implicit statement of value, explicitly stated as a "neutral" fact. As with other aspects of the ideological matrix, progress cannot be acknowledged as value-based, because the "scientific" (highest value) must be valueless. Statements, dogmas, positions, European "choices" can then be imposed upon the tastes of others. European predilections, tendencies, perspectives, become that which is "proper" for all. The idea of progress pervades the European intellect—the European consciousness, as well as the European moral sense. And all who succumb to it are duped by the "magic" by which a chosen way simultaneously becomes "inevitable" change and a European goal becomes "the human goal."

The idea of progress accomplishes all this, so that when someone who describes himself or herself as a "racialist" talks about the "importance of race in civilization,"[11] he or she is merely making sense of the "facts." Once "progress" becomes ideology, once it becomes incorporated into the presupposed matter of culture, there is no way out. It is inextricably bound to European technology, and the technical obsession is the white man's creed; just as is the idea of power over "nonwhites." Wayne MacLeod (the "racialist") is quite right when he points to the weakness in Ashley Montagu's arguments. Montagu, representing the "enlightened" liberal position,[12] argues that technical "advances" are due to "accidental factors." Montagu says that

> cultures differ from one another. . .in the kind of development they have realized. This does not mean that any culture. . .is. . . incapable of realizing or achieving the same degree of development as any other culture, but merely that most cultures have not had the same or similar opportunities to do so, and largely for that reason differ culturally from one another.[13]

Montagu's "apology" for "primitive" cultures assumes the European concept of progress. Cultural "development" depends not so much on "opportunity" as it does on world view. This is what the "Idea of Progress" precludes: the viability of other world-views. But changes are not due merely to "conditions." They occur in greater numbers where they are encouraged, even mandated, by a culture that lives for them and by them. The possibility that European-style progress could be rejected does not occur to Montagu any more than it does to MacLeod. To the European mind there is no such possibility. "Enlightened liberal" and "racialist" alike, *both* have unconsciously universalized the particular. Both think that they are "progressive." For both, progress is a given in experience and assumed to be everywhere. The idea of progress is inherently racialist. Once it is accepted, the "progressive" person must always be identified as Euro-Caucasian.

The Critique of European "Progress"

The ideology of progress indicates a cultural phenomenon that functions as something more than an idea among ideas. As an ideology it becomes a frame of reference, a substratum from which other concepts are created and by which they are judged. It is a permanent criterion of suitability. Progress as ideology refers to the European way of life. It determines much of what is meaningful to them and what is not; what is ethical and what is not. Henry Skolimowski puts it this way:

> The idea of the fulfillment on earth has in time become institutionalized and known as the pursuit of progress, which in its turn has become the driving force of the whole civilization and a justification of a great variety of pursuits and aspirations of man. Indeed, it has become an overriding principle with the force of a moral imperative expressed in one commandment: One must not be against progress.[14]

In this view, the idea, though initially metaphysical-religious, becomes "pragmatic, empiricist, scientific, exploitative and elitist" in the elaboration of European culture.[14]

The function of the absolute and abstract in the European experience is the movement from *utamawazo* to determinants of behavior, to real choices; the relation between what Lovejoy calls the "other worldly" to the "this-worldly." The function of the idea is quite practical. Its abstractness is forgotten—unnecessary once it has been assimilated. Its total meaning becomes linked with the scientific-technical and the power relationships their development suggests.

Science represents something pristine to the European mind, supposedly untouched by cultural predilection. Once progress had been identified with scientific knowledge the character of its present uses were inevitable.

Frances Bacon proclaimed the pursuit of scientific knowledge as being somehow beyond moral judgment. This is an ideological act. Science became morally self-justifying, indeed, "morality" itself. The ideology of progress makes this possible. The "mad scientist" of the European nightmare fantasy is simply "acting out" zealous loyalty to the Baconian-Western creed. Descartes, who became fanatically committed to this creed, took on the task of contributing an "invulnerable" method to the edifice that was being constructed. One must also note the intensity with which he worked at severing "mind" from "body" in the *Meditations*. All such epistemological manipulations contributed to the success of the progress of ideology and the scientific world-view. And both the "Baconian attitude" and Cartesian epistemology were intensifications and developments of possibilities already present in the germinating matrix (*asili*) of the culture.

In Skolimowski's view, "forces which significantly contributed to the formation of our concept of progress" are "the crusading spirit of medieval Christianity," "the white man's mission," "the expansive restlessness of the white man," and his "acquisitive instinct."[15] Skolimowski believes, however, that it is its "interplay" with science that has a "profound influence" on the European world-view and on "our [European] ultimate ideal of progress." And so, this relationship—between science and progress—must be examined. The idea of progress in its properly European context leads inevitably to the technical order. And, in Skolimoski's view, it is the combination of the Baconian influence with that of the Encyclopedists that came to determine Europe's scientific world-view. He skillfully illustrates the way in which the culture, once having "chosen" the path of "scientific progress" continues to "choose" the ideas and theorists (ideologues) by which it will be influenced; i.e., those who are, indeed, compatible with that path. This is what we mean by "Europeanness," the nature of which is defined by the *asili* of the culture. Various ideas may be produced from within European culture, but only those that are supportive of the *utamaroho* and do not contradict the *asili* will survive and will be ultimately determinative. Skolimowski says,

> Did Einstein have a decisive influence in changing our notion of common sense and in reconceptualizing the physical universe that science explores? We are told that in this respect the lesson of Einstein has not yet been fully digested. Quite so. It thus seems as if in spite of his genius, and in spite of the shattering novelty of his ideas, Einstein was pretty irrelevant for our civilization, which is bent on a certain course of progress. For once again, how did he change the course of this civilization? . . . Einstein's influence on culture and civilization at large was negligible because *his* concept of science and his particular advancement of science did not parallel the general idiom of progress. For this reason we have selected from Einstein's science some parts of it, which are relevant to our pursuit of progress. . .and ignored other parts of it.[16]

All ideologies must state choice in terms of necessity; what has been ideologically created in terms of what is given. The functioning of culture as a synthetic whole requires the commitment of people, and that commitment requires the conviction that one way of life is right for them, as opposed to having been chosen by them—even though they *mean* precisely the same thing. But only in the context of the European *utamaroho* does it become necessary to create a category of thought and action (scientific progress) that is said to be void of ideology and belief. Because it is the imposition of that belief that becomes paramount. By dehumanizing science, Europeans have sought to place themselves above others who are not "scientific." Europeans have convinced themselves that the character of their life and culture is not a result of ideological choice, but rather one of universal human needs met by the principles of science. And Skolimowski correctly points out that the idea of "need for invention" should be viewed as a "normative or ideological component of the act of invention." Yet in European culture it is a phrase or idea used to impress others with the inevitability of European-style development. "*Different ideologies define the need for invention in differing ways.*"[17] Yet the ideology of progress is inherently imperialistic and cannot admit of these other possibilities.

How is the concept of "modernity" itself related to the "ruling ideology" of the West? "Progress" in combination with "scientism" acts to encourage the use of the term "modern." "Modern" is, indeed, so much identified with "Western" that it is difficult to see how it can be useful as a tool of analysis or description. In so far as it means anything other than "that which presently exists," it has been tied to European technology and the way of life that accompanies it. Even the term "contemporary" connotes for Europeans a quality possessed by the most advanced evolutionary stage and level of progress. The critique of progress too often identifies "modern man," as the culprit. The identification of European with "modern," whether "good" or "bad," leads away from, rather than towards, meaningful alternatives. Again, it assumes a universal line and the inevitability of European "progress."

Skolimowski views the momentum of European culture from a perspective other than that of the "ruling ideology":

> It is interesting to observe that in the past relatively simple technologies led to splendid and lasting results whereas, in the present, complex and intricate technologies lead to shoddy results. . .the overall balance increasingly shows the progressive trivialization of our lives through increasingly sophisticated technologies.

> In summing up, the story of the inventions of a given society or civilization is intricately woven with the values and social ideals, profoundly influenced by the idea of material progress, have made us favor, if not worship, one kind of invention, namely, the mechanical invention, which is the tool of increasing efficiency acting on physical nature. It is egocentric and megalomaniac on our part to view inventions of other cultures through the telescope of our culture.[18]

It is the particular kind of tyranny of the ideology of progress (its universalization and unidirectional character), in combination with the overwhelming success of Europeans ("the conquerors") that makes the argument all the more plausible—in spite of its inaccuracy—that "European forms are universal." The process of the "mechanization of the cosmos"[19] has displayed development along a consistent theme. The Platonic emphasis, while not on the mechanical tool, mandated the use of "objectification" as the essential "tool" of conceptual rationalism. The etiological and ontological relationship between "objectification" and "mechanization" is important. Intense objectification is a prerequisite for the despiritualization of the universe, and through it the European "world" was made ready for ever increasing materialization. Plato prepared Europe for excessive development in a particular direction; paved the way for the influence of Frances Bacon and for commitment to the idea of progress in its material emphasis. The ideology of progress is indeed a part of Europe's "rational heritage."

Skolimowski says that to the "believers," progress "signifies succeeding stages in the amelioration of the human condition," but in his view, "The metaphysics of progress is based on an exploitative and parasitic form of philosophy. Progress has been a cover-up for Western man's follies in manipulating the external world."[20] He outlines his conclusions regarding "the Legacy of Progress":

(1) We have better medical care. We have eliminated contagious diseases and altogether cope better with illness.

(l) We have destroyed other cultures. We have either treated them as barbarian or savage and therefore unimportant, or we brought them our technology, thereby disrupting their ways of life without giving them our standard of living.

(2) We live longer. We have reduced infant mortality and expanded the individual life.

(2) We have depleted natural resources We have heedlessly exploited the resources of the entire world as if they were infinite or easily replenishable.

(3) We live better. We have a higher standard of living; we live much more comfortably, we eat better, we dress better.

(3) We have caused ecological imbalances. Our superior scientific understanding did not prevent us from radically misreading the behavior of Nature.

(4) We travel faster, we communicate faster. We have more access to things: planes, cars, books, records, reproductions.

(4) We have created unhealthy, if not insane ways of life. We have disengaged the individual from the variety of interactions with nature and other people in which he was naturally engaging in former ways of life.[20]

These are what Skolimowski refers to as the "ambiguous blessings" of progress. (He is writing in 1974 and obviously had no knowledge of the AIDS virus.) Skolimowski continues,

> It is a mistake to think that...science and technology are universal, rational and externally valid forms which can be mixed with different contents. We have made of science and technology the kind of instrument our civilization required for its pursuit of progress; as a result we evolved *Western* (not universal) science and *Western* technology, both being a part of our acquisitive, conquering, materialistic ideology.[21]

Of course, Skolimowski's "we" is a European "we," and as the rest of us know, the political dominance of Europe has allowed for the cultural dominance of Europe. When Europeans speak of "culture" they assume that "technology" means mechanical technology. But cultures have many kinds of "tools," and a people's ideas and spirit are part of their "technology." Superior mechanical technology has led to political superiority, and it is therefore definitive in the European ideology of progress. This is because of the nature of the *asili:* the will-to-power.

For Michael Bradley, "Progress as we have institutionalized it and as caucasoids understand it, is a symptom of undisplaced aggression resulting from psychosexual maladaptation. . . ."[22] He views the Eurocaucasians as suffering from an extreme case of the "Cronos Complex," in which technology and progress are used as "future-limiting" mechanisms, assuring Europeans that they will control and "conquer" the future. Ironically, it is through the European concept of progress and an anti-human, mechanistic worship of technology that their future becomes "unknown" and oppressive; indeed it controls them.

European "progress" has been made at the expense of the quality of human existence. Where is the progress toward greater spirituality, toward human understanding, toward tolerance, toward an appreciation of diversity and plurality, away from aggression? Obviously European "reason" has not performed well in these areas, because the template of the European *asili* does not include a model for the development of humanity, only of its negation, of technological efficiency and of greater capital gain: the tools of power. Human-oriented mechanisms conflict with the driving power force. Socialism, the closest thing to a humanistic paradigm within the European tradition, has taken the shape of another mechanistic order in the ideology of Eastern Europeans. Developments in Eastern Europe, beginning with the "collapse" of the Berlin Wall in 1990, attest to the spiritual inadequacy of European socialism. It is yet another materialist conception and therefore cannot compete with, in fact must ultimately succumb to, the superior materialism of capitalist ideology.

The effects of "progress" in Bradley's view are that now, "Resource wastage and environmental pollution can cripple the future's ability to surpass the achievements of the present controlling lifetime. They are conscious attacks on the future in the interests of present identity-assertion."[23] So that the arrogance of Europeans causes them to even be destructive of their own future. "Progress," says Bradley, "is vindication of all the crises which threaten our survival. It is the materialist conception of hope itself."[24]

Utamawazo, Utamaroho, and "Progress"

Via the idea of progress it is possible to see how the ontological and epistemological definitions of a culture translate into its ideological (value and behavioral) aspects. The assumptions of cause (especially Aristotle's "Final Cause"), of lineality, and the sense of *telos* in the European *utamawazo,* as well as the dependence on abstraction, are all the necessary conceptual ingredients of progress ideology. Its assimilation depends on the mental habits encouraged by these forms of thought. Its acceptance as a predominant molder of group activity is dependent on a frame of mind already or simultaneously conditioned by lineal codification and causalist epistemology. Phenomena must relate to one another within a lineally defined whole, where "causes" precede "effects," and growth implies the incorporation and surpassing of that which has come before in a way that precludes repetition. "Progress" does not recur; it is triumph over past. The need for and feeling of "triumph" is an essential ingredient of the idea of progress. In this view, life is a continuous struggle, based on competition, and meaning is derived from "winning." Hidden behind the so-called universalism and humanism of the concept are the exigencies of an *utamaroho* that feeds on subjugation—surpassing, conquering, winning. "Progress" means "*we* are winning"; "*we* have triumphed over!" The enemy is vaguely felt, not conceived, to be "everything else out there," not only nature, but other people, other ways, ideas, forces, beings. The enemy against which the European competes is everything he or she is not. The idea involves continual movement because the enemy is never totally subdued. "She" seeks to close the gap, "and we must stay ahead of her." Progress is *staying ahead*—it is "defeating" the present.

Contrary to what European philosophy professors teach us, the conceptions of European thought respond to European aesthetic and emotional needs, to the needs of the *utamaroho*; not to a purified "reason." The idea of progress evokes positive sensations from the European self. This is what Lovejoy refers to as "metaphysical pathos."[25] William James talks about the feeling of "absoluteness" in much the same way.[26] The idea of progress achieves this "sensation" by seeming to both create history and to stand "outside" of the history which it creates. Here again the power-need of the European *utamaroho* is being fulfilled. It achieves a unique combination of the illusion of "unchanging-change" thereby providing a dynamic principle (energy source), while at the same time satisfying a sense of the eternal.

The assumption of lineal time is an ontological prerequisite to the idea of progress. Evolutionary development, an ingredient of the idea, necessitates that points be connected; this is the conceptual function of "the line." The written medium is the medium of the line, and it is evidence to the European mind of progress because words accumulate. In this way "more" becomes "better."

Progress is an argument for the discarding of the past. Yet evolutionism, its sibling idea, involves a strange kind of incorporation. Evolution requires the perception of reality as the continual development of a single entity—a single being. Yet while the form is evolving, its essence is being defined. Progress makes "garbage" of the past. It is for this sense of denial, as necessary technological change (as "progress"), that Eric Havelock argues. He characterizes the "pre-Platonic," "nonliterate," "nonhistorical" oral medium of "Homeric" Greece in the following manner:

> The confusion between past and present time guarantees that the past is slowly but continuously contaminated with present as folkways slowly change. The living memory preserves what is necessary for present life. It slowly discards what has become wholly irrelevant. Yet it prefers to remodel rather than discard. New information and new experience are continually grafted on to inherited models.[27]

For Havelock, literacy is the new technology; it represents progress and struggles against the oral sense. It *discards* the past. The concept of "newness"—value in progress ideology—doesn't mean "new" in the sense that a baby is new. It means "different" from that which has been seen before; whereas in the African view every newborn baby is the timeless *re*creation of the human. In progress ideology, what precedes on the line is always destroyed and denied.

Europeans "represent the sequence of time as a line going to the infinite."[28] That is a description of the idea of progress. Uniform and undisturbed flow of time can only be imagined as a line. If other concepts of time are admitted as plausible or operative, the ideology of progress doesn't work. In order for it to work, what must be assumed is a single, infinite, and infinitely divisible time.

In Dorothy Lee's words, the line "underlies our [European] aesthetic apprehension of the given,"[29] and progress is the "meaningful sequence" for Europeans. A people who are not progressive "*go* nowhere." The idea of progress "makes sense" because Europeans think in terms of "climactic historical sequence."[30] They are concerned not with events themselves but with their place within a related series of events.[31] As the idea of purpose permeates European life, so the idea of progress gives the impression of purpose in change.

There has been very little critical work done on the idea of progress; it is so essential to the Eurocentric idea. In 1931, J. D. Bury devoted an entire book to the discussion of *The Idea of Progress*, but his Eurocentric assumptions prevented him from being able to clarify the distinctive "Europeanness" of the concept. Bury's discussion lacks philosophical depth; he says,

> This idea means that civilization has moved, is moving, and will move in a desirable direction. But in order to judge that we are moving in a desirable direction we should have to know precisely what the destination is. To the minds of most people the desirable outcome of human development would be a condition of society in which all the inhabitants would enjoy a perfectly happy existence.[32]

It is certainly tautological to say that people desire happiness and to define happiness as that which people desire. This does not put content into the European view of the desirable, which the idea of progress certainly does. Its peculiarly European flavor is the crucial element in "progress"; for certainly if happiness were really thought to be something that other cultures had long ago achieved— progress or "movement" would be of no consequence. The issue goes deeper, for who is to say that human beings are "moving" towards anything? Bury does not question the fact of movement in lineal time. He makes this assumption because European culture oppresses one with knowledge that is most certainly becoming more and more *something*.

Bury says that obstacles to the development of this idea were not overcome until the sixteenth century.[33] I would put it differently: The necessary cognitive structures had already been set in motion in the archaic West in which a subsequent ideological synthesis could take place. The germs of the idea had been planted and some of its ideological functions were already in operation. Sixteenth-century Europe embraced the idea as a fully-matured concept, because it was also in the process of embracing an individualistic, accumulative, technocratic ethic in the form of materialistic capitalism. Protestantism supported this tendency just as the ideology of progress did. These aspects of European culture reinforced one another, became identified with one another, and grew together; because they were all generated by a common cultural seed (*asili*). Their combined momentum in the sixteenth century merely represented the final unbridled commitment to rational forms. The seeds or germs of all of them are to be found at whichever point there are enough uniquely combined traits to be identified as "European culture." This is the manifestation of the *asili*.

The distinguishable periods in European history are ethnologically a matter of difference in emphasis, intensity, and stage of development. At one point cognitive structures (*utamawazo*) and tendencies (*utamaroho*) exist; at another hardened and definitive cultural facts are present that inescapably shape the forms within which people live. But it is not until the appearance of men like Francis Bacon in the late sixteenth and early seventeenth centuries that "science" triumphed and with it the idea of progress became the unchallenged cultural philosophy of the West. The significance of the Baconian attitude was the formal demise of the tension (albeit ineffective) between European arrogance and the European sense of the supernatural. The scientific pursuit became "religion" and Europeans were no longer embarrassed by their own lack of humility.

It is, of course, with the European "Enlightenment" that the idea becomes full-fledged, respectable ideology. Robin Williams puts it euphemistically:

> In the form in which it had been molded by the Enlightenment, progress was conceived as the beneficent unfolding of man's capacities for reason and goodness. . . .[34]

From an African perspective, the idea represents the unfolding of the European's capacity for unscrupulous imperialism and exploitation of others: It is the supreme rationale. Within the culture, rationalistic epistemology would be totally identified with rationalistic culture; the marriage argued for in Platonism would be finally consummated. Williams continues,

By the late nineteenth century, the concept had been largely assimilated to the values of a complex and expanding industrial order.
Progress could now become a slogan to defend the course of technological innovation and economic rationalization and concentration.[34]

But the ideology of progress defends much more than that, it
becomes a more attractive and sophisticated packaging for the ugly,
raw European *utamaroho*. Nietzsche enthusiastically embraces the
spirit of the idea via his commitment to the ideology of "power" and
his accurate interpretation of the power drive as the essential dominating force within European culture. "Life itself," he says, "I regard
as instinct for growth, for continuance, for accumulation of forces, for
power: where the will to power is wanting there is decline."[35] In
Nietzsche's words it is possible to find an accurate reflection of the
European *utamaroho*. In a very real sense, his work is a "mirror" for
the European.

An Ideology of Imperialism

It is "progress" in its absolutist definition and ideological function that explains to Europeans why it is their duty to exploit, conquer, and control Africans and others who are different from them.
It is an ideology of supremacy, a well-constructed mythology of superiority. The point is that the rationale for an oppressive technical
order, the rational ordering of the universe and the endeavor to dominate, oppress, and destroy majority peoples, unite in a single ideological concept, the European ideology of progress.

Long before the idea of progress was part of the language of
European social theory, Christian ideology was providing the justification for European imperialism and its accompanying white
supremism (see Chaps. I and II). Roger Shinn agrees: ". . . the idea of
progress is a secularization of the biblical view of history."[36] And
Rheinhold Niebuhr says of the European Renaissance: "Its concept of
history as a meaningful process, moving towards the realization of
higher and higher possibilities, is derived from Biblical Christian
eschatology."[37] Christianity and "progress" became bedfellow ideologies as the scienfitic world-view slowly superceded the supremacy
of religion as the dominant mode of sanction. Together Christianity
and the ideology of progress now provide the mythological conceptions and symbolic systems that provide ideological support for
European dominance. Both ideologies are inherently imperialistic.
The imperialistic drive becomes "moral" in the context of these
mythologies. They symbolize Europeans as "human beings" and as

"civilizers"; while the rest of us become only "potentially human"—
"heathen" and "primitive." After using either Christianism or the ideology of progress to transform people of other cultures into
"savages," Europeans can make themselves "morally" responsible for
their "welfare," e.g., imperial control and rape.

The ideology of progress allowed Europeans to speak with
impunity of "uncivilized" and "superior" races in the nineteenth century and later allowed them to speak of "developed," "advanced,"
and "modern" nations. Europeans have no resources of their own,
but, in their view, they have the "expertise" and the "drive" that
allows them to make "proper use" of the resources of others.
Colonialism and neocolonialism in Africa, South African apartheid,
white dominance in Zimbabwe, American treatment of Native
Americans, Jewish settlers on the Gaza strip, the existence of "Israel"
in the land of Palestinians, are all part of one culture, one movement,
one ideology that expresses the attitude, "This place was nothing
before we came here." The ideology of progress vindicates this
European attitude towards our resources and our political integrity.
Euro-Caucasians the world over can never honestly condemn white
control in South Africa, since to them the whites have brought
"progress." Even Marxian theory understands colonialism as having
helped to "progress" Africans from feudalism to capitalism; necessary
lineal progression towards eventual communist revolution. Here
again we have the assumption of the European *utamawazo*. But while
for Marx "progress" stops with the achievement of the communist
state, the ideology of progress says that "progress" is never totally
"possessed"; it is a never-ending process.[38]

"Civilization" and "progress" are synonymous in this ideology;
both are supposed blessings of the European. While Europeans "civ-
ilize" us, they also bring "god," to us. For us to want to be civilized,
to want to find "god," is to want to "progress" toward being white. We
accept the ideology that supports our exploitation. We participate in
our own oppression.

Myths are a crucial aspect of self-determination and development. But they are culture-bound. African myths must explain to
African people why and how we are a great people. When majority
peoples accept the mythology of European progress, we are accepting a system of myths and symbols that explain us negatively. This is
because no single concept represents the *asili* of European culture as
fundamentally as the idea of progress. It is fundamental because of
its ideological strength.

The progress ideology has been continually visible like a thread connecting the various aspects of European culture throughout our discussion. It performs an essential function by helping to give coherence to European forms. In this sense it has a special connection to the *asili* of the culture. We have seen that the ideology of progress justifies the pattern of European behavior towards others and that it is instrumental in the creation of both the European self-image and the dialectically opposed image of others, which combine to make that pattern of behavior possible. The ideology of progress is born out of the European *utamaroho* that seeks and thrives on the power relationship. It provides the definition of superior and inferior beings that the *utamaroho* demands. We have also seen that conceptualization of this ideology assumes the cognitive structures of the European *utamawazo*. It is abstract, absolutist, oppositional, and lineal. It is based on the alienation, devaluation, and control of nature. It presupposes the objectification, despiritualization, and materialization of reality. It is the secularized statement of the Christian mythology of saving the world. It thereby is used to justify contemporary American imperialism. Finally, the ideology of progress imparts "respectability" to European xenophobia and aggression.

In the final analysis, European progress brings economic profit and political and cultural power. Since this is obviously the case, the question becomes, Why should Africans and other majority peoples embrace the European ideology of progress? Europeans have been able to convince us that we are in a "race." We enter the race somehow not realizing that by its very definition, its locus of control, and the nature of its organization, we can *never* win. We are losers even before we start: Since the rules are defined by those who need our resources in order to win. We are afraid to remain distant—to refuse the terms defined by our enemies. We are afraid to organize our own "race" in which *we* set the goals. We never question the degree to which European "progress" carries with it the accoutrements of capitalist-Christian Europeanism. We assume that the decadence of Europe (its crime-filled, drug-laden cities in which, because of spiritual retardation, disintegrated families, and the negative images produced by a capitalist media, alienated children are forced into prostitution) is a natural by-product of "progress." Africans colonized in America are told that "progress" for them means buying-in to the American system. "Black Americans must be a part of the great technological revolution in order to advance" (Ronald Reagan, Tuskegee Convocation, May 10, 1987). But our hope lies in those critical, young Africans who have the intelligence and creativity to ask the African-centered question: Advance towards what?

The reality is that given the European *asili* the ideology of progress is a powerful ideological construct. It works. But it works for Europeans. It brings them power. It justifies their existence as European and provides momentum and direction for their cultural lives and group behavior. It helps them to shape the world in their image. The ideology of progress not only functions for Europeans, but part of its success lies in its ability to seduce "the rest of us," so that we validate our own oppression. We accept its universal applicability, not realizing that its success as an ideology of imperialism is totally dependent on the syntax of "universalism." If we can reject the validity of that syntax, then we can rob it of its power as a tool of European imperialism. The ideology of progress is a European cultural-political *tour-de-force*; the syntax of universalism is its handmaiden.

Power is the ability to define reality and have other people respond to your definition as if it were their own."[1]

— Wade Nobles

Chapter 10

Universalism: The Syntax of Cultural Imperialism

The Tradition

As Europeans present their culture to the world, they do so consistently in universalistic terms. This representation takes the form of a relentless command to universalize. It is our purpose to critically examine the nature of this "universal" that so dominates European rhetoric, using the concept of *asili* to demonstrate the way in which it functions to support and proselytize European ideology. The primary purpose of this chapter is to call attention to the most subtle and ideologically effective manifestation of European cultural imperialism: the use of the semantics of "universalism" by European social theorists and "liberal" ideologues. But first let us briefly recapitulate and enumerate some of the ways the "universal" manifests itself in those patterns of European culture already discussed.

In terms of the European *utamawazo*, it is the "Platonic Abstraction" that represents the universal. It is the nature of the Platonic "forms" that they represent the "whole" and not the "part." The struggle towards and search for the universal is, for the Europeans, a movement towards the ontologically and epistemologically independent. Mircea Eliade has said that it is "sacred space" that becomes the "center of the world" for "religious man" and thereby orients him in the universe; i.e., creates cosmos from chaos.[2] Europeans, we could say are essentially "nonreligious." They therefore become enmeshed in a maze of ontological relativity, lacking a "center" of sacred space. The search for "the universal" is a primary thrust in their attempt to create order, to become centered, and to find their place in the universe.

The "whole" for Plato represents "being" (value and the possibility of knowledge); the "part" or partial is mere "becoming" and meaningless by itself, i.e., dependent. It is the nature of the "rational" that it is associated with universal characteristics. The "particular," therefore, becomes the "irrational" and is associated with mere "opinion." Continuing in the same syntactical mode, but in terms of the ideology of progress, as people become more "rational," they become more "universal." "Culture" is associated with the particular—with opinion and with the irrational. "Civilization" becomes the "universally" valid and adaptable cultural form created by rational human beings. It represents knowledge and, therefore, progress. All of this is the European's attempt to make order out of chaos. It is the European *utamawazo*.

The related Platonic dichotomies of reason/emotion, knowledge/opinion, the whole and the part are involved in the logic of all European value distinctions, and the "universal" and the "particular" (extensions of these) are the "good" and "bad" of European ideology. Nationalism is particularism and, therefore, represents nonvalue in terms of European mental categories. And just as it became necessary for Europeans to represent their culture by the term "civilization," it became necessary to represent their expressions of nationalism as internationalism as well; i.e., their interest as the interest of all people. (The small minority speaking for the overwhelming majority of the world.) This imparts additional value to their cultural commitments in terms of their own system of values, but it also does much more—it acts to support their goals interculturally.

By camoflaging European political interest as universal human goals, Europeans disarm the victims of their imperialism. Culturally-inspired flames of resistance to European aggression are extinguished by a sea of universalistic rhetoric. ("We are seeking the good of humankind, while *you* are acting merely to further the ends of a narrowly defined nationalism.") The circle is, indeed, a vicious one, for the more successfully European culture is imposed on majority cultures, the more convincing becomes the rhetoric, until we, First World "intellectuals"(European-trained), struggle also to represent not our own, but the "universal-humanitarian" interest, which, of course, has already been defined in terms of European value. (We find it "unintelligent" to talk in terms of "Race.")

An example of how this works can be demonstrated by a common contemporary use of the European value dichotomy of abstract (good) and concrete (bad). African (black) children, it is said, are severely handicapped in that they tend to think only in concrete terms and are generally "unable" to think "abstractly." An unfortunate reaction among people of African descent is to seek to *prove* that African (black) children can think just as abstractly as white children. But they are jumping the gun, for the following questions have not been asked: What does it mean to think abstractly? What *value* does it have, if in fact people do think "abstractly"?" What does it mean in terms of the *interest* of the white society? When the charge is made one could conceivably ask: What *kind* of abstraction? If European values are assumed, then one has no choice but to become as "European" as they, for they are most certainly "best."

There is only one way to break the hold, and that is to be able to recognize the phenomenon of European cultural imperalism, no matter what form it takes. This recognition can be facilitated by a critical examination of the concepts that are used to "package" it. Its disguises range from so-called universal religion to "objective scholarship"; from the abstractions of progress, science, and knowledge to the pseudoaltruistic goals of "humanitarianism," "internationalism" and "world peace." Our objective is to make the subtle manifestations of European cultural nationalism more easily discernible.

The early Christian formulation exemplifies the function of European "imperialism." While it is projected as a "world religion," fashioned for the salvation of all people regardless of their cultural origins, it is in fact interpreted as a mandate for the spread of European culture and European control. It preempts other religious formulations in terms of the syntax of European ideology, because they are nationally or culturally defined; while the Christian statement supposedly has universal significance. And yet, of course, the reality is that Christian ideology is clearly defined in terms of the European nationalistic endeavor; that is, in terms of European political interest. Simultaneously, as Europeans march throughout the world "saving souls," the numbers of those who accept the rhetoric of *their* ideology are increasing. Christianity is a "superior" religion because it is "universal"; the indigenous religions of the would-be converts are "inferior" because they are nationalistic and "culturebound." Hence European nationalism goes unrecognized while it spreads and destroys. That is the function of the "universal" in terms of European cultural imperialism. The monotheistic statement corresponds to the objective of universal control—of monolithic control within the West and of European control throughout the world. If there is only one god to obey let it be the Christian "God" of the West; i.e., the European himself. Monotheism conceptually conforms also to the normative structures of the *utamawazo*, characterized as well by the universal imperative. Its political purpose, however, is to discredit other national gods and thereby other nations.

Several African-centered theorists have drawn attention to the way in which the European statement of the standard of a "universal art" serves to impose its aesthetic judgements on African and other majority artistic expression.[3] (See Chap. 3 of this work.) This use of the universal in the cause of European nationalism is classic; it displays a pattern repeated over and over again, so that the imposition of all facets of the value-system is facilitated. It is becoming more and more obvious that to neutralize the effect of the universalistic rhetoric one need merely reject "the universal" as a viable goal, thereby eliminating the force of the rhetoric of European ideology.

Understanding the nature of the European *asili* enables us to explain the various modes of European thought and behavior as issuing from the generative core of the culture. Universalism then becomes one of the themes that contributes to the creation of a cohesive and well-constructed whole. That entity is in this case a culture able to project itself consistently as superior to others and yet normative for them. The need for such a relationship to other cultures is within the European *asili*; within its cultural germ. Universalism, then, becomes part of the natural unfolding of the *asili*.

All manifestations of the universal in the culture find their origin in the character of the *utamaroho*. Europeans use universalistic terms to describe themselves; they are "modern man," "civilized man," and "universal man." It is above all the nature of their *utamaroho* that they project themselves onto the world. They are world saviors and world conquerors; they are world peace-makers. (In 1991, the stated objective of European Americans was to save the world from the "mad man," Saddam Hussein.) They give religion and culture ("civilization") to the world. In this view, their national and cultural creations are those that are best for all people.

It is ultimately the European obsession with unlimited "power over other" that brings universalism into their conceptions. This desire for and definition of power can be found at the base of all of their cultural creations. "Power" for them is not force or energy; it is *control*. The origins of the universal in the European *utamawazo* are precisely the same. Obsessive nationalism represents, for the European mind, the ability to control the universe. By this process the unknown becomes known; the disordered becomes ordered. Nothing is "unknowable." The universal represents independence (that which controls), while the particular represents the dependent (that which is controlled). Let us see how this characteristic of the *utamaroho*, manifested as the theme of universalism, works in terms of liberal ideology; and how the rhetoric of "disinterest" serves the interests of the intellectual expression of European nationalism.

The "Myth of Objectivity" and the Uses of Scientism

An aspect of the contemporary discussion of theoretical anthropology and sociology concerns itself with the question of "objectivity" in the social sciences. European social scientists have found themselves confronted with the question of the epistemological validity of their own methodology and rhetoric; a question, to a large degree, forced upon them by the growing strength of First World self-determinists. In the United States this critique grew out of the radical political movement of students of African descent that initiated in the South in the early 1960s. As this movement matured the students began to question the nature of the Euro-American establishment, including the orthodox left, and its formal and informal decision-making process. Their activism consciously exposed the hypocritical nature of Euro-American politics and pointed to the covert U.S. agenda with regard to the exploitation of African people. The movement grew to college campuses across the country where black students called for "black studies" to be added to their college curricula. White students, inspired by this uncompromising confrontation with "the system," began to expose the covert connections between U.S. imperialists and U.S. academia.

The work of the Frankfurt School, the fairly recent area of "the sociology of knowledge," the social responsibilities symposium in *Current Anthropology* (1964), the series of related "crises" in the ranks of the American Anthropological Association, and documentation of the political nature and objectives of most of European social research abroad have all contributed to the realization of the mythical nature of the "politically detached" social scientist whose work is "free of value-judgement." By no means has the "lie" been exposed, but there is at least enough recognition of the political nature of European social theory that it is becoming more and more difficult for social scientists, or anyone else for that matter, to make claims of "objectivity." How does the scientific view and the myth of objectivity function to further the interests of European imperialism?

> . . .one of the main institutional forces facilitating the survival and spread of the value-free myth was its usefulness in maintaining both the cohesion and the autonomy of the modern university, in general, and the newer social science disciplines, in particular.[4]

We must go much further than Alvin Gouldner does in the above statement. The main cultural force that dictated the creation of the myth and supported its continuance was the fact that it provided pseudoscientific support for the imposition of European ideology.

There has always been a voice—sometimes barely audible—of African (black) social scientists who have pointed to the Eurocentricism in European social theory. They have experienced its ideological strangulation and its inability to accurately reflect the African experience. They have realized that approaching our people as objects has allowed European social scientists to immobilize us and to exploit us. European social science has not helped us to understand who we are. John Gwaltney[5] attempts to lift the "veil of objectivity" and calls for the contribution of "indigenous analysis" to the formulation of theory.[6] In other words, perspective *is* important. As William Willis[7] reminds us, "White rule with its color inequality is the context in which anthropology originated and flourished, and this context has shaped the development of anthropology." Again, Africans are the "objects" both empirically and politically. The ideological connection is clear.

In his article "Objectivity in Anthropology," Jacques Maquet describes the "existential situation" of the anthropologist in colonial Africa in the belief that it is a factor that must be taken into consideration if one is to correctly interpret the anthropologist's conclusions about the area he studies. This emphasis is important because it is diametrically opposed to the stance of European social theory in which theorists strive to "eliminate" themselves—their own particular circumstance—from their analysis. Maquet says that "an unforeseen consequence of the decolonization process is to throw doubt upon the scientific character of anthropology,"[8] because from the perspective of the victim of European colonialism, it is clear that anthropology generally represents a European perspective. This conflicts with the European definition of "science," which does not admit of perspective, therefore calling into question the status of anthropology as a science.

It leads as well to the questioning of the "scientific character" of *any* information gathering and its subsequent interpretation. Maquet concludes that subjectivity is encountered *throughout* the "scientific process." He attempts to redefine the concept of "objectivity." Conventionally, in keeping with Platonic epistemology, it meant "conformity with the object" and independence from the subject. But, says, Maquet, "the content of knowledge is never entirely independent; rather it is the result of the meeting of the subject and the object."⁹ This, he says, is true of "scientific knowlege" generally, for there is always the possibility of different perspectives. Maquet suggests therefore that the only requisite for "objectivity" be that one's observations and conclusions are partly determined by the object; elimination of the subject is *not* necessary.

The implications of Maquet's proposed redefinition are radical in the context of the European *utamawazo*. A change that the phenomenologists have been attempting to effect for over a century. It would mean a complete break from the epistemology that is based on the idea and methodology of "objectification," on which the total separation of "subject" and "object"—of the "knower" from the "known"—is predicated. Ultimately the implications of a radical change in the definition of knowledge or "what it means to know" are not only a change in epistemological methodology, but a change in the European conception of the self, with corresponding changes in the conception of "other" and behavior towards others as well. If the traditional mode of European science—"objectification"—loses its position of primacy on their scale of values, the redefinition of the culture itself theoretically becomes possible. But the *utamaroho* will not allow such a change. Any other conception would be inconsistent with the *asili*. The culture would be in basic conflict and therefore cease to function: It would not "fit" its members. Change would have to occur at the most fundamental level; the level of the *asili*. We are talking about destruction. My suspicion is that neither Maquet nor the phenomenologists are ready for anything that drastic.

European thought is locked into an *utamawazo* in which "science" plays a normative role. But there are questions to be answered: Why does science dominate? And why is science defined Eurocentrically? The ascendancy of science corresponds to other European characteristics and values. It supports a particualr kind of monolith, the assurance of a particular kind of order, and behavior and development in a desired direction. These seem to have been Plato's "reasons." But what the illusion of objectification and the dominance of the scientific mode also succeed in doing is to allow Europeans to conceal their nationalistiic objectives; e.g., their *perspective*. Scientism is science as ideology. It occurs when science becomes morality itself and, therefore, is above moral considerations.

Maquet is not willing to relinquish the dichotomy between subject and object that implies their independence of one another, even though his idea of their "meeting" might imply a partial joining.

The object in its independence from the subject influences the knowledge that the subject has of it, even if the subject has an individual and social situation which limits his possibilities of perception and thus partly determines his knowlege.[9]

It is possible that the concept of "object" as something isolated and distinct is damaging rather than helpful. It seems to prevent or inhibit thought without its use; that is, it might be the case that once the concept becomes hardened in the mind, it determines *all* thought. If the activity of "thinking" were believed to involve feeling rather than being opposed to it, then it would be more like "experiencing" something than distinguishing oneself from it. "Knowing" and "understanding" then become more humanly and existentially meaningful than what has been meant by "scientific knowledge"— defined Eurocentrically (something we are finding more and more inadequate). In Karl Mannheim's words,

> Just as pure logical analysis has severed individual thought from its group situation, so it also separated thought from action. It did this on the tacit assumption that those inherent connections which always exist in reality between thought on the one hand, and group activity on the other, are either insignificant for "correct" thinking or can be detached from these foundations without any resultant difficulties. But the fact that one ignores something by no means puts an end to its existence. Nor can anyone who has not first given himself wholeheartedly to the exact observation of the wealth of forms in which men think they decide *a priori* whether this severance from the social situation and context of activity is always realizable. Nor indeed can it be determined offhand that such a complete dichotomy is fully desirable precisely in the interest of objective, factual knowledge.[10]

Maquet makes "objectivity" possible *if* we take all the perspectives into consideration, a difficult, if not impossible feat.[9] The problem of "object" still presents itself, as long as the European concept of objectivity is maintained. The studies that Maquet suggests would themselves be plagued by the same difficulties that he has so perceptively pointed out in the article. Karl Mannheim says,

> . . . the examination of the object is not an isolated act; it takes place in a context which is coloured by values and collective-unconscious, volitional impulses. In the social sciences it is this intellectual interest, oriented in a matrix of collective activity, which provides not only the general questions, but the concrete hypotheses for research and the thought-models for the ordering of expe-

rience. Only as we succeed in bringing into the area of conscious and explicit observation the various points of departure and of approach to the facts which are current in scientific as well as popular discussion, can we hope. . . to control the unconscious motivations and presuppositions which. . .have brought these modes of thought into existence. A new type of objectivity in the social sciences is attainable not through the exclusion of evaluations but through the critical awareness and control of them.[11]

The danger here is that one becomes committed to the creation of a super-rational human being; a person who gains independence from (i.e., control over) even her epistemological presuppositions. In this view the Platonic conception is not rejected; it is "improved upon." Having found subjectivity (the "person" as irrationality) to have crept into the epistemological methodology of objectification, the goal becomes that of recognizing and controlling this subjective element. This view has very different implications from one that rejects rationality and control as "valued" modes of understanding.

Relying to a degree on Piaget's theory of the development of cognition, Jürgen Habermas argues for the "decentration of an egocentric understanding of the world."[12] It is as though we must mature intellectually and emotionally, learning to separate the "objective" and "social" worlds from the "subjective" world. In this way we can move towards "communicative rationality," which is necessary for a rationally conducted life. And even though this rationality may take a "lifetime" to discern, Habermas is insistent that this be the human objective.[13] He does not reject the vision of rationality, but clings to it, even as he attempts to redefine its meaning. It seems he cannot reject the Platonic model, even while he recognizes its flaws. Habermas has not escaped the European *utamaroho* and therefore needs a universal standard of thought and behavior, which he is convinced will achieve commonality as a basis for moral action. He attempts to circumvent the particularistic aspects of the Western conception of rationality, because of its emphasis on the "cognitive-instrumental."[14] His solution is to discover a more "universal" understanding. Even the most critical Western theorists move towards universalism and rationalism. "Universality" has, within the context of the European *utamawazo*, been the most significant ingredient of "objectivity." It is the myth of scientific objectivity that allows Europeans to speak for all of us. Let us see how the earlier scientists intended European social science to be used.

Claude Henride Saint-Simon

Maquet concludes that social phenomena differ from physical phenomena in that social phenomena may have several meanings and that their meanings are rarely obvious. The meaning of social phenomena can only be ascertained by interpretation; interpretation necessarily brings the personal into the process of social knowledge. And the question arises: Who is the interpreter? His or her perspective is important, and subjectivity comes into play. Factual generalizations synthesize, then, magnify the subjectivity.[15] The point is that social phenomena must be considered specially and differently. Human beings are special.

Claude Henride Saint-Simon didn't see it that way, and it is his distinction to have played a decisive role in the conception and definition of sociology—the academic "father" of anthropology. In his view it is the purpose of the social sciences to apply the "scientific method" of the natural sciences to the study of social phenomena, thereby achieving "truth" and "objective knowledge" with regard to the nature of the social. In Saint-Simon's words,

> Every science, of whatever kind, is nothing but a series of problems to resolve, of questions to analyse, and they do not differ from each other except in the nature of these questions. Thus *the method applicable to some of them should be applicable to all*, for the very reason that it is applicable to some of them; for *this method is an instrument entirely independent of the objects to which it applies and changes nothing in their nature*. Moreover, it is from the application of this method that every science derives its certainty: by this it becomes positive, and ceases to be a conjectural science; and this only happens after centuries of vagueness, error and uncertainties.[16] [Italics added.]

Aside from the questionable methaphysical assumptions implied in Saint-Simon's thought, the question is, Why was it so compelling for Europeans to make social science "positive?" Saint-Simon answers:

> Hitherto, the method of the sciences of observation has not been introduced into political questions; every man has imported his point of view, method of reasoning and judging, and hence there is not yet any precision in the answers, or *universality* in the results. The time has come when this infancy of the science should cease, and certainly it is desirable it should cease, for the troubles of the social order arise from obscurities in political theory.[17] [Italics added.]

One of the reasons for this compulsion is the European need to make everything—all of the culture—every aspect of life, conform to the rationalism of the European cognitive structure (*utamawazo*). But it is not enough to say that this quest for universality is a psycho-intellectual need, a compelling thought-form. It is more than that. It has an ideological (i.e., cultural-political) objective. If there is any doubt, Saint-Simon's writings make it quite clear.

He begins with the belief that by employing the "scientific method" it will be possible to get rid of points of view, of perspective. According to Maquet and Mannheim this is not the case. But if it is accepted as true, then social scientists who employ the method can have their ideological and nationalistic expression pass for "universal objective truth." Used properly this strategy became a formidable cultural/political weapon.

As with Plato, Saint-Simon was no "ivory tower" theorist, constructing theoretical systems for mere intellectual gratification. Like Plato, he was a man with a plan; a design for society. The "scientific principles" ascertained as a result of applying the scientific method to the phenomena of society would serve as guidelines for its reorganization. It is in this context that the European claim to objectivity and, therefore, universal validity must be understood. Saint-Simon is not just a harmless social theorist struggling to fit social phenomena into the European scientific tradition because of the "high valuation" of science in the culture. "Science" in this sense is valued because it can be used as a vehicle of ideological control.

Saint-Simon is a committed European nationalist, concerned with "The Reorganization of the European Community." He wants to build a European confederation that will unite its peoples by "uniformity of institutions, union of interests, conformity of principles, a common ethic and a common education."[18] Saint-Simon is quite human, and being so, his goals and objectives are no more universal nor objective than those of any other human being. They are instead expressions of culturally determined values; ideas of the European self in relation to the "cultural other." They reflect the obsession with power and dominance. In short, sociology is for him a vehicle of European cultural nationalism.[19]

John Stuart Mill

The objectives of European cultural imperialism, i.e., the universal imposition of European order and ideology, required the continual refinement of the social sciences in the tradition of Saint-Simon. Formidable minds were committed to the task of imparting "objectivity" and "universality" to Western social science. John Stuart Mill made an impressive contribution, and in his view,

> The social science (which, by a convenient barbarism, has been termed sociology) . . . is a deductive science, not, indeed, after the model of geometry, but after that of the more complex physical sciences. It infers the law of each effect from the laws of causation on which that effect depends, not however, from the law merely of one cause, as in the geometrical method, but by considering all the causes which conjunctly influence the effect and compounding their laws with one another. Its method, in short, is the concrete deductive method, that of which astronomy furnished the most perfect, natural philosophy a somewhat less perfect, example, and the employment of which, with the adaptations and precautions required by the subject, is beginning to regenerate physiology.[20]

For Mill the inability to predict human behavior has nothing to do with a *qualitative* difference between the social and the natural or the physical. His conclusion in this regard is not influenced by a recognition of the human spirit, but is rather based on what he thinks is a *quantitative* complexity of causal factors.[21] But the desire to predict and to control (the uncontrollable European need to order) compels him to apply the "scientific method" to social phenomena.[22]

And so on the level of theory, that is, superficially, sociology becomes, at best, a collection of insignificant descriptive generalizations, which reflect and encourage a dehumanizing concept of human nature, characteristic of the culture in which the discipline was created. Its epistemological purpose is to give Europeans a feeling of intellectual control that they do not have, in an area that they do not understand. Something else is happening here. The ideology of progress (while on seemingly sound footing when applied to the arena of technology), when viewed critically, reveals the ineptness of Europeans in the social, psychological, moral and spiritual spheres. Europeans needed to be able to "prove" to themselves and others that they also represented the epitome of moral and social progress. It is for this reason that the edifice of European social science was constructed. Most importantly this "social science" provides a vehicle for the exportation of European ideology by giving Europeans the "right" to speak for all people.

Emile Durkheim

The process by which European social science is made to be "objective" is a process of self-delusion. Its architects simply spread misinformation. That's why it becomes clear that it is the practical implications of this process that are its *raison d'etre*. It is not so much that Plato, Saint-Simon, Mill, and countless others were convinced of the truth of what they were saying in any imagined "absolute" sense of that term; but rather that they were convinced of the *form* social theory must take if it was to succeed. They were committed to, what for them, was a "social truth." Emile Durkheim says that one corollary of the "observation of social facts" is that "all preconceptions must be eradicated."[23] It is doubtful that he believed that this was possible, even if desirable. He is consistently concerned that "sentiment" "interferes," an inheritance from the Platonic reason/emotion value dichotomy. Above all "objectification" allowed for the elimination of "subjectivity:"

> . . . the degree of objectivity of a sense perception is proportionate to the degree of stability of its object; for objectivity depends upon the existence of a constant and identical point of reference to which the representation can be referred and which permits the elimination of what is variable, and hence subjective, in it.[24]

"Social phenomena" (human relationships, human emotion, the human spirit) can be treated as objects; as "things." And if not, then let us pretend that they can be. That is the unspoken agreement made by the architects of and adherents to the European social scientific tradition. Durkheim continues,

> . . . social phenomenona are things and ought to be treated as things. . .to treat phenomena as things is to treat them as data, and these constitute the point of departure of science. Now, social phenomena present this character incontestably.
>
> We must, therefore, consider social phenomena in themselves as distinct from the consciously formed representations of them in the mind; we must study them objectively as external things. . .
>
> If this exteriority should prove to be only apparent, the advance of science will bring the disillusionment and we shall see our conception of social phenomena change, as it were, from the objective to the subjective. But in any case, the solution cannot be anticipated; and even if we finally arrive at the result that social phenomena do not possess all the intrinsic characteristics of the thing, we ought first to treat them as if they had.[25]

The phenomenon of European social science itself has indeed

been a costly experiment, if that is how it is to be regarded. Did Durkheim think that it would take place in a vacuum — a politically isolated laboratory? We are presently in the midst of the great "disillusionment"—forced to witness many of its destructive results.

The Political Function of "Objectivity"
A Case Study

The myth of objectivity and the use of the methodology of objectification (scientism) is one aspect of universalism as an expression of the European *utamaroho* and as a tool of Western cultural imperialism. By offering an ethnographic example from contemporary Euro-American society, I can demonstrate how this works.

In 1970, the African and African-American members of the African Studies Association(ASA) challenged the work of the then twelve-year-old organization as being "fundamentally invalid and illegitimate." The ASA represented the American academic establishment. Its members were mainly from the "socio-economic middle stratum of the white colonial minority" just as Maquet describes the "existential situation" of the European anthropologist abroad.[26] The dissenters said that instead of furthering Euro-American interests in Africa, "the study of African life should be undertaken from a Pan-Africanist perspective." These Pan-Africanists acknowledged their own perspective and wanted it, and their participation to influence the ideological thrust of the activities and work of the ASA. In an article entitled "Confrontation at Montreal," Professor John Henrik Clarke said,

> African peoples will no longer permit our people to be raped culturally, economically, politically and intellectually merely to provide European scholars with intellectual status symbols of African artifacts hanging in their living rooms and irrelevant and injurious lectures in their classrooms. . .

> We suspect that this is a new area of academic colonialism and that it is not unrelated to the neocolonialism that is attempting to reenslave Africa by controlling the minds of African people."[27]

The group argued that scholarship was indeed political in its conclusions and uses. They stated their perspective and ideological commitments openly and said that the political interest of the African peoples should determine the character of African studies. The group rejected the offer of token representation made by ASA, and under the leadership of John Henrik Clarke, James Turner, Chike Onwuachi, and others, the African Heritage Studies Association split irrevocably with the ASA.

Now let us look briefly at the method of counterargument used by their opponents. In an article entitled "Politics and Scholarship" published in the ASA journal, *African Studies Review*, Benjamin Nimer begins patronizingly by saying that "two good goals are in collision in African studies in the United States—the fostering of certain black interests and the untrammeled pursuit of scholarship."[28] The word "certain" is a signpost signaling the limitations of the Pan-African position; while scholarship represents the "universal" and therefore that which is valued. This meant that the Pan-Africanists were opposing "scholarship"—an indefensible position. Like "science" and "progress" or "truth," scholarship is something no one wants to tamper with. Who among us, after all, wants to interfere with the "pursuit of science"—or with the course of "progress" on which it takes us. We are encouraged to perceive these to be universal pursuits—not "particular" or "parochial" like Pan-African self-determination. There is no question in Nimer's mind as to who will survive the "collision."

Nimer continues: "untrammeled scholarly inquiry is recognized as rational inquiry in pursuit of truth; and very few people are in principle against the pursuit of truth."

Of course not, because "the pursuit of truth" is nothing but a meaningless abstraction; a rhetorical phrase used to cloud issues, not clarify them. Nimer's article is riddled with these kinds of abstractions—which, interestingly enough, are designed to appeal to the emotions of his audience [the "metaphysical pathos" (Lovejoy) of the European tradition], while pretending to appeal to reason only. By using these terms he succeeds in erecting a wall of rhetorical disinterest, designed to disarm the avowed African nationalist who is admittedly politically and ideologically motivated. But the demystification of the syntax of universalism can prevent us from being intimidated by such terms. We must demand that the writer concretize his abstractions and put meaningful content into them. What exactly *is* "untrammeled scholarship?" *Whose* truth? Certainly Nimer would not accept Fanon's definition of truth.

> Truth is the property of the national cause. . . . Truth is that which hurries on the break-up of the colonialist regime; it is that which promotes the emergence of the nation; it is all that protects the natives, and ruins the foreigners.[29]

Nimer says that the call for African control "can be. . .construed as advocating an undesirable means to justice and the implantation not of truth rationally arrived at, but of dogma."[30] He cannot quarrel with the quest of African Americans for "justice" without embarrassing his own community of liberal academics, but he can condemn their method of pursuing it. His own method assures that *his* argument is not "dogmatic." This position is a familiar echo from the days of the Southern Student Movement of the 60s.

Basically, Nimer is concerned that he and others like him might lose their access to Africa— and their control of the character of African studies. But his argument cannot be stated in terms of a parochial interest, it would lose all of its force. He must argue in terms of "universalism." He must claim his concern to be that African studies continue to represent "truth rationally arrived at" (which means "you must play by our rules"). The position of the Pan-Africanists doesn't have the hypocritical bent characteristic of European rhetoric; they are concerned that African Studies represent an African perspective, and they say so.

The values of European ideology are discernible in Nimer's argument, once we have become adept at recognizing them through the use of the *asili* concept. He says that some people argue that political or social objectives should be primary and that although those espousing this position are often considered to represent "radical" political interests, they can be called "reactionaries" because if successful, "they would take men back to the time before they attained the level of civilization which entails respect for a disciplined search for rational truth."[28]

The entire force of the Western European world-view—the presuppositions of the European *utamawazo*, as well as the themes of European ideology— are behind this statement. The trick is to deal with it in just that way, as though it represented nothing more than European commitment, as opposed to the "universality" on which the force and success of Nimer's argument depends. It is the political effect of the objectivity argument that is of paramount importance. And this is the reason Nimer insists that in spite of the fact that "objective truth" may be unattainable, it is still a standard to be set. Nimer's argument proceeds this way: (1) If the notion of truth has practical meaning and (2) if "scholarship" is the "search for rational truth," then (3) "untrammeled scholarly inquiry" is necessary for the good of society. (It is unnecessary to say that this means scholarly inquiry untrammeled by Pan-Africanism). His argument continues in a very Platonic vein: The good of society is (a) "justice" for all its members and (b) cultivation of human excellence; therefore from the standpoint of the good society whose politics consists of such an ordering of human relations as will maximize the cultivation of human excellence, untrammeled *scholarship* is politically good. [Nimer's italics.][31]

With this view of the good society, "scholarship" cannot be subordinated to other goals. "Scholarship is good in and of itself" —a goal to which we can aspire. It is a *basis* for judgment. "It is for this reason that scholarship should be autonomous from political action in our present world."[32] (Scientism at its best!) In other words, scholarship, like religion, is unquestioned, and so its methodology becomes ideology. Nimer is really saying: How dare these Africans question our authority?

"Failures," says Nimer, "are individual failures."[32] But the point made by the African dissenters was that the ideological commitment and cultural environment of the Western European scholar in Africa has, indeed, been responsible for specific kinds of failures; most probably those which, from Nimer's perspective, would not be recognized as such. The essential thrust of Nimer's statement is counter to that of Jacques Maquet and Kathleen Gough Aberle. Macquet insists on the relevance of the anthropologist's "existential situation," while Aberle points to the fact that:

Anthropologists were of higher social status than their informants; they were usually of the dominant race, and . . .were protected by imperial law. . . . [33]

Of course, it is, in one sense, the "individual" who fails, but the perspective of the individual is most certainly influenced by her culture. And while others may come to realize that ideas are culturally mediated, Nimer must hold fast to the belief that certain epistemological methodologies ensure "purity" and guarantee that scholarship is not contaminated by group interest. He must similarly avoid the concrete and stick to the abstractions that merely indicate the syntax of European argument. His article is a good example of European cultural imperialism as manifested in the rubric of European scholarship. The tacit pivotal issues in Nimer's argument can be stated in terms of objectivity (good) vs. subjectivity (bad); individualism (good) vs. nationalism (bad), where individualism is ironically transformed into universalism. Stanley Diamond, in speaking of the "objectification" of cultural relativism, has stated this process in reverse: "participation in all cultures. . .is scientifically justified as equivalent to participation in none."[34] If we move around the circle in the other direction, "individualism" is understood to represent the lack of specific group interest and therefore to represent the interest of all people. This is a fallacy predicated on mistaken assumptions, but it is habitually used to project European commitment as universal *dis*interest.

This example demonstrates the way in which the myth of "objective" scholarship allows Europeans to claim universality, which, in turn, represents "the good" syntactically in terms of their values and their epistemology. In addition, "objective" scholarship serves to camoflage the proselytization of their own nationalistic interests. It also allows us to see concretely how the Platonic use of the methodology of "objectification" still works, these many centuries hence. Once we have understood the nature of the European *asili*, i.e., as the facade of scientistic argumentation disintegrates under scrutiny, European nationalism will be exposed.

The illusion of objectification in social science facilitates the creation and encouragement of whatever social order to which the theorist is committed. The Platonic epistemology was one aspect. Once his epistemological definitions were accepted as being eternally and universally correct, then the Republic—which corresponded to them and which was their material and ideological embodiment—had also to be accepted. Through the efforts of Saint-Simon and others, by which the illusion of objectification was made part of the definition of a nascent social science, European ideology, European cultural forms, and European value could be projected as having universal validity. With this realization, arguments that demonstrate the nonvalidity of the methodology of objectification become ammunition in the battle against the objectives of European nationalism. Put simply, in the context of European ideology, "objectification" becomes a means of claiming universality where there is none. European cultural imperialism is therefore an inherent part of European scientism.

Implications of European Internationalism

Another expression of the expansionist European *utamaroho*, the need to dominate, and the theme of universalism in the culture has been in the form of the push toward international organization. These are not the only implications that internationalism can have, but we can illustrate some characteristic instances of European internationalism and raise the issue of what the European interpretation of internationalism has meant, especially when understood in terms of the character of the European *utamaroho*. The concept of *asili* insists that we interpret European ideas and behavior in terms of the intense drive for power. Conversely, the power drive is found to be the determinative core of the culture, since all of its forms generate European power.

Western internationalism is not new; it was part of what has been called the Roman vision. Aristides describes it this way:

> Homer said, "Earth common of all," and you have made it come true. You have measured and recorded the land of the entire civilized world; you have spanned the rivers with all kind of bridges and hewn highways through the mountains and filled the barren stretches with posting stations; you have accustomed all areas to a settled and orderly way of life.[35]

Aristides does not say it was only through the contact with the African "Southern Cradle" (Diop) that Rome's nomadic northern ancestors "settled" and "ordered" themselves. That is partly because he defines "order" as "Roman control."

It is worthwhile to look at a lengthy passage from J.B. Bury in which he discusses the idea of the "ecumene" of Alexander and its relationship to the rationale for the building of the Roman empire. In Bury's typically Eurocentric description, we see imperial conquest become "universal brotherhood," imperialists become "saviors," and cultural aggression become the attempt to unite the human race. But we are in a position to interpret these behaviors from the vantage point of the *asili* concept and therefore to recognize them as expressions of European universalism: intolerance of difference, the need to control:

> In the latter period of Greek history, which began with the conquests of Alexander the Great, there had emerged the conception of the whole inhabited world as a unity and totality, the idea of the whole human race as one. We may conveniently call it the ecumenical idea—the principle of the *ecumene* or inhabited world, as opposed to the principle of *polis* or city. Promoted by the vast extension of the geographical limits of the Greek world resulting from Alexander's conquests, and by his policy of breaking down the barriers between Greek and barbarian, the idea was reflected in the Stoic doctrine that all men are brothers, and that a man's true country is not his own particular city but the *ecumene*. It soon became familiar, popularised by the most popular of later philosophies of Greece; and just as it had been implied in the imperial theory of Rome. The idea of the Roman Empire, its theoretical justification, might be a common order, the unification of mankind in a single world-embracing political organism. The term "World," *orbis (terrarum)*, which imperial poets use freely in speaking of the

Empire, is more than a mere poetical or patriotic exaggeration; it expresses the idea, the unrealised ideal of the Empire. There is a stone from Halicarnassus in the British Museum, on which the idea is formally expressed from another point of view. The inscription is of the time of Augustus, and the Emperor is designated as "savior of the community of mankind." There we have the notion of the human race apprehended as a whole, the ecumenical idea, imposing upon Rome the task described by Virgil as *regere imperior populos*, and more humanely by Pliny as the creation of a single fatherland for all peoples of the world.[36]

What sounds good in terms of European rhetoric ("Earth is mother of all; fatherland for all the peoples of the world") is actually an expression of the European world-projection of "self." It is a response to the need to make the world habitable for Europeans; the need to spread European order throughout the universe. The *utamaroho* dictates that Europeans must have unrestricted access to the world. These are the things that Roman "internationalism" meant. As it does for Pan Am Airlines, it meant "making the world comfortable for *us*," i.e., for Europeans, and, above all, making it more convenient. This concept links the ancient and contemporary West.

MacLeod compares the reality of ancient Rome with the dream of the contemporary internationalist:

> What a grandiose age! If we could transpose ourselves back into those times, and see the teeming harbours of the Mediterranean, enriching the empire with an unbelievable quantity of goods; if we could see the sophistication and pursuit of material well-being by the respectable populace, and the resulting progress upon every land; and the concern for peace, security and riches, all presided over by an international government, Rome, that outlawed conflict, that fused nation and nationalities into one human union; any modern rational humanist would, without the least hesitation, conclude that there was a period when mankind achieved nobility. Are these not the same goals that our "humanist one-worlder" is advocating today?[37]

MacLeod's comment is very significant. Writing from an avowed "racialist" perspective, he can see what the self-proclaimed liberal cannot; for the latter is too often preoccupied with abstractions that tend to blur realities. The internationalism of the liberal is concretized in the achievement of the Roman Empire and in the aspirations of the contemporary European hegemony. It is realized in the monolith!

If evidence is needed of the real European objective *vis-a-vis* "internationalism," one need only observe the present movement to build a

European conglomerate of twelve nations considered to be part of the "European Community." This movement is clearly not based on a love of humankind, but rather the pursuit of power. Europe wishes to speak formally with "one voice." We are actually witnessing the atttempt at the formulation of the European "empire." Referred to in an article by Gene Hogberg[38] as the process of "Europeanization," the movement seeks to break down barriers between the twelve European nations, between European ethnicities, and to encourage the growth of a European national consciousness. Ravanna Bey has ably chronicled this process of European "supra nationalism."[39] The 1957 Treaty of Rome was a major step in this process of consolidation, to which amendments were made and approved in 1986 by the European Communities Council of Ministers. The new legislation is called the Single European Act.[40] Of economic significance is the European Currency, a Monetary System, and the use of the European Currency Unit. According to George Kourvetaris, ratification and implementation of the Single European Act and Final Act would replace the present diverse population of Europe with "a mammoth state representing one of the world's most extensive array of populations to fall under the jurisdiction of a single governmental and legal system."[41]

If successful this will merely be a formally institutionalized manifestation of an already existing reality. Saint-Simon, like Plato before him, has been vindicated. His vision has been realized. A European national consciousness is not new. All of European history is the story of the development and reaffirmation of that consciousness. This present process of "Europeanization" means what the collective European objective has always meant: The consolidation of power. This kind of "internationalization" is an expression of intense European nationalism; all the more essential for Europe since Europeans and their descendants actually represent only 10 percent of the world's population. They, like their antecedent slavers before them, live in fear that Africans and other majority peoples will one day speak with "one voice."

Raymond Aron says, in critique of the progress ideology,

> Traditional cultures were *different*, they were not *unequal*. . . . It requires the conjunction at once logical and contradictory, of pride in technology and the egalitarian ideal for the universalistic design of industrial civilization to divide the very humanity it tends to unite.[42]

There is no contradiction for there is no "egalitarian ideal" in the European "universalistic design." It merely imposes a European "yardstick" universally, while silmutaneously *de*lineating access to the European inner circle, thereby using the natural distinctions among people as invidious measurements of worth. The "universalistic design of industrial civilization" is, at best, a response to the demands of technological and rational efficiency.

This is the internationalism of Coca Cola and the international business community (a very "national" business community—writ large!). The International Monetary Fund (IMF) is not "international-ist," it is Euro-American "supranationalist." Theodore Roszak offers a view of the future consistent with this brand of internationalism:

> The ideological rhetoric of the Cold War may continue for some time; but the main course of world affairs will flow toward urban-industrial homogeneity, spreading outward from five or six increas-ingly suave centers of technocratic power. . . .If things continue on the course they now follow, it is likely that for those looking back from a century or so in the future the most prominent feature of our time will be the global consolidation of the artificial environment, carrying with it the cultural dominance of western science and the politics of technocratic elitism.[43]

The "international person" is considered to have undergone the process of "detribalization." She has grown up and no longer relates to the "backwardness" of nationalism. So goes European rhetoric at least. But isn't the internationalization of the business world—the building of a "world business community"—a very lethal kind of nationalism. Jacques Gaston Maisonrouge, president of the IBM World Trade Corporation in 1972, is described as "the prototype of the detribalized man of the twenty-first century."[44] And the position of the business person, *and* the scientific-humanist alike, comes down to what European ideology cannot tolerate —difference; differences are to be done away with.

The internationalist, well-meaning or not, must become sensitive to the expansionist and European nationalist implications of his quest to make the world one. Marcel Griaule makes the following point:

> The staunchest upholders of the cultural superiority of the West are precisely those who, unlike the racialist, proclaim the equality of all mankind and the futility of a qualitative classification of cultures. This egalitarianism can and should, in their view, be interpreted only as a recognition of the right and duty of all mankind to attain to the standard of living and to accept the ways of thinking of the Western societies.

This is no doubt due to the fact that the European, and the American too, even when he got rid of his superiority complex with regard to coloured people, cannot abandon his devout attitude to science, regarded on the one hand as the perogative of his culture and on the other as an entity outside mankind with a life of its own, blindly subjecting stars and infusoria alike to its laws, and inevitably leading to organized happiness.[45]

"Science," says Griaule, is a "vast seismic convulsion" that, as it is expanding and moving towards progress, "breaks down and covers the subtleties and peculiarities which distinguish individuals and nations."[45]

The value dichotomy between "internationalism" and "nationalism" is most often predicated on the assumption that all nationalistic ideologies must be defined in terms of the imperative of cultural aggression. Ironically, this is a concept based on the historical definition and content of Western European "nationalism" and European cultural commitment. It is the commitment to *European* forms that necessarily implies aggression. The aggression is demanded by the *asili.*

Arthur O. Lovejoy criticizes a tendency of "romanticism," which he says originates in the individual ego, becoming collective egotism or "vanity," then "nationalism" or "racism."[46] Clearly Lovejoy is describing idiosyncratic European nationalism and not the politically necessary and healthy cultural nationalism that other cultures must nurture if they are to protect themselves against that same European nationalism. The study of European culture reveals an *asili* that has created a nationalism that becomes cultural imperialism. This is in essence what Lovejoy describes;

The belief in the sanctity of one's idiosyncrasy—especially if it be a group idiosyncrasy, and therefore sustained and intensified by mutual flattery—is rapidly converted into a belief system in its superiority. More than one great people, in the course of the past century and a half, having first made a god of its own peculiarities, good or bad or both, presently suspect that there was no other god. A type of national culture valued at first because it was one's own, and because the conservation of differentness was recognized as a good for humanity as a whole, came in time to be conceived of as a thing which one had a mission to impose upon others, or to diffuse over as large a part of the surface of the planet as possible.[46]

He says that the other side of this tendency originates in resistance to forces such as "democracy and technological progress," which tend to do away with the cultural differences that make human beings interesting and valuable to one another.[47] Here again we can use the concept of *asili* for clarity of analysis and synthesis. The nature of the European *asili* is to seek power over other. "Other" is that which presents itself as threatening because it is not controlled from the European center. The need to obliterate "difference" issues from European xenophobia, the same need to maintain difference of status so that there can be "other" that the self can control. Here we have the formula for the creation of power. In the European *asili*, cultural expression and cultural aggression become synonymous.

By focusing on positive or healthy manifestations of the phenomena of culture, alternative possibilities become visible. If the particular context of the cultural entity is the natural environment in which human beings learn to value one another, then ultimately transcultural (international) respect can only exist to the extent that particular cultural philosophies are compatible with the idea of mutual respect. Nationalism is the love of a people for themselves and their commitment to their group survival. It is the affirmation of the cultural self. It is what motivates the pockets of resistance to European oppression. European nationalism, on the other hand, has meant what Arieli describes as the character of Protestant nationalism; i.e., the mandate to universally impose its European ideas.[48] The political left has traditionally assumed the same invidious distinction between internationalism and nationalism that is characteristic of European ideology. This assumption has led to their general distrust of African nationalism and nationalist ideologies of other majority peoples. European leftists usually discourage nationalism in these groups where possible. This stance is itself an expression of the European *utamaroho*. Just as it is possible for cultural nationalism to take a positive form, it is also possible to define internationalism in such a way that it is not in basic conflict with nationalism. Just as the family unit is not generally thought of as being opposed to the maintenance of cultural unity, so nationalism and internationalism do not have to represent a dichotomy of opposing tendencies. In the African world-view diversity and unity coexist, indeed, are defined in terms of one another. Diversity is the unfolding of the universal principle, while the human intellectual/spiritual mission is the perception of the commonness in all things. If the African *utamawazo* were used to understand the normative relationship of cultural/political entities, we would reach very different conclusions than European thought has taught us. The following statement from Willie Abraham perceptively identifies some of the implications of European internationalism and its relationship to other characteristics of their social theory. Significantly, he suggests the possibility of a desirable internationalism that is not contradicted by nationalism:

> In the eighteenth and nineteenth centuries, a number of theorists thought they could detect the emergence of the truly rational man, a universal man in knowledge and sentiment, freed from his regional and narrow loyalties. His actions were to be based on the idea of the universal brotherhood of man, without differentiation. The hope of the emergence of this kind of man in political life appears to have been set back by the latter half of the nineteenth century and our own century. Those who disliked this international man thought him to be ruthless, too cerebral, too intellectualist, cut off from the warm fullness of life. Those who liked him thought that the resurgence of nationalistic feeling was an atavism or even barbarism. . . Nationalism, even when it reverts to roots, is, of course, not atavism or barbarism. It can be reconciled with internationalism. Indeed, internationalism presupposes nationalism, and the latter ensures that development and progress in the world shall be on a broad front.[49]

In the midst of this profoundly critical and African-centered statement, however, Abraham's idealism gets the better of his good judgement, and he equates the U.N. and the World Bank with "the idea of universal brotherhood." We have learned painfully that these agencies — either well-meaning and powerless, or simply conceived in the interest of European capitalism (like the IMF)—only use the rhetoric of "universal brotherhood."

The Call for a "World Culture"

While the ambitions of European aggression have always been worldwide, the visions of European humanists have inevitably been those of a world culture. The objectives "fit" the cultural *asili*. It is possible to interpret both phenomena as expressions of the theme of universalism in European ideology and as manifestations of the expansionist *utamaroho*.

Woven in and out, and around Lewis Mumford's critically historical analysis of European culture, is the theme of universalism. It influences his interpretation of Plato's objectives and the Roman "accomplishment." In his view, Plato's "real problem was one he did not even consider as a logical possibility." Mumford continues:

> . . . how to create a commonwealth capable of overcoming the limitations of Hellenic society, bridging the division between the slave

and the free; the gap between the Hellenes and the Barbarians, that is all other groups; the disparity between a continent rural life and an expansive mercantile economy tending toward mechanical uniformity. . . . How to turn the new fellowship of the religious mystery into a fellowship for political mastery: that was the problem of problems. . . . Plato never conceived that transformation.[50]

Mumford aligns the self-determinist, isolationist objective with a certain kind of "primitivity" of political vision. He says that Aristotle, like Plato, was concerned with the question: "What size of territory, what numbers, will enable a people to live *to* itself and survive *by* itself. To this Mumford responds:

That question can only be answered on a pre-civilized level; for it is the capacity for entering into a wider world in time and space, through linguistic communication, religious communion, political cooperation, that permits men to pass from the closed society of the tribe to the open society of the commonwealth.[51]

The assumptions inherent in Mumford's statement are that "tribal," kin-based, relatively small, and relatively isolated societies represent an undesirable stage of human moral and political development. Is it that "civilized" societies allow their members to better identify on a human level with those who are different, or is the reality simply that the "open society of the commonwealth" simply forces more people to become more alike? Using this concept of *asili*, this "capacity" of which he speaks can be interpreted, instead, as the demand of an expansionistic *utamaroho*. What Mumford expresses in terms of moral development can be interpreted as the development of peculiarly Western worldwide imperialistic ambition and the kind of organization necessitated by this objective, rather than as inevitable universalism. Mumford explains the reasons for Plato's "failure" in terms of his own objectives of a world culture:

We can now see why Plato failed so completely to regenerate his own culture or to lay down even an ideological basis for renewal. What undermined him, what undermined the Greeks, was their failure to be concerned with the whole life of man and with every member of society. . . . Plato's message was addressed solely to his class and his culture. It called for a radical reorientation to life, and yet it left the chief sacred cows of his world, slavery and class rule, contentedly chewing the cud. Pride of family, pride of city, pride of intellect were all self-defeating. Failing to embrace humanity, the philosophers could not even save themselves.[51]

Mumford has projected his objectives on to Plato. It does not seem, from an African-centered perspective, that Plato "failed to regenerate his own culture" or ideology. In point of fact, he succeeded overwhelmingly in doing just that; "his own culture" is regenerated in the immense political reality that thrives as European culture. Was Plato concerned with "the whole life of man?" Slavery and class rule were not contradictory to his objectives nor to the principles of the society he envisioned any more than it has been in European culture at any stage of its development—or in any of the particular histori- cal forms it has taken. Mumford's dichotomy of "family pride" and the "embracing of humanity" is of questionable value. What does it mean to "embrace humanity?" Does it mean to expand practically? That is what it meant for Alexander and for the Romans. If it means the denial of family, kin and community identification, then in our view it is not desirable. But the compassionate identification with humanness in others is predicated upon, not contradicted by, the sharing of love with those with whom one shares life. To use Sapir's distinction between that which is "genuine" and that which is "spurious"[52] in a new way, love on the level of family and community is potentially "genuine" and naturally realizable and concrete; while the idea of love on a universal level is "spurious," unnatural, and abstract. But, says Mumford, "So much for the vain and fatal parochialism of Hellenic man."[51]

What was lacking was a political and religious ideological state- ment of world conquest. So that while Plato created the formulative structures, European *utamawazo*, the full impact of the aggressive- ness of the European *utamaroho* could not be realized until it was cul- turally supported by a combination of the Judeo-Christian and Roman mandates. We, First World peoples, would have preferred "parochial- ism." Where the Greeks failed, in Mumford's view, did the Romans succeed?

> Politically the new Roman order accomplished in time what the indi- vidual polis had never been able to do: it unified the peoples of this world and brought them the boon of peace and orderly administra- tion. . . . But this unification was superimposed and therefore onesided: not a partnership of equals but a system of patrol. . . . With all Rome's generous show of law, justice, order, the underlying eco- nomic fact was pillage and extortion, and the cornerstone of the whole system was human slavery.[53]

Mumford's characterization of the Roman order is what a European-initiated universal order would inevitably mean. The objective of universalism affects Mumford's vision; "humanitarianism," as always, in the European context, becomes paternalism. He makes that clear:

> ...when the protestant sense of duty was wedded to a rational collective aim, the result was the creation of a new kind of martyr and hero: Cromwell at the head of the Parliamentary armies, Milton sacrificing his ambitions as a poet to perform the office of political secretary; Livingston bringing the Gospel to the remotest tribes of the African jungle; John Brown leading the revolt of slaves at Harpers Ferry; Abraham Lincoln rising to saintly tenderness and charity in his high-principled conduct of a stern war. Better than these, what creed can show?[54]

Mumford's "universal men," framed in an African reference, are anything but heroes. Livingston was quite simply a cultural imperialist facilitating colonial control; Lincoln perhaps displayed courage in terms of Euro-American political history, but was acting in the interest of white people. Cromwell and Milton were simply European nationalists. John Brown was the only one who can be interpreted as acting consistently with African interest, but he should have organized among his own people. He could never be considered an African hero.

Mumford, himself, wishes to distinguish between the universal good society, which is his objective, and the imposition of "irrational" European order.[55] And the "mechanical intercourse" that he disparages results in the internationalism of the business executives (Jacques Gaston Maisonrouge, the "detribalized man"). His recognition of the validity of the "regional" (i.e., cultural) seems to admit of possibilities generally denied in European universalism. But generally Mumford's call for world culture issues from the value dichotomy of universal (good)/regional (bad), which seems in his use to be equated with that between the "human" (good) and the indigenous (bad). This culminates in what is consistently the utopia of the European progressive. The danger this dream poses for other peoples is that in the process of striving for this conceptually remote goal, which seems to contradict the logic of human groupings, its concrete and realizable approximations always take the form of European rule; for they are inevitably European initiated. The "humanizing" forces within European culture, if they do exist would do better to concentrate on changing the culture that produced them; i.e., changing their *asili*– changing themselves. But that would also imply their destruction.

The "world culture" objective protects liberal Europeans from self-examination. It is the method by which these would-be benefactors avoid focusing on their own cultural/historical roots, less these same roots be identified as the source and matrix of systematic exploitation in the world. European intellectuals can justify directing their attention everywhere except on that which is peculiarly "European." Soon they will not have the choice. The critique will come from without, in the form of First World victory.

It is the nature of the *utamaroho* and the character of the European self-image that make us suspicious of any sustained or proclaimed "interest" or involvement of Europeans in other cultures. European anthropology, for instance, has provided undeniable support to the European self-image. It has, at various periods, in different "schools" and colonial situations, ranged from the more overt encouragement and support of European imperialism to the subtle expression of European paternalism, and therefore implied superiority. Because of the character of the *utamaroho*, these things are automatically implied in European relationships with majority peoples. *Such interactions are always initiated, chosen, and dominated by Europeans.*

This is the most difficult thing for the European "progressives" to understand, because it goes so deeply into the nature (*asili*) of the culture and is rooted in centuries of European behavior towards and conceptions of "others." The fact is that the *utamaroho* and self-image are not in any way supported by introspection. When Europeans limit the arena of their considerations to themselves—to their culture alone—they are no longer afforded the image of the power relationship, i.e., the supremacy over "other." They cannot "expand"; they can only transform. They must work with and on themselves. Sociological theory has, for the most part, *not* represented self-criticism or introspection. It has merely been descriptive data-gathering, supportive of an already existing order that assures European power over others. In the authentic critique of Europe, *we* will have to take control.

The only way of negating (short of destroying the culture from without) the inherently paternalistic nature of European interaction with other peoples would be to alter the European self-image, and that would mean changing the character of the *utamaroho* and the values dictated by the ideology: The ideology is, of course, embedded in the nature of the *asili*. That is a frightening truth for the European "humanist"; it's neither pleasurable nor rewarding in any immediate sense. Moreover, it is the most morally difficult task Europeans could undertake. The call for a world culture is an escape from such an unpleasant prospect. It has been, in the main, a way of procrastinating—of putting off a painful, but necessary, ordeal— much as one puts off a tooth extraction, knowing full well that the tooth will eventually have to come out. The issues are how long it will take the decay to cause untenable pain and how extensively it will be allowed to spread. There can be no viable process of European self-criticsm, because this goes against the nature of their *utamaroho.* The decay will spread until the infection is expunged by the world's majority (those external to the culture), otherwise the culture will simply rot.

A case in point: Edward Sapir's answer to the problem of cultural dominance is the call for internationalism that will do away with "spurious" culture or at least with "infatuations with national prestige." The internationalism that he calls for comes admittedly from the model of the international capitalist community. That is not accidental.

Agreeing with Sapir, Kurt Wolff says,

> We have reached a stage where we must realize our "immediate ends" on a world-wide scale, precisely in order to devote our cultural activity to such "remoter ends" as we have come to envisage.[56]

But it is precisely the "immediate," the circumscribed, the indigenous that the Europeans should be concerned with. They must learn to think of themselves as limited beings with limited powers, existing in a culture among cultures. *They* are the problem.

Wolff seeks a united vanguard of radical-anthropologists with political activists and "hippies" to "enter history" and do away with "alienation" and "disenchantment."[57] But this "vanguard" would have its hands full. Their task is nothing less than the destruction of a massive system at its ideological base; the prerequisite to the construction of a new culture. The delusion is that making all people the same will change the nature of European culture. It would in fact leave European culture completely intact, while destroying other valid visions of humanity in the process. We must constantly remember that in order for Europeans to approach others with honesty, they must artificially make them (the others) like themselves. Therefore, in even their infrequent efforts to promote an harmonious environment, they seek to do away with difference. But majority peoples are *not* like Europeans, who are, it must be remembered, only a very small minority.

The "world culture" theme as a projected goal in the literature of progressive European social theory can be interpreted as an escape from self-critique, as antithetical to First World self-determination, and as a further manifestation of the European *utamaraho*, in that the recognition of European malaise and disorder is projected onto the world instead of being lodged in the nature of European culture itself. It is endemic to the *asili*. Unconsciously, this conception of self emerges in the writings of some of the severest critics of European ideology and behavior, so that inevitably their descrptions are no longer of the horrors that Europeans have perpetrated, but of the crimes that "man" has committed. This element of the *utamaroho* is so strong that Europeans not only project their values onto the world, but their weaknesses and failings as well.

Concrete Humane Behavior versus Abstract European Humanism

The moral philosophy or attitude of humanism is regarded as a development of European speculative thought and as being characteristic of the *highest* form of European moral behavior. It is defined as a commitment to things "human," to the eliciting of, to the cultivation of the "human." The humanist is sensitive to "humanness." To the perceptive cultural scientist these phrases would describe a primarily majority culture (not European) world-view and would explain the apparent nature of classical/traditional kin-based societies: (not European culture). But there is another idea associated with European humanism, and that is the implied commitment to and "love of humanity" as an abstract conception. This, in opposition to the natural attachments of family, kingroup, culture, or, as it is derogatively termed, "tribe." If one is a European humanist one loves "Man," with a capital "M."

But it doesn't work out that way, for the demands of the latter have no relationship to the concrete love and identification with other human beings. One represents a very controlled, and purely speculative and theoretical attitude; the other is a reflection of an emotional tie, a sympathetic relationship, a feeling of identification. European humanism is in this regard an extension of the universal imperative in European ideology to conceptual ethics, to speculative moral philosophy. The rhetoric of ethical motivation is placed into the syntax of universalism and "abstraction."

As with the other correlative terms of European value distinctions, this conception of "humanism" is used to place European culture at the top of a scale on which the "least European," i.e., the cultural philosophies that differ most from this abstract norm, are at the bottom. It is the same scale as the one that places Christianity at the top, because it is supposedly monotheistic and universal; the same scale that is used to denounce religion in favor of the "scientific," the same scale by which European forms become the most universally valid and therefore "progressive." According to this scale, this means of valuation, the least European is the "lowest." This is tautological, since it is in fact a European scale.

In terms of European humanism, the higher motives are the more abstract and belong to higher cultures. The "better" and more "moral" interests are the more "universal." Self-interested action represents lower morality. This is the logic of European humanist rhetoric, it does not matter that this obviously does not describe European motivation. In these terms, commitment to or sentiment for one's concrete surroundings represents a low degree of development. R. S. Rattray typifies this view in his description of the Asante of West Africa:

> [the respect which] an Ashanti was taught from an early age to show for the lives and property of others outside his own group was not due to any abstract regard for the "sanctity of the lives" or property of his neighbors; it was due to purely materialistic considerations; a desire for his own preservation and safety; but somewhat similar results were attained, as when man, in a more advanced stage, followed the same course of action from different and higher motives.[58]

Rattray's implied association between the sanctity of proper and "higher motives" reveals his own materialistic and capitalistic "considerations."

We are concerned here specifically with the way in which the rhetorical mode of this aspect of European humanism is used to support the European self-image and how it manifests itself in European expression. Mary Kingsley characterizes the motivations of the West African this way:

> The individual is of supreme importance to himself, and he values his friends and relations; but abstract affection for humanity at large, or belief in the sanctity of lives of people with whom he is unrelated, the African barely posseses.[59]

According to this same "humanistic" attitude referred to in the statements, it is through the exposure to "other" moralities that people can learn to "overcome" their own "tribal" morality. But the above statements are made by European anthropologists with a much more intense and lengthy exposure to "diverse moralities of unfamiliar groups"[60] than the average European will ever have, and their comments are representative, not exceptional, among those made by Europeans who have "knowledge" of other cultures. It is the misconception of the value and possibility of abstraction that gets in their way. But this misconception is not easily avoided, because it is reinforced by the European *utamawazo* and other aspects of European ideology.

In both descriptions the implication is that Africans are some-how morally deficient because they do not have these "abstract con-ceptions." What is significant is that in neither case is the actual behavioral pattern of the persons being called into question. This is a manifestation of the hypocritical character of the European system of morality and the rhetorical and purely verbal form that their ethics are able to assume. By no stretch of the imagination can these social scientists say that they have observed Europeans generally exhibit-ing a more profound regard for the "sanctity of human life," nor greater affection for other human beings, than the Africans whom they observed. But that is not the point; not for a person who has been trained to think in terms of European modalities. Such a person will more than likely manifest the subtle and intellectual expression of European cultural nationalism.

Within the logic of European humanism one can talk about "morality" that is not reflected in behavior. One is considered to be highly moral if the language that one uses is couched in the syntax of abstraction and of universality; that is, of disinterest. This makes no sense in other cultures where morality is concerned with behavior only and is meaningless unless it is indicative of a behavioral norm. Which is the more "human"—the way of life that dictates respectful behavior or the one that attempts to encourage an "abstract affection for humanity at large," which has no relationship to behavior and to which the individual cannot relate? The answer lies in part in a com-parison of behavior toward unrelated peoples. It is European exploita-tion and aggressive behavior towards others that is consistent with abstraction as a normative goal. It has been to the detriment of other peoples that their conceptions have not allowed them to act with as intense and sustained hostility as Europeans have. It is their very humanity that has obstructed their political vision. (Via European "double-think" Africans became xenophobic and Europeans Xenophilic!) This is the lesson to be learned from the Gikuyu legend concerning the coming of the Europeans[61] and Ayi Kwei Armah's poetic statement "A Ruinnous Openness" (See Chap. 5).[62]

It has been pointed out that the more abstract the conceptualization, the greater the difference between verbalized moral "attitudes" and concrete acts. Stanley Diamond demonstrates this distinction between verbalized abstraction and concrete behavior as manifested in the morality of European and majority cultures, respectively, in the following quote:

> Among the Winnebago . . . no mere mouthing of an ideal of love can gain an individual either admiration or respect in the absence of the appropriate behavior. Consonant with this attitude is the degree of love insisted upon: one cannot love everybody equally. Above all, say the Winnebago: "Do not love your neighbor as you love those of your own house. Only if you are wicked will you love other people's children more than your own. . . ." To love everyone alike is impossible, and a statement to that effect would not only be insincere, but unjust, because it would lead to the neglect of those whom one ought to love most, if one is to learn to love at all. In this mode of cognition, one deserves neither credit nor discredit for giving expression to normal human emotions. It is in the context, the concrete effects that count. It is wicked to love other people's children as much as your own. . . "it is wicked to love your enemy while he is your enemy."[63]

And Frantz Fanon admonishes African and other majority peoples to:

> Leave this Europe where they are never done talking of Man, yet murder men everywhere they find them, at the corner of every one of their own streets, in all the corners of the globe. For centuries they have stifled almost the whole of humanity in the name of a so-called spiritual experience. Look at them today swaying between atomic and spiritual disintegration.
>
> . . . That same Europe where they never stopped proclaiming that they were only anxious for the welfare of Man: today we know with what suffering humanity has paid for every one of their triumphs of the mind.[64]

In terms of the *asili* concept, universalism and abstraction take on very specific meaning when they are expressed as aspects of European humanism. Using *asili* as a conceptual tool, we can explain why "humanism" has a very different meaning when used with reference to the African world-view. African culture traditionally is human-centered, and one's humanity is considered to be primarily a spiritual phenomenon. Yet this is neither rhetorical nor reflective nor abstract.

Such concepts are continually abstracted through symbolic expressions of many kinds, *and* they are ritualized. But they are also lived and felt, and that is very much a part of what "humanism" means in the African context.

The intellectualist posture of European humanism often allows scientists to become confused and to confuse others as to their own motivations and the real nature of their activities. As a representative example of how the projection of European self-interest can be made to sound like a universalistic interest in "humanity," read Ralph Beals' book, *The Politics of Social Research*. In it, Beals describes the "anthropological concern" of "anthropologists throughout the world," but, of course, anthropologists do not come from "throughout the world." They have come overwhelmingly from the West and have, therefore, represented European culture. It is their *continued access* to majority cultures with which they are concerned. The same concern as that of the U.S. Government and the International Business Community. How is this access to be assured? Again we are asked to believe that all of these concerns are based on the commitment to "untrammeled" scholarly inquiry and a desire to understand "human nature." The concrete results and relationship of this "inquiry" to European government and capitalist interests lead us to believe that the commitment has been to something much more immediate and closer to home.

The anthropologist, says Beals, "should not represent hypotheses or personal opinions as scientifically validated principles."[65] The words are easily pronounced and more easily written, but do European social scientists understand the implications of that statement? Their works, including Beal's "inquiry," would indicate that they do not.

Beals explains some of the objectives of social research:

Ultimately it was hoped to establish a computer-based model that would permit the rapid prediction of various types of outcomes of social change and conflict situations and the assessment of the effectiveness of different action programs in resolving or averting conflicts.[66]

This, indeed, is what the "advancement of science" means. Its significance is neither noble nor transcendent. Rather it is quite pragmatic, "profane," and provincial—designed for the sake of prediction and control of revolutionary movements. Beals is also pragmatically concerned that the social sciences are provided "with the proper conditions and funds to do the job."

To Science he [the anthropologist] has the responsiblity of avoiding any actions or recommendations that will impede the advancement of scientific knowledge. In the wake of his own studies he
must undertake to leave hospitable climate for future study. . . . [65]

His own "inquiry" was initiated as a study for the American
Anthropological Association "into the ethics and responsibilities of
social scientists." These are some of his "findings":

Empathy is a most valuable quality for the investigator but, when
extended to involvement in actions, it may cause difficulties for
current research and hinder access to the field for future investigations.[67]

(Beals calls this the possibility of "over-identification.")

"Primitivism"—praising the "primitive" is an affront to national
pride. . . all social scientists concerned with development problems may easily fall under criticism if they are careless in terminology or too blatantly use their own standards as the measures of
progress or development. Such terms as "backward" or even "unde-
veloped" may be regarded as perjorative if not clearly qualified. . .

Increasingly the relevance of social research is being questioned
abroad. It is noteworthy that this question is asked least often in
those countries with an active group of local social scientists, where
the public has greater understanding of scholarly and scientific
procedures.[68]

His book represents neither European self-criticism nor self-
reflection. Rather it fits the over-all pattern of mainstream European
social theory and reads like a manual for successful rapport in the
field. It avoids any really meaningful statements and therefore succeeds in saying nothing that could not have been said without extensive "study." My purpose is not to criticize this work as an isolated
instance, but rather to illustrate a dominant theme in the stance of
European intellectual-liberalism. This is one way in which the
European concept of "humanism" is used to circumvent concrete
issues and implications of behavior. The syntax of the concept itself—
its universalism and abstractnesss—allows this to happen. A "humanist" in this conception becomes a social scientist who studies other
societies for the "sake of human welfare"; but, Beals warns, he must
avoid "over-identification," i.e., not *too* much "humanism."
      This use of the abstract "humanist" rhetoric can result in the

most pernicious manifestation of European cultural imperialism, simply because, if misunderstood, it gives the impression of representing the opposite of nationalistic self-interest, in the form of humanitarian "altruism," while serving to sustain and proselytize European ideology. This brand of "humanism" is considered to represent the most progressive form of morality and is all the more detrimental from an African perspective, as it is most attractive to European intellectuals and scholars who give the impression of looking critically at their own culture. It is these individuals who are in the best position to influence First World nationalists, because it is they who gain easiest access. It is not surprising that it is the avowed European white nationalist, the separatist, who rejects the humanistic rhetoric and is usually more straightforward in representing his intentions.

The abstract concept of the "good person" is consistent with the European *utamawazo*. He is the "universal man," in that he is committed to the welfare of all and identifies with no particular group of people. He is not parochial; he is "international." He is not motivated by limiting and constraining emotional attachments, therefore he is liberated through reason and intellect so that he can identify with the "universal suffering of man." He doesn't love people, he loves "humanity." He does what he does out of a commitment to abstract ideals. He has risen above nationalism; he is internationalist. This is the syntax of the European rhetorical ethic. But Europeans resemble this description no more than do majority peoples. The successful promulgation of the European empire is, in fact, due to the intensity of their nationalistic or particularistic commitment and to the uniquely inhumane definition of their national cause.

Universalism in the European concept of humanism is the translation of scientific-rationalism into the area of conceptual ethics. An implication of "progressivism" in Dwight MacDonald's critical use of the term[69] is that morality can be derived from independent rationality and that superior people do not form moral opinion from their own human associations. The result is a very nonhuman concept of morality. Dwight MacDonald defines a radical approach to morality that is inconsistent with the European *asili*. "It rather defines a sphere which is outside the reach of scientific investigation, and whose value judgements cannot be proved (though they can be demonstrated in appropriate and completely unscientific terms); that is the traditional sphere of art and morality."[70]

Plato fought hard and successfully against such a possibility. Once the primacy of abstract, universal goals was established, an entire system of rational conceptual ethics could be constructed based on that premise—a system without "normative implications" (Stanley Diamond). Intraculturally, that is the function of the "rhetorical ethic": it agrees syntactically with the "rules" of the European *utamawazo* and is no more in tune with human nature or with the spiritual universe than is that cognitive structure.

Stanley Diamond has said,

> The result to which relativism logically tends and which it never quite achieves is to detach the anthropologist from all particular cultures. It does not provide him with a moral center.[71]

As a result the anthropologist's "self-knowledge," "engagement" and "involvement" are discouraged. In general, the abstractification of morality tends to create an unreal context for commitment, and the emphasis on the transcultural can result in a deemphasis of the concrete and immediate. It can be a form of dehumanization. It leads to what Wade Nobles calls a "transubstantive error." Transubstantive errors are literally "mistakes of meaning." They occur when the cultural manifestations of two groups of people are similar, yet the cultural substance, which gives the manifestations meaning, is different. The knower of one culture will attribute meaning, for instance, to the behavior of a member of another culture utilizing his/her own cultural substance. To the extent that the cultural substance of the groups differs, the knower will erroneously interpret the behavior in terms of his/her own perspective and thereby commit a "transubstantive error."[72]

Europeans are not the only ones who make "transubstantive errors"; although they may be the only ones who make them intentionally. We, Africans, and other primary peoples also make such errors when we trust Europeans and treat them as "family," taking them at their word. The concept of *asili* has been created to prevent us from making these mistakes. Using it, we can interpret European culture in terms of its own nature.

The ultimate goal of the cultural/political survival of all peoples does not necessarily imply the denial of culture by an affirmation of the transcultural experience. It is a question of strategy and behavior, of where you start from, and of what possibilities are thereby left to you. The stated desire to "rise above culture," to universalize commitment, has most often resulted in an ineptness at political mobilization and a failure to change European society.

European epistemological predilections, in combination with the European *utamaroho* (energy-force), generate two closely related styles of thought that are generally connected under the rubric of "humanism." On the one hand we have a tradition that is incapable of extricating itself from the behavior it purports to criticize, and succeeds in a hypocritical stance, merely paying lip-service to moral-sounding abstractions about humanistic behavior, while being immobilized politically. At the other end of this very limited spectrum are the "progressives" who run into a strangely related set of problems. Karl Marx offered an analysis of history and of capitalist society. Most of those who have accepted his analysis have raised it to the level of ideology; they have made of his analysis an "ism." In so doing they have succumbed to the European world-view, in which science becomes religion (scientism) and universalism is expressed as "internationalism" (the obliteration of cultural difference), in which "revolutionaries" are expected to commit themselves to the universal goal of a classless society. Ironically Marxian analysis, because of its narrow materialism, only inspires viable revolution when it is rooted in cultural circumstances, where it can be supplemented by more spiritualistic world-views and therefore nurtured. The resultant movements arise, therefore, from the specific historical experiences of the people involved. The more intellectualized, abstract, and universal its application, the less its viability as an effective organizing tool.

The most "liberal" and "progressive" Europeans take the position that they are best qualified to lead the rest of us in our war against *their* people. Of course, enemies become necessarily abstracted as "forces" and not cultural beings in order to support their position of continued superiority as our leaders. But Europeans are least able to universalize authentically, since their world-view is myopic, while the African world-view is more genuinely "universal" in that it is "global," wholistic, and synthetic. But we have no need to speak for everyone. Roszak has this to say:

> Marx failed to see that—once having endorsed the fundamental values of industrialism—his socialist alternative might have no choice but to let its dynamic capitalist competitor pace it along the course of history. The two centers may bear different banners, but they are in the same race. . .it becomes somewhat difficult to tell them apart.[73]

The most profound critique of Marxism, however, comes from "the Black radical tradition," as Cedric J. Robinson tells us. And his work probably represents the apogee of that tradition; a synthesis of the African-centered critique in this regard. Robinson understands that "Marxism, the dominant form that the critique of capitalism has assumed in Western thought, incorporated theoretical and ideological weaknesses which stemmed from the same social forces which provided the basis of capitalist formation."[74] Marxism, therefore, while providing an effective analytical vocabulary for the critique of capitalism, failed to place its origins firmly within the specificity of European experience. Marx's critique would, as a result, ultimately lack viability from an African frame of reference, because his own thought was "forged from the same metaphysical conventions" as that of Hegel, Darwin, and Spencer.[75] And while Marxism claims to be "intenationalist," it, as well as capitalism, Robinson argues, grows out of European nationalist sentiment.[76]

This is to be expected, since sensitivity to the characteristics of "humanness" is not implied in the European concept of humanism. A culture responsible to human needs is more to the point, and this ideological commitment does not require universalism or abstraction. European humanism has issued from the tradition of European rationalism. It suffers from the same insensitivity to spirituality as the culture does generally. It is in that sense consistent with the European *utamaroho*. European humanism has not been properly distinguished from the European scientific tradition. Science in European thought is defined mechanistically not humanistically. If humanism is defined as the recognition of the possibility of spirituality in human beings, and in terms of concrete behavior, then European "abstract" humanism is not a viable means to a more human society. True "humanism" is spiritual, not rational, which places it outside of the West not in. It involves more of the transcendence and wholism characteristic of the African world-view than the "universalism" of European thought.

Universalism and the European *Asili*

Universalism in European definition is an expression of the *asili* of European culture. The seed (*asili*) of the culture gives birth both to the intellectualist, liberal-humanist tradition and to the pattern of European behavior towards others. These patterns of thought and behavior are therefore related. By focusing on the concept of *asili*—the essential ideological core of European culture—we are able to demonstrate and to understand how the modalities of behavior and thought cohere in a consistent cultural construct, thereby giving force to one another. This is an essential step in the political analysis of European interest, which in turn leads to an understanding of the inherent nature of the European attitude towards other cultures and of the behavior that attitude directs. *Asili* allows us to link apparently "benevolent" European behavior with obviously destructive

European behavior; and further, to understand how the "humanistic" posture becomes a debilitating ideological weapon complementing the overtly aggressive and violent behavior discussed in Chap. 8. In one instance the weapons are visible, tangible, and physically destructive; in another they are difficult to discern— subtle and spiritually and ideologically destructive.

It is very helpful to examine an example of one of these more subtle expressions of European nationalism. In her discussion of "Three Thousand Years of Racism," Merlin Stone universalizes the phenomenon of "racism" into an historical "process" and tells us to remember that there are "moral qualities in all peoples" and that "no race or ethnic group has been totally morally and ethically perfect."[77] She barely mentions African descendants in her "study." The result is two-fold: If one accepts her analysis (description), she, herself, becomes one of the "good guys," separated from "3000 " years of racist behavior, and our justifiable rage is diffused as we come to "understand" ourselves as only insignificant, if unfortunate, targets of a universal process that has significantly victimized "darker" Europeans![78] She tells us to combat racism by the study of "the ethics and morals of pre- and non-Christian religions,"[77] and by "Explaining that the earliest known cultural accomplishments of humankind were those initiated and developed by darker skinned peoples...."[79] (She is vague as to the identity of these "peoples.") Yet blatantly missing from her bibliography are the very people who have committed their lives to this endeavor; from Edward Wilmot Blyden to Cheikh Anta Diop, Duse Muhammad, Yosef Ben Jochannan, John Henrik Clarke, and a host of other scholar/warriors from the African Diaspora.

We cannot mobilize for effective resistance to our physical destruction unless we are ideologically liberated. What impedes that liberation is cultural imperialism. European "universalism" and its attendant spurious "humanism" are very dangerous and effective forms of European cultural imperialism.

Universalism, when translated scientistically, becomes objectification. The illusion of objectivity promotes the myth of universalistic commitment, that is, it is a stance that disavows political or group interest. It thereby services group interest more subtly by calling it something other than what it is. We can conclude that this universalism semantically represents European value, is not a universally valid goal, and, as an "imperative" serves the interest of European cultural imperialism in the following manner: Once individuals are persuaded that universal characteristics are the proper human goals, European patterns and values can be presented as universal, while others are labelled as "particular." Then European ideology can be proselytized without the appearance of imposition, invasion, conquest, exploitation, or chauvinism.

The European claim to "universalism" is a formidable weapon, and victims of European aggression can successfully combat it if they /we proceed as follows:

1. refuse to accept "universality" as either humanly possible or desirable.

2. critically assess all universalistic concepts, including monotheism, scientific objectivity, progressivism, abstract humanism; and reject them when they are found to represent European values only and to conflict with conceptualizations based on our own ideologies.

3. accept nationalism, that is, cultural commitment, as a potentially positive, liberating, and constructive expression of human energy, depending on the specific content and definition that is given.

If we are mindful of these cultural facts, European self-interest expressed as "universalism" will become highly visible as an expression of European nationalism and cultural commitment and will thereby lose its intellectual and ideological effectiveness. We will be able to recognize ourselves as victors. For it is now clear that European universalism acts to *fulfill* the expansionist *utamaroho*, as it serves the ideological function of *utamawazo* (cognitive structure) and the power needs of the *asili* (cultural essence). Rather than being understood, then, as the new nonpartisan morality of an international order, we must interpret universalism, in its European context, in terms of the particularity of the European *asili*. It is the quintessential statement of European nationalism.

CONCLUSION

*It was not always so. The desert was made the
desert, turned barren by a people whose spirit is
itself the seed of death. Each single one of them is a
carrier of destruction. The spirit of their coming
together, the purpose of their existence, is the
spread of death over all the earth. An insatiable
urge drives them.*
— *Ayi Kwei Armah*

Conclusion

Yurugu,
The Incomplete Being

What It All Means

The concept of *asili* has been used throughout this study in the search for pattern, consistency, and logos. It is a concept that seeks to identify the germinating principle of the culture and to explain its forms in terms of their ideological source. The concept of *asili* helps us to understand that the distinctive character of Europeaness lies precisely in Europe's resistance to exotic ideas or the ability to incorporate them in such a way that the *asili* is reinforced. The scattered disssonant voices of the European tradition are made ineffective through the power of the *asili*, itself power-seeking.

Europe and its diaspora emerges, then, as a monolith; as formidable, persistent, and unidirectional. Its culture has the driving force of a machine. The cultural scientist must ask: How does this machine function? Why is it so successful in achieving its objective? Wherein lies its uniqueness? (Other cultures have at times exhibited aggression, intense technological orientation, imperialistic behavior, and other characteristics associated with European development, but they have never been as successful in these pursuits as Europeans have collectively. These tendencies never combined or sustained themselves in other cultures as they have in the West.)[1] The answers lay within the way in which the dominant modes of the culture combine; the way in which they interrelate with and reinforce one another. This synogistic effect, in turn, has as its source the ideological premise of the culture, i.e., the logos of its *asili*. Having used this concept to facilitate our study, we conclude that the success of European culture depends on the symphonic meshing of its dominant modalities around the theme of power.

The Workings of Yurugu

Yurugu, originally named Ogo, is described in Dogon mythology as acting with "anxiety and impatience." He is "incessantly restless," in search of the secrets of Amma (the creative principle), of which he wants to "gain possession." He is known for his aggressiveness and incompleteness.[2] He is in a state of solitude, having been deprived of his female principle; he is also impotent.[3] When Yurugu, "the pale fox," reaches his final form of development, he is "the permanent element of disorder in the universe," the "agent of disorganization." He was "marked" from birth for failure, to remain forever incomplete; to search perpetually for his female principle. He is not only the agent of cosmic disorder, but also of psychological individualization.[4]

Perhaps we should begin with the despiritualization of the world and its effect on day-to-day life. This is meant in an existential, ontological sense, not in a strict theological sense. In essence, Europeans have denied themselves the possibility of transcendence. This is central because many of their creations are explicable as surrogates for transcendence. The objective becomes that of attaining a sense of the divine, an awareness of the sacred dimension, the experience of eternality, which implies the suspension of ordinary time and profane space, along with the capacity to exceed the boundaries of a conceptually limited ego. Abstract categories of thought, conceptual absolutes, the syntax of universalism become the means by which they are able to achieve the illusion of transcendence. But the culture forecloses on the consequences of faith and love, while inhibiting their precondition; i.e., spirituality. The universe loses its richness as it is tranformed into lifeless matter; the supernatural is reduced to the "natural," which means to them, the merely biological or physical. Consequently, time can only be lineal; space, three-dimensional; and material causality, the ultimate reality. In European religious thought the human and the divine are hopelessly split; there is no sacred ground on which they meet. In such a setting, the exaggerated material priorities of the culture are simply a result of the praxis of its participants, of the limiting realities offered by the culture. The resultant materialism further despiritualizes the culture. So the circle is joined; and European culture gives the appearance of being a self-perpetuating system.

Let me explain further what I mean by the process of "despiritualization"; how it occurs, why it is compelling. The answers lay in the fact that only by obviating spirit can the world be made to appear rational. The illusion of the appropriateness of the supremacy of the rational mode requires an effectively despiritualized universe. It is a process by which the human being is split into rational and irrational (emotional) tendencies. These are thought to represent warring factions of her/his being. The rational self offers the possibility of knowledge (control), while the emotional self is a constant threat to the loss of control. The possibility of knowledge can only be realized when the rational self is in control of that part of the self that interferes with the rational pursuit. In this view the human being becomes properly rational, only improperly, immaturely emotional. Other cultures are experienced as the emotional, uncontrolled self. This control of the emotions begins to imply the elimination of feeling, since the definition of knowledge is that which has been decontaminated of emotional response. Since this definition comes to dominate and supplant all others, Europeans learn to value unemotional behavior. It is by being cold, uninvolved, "rational" that they gain respect; this is referred to as the achievement of "objectivity."

But affective sensibility and response are crucial for the apprehension of spiritual truths; a prerequisite for the realization of the human spirit and for the mode of participation. Rationalism and its ascendance to the position of a dominant cultural mode, then dehumanizes humanity as it consciously despiritualizes the universe. "Abstractification" (Kovel's term), a critical part of this process, helps to remove the contemplated "object" from the human context, thereby making it remote from the "knowing self." What is not near cannot be felt. The more intensified this process becomes, the more European intellect focuses on the things and objects it has created through "abstractification" and objectification, and the less is understood of what is truly human, as it escapes perception. Since this activity of "knowing" (or controlling) is a means of experiencing power, definitions are very important; naming, identifying and delineating things conceptualizes them as claimed objects—a part of the empire. What is said to be "human" then becomes knowable by rationally dehumanizing it: That is, it is made to fit into the system that the "knower" controls by the definition he or she gives it. Thus spirit is "defined" out of existence.

In terms of the reality that transcends that system, of course, the spirit is there, and it suffers, contorts, and atrophies through neglect and ignorance. It is impossible, after all, to ignore the spirit without ignoring the "person." Consequently, such rationality helps to create a certain kind of person ("individual"). Even as Europeans seek to effectively despiritualize their surroundings, they are aware of the spiritual aspect of existence. But given the premises of their rationalisitic epistemology, it must remain forever unknowable, unattainable. Spirituality represents a constant threat to the ordered system they have constructed. They therefore suffer from a chronic fear of spiritual implications; they distrust spirituality and humanness in people and in cultures. They must pretend that these phenomena do not exist, and therefore are embarrassed by their manifestations. (This, for instance is why African ritual has a tendency to make Europeans uncomfortable or causes them to overreact.) European science serves as the supremely valued activity, replacing "religion" (spiritual knowledge) as the primary means by which anxiety is relieved. It succeeds only to the degree that it is able to despiritualize the world.

The result of this many-faceted process is that all of these mechanisms are breaking down since the problem is spiritual in nature and demands another perspective on existence, another world-view. As formalized religion has taken on the character of the over-all culture, as it has become increasingly institutionalized, it has ceased to be a repository of spiritual wisdom and is unable to function as a source of spiritual-emotional well-being. "Religion" is thought also to be properly rational, and the presence of the metarational in religious belief and activity is labelled as improper to human beings; this thinking reaches its height in Protestantism. The natural cultural function of religion is a vehicle through which one's world and one's people become special and life sacred. As European religion becomes more rationalistic, it loses the ability to sacralize the profane, while simultaneously intensifying the political wasteland of European experience. Indeed, the advent of European religion is the pronouncement of its historicity.[5] This necessarily limits it to mundane space and time; to temporal categories. Secularization and desacralization are by-products of the process of rational ordering. There is no source of conflict with this process from "religious" quarters, since formalized European religion has itself been secularized. If nothing is sacred, then no act is sacrilegious. The result is a world-view that encourages attitudes of arrogance and disrespect; attitudes that are in the modality of imposed order, control, and power.

Conversely, humility, respect and a reverence for the natural order are in the modality of harmony and balance.

What effect does this have on the "self" and other European selves to which the world is forced to relate? It is a "self," or an "ego," for which no reservoirs of spiritual sustenance are provided, yet it is faced daily with the granite surface of a materialized world. This ego loses spirituality and frequently becomes deformed, or it maintains its spirituality and goes "insane" as the culture defines "insanity." By controlling the emotions and dulling the senses, "it" (the ego) is able to project "itself" and is in a better position to seek the domination of others. This attitude is supported by a rationalistic epistemology, which, as we have seen, requires that the "self" be split and that its emotional ground be denied. Yet that which is denied represents precisely the aspects of the human soul that allow one "self" to join with another. It is spirit that allows for participation, identification, and love; all are devalued modes in this minority. But they are the valid repositories of authentic morality and creative aesthetic experience.

Intraculturally, there is no basis for morality. Instead, there is merely a competitive ethic. The well-being and "success" of each disparate "self" (or ego) is threatened by that of others. Instead of being dependent on their well-being, European social structures depend, for their proper, efficient functioning, on mutual aggression, distrust, and competitiveness; i.e., fundamentally hostile relationships. If love were to enter into these microsystems they would break down. But they are ensured against this occurrence, since they breed for cold calculation and reward competitiveness and aggression. In a recent psychological test, the "male" personality was described as "aggressive, assertive, ambitious, competitive, dominant, forceful, independent, self-reliant"; while the "female" personality was "affectionate, compassionate, gentle, loving toward children, loyal, sensitive, sympathetic, understanding, warm."[6] Obviously, the "male" characteristics correspond to the European self-image. They represent those behavioral tendencies that are valued in the culture and are necessary for success in its systems. The so-called female traits are those with which the culture does not wish to identify. They are liabilities in a materialized world, all right for those who are to remain in the home, but not for the leaders and bread winners. Imbalance enters the picture.

In this hostile arena of competing selves, Europeans guard their separateness jealously, under the illusion that they are guarding their persons, their worth or being. Their "freedom" is thought to lie in the ability to be distinct. They are taught to think of themselves as the "free-est" of people; a powerful agent of change. But the European concept of individual freedom is only a reflection of the conceptually delimited European "self" (ego), which, in painful isolation, becomes increasingly passive.[7] The capacity for action has been defined only in terms of a power relationship; i.e., either I am dominant, or I am dominated—which again inhibits love. Moreover, along with spirit, the mode of participation is devalued, since this "rational psyche" has little basis from which to identify and merge with "other." The result is that European forms do not allow for the active participation of the mature self. You play according to the rules, or you don't play; and you guard your reactions or you will be rejected as "unsophisticated"—as subhuman. The creative and performing arts, normally vehicles of transcendence, in the West are most often reflections of the European *utamawazo;* i.e., analytical, impersonal and secular. And since European art is primarily an individual rather than a communal experience (the two become oppositions in the West), those few exceptions who manage to perceive and express a vision of a different reality can only communicate it to others like themselves. The culture as a whole remains untouched.

It is possible to start from any one aspect of the culture and generate its other aspects. And, what is more, these links do not follow one fixed order. They are so closely and so well related that the relationship may be explained in any number of ways. But there is a level on which they all become the same. They cohere and merge; they come together on the level of the *utamaroho* and ideology in the originating *asili.* Through an understanding of the European *utamaroho* and the *asili,* which demands it, every theme becomes one; every mechanism a method of engaging in the same valued activity, of achieving the same goal. The various modes of European culture are integrated by its ideological premise.

Utamaroho in Disequilibrium

The immortal gods have willed the Roman to rule all nations.
Cicero: Phillipics: 333

Utamaroho (the energy source of the culture) is the force that determines collective behavior. It manifests as the collective affective being (personality) of the members of the culture, tending to standardize their tastes and behaviors. It is the vital quality of the culture and is uniquely defined according to the needs of the *asili,* which it helps to fulfill. The phenomenon of the European *utamaroho* demands ethnological attention. Once its essential character is understood, it becomes relatively easy to "make sense" of the pattern of European development. What are the characteristics euphemistically associated with this *utamaroho*? "Spirit of adventure"; "the love of challenge and exploration"; "the conquering mood"; "a certain inventiveness, ingenuity and restlessness"; "ambition"; "love of freedom." These phrases signify the misinterpretation of an intensely devastating spiritual disease.

Twisted by the ideological demands of the culture into valued characteristics, they are made to seem positive, superior, even healthy. They are, instead, manifestations of a cultural ego in disequilibrium. Created in a spiritless context, the European *utamaroho* lacks the balance that comes from an informed experience of the whole self. The self that then emerges—defined in disharmony—seeks further to despiritualize its surroundings. The effectively despiritualized context it creates redefines an *utamaroho* that is in essential imbalance, in basic disequilibrium. Chronically insufficient and spiritually inadequate, this *utamaroho* ever seeks spiritual fulfillment, a harmonious condition. Europe is a cultural statement of Yurugu (see Author's Note, p. i), the male being, arrogant and immature, who caused his own incompleteness, and so is locked into a perpetually unfulfilled search for the female twin-soul that would make him whole, the part of himself he has denied.

The European *utamaroho* is seeking the self it lacks. But the possibility of spirituality as a recognized and valued dimension of experience has been denied to Europeans by the presuppositions and definitions of their *utamawazo,* by their world-view, and perhaps, as in the case of Yurugu, by the circumstances of their birth. They, therefore, interpret their needs to lie elsewhere; an error that sets in motion the process of European development. Because assessment of their needs is blurred by what Theodore Roszak has called "single vision," because they search in the wrong dimension of human experience, and because they are, by definition, deficient (Yurugu), their search is unending. The more unsatisfying the pursuit, the greater is the assurance of the continued existence of an *utamaroho* in disequilibrium; an unfulfilled spirit. The unchanging character of the European *utamaroho* and the unidirectional driving force of the culture are therefore guaranteed. Its "success" and failure are inseparable and causally linked.

This search is, after all, the expression of a universal human need; it is the need for peace (completion, wholeness). But the European has been misled by the ideological architects of his culture. He has been taught to identify "peace" with rational order, rather than with harmony. Rational order and harmonious order are very different. They represent two radically different modalities of being. Remember that for Plato "justice" in the individual and in the State is achieved by the rational ordering of conflicting elements; that is, through the control of the irrational by the rational. The struggle to control can never lead to harmony—the essence of spiritual well-being. Rational ordering is predicated on the assumption of conflict and opposition and, in European intensity, becomes a sublimated form of violence. Rational order can never be more than a creation of human beings in partial recognition of who they are; that is, in partial recognition of their cosmic significance. Rational order is the order of lesser beings, in this sense. Through it, they can only experience a part of what is possible. If they limit themselves to this order, which they have created, they and their world become distorted, which is how the *asili* was initiated, through a distortion of nature.

The apprehension of harmony requires the ability to "feel" for and intuit a pre-existing order, pre-existing not in a temporal sense; but in the sense that its existence is more comprehensive than that which we can rationally consume or generate. Greater than we are, its discovery takes us beyond ourselves, and yet is ourselves (but not as persons are thought to think of themselves in the West). Its perception requires, at least for the moment, transcendence beyond the cognitively rational self. The experience of harmony is lodged in the recognition of spirit, to which human intuitive response and interaction are guideposts. It is predicated on interdependence. It is the sense of this cosmic harmony that typically has lent majority cultures their human and moral order; herein lies the philosophical profundity of African thought.[8] Human-made rational order has its place but is only meaningful when understood to be a small part of an ordered whole. It is only on the level of spirit that rationality can be positively integrated into the human context. When that level is not reached, that which is rationally ordered merely succeeds in distorting the environment and impairing the spirit.

The European *utamaroho* translates the search for fulfillment into fanatical expansionism. The expansionism endemic to European culture is constantly reinforced by the insatiable desire for complete rational order; which, in concrete terms, comes to mean the European ordering of the world. For the European *utamaroho* order comes to mean European control, since it is by projecting the rational self that the world becomes ordered—a cultural definition that helps to create a unique *utamaroho*; an *utamaroho* that demands exactly this cultural view. Only by destroying the order inherent in the cosmos can this *utamaroho* regenerate itself. Projection of ego is substituted for

fulfillment of self. This *utamaroho* eternally seeks an emotional satisfaction it cannot experience.

The ideology of progress is but an expression of this *utamaroho.*
It is predicated on the destruction of a harmonious, organic order and
seeks to replace it with a rational and mechanical one. This ideology
proffers a goal that can never be realized, for the sake of which human
beings consume as they destroy. Technological rationalization and
exploitative capitalistic enterprise are the social activities correlated
with this ideology and the *utamaroho* that created it. Global imperialism (the destruction and consumption, or reordering of other cultures) is the form of intercultural behavior the *utamaroho* demands.
The syntax of universalism is the ideological and cognitive manifestation of this expansionistic *utamaroho.*

It is important to understand the relationship between expansionism and control, since they give shape to the dynamics of the
European *utamaroho.* "To control," for this *utamaroho*, means to render passive. Once a thing, person, or culture can be "acted upon" at
will by the European self (ego), that self is considered to have
expanded. Expansionism is the increase of its domain. Hence the
European concept of "power," is the ability to manipulate and control—to make passive as an agent of change. It is power "over," not
power "through."

Power as Logos

This concept of power, then, born out of the nature of the
European *utamaroho,* becomes the pivotal term in European ethnology; i.e., the nature of its center, its *asili.* The chronic disharmony and
imbalance of the *utamaroho* perverts spirit into lust. As emotional
security is sought via material control, the need for fulfillment
becomes the ceaseless will-to-power; i.e., the self-realization of the
asili. The nature of the *utamaroho* is itself the guaranteed source of
continued energy to be put at the service of the European quest for
greater and greater power. And this power-drive becomes the
"premise" of the culture—that fundamental aspect on which all others depend. It is the European *asili.* All European forms cohere in its
dominant ideology. It has been the objective of this entire discussion
to demonstrate the historical and synchronic depth and pervasive-
ness of this ideological force, which the concept of *asili* has enabled
us to recognize. Beginning with the premise of the need for power as
it has been defined, the dominant modes of expressions of European
thought and behavior become ethnologically explainable. The *asili* in
which the will-to-power originates demands as well that the world be

redefined in terms of power-relationships; every characteristic and theme discussed can be understood as a mechanism designed to achieve the illusion or actuality of European control.

It is not simply the aspects of the culture taken in isolation that give them European definition. On a nonideological level, and alongside other themes and values, they are to be found in all cultures. It is the concept of power lying at the ideological base of the culture that mandates the artificial "splits" that characterize the *utamawazo*. It is the mode of power and dominance that requires abstraction to be separated from concrete thought, which then become the two sides of a value dichotomy. The "true" European becomes committed, then, to the universalization of this value dichotomy; reifying one of its terms (abstraction), while he demeans the other (concrete thought). These are all steps in the "power process," which in terms of thought issues from the *utamawazo,* the cognitive manifestation of the *asili.* It is the mode of power that eliminates the possibility of conceptual unities. It is in the mode of balance and harmony, on the other hand, that unity can be perceived even in ambiguity, contrast, and inconsistency, where the European mind sees merely a battery of irreconcilable opposites (paradoxes).

European culture unfolds as a series of (1) definitions in which the world is consistently, and on every level, divided into the "conquering self" and the "controllable other"; and (2) mechanisms by which this self is assured emotional remoteness from the dominated object. This is the origin of the "impersonalism" Diamond recognizes and Roszak has called the "alienating dichotomy."[9] The cognitive self is split into that which controls and that which is or should be controlled, and this projects into a self-image in which the Europeans become the "destroying saviors." "Others" are simply imagined to be like that part of themselves that is to be controlled; that part of themselves that is "object." Just as they must not allow themselves to be defined by that irrational/emotional part of themselves, seeking always to decrease its potential, so the culture as a whole gains power by denying these "others" the capacity for self-definition.

Since all spirituality conflicts with the European concept of power, the possibility of spirit threatens its achievement. On a personal level this makes love relationships even conceptually problematical, since love and power, as they are understood in the West, are opposites; love representing loss of self and therefore of control, while power demands control of self and emotional remoteness. It is on an intercultural level that the expression of the European *utamaroho* becomes most evident. As we have seen, in the European understanding, power is predicated on destruction. The maintenance of the European *utamaroho* requires the destruction of other peoples. They are the ideal objects of European power since they are most remote from the European self-image. With the redefinition of "humanness" in terms of "rationality" (European power), other people become subhuman; they must therefore be controlled (culturally destroyed). This can be done without the moral disruption of European culture, since with the help of objectification such destruction is either not experienced or elaborately rationalized.

While the *utamaroho* demands the destruction of others, it is simultaneously dependent on the existence of the "cultural other" for its definition and functioning. It is, after all, the European *utamaroho* that is least self-sufficient. Without "other" there is no possibility of power. It is in this sense that European culture can never be self-reliant or even constructively isolationist. Europe itself is barren, depending on the resources (spiritual as well as material) of others for its existence. In accordance with the historical record of European intercultural behavior, capitalism demonstrates this well; it is acquisitive and exploitative in principle. It must ever seek new markets to control, new resources to exploit. It can never be a system at rest. Communalism and the African world-view, on the other hand, are predicated on balance and interrelationship, on the eternality of the moment.

Ontologically, the European experience demands that the universe become an aggregation of distinctly disparate beings, eternally independent of one another. The cosmos is reduced simply to the superhuman, rational, European cultural ego, and all other forms of life are despiritualized. This justifies our exploitation; use without replenishment, without regard for natural order or being.

Universalism, in European thought, is the translation of the omnipotence-ideal into a mental category, and ideological and ethical mandates. All modes of the *utamawazo* and ideology state the normative imperative of universal forms and act to create the illusion of total control. Science, representing the epitome of rational control and manipulation to the European mind, becomes, as Kovel says, a primary means of power. Scientism is but its universalistic expression. Since the desire for power—i.e., ever expanding control—is the basis of European culture, its values must necessarily be presented as universal values. The characteristics of the European *utamawazo*—its intense rationalism, analysis, objectification, and lineality—all contribute to the illusion of intellectual power and therefore to the achievement of material power. They are the mech-

anisms of mental control and manipulation necessary for the epistemological transformation of the world into something that does not
question the European *asili,* but complements the European *uta-maroho*, and guarantees white supremacy.

The ideology of progress is a power ideology. It states the desirability of total control of the environment through an increasingly
rationalized technical order, at the same time providing the moral justification for universal European supremacy. European religion is an
aspect of this progress ideology; shaped by the *utamawazo* and *uta-maroho*, it also morally supports the dominance of European forms
by mandating the universal imposition of the culture. Even European
scientific humanism acts to enhance the illusion of power for the benefit of the *utamaroho*. This exalted ethical statement is a perversion
of that which is morally valid. "Abstract love" is the absence of love.
Like the Christian concept of "agape," it is love uncontaminated by
humanness. Through rationalism and abstractification, European
humanism helps to remove the moral agent from the human context.
What is considered moral action loses existential meaning. The ultimate result is the ascendency of European definitions, which helps
the European to become, once again, the protagonist. There is no
aspect of intercultural behavior in which the *utamaroho* will allow
the European to be "taught" by majority peoples or to participate as
a noncompeting equal. (This is why the idea of Africans seeking
"equality" "from" Europeans is an apolitical approach to reality.
Equally absurd is the attempt to "enlighten" or "change" them.) The
success of the culture is due to the fact that nothing within it ideologically conflicts with the quest for power. So-called European
humanism, at best, redirects the power drive by emphasizing its intellectual expressions; and humanitarianism becomes paternalism, a
disguised form of European supremacy. The culture itself is designed
to be a dehumanizing force; European humanism is a contradiction
in terms.

All modes of European behavior and dominant styles of action
act to increase and ensure material control. Protestantism is the ultimate ethical statement of the individual behavioral pattern necessary for control on all levels. In terms of the logic of the culture, all
of these cultural phenomena become mechanisms of power, which in
turn feed an already deformed *utamaroho*. The power ideology that
defines the total culture keeps it off-balance. The culture itself—
always "progressing," never "progressed"—is unidirectional, one
dimensional, fanatical, and atrophied; a culture that must consume
others. But ultimately this ideology is incoherent; it literally lacks

human meaning. It is the compulsiveness, the drive, the insatiable appetite of the culture that are its distinguishing features (Kovel speaks of a "cosmic yearning," an "endless striving," a "bottomless longing"). It is as well-constructed as a power machine can be. Its *asili* guarantees power over "others." In this respect, Spengler is right. The culture is Faustian. For success it has sacrificed "soul." What is left is profane. Aesthetically, and in terms of self-image, it identifies as white. Europe is the cultural home of a people who identify as one race; i.e., banding together for survival and destruction of others. They would destroy each other if there were not others to destroy. They fear and hate blackness, which they associate with spiritual power—a power which they can neither possess, create, nor control.

Imposing the Cultural Self

Here is an example of European nationalism:

> A cooperative attitude of unity must eventually take place amongst all western peoples for the naked purpose of survival. In this age of anti-westernism the ideal of common brotherhood must take root amongst Americans, Scandinavians, South Africans, Australians, or whatever.[10]

Explicit statements such as this one are not hard to identify, and they resemble nationalistic expression of other cultures, only the names are different. European nationalism generally, however, finds more indirect and complex means of expression. It is the commitment to sustain the conventional definitions and themes of European culture. We have identified these, as mechanisms by which power and supremacy are maintained. Since the success of the culture conflicts with the survival of other cultures as self-defining entities, European nationalism becomes cultural imperialism and therefore denies the validity of the self-determination of other cultures. With an understanding of the European *asili*, the ideology of the culture and its nationalistic expression become more visible. This new visibility makes the European assault easier to assess and to combat ideologically and politically.

As a single phenomenon, European cultural imperialism is the attempt to proselytize, encourage, and project European ideology. The *asili* is imperialistic by definition. The cultural self is spread in order to control others, and by controlling others the culture spreads itself. European nationalism implies European expansionism, that, in turn, mandates European imperialism. European nationalistic expression takes the form of rhetoric or behavior which seeks to increase European power. In this sense, the European *utamaroho* is by definition nationalistic. The culture is inherently expansionistic; it seeks not self-determination, but imperial dominion (for that, as Cicero has so aptly put it, is European self-expression). Above all it seeks the universal imposition of European ideology, and the most effective means of achieving this has been by packaging it in what appear to be non-valuative terms. We can now enumerate the general categories into which the various manifestations and forms of European cultural imperialism fall. The various chapters of this study are replete with specific examples of each of these forms of expression.

The Forms of Expression of European Cultural Nationalism

European imperialism/expansionism:

All cultural statements and styles of behavior that aid this objective. Included in this form of expression are all wars in which the Europeans have been involved, as well as such cultural mechanisms as the rhetorical ethic.

Theories of white supremacy:

This includes the systematic attempt to destroy positive self-images of African and other majority peoples.

Theories of European supremacy:

This is exemplified by the ideology of progress, the Judeo-Christian formulation, unilinear cultural evolution, etc.

All vehicles used to promote theories of white and European supremacy:

This would include the use of their popular media to depict European invaders as morally heroic victims of non-European "savagery" and brutality; such mechanisms as I.Q. testing; the dominant thrust of European social theory and European speculative philosophy.

The defamation of all African and other majority nationalisms, cultural and ethnic identification, and attempts at self-definition.

European humanism:

This is nationalistic insofar as it tends to promote European forms, the European *utamawazo,* a scientific-rational view of the human, the mythology of European intellectual superiority, and superficial interculturalism.

Liberal ideology:

This is characterized by a deemphasis of European limitations and deficiencies, by the attempt to place them on a nonideological level, as well as the attempt to co-opt critical thought (that is, to make it ineffective). This acts to maintain the culture with the same ideological commitment and in the same power position vis-à-vis other cultures.

The devaluation of spirit:

This can take the form of the debasement of spirituality in other peoples and other cultures, and the attempt to spread cynicism—convincing others that there is no spiritual reality. When successful, this is a very powerful weapon of European cultural imperialism.

The celebration of material power:

Along with the devaluation of spirit, when effective, this succeeds in reducing everything to European hegemony.

As a general rule for identifying expressions of European cultural imperialism, statements must always be put into the context of European ideology; that is, they must be interpreted in terms of the European *asili*. It is here that they become statements of nationalistic commitment, and only in this setting can their relationship to our political interests be determined.

Towards a Vision of the Human Spirit

Ayi Kwei Armah writes:

> What a scene of carnage the white destroyers have brought here,
> What a destruction of bodies, what a death of souls!
>
> Against this what a vision of creation yet unknown,
> higher, much more profound than all erstwhile creation!
> What a hearing of the confluence of all the waters of life
> flowing to overwhelm the ashen desert's blight!
> What an utterance of the coming together of all the peoples of our
> way, the coming together of all people of the way.[11]
>
> Their news was also of relationships of a beauty still to be realized,
> of paths to be found.
> Their news was of the way, the forgotten and the future way.[12]
>
> All beauty is in the creative purpose of our relationships;
> all uglyness is in the destructive aims of the destroyer's arrangements.

The mind that knows this, the destroyers will set traps for it,
but the destroyers' traps will never hold that mind.
The group that knows this and works knowing this,
that group itself is a work of beauty, creation's work.[13]

The image of the West with which the world has been bombarded is one that has served the purposes of continued European political and cultural/ideological domination. European cultural imperialism has done a formidable job. Since Plato the intellectual energies of Europeans have been devoted to convincing themselves and others of their superiority. As a result, the European tradition is a bastion of propaganda, and those who do not share European commitments have been forced to occupy themselves with denying the validity of this portrait; i.e., with refuting its inherent arguments and with offering a different view of the meaning of European development.

But in this endeavor there is a danger of becoming "possessed" ourselves by the very definitions that we have denied. Now that we have broken the power of their ideology, we must leave them and direct our energies toward the recreation of cultural alternatives informed by ancestral visions of a future that celebrates our Africaness and encourages the best of the human spirit. Each of the cultures historically victimized by Europe must reclaim its own image. As for those of us who are African, our salvation (redemption) lies in our ancientness and connectedness; not in a romanticized glorification of the past, but in a return to the center in which all contradictions are resolved and from which the spiral of development can continue with clarity. From the center, ikons can be retrieved in our image that will allow us to tap the energy of the collective conscious will of our people.

It is our destiny not to flee the predators' thrust
not to seek hiding places from destroyers left
triumphant; but to turn against the predators advancing,
turn against the destroyers, and bending all our
soul against their thrust, turning every strategem
of the destroyers against themselves, destroy them.
That is our destiny: to end destruction - utterly;
to begin the highest, the profoundest work of creation, the work
that is inseparable from our way, inseparable
from the way.

— Ayi Kwei Armah

Notes

Introduction

1. Chinweizu, *The West and the Rest of Us*, Nok Publishers, Lagos, 1978, p. xiv; Carter G. Woodson, *The Mis-Education of The Negro*, AMS Press, New York, 1977.
2. Chinweizu, Onwuchekwa Jemie, and Ihechukwu Madubuike, *Toward the Decolonization of African Literature*, Vol. I, Howard University Press, Washington, D.C., 1983; Iva Carruthers, "War on African Familyhood," in *Sturdy Black Bridges*, Roseann Bell, Betty Parker, and Beverly Guy-Sheftall (eds.), Anchor Press, Garden City, N.J., 1979.
3. Kathleen Gough, "Anthropology and Imperialism," in *Monthly Review*, April 1968, pp. 12–23.
4. Dona Marimba Richards, "From Anthropology to African-centered Cultural Science," unpublished paper. New York, 1984.
5. Wade Nobles, *Africanity and the Black Family*, Black Family Institute Publications, Oakland, Ca., 1985, p. 103.
6. Leonard Barrett, *Soul-Force: African Heritage in Afro-American Religion*, Doubleday, Garden City, N.J., 1974, p. 6.
7. Willie Abraham, *The Mind of Africa*, University of Chicago Press, Chicago, 1962, p. 27.
8. Raymond Betts, (ed.) *The Ideology of Blackness*, D.C. Heath and Company, Lexington, Mass., 1971, p. v.
9. Barrett, p. 6.
10. Morris Opler, "Themes as Dynamic Forces in Culture," in *American Journal of Sociology*, Vol. 51, 1945, p. 98.
11. Robin Williams, *American Society*, 3rd ed., Alfred A. Knopf, New York, 1970, p. 22.
12. Edward T. Hall, *Beyond Culture*, Anchor Press, Garden City, N.J., 1976, p. 42.
13. Clifford Geertz, *The Interpretation of Cultures*, Basic Books, New York, 1979.
14. Wade Nobles, "African Consciousness and liberation Struggles: Implications for the Development and Construction of Scientific Paradigms, Part I," *Journal of Black Studies*, Vol. I, November 3, 1985, San Francisco State University, Black Studies Department.
15. Hunter Adams, "Strategies Toward the Recovery of Meta-Conscious African Thought," lecture at City College in New York, 6 June 1987; Molefi Kete Asante, *Afrocentricity: The Theory of Social Change*, rev. ed., Africa World Press, Trenton, 1986; orig. published 1980.

16. Robert Armstrong, *Wellspring: On the Myth and Source of Culture*, University of California Press, Berkeley, 1975, p. 94.

17. Ibid, p. 96.

18. Professor Ibrahim Sherif (African Studies, Rutgers University) and Professor Jaffer Kassimali (African and Puerto Rican Studies, Hunter College) have helped me with the construction of these terms.

19. Gregory Bateson, *Naven*, Stanford University Press, Stanford, 1958, p. 25.

20. Ibid, p. 220.

21. Ibid, p. 115.

22. Ibid, p. 311.

23. Ibid, p. 212.

24. Julian Jaynes, *The Origin of Consciousness in the Breakdown of the Bicameral Mind*, Houghton Mifflin, Boston 1976, p. 439.

25. Nobles, pp. 104–105.

26. M. Karenga, *Kawaida Theory*, Kawaida Publications, Inglewood, N.J., 1980, p. 90.

27. Eli Sagan, *The Lust to Annihilate: A Psychoanalytical Study of Violence in Ancient Greek Culture*, Psychohistory Press, New York, 1985; Joel Kovel, *White Racism: A Psychohistory*, Vintage, New York, 1971.

28. Norman Cantor, *Western Civilization: Its Genesis and Destiny*, Vol. I, Scott, Foresman, Atlanta, 1969, p. 3.

29. Ibid, p. 4.

30. Ibid, p. 5.

31. Ibid, p. 8.

32. Quoted in George O. Adams, "The Idea of Civilization," in *Civilization*, University of California Press, Berkeley, 1975, p. 45.

33. Oswald Spengler, *The Decline of the West*, Vol. I, Alfred A. Knopf, New York, 1928, p. 3.

34. Max Weber, *The Protestant Ethic and the Spirit of Capitalism*, rev. ed., Charles Scribner's Sons, New York, 1958, p. 13.

35. Stanley Diamond, *Search for the Primitive*, Transaction Press, New Brunswick, N.J., 1974, p. 118.

36. Dona Marimba Richards, "Toward the Demystification of Objectivity," in *Imhotep, Journal of Afrocentric Thought*, Vol. I, No. 1, Department of African American Studies, Temple University, 1989.

37. Nobles, p. 104.

38. Asante, *Afrocentricity: The Theory of Social Change*, Africa World Press, Trenton, 1986.

39. Ibid.

Part I - Thought and Iconography

Chapter 1 - *Utamawazo*:
The Cultural Structuring of Thought

1. Plato, *Timaeus*, The Dialogues of Plato, Vol.I, trans. Benjamin Jowett, Random House, New York, 1937, p. 10; George James, *Stolen Legacy*, Julian Richardson, San Franscisco, 1976; Theophile Obenga, "African Philosophy of the Pharoanic Period," in *Egypt Revisited*, 2nd ed., Ivan Van Sertima (ed.), Transaction, New Brunswick, 1989.
2. Eric Havelock, *Preface to Plato*, Grosset and Dunlap, New York, 1967, p. 200.
3. Ibid, p. 236.
4. Fritjof Capra, *The Tao of Physics*, Bantam Books, New York, 1977, p. 9.
5. Plato, *The Republic*, Bk. IV:431, The Dialogues of Plato, Vol. I, trans. Benjamin Jowett, Random House, New York, 1937.
6. Paul Goodman, "Polarities and Wholeness: Gestalt Critique of 'Mind,' 'Body,' 'External World,'" in *Sources*, Theodore Roszak (ed.), Harper and Row, New York, 1972.
7. Iva Carruthers, "Africanity and the Black Woman," in *Black Books Bulletin*, 1980, Vol. VI, No. 4.
8. Robert Armstrong, *Wellspring: On the Myth and Source of Culture*, University of California Press, Berkeley, 1975, p. 115.
9. Ibid, p. 116.
10. Ibid, p. 117.
11. Page duBois, *Centaurs and Amazons: Women and the Pre-history of the Great Chain of Being*, University of Michigan Press, Ann Arbor, 1982, p. 16.
12. Vernon Dixon, "World Views and Research Methodolgy," in *African Philosophy*, Lewis King, Vernon Dixon, and Wade Nobles (eds.), Fanon Center Publications, Los Angeles, 1976.
13. duBois, p. 2.
14. Dixon.
15. duBois, p. 5.
16. duBois, p. 9.
17. Stanley Diamond, *Search for the Primitive*, Transaction Press, New Brunswick, N.J., 1974, p. 183.
18. Frances Cress Welsing, *The Isis Papers: The Keys to the Colors*, Third World Press, Chicago, 1991, pp. 1–14.
19. Havelock, Ch. 11.
20. Dixon, p. 55.
21. Havelock, p. 223.
22. Theodore Roszak, *Where the Wasteland Ends*, Doubleday, New York, 1972, p. 68.
23. Plato, *Theatetus*, trans. Francis Cornford, The Liberal Arts Press, New York, 1959, p. 184.

24. Richard King, "African Origins of Psychobiology," lecture at City College, New York, 1987.
25. duBois, p. 132.
26. Ibid, p. 138.
27. Plato, *Phaedrus*, p. 264c, quoted in duBois, p. 138.
28. duBois, p. 138.
29. Quoted in duBois, p. 139.
30. Jurgen Habermas, *Reason and the Rationalization of Society* Vol. I, Beacon Press, Boston, 1984, p. 68.
31. Richard King, "African Origins of Psychobiology," lecture at City College, New York, 1987.
32. Francis Cornford, *Plato's Theory of Knowledge*, Bobbs Merrill Educational Publishing, Indianapolis, 1957, p. 102.
33. Plato, *Theatetus*, trans. Francis Cornford, Liberal Arts Press, New York, 1959, p. 102.
34. Plato, *Timeaus*, p.12.
35. Friedrich Juenger, *The Failure of Technology*, Henry Regnery Co., Chicago, 1956, p. 107.
36. Havelock, p. 197.
37. Michael Bradley, *The Iceman Inheritance*, Warner Books, New York, 1978.
38. Carl Sagan, *The Dragons of Eden*, Ballantine Books, New York, 1977.
39. Henri Frankfort and H.A. Frankfort, "Myth and Reality," in *The Intellectual Adventure of Ancient Man*, Frankfort et al. (eds.), University of Chicago Press, Chicago, 1977, pp. 14, 20, 21.
40. Habermas, p. 70.
41. Ibid, p. 74.
42. Diamond, p. 192.
43. Havelock, p. 230.
44. J.B. Levi, *The Ancient Egyptian Language: Pathway to Africa*, unpublished paper, 1984.
45. Frankfort and H.A. Frankfort, pp. 3–27.
46. Havelock, pp. 190–210.
47. Amos Wilson, "The Mis-education of Black Students," lecture at Hunter College, New York, April 29, 1988.
48. Plato, *Republic*, Bk X:605.
49. Havelock, p. 208.
50. Habermas, p. 70.
51. Edward T. Hall quoted in J. Brown, "Plato's Republic as an Early Study of Media Bias and a Charter for Prosaic Education," in *American Anthropologist*, 1973, Vol. 74, No. 3.
52. Diamond, p. 192.
53. R.A. Schwaller De Lubicz, *Symbol and the Symbolic*, trans. Robert and Deborah Lawlor, Autumn Press, Brookline, Mass., 1978, p. 55.
54. Ibid, p. 44.
55. Ibid, p. 27.
56. Diamond, pp. 3–4.
57. H.L. Searles, *Logic and Scientific Methods*, 2nd ed., Ronald Press, New York, 1956, p. 4.

58. Habermas, p. 69.
59. Edward T. Hall, *Beyond Culture*, Anchor Press, New York, 1977, p. 9.
60. Havelock, p. 182.
61. Dorothy Lee, *Freedom and Culture*, Prentice Hall, Englewood Cliffs, N.J.,
    1959, p. 117.
62. Ibid, p. 91.
63. John S. Mbiti, *African Religions and Philosophies*, Anchor Press, New York,
    1970, pp. 127–129.
64. Mircea Eliade, *The Sacred and the Profane*, Harcourt Brace, New York, 1959,
    p. 21.
65. Dona Marimba Richards, "European Mythology: The Ideology of Progress,"
    in *Black Contemporary Thought*, Molefi Asante and Abdulai Vandi (eds.),
    Sage Publlications, Los Angeles, 1985, p. 218.
66. Juenger, pp. 35–36.
67. Ibid, p. 39.
68. Ibid, p. 46.
69. Ibid, p. 48.
70. Marshall McLuhan, *Understanding Media*, McGraw-Hill, New York, 1967,
    p. 57.
71. Edmund Carpenter, "The New Languages," in *Explorations in
    Communication*, Edmund Carpenter and Marshall McLuhan (eds.),
    Beacon Press, Boston, 1960, p. 162.
72. Mircea Eliade, *The Myth of the Eternal Return*, Harcourt Brace, New York,
    1954, p. xi.
73. James, pp. 114–130.
74. Aristotle, *Introduction to Aristotle*, Richard McKeon (ed.), Modern Library,
    New York, p. 248.
75. De Lubicz, p. 78.
76. Frankfort and Frankfort, pp. 15, 20.
77. Cedric X. Clark, "Some Implications of Nkrumah's 'Consciencism' for
    Alternative Coordinates in Non-European Causality," in *African
    Philosophy*, Lewis M. King, Vernon J. Dixon, and Wade W. Nobles (eds.),
    Fanon Center Publication, Los Angeles, pp. 117–118.
78. Leonard Barrett, *Soul Force*, Doubleday, Garden City, N.J., 1974, Ch. 2.
79. Clark, p. 118.
80. Carl Spight, "Towards Black Science and Technology," in *Black Books
    Bulletin*, Fall 1977, Vol. I, No. 3, pp. 6–11, 49.
81. Hunter Adams, "African Observers of the Universe," in *Journal of African
    Civilizations*, 1979, Vol. I, No. 2.
82. Quoted in Adams, p. 5.
83. Quoted in Adams, p. 6.
84. De Lubicz, p. 91.
85. Hall, p. 11.
86. Ibid, p. 243.
87. Aristotle, *Metaphysics*, 1005B, quoted in Dixon, "World Views and Research
    Methodology," p. 75.
88. Dixon, pp. 75–76.
89. Havelock, p. 226.

90. Francis Yates, *Giordano Bruno and the Hermetic Tradition*, University of Chicago Press, Chicago, 1978.
91. Diamond, p. 193.
92. Ibid, p. 194.
93. Alvin Gouldner, *Enter Plato*, Basic Books, New York, 1965.
94. Lewis Richards, *Ancient Greek Literature in Translation*, Vol. II, Chicago, 1986, p. 372.
95. Ibid, p. 64.
96. Gouldner, p. 190.
97. Arthur O. Lovejoy, *The Great Chain of Being*, Harvard University Press, Cambridge, 1966, p. 12.
98. Ibid, p. 45.
99. Norman Brown, *Life Against Death*, Wesleyan University Press, Middleton, Conn., 1959, p. 274.
100. William James, *The Writings of William James*, John H. McDermott (ed.), Random House, New York, 1968, pp. 498–500.
101. Ibid, p. 431.
102. Willie Abraham, *The Mind of Africa*, University of Chicago Press, Chicago, 1962, p. 19.
103. B. Edwards, *Drawing on the Right Side of the Brain*, J.P. Tarcher, Los Angeles, 1979, p. 29.
104. Hunter Adams, "Strategies. Toward the Recovery of Meta-Conscious African Thought," lecture at City College of New York, 6 June, 1987.
105. Julian Jaynes, *The Origin of Consciousness in the Breakdown of the Bicameral Mind*, Houghton Mifflin, Boston, 1982, p. 47.
106. Ibid, pp. 59–65.
107. Ibid, p. 66.
108. Ibid, pp. 69, 72, 73.
109. Ibid, pp. 103–104.
110. Ibid p. 93.
111. Ibid, p. 79.
112. Ibid, pp. 104–105.
113. Ibid, pp. 101–103.
114. Ibid p. 221.
115. Ibid, p. 106.
116. Ibid, pp. 439–440.
117. Erich Neumann, "On the Moon and Matriarchal Consciousness," in *Fathers and Mothers: Five Papers on the Archetypal Background of Family Psychology*, Spring Publications, Zurich, 1973, p. 46.
118. Ibid, p. 48.
119. Hall, p. 191.
120. David Bidney, "The Concept of Meta-Anthropology and its Significance for Contemporary Anthropological Science," in *Ideological Differences and World Order*, F.S.C. Northrop (ed.), Yale University Press, New Haven, 1949, p. 325.
121. Gouldner, p. 191.
122. Ibid, p. 121.
123. Ibid, p. 306.

124. Katherine George, "The Civilized West Looks at Primitive Africa: 1400–1800," in *The Concept of the Primitive*, Ashley Montagu (ed.), The Free Press, New York, 1968, pp. 178, 182.

125. Rheinhold Niebuhr, *The Nature and Destiny of Man*, Vol. I, Charles Scribner's Sons, New York, 1937, pp. 26–27.

126. Ibid, p. 26.

127. Roszak, *Where The Wasteland Ends*, p. 164.

128. Ibid, pp. 170, 173.

129. Ibid, p. 168.

130. Ibid, p. 248.

131. Lovejoy, *The Great Chain of Being*, p. 21.

132. Ibid, p. 327.

133. Ibid, p. 59.

134. Ibid, pp. 183, 63.

135. Ibid, pp. 58–59.

136. Ibid, p. 199.

137. Ibid, p. 187.

138. duBois, p. 13.

139. Niebuhr, p. 14.

140. Abraham, *The Mind of Africa*, p. 42.

141. Ibid, p. 24.

142. Ibid, pp. 15–16.

143. Ibid, p. 48, pp. 61, 51.

144. Havelock, *Preface to Plato*, p. 205.

145. Ibid, p. 197.

146. Plato, *Laws*, Bk. IX:875C. The Dialogues of Plato, trans. Benjamin Jowett, Random House, New York, 1937, p. 620.

147. Lovejoy, p. 324.

148. Ibid, p. 198.

149. Juenger, *The Failure of Technology*, p. 155.

150. Lovejoy, p. 328.

151. Ibid, p. 329.

152. Ibid, pp. 331–332.

153. Ibid, p. 333.

154. Dixon, "World Views..." p. 57.

155. Ibid, p. 56.

156. R.A. Schwaller De Lubicz, *The Sacred Science*, Inner Traditions, New York, 1982, p. 9.

157. Ibid, p. 18.

158. Ayi Kwei Armah, *Two Thousand Seasons*, Third World Press, Chicago, 1979, p. 4.

159. Capra, pp. 10–11.

160. Ibid, p. 7.

161. Ibid, p.9.

162. Ibid, p. 6.

163. Vine Deloria, *God Is Red*, Delta Book, New York, 1957, p. 102.

164. Ibid, p. 103.

165. Ibid, p. 175.

166. Frankfort and Frankfort, p. 4.

167. Jennifer Brown, "Plato's Republic as an Early Study of Media Bias and a Charter for Prosaic Education," *American Anthropologist*, Vol. 74, No. 3, 1973, p.673.

168. Armah, p. 321.

Chapter 2 - Religion and Ideology

1. Mircea Eliade, *The Sacred and the Profane*, trans. Williard R. Trask, Harcourt Brace, New York, 1959.

2. John G. Jackson, "Egypt and Christianity," in *Journal of African Civilizations*, Vol. IV, No. 2, Nov. 1982, pp. 65–80; Yosef Ben-Jochannan, *African Origins of Major "Western Religions,"* Alkebu-Lan Books, New York, 1973; J.M. Robertson, *Pagan Christs,* University Books, New York, 1967; Gerald Massey, *Ancient Egypt: Light of the World*, rev. ed., Random House, New York, 1973; T.W. Doane, *Bible Myths; And Their Parallels in Other Religions*, University Books, New Hyde Park, New York, 1971.

3. Clifford Geertz, "Religion as a Cultural System," in *Anthropological Approaches to the Study of Religion*, Michael Banton (ed.), Praeger, New York, 1966).

4. Plato, *Republic*, Bk. VII: 531, 525, trans. Benjamin Jowett, Random House, New York, 1977.

5. George Steiner, *Language and Silence*, Atheneum, New York, 1967.

6. Arthur O. Lovejoy, *The Great Chain of Being*, Harvard Universtiy Press, Cambridge, 1966, p. 42.

7. In European culture, this conservative function must be self-conscious, mechanical, and exacting in order to stabilize the culture and maintain its ideological thrust, since a crucial aspect of the ideology is constant superficial change. In traditional, classical African and other non-European cultures, this relationship between stasis and creativity is a much more organic one, i.e, until the intrusion of Europe.

8. Hugh J. Schonfield, *The Passover Plot*, Bantam, New York, 1967, p. 16.

9. Ibid, p. 195.

10. Terence Penelhum, *Religion and Rationality*, Random House, New York, 1971, p. 6.

11. Oswald Spengler, *The Decline of the West*, Vol. II, Alfred A. Knopf, New York, 1928, p. 219.

12. Rheinhold Niebuhr, *The Nature and Destiny of Man*, Vol. II, Charles Scribner's Sons, New York, 1946, p. 42.

13. Schonfield, p. 8.

14. Ibid, p. 4.

15. Ibid, p. 211.

16. Arthur E. R. Boak, *A History of Rome to 565 A.D.,* 4th ed., Macmillan, New York, 1955, p. 393.

17. Norman Baynes, "Constantine The Great and the Christian Church," in *The Proceedings of the British Academy*, Vol. XV, Humphrey Milford, London, 1929, p. 3.

18. Eusebius "The Conversion of Constantine," in *History of Western*

Civilization, Topic IV, Christianity in the Ancient World, University of Chicago Press, Chicago, 1956, p. 9; orig. published 324 A.D.

19. Ibid, pp. 13–14.
20. Boak, p. 432.
21. Timothy Barnes, *Constantine and Eusebius*, Harvard University Press, Cambridge, 1981.
22. Ibid, p. 210.
23. Boak, p. 433.
24. Ibid, p. 434.
25. Eusebius, pp. 10–11.
26. Boak, p. 502.
27. Baynes, *Constantine The Great,* p. 15.
28. Ibid, p. 17.
29. Ibid, p. 20.
30. Ibid, p. 19.
31. Ibid, p. 31.
32. Ibid, p. 26.
33. Aristides in William H. McNeill, *History of Western Civilization: Selected Readings*, University of Chicago Press, Chicago, 1953, p. 31.
34. Baynes, *Constantine The Great,* p. 5.
35. Ibid, p. 36.
36. Ibid, p. 3.
37. Jackson, pp. 65–80.
38. Elaine Pagels, *The Gnostic Gospels*, Vintage, New York, 1981, p. 5.
39. Ibid, p. 4.
40. Schonfield, p. 4.
41. Pagels, p. 7.
42. Ibid, p. 8.
43. Ibid, p. 12.
44. Ibid, p. 14.
45. Ibid, p. 17.
46. Ibid, p. 30.
47. Ibid, p. 32.
48. Ibid, p. 56.
49. Ibid, p. 48–49.
50. Ibid, p. 51.
51. Ibid, pp. 44, 46, 47, 52.
52. Dona Marimba Richards, "Let the Circle Be Unbroken: The Implications of African-American Spirituality," in *Presence Africaine*, Nos. 117/118, 1981, pp. 247–292.
53. Spengler, *Decline of the West*, Vol. II, p. 217.
54. Norman Baynes, *The Political Ideas of St. Augustine's De Civitate Dei*, George Philip and Son, London, 1949, pp. 89.
55. Ibid, p. 7.
56. Augustine, *City of God*, in The Basic Writings of St. Augustine, Vol. II, Whitney J. Oates (ed.), Random House, New York, 1948, p. 86.
57. Baynes, "Political Ideas," p. 13.
58. Niebuhr, Vol. I, p. 216.

59. Baynes, "Political Ideas," p. 14.

60. Augustine, p. 491.

61. Carlton W. Molette III, "Afro-American Ritual Drama," in *Black World*, Vol. XXII, No. 6, 1973, pp. 54–56

62. Rheinhold Niebuhr, *The Nature and Destiny of Man* Vol. I, p. 216.

63. John S. Mbiti, *African Religions and Philosophies*, Doubleday, Garden City, N.J., 1970, p. 5.

64. Jomo Kenyatta, *Facing Mt. Kenya*, Vintage, New York, 1965, p. 232.

65. L.J. Cheney, *A History of the Western World*, Mentor, New York, 1959, p. 89.

66. William H. McNeill, *History of Western Civilization: Selected Readings*, University of Chicago Press, Chicago, 1953, pp. 337–338.

67. Philip Curtin, *The Image of Africa*, University of Wisconsin Press, Madison, 1964, p. 299.

68. Ibid, p. 415.

69. Ibid, p. 420.

70. Thomas F. Gossett, *Race: The History of an Idea in America*, Schocken, New York, 1965, pp. 30–31.

71. Katherine George, "The Civilized West Looks at Primitive Africa: A Study in Ethnocentrism," in *The Concept of the Primitive*, Ashley Montagu (ed.), The Free Press, New York, 1968, p. 182.

72. Paul Jacobs et al, *To Serve the Devil*, Vol. II, Vintage, New York, 1971, p. 19.

73. Ibid, Vol. I, p. 19.

74. William Howitt, *Colonization and Christianity*, Green and Longman, London, 1838, pp. 19–20.

75. Chapman Cohen, *Christianity, Slavery and Labour*, 4th ed., Pioneer Press, London, 1931, p. 46.

76. Chapman Cohen, *War, Civilization and the Churches*, Pioneer Press, London, 1930, pp. 56–57.

77. W.E.B. DuBois, *The World and Africa*, International Publishers, New York, 1965, p. 51.

78. E.D. Morel, *The Black Man's Burden*, rev. ed., Monthly Review Press, New York, 1969, pp. 15–16.

79. *Special Forces Handbook*, Commandant Army Special Warfare School, Fort Bragg, N.C., 1965, back cover.

80. Quoted in Cohen, *War, Civilization and the Churches*, p. 66.

81. Cohen, *Christianity, Slavery, and Labor*, p. 44.

82. Ibid, p. 28.

83. Chinweizu, *The West and the Rest of Us*, Nok Publisher, Lagos, 1978, p. 137.

84. Ibid, p. 49.

85. Ibid, pp. 76–77.

86. Ibid, pp. 128–129.

87. Jacobs et al, p. 26.

88. H.R. Ellis Davidson, *Gods and the Myths of Western Europe*, Penguin, New York, 1964, p. 48.

89. Ibid, p. 49.

90. Ibid, p. 70.

91. Ibid, p. 71.

92. Ibid, p. 54.

93. George Dumezil, *The Destiny of the Warrior*, University of Chicago Press, Chicago, 1970, pp. 46–47.

94. Ibid, p. 47.

95. Davidson, p. 14.

96. *Random House Dictionary*, unabridged ed., New York, 1971, p. 655.

97. Ibid, p. 1036.

98. Davidson, p. 14.

99. Mircea Eliade, *A History of Religious Ideas*, Vol. I, trans. Williard R. Trask, University of Chicago Press, Chicago, 1978, p. 187.

100. Cheikh Anta Diop, *The Cultural Unity of Black Africa*, Third World Press, Chicago, 1979, p. 29.

101. Eliade, *A History of Religious Ideas*, Vol. I, p. 187.

102. Ibid, p. 188.

103. Ibid, pp. 189, 190, 197.

104. Rosemary Radford Ruether, *Sexism and God-Talk: Toward a Feminist Theology*, Beacon Press, Boston, 1983, p. 53.

105. Ibid, p. 54.

106. Pagels, p. 57.

107. Ibid, p. 59.

108. Ibid, p. 61.

109. Ibid, p. 59.

110. Ibid, p. 68.

111. Ibid, pp. 71–72.

112. Ibid, p. 73.

113. Ibid, p. 75.

114. Ibid, p. 79.

115. Ibid, p. 83.

116. Page duBois, *Centaurs and Amazons: Women and the Pre-History of the Great Chain of Being*, University of Michigan Press, Ann Arbor, 1982, p. 136.

117. Ibid, p. 140.

118. Plato, *Republic*, Bk: 90e–91a, qouted in Page duBois, p. 135.

119. E.I. Allen, *Guidebook to Western Thought*, English Universities Press, London, 1957, p. 15.

120. Niebuhr, Vol. I, p. 13.

121. Thomas Aquinas, *Summa contra Gentiles*, Chapter XV, London, 1923.

122. Gottfried Wilhelm Leibniz, *Principles of Nature and of Grace, Founded on Reason, Leibniz: Philosophical Writing*, trans. Mary Morris, E.P. Dutton, New York, 1934, p. 27.

123. Robert Lowie, Primitive Religion, Liveright, New York, 1970. p. xiii.

124. William James, *The Varieties of Religious Experience*, Longmans, Green and Company, New York, 1919, p. 4.

125. See Peter Berger, *A Rumor of Angels*, Doubleday, Garden City, N.J., 1970, p. 39.

126. William James, p. 4.

127. Arthur E. Boak says, "The acceptance of Christianity was more rapid and complete in the cities than throughout the countryside. This gave rise to the use of the term pagan (from Latin Paganua, "rural," in the sense of

"barbarian") to designate non-Christians; a usage which had become official by 370 A.D. Between the fifth and ninth centuries paganism virtually disappeared within the boundaries of the Empire." (*A History of Rome to 565 A.D.*, p. 502.)

128. Kofi Awoonor, *The Breast of the Earth*, Doubleday, Garden City, N.J., 1975, pp. 28, 30.
129. Ibid, p. 26.
130. Ibid, p. 27.
131. Ibid, pp. 28, 30.
132. Ibid, p. 30.
133. Niebuhr, Vol. I, p. 24.
134. Lynn White, "The Historical Roots of Our Ecological Crisis," in *The Subversive Science,* Paul Shepard and Daniel McKinley (eds.), Houghton Mifflin, Boston, 1969, p. 345.
135. Eliade, *A History of Religious Ideas*, Vol. I, p. 354.
136. Reuther, Ch. 2.
137. Ibid, p. 76.
138. Eliade, *The Sacred and the Profane*, p. 116.
139. Ibid, p. 118.
140. Ibid, p. 11.
141. Ibid, p. 12.
142. Ibid, p. 13.
143. White, pp. 347–348.
144. Ibid, p. 349.
145. Ibid, p. 350.
146. Ibid, p. 346.
147. Niebuhr, Vol. I, p. 217.
148. The Broadway show *Pippin* was much more accurate in this regard than Niebuhr.
149. Niebuhr, Vol. I, p. 215, footnote 5.
150. Ibid, p. 214.

Chapter 3 - Aesthetic: The Power of Symbols

1. Max Weber, *The Protestant Ethic and the Spirit of Capitalism*, trans. Talcott Parsons, Charles Scribner's Son, New York, 1958, p. 15.
2. Immanuel Kant, *Critique of Judgement*, Vintage, New York, 1951, pp. 54–55.
3. Ibid, pp. 67–68.
4. Willlie Abraham, *The Mind of Africa*, University of Chicago Press, Chicago, 1962, p. 111.
5. Kofi Awoonor, *The Breast of the Earth*, Doubleday, Garden City, N.J., 975, p. 53.
6. Ibid, p. 55.
7. P.A. Sorokin, *The Crisis of Our Age*, E.P. Dutton, New York, 1941, p. 56.
8. Ibid, p. 58.
9. Daiseti Suzuki, "Buddhist Symbolism," in *Explorations in Communications*, Edmund Carpenter and Marshall McLuhan (eds.), Beacon Press, Boston, 1960, p. 38.
10. Ibid, p. 39.

11. Wade Nobles, "Ancient Egyptian Thought and the Development of African (Black) Psychology," in *Kemet and the African World View*, Maulana Karenga and Jacob Carruthers (eds.), University of Sankore Press, Los Angeles, 1986, p. 100.

12. Suzuki, p. 40.

13. Abraham, p. 193.

14. Robert Armstrong, *Wellspring: On the Myth and Source of Culture*, University of California Press, Berkeley, 1975, p. 120.

15. Aziza Gibson-Hunter, personal conversation, 1987.

16. Robert Goldwater, "The Western Experience of Negro Art," in *Colloquium on the Function and Significance of African Negro Art in the Life of African Culture*, Vol I, Society of African Culture and UNESCO, 1966, p. 342.

17. Ortiz Walton, "A Comparative Analysis of the African and Western Aesthetic," in *The Black Aesthetic*, Addison Gayle, Jr. (ed.), Doubleday, Garden City, N.J., 1972, pp. 154–155.

18. Ibid, p. 156.

19. Weber, pp. 14–15.

20. Walton, "Rationalism and Western Music," in *Black World*, Vol. XXII, No. 1, November 1973, p. 55.

21. Walton, "A Comparative Analysis of the African and Western Aesthetic," pp. 159.

22. See Leonard Barrett, *Soul-Force*, Doubleday, Garden City, N.J., 1974, p. 83; Naim Akbar, "Rhythmic Patterns in African Personality," in *African Philosophy: Paradigms for Research on Black Persons*, Lewis King, Vernon Dixon, and Wade Nobles (eds.), Fanon Center Publications, Los Angeles, 1976; and Kariamu Welsh-Asante, "Rhythm as Text and Structure in African culture," in *The Griot*, Fall 1990, on the significance of rhythm in African cosmology. This point is well made by Joseph Okpaku in *New African Literature*, Vol. I, Thomas Crowell, New York, 1970, p. 18.

23. Quoted in Okpaku, p. 18.

24. Carlton Molette, "Afro-American Ritual Drama," in *Black World*, Vol. XXII, No. 6,1973, p. 9.

25. Dona Marimba Richards, "The Implications of African American Spirituality," in *African Culture*, Molefi Asante and Kariamu Welsh Asante, (eds.), Greenwood Press, Westport, Conn. 1985, p. 213.

26. Molette, pp. 10–12; also Stanley Diamond, *In Search of the Primitive*, Transaction Press, New Brunswick, N.J., 1974, pp. 197–199.

27. René Wassing, *African Art*, Harry N. Abrams, Inc., New York, 1968, p. 5.

28. Armstrong, p. 114.

29. Madison Grant, *The Passing of the Great Race*, Charles Scribner's Sons, New York, 1921, pp. 229–230.

30. Addison Gayle, Jr., "Cultural Strangulation: Black Literature and the White Aesthetic," in *The Black Aesthetic*, Addison Gayle, Jr., (ed.) Doubleday, Garden City, N.J., 972, p. 40.

31. Ibid, p. 41.

32. *Maafa* is Kiswahili for "Great Disaster." This term refers to the era of the European slave trade and its effect on African people: over 100 million people lost their lives and their descendants were then systematically

and continuously assaulted through institutionalized anti-Africanism.

33. Gayle, p. 42.
34. Joel Kovel, *White Racism: A Psychohistory*, Vintage, New York, 1971, p. 107.
35. Giovanni Gentile, *The Philosophy of Art*, Ithaca: New York, 1972, p. 279.
36. Molefi Asante, *Afrocentricity: The Theory of Social Change*, Africa World Press, Trenton, 1988, p. 46.
37. Aristotle, *The Rhetoric and Poetics of Aristotle*, trans., Friedrich Solmesen, Random House, New York, 1954, p. 235.
38. Gentile, p. 14.
39. Armstrong, pp. 14–15.
40. A question posed by the children of the African Heritage Afterschool Program in Harlem, New York.
41. Okpaku, p. 14.
42. Johari Amini, "Re-Definition: Concept As Being," in *Black World*, Vol. XXII, No. 7, 1972, p. 11.
43. Gayle, p. 42.
44. Matila Ghyka, "The Pythagorean and Platonic Scientific Criterion of the Beautiful in Classical Western Art," in *Ideological Differences and World Order*, F.S.C. Northrop (ed.), Yale University Press, New Haven, 1949, p. 99.
45. Germaine Dieterlen and Marcel Griaule, "The Dogon," in *African Worlds*, Daryll Forde (ed.), Oxford University Press, London, 1954.
46. Ghyka, p. 100.
47. Ibid, p. 92.
48. Ibid, p. 93.
49. Plato, *Symposium*: 211, The Dialogues of Plato, Vol. I, trans., Benjamin Jowett, Random House, New York, 1937, p. 355.
50. Plato, *Philebus*: 51, The Dialogues of Plato, Vol. II, trans., Benjamin Jowett Vol. II, Random House, New York, 1937, p. 386.
51. Quoted in Ghyka, p. 112.
52. Ghyka, p. 94.
53. Kariamu Welsh-Asante, "Commonalities in African Dance: An Aesthetic Foundation," in *The African Culture*, Molefi Asante and Kariamu Welsh-Asante (eds.), Greenwood Press, Westport, 1985, p. 78.
54. Aziza Gibson-Hunter, personal conversation, 1988.
55. Asante, *Afrocentricity,* Africa World Press, Trenton, 1988.
56. Amos Wilson, an African psychologist, offers this concept of the "creation" of the person, in *Black on Black Violence*, Afrikan World Infosystems, New York, 1990, p. 55.

Part II - Image and National Consciousness

Notes to Chapter 4 - Self-Image

1. E.D. Morel, *The Black Man's Burden*, Monthly Review Press, New York, 1969, p. 3.
2. Joel Kovel, *White Racism: A Psycho-History*, Vintage, New York, 1971, p. 104.
3. Ibid, p. 287.
4. Jurgen Habermas, *The Theory of Communicative Action: Reason and the Rationalization of Society*, Vol. I, trans. Thomas McCarthy, Beacon Press, Boston, 1954, p. 43.
5. Ibid, p. 44.
6. Ibid, p. 54.
7. Ibid, p. 42.
8. Eric Havelock, *A Preface to Plato*, Grossett and Dunlap, New York, 1963, p. 199.
9. Ibid, p. 219.
10. Iva Carruthers, "War on African Familyhood," in *Sturdy Black Bridges*, Roseann P. Bell, Betty Parker, and Beverly Guy-Sheftall. (eds.), Anchor Press, Garden City, N.J., 1979, pp. 8–17.
11. Rosemary Radford Ruether, *Sexism and God-Talk*, Beacon Press, Boston, 1983, p. 44.
12. Susan Brownmiller, *Against Our Will*, Bantam, New York, 1976, p. 4.
13. Erich Neumann, "On the Moon and Matriarchal Consciousness," in *Fathers and Mothers: Five Papers on the Archetypal Background of Family Psychology*, Spring Publications, Zurich, 1973, p. 55.
14. Ifi Amadiume, *Afrikan Matriarchal Foundations*, Karnak House, London, 1987.
15. Iva Carruthers, "Africanity and the Black Woman," in *Black Books Bulletin*, 1980, Vol. 6, No. 4, pp. 14–20.
16. Plato, *Symposium*, The Dialogues of Plato, Vol. I, trans. Benjamin Jowett, Random House, New York, p. 185:192.
17. Willlie Abraham, *The Mind of Africa*, University of Chicago Press, Chicago, 1962, p. 31.
18. Michael Bradley, *The Iceman Inheritance*, Warner Books, New York, 1978, p. 123.
19. Harry Elmer Barnes, *An Intellectual and Cultural History of the Western World*, Vol. I, 3rd ed., Dover, New York, 1965, p. 43.
20. Ibid, p. 53.
21. Hugh A. MacDougall, *Racial Myth in English History*, Harvest House, Montreal, 1982, p. 91.
22. Quoted in Paul Jacobs et al, *To Serve the Devil*, Vol. II, Vintage, New York, 1971, pp. 333–335.
23. Merlin Stone, *Three Thousand Years of Racism*, New Sibylline Books, New York, 1981, p. 21.
24. Aristides, "To Rome," in *History of Western Civilization: Selected Readings*,

Supplement, University of Chicago Press, Chicago, 1958, pp. 18, 19, 23, 24.

25. Kovel, pp. 133, 144, 182.

26. Norman Cantor, *Western Civilization: Its Genesis and Destiny*, Vol. I, Scott, Foresman, Atlanta, 1969, p. 4.

27. Philip Curtin, *The Image of Africa*, University of Wisconsin Press, Madison, 1964, p. 415.

28. Ibid.

29. Kovel, pp. 164–165.

30. Yehoshua Arieli, *Individualism and Nationalism in American Ideology*, Penguin Books, Baltimore, 1966, pp. 250–251.

31. Aristides, Section 88, pp. 31–32.

32. Mircea Eliade, *The Sacred and the Profane*, Harcourt Brace, New York, 1959, p. 116ff.

33. Aristides pp. 38–39.

34. Curtin, p. 303.

35. Aristides, p. 43.

36. Leon Poliakov, *The Aryan Myth: A History of Racist and Nationalist Ideas in Europe*, trans. Edmund Howard, New American Library, New York, 1974, p. 82.

37. MacDougall, p. 344.

38. Poliakov, pp. 82–83.

39. Ibid, p. 14.

40. Ibid, p. 15.

41. Ibid, p. 20.

42. Quoted in Poliakov, p. 18.

43. Ibid, p. 18.

44. Quoted in Poliakov, p. 25.

45. Ibid, p. 25.

46. Cheikh Anta Diop, *The Cultural Unity of Black Africa*, Third World Press, Chicago, 1978.

47. MacDougall, p. 11.

48. Ibid, p. 26.

49. Ibid, p. 31.

50. Ibid, p. 2.

51. Quoted in MacDougall, p. 44.

52. Ibid, p. 44.

53. Ibid, p. 46.

54. Ibid, p. 49.

55. Ibid, p. 91.

56. Ibid, p. 82.

57. Immanuel Kant, Critique of Practical Reason, Bobbs-Merrill, Indianapolis, 1956.

58. Quoted in MacDougall, p. 92.

59. Ibid, p. 93.

60. Quoted in Poliakov, p. 27.

61. Quoted in MacDougall, p. 98.

62. Ibid, p. 99.

63. Dona Marimba Richards, "European Mythology: The Ideology of Progress," in *Black Contemporary Thought*, Molefi Kete Asante and Abdulai S. Vandi (eds.), Sage Publications, Beverly Hills, 1980.
64. MacDougall, p. 89.
65. Ibid, p. 90.
66. Ibid, p. 99.
67. Quoted in MacDougall, p. 100.
68. Ibid, p. 121.
69. Kovel, p. 166.
70. William Hepworth Dixon, *White Conquest*, Chatto & Windus, London, 1876, pp. 368–371.
71. Joseph Arthur Gobineau, *Selected Political Writings*, Michael D. Biddiss (ed.), Harper & Row, New York, 1970, p. 84.
72. Ibid, p. 136.
73. Wayne MacLeod, *The Importance of Race in Civilization*, Noontide Press, Los Angeles, 1968, p. 6.
74. Ibid, pp. 6–7.
75. Ibid, pp. 22–23.
76. Ibid, pp. 28, 45, 71.
77. Lothrop Stoddard, *The Rising Tide of Colour*, Charles Scribner's Sons, New York, 1920, p. 3.
78. Ibid, pp. 102–103.
79. Ibid, p. 145.
80. For a contemporary statement of this concern over European comparative infertility, see Ben J. Wattenberg, *The Birth Dearth*, Pharos Books, New York, 1987.
81. Stoddard, p. 148.
82. Ibid, p. 149.
83. For more ethnographic material of this sort, see Barry Schwartz and Robert Disch, eds., *White Racism*, Laurel, New York, 1970, especially, "The Ideology of White Supremacy," by James Vander Zanden. See also both volumes of Paul Jacobs et al., *To Serve the Devil*. Of course, the writings of the white nationalists themselves should be read.
84. P.W. Botha, "Why We Hate Blacks," in *The Shield*, the official African American newspaper of Hunter College. Reprinted from the South African newspaper, *Sunday Times*, Aug. 18, 1985, in the by-line of David G. Maillu, p. 4.

CHAPTER 5 - Image of Others

1. Paul Jacobs et al, *To Serve the Devil*, Vol. II, Vintage, New York, 1971, p. 42.
2. Edward Tylor, *The Origins of Culture*, Vol. I, Harper and Brothers, 1958.
3. Ashley Montagu, "The Concept of 'Primitive' and Related Anthropological Terms: A Study in the Systematics of Confusion," in *The Concept of the Primitive*, Ashley Montagu, (ed.) The Free Press, New York, 1968, p. 4.
4. Harry Elmer Barnes, *An Intellectual and Cultural History of the Western World*, Vol. I, Dover, New York, 1965, p. 41.
5. Gobineau, *Selected Political Writings*, Michael D. Biddiss (ed.), Harper & Row, New York, 1970, pp. 135–138.

6. Lothrop Stoddard, *The Rising Tide of Colour*, Charles Scribner's Sons, New York, 1920, pp. 91–92.

7. Ibid, pp. 100–101.

8. Joel Kovel, *White Racism: A Psycho-History*, Vintage, New York, 1971, p. 107.

9. Merlin Stone, *Three Thousand Years of Racism*, New Sibylline Books, New York, 1981, p. 20.

10. Quoted in Vulindlela Wobogo, "Diop's Two Cradle Theory and the Origin of White Racism," in *Black Books Bulletin*, Vol. 4, No. 4, Winter, 1976, p. 26.

11. Madison Grant, *The Passing of the Great Race*, Charles Scribner's Sons, New York, 1921, pp. 53–54.

12. Stoddard, p. 17.

13. Ibid, p. 90.

14. P.W. Botha, "Why We Hate Blacks," in *The Shield*, the official African American newspaper of Hunter College. Reprinted from the South African newspaper, *Sunday Times*, August 18, 1985, in the by-line of David G. Maillu, p. 4.

15. Kovel's terms: Joel Kovel, *White Racism: A Psycho-History*, Morningside edition, Columbia University Press, New York, 1984, p. xi.

16. Ben J. Wattenberg, *The Birth Dearth*, Pharos Books, New York, 1987.

17. Ibid, p. 113.

18. Ibid, p. 115.

19. Ibid, p. 98.

20. Ibid, p. 33.

21. Ibid, p. 89.

22. Ibid, p. 45, Chart 4J.

23. Ibid, p. 67.

24. Ibid, p. 97.

25. Ibid, pp. 97–98.

26. Ibid, p. 99.

27. Ibid, p. 168.

28. James Pope-Hennesy, *Sins of the Father*, Capricorn, New York, 1969, p. 47.

29. Quoted in James W. Vander Zanden, "The Ideology of White Supremacy," in *White Racism*, Barry N. Schwartz and Robert Disch (ed.), Laurel, New York, 1970, p. 128.

30. Paul Jacobs,et al., *To Serve the Devil*, Vol. II, Vintage, New York, 1971, p.176, footnote.

31. Wayne MacLeod, *The Importance of Race in Civilization*, Noontide Press, Los Angeles, 1968, p. 73.

32. Ibid, p. 3.

33. Stone, p. 4.

34. Quoted in Marvin Harris, *The Rise of Anthropological Theory*, Thomas Y. Crowell, New York, 1968, p. 69.

35. Quoted in George Stocking, *Race, Culture and Evolution*, The Free Press, New York, 1968, p. 113.

36. Quoted in Harris, p. 87.

37. Ibid, p. 88.

38. Quoted in J.M. Ita, "Frobenius, Senghor and The Image of Africa," in *Modes of Thought*, Robin Horton and Ruth Finnegan (eds.), Faber and Faber,

London, 1973, p. 310 from Hegel, *Die Philosophie der Gerschichte*, Reclam Vertarg Stuttgart, 1961, p. 155.

39. Arnold Toynbee, *A Study of History*, Oxford University Press, London, (1934), 1961.

40. Arthur O. Lovejoy, *The Great Chain of Being*, Harvard University Press, Cambridge, 1966, p. 194.

41. Ibid, p. 88.

42. Ibid, p. 187.

43. Paul Jacobs et al,Vols. I and II.

44. Ibid, Vol. I, p. 13.

45. Ibid, Vol. II, p. 38.

46. Ibid, Vol. II, p. 37.

47. Ayi Kwei Armah, *Two Thousand Seasons*, Third World Press, Chicago, 1979, p. 3.

48. Cheikh Anta Diop, "Interview," in *Black Books Bulletin.*, Vol. IV, No. 4, 1976, pp. 30–37.

49. MacLeod, p. 73.

50. Johari Amini, "Re-Definition: Concept as Being," in *Black World*, 1972, Vol. XXII, No. 7, p. 6.

51. Ibid, p. 10.

52. James Baldwin, *Notes of a Native Son*, Beacon Paperback, Beacon Hill, 1957, p. 30.

Part III - Behavior and Ethics

Notes on Chapter 6 - Rhetoric and Behavior

1. William Strickland, "Watergate: Its Meaning for Black America," in *Black World*, 1973, Vol. XXIII, No. 2, p. 7.

2. A.R. Faraz, *The City Sun*, December 6-9, 1986, New York.

3. Carol Ember and Melvin Ember, *Anthropology*, Appleton-Century-Crofts, New York, 1973, p. 29.

4. Eric Hoebel, *Anthropology: The Study of Man*, 3rd ed., McGraw-Hill, New York, 1966, p. 29.

5. Ibid, p. 23.

6. Paul Jacobs et al, *To Serve the Devil*, Vol. I, Vintage, New York, 1971, p. 12.

7. Eric Havelock, *Preface to Plato*, Grosset and Dunlap, New York, 1967, p. 158.

8. Joel Kovel, *White Racism*, Vintage, New York, 1971, p. 146.

9. Ibid, p. 145.

10. *Kierkegaard's Attack Upon Christendom* (1854-1855), trans. Walter Lowrie, Princeton University Press, Princeton, 1944, pp. 304–305.

11. Oswald Spengler, *The Decline of the West*, Vol. II, Alfred A. Knopf, New York, 1928, pp. 216–217.

12. Ayn Rand on *Speaking Freely*, NBC, August 12, 1972.

13. Friedrich Nietzsche, "The Anti Christ," in *Works of Friedrich Nietzsche*, Vol. XI, trans. Thomas Common, Alexander Tille (ed.), Macmillan, New York, 1924, p. 240.

14. Ibid, p. 242.
15. Chapman Cohen, *Christianity, Slavery and Labour*, Pioneer Press, London, 1931, p. 117.
16. Robin Williams, *American Society: A Sociological Interpretation*, 3rd ed., Alfred A. Knopf, New York, 1970, p. 463.
17. Ibid, pp. 462–463.
18. Wayne MacLeod, *The Importance of Race in Civilization*, Noontide Press, Los Angeles, 1968, p. 96.
19. Williams, p. 499.
20. Yehoshua Arieli, *Individualism and Nationalism in American Ideology*, Penguin Books, Baltimore, 1966, p. 256.
21. Williams, p. 491.
22. Norman F. Cantor, *Western Civilization: Its Genesis and Destiny*, Vol. II, Scott, Foreman, Glenview, Ill.,1970, p. 626.
23. Ibid, p. 624.
24. Frances Cress Welsing, "A Conversation with Dr. Welsing," in *Essence Magazine*, October, 1973, p. 51.

Notes on Chapter 7 - Intracultural Behavior

1. Robin Williams, *American Society: A Sociological Interpretation*, 3rd ed., Alfred A. Knopf, New York, 1970, p. 26.
2. Ibid, p. 27.
3. Ibid, p. 37.
4. Ibid, p. 28.
5. Emile Durkheim, *Suicide*, The Free Press, Glencoe, Ill., 1951, Ch. 1, Book III.
6. Williams, pp. 495, 497.
7. Ibid, pp. 495, 483.
8. Dorothy Lee, *Freedom and Culture*, Prentice-Hall, Englewood Cliffs,N.J., 1959, p. 53.
9. Ibid, pp. 54–55.
10. Ibid, pp. 55–57.
11. Ibid, p. 131.
12. Norman O. Brown, *Life Against Death*, Wesleyan University Press, Middletown, Conn., 1959, p. 53.
13. Ibid, p. 50.
14. Paul Goodman, "Polarities and Wholeness: A Gestalt Critique of 'Mind,' 'Body,' and 'External World,'" in *Sources*, Theodore Roszak (ed.), Colophon, New York, 1972, p. 139.
15. Ibid, p. 140.
16. Lee, p. 132.
17. Vernon Dixon, "World Views and Research Methodology," in *African Philosophy: Assumptions and Paradigms for Research on Black Persons*, Lewis King, Vernon Dixon, and Wade Nobles (eds.), Fanon Center Publications, Los Angeles, 1976, p. 63.
18. Ibid, p. 62.
19. Ibid, p. 58.
20. Carlton W. Molette III, "Afro-American Ritual Drama," in *Black World*, Vol. XXII, No. 6, April, 1973.

21. Lee, p. 133.
22. Ibid, p. 134.
23. Ibid, p. 63.
24. Ibid, pp. 137–138.
25. Ibid, p. 20.
26. See Stanley Diamond, *In Search of the Primitive*, Transactions Books, New Brunswick, N.J., 1974, pp. 68, 172.
27. Lee, pp. 20–21.
28. Ibid, p. 22.
29. For a contrasting view of the individual, see Lee, pp. 23–25.
30. Joel Kovel, *White Racism*, Vintage, New York, 1971, pp. 160–161.
31. Lee, p. 5.
32. Diamond, p. 160.
33. Ibid, p. 166.
34. Quoted in Diamond, p. 166.
35. Ibid, p. 167.
36. Max Weber, *The Protestant Ethic and the Spirit of Capitalism*, trans. Talcott Parsons, Charles Scribner's Sons, New York, 1958, p. 27.
37. Lewis Mumford, *The Condition of Man*, Harcourt Brace, New York, 1944, pp. 159-160.
38. Ibid, p. 183.
39. Ibid, p. 199.
40. Ibid, p. 201.
41. Kovel, pp. 150–151.
42. John G. Jackson, "Egypt and Christianity," in *Journal of African Civilizations*, 1982, Vol 4, No. 21, pp. 65–80; John G. Jackson, *Christianity Before Christ*, American Atheist Press, Austin, 1985; Gerald Massey, *Ancient Egypt: Light of the World,* Samuel Weiser, New York, 1973; orig. pub. 1907.
43. Mumford, p. 185.
44. Ibid p. 188.
45. Kovel, p. 150.
46. Mumford, p. 189.
47. Ibid, p. 192.
48. Ibid, p. 198.
49. Ibid, pp. 189, 197.
50. Ibid, p. 196.
51. Ibid, p. 197.
52. Ibid, p. 194.
53. Mircea Eliade, *The Sacred and the Profane*, Harcourt Brace, New York, 1959, pp. 22–24.
54. Kovel, p. 137.
55. Ibid, p. 151.
56. Brown, *Life Against Death*, p. 202.
57. It was Luther himself who thought this information significant enough to be recorded; see Kovel, p. 131.
58. Mumford, p. 187.
59. Ibid p. 198.
60. Ibid p. 188.

61. William Strickland, "Watergate: Its Meaning for Black America," in *Black World*, Vol. XXIII, No. 2, 1973, p. 9.
62. Eli Sagan, *The Lust to Annihilate: A Psychoanalytical Study of Violence in Ancient Greek Culture*, Psychohistory Press, New York, 1979, p. 4.
63. Sagan, p. 3.
64. Ibid, p. 23.
65. Ibid, p. 35.
66. Ibid, p. 36.
67. Ibid, p. 37.
68. Ibid, pp. 41–42.
69. Ibid, p. 59.
70. Ibid, p. 60.
71. Ibid, p. 216.
72. Kovel, p. 129.
73. Ibid, p. 167.
74. Alexis Kagame, *La Philosophie Bantu-Rwandaise de l'Etre*, Arsom, Bruxelles, 1956.
75. Williams, p. 493.
76. Theodore Roszak, ed., Introduction to *Sources*, Harper and Row, Colophon, New York, 1972, p. xvii.
77. Williams, p. 501.
78. See Kovel, pp. 114–115, for an extended discussion of this point.
79. Ibid p. 116.
80. Williams, p. 471.
81. Willlie Abraham, *The Mind of Africa*, University of Chicago Press, Chicago, 1962, p. 34.
82. Ibid, p. 193.
83. Ibid, p. 31.
84. Kovel, p. 158.
85. Williams, p. 465.
86. Ibid, p. 488.
87. Kovel, p. 156.
88. Ibid, pp. 158–159.
89. Ibid, p. 132.
90. Ibid, p. 133.
91. Ibid, p. 130.
92. A.I. Hallowell, "Ojibwa Ontology, Behavior, and World View," in *Primitive Views of the World*, Stanley Diamond (ed.) Columbia University Press, New York, 1966, p. 50.
93. Brown, *Life Against Death*, p. 42.
94. Ibid pp. 45, 48, 52–53.
95. Ibid, p. 54.
96. Michael Bradley, *The Iceman Inheritance*, Warner Books, New York, 1978, p. 130-131.
97. Plato, *Symposium* The Dialogues of Plato, Vol. I, trans., Benjamin Jowett, Random House, New York, 1937, p. 334.
98. Edward T. Hall, *Beyond Culture*, Anchor Press, Garden City, N.J., 1977, p. 234.

99. Ibid, p. 235.
100. Ibid, p. 238.
101. Strickland, p. 9.

Notes on Chapter 8 - Behavior Toward Others

1. See Norman Cantor, *Western Civilization: Its Genesis and Destiny*, Vol. I, Scott, Foresman, Atlanta, 1969, Part II, Ch. 12, Sect. VII for an example of this argument.
2. Joel Kovel, *White Racism*, Vintage, New York, 1971, p. 108.
3. Claude Henri de Saint-Simon, *Social Organization, The Science of Man, and Other Writings*, trans. and ed. Felix Markham, Harper Torchbooks, New York, 1964, p. 49.
4. Kovel, p. 181.
5. W.E.B. DuBois, *The World and Africa*, International Publishers, New York, 1965, p. 23.
6. Alphonso Pinckney, *The American Way of Violence*, Vintage, New York, 1972, p. 69.
7. Johari Amini, "Re-Definition: Concept as Being," in *Black World*, Vol. XXI, No. 7, 1972, p. 7.
8. Kovel, p. 96.
9. Paul Jacobs et al, *To Serve the Devil*, Vol. II, Vintage, New York, 1971, p. 335.
10. Jomo Kenyatta, *Facing Mt. Kenya*, Vintage, New York, 1965, p. 37.
11. Ibid, p. 23.
12. Ibid, p. 41.
13. Chapman Cohen, *Christianity, Slavery and Labour*, 3rd ed., Pioneer Press, London, 1931, p. 121.
14. Quoted in Chinweizu, *The West and the Rest of Us*, Nok Publishers, Lagos, 1978, p. 64.
15. Cohen, p. 118.
16. Ibid, p. 122.
17. *The World at War*, WOR-TV, New York, March 2, 1974.
18. Mokubung Nkomo, "Education for Blacks in South Africa: Fact vs. Fiction," in *Interracial Books for Children Bulletin*, Vol. XVI, Nos. 5 and 6, Council on Interracial Books for Children, New York, 1985, p. 5.
19. NYPIRG and South Africa Perspectives, Africa Fund, American Committee on Africa, January 1984.
20. South Africa Perspectives, Africa Fund, American Committee on Africa, January 1984.
21. NYPIRG.
22. Committee in Solidarity with Free Grenada, November 1, 1983.
23.. "War on Nicaragua," *Frontline*, PBS, April 21, 1987.
24. Amini, p. 7.
25. Kofi Awoonor, *The Breast of the Earth*, Doubleday, New York, 1975, pp. 21, 23.
26. Ibid, pp. 23, 25.
27. Ibid, pp. 25, 27.
28. Ibid, pp. 25, 28.
29. Carter G. Woodson, *The Mis-Education of the Negro*, Associated Publishers,

Washington, D.C., 1977; p. xiii.

30. E.D. Morel, *The Black Man's Burden*, Monthly Review Press, New York, 1969, p. 8.

31. Wayne MacLeod, *The Importance of Race in Civilization*, Noontide Press, Los Angeles, 1968, p. 86.

32. Jacobs, Vol. II.

33. Chinweizu, p. xiv.

34. Jacobs, Vol. II.

35. James H. Jones, *Bad Blood: The Tuskegee Syphilis Experiment*, The Free Press, New York, 1981, p. 1.

36. Ibid, p. 2.

37. Ibid, p. 3.

38. Ibid, p. 4.

39. Ibid, p. 4.

40, Ibid, p. 4.

41. Ibid, pp. 6, 10.

42. Louis Wender, quoted in Jones, p. 27; Bruce McVey, quoted in Jones, p. 26.

43. A physician from Virginia, quoted in Jones, p. 26.

44. Jones, p. 48.

45. Robert Jay Lifton, *The Nazi Doctors: Medical Killing and the Psychology of Genocide*, Basic Books, New York, 1986; John Cookson and Judith Nottingham, *A Survey of Chemical and Biological Warfare*, Monthly Review Press, New York, 1969.

46. Jones, p. 48.

47. David Dickson, "AIDS: Racist Myths, Hard Facts," in *AfricAsia*, No. 41., Panos Institute, London, May 1987.

48. Frances Cress Welsing, "To Whom it May Concern," Letter to the African Descendant Community, February 25, 1987.

49. William Campbell Douglass, "Who Murdered Africa," in *Health Freedom News*, September 1987.

50. WHO (World Health Organization), Vol. 47, 1972.

51. Douglass, p. 42.

52. Barbara Justice, "AIDS and Genocide," lecture at Hunter College, May 1990.

53. Jack Felder, *AIDS: United States Germ Warfare at its Best, with Documents and Proof*, published by the author, 1989; Alan Cantwell, Jr., *AIDS and the Doctors of Death*, Aries Press, Los Angeles, 1988.

54. D.K. Keoch and A.O. Obel, "Efficacy of KEMRON (low dose oral natural human interferon alpha) in the Management of HIV-1 Infection and Acquired Immune Deficiency Syndrome (AIDS)," in *East African Medical Journal*, July 1990, Vol. 67, No. 7, July 1990, Special Supplement No. 2, pp. 64–70.

55. Dana Alston, ed. *We Speak for Ourselves/Social Justice, Race and Environment*, The Panos Institute, Washington, D.C., 1990, pp. 9, 32, 33.

56. Kovel, p. 8.

57. Ibid, p. 148.

58. Ibid, p. 95.

59. Frances Cress Welsing, "A Conversation with Dr. Welsing," in *Essence Magazine*, October 1973.

60. Bobby Wright, *The Psychopathic Racial Personality and Other Essays*, Third World Press, Chicago, 1985, p. 2.
61. Ibid, p. 7.
62. Ibid, p. 6.
63. Frances Cress Welsing, *The Isis Papers: The Keys to the Colors*, Third World Press, Chicago, 1991, p. 4.
64. Ibid, p. 5.
65. Ibid.
66. Ibid, p. 6.
67. Ibid, pp. 7–8.
68. Ibid, p. 10.
69. Ibid, p. 12.
70. Ibid.
71. Kovel, p. 49.
72. Ibid, p. 277.
73. Ibid, p. 273.
74. Ibid, p. 284.
75. Ibid, p. 11.
76. Ibid, p. 44.
77. Ibid, p. 47.
78. Ibid, pp. 49–50`.
79. Ibid, p. 9.
80. Ibid, p. 95.
81. Ibid, p. 107.
82. Ibid, p. 108.
83. Sigmund Freud, *Totem and Taboo*, trans. James Strachey, W. W. Norton, New York, 1950.
84. Ibid, p. 1.
85. Michael Bradley, *The Iceman Inheritance*, Warner Books, New York, 1978, p. 125.
86. Ibid, p. 67.
87. Ibid, p. 122.
88. Ibid, p. 90.
89. Ibid, p. 109.
90. Cheikh Anta Diop, *The Cultural Unity of Black Africa*, Third World Press, Chicago, 1978, p. 76.
91. Bradley, p. 123.
92. Ibid, p. 175.
93. Ibid, p. 112.
94. Ibid, p. 14.
95. Ibid, p. 18.
96. Diop quoted in Iva Carruthers, "War on African Familyhood," in *Sturdy Black Bridges*, Roseann Bell, Betty Parker, and Beverly Guy-Sheftall, eds., Anchor Press, Garden City, N.J.,1979, pp. 8–17, see especially p. 10.
97. Diop, p. 167.
98. Ibid, p. 195.
99. Vulindlela Wobogo, "Diop's Two Cradle Theory and the Origin of White Racism," in *Black Books Bulletin*, Vol. 4, No. 4, Winter, 1976, p. 21.

100. Richard King, *African Origins of Biological Psychiatry*, Seymour-Smith, Germantown, Tenn., 1990, p. 35.

101. Richard King, "African Origins of PsychoBiology," lecture at City College of New York, 1987.

102. King, *African Origins*, pp. 31–32.

103. Ibid, p. 32.

104. Marguerite Lerner, *Color and People: The Story of Pigmentation*, Lerner Publications, Minneapolis, 1971, p. 13.

105. King, Ch.1–3.

106. Ibid, pp. 13–14.

107. *Children of Eve*, PBS Documentary, 1987.

108. King, p. 57.

109. Ibid, pp 58–59.

110. Ibid, p. 64.

111. Ibid, p. 63.

112. Edward T. Hall, *Beyond Culture*, Anchor, Garden City, N.J., 1976, p. 239.

113. King, p. 64.

114. Frank Sullowway, *Biologists of the Mind*, Basic Books, New York, 1979, p. 361.

115. Carl Jung, *Memories, Dreams and Reflections*. Aniela Jaffé (ed.), trans. Richard and Clara Winston, Pantheon, New York, 1968.

116. *1st National Conference on Global White Supremacy*, presentation by Joseph Baldwin, Chicago, Oct. 12, 1990.

117. Ashley Montagu, "The Concept of 'Primitive' and Related Anthropological Terms: A Study in the Systematics of Confusion," p. 161.

118. See Charles A. Beard's, Introduction, to J.B. Bury, *Idea of Progress*, Dover, New York, 1955, p. xviii.

119. Marvin Harris, *The Rise of Anthropological Theory*, Thomas Y. Crowell, New York, 1968, p. 146.

120. Robin Williams, *American Society: A Sociological Interpretation*, Alfred A. Knopf, New York, 1970, p. 501.

121. Kovel, pp. 154–155.

122. Johari Amini, p. 6.

Part IV - Ideology

Chapter 9 - Progress as Ideology

1. See Beard's Introduction to J.B. Bury, *The Idea of Progress*, Dover, New York, 1955, p. xxviii.
2. Ibid, p. 11.
3. Theodore Roszak, ed., *Sources*, Colophon, New York, 1972.
4. E.O. Bassett, "Plato's Theory of Social Progress," in *International Journal of Ethics*, XXVIII, 1927-1928, p. 476.
5. Arthur O. Lovejoy and George Boas, *Primitivism and Related Ideas in Antiquity*, Octagon Books, New York, 1965, p. 168.
6. Karl Popper, *The Open Society and Its Enemies*, Vol. II, 5th ed., Princeton University Press, Princeton, 1966, pp. 4-5.
7. Joel Kovel, *White Racism: A PsychoHistory*, Vintage, New York, 1971, p. 125.
8. Ibid, p. 128.
9. Aristides, "To Rome," in *History of Western Civilization: Selected Readings*, Supplement, University of Chicago Press, Chicago, 1958, p. 40.
10. Charles Beard's Introduction to J.B. Bury, *The Idea of Progress*, Dover, New York, 1955, p. xx.
11. See Wayne MacLeod, *The Importance of Race in Civilization*, Noontide Press, Los Angeles, 1968.
12. Ashley Montagu, "The Concept of 'Primitive' and Related Anthropological Terms: A Study in the Systematics of Confusion," in *The Concept of the Primitive*, Ashley Montagu (ed.), The Free Press, New York, 1968, pp. 3-4.
13. Ibid, p. 4.
14. Henryk Skolimowski, "The Scientific World View and the Illusions of Progress," in *Social Research*, Vol. 41, No. 1, 1974, p. 53.
15. Skolimowski, pp. 56–57.
16. Ibid, pp. 59–60.
17. Ibid, pp. 70–71.
18. Ibid, p. 72.
19. Ibid, p. 75.
20. Ibid, pp. 77–78.
21. Ibid, p. 82.
22. Michael Bradley, *The Iceman Inheritance*, Warner Books, New York, 1978, p. 12.
23. Ibid, p. 18.
24. Ibid, p. 4.
25. Arthur O. Lovejoy, *The Great Chain of Being*, Harvard University Press, Cambridge, 1966, pp. 10–14.
26. William James, *The Writings of William James*, John J. McDermott. (ed.), Modern Library, New York, 1968, pp. 498–499.
27. Eric Havelock, *Preface to Plato*, Grossett and Dunlap, New York, 1967, p. 122.
28. Friedrich Juenger, *The Failure of Technology*, Henry Regnery, Chicago, 1956, pp. 39–40.
29. Dorothy Lee, *Freedom and Culture*, Prentice Hall, Eglewood Cliffs, N.J., 1959,

p. 110.

30. Ibid, p. 91.

31. Ibid, p. 94.

32. Bury, p. 2.

33. Ibid, p. 7.

34. Robin Williams, *American Society*, Alfred A. Knopf, New York, 1970, p. 469.

35. Friedrich Nietzsche, "The Anti-Christ," *The Works of Nietzsche*, Vol. XI, trans. and ed. Alexander Tille, Macmillian, New York, 1924, p. 241.

36. Roger Shinn, "Perilous Progress in Genetics," *Social Research*, Vol. 41, No. 1, 1974, p. 83.

37. Rheinhold Niebuhr, *The Nature and Destiny of Man*, Vol. II, Charles Scribner's Sons, New York, 1946, p. 154.

38. For the quintessential critique of Marxist theory and praxis, in relation to the European and African experiences, see Cedric J. Robinson, *Black Marxism: The Making of the Black Radical Tradition*, Zed Press, London, 1983.

Notes on Chapter 10 - Universalism: The Syntax of Cultural Imperialism

1. Wade Nobles, *Africanity and the Black Family*, Black Family Research Institute Publications, Oakland, 1985, p. 107.

2. Mircea Eliade, *The Sacred and the Profane*, Harcourt Brace, New York, 1959, p. 22.

3. Johari Amini, "Re-Definition: Concept as Being," in *Black World*, 1972, Vol. XXI, No. 7; Molefi Asante, *The Afrocentric Idea*, Temple University Press, Philadelphia, 1987.

4. Alvin W. Gouldner, "Anti-Minotaur: The Myth of a Value-Free Social Science," in *The New Sociology*, Irving Horowitz (ed.), Oxford University Press, New York, 1964, p. 199.

5. John Gwaltney, *Dryslong: A Self Portrait of Black America*, Vintage, New York, 1981, p. 26.

6. Ibid, p. 27.

7. William S. Willis, "Skeletons in the Anthropological Closet," in *Reinventing Anthropology*, Dell Hymes (ed.), Vintage, New York, 1974, p. 122.

8. Jacques Maquet, "Objectivity in Anthropology," in *Current Anthropology*, Vol. 5, No. 1, 1964, p. 53.

9. Ibid, p. 54.

10. Karl Mannheim, *Ideology and Utopia*, Harcourt Brace, New York, 1936, p. 4.

11. Ibid, p. 5.

12. Jurgen Habermas, *Reason and the Rationalization of Society*, Vol. I, Beacon Press, Boston, 1984, p. 69.

13. Ibid, p. 43.

14. Ibid, p. 74.

15. Maquet, pp. 51–52.

16. Claude Henri de Saint-Simon, *Social Organization, the Science of Man, and Other Writings*, trans. and ed. Felix Markham, Harper Torchbooks, New York, 1964, pp. 39–40.

17. Ibid, p. 40.

18. Ibid, p. 49.
19. See Saint-Simon, p. 49, quoted in Chap. 8 of this work.
20. John Stuart Mill, *John Stuart Mill's Philosophy of Scientific Method*, Ernest Nagel (ed.) Hafner, New York, 1950, p. 332.
21. Ibid, p. 312.
22. See Mill's discussion, Ibid. p. 313.
23. Emile Durkheim, *The Rules of the Sociological Method*, The Free Press, New York, 1964, p. 31.
24. Ibid, p. 44.
25. Ibid, pp. 27–28.
26. Maquet, p. 51.
27. John Henrik Clarke, "Confrontation at Montreal," in *Negro Digest*, Vol. XIX, No. 4, 1970, p. 10.
28. Benjamin Nimer, "Politics and Scholarship in the United States," in *African Studies Review*, Vol. XIII, No. 3, 1970, p. 353.
29. Frantz Fanon, *The Wretched of the Earth*, Grove Press, New York, 1963, p. 40.
30. Nimer, p. 323.
31. Ibid, p. 357.
32. Ibid, p. 358.
33. Kathleen Gough Aberle, "New Proposals for Anthropologists," in *Current Anthropology*, Vol. IX, No. 5, 1968, p. 403.
34. Stanley Diamond, *In Search of the Primitive*, Transaction Press, New Brunswick, 1974, p. 111.
35. Aristides, "To Rome," in *History of Western Civilization: Selected Readings*, Supplement, University of Chicago Press, Chicago, 1958, p. 42.
36. J.B. Bury, *The Idea of Progress*, Dover, New York, 1955, pp. 23–24.
37. Wayne MacLeod, *The Importance of Race in Civilization*, Noontide Press, Los Angeles, 1968, p. 89.
38. Gene Hogberg, *Plain Truth Magazine*, March/April, 1972.
39. For an excellent discussion of contemporary European supra nationalism, see Ravanna Bey, "Supra Nationalism and the European Community," unpublished paper, association of Afrikan Historians, January 1990, Inner City Studies, Chicago.
40. Hogberg, p. 2.
41. George Kourvetaris, *The Journal of Social, Political, Economic Studies.* Summer, 1986.
42. Raymond Aron, *Progress and Disillusion*, Praeger, New York, 1968, p. 164.
43. Theodore Roszak, ed., *Sources*, Colophon, New York, 1972, p. 49.
44. *Plain Truth Magazine* March/April, 1987, p. 35.
45. Marcel Griaule, "The Problem of Negro Culture," in *Interrelation of Culture*, UNESCO, 1953, p. 352.
46. Arthur O. Lovejoy, *The Great Chain of Being*, Harvard University Press, Cambridge, 1966, p. 313.
47. Ibid, p. 312.
48. Yehoshua Arieli, *Individualism and Nationalism in American Ideology*, Penguin Books, Baltimore, 1966, pp. 249–250.
49. Willie Abraham, *The Mind of Africa*, University of Chicago Press, Chicago, 1962, p. 153.

50. Lewis Mumford, *The Condition of Man*, Harcourt Brace, New York, 1944, p. 31.
51. Ibid, p. 32.
52. Edward Sapir, "Culture, Genuine and Spurious," in *Edward Sapir, Culture, Language and Personality: Selected Essays,* David G. Mandelbaum (ed.), University of California, Berkeley, 1970, pp. 78–119.
53. Mumford, p. 39.
54. Ibid, p. 200.
55. Ibid, p. 403.
56. Kurt Wolff, "This Is the Time for Radical Anthropology," in *Reinventing Anthropology*, Dell Hymes (ed.), Vintage, New York, 1974, p. 101.
57. Ibid, pp. 113–115.
58. R.S. Rattray, *Ashanti Law and Constitution*, Oxford, London, 1929, p. 291.
59. Mary Kingsley, *West African Studies*, Barnes and Nobles, New York, 1964, p. 150.
60. Gouldner, p. 47.
61. Jomo Kenyatta, *Facing Mt. Kenya*, Vintage, New York, n.d., p. 41.
62. Ayi Kwei Armah, *Two Thousand Seasons*, Third World Press, Chicago, 1979, p. 3.
63. Diamond, p. 163.
64. Fanon, p. 252.
65. Ralph Beals, *The Politics of Social Research*, Aldine Publishing Co., Chicago, 1969, p. 197.
66. Ibid, p. 197.
67. Ibid, p. 5.
68. Ibid, p. 40.
69. Quoted in Roszak (ed.) *Sources,* pp. x–xi.
70. Ibid, p. xi.
71. Diamond, p. 110.
72. Nobles, p. 109.
73. Roszak, pp. xii–xiv.
74. Cedric J. Robinson, *Black Marxism: The Making of the Black Radical Tradition*, Zed Press,London, 1983, p. 9.
75. Ibid, p. 19.
76. Ibid, p. 67ff.
77. Merlin Stone, *Three Thousand Years of Racism*, New Sibylline Books, New York, 1981, p. 26.
78. This later analysis is a collective product of the participants in a seminar on "White Racism" held at Hunter College in Spring, 1991.
79. Stone, p. 25.

Conclusion - Yurugu: The Incomplete Being

1. See Joel Kovel, *White Racism: A Psychohistory*, Vintage, New York, 1971, p. 130.
2. Marcel Griaule and G. Dieterlen, *The Pale Fox*, Continuum Foundation, Chino Valley, 1986, pp. 198–199.
3. Ibid, p. 285.
4. Ibid, p. 290.
5. Theodore Roszak, *Where the Wasteland Ends*, Doubleday, Garden City, N.J., 1972, p. 131.
6. *Of Men and Women*, NBC-TV, Jan. 9, 1975.
7. Stanley Diamond, *In Search of the Primitive*, Transaction Books, New Brunswick, N.J., 1974, p. 51.
8. Leonard Barrett, *Soul-Force*, Anchor Press, Garden City, N.J., 1974, p. 17.
9. Roszak, p. 168.
10. Wayne MacLeod, *The Importance of Race in Civilization*, Noontide Press, Los Angeles, 1968, p. 72.
11. Ayi Kwei Armah, *Two Thousand Seasons*, Third World Press, Chicago, 1984, p. 321.
12. Ibid, p. 7.
13. Ibid, p. 321.

Bibliography

African Authors

Abraham, Willie E., *The Mind of Africa*, Chicago: University of Chicago Press, 1962.

Adams, Hunter H., "Strategies Toward the Recovery of Meta-Conscious Thought," Lecture at City College, New York, June 1987.

———, "African Observers of the Universe," *Journal of African Civilizations*, Vol. I, No. 2, November 1979; 1–20.

Akbar, Na'im, "Rhythmic Pattern in African Personality," *African Philosophy: Assumptions and Paradigms for Research on Black Persons,* Lewis M. King, Vernon J. Dixon, Wade W. Nobles (eds.), Los Angeles: Fanon Center Publications, 1976; 175–189.

Akoto, Kwame Agyei, *Nation-Building: Theory and Practice in Afrikan-Centered Education*, Washington. D.C.: Pan Afrikan World Institute, 1992.

Amadiume, Ifi, *Afrikan Matriarchal Foundations*, London: Karnak House, 1987.

Amini, Johari, "Re-Definition: Concept as Being," *Black World*, Vol. XXI, No. 7, May 1972; 4–12.

Anyanwu, K.C., *The African Experience in the American Marketplace*, Smithtown, N.Y.: Exposition Press, 1983.

Armah, Ayi Kwei, *Two Thousand Seasons*, Chicago: Third World Press, 1979.

———, *The Healers*, London: Heinemann, 1979.

Asante, Molefi Kete, *The Afrocentric Idea*, Philadelphia: Temple University Press, 1987.

———, *Afrocentricity: The Theory of Social Change*, Trenton: Africa World Press, 1988.

————, *Kemet, Afrocentricity, and Knowledge,* Trenton: Africa World Press, 1990.

Awoonor, Kofi, *The Breast of the Earth,* New York: Doubleday, Anchor, 1975.

Baldwin, James, *Notes of a Native Son,* Beacon Hill: Beacon Paperback, 1957.

Baldwin, Joseph, "Psychological Aspects of European Cosmology in American Society," *Western Journal of Black Studies;* Vol. 9, No.4, l985; 216–223.

Barrett, Leonard, *Soul-Force: African Heritage in Afro-American Religion,* Garden City, N.Y.: Doubleday, 1974.

Ben-Jochannan, Yosef, *African Origins of the Major 'Western Religions,'* New York: Alkebu-Lan Books, 1973.

Betts, Raymond (ed.), *The Ideology of Blackness,* Lexington, Mass.: D.C. Health and Company, 1971.

Braithwaite, Edward, *Folk Culture of the Slaves in Jamaica,* London: New Beacon Books, 1970.

Carruthers, Iva, "Africanity and the Black Woman," *Black Books Bulletin,* Vol. 6, No. 4, 1980; 14- 20.

————, "War on African Familyhood," *Sturdy Black Bridges,* Roseann Bell, Betty Parker, Beverly Guy-Sheftall (eds.), Garden City, N.Y.: Anchor Press, 1979; 8–17.

Chinweizu, *Decolonising the African Mind,* Lagos: Pero Press, 1987.

————, *The West and the Rest of Us,* Lagos: Nok Publishers, 1978.

————, Onwuchekwa Jemie and Ihechukwu Madubuike, *Toward the Decolonization of African Literature,* Vol. I, Washington, D.C.: Howard University Press, 1983.

Clark, Cedric X., "Some Implications of Nkrumah's 'Consciencism' for Alternative Coordinates in Non-European Causality," *African Philosophy: Assumptions and Paradigms for Research on Black Persons,* Lewis M. King, Vernon J. Dixon, Wade W. Nobles (eds.), Los Angeles: Fanon Center Publication, 1976; 103-119.

Clarke, John Henrik, "Confrontation at Montreal," *Negro Digest,* Vol. XIX, No. 4, 1970.

————, *African World Revolution,* Trenton: Africa World Press, 1991.

Diop, Cheikh Anta, "Africa: Cradle of Humanity," *Nile Valley Civilizations*, Ivan Van Sertima (ed.), New Brunswick: Journal of African Civilizations, 1985; 23–28.

———, *The Cultural Unity of Black Africa*, Chicago: Third World Press, 1979.

———, Interview, *Black Books Bulletin*, Vol. 4, No. 4, Winter 1976; 30–37.

Dixon, Vernon J., "World Views and Research Methodology," *African Philosophy: Assumptions and Paradigms for Research on Black Persons*, Lewis M. King, Vernon J. Dixon and Wade W. Nobles (eds.), Los Angeles: Fanon Center Publications, 1976; 51–102.

DuBois, W.E.B., *The World and Africa*, New York: International Publishers, 1965.

Fanon, Frantz, *The Wretched of the Earth*, New York: Grove Press, 1963.

Felder, Jack, *AIDS: United States Germ Warfare*, New York: Felder, 1989.

Gayle, Addison, Jr., *The Black Aesthetic*, Garden City: Doubleday, 1972.

Gibson-Hunter, Aziza, "An Afrocentric Creative Process: Feeling and Form," unpublished paper, Washington D.C.: 1985

Gwaltney, John, *Dryslongo: A Self Portrait of Black America*, New York: Vintage, 1981.

Harrison, Paul Carter, *The Drama of Nommo*, New York: Grove Press, 1972.

Ita, J.M., "Frobenius, Senghor and the Image of Africa," *Modes of Thought*, Robin Horton and Ruth Finnegan (eds.), London: Faber and Faber, 1973; 306–336.

Jackson, John G., *Christianity Before Christ*, Austin: American Atheist Press, 1985.

———, "Egypt and Christianity," *Journal of African Civilizations*, Vol. 4, No. 2, November 1982; 65–80.

James, George, *Stolen Legacy*, New York: Philosophical Library, 1954.

Jones, James H., *Bad Blood: The Tuskegee Syphilis Experiment*, New York: The Free Press, 1981.

Kagame, Alexis, *La Philosophie Bantu-Rwandaise de l'etre*, Bruxelles: Arsom, 1956.

Kambon, Kobi Kazembe Kalongi, *The African Personality in America: An African-Centered Framework*, Tallahassee: Nubian Nation Publications, 1992.

Karenga, Maulana, *Kawaida Theory,* Inglewood: Kawaida Publications, 1980.

Kenyatta, Jomo, *Facing Mt. Kenya*, New York: Vintage, 1965.

King, Richard, "African Origins of Psychobiology," Lecture at City College, New York, 1987.

————, *African Origins of Biological Psychiatry,* Germantown, Tn.: Seymour-Smith, 1990.

Koech, D.K. and A.O. Obel, "Efficacy of KEMRON (Low dose oral natural human interferon alpha) in the Management of HIV-1 Infection and Acquired Immune Deficiency Syndrome (AIDS)," *East African Medical Journal*, Vol. 67, No. 7, July 1990, Special Supplement; 64-70.

Levi, Josef B., *The Ancient Egyptian Language: Pathway to Africa,* Unpublished Paper, 1984.

Mbiti, J. S., *African Religions and Philosophies*, New York: Anchor Press, Doubleday, 1970.

Molette, Carlton W. III, "Afro-American Ritual Drama," *Black World*, Vol. XXII, No. 6, April 1973; 9-12.

Myers, Linda James, *Understanding an Afrocentric World View*, DuBuque: Kendall/Hunt, 1988.

Nkomo, Mokubung, "Education for Blacks in South Africa: Fact vs. Fiction," *Interracial Books for Children Bulletin*, Vol. XVI, Nos. 5 & 6, New York: Council on Interracial Books for Children, 1985; 5–9.

Nobles, Wade, *Africanity and the Black Family*, Oakland, Ca.: Black Family Institute Publications, 1985.

————, "Ancient Egyptian Thought and the Development of African (Black) Psychology," *Kemet and the African World View,* Maulana Karenga and Jacob Carruthers (eds.), Los Angeles: University of Sankore Press, 1986; 100–118.

Obenga, Theophile, "African Philosophy of the Pharoanic Period," *Egypt Revisited*, 2nd ed., Ivan Van Sertima (ed.), New Brunswick: Transaction Press, 1989; 286–324.

Okpaku, Joseph, *New African Literature*, New York: Thomas Y. Crowell, Apollo Edition, 1970.

Pinckney, Alphonso, *The American Way of Violence*, New York: Vintage, 1972.

Richards, Dona Marimba, "From Anthropology to African-centered Cultural Science," Unpublished Paper, New York, 1984.

————, "The African 'Aesthetic' and National Consciousness," *The African Aesthetic: Keeper of the Traditions*, Kariamu Welsh-Asante (ed.), Westport: Greenwood Press, l993.

————, "European Mythology: The Ideology of Progress," *Black Contemporary Thought*, Molefi Kete Asante and Abdulai Vandi (eds.), Los Angeles: Sage Publications, 1985; 59–79.

————, *Let the Circle Be Unbroken: The Implications of African Spirituality in the Diaspora*, Trenton: Red Sea Press, 1989.

————, Toward the Demystification of Objectivity," Imhotep, *Journal of Afrocentric Thought*, Vol. I, No. 1, Dept. of African American Studies, Temple University, 1989.

————, "The Implications of African-American Spirituality," *African Culture: Rhythms of Unity*, Molefi Kete Asante and Kariamu Welsh-Asante (eds.), Westport: Greenwood Press, 1985; 207–232.

————, "The Ideology of European Dominance," *Presence Africaine*, No. III, 3rd Quarterly, 1979; 3–18. Also in *The Western Journal of Black Studies*, Vol 3, No. 4, Winter 1979; 244–250.

Robinson, Cedric J., *Black Marxism: The Making of the Black Radical Tradition*, London: Zed Press, 1983.

Spight, Carl, "Towards Black Science and Technology," *Black Books Bulletin*, Vol. 5, No. 3, Fall 1977; 6–11, 49.

Strickland, William, "Watergate: Its Meaning for Black America," *Black World*, Vol. XXIII, No. 2, December 1973; 9–14.

Walton, Ortiz, "A Comparative Analysis of the African and Western Aesthetic," *The Black Aesthetic*, Addison Gayle, Jr. (ed.), Garden City: Doubleday, 1972; 154–164.

————, "Rationalism and Western Music," *Black World*, Vol. XXII, No. 1, Nov. 1973; 54-57.

Welsh-Asante, Kariamu, "Commonalities in African Dance: An Aesthetic Foundation," *The African Culture: Rhythms of Unity,* Molefi Kete Asante and Kariamu Welsh-Asante (eds.), Westport: Greenwood Press, 1985; 71–82.

Welsing, Frances Cress, "To Whom it May Concern," Letter to the African Descendant Community, Washington D.C. February 1987.

————, *The Isis Papers: Keys to the Colors*, Chicago: Third World Press, 1990.

————, "A Conversation with Dr. Welsing," *Essence,* October 1973.

Willis, William S., "Skeletons in the Anthropological Closet," *Reinventing Anthropology*, Dell Hymes (ed.), New York: Vintage, 1974; 121-152.

Wilson, Amos, "The Mis-Education of Black Students," Lecture at Hunter College, New York City, April 1988.

————, *Black on Black Violence: The Psychodynamics of Black Self-Annihilation in the Service of White Domination,* New York: Afrikan Infosystems, 1990.

Wobogo, Vulindlela, "Diop's Two Cradle Theory and the Origin of White Racism," *Black Books Bulletin,* Vol. 4, No. 4, Winter 1976; 20-29, 72.

Woodson, Carter G., *The Mis-Education of the Negro*, New York: AMS Press, 1977; orig. published 1933.

Wright, Bobby, *The Psychopathic Racial Personality and Other Essays,* Chicago: Third World Press, 1984.

Non-African Authors

Aberle, Kathleen Gough, "New Proposals for Anthropologist," *Current Anthropology*, Vol. 9, No. 5, 1968.

Adams, George P., "The Idea of Civilization," *Civilization*, Berkeley: University of California Press, 1959.

Allen, E I, *Guidebook to Western Thought*, London: English Universities Press, 1957.

Alston, Dana (ed.), *We Speak for Ourselves: Social Justice, Race, and Environment*, Washington, D.C.: The Panos Institute, 1990.

Aquinas, St. Thomas, *The Summa Contra Gentiles*, Chapter XV, London, 1923.

Arieli, Yehoshua, *Individualism and Nationalism in American Ideology*, Baltimore: Penguin Books, 1966.

Aristides, *History of Western Civilization*, Selected Readings, Supplement, Chicago: University of Chicago Press, 1958.

Aristotle, *The Rhetoric and Poetics of Aristotle*, Introduction and Notes by Friedrich Solmesen, New York: Random House, Modern Library Edition, 1954.

Armstrong, Robert, *Wellspring: On the Myth and Source of Culture*, Berkeley: University of California Press, 1975.

Aron, Raymond, *Progress and Disillusion*, New York: Praeger, 1968.

Augustine, *City of God, The Basic Writings of Saint Augustine*, Vol. II, Whitney J. Oates (ed.), New York: Random House, 1948; 3–663.

Barnes, Harry Elmer, *An Intellectual and Cultural History of the Western World*, Vol. I, 3rd ed., New York: Dover, 1965.

Barnes, Timothy, *Constantine and Eusebius*, Cambridge, Mass.: Harvard University Press, 1981.

Bassett, E.O., "Plato's Theory of Social Progress," *International Journal of Ethics*, Vol. XXXVIII, 1927–1928.

Bateson, Gregory, *Naven*, Stanford: Stanford University Press, 1958.

Bauer, Marion and Ethel Oeyser, *How Music Grew*, New York: Putnam, 1939.

Baynes, Norman, "Constantine The Great and the Christian Church," *The Proceedings of the British Academy,* Vol. XV, London: Humphrey Milford, 1929.

————, *The Political Ideas of St. Augustine's De Civitate Dei,* London: George Philip and Son, London, 1949.

Beals, Ralph, *The Politics of Social Research,* Chicago: Aldine Publishing Company, 1969.

Beard, Charles A., *The Idea of Progress,* New York: J.B. Bury, Dover, 1955.

Berger, Peter, *A Rumor of Angels,* Garden City: Doubleday, 1970.

Bidney, D., "The Concept of Meta-Anthropology and its Significance for Contemporary Anthropological Science," *Ideological Differences and World Order,* F.S.C. Northrop (ed.), New Haven: Yale University Press, 1949; 323–355.

Boak, Arthur, E.R., *A History of Rome to 565 A.D.,* 4th ed., New York: MacMillan, 1955.

Botha, P.W., "Why We Hate Blacks,"*The Shield,* the official Black Newspaper of Hunter College. Reprinted from the South African Newspaper, *Sunday Times,* Aug. 18, 1985, under the by-line of David G. Maillu.

Bradley, Michael, *The Iceman Inheritance,* New York: Warner Books, 1978.

Brown, J., "Plato's Republic as an Early Study of Media Bias and a Charter for Prosaic Education," *American Anthropologist,* Vol. 74, No. 3, June 1972; 672–675.

Brown, Norman O., *Life Against Death,* Middleton: Wesleyan University Press, 1959.

Brownmiller, Susan, *Against Our Will,* New York: Bantam, 1976.

Bury, J.B., *The Idea of Progress,* New York: Dover, New York, 1955.

Cantor, Norman, *Western Civilization: Its Genesis and Destiny,* Vols. I & II, Atlanta: Scott, Foresman, 1969.

Cantwell, Alan Jr., *AIDS and the Doctors of Death,* Los Angeles: Aries Press, 1988.

Capra, Fritjof, *The Tao of Physics,* New York: Bantam Books, New York, 1977.

Carpenter, Edmund, "The New Languages," *Explorations in Communication*, Edmund Carpenter and Marshall McLuhan (eds.), Boston: Beacon Press, 1960; 162–179.

Cheney, L.J., *A History of the Western World*, New York: Mentor, 1959.

"Children of Eve," PBS 1987.

Cicero, *Phillipics*, 333.

Cohen, Chapman, *Christianity, Slavery and Labour*, 4th ed., London: Pioneer Press, 1931.

————, *War, Civilization and The Churches*, London: Pioneer Press, 1930.

Cookson, John and Judith Nottingham, *A Survey of Chemical and Biological Warfare*, New York: Monthly Review Press, 1969.

Cornford, Francis M., *Plato's Theatetus*, New York: The Library of Liberal Arts, 1959.

————, *Plato's Theory of Knowledge*, Indianapolis: Bobbs Merrill Educational Publishing, 1957.

Curtin, Philip, *The Image of Africa*, Madison: University of Wisconsin Press, 1964.

Davidson, H.R. Ellis, *Gods and Myths of Northern Europe*, New York: Penguin, 1964.

Deloria, Vine, *God is Red*, New York: Dell Publishing, Delta Book, 1957.

Deuteronomy, 13:6–13:10, 13:12, 13, 15, 16.

Diamond, Stanley, *Search for the Primitive*, New Brunswick: Transaction Press, 1974.

Dixon, William Hepworth, *White Conquest*, London: Chatto & Windus, 1876.

Doane, T. W., *Bible Myths: and Their Parallels in Other Religions*, New Hyde Park, New York: University Books, 1971.

duBois, Page, *Centaurs and Amazons: Women and the Pre-History of the Great Chain of Being*, Ann Arbor: University of Michigan Press, 1982.

Douglass, William Campbell, "Who Murdered Africa," *Health Freedom News*, September 1987.

Dumezil, George, *The Destiny of the Warrior*, Chicago: University of Chicago Press, 1970.

Durkheim, Emile, *The Rules of the Sociological Method*, New York: The Free Press, 1964.

————, *Suicide*, Glencoe, Illinois: The Free Press, 1951.

Edwards, B., *Drawing of the Right Side of the Brain*, Los Angeles: J.P. Tarcher, 1979.

Eliade, Mircea, *A History of Religious Ideas*, Vol. I, trans. Willard R. Trask, Chicago: University of Chicago Press, 1978.

————, *The Sacred and the Profane*, trans. Willard R. Trask, New York: Harcourt Brace, 1959.

————, *The Myth of the Eternal Return*, trans. Willard R. Trask, New York: Bollingen, 1954.

Ember, Carol and Melvin Ember, *Anthropology*, New York: Appleton-Century-Crofts, 1973.

Eusebius, "The Conversion of Constantine," *History of Western Civilization, Topic IV, Christianity and the Ancient World*, Chicago: University of Chicago Press, 1956.

————, *The History of the Church*, trans., G.A. Williamson, New York: Penguin Books, Penguin Classics, 1965.

Foucault, Michael, *Madness and Civilization: A History of Insanity in the Age of Reason*, New York: Pantheon, 1965.

Frankfort, H. and H.A., "Myth and Reality," *The Intellectual Adventure of Ancient Man*, Franfort et al (eds.), Chicago: University of Chicago Press, 1946; 3–27.

Freud, Sigmund, *Totem and Taboo: Some Points of Agreement Between the Mental Lives of Savages and Neurotics*, trans. James Strachey, New York: W.W. Norton & Co., 1950.

Geertz, Clifford, *The Interpretation of Cultures*, New York: Basic Books, 1979.

————, "Religion as a Cultural System," *Anthropological Approaches to the Study of Religion*, Michael Banton (ed.), New York: Praeger, 1966; 1–46.

Gentile, Giovanni, *The Philosophy of Art*, Ithaca, New York: Cornell University Press, 1972.

George, Katherine, "The Civilized West Looks at Primitive Africa: 1400–1800," *The Concept of the Primitive,* Ashley Montagu (ed.), New York: The Free Press, 1968; 175–193.

Ghyka, Matila, "The Pythagorean and Platonic Scientific Criterion of the Beautiful in Classical Western Art," *Ideological Differences and World Order*, F.S.C. Northrop (ed.), New Haven: Yale University Press, New Haven, 1949; 90–116.

Gobineau, *Selected Political Writings*, Michael D. Biddiss (ed.), New York: Harper & Row, 1970.

Golding, William, *Lord of the Flies,* New York: Putnam, New York, 1959.

Goldwater, Robert, "The Western Experience of Negro Art," *Colloquium on the Function and Significance of African Negro Art in the Life of African Culture*, Vol. I, Society of African Culture and UNESCO, 1966; 342.

Goodman, Paul, "Polarities and Wholeness: A Gestalt Critique of 'Mind',' Body' and 'External World,'" *Sources*, Theodore Roszak (ed.), New York: Harper and Row, Harper Colophon, 1972; 138–156.

Gossett, Thomas F., *Race: The History of an Idea in America*, New York: Schocken, 1965.

Gough, Kathleen, "Anthropology and Imperialism," *Monthly Review*, April 1968; 12–23.

Gouldner, Alvin W., "Anti-Minotaur: The Myth of a Value-Free Social Science," *The New Sociology,* Irving Horowitz (ed.), New York: Oxford University Press, 1964; 196–217.

———, *Enter Plato,* New York: Basic Books, 1956.

Grant, Madison, *The Passing of The Great Race*, New York: Charles Scribner & Sons, 1921.

Griaule, Marcel , "The Problem of Negro Culture," *Interrelations of Culture,* UNESCO, 1953.

——— and G. Dieterlen, *The Pale Fox*, Chino Valley: Continuum Foundation, 1986.

———, "The Dogon," *African Worlds*, Daryll Forde (ed.), London: Oxford University Press, 1954; 83–110.

Habermas, Jurgen, *The Theory of Communicative Action: Reason and the Rationalization of Society,* Vol. I, trans. Thomas McCarthy, Boston: Beacon Press, 1954.

Hackforth, R., *Plato's Phaedrus,* New York: The Library of Liberal Arts, 1952.

Hall, Edward T., *Beyond Culture,* Garden City, N.Y.: Anchor Press, 1976.

Hallowell, A.I., "Ojibwa Ontology, Behavior, and World View," *Primitive Views of the World,* Stanley Diamond (ed.), New York: Columbia University Press, 1966; 49–82.

Harris, Marvin, *The Rise of Anthropological Theory,* New York: Thomas Y. Crowell, 1968.

Havelock, Eric, *Preface to Plato,* New York: Grossett and Dunlap, 1967.

Hoebel, A.E., *Anthropology: The Study of Man,* 3rd ed., New York: McGraw-Hill, 1966.

Howitt, William, *Colonization and Christianity,* London: Green and Longman, 1838.

Jacobs, Paul and Saul Landau with Eve Pell, *To Serve the Devil,* Vols. I & II, New York: Vintage, 1971.

James, William, *The Writings of William James,* John J. McDermott (ed.), New York: Random House, 1968.

————, *The Varieties of Religious Experience,* New York: Longmans, Green and Company, 1919.

Jaynes, Julian, *The Origin of Consciousness in the Breakdown of the Bicameral Mind,* Boston: Houghton Mifflin, 1976.

Juenger, Friedrich, *The Failure of Technology,* Chicago: Henry Regnery Co., 1956.

Jung, Carl G., *Memories, Dreams, Reflections,* Aniela Jaffé (ed.), trans. Richard and Clara Winston, New York: Pantheon, 1968.

Kant, Immanuel, *Critique of Judgement,* New York: Hafner, 1951.

Kazanzakis, Nikos, *The Last Temptation of Christ,* trans. P.A. Bien, New York: Bantam Books, 1961.

Kierkegaard, *Attack Upon Christendom,* trans., Walter Lowrie, Princeton: Princeton University Press, 1944.

Kingsley, Mary, *West African Studies,* New York: Barnes and Noble, 1964.

Kovel, Joel, *White Racism: A Psychohistory,* New York: Vintage, 1971; and New York: Morningside edition, Columbia University Press, 1984.

Lee, Dorothy, *Freedom and Culture*, Englewood Cliffs: Prentice Hall, 1959.

Leibniz, Gottfried, *Leibniz: Philosophical Writings,* trans. Mary Morris, New York: E.P. Dutton, 1934.

Lerner, Marguerite, *Color and People: The Story of Pigmentation*, Minneapolis: Lerner Publications, 1971.

Lifton, Robert Jay, *The Nazi Doctors: Medical Killing and the Psychology of Genocide*, New York: Basic Books, 1986.

Lovejoy, Arthur O., *The Great Chain of Being*, Cambridge: Harvard University Press, 1966.

—— and George Boas, *Primitivism and Related Ideas in Antiquity,* New York: Octagon Books, 1965.

Lowie, Robert, *Primitive Religion,* New York: Liveright, 1970; orig. published 1924.

Lowith, K., *Meaning in History,* Chicago: University of Chicago Press, 1949.

MacDougall, Hugh A., *Racial Myth in English History,* Montreal: Harvest House, 1982.

MacLeod, Wayne, *The Importance of Race in Civilization*, Los Angeles: Noontide Press, 1968.

McCasland, Vernon S., *Religions of the World*, New York: Random House, 1969.

McKeon, R. (ed.), *Introduction to Aristotle,* New York: Random House, Modern Library, 1947.

McLuhan, Marshall, *Understanding Media*, New York: McGraw-Hill, 1967.

McNeill, William H., *History of Western Civilization: Selected Readings*, Handbook, Chicago: University of Chicago Press, 1953.

Mannheim, Karl, *Ideology and Utopia,* New York: Harcourt Brace, 1936.

Maquet, Jacques, "Objectivity in Anthropology," *Current Anthropology,* Vol. 5, No. 1, 1964.

Massey, Gerald, *Ancient Egypt: The Light of the World*, New York: Samuel Weiser, 1973; orig. published 1907.

Mill, John Stuart, *John Stuart Mill's Philosophy of Scientific Method*, Ernest Nagel (ed.), New York: Hafner, 1950.

Montagu Ashley (ed.), *The Concept of the Primitive*, New York: The Free Press, 1968.

————, "The Concept of the 'Primitive' and Related Anthropological Terms: A Study in the Systematics of Confusion," *The Concept of the Primitive*, Ashley Montagu (ed.), New York: The Free Press, 1968; 148–168.

Morel, E. D., *The Black Man's Burden*, New York: Monthly Review Press, 1969.

Mumford, Lewis, *The Condition of Man,* New York: Harcourt Brace, 1944.

Neumann, Erich, "On the Moon and Matriarchal Consciousness," *Fathers and Mothers,* Five Papers on the Archetypal Background of Family Psychology, Spring Publications, Zurich, 1973; 40–63.

Niebuhr, Rheinhold, *The Nature and Destiny of Man*, Vols. I & II, New York: Charles Scribner's Sons, 1946.

Nietzche, Friedrich, "The Anti-Christ," *Works of Friedrich Nietzche*, Vol. XI, trans. Thomas Common, Alexander Tille (ed.), New York: MacMillan, 1924; 235–351.

Nimer, Benjamin, "Politics and Scholarship in the United States," *African Studies Review,* Vol. XIII, 1970.

Opler, Morris, "Themes as Dynamic Forces in Culture," *American Journal of Sociology,* Vol. 51, 1945.

Pagels, Elaine, *The Gnostic Gospels*, New York: Random House, Vintage, 1981.

Penelhum, Terence, *Religion and Rationality*, New York: Random House, 1971.

Plato, *The Dialogues of Plato*, Vols. I & II, trans. B. Jowett, New York: Random House, 1937.

Poliakov, Leon, *The Aryan Myth: A History of Racist and Nationalist Ideas in Europe*, trans., Edmund Howard, New York: New American Library, 1974.

Pope-Hennesy, James, *Sins of the Fathers,* New York: Capricorn, 1969.

Popper, Karl, *The Open Society and its Enemies*, Vol. II, 5th ed., Princeton: Princeton University Press, 1966.

Rand, Ayn, Interview, *Speaking Freely,* NBC, August 1972.

Rattray, R.S., *Ashanti Law and Constitution*, London: Oxford, 1929.

Robertson, J.M., *Pagan Christs,* New Hyde Park, New York: University Books, 1967.

Rostovtzeff, Mikhail Ivanovich, *The Social and Economic History of the Roman Empire*, Oxford: Clarendon Press, 1957.

Roszak, Theodore, *Where the Wasteland Ends,* New York: Doubleday, 1972.

———— (ed.), *Sources,* New York: Harper & Row, Colophon, 1972.

Ruether, Rosemary Radford, *Sexism and God-Talk: Toward a Feminist Theology,* Boston: Beacon Press, 1983.

Sagan, Carl, *The Dragons of Eden,* New York: Ballantine Books, 1977.

Sagan, Eli, *The Lust to Annihilate: A Psychoanalytical Study of Violence in Ancient Greek Culture,* New York: Psychohistory Press, 1979.

Saint-Simon, Claude Henri de, *Social Organization, the Science of Man, and Other Writings,* trans. Felix Markham (ed.), New York: Harper Torchbooks, 1964.

Sapir, Edward, "Culture, Genuine and Spurious," *Edward Sapir, Culture, Language and Personality: Selected Essays,* David G. Mandelbaum (ed.), Berkeley: University of California Press, 1970; 78-119.

Schonfield, Hugh J., *The Passover Plot,* New York: Bantam, 1967.

Schwaller De Lubicz, R A, *The Sacred Science*, New York: Inner Traditions, 1982.

————, *The Temple in Man*, trans. Robert and Deborah Lawlor, Brookline, Mass.: Autumn Press, 1978; orig. published 1949.

————, *Symbol and the Symbolic*, trans. Robert and Deborah Lawlor, Brookline, Mass.: Autumn Press, 1978; orig. published 1949.

Schwartz, Barry and Robert Disch (eds.), *White Racism*, New York: Laurel, 1970.

Searles, H. L., *Logic and Scientific Methods,* 2nd ed., New York: The Ronald Press, 1956.

Shinn, Roger, "Perilous Progress in Genetics," *Social Research*, Vol. 41, No. 1, 1974; 83–103.

Skolomowski, Henryk, "The Scientific World View and the Illusions of Progress," *Social Research,* Vol. 41, No. 1, 1974; 52–82.

Sorokin, P.A., *The Crisis of Our Age*, New York: E.P. Dutton, 1941.

South Africa Perspectives, Africa Fund, American Committee on Africa, January, 1984.

Special Forces Handbook, ST31-180, Boulder, Colorado: Panther Publications, January 1965; Back Cover.

Spengler, Oswald, *The Decline of the West,* Vols. I & II, New York: Alfred A. Knopf, 1928.

Stein, Howard, *The Psychoanthropology of American Culture,* New York: The Psychohistory Press, 1985.

Steiner, George, *Language and Silence*, New York: Atheneum, 1967.

Stocking, George W., *Race, Culture, and Evolution*, New York: The Free Press, 1968.

Stoddard, Lothrop, *The Rising Tide of Colour*, New York: Charles Scribner's Sons, 1920.

————, *Clashing Tides of Colour*, New York: Charles Scribner's Sons, 1935.

Stone, Merlin, *Three Thousand Years of Racism*, New York: New Sibylline Books, 1981.

The Strecker Memorandum, Los Angeles: The Strecker Group, 1988.

Sulloway, Frank, *Biologists of the Mind*, New York: Basic Books, 1979.

Suzuki, Daiseti, "Buddhist Symbolism," *Explorations in Communications,* Edmund Carpenter and Marshall McLuhan (eds.), Boston: Beacon Press, 1960; 36–42.

Toynbee, Arnold, *The Study of History*, London: Oxford University Press, 1961; orig. published 1934.

Tylor, Edward, *The Origins of Culture*, Vol. I, New York: Harper and Brothers, 1958.

————, *Primitive Culture,* 7th ed., New York: Brentano, 1924; orig. published 1871.

Vander Zanden, James W., "The Ideology of White Supremacy," *White Racism,*
    Barry N. Schwartz and Robert Disch (eds.), New York: Laurel, 1970;
    121–139.

Vernon, John, *The Garden and the Map: Schizophrenia in Twentieth Century
    Literature and Culture*, Urbana: University of Illinois Press, 1973.

"War on Nicaragua," *Frontline,* PBS, April 1987.

Wassing, Rene, *African Art,* New York: Harry N. Abrams, Inc., 1968.

Wattenberg, Ben J., *The Birth Dearth,* New York: Pharos Books, 1987.

Weber, Max, *The Protestant Ethic and the Spirit of Capitalism*, New York: Charles
    Scribner and Sons, 1958.

White, Lynn, "The Historical Roots of Our Ecological Crisis," *The Subversive
    Science*, Paul Shepard and Daniel McKinley (eds.), Boston: Houghton
    Mifflin, 1969; 341–350.

Williams, Robin, *American Society: A Sociological Interpretation*, 3rd ed., New
    York: Alfred A. Knopf, 1970.

Wolff, Kurt, "This is the Time for Radical Anthropology," *Reinventing
    Anthropology*, Dell Hymes (ed.), New York: Vintage, 1974; 99–118.

Yates, F, *Giordano Bruno and the Hermetic Tradition*, Chicago: University of
    Chicago Press, 1978.

INDEX

Index of African Names

Index of Non-African Names